THE
HUMAN
BODY
BOOK

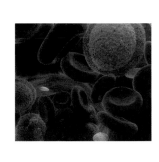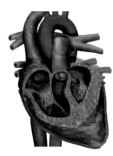

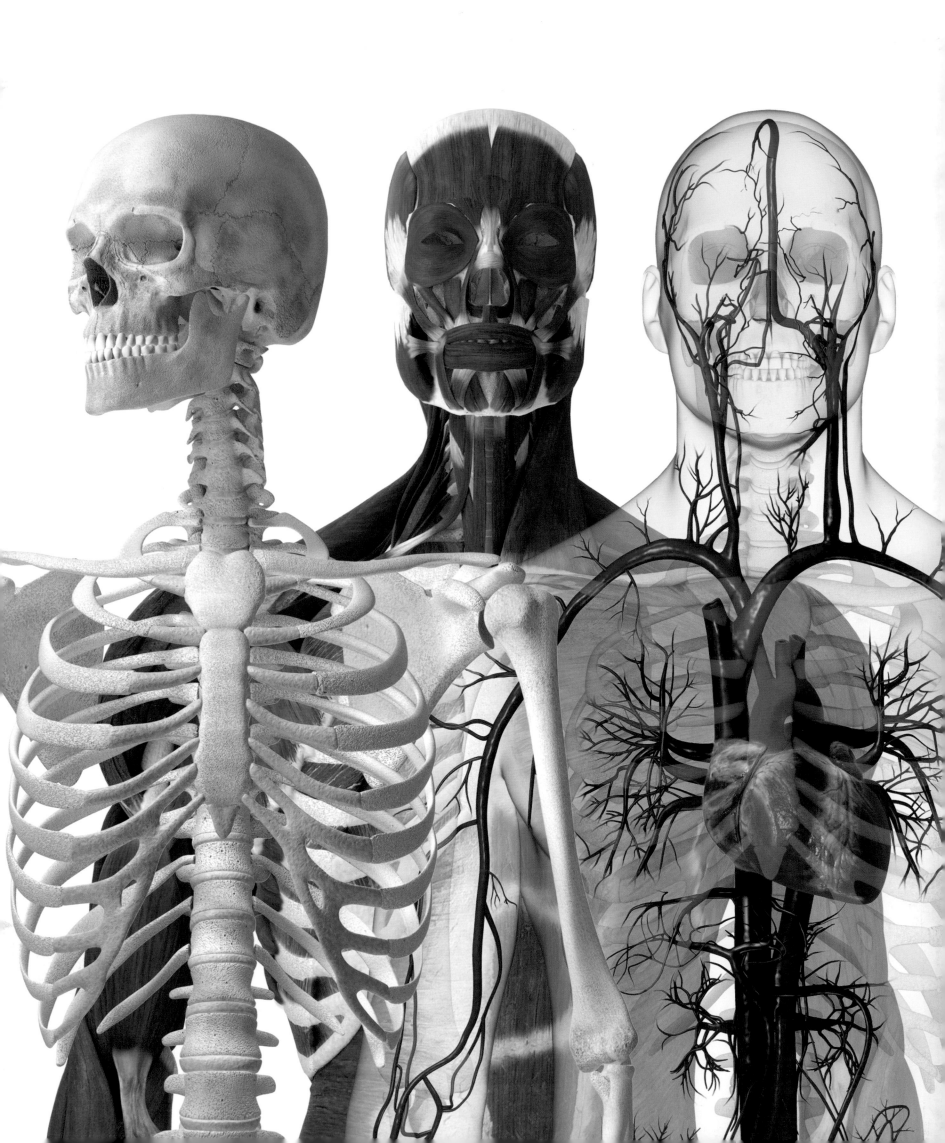

THE HUMAN BODY BOOK

STEVE PARKER

FOREWORD BY
PROFESSOR ROBERT WINSTON

CONTENTS

LONDON, NEW YORK, MELBOURNE,
MUNICH, AND DELHI

PROJECT EDITOR Rob Houston
PROJECT ART EDITOR Maxine Lea

EDITORS Ruth O'Rourke, Rebecca Warren,
Mary Allen, Sean O'Connor, Kim Bryan,
Tarda Davidson-Aitkins, Jane de Burgh,
Salima Hirani, Miezan van Zyl

DESIGNERS Matt Schofield, Kenny Grant,
Francis Wong, Anna Plucinska

MANAGING EDITOR Sarah Larter
MANAGING ART EDITOR Philip Ormerod
PUBLISHING MANAGER Liz Wheeler
REFERENCE PUBLISHER Jonathan Metcalf
ART DIRECTOR Bryn Walls

PICTURE RESEARCHER Louise Thomas
JACKET DESIGNER Lee Ellwood
DTP DESIGNER Laragh Kedwell
PRODUCTION CONTROLLER Tony Phipps
EDITORIAL ASSISTANTS
Tamlyn Calitz, Manisha Thakkar
INDEXER Hilary Bird
PROOF-READER Andrea Bagg

CONTRIBUTORS Mary Allen,
Andrea Bagg, Jill Hamilton, Katie John,
Janet Fricker, Jane de Burgh, Claire Cross

MEDICAL CONSULTANTS Dr Sue Davidson,
Dr Penny Preston, Dr Ian Guinan

ILLUSTRATORS

CREATIVE DIRECTOR Rajeev Doshi
3D ARTISTS Olaf Louwinger
Gavin Whelan, Monica Taddei

ADDITIONAL ILLUSTRATORS Peter Bull Art Studio,
Kevin Jones Associates, Adam Howard

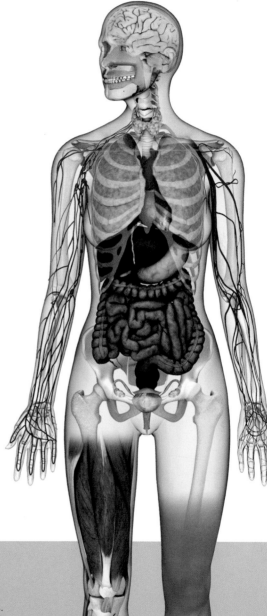

DVD system requirements:

PC: Windows 98, 2000, or XP; Intel or AMD
processor; soundcard; 24-bit colour display;
screen resolution 1024 × 768
Macintosh: OS X; G4, G5, or Intel processor;
soundcard; 24-bit colour display,
screen resolution 1024 × 768

The Human Body Book provides information on a wide
range of medical topics, and every effort has been made to
ensure that the information in this book is accurate. The
book is not a substitute for medical advice, however, and
you are advised always to consult a doctor or other health
professional on personal health matters.

Some of the text in this book has been adapted from *The
Human Body* by Dr Tony Smith, first published in 1995.

This edition produced for The Book People Ltd,
Hall Wood Avenue, Haydock, St Helens WA11 9UL.

First published in Great Britain in 2007 by
Dorling Kindersley Limited, 80 Strand, London WC2R 0RL
A Penguin Company

Copyright © 2007 Dorling Kindersley Limited
2 4 6 8 10 9 7 5 3 1

A CIP catalogue record for this book
is available from the British Library

ISBN 978-1-8561-3007-3

Colour reproduction by GRB Editrice s.r.l in London, UK
Printed and bound in China by Hung Hing

See our complete catalogue at www.dk.com

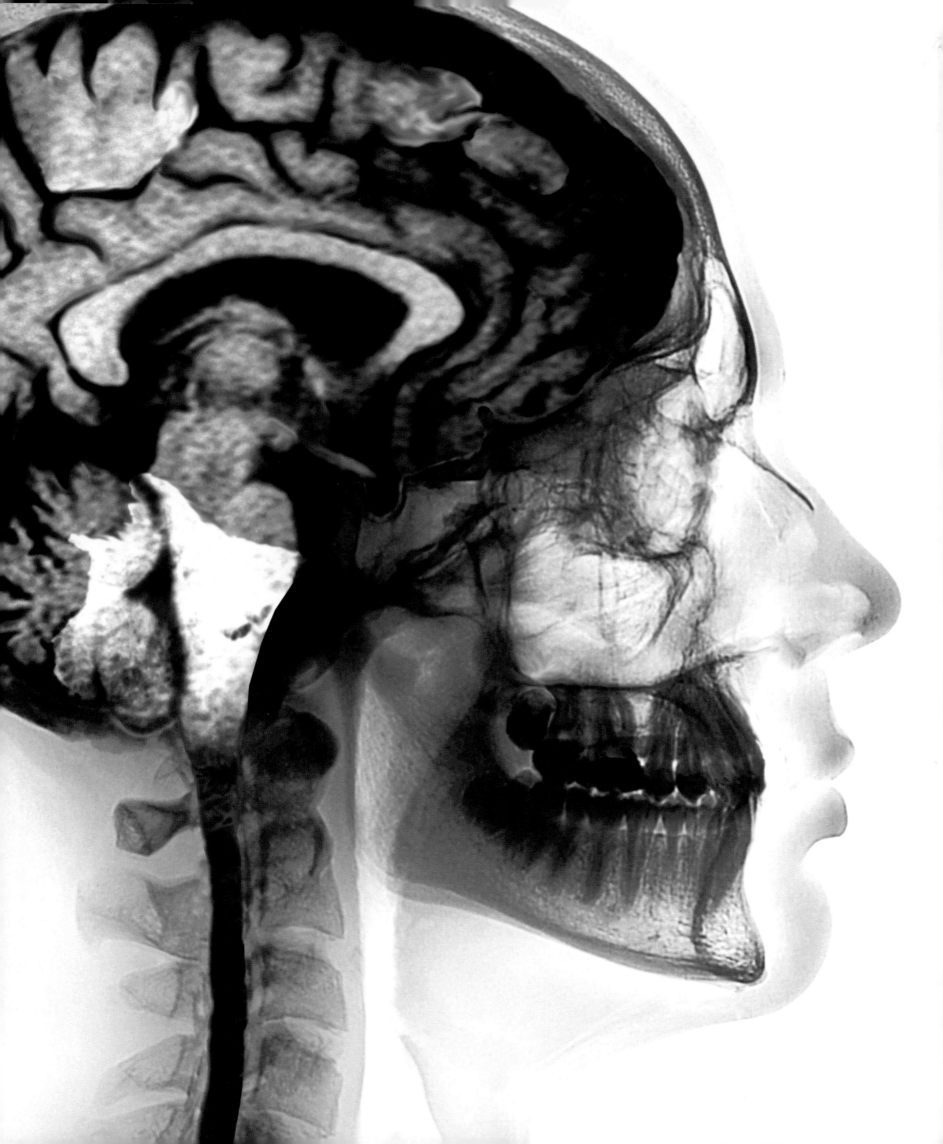

FOREWORD

This amazing book shows the detailed structure inside the human body as never seen before. It is only possible to produce these pictures because of major advances in technology. Although we have used dissection for several hundred years, new techniques help us to reveal what lies under our skin in meticulous detail. Being able to see ourselves in this way was first made possible by computed tomography – X-rays that slice through the body, photographing it in sections. These images can then be combined using advanced computing, making it possible to construct accurate, elegant, three-dimensional images. More recently, tomographic techniques have been used with magnetic resonance scanning, which carries no risks. If your body is placed inside a massive magnet strong enough to rip the wristwatch from your arm, all the molecules in the tissues are harmlessly lined up like a needle in a compass. When radio waves are then directed at the magnetized tissues, different tissue structures vibrate in different ways. These vibrations can be detected and, after computation, it is again possible to produce a three-dimensional image. Consequently, we can now produce images of human anatomy with great accuracy. Of course, some pictures in this book are drawings of what is seen down a microscope. The combination of microscopic anatomy and the three-dimensional images is highly instructive, and this book allows people to more than glimpse at the unique wonders inside the body. It will appeal not only to adults and young people, who are just interested in how the body works, but also to those, like nurses or physiotherapists, for whom it has more professional relevance. How much more thrilling learning anatomy would have been when I was a medical student 40 years ago if we had been able to see beautiful, accurate images like these.

PROFESSOR ROBERT WINSTON

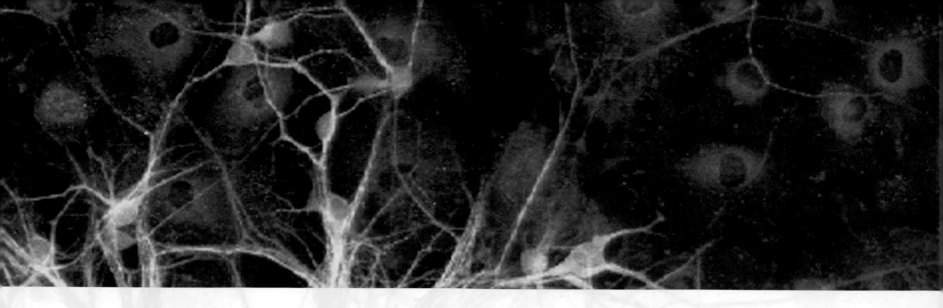

INTRODUCTION

The number of humans in the world is racing towards seven billion (7,000,000,000). More than 250 babies are born every minute, while 150,000 people die daily, with the population increasing by almost three humans per second. Each of these people lives, thinks, worries, and daydreams with, and within, that most complex and marvellous of possessions – a human body. An enduring feature of this body and its behaviour is self-curiosity. We continually look inside ourselves, in enormous and ever-increasing detail, in order to comprehend the action within. This book aims to quench aspects of our curious nature by revealing every aspect of the human body.

LEVELS OF ORGANIZATION

To understand the inner structure and workings of the human body this book takes the "living machine" approach, borrowed from sciences such as engineering. This views the body as a series of integrated systems. Each system carries out one major role or task. In the cardiovascular system, for example, the heart pumps blood through vessels, to supply every body part with essential oxygen and nutrients. The systems are, in turn, composed of main parts known as organs. The stomach, intestines, and liver are organs of the digestive system. Moving through further levels in the hierarchy, the organs consist of tissues, and tissues are made up of cells.

Cells are often called the microscopic building blocks of the body. However, they are far from passive bricks in a wall – they are active and dynamic, they continually grow and specialize, function,

die, and replenish themselves, by the millions every second. The whole body contains about 100 million million cells, of at least 200 different kinds. Science is increasingly able to delve deeper than cells, to the organelles within them, and onwards and inwards, to the ultimate components of ordinary matter – molecules and atoms.

ANATOMY

The study of the body's structure, and how its cells, tissues, and organs are assembled, is known as human anatomy. Its elements are often shown in isolation, using techniques such as cutaways, cross-sections, and "exploded" views, which provide clarity and understanding. But in reality, the inside of the body is a crowded place. Tissues and organs push and press against one another. There is no free space, and no stillness either. Body parts shift continually in relation to each other, as we move about, breathe, pump blood, shift digestive matter, and eat. For example, swallowed food does not simply fall down inside the gullet (oesophagus). The gullet is normally pressed flat by internal chest pressure so that food must be forced down into the stomach by waves of muscular contraction.

PHYSIOLOGY

The anatomical drawing of a large factory or office would show the arrangement of rooms, location of machinery and furniture, and service ducts for electricity, water, and air-conditioning. It is a static snapshot of structure and layout. For a rounded understanding,

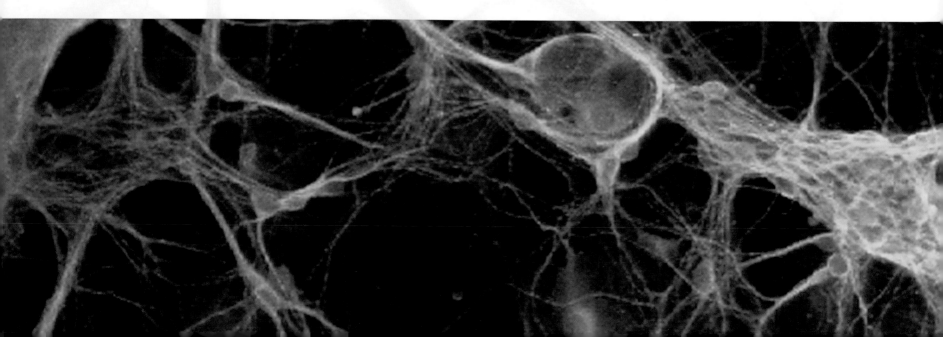

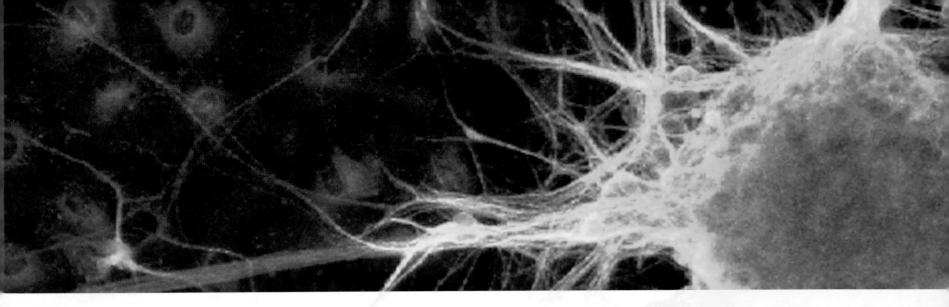

we need to see the premises in action, with people, goods, and information on the move. Similarly, human anatomy is combined with its twin, physiology, which is the study of the body's workings and how it functions. Physiology focuses on the dynamic chemical minutiae at atomic, ionic, and molecular level. It investigates the workings of such processes as enzyme action, hormone stimulation, DNA synthesis, and how the body stores and uses energy from food. As researchers stare harder and closer, more biochemical pathways are unravelled, and more physiological secrets are unlocked. Much of this work is directed at preventing, treating, or alleviating disease, and allows us to appreciate the latest wonder drug, or take a medication that makes us feel better.

HEALTH AND ILLNESS

Medical science amasses mountains of evidence every year for the best ways to stay healthy and avoid disease. At present, an individual's genetic inheritance, which is a matter of chance, is the given starting point for maintaining health and wellbeing. In coming years, treatments such as pre-implantation genetic diagnosis (PGN) – carried out as part of assisted reproductive techniques, such as in vitro fertilization (IVF) – and gene therapy could remove or negate some of these chance elements. Many aspects of upbringing have a major impact on health. Factors such as diet, whether it is too rich, bringing with it the risk of obesity or too poor leading to malnutrition, particularly affect children, as their bodies are still developing. The body can be affected by many different types of

disorder, such as infection by a virus or bacteria, injuries resulting from an accident or long-term repetitive activities, inherited faulty genes, or exposure to toxins in the environment.

ABOUT THIS BOOK

The pages that follow describe the structures and workings of the human body at all levels. First, the hierarchy of organization is described, from molecules such as DNA, to organelles and cells, to tissues and organs. Then the approach is basically functional, focusing on each major system in turn. Every section opens with an overview of its system, and subsequently explores its organs and tissues, to examine how they work and what they do.

At the end of each section common ailments relating to the system are explored. A variety of problems is discussed, including those caused by genetic variation, ageing, infection, and injury.

The running order of the sections that follow moves from support and movement (bones and muscles), through control and coordination (nerves and hormones), to basic life support, protection, and nourishment (heart, lungs, skin, immunity, digestion, and waste disposal). The final section examines reproduction, inheritance, and the ageing process.

COMMUNICATION NETWORK
This microscopic image of nerve cells (neurons) shows the thin strands (axons and dendrites) that connect the cell bodies. Neurons transmit electrical signals around the body, especially the brain and spinal cord; each one connects with hundreds of others to form a dense network.

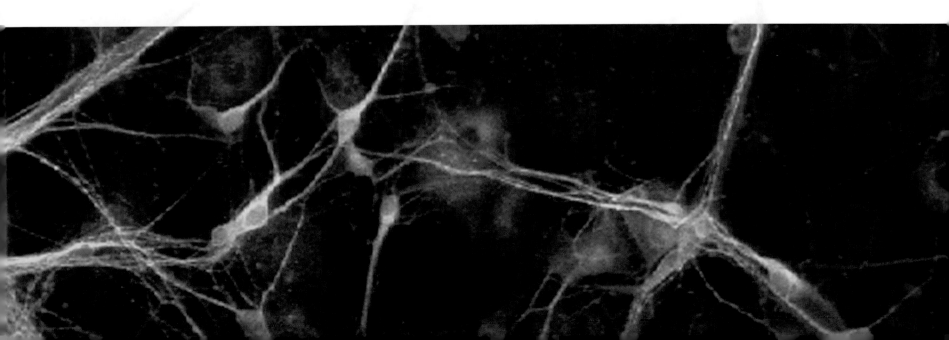

IMAGING THE BODY

IMAGING IS VITAL TO DIAGNOSE ILLNESS, UNRAVEL DISEASE PROCESSES, AND EVALUATE TREATMENTS. MODERN TECHNIQUES PROVIDE DETAILED INFORMATION WITH MINIMUM DISCOMFORT TO THE PATIENT AND HAVE LARGELY REPLACED SURGERY IN ESTABLISHING THE PRESENCE AND EXTENT OF DISEASE. MICROSCOPY HAS ALSO HELPED ADVANCE BIOLOGICAL RESEARCH.

The invention of the X-ray made the development of non-invasive medicine possible. Without the ability to see inside the body, many internal disorders could only be found after major surgery. Computerized imaging now helps doctors make early diagnoses, which in many cases greatly increase the likelihood of recovery. Computers process and enhance raw data to aid our visual ability, for example by coding and re-interpreting subtle shades of grey from an X-ray or scan into distinguishable colours. While enhanced images are valuable, sometimes direct observation is essential. Viewing techniques have also become less invasive with the development of instruments such as the endoscope (see opposite). This book makes extensive use of imagery from real bodies, as well as artistically conceived illustrations.

MICROSCOPY

Light microscopy (LM) uses magnifying lenses to focus light rays. In light microscopy, light passes through a thin section of material and enlarges it up to 2,000 times. Higher magnifications are achieved with beams of subatomic particles called electrons. In scanning electron microscopy (SEM) the beam runs across a specimen coated with gold film. Electrons bounce off the surface contours, to create a three-dimensional image.

SEM OF TUMOUR BLOOD SUPPLY
This freeze-fracture image, in which the specimen is frozen and then cracked open before being scanned, shows a blood vessel with blood cells growing into a melanoma (skin tumour).

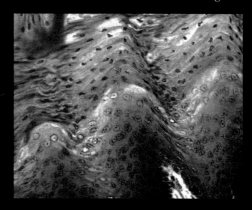

TEM OF MITOCHONDRION
In transmission electron microscopy (TEM), enlargements of several million times are possible. This coloured image shows a mitochondrion within a cell, magnified about 12,000 times.

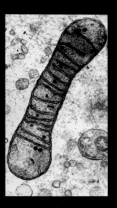

LM OF TONGUE PAPILLAE
This light photomicrograph shows the tiny pimples, or papillae, on the tongue. Specimens for LM are usually stained with chemicals to colour structures, such as cell nuclei.

ANGIOGRAM
In this image, a contrast medium, which is coloured red, has been injected into the arteries of the shoulder, neck, and lower head. Bones show up white. This type of X-ray image is called an angiogram.

X-RAY

Like light rays, X-rays are electromagnetic energy, but of very short wavelength. When passed through the body to strike photographic film, they create shadow images (radiographs). Dense structures such as bone absorb more X-rays and show up white, while soft tissues, such as muscle, appear as shades of grey. To view hollow or fluid-filled structures clearly, these must first be filled with a substance that absorbs X-rays (a contrast medium). To view the oesophagus, for example, the patient swallows barium, which is insoluble.

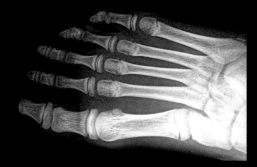

PLAIN X-RAY OF FOOT
A plain X-ray is especially useful for viewing dense tissue, such as bone. This image shows the foot bones of a nine-year-old. The gaps near the bone ends indicate areas of cartilage where the bones are still growing.

MRI AND CT SCANNING

Computerized tomography (CT) and magnetic resonance imaging (MRI) reveal detail about many tissue types. CT scans use weak levels of X-rays to produce an image. In CT, an X-ray scanner rotates around the patient as a computer records the levels of electromagnetic energy absorbed by tissues of different densities. A cross-section is built from layers of data. In MRI, a person lies in a magnetic chamber, which causes hydrogen atoms in the body to align. A pulse of radio waves is released, throwing the atoms out of alignment. As they realign, they emit radio signals, which are used to create an image.

MRI SCAN OF HEAD
A digitally enhanced MRI scan of the head shows tissues of the brain and spinal cord in orange and yellow, while muscle and bone are coded in blue.

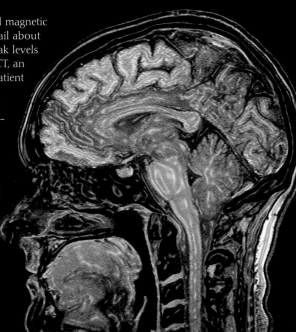

ARTERY SCAN
The layered images produced by a CT scan can be built into a three-dimensional image on a computer. This image reveals the interior of a narrowed carotid artery.

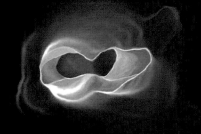

CT SCAN OF LUNGS
In a horizontal slice through the chest, the spongy tissues and airways of the healthy lungs (oranges and yellows) show up quite distinctly from their denser surroundings. The heart and major blood vessels between the lungs are mid-blue, and the vertebrae (backbones), ribs, and sternum (breastbone) are dark blue.

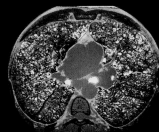

RADIONUCLIDE AND PET SCANNING

In radionuclide imaging, a radioactive substance is injected into the body and is absorbed by the area to be imaged. As the substance decays it emits gamma rays, which a computer forms into an image. Positron emission tomography (PET) is a type of radionuclide scanning that uses injected chemicals, which emit radioactive particles called positrons. PET provides data about function rather than detailed anatomy, by recording features such as nerve activity.

RADIONUCLIDE BONE SCAN
In this scan the bone (blue) has absorbed the radionuclide more than other tissue has. This method can reveal increased cell activity that could indicate cancer.

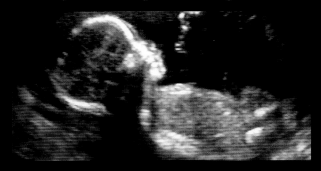

PET SCAN
These side views of the brain reveal its activity. The upper image was taken as the subject listened to spoken words; the auditory cortex is highlighted. The lower image shows the subject both listening to and repeating the words; a motor area of the brain becomes active to control the muscles of speech.

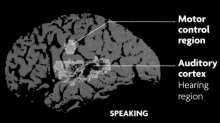

Auditory cortex
Hearing region

LISTENING

Motor control region

Auditory cortex
Hearing region

SPEAKING

ULTRASOUND

Sound waves of very high frequency (too high-pitched for us to hear) are emitted by a device called a transducer as it is passed over the body part being examined. The sound waves echo back to the transducer according to the density of the tissues they encounter. A computer analyses the reflections and creates an image. Ultrasound is used to monitor fetal development in the uterus. This technique is regarded as extremely safe because no radiation is used.

FETAL ULTRASOUND
A fetus of about six months, surrounded by amniotic fluid, is clearly visible in this image.

A modified form, echocardiography, shows the heart beating in real time.

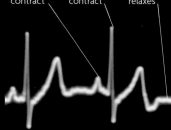

ENDOSCOPY

A variety of telescope-like endoscopes are inserted through natural orifices or incisions to produce images of the body's interior. Some types are rigid but many are flexible, utilizing fibreoptic technology, and can be bent and controlled as they are guided along. They carry their own light source and may be equipped with tubes to introduce or remove fluids or gases, blades for surgery, forceps to take samples (biopsy), and perhaps a laser to cauterize damaged tissue. Endoscopes have been developed to fit different body parts – a bronchosope for the airways, a gastroscope for the oesophagus and stomach, a laparoscope for the abdomen, and a proctoscope for the lower bowel.

TRACHEA
A bronchoscope image of the interior trachea (windpipe) shows the hoops of cartilage that prevent it collapsing.

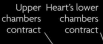

ELECTRICAL ACTIVITY

Sensor pads applied to the skin detect electrical signals coming from active muscles and nerves. The signals are coordinated, amplified, and displayed as a real-time trace, usually a spiky or wavy line. This technique includes electrocardiography (ECG) of the heart (see below) and electro-encephalography (EEG) of the brain's nerve activity.

Upper chambers contract

Heart's lower chambers contract

Heart muscle relaxes

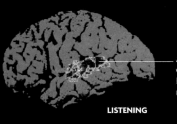

SKELETAL

EXPLORED ON PAGES 34–53

The skeleton is a solid, moveable framework that supports the body. Its bones work as levers and anchor plates to allow for movement. Bones also work for other body systems – blood cells develop in their fatty inner tissue (red marrow), for example. The body draws from mineral stores in bones during times of shortage, such as when calcium is needed for healthy nerve function.

COMPONENTS

- Skull, spine, ribs, and breast bone (axial skeleton)
- Limb bones, shoulders, and hips (appendicular skeleton)
- Ligaments

MUSCULAR

EXPLORED ON PAGES 54–65

Muscles work with the skeleton, providing the pulling force for movement, from powerful to intricate. Involuntary muscles work largely automatically to control internal processes, such as blood distribution and digestion. Muscles rely on nerves to control them and blood to supply them with oxygen and energy.

COMPONENTS

- Skeletal muscles (attached to bones)
- Smooth muscle within organs
- Tendons
- Cardiac muscle of heart

NERVOUS

EXPLORED ON PAGES 66–101

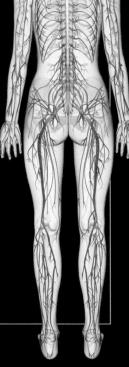

The brain is the seat of both consciousness and creativity and, through the spinal cord and nerve branches, it controls all body movements with its motor output. The brain also receives sensory information from outside the body and within. Yet much of the brain's second-by-second activity is carried out unconsciously as it works with endocrine glands to monitor and maintain other body systems.

COMPONENTS

- Brain
- Spinal cord
- Peripheral nerves
- Sense organs

ENDOCRINE

EXPLORED ON PAGES 102–11

The glands and cells of the endocrine system produce chemical messengers called hormones, which circulate in blood and other fluids. In response to physiological feedback, they maintain an optimal internal environment. Hormones also govern long-term processes such as growth, the changes that take place during puberty, and reproductive activity. The endocrine system is linked closely to the nervous system via the brain, allowing for dual monitoring and control of all other systems.

COMPONENTS

- Pituitary gland
- Hypothalamus
- Thyroid gland
- Thymus gland
- Heart
- Stomach
- Pancreas
- Intestines
- Adrenal glands
- Ovaries (in female)
- Testes (in male)

MALE

CARDIOVASCULAR

EXPLORED ON PAGES 112–27

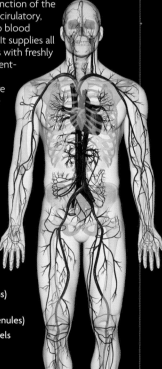

The most basic function of the cardiovascular, or cirulatory, system is to pump blood around the body. It supplies all organs and tissues with freshly oxygenated, nutrient-rich blood. Any waste products are removed with the blood as it leaves. The circulatory system also transports other vital substances, such as nutrients, hormones, and immune cells.

COMPONENTS

- Heart
- Blood
- Major vessels (arteries and veins)
- Minor vessels (arterioles and venules)
- Microscopic vessels (capillaries)

RESPIRATORY

EXPLORED ON PAGES 128–43

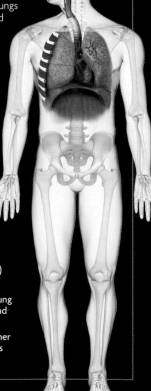

The respiratory tract and its movements, powered by breathing muscles, carries air into and out of the lungs. Deep in the lungs gases are exchanged – vital oxygen is absorbed from the air and carbon dioxide is passed into it before the air is carried back out of the body. A secondary function of this system is vocalization.

COMPONENTS

- Nasal and other air passages in the skull
- Throat (pharynx)
- Windpipe (trachea)
- Lungs
- Major and minor lung airways (bronchi and bronchioles)
- Diaphragm and other respiratory muscles

SKIN, HAIR, AND NAILS

EXPLORED ON PAGES 144–53

The skin, hair, and nails form the body's outer protective covering, and are together termed the integumentary system. They repel physical damage and hazards such as microorganisms and radiation. The skin also regulates body temperature by sweating when too hot. The layer of subcutaneous fat under the skin acts as an insulator, an energy store, and a physical shock absorber.

COMPONENTS

- Skin
- Hair
- Nails
- Subcutaneous fat layer

LYMPHATIC AND IMMUNE

EXPLORED ON PAGES 154–69

The immune system's intricate interrelationships of physical, cellular, and chemical defences provide vital resistance to many threats, including infectious diseases and malfunctions of internal processes. The slowly circulating lymph fluid helps to distribute nutrients and collect waste. It also delivers immunity-providing white blood cells when needed.

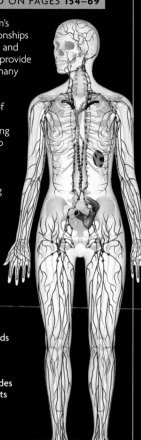

COMPONENTS

- White blood cells (such as lymphocytes)
- Antibodies
- Spleen
- Tonsils and adenoids
- Thymus gland
- Lymph fluid
- Lymph vessels, nodes ("glands"), and ducts

BODY SYSTEMS

THE HUMAN BODY'S SYSTEMS WORK TOGETHER AS A TRUE COOPERATIVE – EACH ONE FULFILS ITS OWN VITAL FUNCTION, BUT ALL WORK TOGETHER TO MAINTAIN HEALTH AND EFFICIENCY.

Just like every other living thing, the prime biological aim of the human body is to replace itself with viable offspring. However, it is far from being simply a gene-carrier, a reproductive system with extra supporting parts "added on". In fact, and somewhat ironically, the reproductive system is the only one that is not required for basic survival. The exact number and extent of the body's systems is debated – the muscles, bones, and joints are sometimes combined as the musculoskeletal system, for instance. Although these systems can be described as separate entities, each depends on all others for physical and physiological support. Most systems have some "general" body tissues such as the connective tissues which delineate, support, and cushion many organs.

DIGESTIVE

EXPLORED ON PAGES 170–91

The digestive tract's nine metres or so of tubing, which varies in size between the mouth and the anus, has a complex range of functions. It chops and chews food, stores and then digests it, eliminates waste products, and passes the nutrients to the major gland, the liver, which makes optimal use of the various digestive products. Healthy digestion depends on the proper functioning of the immune and nervous systems, and psychological state also greatly affects digestion.

COMPONENTS

- Mouth and throat (pharynx)
- Oesophagus
- Stomach
- Pancreas
- Liver
- Gallbladder
- Small intestine (duodenum, jejunum, and ileum)
- Large intestine (colon, appendix, and rectum)
- Anus

URINARY

EXPLORED ON PAGES 192–99

The formation of urine by the kidneys eliminates wastes and excess substances from the blood, helping to maintain the body's correct balance of water, fluids, salts, and minerals. Urine production is controlled by several hormones and is influenced by blood flow and pressure, the quantities of incoming water and nutrients, fluid loss (through sweating and bleeding, for instance), external conditions (especially temperature), and regular bodily cycles (such as sleeping and waking).

COMPONENTS

- Kidneys
- Ureters
- Bladder
- Urethra

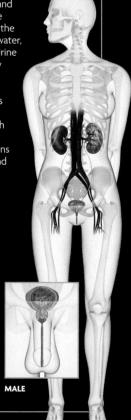

MALE

REPRODUCTIVE

EXPLORED ON PAGES 200–37

Unlike any other system, the reproductive system differs dramatically between female and male, it functions only for part of the human life span, and it can be surgically removed without threatening life. The production of sperm in the male is continual while the female production of ripe eggs is cyclical. In the male, both sperm and urine use the urethra as an exit tube at different times.

COMPONENTS

Female:
- Ovaries, fallopian tubes, and uterus
- Vagina and external genitalia
- Breasts

Male:
- Testes, spermatic ducts, seminal vesicles, urethra, and penis
- Prostate and bulbourethral glands

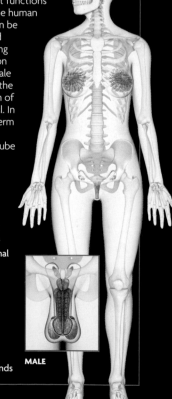

MALE

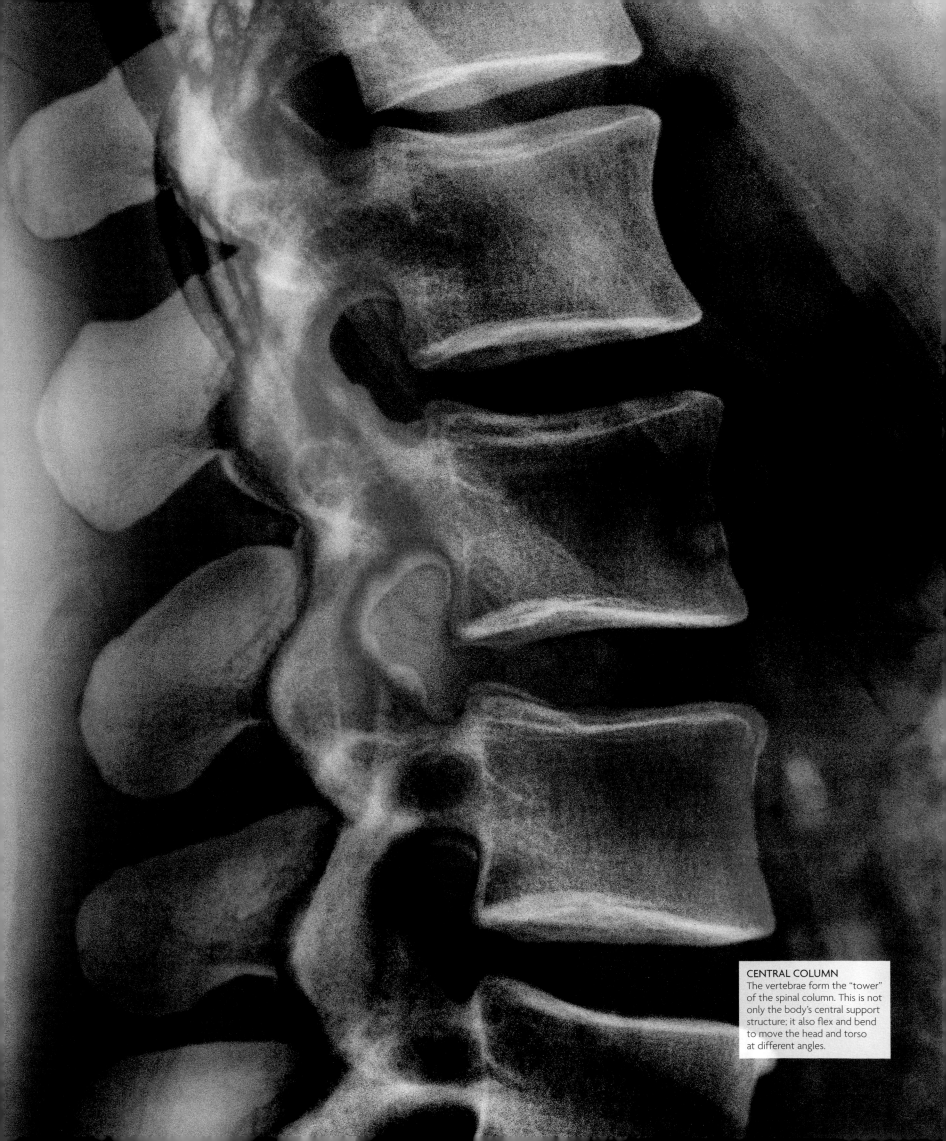

CENTRAL COLUMN
The vertebrae form the "tower" of the spinal column. This is not only the body's central support structure; it also flex and bend to move the head and torso at different angles.

SUPPORT AND MOVEMENT

THE BODY'S MUSCLES, BONES, AND JOINTS PROVIDE A SUPPORTIVE FRAMEWORK CAPABLE OF AN ENORMOUS RANGE OF DYNAMIC MOTION. MUSCLES AND BONES ALSO HAVE NUMEROUS INTERACTIONS WITH OTHER BODILY SYSTEMS, ESPECIALLY THE NERVES FOR CONTROL AND COORDINATION, AND THE BLOOD, WHICH SUPPLIES THE ENERGY-HUNGRY MUSCLES WITH THEIR ESSENTIAL REQUIREMENTS.

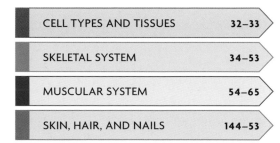
The body's muscular system is never still. Even as the body sleeps, breathing continues, the heart beats, and the intestines squirm. Most muscles relax during sleep, but some contract occasionally to shift the body into a new position. This avoids squashing nerves and vessels, which could cause blood deprivation and damage, thereby safeguarding all body systems.

MUSCLE TEAMWORK

Apart from simple movements, such as the blink of an eye, actions are the result of multiple muscle contractions. A subtle movement such as a smile, for example, involves 20 facial muscles. Writing utilizes more than 60 muscles in the arm, hand,

STAYING SUPPLE
Our potential for movement, and the health of the skeletal and muscular systems, is maximized by regular "3 S" exercises, for strength, stamina, and suppleness. Warm-ups and warm-downs avoid sudden strain that could cause injury.

and wrist. As the arm moves, muscles in the shoulder come into play, while the shifting weight load on the main torso uses yet more muscles to balance the body. The other muscles do not simply relax. They maintain tension, so that their opposing partners have some resistance to pull against, in a continuing sequence of split-second give-and-take.

STRESS AND FLEXIBILITY

Bones are slightly flexible so they can absorb normal stress without cracking or snapping. Sensory systems built into

muscles, bones, and joints also protect against injury. Microsensors within them, and inside associated parts, such as tendons and ligaments, gauge tensions and pressures. Nerve messages feed the brain and provide warning, registering stress to the bones as discomfort or pain. Awareness of the pain stimulates action by the body.

POSTURE AND FEEDBACK

Feedback signals also provide the brain with information about the body's posture and the detailed positions of its parts, which is known as the proprioceptive sense. In this way we "know", without having to look, or feel, that the fingers are clenched or a knee is bent. When learning a new motor skill, the eyes watch the movement's progress, and the skin feels it, as the brain adjusts its muscle control through trial and error. With practice, the motor nerve patterns and their proprioceptive feedback become well-tuned and established. Eventually the movement becomes automatic. It is organized by part of the lower rear brain called the cerebellum, and we no longer need to concentrate on it.

MUTUAL HEALTH

The interdependence of muscles, bones, and joints not only allows them to function but also keeps them healthy. During vigorous exercise, two-thirds of the heart's output of

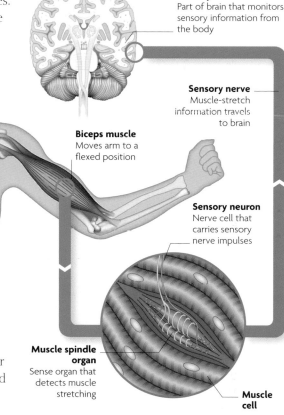

Sensory cortex
Part of brain that monitors sensory information from the body

Sensory nerve
Muscle-stretch information travels to brain

Biceps muscle
Moves arm to a flexed position

Sensory neuron
Nerve cell that carries sensory nerve impulses

Muscle spindle organ
Sense organ that detects muscle stretching

Muscle cell

SENSORY FEEDBACK
Nerve endings form tiny sense organs (muscle spindle organs) within the muscles. Specialized to respond to tension or stretching, they fire signals along nerve fibres to the brain. The signals arrive at the sensory cortex, where they inform the brain about what is happening.

blood goes to the muscles, compared to only one-fifth at rest, giving the heart muscle a workout. Muscles exercised to extremes can exert so much force on a bone that it breaks. Conversely, weak muscles do not put bones under regular pressure, and so the bone starts to weaken and waste.

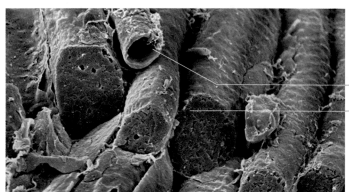

Blood vessel

Muscle fibre

MUSCLE FIBRES
This false-colour electron micrograph of muscle tissue shows the cut ends of several hair-like myofibres, which are large cells. Each fibre has within it bundles of even slimmer myofilaments.

INFORMATION PROCESSING

THE HUMAN BODY IS ALIVE WITH INFORMATION. BEING A COMPLEX, DYNAMIC MECHANISM, ITS INTERACTING AND INTERDEPENDENT PARTS REQUIRE CONTROL AND COORDINATION. THIS IS DONE BY PASSING INFORMATION BETWEEN THEM. TWO BODY SYSTEMS ARE RESPONSIBLE FOR COMMAND-CONTROL AND DATA MANAGEMENT – THE NERVOUS AND ENDOCRINE SYSTEMS.

Information processing involves inputs, evaluation, and decision-making, followed by outputs. The body has inputs from the various senses such as sight and hearing. Its brain is the "CPU" (central processing unit), whose outputs control the physical actions of muscles and the chemical responses of glands. Both nerves and hormones are involved in data management.

ELECTRICAL AND CHEMICAL PATHWAYS

The "language" of the nervous system is tiny electrical impulses. They are small and fast – each just one-tenth of a volt in strength and lasting hardly one-thousandth of a second – and numerous. Every second, millions pass through the network of long, pale, string-like pathways we call nerves. Information from the senses flows to the brain as electrical impulses. Here, it is sifted, analysed, and evaluated, causing millions more signals to pass around and within the brain between its numerous, complex areas. Decisions are reached and command messages are produced in the form of electrical impulses. The brain's electrical output travels along motor nerves to the muscles to stimulate and coordinate their contractions for movements. Different information carriers – hormones – instruct the endocrine glands on the timing and quantity of secretion required for the desired effect. More than 50 hormones circulate in the bloodstream. The specific molecular structure of each hormone

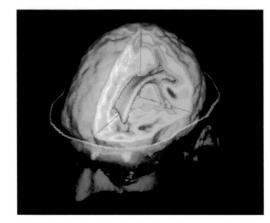

BRAIN ACTIVITY
This image is a three-dimensional, functional MRI scan showing brain activity during speech. Red indicates areas of high activity, yellow indicates medium activity, while green indicates low activity.

stimulates only cells with suitable receptors on their surface, instructing the cells to carry out certain procedures. In general, nerves work fast – within fractions of a second. Most hormones function over longer times – within minutes, days, or even months. Long-lasting effects, as in growth hormone for example, occur because the hormone is continuously secreted over many years; an individual dose would last only a few days.

BODY-CLOCK INPUT

The body has built-in rhythms of activity. People in experimental "timeless" surroundings (of constant light, temperature, food availability, and other conditions) still tend to sleep, wake, eat, become alert, and move about in a roughly 24-hour cycle. A small part of the brain known as the

suprachiasmatic nucleus, located just above the place where the visual, or optic, nerves meet (see p.79), is the "body clock". It is continually adjusted by external cues, such as light levels and temperature fluctuations, and our mental acknowledgment of clock times. In turn, it feeds information to many brain parts that deal with cyclical activities, such as hormone release, tissue repair, body temperature control, urine production, and digestive matters. In this way, the natural rhythms of the body are coordinated.

THE IMPORTANCE OF INPUT

As can be seen by the workings of the body clock, feeding information into the brain's processing centres relies on more than the five senses. The continuing environmental adjustment of the body clock is one example

SELECTIVE FOCUS
The nose detects smells continuously and sends endless streams of nerve signals to the brain. However, we can choose to ignore this information, or to focus on it, as part of the mind's selective awareness of incoming data.

of more subtle and complex sensory input. Within the body, there are thousands of microreceptors that continually monitor variables, such as blood pressure, body temperature, and levels of important chemicals, for example oxygen, waste carbon dioxide, and blood glucose. These data feed to "automatic" or subconscious parts of the brain, which make decisions that do not register in the conscious mind. In this way a huge amount of information processing occurs, of which we are hardly ever aware.

DAILY CYCLES
Hormone levels follow a 24-hour cycle. Melatonin, the "sleep hormone", both maintains and is affected by the rhythm control system. Aldosterone affects urine production. Cortisol is involved in many tasks, from influencing glucose levels to promoting healing and alleviating stress.

KEY
- Aldosterone
- Melatonin
- Cortisol

(Graph axes: HORMONE CONCENTRATION vs TIME (HOURS); DAY NIGHT DAY NIGHT; 12:00 18:00 00:00 06:00 12:00 18:00 00:00 06:00 12:00)

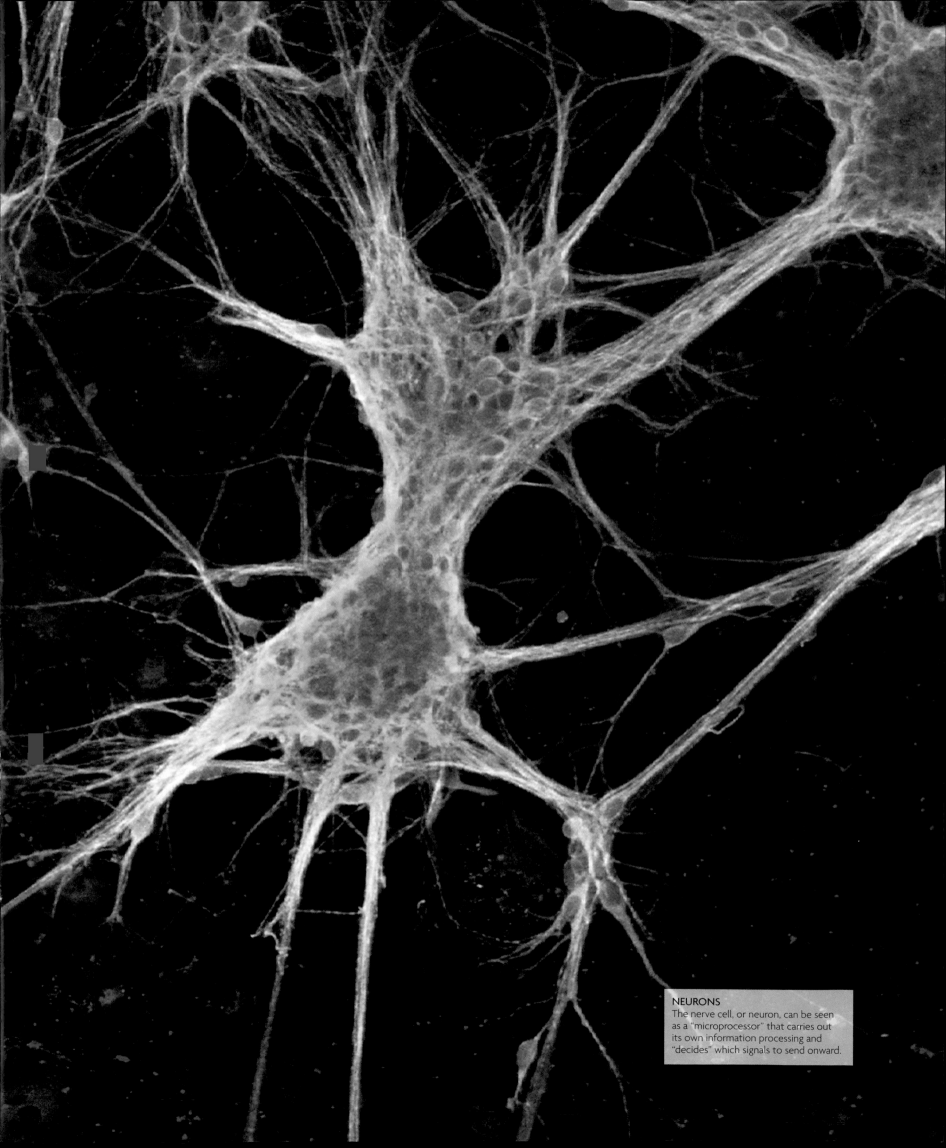

NEURONS
The nerve cell, or neuron, can be seen as a "microprocessor" that carries out its own information processing and "decides" which signals to send onward.

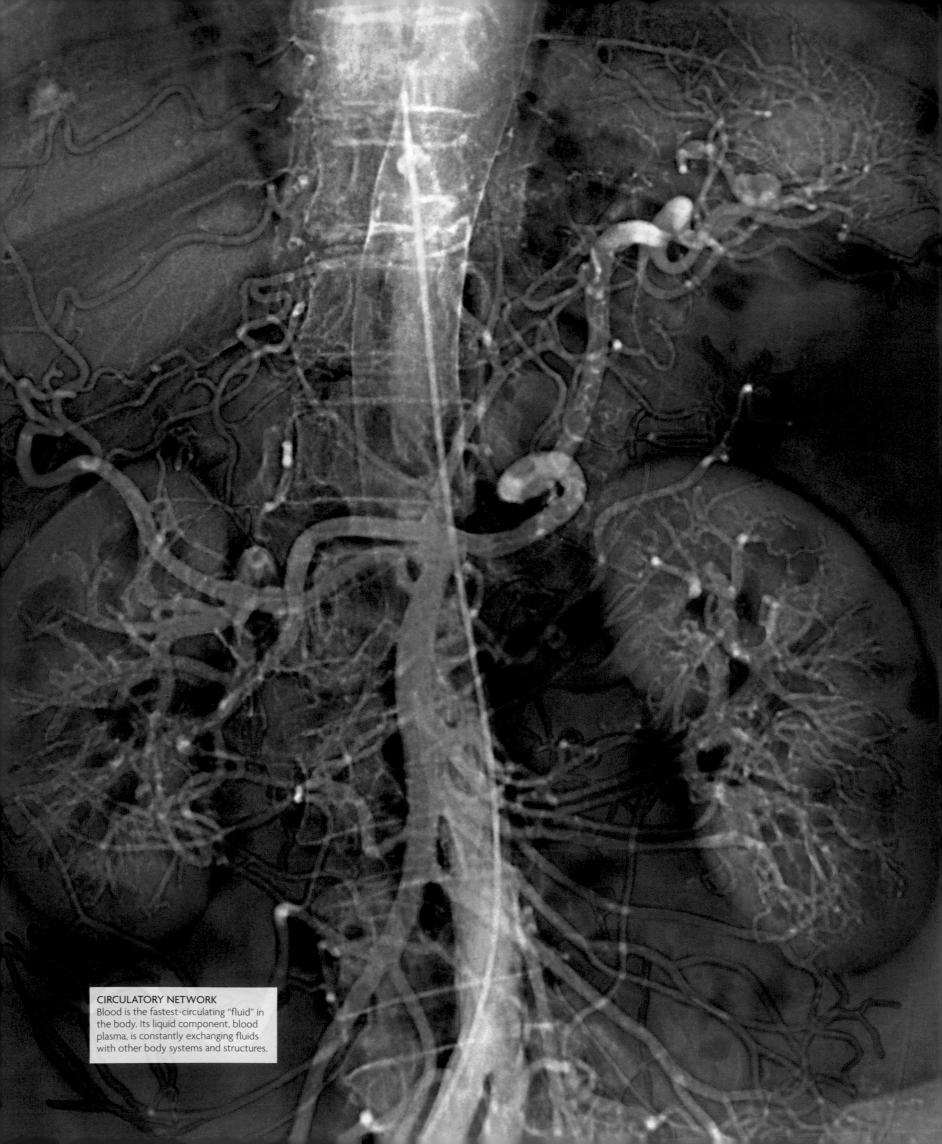

CIRCULATORY NETWORK
Blood is the fastest-circulating "fluid" in the body. Its liquid component, blood plasma, is constantly exchanging fluids with other body systems and structures.

THE FLUID BODY

ROUGHLY TWO-THIRDS OF THE BODY IS COMPOSED OF WATER AND THE VARIOUS
ESSENTIAL SUBSTANCES DISSOLVED WITHIN IT. THESE FLUIDS HAVE INNUMERABLE
VITAL ROLES WITHIN MANY BODY SYSTEMS. THEY ARE FOUND IN CELLS, AROUND
THE BODY'S TISSUES AND, MOST OBVIOUSLY, IN BLOOD AND LYMPH.

| CARDIOVASCULAR SYSTEM | 112–27 |
| LYMPH AND IMMUNITY | 154–69 |

Most body parts are largely composed
of water. Tissues are 70–80 per cent fluid,
which means that organs such as the
brain and intestines are typically three-
quarters water. Blood plasma is over
90 per cent water, while bones contain
almost 25 per cent. Fat has 10–15 per
cent water in its composition.

FLUID COMPARTMENTS
The body's different fluids can be
grouped into physiological categories
that are known as compartments.
There are two major fluid
compartments – intracellular and
extracellular. Intracellular fluid (also
known as cytoplasm) is found within the
body's cells. Extracellular fluid accounts
for all other fluids in the body. Its
subcompartments are: interstitial fluid,
which occupies the spaces between cells and
tissues; blood plasma and lymph; the fluids
found in bones, joints, and dense connective
tissue; and transcellular fluid which includes
saliva and other digestive juices, mucus,
sweat, and urine.

FUNCTIONS OF FLUIDS
Water is an excellent solvent. Thousands of
substances that are dissolved in it are used
in the body's biochemical reactions. These
reactions are the very basis of life. Water is

Blood plasma
The pressure produced by the
heart's pumping squeezes blood
plasma through capillary walls.

BLOOD PLASMA AND LYMPH CYCLE
Blood plasma leaks out from capillaries
to become interstitial fluid. Some
of this drains into lymph vessels and
becomes lymph fluid. Eventually this
fluid is returned to blood circulation, as
lymphatic vessels empty into large veins.

Lymph
Lymph vessels collect and
circulate the fluid, then route it
back into the blood circulation.

Interstitial fluid
The fluid, now under little
pressure, flows randomly and
slowly around cells and tissues.

also an effective transport system. It moves
around the body distributing nutrients and
collecting and delivering waste materials.
Fluids spread heat from active parts of
the body, such as exercising muscles, to
cooler areas, and in doing so they aid in
thermoregulation. The body uses fluids as
shock absorbers to cushion sensitive areas
such as the brain, the eyes, and the spinal
cord. Fluids also work as lubricants within
the body, so that tissues and organs slip
past each other with minimal friction. Small
amounts of specific fluids that specialize in
this role include the pleural fluid around the
lungs, the pericardial fluid around the heart,
and the synovial fluid inside joints.

BLOOD AND LYMPH
The blood and lymph circulatory
systems are closely linked because they
are constantly swapping fluids. Blood
plasma, the fluid in which blood cells
are suspended, transports red blood
cells (which carry oxygen and remove
carbon dioxide) around the body. Blood
plasma leaks from capillaries into the
tissues around them, becoming interstitial
fluid. Most of this leaked fluid is reabsorbed
into the blood, but
some of it is drawn into
the capillaries of the
lymphatic system where
it is used as lymph fluid.

This transports white blood cells (which
produce antibodies to fight infection and
disease) around the body. After flowing
through the lymphatic system, lymph
drains back into the blood stream once
again to be used as blood plasma.

BALANCE AND RECYCLING
The average adult body contains about 40
litres (70 pints) of water. Every day, water is
lost from the body in the form of urine,
sweat, water vapour from the lungs,
and in faeces. Water is used up and also
produced by the body in biochemical
reactions. For example, the glands
producing saliva and digestive juices. To
maintain a healthy balance of fluids, we
need to drink at least 2 litres (3½ pints)
of water per day. But if it were not for the
body's amazing water conservation and
recycling measures (such as recycling
blood plasma as lymph, and vice versa),
we would need to consume at least 100
times more water than the recommended
amount every day.

COMPONENTS OF BLOOD PLASMA

Blood cells are transported by blood plasma,
a liquid that accounts for about 55 per cent of
blood volume and is itself about 90 per cent
water. It contains many important substances.

PLASMA PROTEINS	Such as albumins (stop water leaking into the tissues), fibrinogen (involved in blood clotting), and globulins (such as antibodies).
ELECTROLYTES	Mainly mineral salts, that form ions when dissolved, principally sodium, chloride, potassium, calcium, and phosphate.
HORMONES	Like insulin and glucagon (regulate blood-glucose levels), thyroid hormones (control rate of cell metabolism), and sex hormones.
NUTRIENTS	Such as glucose (for energy), amino acids, and lipids, such as cholesterol and triglycerides (for cellular components and energy).
WASTES	Such as carbon dioxide, lactic acid, creatinine, and uric acid. These are transported out of the blood circulation by the kidneys.

1.4L (2½ PINTS) LYMPH

16.6L (29¼ PINTS)
INTERSTITIAL FLUIDS

20.3L (35¾ PINTS)
INTRACELLULAR
FLUIDS

1.1L (2 PINTS)
BLOOD IN ATERIES

4.15L (7¼ PINTS)
BLOOD IN VEINS

0.28L (½ PINTS)
BLOOD IN CAPILLARIES

VOLUMES OF MAJOR BODY FLUIDS
The fluids within cells (intracellular fluids) and around
cells and tissues (interstitial fluids) form the greatest
proportion of body liquids. This chart ignores many
other fluids, such as saliva and other secretions,
and fluid in bones, joints, and connective tissues.

EQUILIBRIUM

THE BODY'S CELLS AND TISSUES ARE DELICATE AND EASILY DISRUPTED. THEY ONLY FUNCTION WELL IF ALL ASPECTS OF THEIR CHEMICAL AND PHYSICAL ENVIRONMENT ARE CONTINUOUSLY ADJUSTED TO KEEP THEM STABLE AND IN EQUILIBRIUM. SEVERAL BODY SYSTEMS WORK TOGETHER TO MAINTAIN A BALANCED ENVIRONMENT, A PROCESS CALLED HOMEOSTASIS.

Chemical changes that occur inside every cell are attuned to specific conditions: body fluid concentration, oxygen levels, glucose and vital supplies, acid-alkali balance, and external circumstances, such as temperature and pressure. The body must maintain these internal conditions within certain limits, or its biochemical pathways go awry, waste builds up, energy runs out, and the resulting adverse effects rapidly spread.

HOMEOSTATIC SYSTEMS

Several body systems contribute to homeostasis. The respiratory system ensures that the body has a constant supply of oxygen, which is consumed when liberating

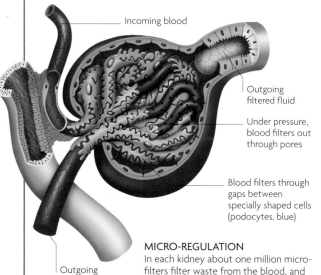

Incoming blood

Outgoing filtered fluid

Under pressure, blood filters out through pores

Blood filters through gaps between specially shaped cells (podocytes, blue)

Outgoing blood

MICRO-REGULATION
In each kidney about one million micro-filters filter waste from the blood, and regulate the amount of water, salts, and minerals it contains.

energy from nutrients, and cannot be stored in the body in any quantity. The digestive system takes in and processes nutrients, some of which are used for the repair and maintenance of old cells and tissues. The circulatory system ensures that oxygen and nutrients are distributed throughout the body, as well as gathering waste products, which are removed by the urinary and respiratory systems. The integumentary system (skin, hair, and nails) buffers the body's interior against the ever-varying external environment and fluctuations in temperature, moisture levels, and radiation.

CONTROL AND FEEDBACK

The body's two major control systems, nerves and hormones, are mainly responsible for coordinating homeostatic mechanisms using feedback loops. For example, if water levels fall slightly in the tissues, blood and other fluids become more concentrated. Various sensors monitor this, switch on, and feed back information to alert the brain. The brain's homeostatic centres trigger a sequence of regulating actions. Hormonal control of urinary excretion is adjusted to conserve water and nervous activity produces a thirst urge in our conscious awareness, so we take a drink to replenish water levels. The sensors detect the changes as fluid concentrations return towards normal, then they switch off until the next time they are needed. In this way, constant monitoring of internal conditions maintains a stable internal environment, so that cells and tissues can function with maximum efficiency.

THERMOREGULATION

One facet that demonstrates the intricacy of internal homeostasis and is obvious from the outside is thermoregulation – the maintenance of an approximately constant body temperature. The principle is much the same as a thermostat-equipped heater. When the thermostat sensor detects a fall

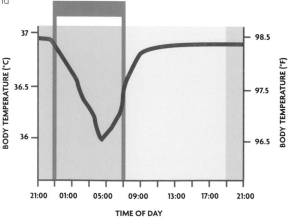

SLEEP

BODY TEMPERATURE (°C)

37

36.5

36

BODY TEMPERATURE (°F)

98.5

97.5

96.5

21:00 01:00 05:00 09:00 13:00 17:00 21:00
TIME OF DAY

DYNAMIC EQUILIBRIUM
The body's normal core temperature is about 37°C (98.6°F) when awake and active, falling to about 36°C (96.8°F) when asleep. Because the equilibrium point alters according to circumstances, it is called dynamic equilibrium.

in temperature, it switches on the heating; as the temperature reaches its required set point, it is switched off. In the body, active muscles generate heat, which is dissipated to all parts by blood flow. But a temperature variation of much more than 1°C (2°F) starts to affect the chemical reactions inside cells. Protein molecules, in particular – which include enzymes that control rates of reactions – are very heat-sensitive. They begin to distort and lose their complex three-dimensional structure when too warm. The body's temperature-sensing nerve endings trigger the thermostatic processes.

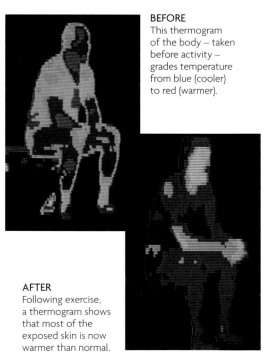

BEFORE
This thermogram of the body – taken before activity – grades temperature from blue (cooler) to red (warmer).

AFTER
Following exercise, a thermogram shows that most of the exposed skin is now warmer than normal.

Blood vessels in the skin widen to allow greater blood flow, which leads to increased heat loss to the surrounding air, while perspiration also occurs, so that warmth is drawn from the body by evaporation of watery sweat. In these ways, both the physical and chemical conditions inside the body are kept relatively stable, and an ongoing equilibrium is maintained.

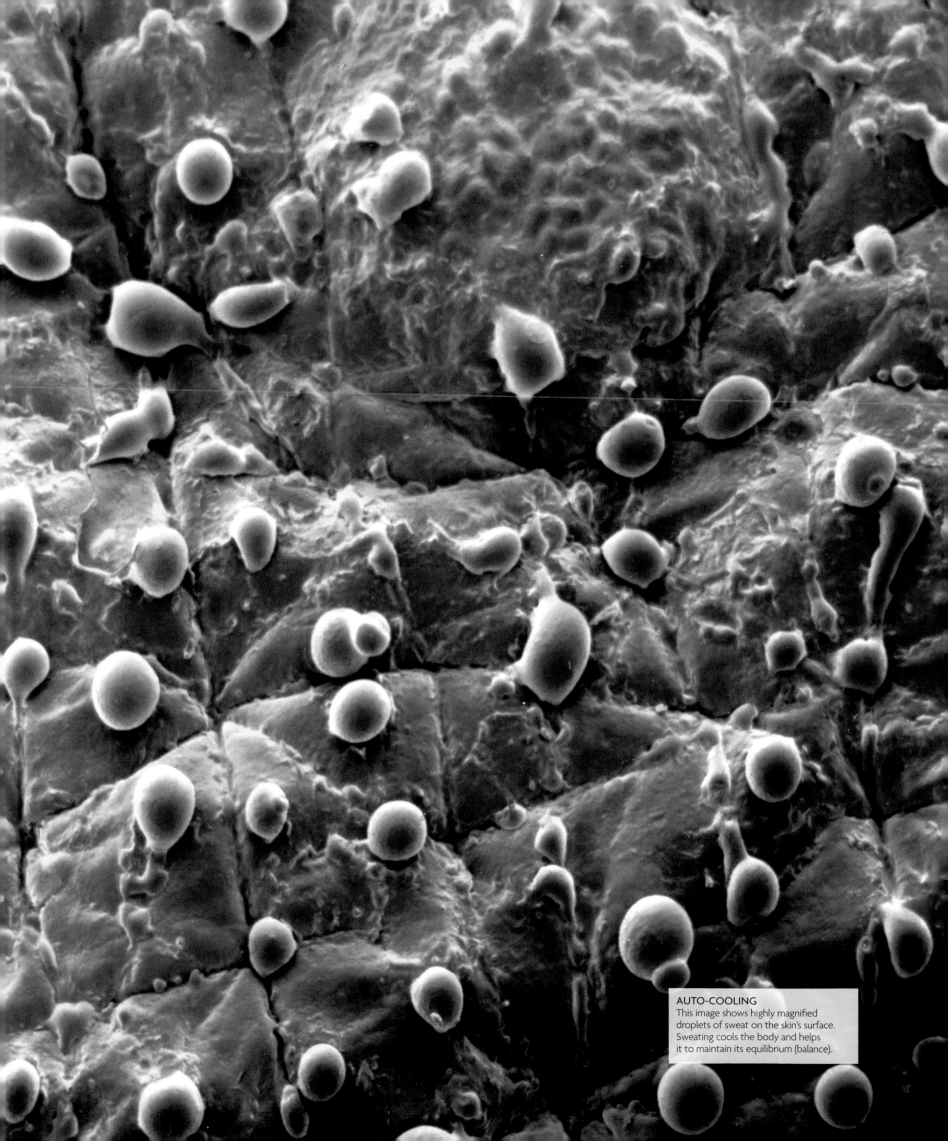

AUTO-COOLING
This image shows highly magnified droplets of sweat on the skin's surface. Sweating cools the body and helps it to maintain its equilibrium (balance).

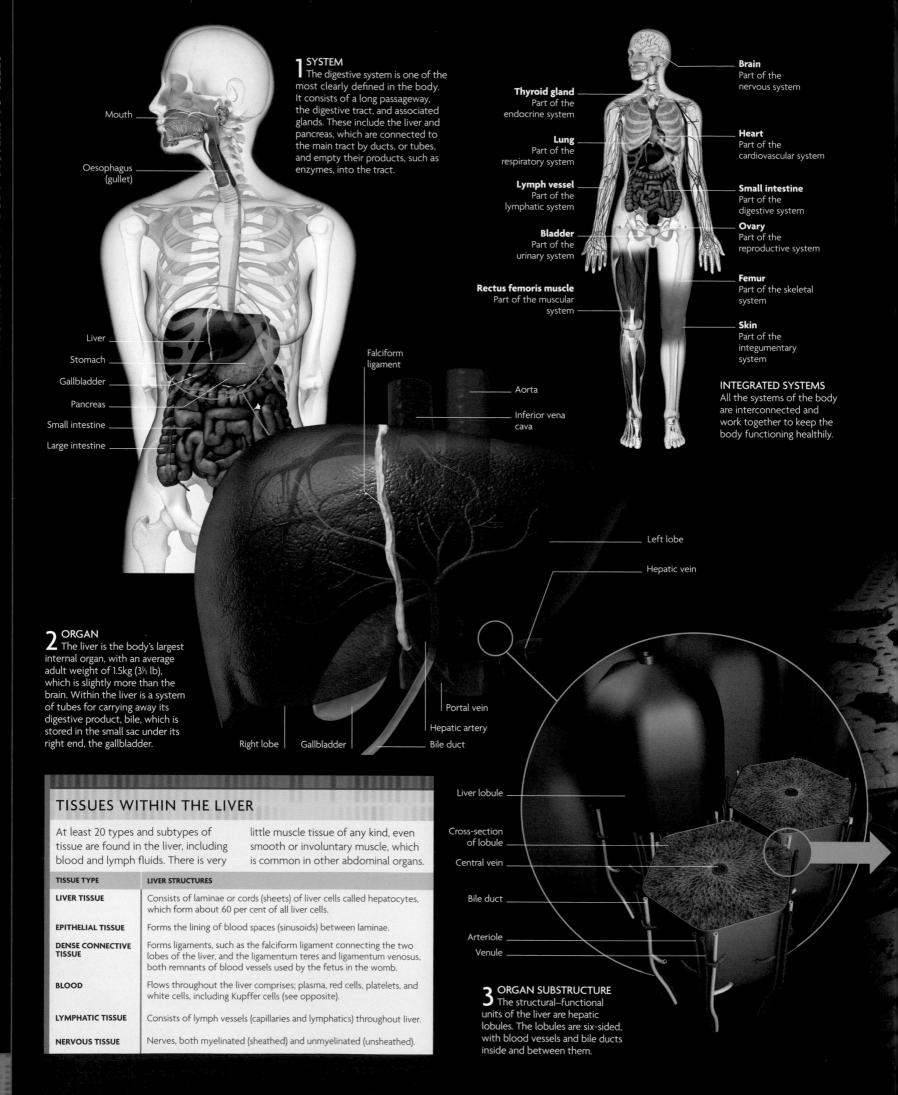

1 SYSTEM

The digestive system is one of the most clearly defined in the body. It consists of a long passageway, the digestive tract, and associated glands. These include the liver and pancreas, which are connected to the main tract by ducts, or tubes, and empty their products, such as enzymes, into the tract.

Mouth

Oesophagus (gullet)

Liver

Stomach

Gallbladder

Pancreas

Small intestine

Large intestine

Falciform ligament

Aorta

Inferior vena cava

Right lobe

Gallbladder

Portal vein

Hepatic artery

Bile duct

Brain
Part of the nervous system

Thyroid gland
Part of the endocrine system

Lung
Part of the respiratory system

Lymph vessel
Part of the lymphatic system

Bladder
Part of the urinary system

Heart
Part of the cardiovascular system

Small intestine
Part of the digestive system

Ovary
Part of the reproductive system

Rectus femoris muscle
Part of the muscular system

Femur
Part of the skeletal system

Skin
Part of the integumentary system

INTEGRATED SYSTEMS

All the systems of the body are interconnected and work together to keep the body functioning healthily.

2 ORGAN

The liver is the body's largest internal organ, with an average adult weight of 1.5kg (3⅓ lb), which is slightly more than the brain. Within the liver is a system of tubes for carrying away its digestive product, bile, which is stored in the small sac under its right end, the gallbladder.

Left lobe

Hepatic vein

Liver lobule

Cross-section of lobule

Central vein

Bile duct

Arteriole

Venule

TISSUES WITHIN THE LIVER

At least 20 types and subtypes of tissue are found in the liver, including blood and lymph fluids. There is very little muscle tissue of any kind, even smooth or involuntary muscle, which is common in other abdominal organs.

TISSUE TYPE	LIVER STRUCTURES
LIVER TISSUE	Consists of laminae or cords (sheets) of liver cells called hepatocytes, which form about 60 per cent of all liver cells.
EPITHELIAL TISSUE	Forms the lining of blood spaces (sinusoids) between laminae.
DENSE CONNECTIVE TISSUE	Forms ligaments, such as the falciform ligament connecting the two lobes of the liver, and the ligamentum teres and ligamentum venosus, both remnants of blood vessels used by the fetus in the womb.
BLOOD	Flows throughout the liver comprises; plasma, red cells, platelets, and white cells, including Kupffer cells (see opposite).
LYMPHATIC TISSUE	Consists of lymph vessels (capillaries and lymphatics) throughout liver.
NERVOUS TISSUE	Nerves, both myelinated (sheathed) and unmyelinated (unsheathed).

3 ORGAN SUBSTRUCTURE

The structural–functional units of the liver are hepatic lobules. The lobules are six-sided, with blood vessels and bile ducts inside and between them.

BODY SYSTEMS TO CELLS

BROADLY SPEAKING, EACH SYSTEM CAN BE SEEN AS A HIERARCHY OF LARGE COMPONENTS COMPOSED OF SMALLER ONES. THE SYSTEM ITSELF IS AT THE TOP OF THE HIERARCHY; NEXT ARE ITS ORGANS; BELOW THESE ARE THE TISSUES THAT MAKE UP THE ORGANS; AND AT THE BOTTOM OF THE HIERARCHY ARE THE CELLS THAT THE TISSUES ARE MADE FROM.

A system of the body is usually regarded as a collection of organs and parts designed for one important task. The systems are integrated and interdependent, but each has its own identifiable components and boundaries. The main parts of a system are its organs and tissues. (In the circulatory system, the heart is the essential organ and pumps the liquid tissue, blood, around the body.) Most organs are composed of different tissues. The brain, for example, contains not only nervous tissue but also connective and epithelial (covering or lining) tissues. In turn, a tissue is a group of microscopic cells, all similar in structure and carrying out the same specialized function (see pp.32–33).

MICRO-SECTION
In this magnified section of liver tissue the cells (pinkish purple) and their nuclei (dark purple) are visible. The white circular areas are fatty deposits that have built up in the tissue.

Kupffer cell
Also known as a hepatic macrophage; a type of white blood cell specific to the liver; engulfs and digests old worn-out blood cells and other debris

4 TISSUE
The unique tissue of the liver consists of branching sheets, or laminae, of liver cells (hepatocytes) arranged at angles. These are permeated by fluids and microscopic branches of two main kinds of tubes: blood vessels and bile ducts.

Cytoplasm

Cell membrane

Nucleus

Mitochondrion

5 CELL
The fundamental living unit of all tissues, a typical cell is capable of obtaining energy and processing nutrients. The hepatocytes of the liver are an example of body cells, containing most types of the miniature structures, called organelles, inside them.

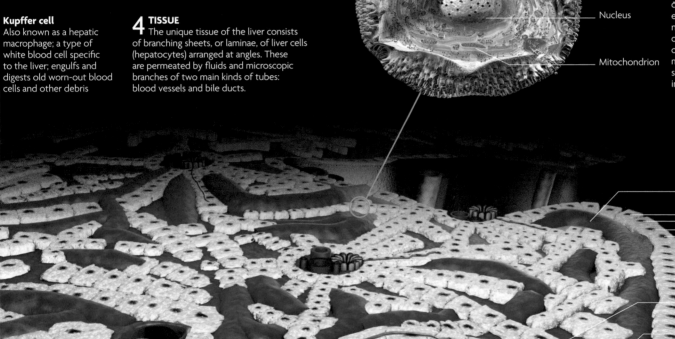

Sinusoid
A blood vessel with many pores that allow for the exchange of oxygen and nutrients

Hepatocytes

Bile canaliculus
Smallest branch of bile duct; snakes between hepatocytes

Bile duct
Collects bile fluid, made by hepatocytes, from canaliculi

Branch of hepatic portal vein

Branch of hepatic artery

Lymph vessel

Red blood cell

Central vein
Has its own endothelial cells forming its inner lining

White blood cell

Fat-storing cell

Vacuole
A sac that stores and transports ingested materials, waste products, and water

Nucleolus
The region at the centre of the nucleus that plays an important role in ribosome production

Nucleus
The cell's control centre, containing chromatin and most of the cell's DNA

Nuclear membrane
A two-layered membrane with pores through which substances enter and leave the nucleus

Cytoskeleton
Internal framework of the cell, comprised of microfilaments and hollow microtubules

Nucleoplasm
The fluid within the nucleus in which nucleolus and chromosomes float

Microfilament
Provides support for the cell; sometimes linked to the cell's outer membrane

Mitochondrion
The site of fat and sugar digestion in the cell; produces energy

Cytoplasm
Jelly-like fluid in which organelles float; primarily water but also contains enzymes and amino acids

Microtubules
Part of the cell's cytoskeleton; aid movement of substances through the watery cytoplasm

Centriole
Composed of two cylinders of tubules; essential to cell reproduction

Microvilli
Projections found on some cells; they increase the cell's surface area, helping absorption of nutrients

Released secretions
Secretions are released from the cell by exytosis – a vesicle merges with the cell membrane and releases its contents

Ribosome
Small structure that functions in protein assembly

Secretory vesicle
Sac that contains various substances, such as enzymes, that are produced by the cell and secreted at the cell membrane

Lysosome
Produces powerful enzymes that aid in digestion and excretion of substances and worn-out organelles

Cell membrane
Encloses contents of the cell, regulating the flow of substances into and out of the cell

Rough endoplasmic reticulum
Folded membranes extending throughout cell, studded with ribosomes; help transport materials through cell; site of much protein manufacture

Golgi complex
Organelle that processes and repackages proteins produced in rough endoplasmic reticulum for release at cell membrane

Smooth endoplasmic reticulum
Network of tubes and flat, curved sacs that helps to transport materials through cell; site of calcium storage; main location of fat metabolism

Peroxisome
Makes enzymes that oxidize some toxic chemicals

INSIDE A CELL
This generalized body cell shows all the tiny structures (organelles), each with a particular task. Liver cells may be the closest equivalent to such a "general" cell. A large number of an organelle indicates the cell's chief role.

THE CELL

THE CELL IS THE BASIC STRUCTURAL AND FUNCTIONAL UNIT OF THE BODY. IT IS THE SMALLEST PART CAPABLE OF THE PROCESSES THAT DEFINE LIFE, INCLUDING REPRODUCTION, MOVEMENT, RESPIRATION, DIGESTION, AND EXCRETION – ALTHOUGH NOT EVERY CELL HAS ALL OF THESE ABILITIES.

CELL ANATOMY

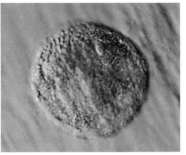

EMBRYONIC STEM CELL
All cells develop from one of two types of undifferentiated cell (stem cells), somatic or embryonic.

Most cells are microscopic – a typical cell is 20–30μm in diameter, which means 40 in a row would stretch across a full stop. Very specialized, long, thin cells include neurons (nerve cells) and muscle fibre cells (myofibres), which may extend more than 30cm (12in) but are incredibly thin. Most cells are bounded by an outer flexible "skin", the cell, or plasma, membrane. Inside is an array of structural components known as organelles, each with a characteristic shape, size, and function. These organelles do not float about at random. The cell is highly organized, with many interior chambers and compartments linked by sheets and membranes and held in place by a flexible, lattice-like, ever-changing "skeleton" of even tinier tubules and filaments.

CELL MEMBRANE

Several features allow the membrane to fulfil its dual responsibilities of protecting the cell within and permitting movement of materials into and out of the cell. The primary component of this membrane is a double layer of phospholipid molecules. Each phospholipid has a water-loving (hydrophilic) head group and two hydrophobic tails. The two layers are arranged with the heads on both the outside and inside of the cell membrane, and the tails in between. The phospholipids are interspersed with protein molecules and carbohydrate chains that allow the cell to be recognized by other body cells.

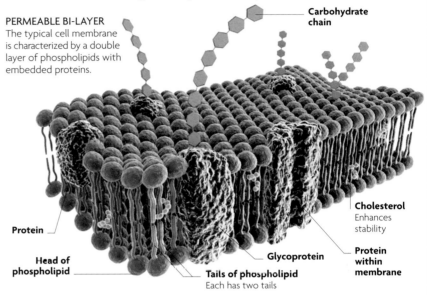

PERMEABLE BI-LAYER
The typical cell membrane is characterized by a double layer of phospholipids with embedded proteins.

Carbohydrate chain

Protein

Head of phospholipid

Tails of phospholipid
Each has two tails

Glycoprotein

Cholesterol
Enhances stability

Protein within membrane

MEMBRANES OF ORGANELLES

Membranes abound in the cell: they separate and divide the cytoplasm into sections and control the passage of materials between these regions; act as attachment points for ribosomes and other structures and as storage areas; and they shape channels along which substances move. Several important organelles are enclosed in their own membrane.

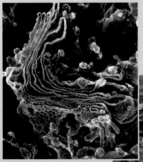

GOLGI COMPLEX
Within this stack of flattened membranous sacs protein from the endoplasmic reticulum is modified and repackaged.

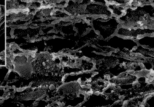

ENDOPLASMIC RETICULUM (ER)
A series of highly folded and curved ER membranes usually encloses one continuous labyrinthine space.

MITOCHONDRION
The inner membrane is folded in shelf-like, incomplete partitions to increase the surface area for releasing energy from sugars and fats. The outer membrane of a mitochondrion is smooth and featureless.

TRANSPORT

The transfer of materials through the cell membrane occurs by one of three processes. Small molecules such as glycerol, water, oxygen, and carbon dioxide cross the membrane by diffusion. Molecules that cannot cross the phospholipid layer must cross by facilitated diffusion. When substances (including minerals and nutrients) are in lower concentration on the outside of the cell than on the inside, they must be conveyed by active transport, requiring energy.

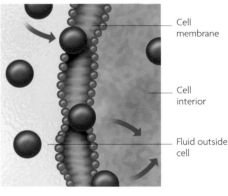

Cell membrane

Cell interior

Fluid outside cell

DIFFUSION
Many molecules naturally move from an area where they are in high concentration to one in which their numbers are fewer. This process is known as diffusion.

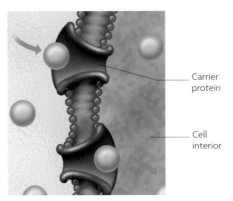

Carrier protein

Cell interior

FACILITATED DIFFUSION
A carrier protein binds with a specific molecule, such as glucose, outside the cell, then changes shape and ejects the molecule into the cell.

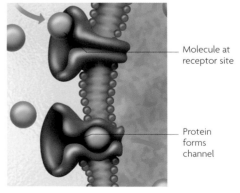

Molecule at receptor site

Protein forms channel

ACTIVE TRANSPORT
Molecules bind to a receptor site on the cell membrane, triggering a protein, which changes into a channel through which molecules travel.

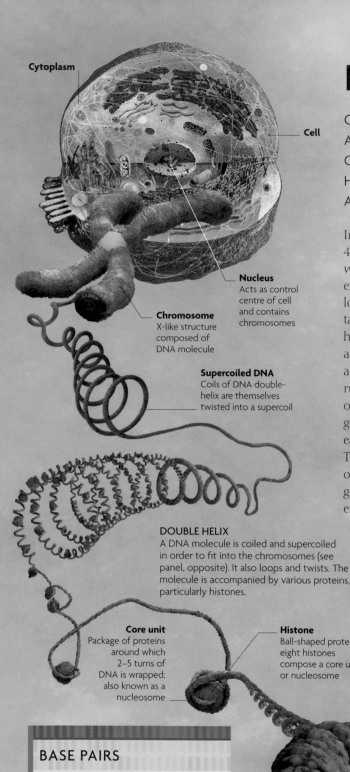

Cytoplasm

Cell

Nucleus
Acts as control
centre of cell
and contains
chromosomes

Chromosome
X-like structure
composed of
DNA molecule

Supercoiled DNA
Coils of DNA double-
helix are themselves
twisted into a supercoil

DNA

OFTEN REFERRED TO AS THE MOLECULE OF LIFE, DNA (DEOXYRIBONUCLEIC ACID) IS FOUND IN ALMOST ALL LIVING THINGS. IT ACTS AS A TYPE OF CHEMICAL CODE THAT CONTAINS INSTRUCTIONS, KNOWN AS GENES, FOR HOW THE BODY AND ALL ITS DIFFERENT PARTS GROW, DEVELOP, FUNCTION, AND MAINTAIN THEMSELVES.

In nearly all human cells, DNA is packaged into 46 X-shaped elements called chromosomes, which are situated in the cell's nucleus. DNA's enormous list of instructions takes the form of long, thin molecules, one per chromosome, each taking the shape of a double-helix. Each double-helix has two long, corkscrew-like strands, which act as "backbones" for the molecule, twining around each other. These are held together by rungs, like a twisted ladder. The rungs are made of pairs of chemicals called bases: adenine (A), guanine (G), thymine (T), and cytosine (C). In each rung, A always pairs with T, and G with C. This structure gives DNA its two key features: the order of the bases contains the chromosome's genetic code, while the way the bases cross-link enables DNA to make exact copies of itself.

DNA UNDER THE MICROSCOPE
This scanning tunnelling micrograph (STM) of DNA, magnified about one million times, shows the twists of the helix as a series of yellow peaks on the left.

DOUBLE HELIX
A DNA molecule is coiled and supercoiled in order to fit into the chromosomes (see panel, opposite). It also loops and twists. The molecule is accompanied by various proteins, particularly histones.

Core unit
Package of proteins
around which
2–5 turns of
DNA is wrapped;
also known as a
nucleosome

Histone
Ball-shaped protein;
eight histones
compose a core unit,
or nucleosome

Helical repeat
DNA helix twists
once for every 10.4
rungs of base pairs

Thymine

Adenine

Guanine

Adenine–thymine link
Adenine always forms a
base pair with thymine

Cytosine

Guanine–cytosine link
Guanine always forms a
pair with cytosine

DNA backbone
Constructed of
alternating units
of deoxyribose
(a form of sugar)
and phosphate
chemicals

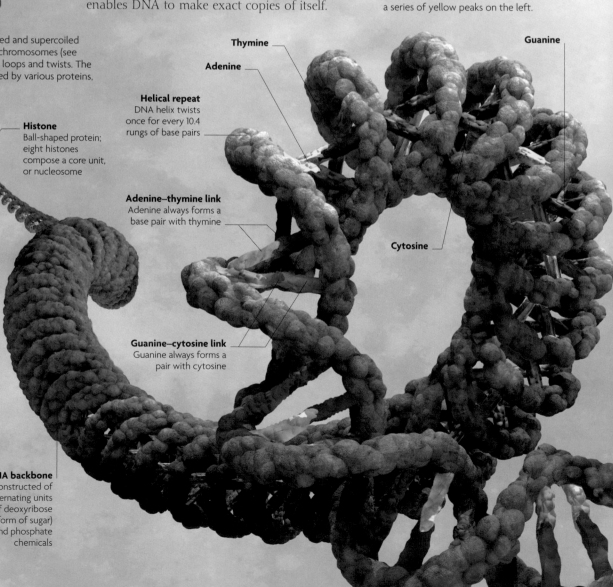

BASE PAIRS

The four bases can pair in only two configurations due to their chemical structures. Adenine and thymine each have two positions for forming hydrogen bonds and so fit together, while guanine and cytosine each have three hydrogen-bond locations.

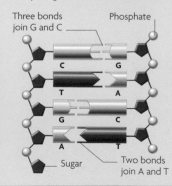

Three bonds
join G and C

Phosphate

C G

T A

G C

A T

Sugar

Two bonds
join A and T

HOW DNA WORKS

One of DNA's key functions is to provide the information to build proteins. Some proteins are the body's major structural molecules, others form enzymes, which control chemical reactions within the body. Manufacture of proteins occurs in two main phases, transcription and translation. In transcription, information is taken from the DNA and copied to an intermediate type of molecule called mRNA (messenger ribonucleic acid). This is built from nucleotide units in a similar way to DNA. The mRNA moves out of the cell's nucleus to protein assembly units called ribosomes. In the translation phase, the mRNA acts as a template for the formation of units of protein, known as amino acids. There are about 20 different amino acids. Their order is specified by lengths of mRNA three bases long, called triplet codons. The order of bases in each codon is the code for a particular amino acid (hence the term genetic code). The mRNA carries instructions to make a specific protein from a sequence of amino acids.

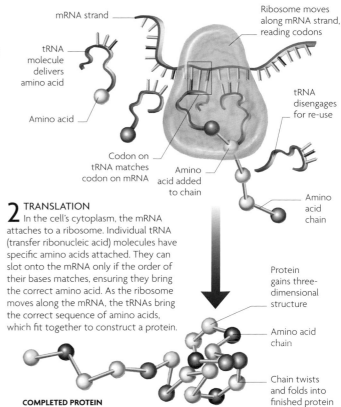

Nucleotide (one base, one sugar, and one phosphate)

mRNA builds according to DNA code

DNA strands separate

Unattached RNA nucleotide

1 TRANSCRIPTION
In the cell's nucleus, the DNA strands temporarily separate, with one acting as the template for the formation of mRNA. Separate RNA nucleotides with the correct bases lock onto the exposed DNA bases in cross-linked fashion, thereby forming a mirror image of the DNA's information.

mRNA strand

tRNA molecule delivers amino acid

Amino acid

Ribosome moves along mRNA strand, reading codons

tRNA disengages for re-use

Codon on tRNA matches codon on mRNA

Amino acid added to chain

Amino acid chain

Protein gains three-dimensional structure

Amino acid chain

Chain twists and folds into finished protein

2 TRANSLATION
In the cell's cytoplasm, the mRNA attaches to a ribosome. Individual tRNA (transfer ribonucleic acid) molecules have specific amino acids attached. They can slot onto the mRNA only if the order of their bases matches, ensuring they bring the correct amino acid. As the ribosome moves along the mRNA, the tRNAs bring the correct sequence of amino acids, which fit together to construct a protein.

COMPLETED PROTEIN

COILS AND SUPERCOILS

DNA's multi-coiled structure allows an incredible length to be packed into a tiny space. The single length of DNA in a typical chromosome, if unwound, would stretch about 5cm (2in). There are 46 chromosomes in the nucleus of each cell. (A few cell types, such as mature red blood cells, lack DNA.) When cells are not dividing, the DNA is loosely coiled and winds around the nucleus, forming a tangled-looking structure called chromatin. This allows portions to be available for protein assembly and other functions. As a cell prepares to divide, its DNA coils into supercoils, which are shorter and denser, and visible as the typical chromosome "X" shapes.

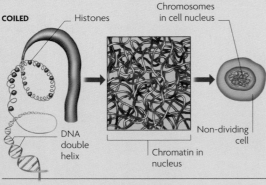

COILED

Histones

Chromosomes in cell nucleus

DNA double helix

Chromatin in nucleus

Non-dividing cell

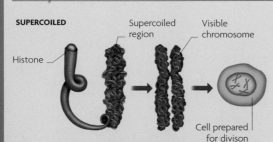

SUPERCOILED

Supercoiled region

Visible chromosome

Histone

Cell prepared for divison

WHAT ARE GENES?

A gene is generally regarded as a unit of DNA needed to construct one protein. It consists of all the sections of DNA that code for all the amino acids for that protein. These sections are not necessarily on the same strand of DNA or even on the same chromosome. There may be many strands of DNA, each containing the code for one portion of the protein. Typically, lengths of DNA called introns and exons are both transcribed (see below) to form immature mRNA. The parts of mRNA made from the introns are then stripped out by the cell's molecular machinery, leaving mature mRNA for translation. There are also regulatory DNA sequences that code for their own proteins, affecting the gene transcription rate.

EYE COLOUR
Iris colour is affected by at least three genes, called bey 1 and bey 2 on chromosome 15, and gey on chromosome 19.

PARTS OF A GENE
Regions called introns and exons both transcribe to form mRNAs for different portions of a protein. The lengths made from introns are then spliced out chemically, to leave exon-only portions, which go on to make the protein.

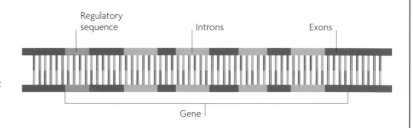

Regulatory sequence

Introns

Exons

Gene

RANGE OF GENE SIZE
Genes vary enormously in their size, which is usually measured in numbers of base pairs. Small genes may be just a few hundred base pairs long, while others are measured in millions of base pairs. The gene for beta-globin is one of the smallest. It codes for part of the haemoglobin molecule. It is compared, right, with a larger gene.

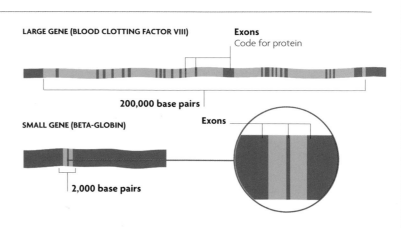

LARGE GENE (BLOOD CLOTTING FACTOR VIII)

Exons
Code for protein

200,000 base pairs

SMALL GENE (BETA-GLOBIN)

Exons

2,000 base pairs

THE GENOME

A GENOME IS THE FULL SET OF GENETIC INSTRUCTIONS FOR A LIVING THING, CONTROLLING ITS DEVELOPMENT FROM A SINGLE CELL INTO A COMPLEX, ADULT BODY. THE HUMAN GENOME CONSISTS OF AN ESTIMATED 30,000–35,000 GENES, CARRIED ON THE DOUBLE SET OF 46 CHROMOSOMES FOUND IN NEARLY EVERY KIND OF BODY CELL.

CHROMOSOMES AND DNA

The Human Genome Project, a multinational effort to map the sequence of the human genome, was completed in 2003. This research led to the identification of more than 30,000 individual human genes within 46 chromosomes that collectively includes 3.2 billion base pairs. Although much DNA does not provide codes for individual genes, known as non-coding and "junk" DNA, it may still regulate their function. Junk DNA differs from non-coding DNA in that its structure does not resemble that of genes. Mapping of the genome makes it possible for medical researchers to know which genes are involved in certain metabolic processes.

KARYOTYPE
A "group photograph" of all chromosomes from a cell, arranged in their pairs in a standard order, is known as a karyotype. It reveals if there are extra, missing, broken, or oddly banded chromosomes. This example is from a male (note the large curved "X" and small "Y" at bottom, right).

3%
Coding DNA (genes)

23%
Non-coding DNA

74%
Junk DNA

USEFUL AND "USELESS"
Only 3% of the genome's DNA is estimated to carry data to make proteins and other substances. Some non-coding and "junk" DNA may have unknown uses, such as guiding how fast other genes make products.

CHROMOSOMES
This scanning electron microscope image shows the coils and supercoils of a DNA double helix within each chromosome, shaped like a large fluffy brush.

CHROMOSOME COMPLEMENT
The full set of chromosomes in a human cell numbers 46. These consist of 22 equivalent pairs, one of each pair derived from the mother and one from the father. They are numbered from 1 (largest) to 22 (smallest). The 23rd pair is the sex chromosomes, XX signifying female and XY (as here) male. When coloured by chemical stains, dark and pale stripes called banding patterns show up on each chromosome. These allow researchers to "map" the locations of particular genes within the chromosome.

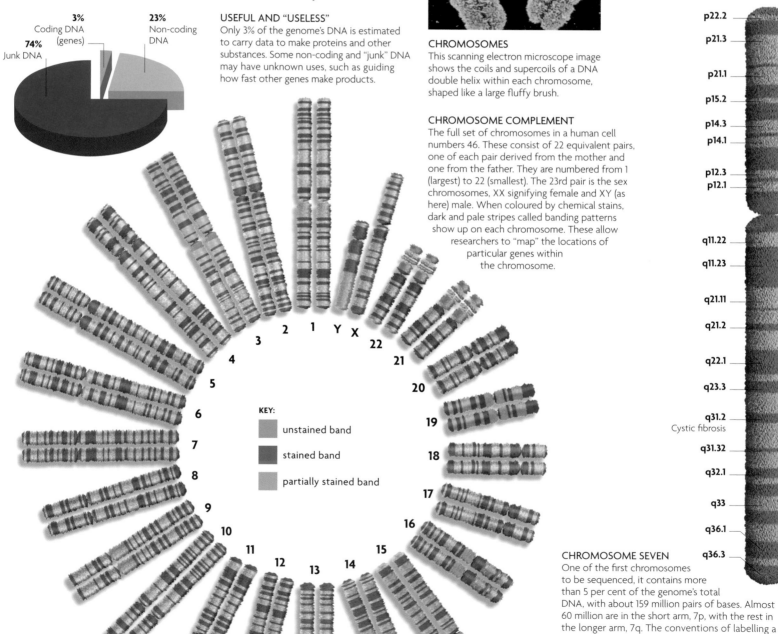

KEY:
- unstained band
- stained band
- partially stained band

Chromosome labels: 1, 2, 3, 4, 5, 6, 7, 8, 9, 10, 11, 12, 13, 14, 15, 16, 17, 18, 19, 20, 21, 22, Y, X

Chromosome seven band labels:
p22.2, p21.3, p21.1, p15.2, p14.3, p14.1, p12.3, p12.1, q11.22, q11.23, q21.11, q21.2, q22.1, q23.3, q31.2 (Cystic fibrosis), q31.32, q32.1, q33, q36.1, q36.3

CHROMOSOME SEVEN
One of the first chromosomes to be sequenced, it contains more than 5 per cent of the genome's total DNA, with about 159 million pairs of bases. Almost 60 million are in the short arm, 7p, with the rest in the longer arm, 7q. The conventions of labelling a chromosome make it possible to find the site of the gene if you know its "address". The cystic fibrosis gene (CFTR), for example, is located at 7q31.2.

CHROMOSOME		
NO.	GENES	EXAMPLES OF GENE FUNCTIONS
1	3,100	Pancreatic secretion; tumour suppression; type of collagen; coagulation factor V (F5)
2	1,900	Red hair colour; growth of bone and cartilage (BMPR2)
3	2,000	Rhodopsin retinal pigment (RHO); smell (olfactory receptors); DNA repair (MLH1)
4	1,200	Red hair colour (HCL2); coagulation factor XI; dentin (DSPP)
5	1,300	Taste receptor; growth hormone receptor; embryonic development (NIPBL)
6	1,500	Control of light-sensing pigments (RDS); iron balance (HFE); immune system (HLA-B)
7	1,500	Type of collagen; colour blindness (blue/yellow); growth-rate controlling factor
8	1,000	Fibroblast growth factor receptor 1; fat transport and breakdown (LPL)
9	1,100	Blood group; removal of excess cholesterol (ABCA1)
10	1,100	Fibroblast growth factor receptor 2; tumour suppression (PTEN)
11	1,800	Albinism (OCA1); beta haemoglobin (HBB); parathyroid hormone; calcitonin
12	1,400	Interferon; type of collagen; regulate muscle proteins (PPP1R12A)
13	550	Cholesterol-lowering factor; coagulation factors VII and X
14	1,300	Thyroid-stimulating hormone factor; coagulation factor C
15	950	Brown and blue eye colour (Bey 1/Bey 2); brown hair colour (HC13); albinism (OCA2)
16	1,100	Alpha haemoglobin; skin colour – melanin (MC1R); breakdown of fatty acids (MLYCD)
17	1,500	Growth hormone; tumour suppression (FLCN); urea production in liver (NAGS)
18	400	Controlling inflammation (MEFV); tumour suppression (SMAD4)
19	1,700	Green eye colour (Gey 1); brown hair colour (HCL1); protection of nerve cells (PRX)
20	700	Embryonic development (JAG1); nervous system function (PRNP)
21	350	Calcium channels in cardiac muscle and ears (KCNE1)
22	700	Tumour suppression (CHEK2); normal nerve function (NEFH)
X	1,300	Colour blindness (red/green); maternal–fetal interface role; brain development (CDKL5)
Y	300	Sex determination; skeletal development (SHOX), also present on X chromosome

MITOCHONDRIAL GENES

Mitochondria have their own DNA (also known as mtDNA), RNA, and ribosomes, and therefore can make many of their own proteins. Unlike nuclear DNA, which is arranged on chromosomes, the mitochondrial DNA molecule forms circular, double-stranded chains that are 16,500 base pairs in length. Each chain has 37 genes, 13 that code for proteins, 22 for transfer RNAs, and 2 for ribosomal RNAs. There are more than 1,000 identical molecules of mtDNA in humans. Mitochondrial DNA has been used to study genetic relationships because it has a high mutation rate and is inherited primarily through the mother, thereby making it possible to trace specific genetic lines.

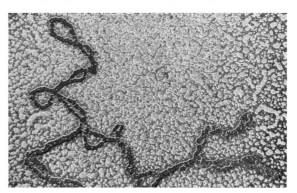

MITOCHONDRIAL NUCLEOID
Known as a nucleoid, mitochondrial DNA forms a closed loop, unlike other, open-ended, DNA. This electron microscope image shows several circular loops and reveals that the molecule is often twisted.

GENETIC CONTROL OF CELLS

Not all genes are active and working in all cells. The process by which a gene is able to make its protein or other substance is known as gene expression. Some types of genes are "switched on" and express themselves in most cells. These are genes concerned with basic life processes and "housekeeping", such as breaking down glucose sugar for energy and building cellular membranes. Other genes are switched off; these are for making specialized products, such as hormones, or particular proteins, like the actin and myosin filaments that pack muscle cells. Cell specialization involves certain genes being switched on or off, according to exposure to chemicals such as growth factors and regulators – products of other genes.

CELLULAR DIFFERENTIATION
The first cells produced by divisions of a fertilized egg are "generalized". As they build in numbers, preprogrammed instructions begin to act. Patterns of intercellular contacts and the chemical environment inform cells in certain parts of an embryo to differentiate and become tissues such as nerves, muscle, and skin.

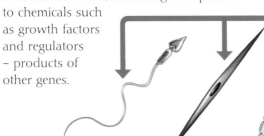

PRECURSOR CELL

PRECURSOR CELL
This can become any of a variety of cells. Some lines of offspring cells retain the ability to specialize, while others go on to become specialists

SPERM CELL
Packed with mitochondria to supply fuel

MUSCLE CELL
Long, thin cells packed with contractile proteins

NERVE CELL
Extreme specialization in shape and connections

EPITHELIAL CELL
Programmed to multiply rapidly and then die

FAT CELL
Stores energy in case diet does not meet energy requirements

STEM CELLS

A stem cell is a "beginner" or undifferentiated cell, which retains the ability both to keep dividing for self-renewal of its population, and to become specialized in certain conditions. Embryonic stem cells occur in the early embryo, and have the ability to differentiate into any of the 200-plus types of specialized cells in the eventual body. Adult stem cells occur in certain tissues where they multiply rapidly as part of ongoing maintenance. In the bone marrow they produce millions of different blood cells every second.

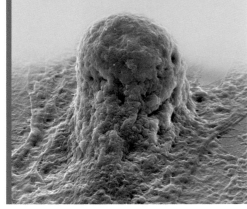

CELL TYPES AND TISSUES

MORE THAN 200 TYPES OF SPECIALIZED CELL POPULATE THE HUMAN BODY. THEY DEVELOP WITH THEIR OWN KIND TO FORM CLOSELY KNIT CONFIGURATIONS, WHICH ARE CLEARLY RECOGNIZABLE AS SPECIFIC TYPES OF TISSUE. IN SOME CASES, TISSUES ARE MADE OF SEVERAL TYPES OF CELLS.

TISSUE TYPES

The cells that form tissue all have much the same structure and perform the same function. Classically there are four primary tissue types, derived from specific cell layers in the early embryo: epithelial, connective, muscle, and nerve. Blood, bone, cartilage, tendons, and ligaments are forms of connective tissue. The epidermis and the tissues that line almost every organ are all types of epithelial tissues. Muscle and nerve tissues, of course, form muscles and nerves.

NERVE TISSUE

An immunofluorescent microscope image showing glial cells that support message-conducting nerve cells (neurons) in nerve tissue, and are known as neuroglia. Among these are astrocytes (light green spider-like forms). These supply neurons with nutrients.

White matter Contains long, wire-like insulated nerve fibres

Grey matter Contains nerve-cell bodies and support cells

CROSS-SECTION OF BRAIN FROM THE FRONT

LOOSE CONNECTIVE TISSUE

Some connective tissue (in parts of the lower layer of skin, for example) is made up of cells that are loosely embedded in fibres. Here, the nuclei of fibroblast cells (dark spots) can be seen among fibres of elastin (dark lines) and collagen (broad purple stripes).

Connective dermal tissue Connects dermis of skin (pictured) to underlying organs

CELL TYPES

Cells come in many shapes and sizes, depending on their specialized functions within tissues. Speed of cell division also varies. It is most rapid in epithelial (covering and lining) cells, which are subjected to physical abrasion and wear, and which must continually replace themselves. It is slow or even non-existent in structurally complex cells such as nerve cells (neurons).

Epithelial cells These cells form skin, cover most organs, and line hollow cavities. The cells shown here are from the top surface of the intestinal tract.

Smooth muscle cell The large, elongated, spindle-like cells of smooth muscle are known as muscle fibres. The shape allows for contraction by means of sliding strands of protein inside.

Photoreceptor cell A cone cell is a type of light-sensitive cell that is found in the retina of the eye. Cone cells are activated by bright light and are responsible for colour perception.

Nerve cell Each cell has a configuration of short extensions (dendrites) to receive nerve signals, and a long "wire" (axon) to send signals to other cells.

Red blood cell The red cell (erythrocyte) is a bag of oxygen-carrying haemoglobin molecules. Its double-dished (biconcave) shape allows for rapid, maximal oxygen absorption.

Sperm cell Each sperm has a head that carries the paternal set of genetic material, and a long, whip-like tail which propels it towards the egg.

Adipose (fat) cell The main adipose cells, adipocytes, are bulky and crammed with droplets of fat (lipids), which store energy in case the diet cannot meet requirements.

Ovum (egg) cell These giant cells contain the maternal complement of genetic material, and energy resources for the first cell divisions that shape the early embryo.

Elastic cartilage Light and bendy; holds the larynx open

Hyaline cartilage Tough yet flexible; the most common type of cartilage

LARYNX

ELASTIC CARTILAGE

Cartilaginous tissues (types of connective tissue) have varying properties depending on cell proportions and type of tissue structure. This microscope image of an epiglottis reveals rounded cells (chondrocytes) in fibres of elastin, making it lightweight, flexible, and strong.

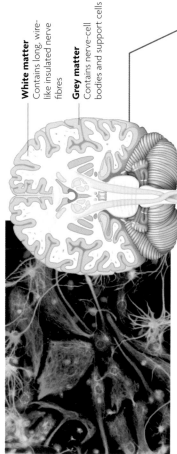

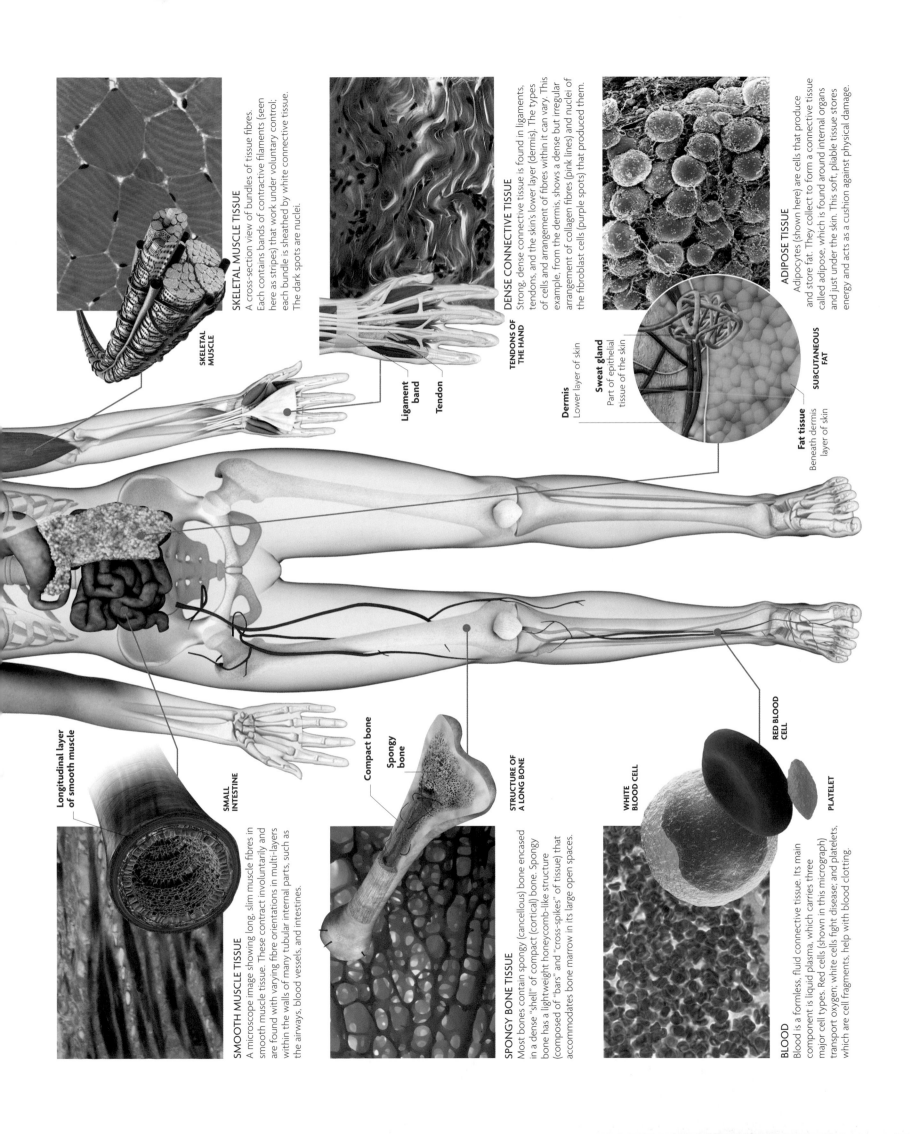

SKELETAL MUSCLE TISSUE

A cross-section view of bundles of tissue fibres. Each contains bands of contractive filaments (seen here as stripes) that work under voluntary control: each bundle is sheathed by white connective tissue. The dark spots are nuclei.

SKELETAL MUSCLE

Ligament band

Tendon

TENDONS OF THE HAND

DENSE CONNECTIVE TISSUE

Strong, dense connective tissue is found in ligaments, tendons, and the skin's lower layer (dermis). The types of cells and arrangement of fibres within it can vary. This example, from the dermis, shows a dense but irregular arrangement of collagen fibres (pink lines) and nuclei of the fibroblast cells (purple spots) that produced them.

Dermis
Lower layer of skin

Sweat gland
Part of epithelial tissue of the skin

Fat tissue
Beneath dermis layer of skin

SUBCUTANEOUS FAT

ADIPOSE TISSUE

Adipocytes (shown here) are cells that produce and store fat. They collect to form a connective tissue called adipose, which is found around internal organs and just under the skin. This soft, pliable tissue stores energy and acts as a cushion against physical damage.

SMOOTH MUSCLE TISSUE

A microscope image showing long, slim muscle fibres in smooth muscle tissue. These contract involuntarily and are found with varying fibre orientations in multi-layers within the walls of many tubular internal parts, such as the airways, blood vessels, and intestines.

Longitudinal layer of smooth muscle

SMALL INTESTINE

SPONGY BONE TISSUE

Most bones contain spongy (cancellous) bone encased in a dense "shell" of compact (cortical) bone. Spongy bone has a lightweight honeycomb-like structure (composed of "bars" and "cross-spikes" of tissue) that accommodates bone marrow in its large open spaces.

Compact bone

Spongy bone

STRUCTURE OF A LONG BONE

BLOOD

Blood is a formless, fluid connective tissue. Its main component is liquid plasma, which carries three major cell types. Red cells (shown in this micrograph) transport oxygen; white cells fight disease; and platelets, which are cell fragments, help with blood clotting.

RED BLOOD CELL

WHITE BLOOD CELL

PLATELET

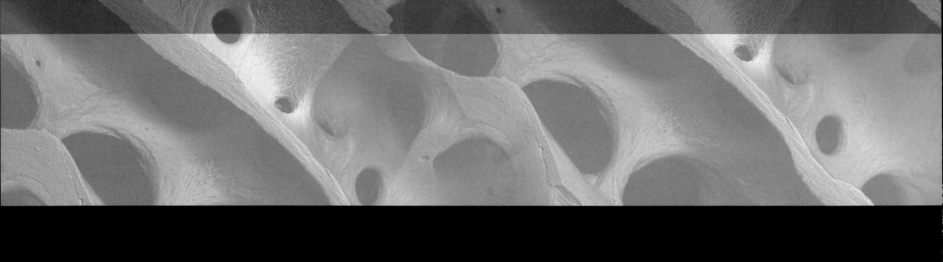

WITH ITS HIGHLY ENGINEERED JOINTS, THE LIVING SKELETON
IS INTIMATELY CONNECTED WITH THE MUSCULAR SYSTEM. IT
PROVIDES A FRAMEWORK OF STIFF LEVERS AND STABLE PLATES
THAT PERMITS A MULTITUDE OF MOVEMENTS. THE SKELETON

SKELETAL SYSTEM

SKELETON

THE SKELETON MAKES UP ALMOST ONE-FIFTH OF A HEALTHY BODY'S WEIGHT. THIS FLEXIBLE INNER FRAMEWORK SUPPORTS ALL OTHER PARTS AND TISSUES, WHICH WOULD COLLAPSE WITHOUT SKELETAL REINFORCEMENT. THE SKELETON ALSO PROTECTS CERTAIN ORGANS, SUCH AS THE DELICATE BRAIN INSIDE THE SKULL. IN ADDITION, BONES ARE RESERVOIRS FOR IMPORTANT MINERALS, ESPECIALLY CALCIUM, AND ALSO MAKE NEW CELLS FOR THE BLOOD.

The average skeleton has 206 bones. There are natural variations: about one individual in 20 has an extra rib. The number of small bones fused into the skull also varies. Bone is an active tissue, and even though it is about 22 per cent water, it has an extremely strong yet lightweight and flexible structure. A similar frame made of high-technology composite materials could not match the skeleton's weight, strength, and durability. The skeleton also has the advantage of being able to repair itself if damaged. It can also remodel its bones to thicken and strengthen them in areas of extra stress, as seen in some activities such as horse riding and weight lifting. The two major divisions of the skeleton are called the axial and appendicular skeletons. The axial skeleton consists of the skull, vertebral (spinal) column, ribs, and sternum. The appendicular skeleton includes the bones of the shoulder, arm, wrist, and hand, andthe hips, legs, ankles, and feet. Of the 206 bones, 80 are in the axial skeleton, with 64 in the upper appendicular and 62 in the lower appendicular skeleton.

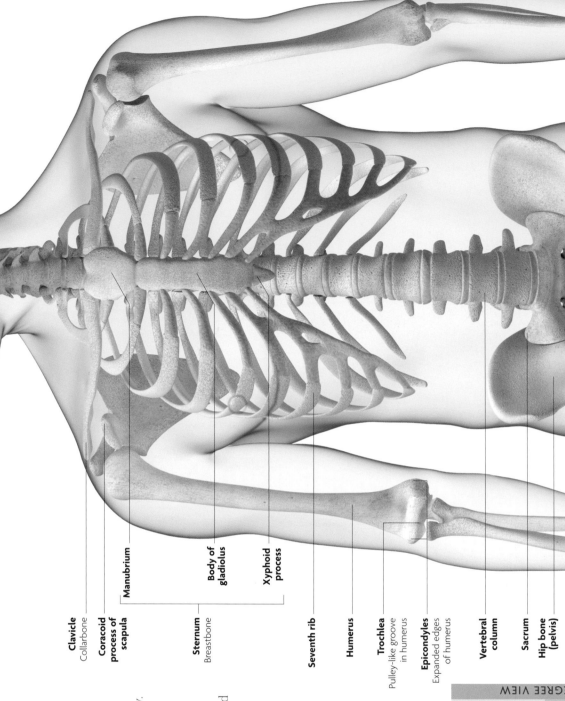

Cranium
Skull

Mandible
Jawbone

Clavicle
Collarbone

Coracoid process of scapula

Manubrium

Body of gladiolus

Xyphoid process

Sternum
Breastbone

Seventh rib

Humerus

Trochlea
Pulley-like groove in humerus

Epicondyles
Expanded edges of humerus

Vertebral column

Sacrum

Hip bone (pelvis)

Radius

Ulna

Carpals
Wrist bones

360-DEGREE VIEW

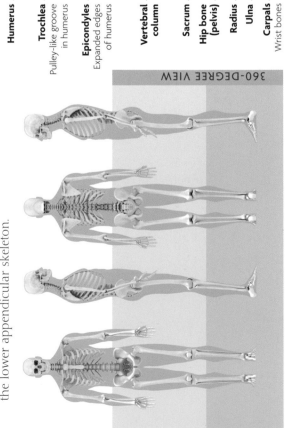

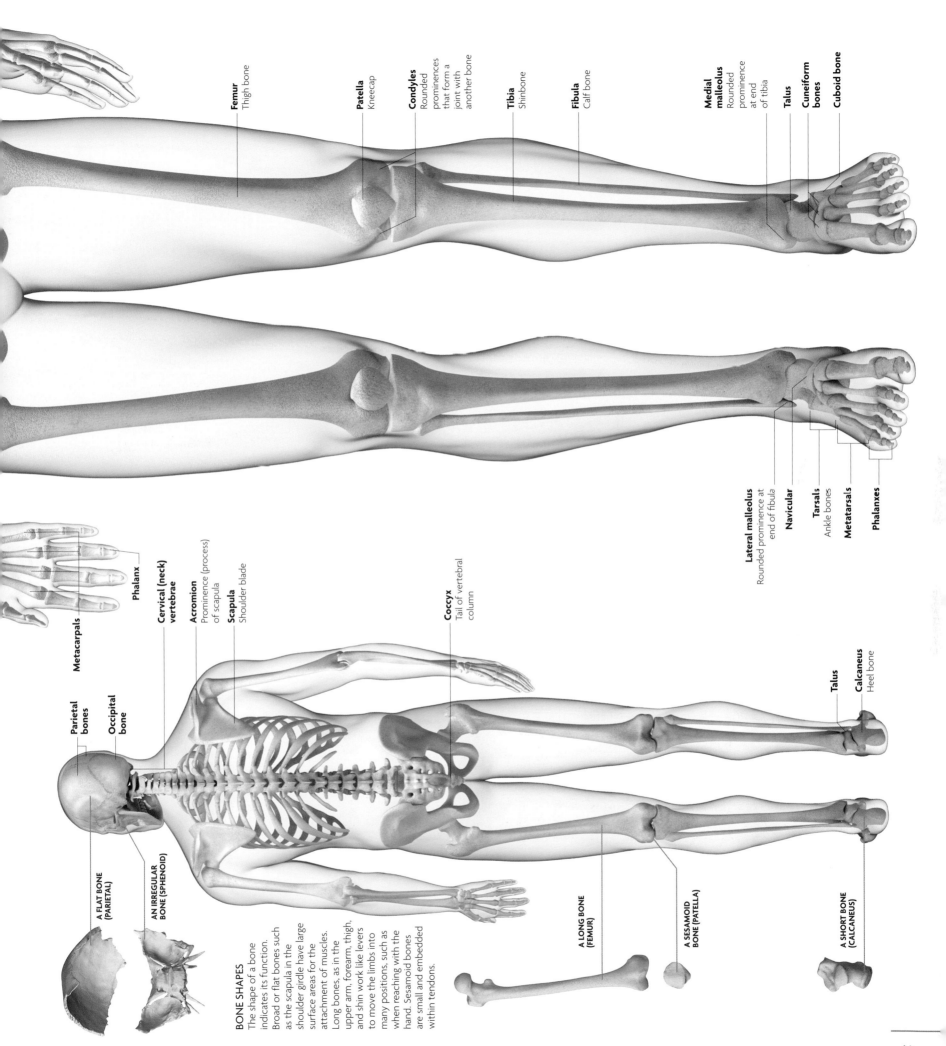

Femur
Thigh bone

Patella
Kneecap

Condyles
Rounded prominences that form a joint with another bone

Tibia
Shinbone

Fibula
Calf bone

Medial malleolus
Rounded prominence at end of tibia

Talus

Cuneiform bones

Cuboid bone

Lateral malleolus
Rounded prominence at end of fibula

Navicular

Tarsals
Ankle bones

Metatarsals

Phalanxes

Metacarpals

Phalanx

Cervical (neck) vertebrae

Acromion
Prominence (process) of scapula

Scapula
Shoulder blade

Coccyx
Tail of vertebral column

Talus

Calcaneus
Heel bone

Parietal bones

Occipital bone

BONE SHAPES

The shape of a bone indicates its function. Broad or flat bones such as the scapula in the shoulder girdle have large surface areas for the attachment of muscles. Long bones, as in the upper arm, forearm, thigh, and shin work like levers to move the limbs into many positions, such as when reaching with the hand. Sesamoid bones are small and embedded within tendons.

A FLAT BONE (PARIETAL)

AN IRREGULAR BONE (SPHENOID)

A LONG BONE (FEMUR)

A SESAMOID BONE (PATELLA)

A SHORT BONE (CALCANEUS)

BONE STRUCTURE

BONE IS A TYPE OF CONNECTIVE TISSUE THAT IS AS STRONG AS STEEL, BUT AS LIGHT AS ALUMINIUM. IT IS MADE OF SPECIALIZED CELLS AND PROTEIN FIBRES. NEITHER IMMOBILE NOR DEAD, BONE CONSTANTLY BREAKS DOWN AND REBUILDS ITSELF. EACH BONE ADJUSTS ITS SIZE AND SHAPE DURING THE GROWING PROCESS, AFTER AN INJURY, AND IN RESPONSE TO STRESS.

STRUCTURE OF A BONE

Along the central shaft of a long bone (such as the femur, tibia, or humerus) is the medullary canal or marrow cavity. This contains red bone marrow, which produces blood cells; yellow marrow, which is mostly fatty tissue; and plentiful blood vessels. Surrounding the marrow cavity is a layer of spongy (cancellous) bone, the honeycomb-like cavities of which also contain marrow. Around this is a shell-like layer of compact (cortical) bone, which is hard, dense, and strong. Small canals connect the marrow cavity with the periosteum – a membrane covering the bone surface. Bone tissue is made of specialized cells and protein fibres, chiefly collagen, woven into a matrix of water, mineral crystals and salts, carbohydrates, and other substances. Bone cells include osteoblasts, which calcify bone as it forms; osteocytes, which maintain healthy bone structure; and osteoclasts, which absorb bone tissue where it is degenerating or not needed.

COMPACT BONE
Compact, or cortical, bone is composed of tiny rod-like cells called osteons. Under a microscope, these can be seen bundled tightly together, an arrangement that provides great strength.

Blood vessel
Rich network of blood vessels nourishes bone

INSIDE A BONE
Long bones, for example those in the leg, have most types of bone tissue. The ratio of compact to spongy bone varies with age and activity, reflecting the physical stresses placed on the bone.

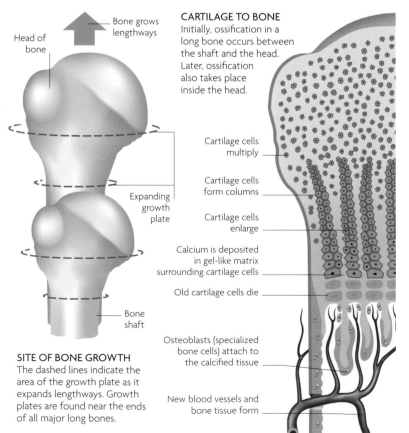

Periosteum
Thin, fibrous membrane covering entire bone surface (except in joints)

Compact bone
Bone gets its strength from this hard, shell-like tissue

BONE CELLS

Healthy bones depend on three types of cells, formed (along with blood cells) in the marrow. Osteoblasts at first manufacture bone as the skeleton grows. They then turn into osteocytes, which sustain the surrounding bone tissue. Osteoclasts are large cells with several nuclei that break down unwanted or unhealthy bone.

OSTEOCYTE IN BONE
This greatly magnified picture shows an osteocyte bone cell within a tiny cavity (lacuna) in compact bone.

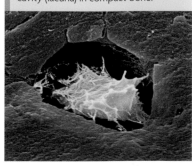

BONE GROWTH

During development in the womb and infancy, most bones develop from structures made of cartilage. Ossification is the process by which the cartilage tissue of these structures is converted into bone tissue by the deposition of mineral salts and crystals, mainly phosphates and carbonates of calcium. Much of the increase in height during childhood comes from lengthening long bones. Near each end of a long bone is an area known as the growth plate, where lengthening and ossification both occur. Cartilage cells (see opposite) multiply here and form columns towards the bone shaft. As the cartilage cells enlarge and die, the space they occupied is filled by new bone cells. In this way the growth plate moves along the lengthening bone shaft, remaining between the shaft and the head of the bone.

Bone grows lengthways

Head of bone

Expanding growth plate

Bone shaft

SITE OF BONE GROWTH
The dashed lines indicate the area of the growth plate as it expands lengthways. Growth plates are found near the ends of all major long bones.

CARTILAGE TO BONE
Initially, ossification in a long bone occurs between the shaft and the head. Later, ossification also takes place inside the head.

Cartilage cells multiply

Cartilage cells form columns

Cartilage cells enlarge

Calcium is deposited in gel-like matrix surrounding cartilage cells

Old cartilage cells die

Osteoblasts (specialized bone cells) attach to the calcified tissue

New blood vessels and bone tissue form

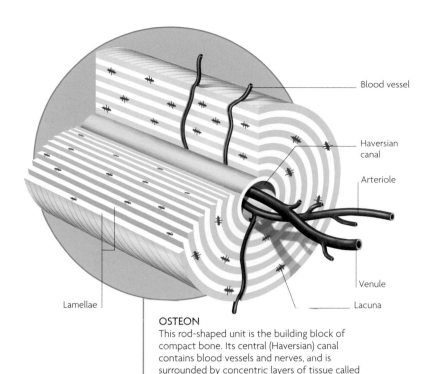

Blood vessel

Haversian canal

Arteriole

Venule

Lacuna

Lamellae

OSTEON
This rod-shaped unit is the building block of compact bone. Its central (Haversian) canal contains blood vessels and nerves, and is surrounded by concentric layers of tissue called lamellae. Gaps (lacunae) in the tissue contain osteocyte cells, which keep bones healthy.

CARTILAGE
Cartilage is a tough, highly adaptable form of connective tissue. It consists of a gel-like matrix containing many chemicals, such as proteins and carbohydrates. In this are embedded various types of fibres, and cells called chondrocytes that make and maintain the whole tissue. The chondrocytes occupy small cavities or spaces, known as lacunae. Cartilage does not usually have any blood vessels – instead it receives nutrients and oxygen by diffusion, and wastes move by the same process in the opposite direction. There are several kinds of cartilage, including hyaline cartilage, fibrocartilage, and elastic cartilage, which are classified according what proportion of matrix jelly, chondrocytes, and fibre they have. The most flexible is elastic cartilage due to its high proportion of elastin fibres and relatively little matrix. It provides lightweight, flexible support at sites such as the outer ear flap, epiglottis, and larynx.

HYALINE CARTILAGE
Dense collagen fibres make this cartilage extra tough and resistant. It covers bone ends in joints, attaches ribs to the sternum, and is also found in the trachea and nose.

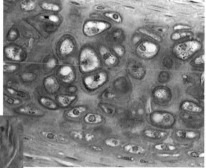

Osteon

Bone marrow
Tissue filling a bone's central cavity; at first (as shown here) long bones have red marrow – later this turns into yellow marrow

FIBROCARTILAGE
This is mostly dense bundles of collagen fibres, with little gel-like matrix. It is found in the jaw, knee meniscus, and intervertebral discs.

Spongy bone
Latticework structure consisting of bony spikes (trabeculae), arranged along lines of greatest stress

Vein

Epiphysis
Expanded head of bone containing mainly spongy bone tissue

Bone shaft
Long shaft is mostly marrow and compact bone

Artery

BLOOD FACTORY

Red bone marrow contains haemopoietic tissue, the chief function of which is to produce all three main kinds of blood cell: red; white; and platelets. At birth, red marrow is present in all bones, but with increasing age, in the long bones it gradually becomes yellow marrow and loses its blood-making capacity.

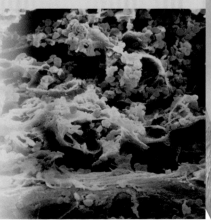

BLOOD CELL FORMATION
This microscopic image shows red marrow dotted with red blood cells destined for the bloodstream.

JOINTS

THE SITE AT WHICH TWO BONES LINK IS CALLED A JOINT OR AN ARTICULATION. JOINTS CAN BE CLASSIFIED ACCORDING TO THEIR STRUCTURE AND BY THE TYPES OF MOVEMENT THEY ALLOW. THE BODY HAS MORE THAN 300 DIFFERENT JOINTS.

SYNOVIAL JOINTS

The body's most numerous, versatile, and freely moving joints are known as synovial joints. They can work well for many decades if used well and often, but not overused. Synovial joints are enclosed by a protective outer covering – the joint capsule. The capsule's inner lining, called the synovial membrane, produces slippery, oil-like synovial fluid that keeps the joint well lubricated so that the joint surfaces in contact slide with minimal friction and wear. There are around 230 synovial joints in the body.

TYPES OF SYNOVIAL JOINT
A synovial joint's range of movement is determined by the shape of its articular cartilage surfaces (see p.41) and how they fit together.

SEMIMOVABLE AND FIXED JOINTS

Not all joints have a wide range of movement. Some allow for growth or for greater stability. The bones in these joints are usually linked by cartilage or tough fibres made of substances such as the protein collagen. In the fixed joints of the skull, once growth is complete, the separate bone plates are securely connected by interlocking fibrous tissue, forming suture joints.

Suture

FIXED JOINT
The adult skull's suture joints show up as wiggling lines. In infancy, these joints are loosely attached to allow for expansion of the rapidly growing brain.

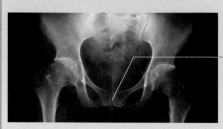

Pubic symphysis

SEMIMOVABLE JOINT
In partly flexible joints bones are linked by fibrous tissue or cartilage, as in the pubic symphysis.

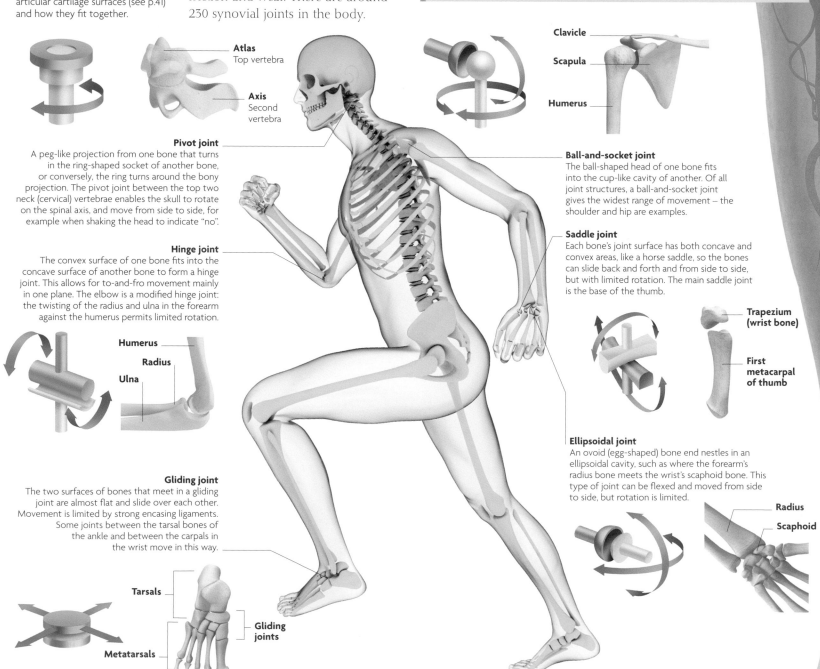

Atlas
Top vertebra

Axis
Second vertebra

Pivot joint
A peg-like projection from one bone that turns in the ring-shaped socket of another bone, or conversely, the ring turns around the bony projection. The pivot joint between the top two neck (cervical) vertebrae enables the skull to rotate on the spinal axis, and move from side to side, for example when shaking the head to indicate "no".

Hinge joint
The convex surface of one bone fits into the concave surface of another bone to form a hinge joint. This allows for to-and-fro movement mainly in one plane. The elbow is a modified hinge joint: the twisting of the radius and ulna in the forearm against the humerus permits limited rotation.

Humerus
Radius
Ulna

Gliding joint
The two surfaces of bones that meet in a gliding joint are almost flat and slide over each other. Movement is limited by strong encasing ligaments. Some joints between the tarsal bones of the ankle and between the carpals in the wrist move in this way.

Tarsals
Gliding joints
Metatarsals

Clavicle
Scapula
Humerus

Ball-and-socket joint
The ball-shaped head of one bone fits into the cup-like cavity of another. Of all joint structures, a ball-and-socket joint gives the widest range of movement – the shoulder and hip are examples.

Saddle joint
Each bone's joint surface has both concave and convex areas, like a horse saddle, so the bones can slide back and forth and from side to side, but with limited rotation. The main saddle joint is the base of the thumb.

Trapezium (wrist bone)
First metacarpal of thumb

Ellipsoidal joint
An ovoid (egg-shaped) bone end nestles in an ellipsoidal cavity, such as where the forearm's radius bone meets the wrist's scaphoid bone. This type of joint can be flexed and moved from side to side, but rotation is limited.

Radius
Scaphoid

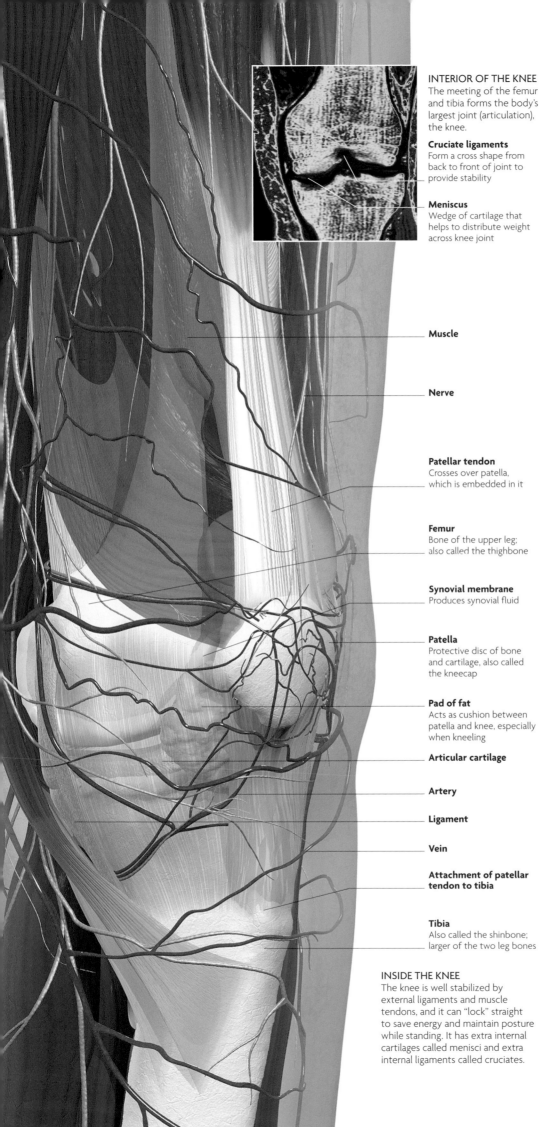

INTERIOR OF THE KNEE
The meeting of the femur and tibia forms the body's largest joint (articulation), the knee.

Cruciate ligaments
Form a cross shape from back to front of joint to provide stability

Meniscus
Wedge of cartilage that helps to distribute weight across knee joint

Muscle

Nerve

Patellar tendon
Crosses over patella, which is embedded in it

Femur
Bone of the upper leg; also called the thighbone

Synovial membrane
Produces synovial fluid

Patella
Protective disc of bone and cartilage, also called the kneecap

Pad of fat
Acts as cushion between patella and knee, especially when kneeling

Articular cartilage

Artery

Ligament

Vein

Attachment of patellar tendon to tibia

Tibia
Also called the shinbone; larger of the two leg bones

INSIDE THE KNEE
The knee is well stabilized by external ligaments and muscle tendons, and it can "lock" straight to save energy and maintain posture while standing. It has extra internal cartilages called menisci and extra internal ligaments called cruciates.

INSIDE A JOINT

The bone ends in a synovial joint are covered and protected by a type of cartilage called articular cartilage, which is smooth and slightly compressible. Surrounding the joint is the joint capsule, which is made of strong connective tissue and is attached to the bone ends. Its delicate inner lining, the synovial membrane, continuously secretes viscous synovial fluid into the synovial cavity to keep the joint well oiled. The fluid also nourishes the cartilage with fats and proteins, and is constantly reabsorbed. Fibrous thickenings of the capsule called ligaments are anchored to bones at each end. They prevent the bones moving too far or in unnatural directions. Muscles around the joint, and connected to its bones by tendons, tense for stability and contract to produce movement.

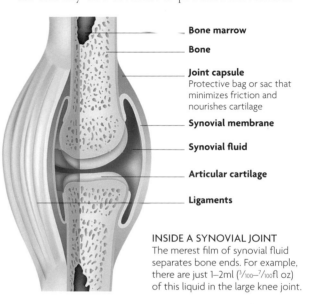

Bone marrow

Bone

Joint capsule
Protective bag or sac that minimizes friction and nourishes cartilage

Synovial membrane

Synovial fluid

Articular cartilage

Ligaments

INSIDE A SYNOVIAL JOINT
The merest film of synovial fluid separates bone ends. For example, there are just 1–2ml ($^3/_{100}$–$^7/_{100}$fl oz) of this liquid in the large knee joint.

CARTILAGE AS A SHOCK ABSORBER

The articular cartilage that coats the bone ends in a synovial joint is also known as hyaline cartilage (see p.39). When sudden knocks or vibrations jolt the joint, this cartilage works as a shock absorber to dissipate some of the force of the impact and so prevent jarring damage to the much stiffer bones. In certain joints the cartilage has tougher fibres. Examples include the fibrocartilaginous pads, called intervertebral discs, between the vertebrae of the backbone. Fibrocartilage also occurs in the jaw and wrist joints and the menisci in the knee.

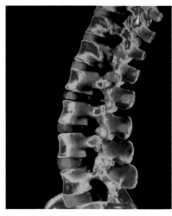

SPINAL CARTILAGE
The fibrocartilage discs between the vertebrae play an important role in stabilizing and cushioning the spinal column.

SKULL

THERE ARE, IN TOTAL, 29 BONES IN THE HUMAN HEAD – 22 BONES FORM THE SKULL ITSELF, WITH 21 OF THESE, EXCLUDING THE LOWER JAW, OR MANDIBLE, FUSED INTO A SINGLE, FIRM STRUCTURE. THE REMAINING BONES ARE THE HYOID BONE IN THE UPPER FRONT OF THE NECK AND THREE PAIRS OF TINY EAR BONES, CALLED OSSICLES, ONE SET LOCATED IN EACH MIDDLE EAR.

SKULL

Two groups of bones make up the skull. The upper set of eight bones forms the dome-like cranium (cranial skull or cranial vault), which encloses and protects the brain. The other 14 bones make the skeleton of the face. Twenty-one of the 22 bones become strongly fused during growth at faint joint lines, called sutures. The lower jaw, or mandible, remains unfixed and is linked to the rest of the skull at the two jaw, or temporomandibular, joints.

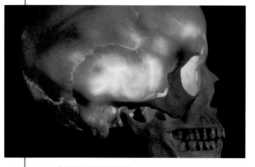

SKULL SUTURES
Lines on the skull's surface, highlighted here by backlighting, are the fused margins of the skull bones.

SINUSES

The four pairs of sinuses, known as paranasal sinuses, are air-filled cavities within the skull bones. They are named after the bones in which they are located: maxillary, frontal, sphenoidal, and ethmoidal sinuses. The first three pairs have fairly well-defined shapes. The ethmoidal sinuses are more honeycomb-like and variable.

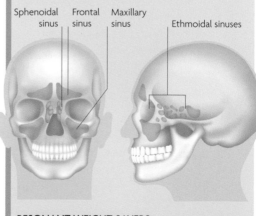

Sphenoidal sinus / Frontal sinus / Maxillary sinus / Ethmoidal sinuses

RESONANT WEIGHT-SAVERS
The sinuses help to lighten the skull's overall weight, and also act as resonating chambers to give each person's voice an individual character.

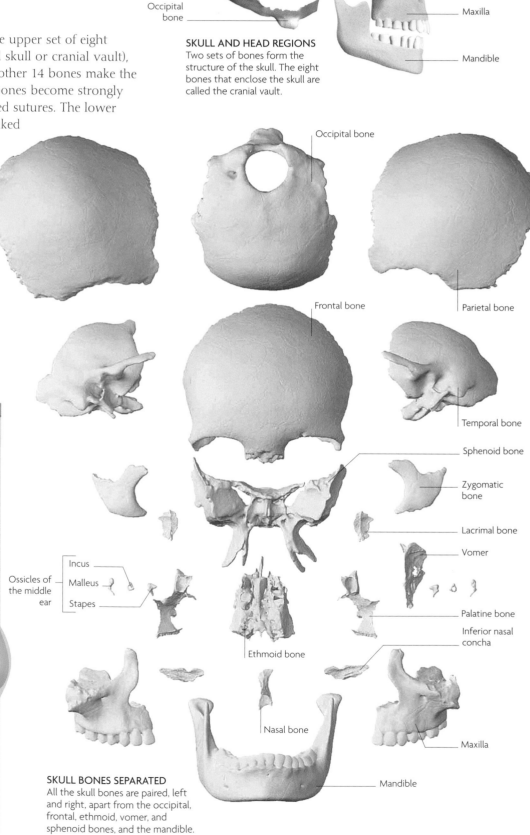

SKULL AND HEAD REGIONS
Two sets of bones form the structure of the skull. The eight bones that enclose the skull are called the cranial vault.

Parietal bone / Frontal bone / Ethmoid bone / Temporal bone / Lacrimal bone / Nasal bone / Zygomatic bone / Sphenoid bone / Maxilla / Occipital bone / Mandible

Occipital bone / Frontal bone / Parietal bone / Temporal bone / Sphenoid bone / Zygomatic bone / Lacrimal bone / Vomer / Palatine bone / Inferior nasal concha / Maxilla / Mandible / Nasal bone / Ethmoid bone

Ossicles of the middle ear: Incus / Malleus / Stapes

SKULL BONES SEPARATED
All the skull bones are paired, left and right, apart from the occipital, frontal, ethmoid, vomer, and sphenoid bones, and the mandible.

SPINE

THE SPINE IS ALSO KNOWN AS THE SPINAL OR VERTEBRAL COLUMN, OR SIMPLY "THE BACKBONE". THIS STRONG YET FLEXIBLE CENTRAL SUPPORT HOLDS THE HEAD AND TORSO UPRIGHT, YET ALLOWS THE NECK AND BACK TO BEND AND TWIST.

SPINE FUNCTION

The spine consists of 33 ring-like bones called vertebrae. The bottom nine vertebrae are fused into two larger bones termed the sacrum and the cocyx, leaving 26 movable components within the spine. These components are linked by a series of mobile joints. Sandwiched between the bones in each joint is the intervertebral disc, a springy pad of tough, fibrous cartilage that squashes slightly under pressure to absorb shocks. Strong ligaments and many sets of muscles around the spine stabilize the vertebrae and help to control movement. The spinal column also protects the spinal cord and allows nerve roots to exit through spaces in the vertebrae (see p.81).

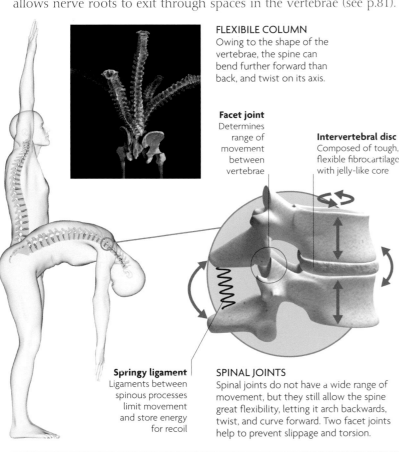

FLEXIBILE COLUMN
Owing to the shape of the vertebrae, the spine can bend further forward than back, and twist on its axis.

Facet joint
Determines range of movement between vertebrae

Intervertebral disc
Composed of tough, flexible fibrocartilage with jelly-like core

Springy ligament
Ligaments between spinous processes limit movement and store energy for recoil

SPINAL JOINTS
Spinal joints do not have a wide range of movement, but they still allow the spine great flexibility, letting it arch backwards, twist, and curve forward. Two facet joints help to prevent slippage and torsion.

HYOID BONE

The single U-shaped hyoid bone is located at the root of the tongue, just above the larynx. It is one of the few bones in the body that does not join directly to another bone. It is held in position by muscles and by the strong stylohyoid ligament on each side of the bone, which links to the styloid process of the skull's temporal bone. The hyoid stabilizes several sets of muscles used in swallowing and speech.

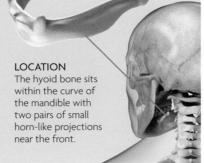

LOCATION
The hyoid bone sits within the curve of the mandible with two pairs of small horn-like projections near the front.

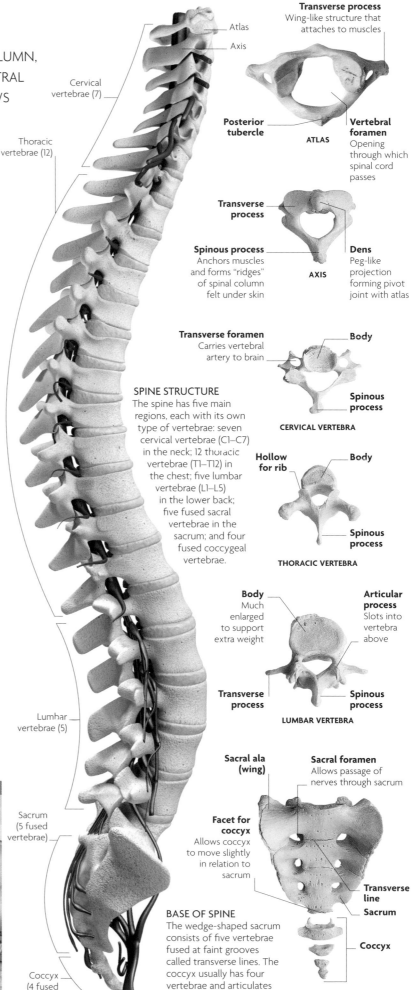

Atlas

Axis

Cervical vertebrae (7)

Thoracic vertebrae (12)

SPINE STRUCTURE
The spine has five main regions, each with its own type of vertebrae: seven cervical vertebrae (C1–C7) in the neck; 12 thoracic vertebrae (T1–T12) in the chest; five lumbar vertebrae (L1–L5) in the lower back; five fused sacral vertebrae in the sacrum; and four fused coccygeal vertebrae.

Lumbar vertebrae (5)

Sacrum (5 fused vertebrae)

Coccyx (4 fused vertebrae)

Transverse process
Wing-like structure that attaches to muscles

Posterior tubercle

ATLAS

Vertebral foramen
Opening through which spinal cord passes

Transverse process

Spinous process
Anchors muscles and forms "ridges" of spinal column felt under skin

AXIS

Dens
Peg-like projection forming pivot joint with atlas

Transverse foramen
Carries vertebral artery to brain

Body

Spinous process

CERVICAL VERTEBRA

Hollow for rib

Body

Spinous process

THORACIC VERTEBRA

Body
Much enlarged to support extra weight

Articular process
Slots into vertebra above

Transverse process

Spinous process

LUMBAR VERTEBRA

Sacral ala (wing)

Sacral foramen
Allows passage of nerves through sacrum

Facet for coccyx
Allows coccyx to move slightly in relation to sacrum

Transverse line

Sacrum

BASE OF SPINE
The wedge-shaped sacrum consists of five vertebrae fused at faint grooves called transverse lines. The coccyx usually has four vertebrae and articulates with the sacrum.

Coccyx

SACRUM AND COCCYX

RIBS, PELVIS, HANDS, AND FEET

THE RIBS AND HIPBONE (PELVIS) GUARD VITAL CHEST AND ABDOMINAL ORGANS, AND THEY DEMONSTRATE THE SKELETON'S TWIN FUNCTIONS OF SUPPORT AND PROTECTION. THE PELVIS PROVIDES SURFACES FOR ANCHORING THE POWERFUL HIP AND THIGH MUSCLES. THE WRISTS, HANDS, ANKLES, AND FEET, WHICH TOGETHER CONTAIN MORE THAN HALF OF ALL THE BONES IN THE BODY, ARE VITAL FOR COORDINATED MOVEMENT.

RIBCAGE

Most people have 12 pairs of ribs, but about 1 in 20 is born with one or more extra pairs. All ribs attach to the spinal column at the rear. The upper seven pairs of "true ribs" link directly to the breatbone (sternum) by their cartilage extensions (costal cartilages). The next two or three pairs of "false ribs" connect to the cartilages of the ribs above. The remaining "floating ribs" do not link to the sternum. The whole ribcage is flexible because the ribs tilt.

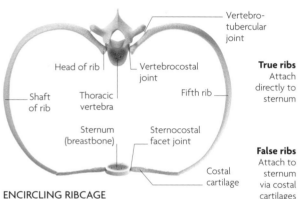

ENCIRCLING RIBCAGE
Each rib links to its corresponding chest (thoracic) vertebra at two points. Flexible costal cartilage attaches ribs to the sternum, allowing the ribcage to change volume during breathing.

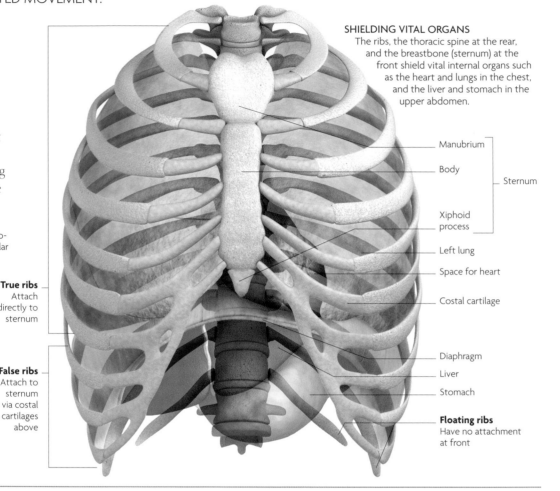

Vertebro-tubercular joint

Head of rib

Vertebrocostal joint

Shaft of rib

Thoracic vertebra

Fifth rib

Sternum (breastbone)

Sternocostal facet joint

Costal cartilage

True ribs
Attach directly to sternum

False ribs
Attach to sternum via costal cartilages above

SHIELDING VITAL ORGANS
The ribs, the thoracic spine at the rear, and the breastbone (sternum) at the front shield vital internal organs such as the heart and lungs in the chest, and the liver and stomach in the upper abdomen.

Manubrium

Body

Sternum

Xiphoid process

Left lung

Space for heart

Costal cartilage

Diaphragm

Liver

Stomach

Floating ribs
Have no attachment at front

PELVIS

Often referred to as the hipbone, the pelvis is a bowl-like structure consisting of the left and right innominate bones or ossa coxae, and the wedge-shaped sacrum and coccyx, which makes up a "tailbone" at the rear. Each innominate bone has three fused bony elements: the large, flaring ilium at the rear, which forms the hipbone you can feel under the skin; the ischium at the lower front; and the pubis above it. There are paired sacroiliac joints at the rear and the pubic symphysis, a semi-movable joint made of fibrocartilage, at the front. The shape of the pelvis is shallower and wider in females, with a larger gap, or pelvic inlet, and a greater pelvic outlet, to allow a baby to pass through at birth.

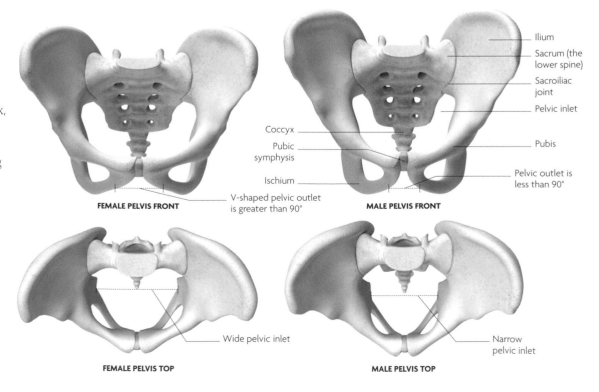

Ilium

Sacrum (the lower spine)

Sacroiliac joint

Pelvic inlet

Coccyx

Pubic symphysis

Pubis

Ischium

Pelvic outlet is less than 90°

FEMALE PELVIS FRONT

V-shaped pelvic outlet is greater than 90°

MALE PELVIS FRONT

Wide pelvic inlet

Narrow pelvic inlet

FEMALE PELVIS TOP

MALE PELVIS TOP

WRIST AND HAND

The wrist is made up of the eight carpal bones, arranged approximately in two rows of four. They are linked to each other chiefly by plane or gliding joints (see p.40), and to the forearm bones by the radiocarpal joint. The palm of the hand contains five metacarpal bones. Each of these joins at its outer end to the finger bone (phalanx), of which there are two in the thumb (first digit, or pollex) and three each in the other four digits. The entire structure is moved by more than 50 muscles, including several in the forearm, to provide great flexibility and delicate manipulation.

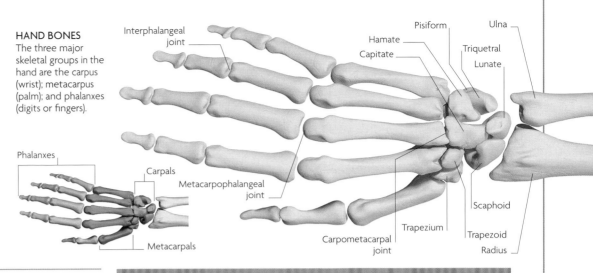

HAND BONES
The three major skeletal groups in the hand are the carpus (wrist); metacarpus (palm); and phalanxes (digits or fingers).

Interphalangeal joint · Pisiform · Ulna · Hamate · Triquetral · Capitate · Lunate

Phalanxes · Carpals · Metacarpophalangeal joint · Trapezium · Scaphoid · Carpometacarpal joint · Trapezoid · Radius · Metacarpals

ANKLE AND FOOT

The ankle and foot have a similar bone arrangement to the wrist and hand (see above), except there are only seven tarsal (ankle) bones. The build of the ankle and foot bones is heavier, for strength and weight-bearing stability at the expense of precision and mobility. The sole of the foot is supported by the five metatarsal bones. As in the hand, the hallux (first digit or big toe) has two phalanxes (toe bones), and the others have three each. The bony prominence commonly called the "heel bone" is formed by the calcaneus.

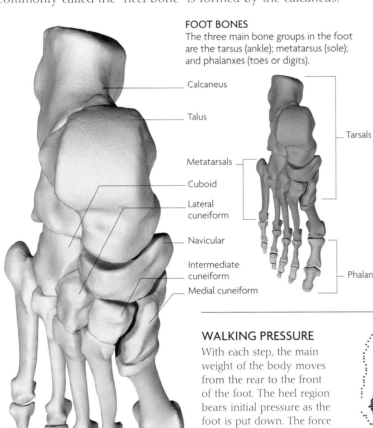

FOOT BONES
The three main bone groups in the foot are the tarsus (ankle); metatarsus (sole); and phalanxes (toes or digits).

Calcaneus · Talus · Tarsals · Metatarsals · Cuboid · Lateral cuneiform · Navicular · Intermediate cuneiform · Medial cuneiform · Phalanxes

LIGAMENTS

Ligaments are strong bands or straps of fibrous tissue that provide support to bones and link bone ends together in and around joints. They are made of collagen – a tough, elastic protein. A large number of ligaments bind together the complex wrist and ankle joints. Each one is named after the bones it links; for example, the calcaneofibular ligament links the calcaneus and the fibula. The foot ligaments store energy as they stretch when the foot is planted and then impart it again as they recoil and shorten to put a "spring in the step". This saves an enormous amount of energy when walking. Ligaments are susceptible to a wide range of injury as a result of the stresses and strains placed on them, especially during sport.

Fibula · Tibia · Calcaneofibular ligament · Calcaneus · Tibiofibular ligament · Ligaments connecting tarsals and metatarsals

ANKLE LIGAMENTS
More than a dozen ligaments bind the foot's tarsal bones to each other, and ligaments run from the tarsals to the fibula, tibia, and metatarsals (viewed here from outer side).

WALKING PRESSURE

With each step, the main weight of the body moves from the rear to the front of the foot. The heel region bears initial pressure as the foot is put down. The force passes along the arch, which flattens slightly, then recoils to transfer the energy and pressure to the ball of the foot, and finally to the big toe for the push-off.

LOAD AREAS ON THE FOOT
These footprint impressions show (from left to right) how the body's weight transfers from the heel to the ball to the big toe when walking.

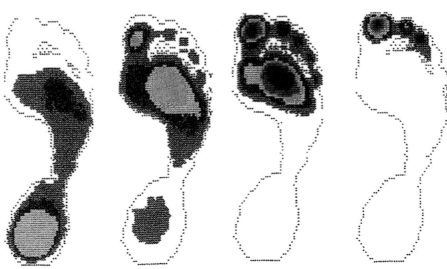

BONE DISORDERS

BONE STRENGTH GRADUALLY DECREASES WITH AGE AND, TOGETHER WITH INCREASED RISK OF FALLS, MAKES FRACTURES MORE COMMON IN THE ELDERLY. HOWEVER, FRACTURES ARE ALSO COMMON EARLY IN LIFE AS CHILDREN ARE LESS AWARE OF RISKS. OTHER FACTORS THAT INFLUENCE BONE HEALTH ARE NUTRITIONAL AND HORMONE DEFICIENCIES, LACK OF EXERCISE AND BEING OVERWEIGHT.

FRACTURE

BROKEN BONES – FRACTURES – RANGE FROM A MINOR CRACK IN THE BONE SURFACE TO A SPLIT PARTWAY THROUGH THE BONE, TO A COMPLETE BREAK.

Fractures may be caused by a sudden impact, by compression, or by repeated stress. A displaced fracture occurs when the broken surfaces of bone are forced from their normal positions. There are various types of displaced fracture, depending on the on the angle and strength of the blow. A compression fracture occurs when spongy bone, such as in the vertebrae, is crushed. Stress fractures are caused by prolonged or repeated force straining the bone; they occur in long-distance runners and in the elderly, in whom minor stress, such as coughing, may cause a fracture. Nutritional deficiencies or certain chronic diseases such as osteoporosis, which can weaken bone, may increase the likelihood of fractures. If a broken bone remains beneath the skin, the fracture is described as closed or simple, and there is a low risk of infection. If the ends of the fractured bones project through the skin, the injury is described as open or compound, and there is a danger of dirt entering the bone tissue and causing microbial contamination.

Bone repair

Despite its image as dry, brittle, and even lifeless, bone is an active tissue with an extensive blood supply and its own restorative processes. After a fracture, blood clots as it does elsewhere in the body. Fibrous tissue, and then new bone growth, bridge the break and eventually restore strength. However, medical treatment is often required to ensure that the repair process is effective and the result is not misshapen. If the bones are displaced, manipulation to restore their normal position – known as reduction – may be performed under anaesthesia. The bone will also be immobilized to allow the ends to heal correctly.

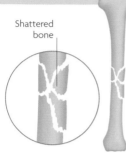
Shattered bone

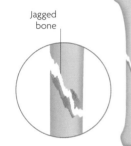

COMMINUTED FRACTURE
A direct impact can shatter a bone into several fragments or pieces. This type of fracture is likely to occur during a road traffic accident.

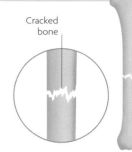
Cracked bone

TRANSVERSE FRACTURE
A powerful force may cause a break across the bone width. The injury is usually stable; the broken surfaces are unlikely to move.

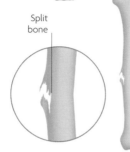
Split bone

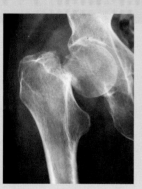
Jagged bone

GREENSTICK FRACTURE
A crack on one side of a long bone caused by the bone bending under force. This common in children, whose bones are flexible.

SPIRAL FRACTURE
A sharp, twisting force may break a bone diagonally across the shaft. The jagged ends may be difficult to reposition.

COMMONLY INJURED BONES

Typical breaks vary depending on age and activity levels. Elbow fracture is common in childhood; the humerus (upper arm bone) breaks just above the elbow joint often as a result of a fall during play. A young person is likely to injure a lower leg bone during activity, especially team sports. With age, bones naturally become "thinner" – weaker and more brittle – and they are more likely to fracture with only minimal force. The hip joint is especially vulnerable, and fracture is often the consequence of a fall. Another common injury in the elderly is Colles' fracture, which affects the wrist; it is usually caused by an outstretched arm trying to break a fall.

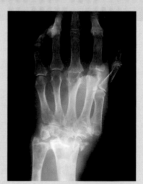

HIP FRACTURE
Common in the elderly, this is a break in the femur just below its ball-shaped head.

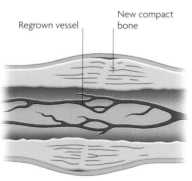

COLLES' FRACTURE
Flexing a hand to cushion a fall may break the end of the radius and the tip of the ulna.

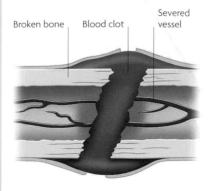
Broken bone   Blood clot   Severed vessel

IMMEDIATE RESPONSE
Blood leaks from the blood vessel and clots. White blood cells gather at the area to scavenge damaged cells and debris.

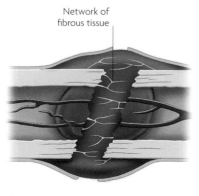
Network of fibrous tissue

AFTER SEVERAL DAYS
Fibroblast cells construct new fibrous tissue across the break. The limb is immobilized, usually in a plaster cast or splint.

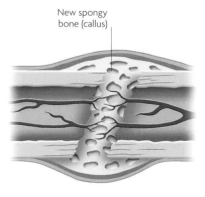
New spongy bone (callus)

AFTER 1–2 WEEKS
Bone-building cells (osteoblasts) multiply and form new bone tissue. Initially spongy, the tissue infiltrates the site as a callus.

Regrown vessel   New compact bone

AFTER 2–3 MONTHS
Blood vessels reconnect across the break. The callus reshapes while new bone tissue is "remodelled" into dense, compact bone.

SPINAL FRACTURES

MOST MAJOR SPINAL INJURIES OCCUR AS A RESULT OF SEVERE FORCES OF COMPRESSION, ROTATION, OR FLEXING BEYOND THE SPINE'S NORMAL RANGE OF MOVEMENT.

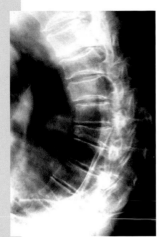

Many injuries to the spine are minor and cause only slight bruising. However, a severe fall or an accident may dislocate or fracture one or more of the vertebrae. If the spinal cord or nerves are damaged, a loss of sensation or function may result; paralysis may occur if the damage is severe, particularly in the neck region. Bone disease, for example osteoporosis, can affect the spine and increase the likelihood of fractures. The outcome of a spinal fracture depends on whether it is stable (unlikely to shift) or unstable, in which case damage to the spinal cord or nerves is more likely.

COMPRESSION FRACTURE
The area in red on this X-ray shows a fractured vertebra that has collapsed. This type of fracture often occurs in the elderly.

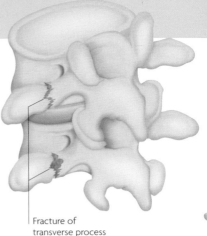

Fracture of transverse process

STABLE FRACTURE
Fracture of a transverse process is usually minor because the vertebra remains stable – it does not shift from its normal position to cause nerve damage. Lumbar vertebrae are the type most commonly affected.

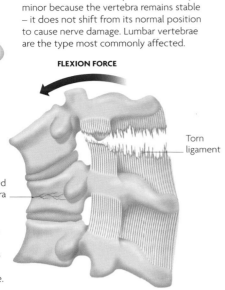

FLEXION FORCE

Torn ligament

Compressed vertebra

UNSTABLE FRACTURE
If ligaments tear during extreme flexion or rotation, vertebrae may be forced out of normal alignment. This threatens the spine's stability and may result in permanent spinal cord or nerve damage.

SCIATICA

PRESSURE ON THE ROOTS OF THE SCIATIC NERVE CAUSES PAIN IN THE BUTTOCK AND THE BACK OF THE THIGH.

The sciatic nerve is the largest nerve in the body, and pressure on its roots may cause pain to radiate down the entire leg. In severe cases, pain may be accompanied by weakness of the leg muscles. The source of the pressure on the sciatic nerve roots (junctions with the spinal cord) is usually a prolapsed intervertebral disc. Other causes include muscle spasm, sitting awkwardly for a long time, and, in older people, osteoarthritis. Rarely, a tumour may be the cause.

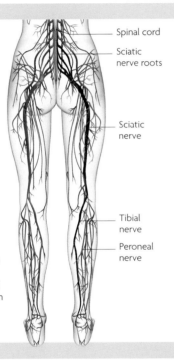

Spinal cord

Sciatic nerve roots

Sciatic nerve

Tibial nerve

Peroneal nerve

SCIATIC NERVE
The large sciatic nerve in the thigh sends branches down the leg and into the foot from its roots within the spinal cord.

WHIPLASH

SUDDEN BENDING OF THE SPINE CAUSES INJURY TO THE CERVICAL VERTEBRAE.

Whiplash injury is usually the result of a car accident. If hit from behind, a vehicle jerks forward, causing a rapid motion of the head first backwards and then forwards. The whip-like, backward motion hyperextends the cervical vertebrae, and this movement is quickly followed by flexion of the vertebrae as the head's momentum carries it forwards and causes the chin to arc down to the chest. The effect of this violent motion is spraining of the ligaments attached to the cervical vertebrae, or partial dislocation of a cervical joint, or both.

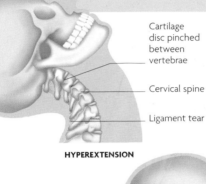

Cartilage disc pinched between vertebrae

Cervical spine

Ligament tear

HYPEREXTENSION

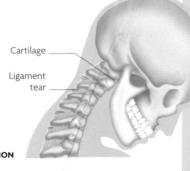

Cartilage

Ligament tear

FLEXION

DISC PROLAPSE

A PROLAPSED (ALSO KNOWN AS HERNIATED OR "SLIPPED") DISC IS A PROTRUSION FROM ONE OF THE SHOCK-ABSORBING PADS BETWEEN THE VERTEBRAE.

The cushion-like cartilage discs or pads that separate adjacent vertebrae have a hard outer covering and a jelly-like centre. An accident, wear and tear, or excessive pressure when lifting awkwardly may rupture the outer layer. This forces some of the core material to bulge out or prolapse. The prolapsed (or herniated) portion may cause pressure on the nearby spinal nerve root. Symptoms of disc prolapse include dull pain, muscle spasm and stiffness in the area of the back affected, and pain, tingling, numbness, or weakness in the body part supplied by the nerve – usually the leg or, with a prolapse higher in the spinal column, the arm. The term "slipped disc" is misleading as it is not the whole disc that slides out of position.

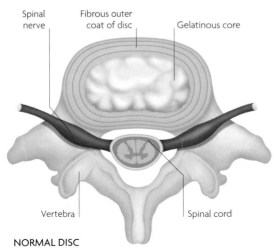

Spinal nerve

Fibrous outer coat of disc

Gelatinous core

Vertebra

Spinal cord

NORMAL DISC
The outer casing or capsule of the intervertebral disc is intact and completely encloses its gelatinous core. The disc sits between the bodies, or centra, of adjacent vertebrae.

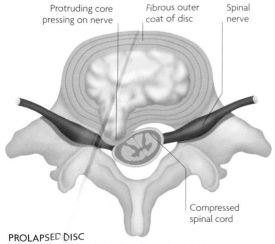

Protruding core pressing on nerve

Fibrous outer coat of disc

Spinal nerve

Compressed spinal cord

PROLAPSED DISC
A weak site in the outer casing allows the gelatinous core material to bulge through as the disc is compressed. The resulting pressure on the spinal nerve causes pain.

SPINAL CURVATURE

KYPHOSIS AND LORDOSIS INVOLVE EXAGGERATED CURVATURE OF THE UPPER AND LOWER PARTS OF THE SPINE.

The spinal column, or backbone, has two main natural curves. These are the thoracic curve to the rear in the chest region, and the lumbar curvature to the front in the lower back. Increased thoracic curvature, causing a rounded, or humped, upper back, is called kyphosis. Lordosis is exaggerated lumbar curvature that produces a hollow in the small of the back. The conditions may occur together as one tends to compensate the other. Causes include bone or joint problems, such as osteoarthritis or osteoporosis, poor posture, and being overweight.

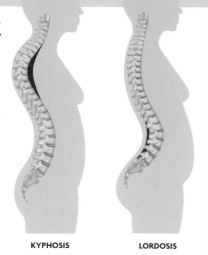

KYPHOSIS **LORDOSIS**

TYPES OF CURVATURE OF THE SPINE
Kyphosis accentuates the upper spinal column while lordosis affects the lower region (normal curvatures are shown in red).

OSTEOMYELITIS

INFECTION OF A BONE, USUALLY BY BACTERIA, CAN LEAD TO PAINFUL, WEAK, AND DAMAGED BONE TISSUE.

Osteomyelitis generally affects young and elderly people, although it can occur in those with reduced immunity, for example people on immunosuppressive drugs, or with a condition such as sickle-cell anaemia. In children, the vertebrae or long limb bones are most frequently affected and, in adults, the vertebrae or pelvis. In acute osteomyelitis, the causative bacteria may be *Staphylococcus aureus*. Symptoms include swelling, pain, and a fever. The chronic form may be caused by tuberculosis, which does not produce swelling or fever.

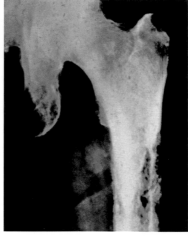

INFECTED FEMUR
A region of the leg infected by osteomyelitis (darker area, lower right) can be seen clearly in the shaft of the femur (thighbone).

OSTEOPOROSIS

MORE COMMON WITH INCREASED AGE, OSTEOPOROSIS IS LOSS OR THINNING OF BONE TISSUE THAT MAKES BONES WEAKER, MORE BRITTLE, AND MORE LIKELY TO BREAK.

In order for healthy bone growth and repair to occur, bone tissue is continually being broken down and replaced. Sex hormones are essential to initiate and maintain this process and with the decline in production of sex hormones in both sexes after middle age, bones become notably thinner and more porous. Oestrogen levels fall rapidly in women after the menopause, which can lead to severe thinning, or osteoporosis. The decline in testosterone in men is gradual

and, in general, males are less prone to osteoporosis. Exercise is an essential component in maintaining bone health, and a lack of activity is a predisposing factor to developing osteoporosis. The decreased density of osteoporotic bones means they are more likely to fracture. Crush fractures in the spine can cause spinal curvature; hip or wrist fractures may occur after minor falls. Other factors that influence the development of osteoporosis include smoking, corticosteroid treatment, rheumatoid arthritis, an overactive thyroid, and long-term kidney failure.

STRUCTURE OF NORMAL BONE
The outer periosteum encloses a band of hard, cortical bone. Within this is a layer of spongy, or cancellous, bone. Hard bone is composed of osteons, which are tightly packed, concentric layers (lamellae) formed by osteocytes.

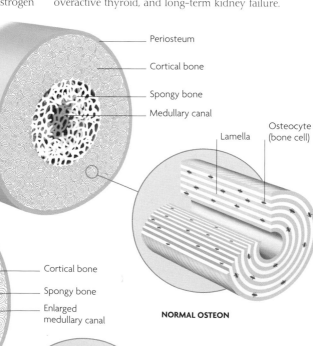

Periosteum
Cortical bone
Spongy bone
Medullary canal
Lamella
Osteocyte (bone cell)

Cortical bone
Spongy bone
Enlarged medullary canal

NORMAL OSTEON

Lamella
Gap

OSTEOPOROTIC OSTEON

STRUCTURE OF OSTEOPOROTIC BONE
The mineral density (mainly calcium and phosphorus) is reduced from two-thirds to one-third. The medullary canal through the bone's centre is enlarged, while gaps in the lamellae contribute to the bone's fragility.

WHY OSTEOPOROSIS OCCURS

Bone tissue is built up by the deposition of minerals (mainly calcium salts) on a framework of collagen fibres. It is continually broken down and rebuilt in order to allow growth and repair. Osteoporosis develops when the rate at which fibres, minerals, and cells are broken down becomes much greater than the formation of new tissue.

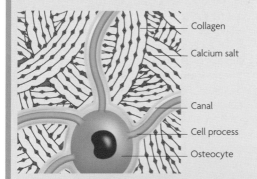

Collagen
Calcium salt
Canal
Cell process
Osteocyte

NORMAL BONE
Osteocytes (bone-maintaining cells) form collagen fibres and aid calcium deposition. Calcium moves in canals between bone and blood in response to hormones.

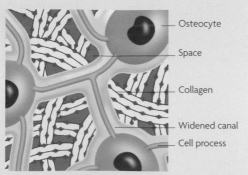

Osteocyte
Space
Collagen
Widened canal
Cell process

OSTEOPOROTIC BONE
In osteoporosis, the collagen framework and deposited minerals are broken down faster than they form. The canals widen, new spaces appear, and bone weakens.

OSTEOMALACIA

A LOSS OF CALCIUM AND PHOSPHORUS, OFTEN AS THE RESULT OF VITAMIN D DEFICIENCY, CAN CAUSE WEAK BONES.

In osteomalacia, bones are weakened by a loss of minerals, most notably calcium. Other symptoms include bone tenderness and deformity. The main cause is a shortage of vitamin D, which is essential to enable the body to absorb calcium and phosphorus. Vitamin D is obtained from food and also by the action of sunlight on skin. Inadequate supplies can be due to lack of sunlight, an unbalanced diet, or disorders that affect absorption of the vitamin, such as coeliac disease, and it can also occur as a result of some kidney diseases. In children, the condition is known as rickets.

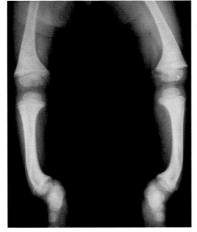

RICKETS
This X-ray shows the legs of a child diagnosed with rickets. The characteristic bowing of the legs at the knees can become a permanent disability if the disorder occurs early in the child's development.

PAGET'S DISEASE

THIS ABNORMALITY IN THE BALANCE OF BONE FORMATION AND BREAKDOWN CAUSES BONE DISTORTION.

Paget's disease, also known as osteitis deformans, can affect any bone in the skeleton, although it occurs most commonly in the pelvis, collarbone, vertebrae, skull, and leg bones. The bone tissue is broken down at an increased rate and is replaced rapidly by abnormal bone. The affected bone becomes weakened, distorted, and is often painful, and may become more liable to fracture. If the enlarged bone presses on a nerve, there may be numbness, tingling, weakness, and loss of function. Rare in young people, the condition becomes increasingly common over the age of 50 years.

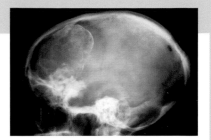
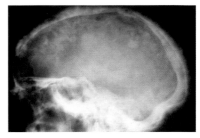

BONE THICKENING
A normal skull (top) is compared with an affected skull (bottom). Areas of increased bone density are seen as white patches. The bone distortion may cause hearing loss if the auditory nerve is compressed.

BONE CANCER

CANCER IN A BONE MAY BE PRIMARY, THAT IS FORMING IN THE BONE ITSELF; MORE OFTEN IT IS SECONDARY, HAVING SPREAD FROM ELSEWHERE IN THE BODY.

Primary cancer

A malignant, or cancerous, tumour that originates within a bone is described as primary. Cancers that start in bone are most likely to occur in children and adolescents. Osteosarcoma, which affects long bones, such as the femur (thighbone), is the most common type of primary bone cancer. The affected leg may be painful and swollen and is susceptible to fracture. Another primary bone cancer, chondrosarcoma, occurs mainly in the pelvis, ribs, and breastbone.

Secondary cancer

More frequent than primary bone cancers, secondary tumours in bone are the result of cancer cells spreading from a primary tumour elsewhere in the body. This type of bone cancer is known as metastatic. Secondary bone cancer is more likely to occur in older people, mainly because this age group is likely to have cancer elsewhere. Cancers most likely to spread to bone are breast, lung, thyroid, kidney, and prostate cancer, but sometimes the primary site is unknown. Symptoms include gnawing pain that is worse at night, and swelling and tenderness at the site. The most commonly affected areas are the skull, sternum, pelvis, vertebrae, ribs and, less often, the top of the femur and humerus.

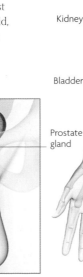

PROSTATE GLAND
In men, the prostate gland at the base of the bladder makes secretions for sperm. Prostate cancer often spreads to bones around the body.

SECONDARY CANCER
Cancerous cells travel to bones through the blood circulation. The breast, lung, thyroid, kidney, bladder, and (in males) prostate gland are the most common primary sites linked to bone metastases.

Thyroid gland

Lung

Breast

Kidney

Bladder

Prostate gland

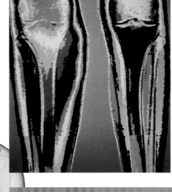

Tumour

OSTEOSARCOMA
This primary bone tumour is seen just above the knee at the lower end of the femur (the dark blue area at the upper left of this scan). Externally, the leg would appear swollen and distorted.

BONE TUMOURS

Tumours in bone may be either benign (non-cancerous) or malignant (cancerous). Benign tumours and non-invasive malignant tumours do not spread to other parts of the body. The most common sites for non-cancerous growths are the long bones of the limbs, such as the femur (thighbone), and the bones in the hands. Such tumours tend to occur during childhood or adolescence, and are very rare after the age of 40 years. There may be pain, enlargement, and deformity at the location of the tumour, and the weakened bone is more likely to fracture.

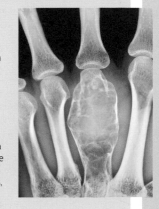

METACARPAL TUMOUR
An X-ray showing a large, non-cancerous tumour on a metacarpal (hand bone). The tumour causes swelling and may press on nearby nerves, blood vessels, and tendons.

JOINT DISORDERS

JOINTS ARE DESIGNED TO WORK IN SPECIFIC WAYS, AND ANY MOVEMENT BEYOND THE NORMAL RANGE, OR IN AN UNNATURAL DIRECTION, CAN RESULT IN INJURY. COMMON CAUSES INCLUDE A DIRECT BLOW OR FALL, AND INJURY DURING PHYSICAL ACTIVITIES SUCH AS SPORT. THE PROBLEMS CAN ALSO STEM FROM OVERUSE. CONGENITAL DEFECTS MAY CAUSE JOINT PROBLEMS (SEE ALSO PP.52–53).

LIGAMENT INJURIES

IF A JOINT IS FORCED BEYOND ITS NATURAL RANGE, THE LIGAMENTS THAT ARE NORMALLY ABLE TO PREVENT EXCESSIVE MOVEMENT MAY BE STRAINED OR TORN.

Ligaments are strong, flexible bands of fibrous tissue, linking bone ends together around a joint. If the bones within a joint are pulled too far apart, often as a result of a sudden, unexpected, or forceful movement, the fibres of the ligaments may overstretch or tear. This commonly results in swelling, pain, and muscle spasm. A joint "sprain" is usually due to partial tearing of a ligament. Rest, ice, compression, and elevation of the joint are the usual treatments if a sprain is not serious. If the injury is severe, it may result in joint instability or dislocation, which requires medical intervention.

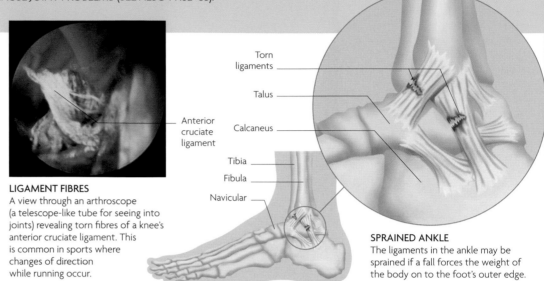

LIGAMENT FIBRES
A view through an arthroscope (a telescope-like tube for seeing into joints) revealing torn fibres of a knee's anterior cruciate ligament. This is common in sports where changes of direction while running occur.

Anterior cruciate ligament

Torn ligaments
Talus
Calcaneus
Tibia
Fibula
Navicular

SPRAINED ANKLE
The ligaments in the ankle may be sprained if a fall forces the weight of the body on to the foot's outer edge.

TORN CARTILAGE

CARTILAGE COVERS THE BONE ENDS IN MANY JOINTS, BUT THE TERM "TORN CARTILAGE" USUALLY REFERS TO THE KNEE IN PARTICULAR.

The knee joint contains pad-like curved "discs" of cartilage called menisci. These are almost C-shaped and made of tough fibrous cartilage. The discs are sited between the lower end of the femur and upper end of the tibia, with the medial cartilage on the knee's inner side and the lateral cartilage on the outside. These menisci stabilize the joint, helping it to "lock" straight while standing, and cushion the bones. A meniscus may be crushed or torn by rapid twisting of the knee, often while playing sport. If painful, surgery can remove the damaged piece of cartilage.

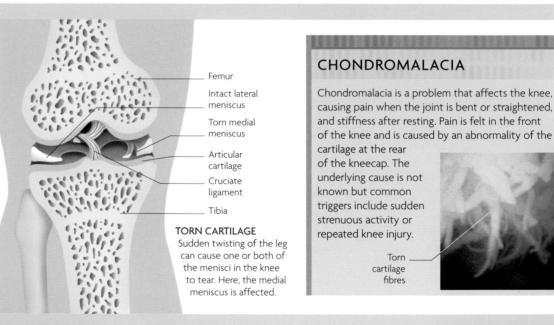

Femur
Intact lateral meniscus
Torn medial meniscus
Articular cartilage
Cruciate ligament
Tibia

TORN CARTILAGE
Sudden twisting of the leg can cause one or both of the menisci in the knee to tear. Here, the medial meniscus is affected.

CHONDROMALACIA

Chondromalacia is a problem that affects the knee, causing pain when the joint is bent or straightened, and stiffness after resting. Pain is felt in the front of the knee and is caused by an abnormality of the cartilage at the rear of the kneecap. The underlying cause is not known but common triggers include sudden strenuous activity or repeated knee injury.

Torn cartilage fibres

FROZEN SHOULDER

FROZEN SHOULDER REFERS TO PAIN AND RESTRICTED MOVEMENT BROUGHT ON BY INFLAMMATION IN THE JOINT.

The cause of frozen shoulder, or adhesive capsulitis, may be linked to injury or overuse of the joint, or immobilization after an arm bone fracture or a stroke, but sometimes there is no obvious cause. The pain can be severe and may result in loss of all arm and shoulder movements. Analgesics and anti-inflammatories may ease the condition, along with physiotherapy, but the condition usually gets better with time.

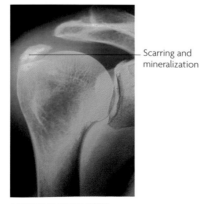

Scarring and mineralization

ADHESIVE CAPSULITIS
Scar tissue and mineral deposits, a typical sign of frozen shoulder, can be seen in the right shoulder joint shown in this X-ray.

BUNION

A BUNION CONSISTS OF INFLAMED, THICKENED SOFT TISSUE AND BONY OVERGROWTHS AT THE BASE OF THE BIG TOE.

A bunion is usually caused by hallux valgus, in which the big toe bends in towards the other toes. The condition is more common in women and tends to run in families. The metatarsal (foot bone) of the big toe, angles towards the body's midline, but the phalanxes (toe bones) angle the other way. A bunion makes walking painful. If severe, it can be corrected by surgery, in which some bone is removed to realign the toe.

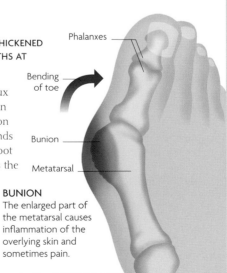

Phalanxes
Bending of toe
Bunion
Metatarsal

BUNION
The enlarged part of the metatarsal causes inflammation of the overlying skin and sometimes pain.

DISLOCATED JOINTS

A DRASTIC SHIFT OF BONE ENDS OUT OF THEIR NORMAL POSITION WITHIN A JOINT IS CALLED A DISLOCATION.

Often painful, a dislocation can be partial, in which only part of the bone is misplaced, or complete, such as in a dislocated shoulder where the humerus is totally out of its socket. A dislocation is often the result of a fall or sports injury. Rarely, the dislocation may also damage nerves, adjacent blood vessels, and other soft tissues, which rapidly swell and become painful. The affected area may have a different appearance from the normal joint on the other side of the body. Some people have joints that are prone to dislocation because of slight natural variations in the shapes of the bone ends, or laxity of the ligaments, which can be inherited.

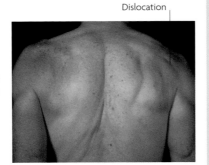

Dislocation

DISLOCATED SHOULDER
The area around the right shoulder joint appears swollen and misshapen compared with the normal shoulder on the left.

BURSITIS

INFLAMMATION OF THE BURSA, THE CUSHIONING PAD AT OR NEAR A JOINT, CAUSES PAIN, REDNESS, AND SWELLING.

A bursa is a fluid-filled sac that acts as a cushioned lubricating pad around a joint. It reduces the effect of friction and wear between muscle, tendon, and bone. Prolonged or repeated pressure, or sudden excessive stress at a joint, can cause a bursa to become inflamed and swollen. This may happen at various places in the body but is most likely to occur at the knee and elbow. Predisposing factors to bursitis include rheumatoid arthritis, gout, or previous joint injury. In rare cases, bursitis is due to bacterial infection. Treatment includes rest and anti-inflammatory medication, and possibly draining excess synovial fluid from the bursa by aspiration. Sometimes a corticosteroid drug may be injected into the site.

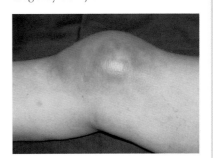

SWOLLEN KNEE
Swelling and tenderness in the bursa of the knee joint is often due to repeated kneeling and traditionally named "housemaid's knee".

HIP DISORDERS IN CHILDREN

Although most bone and joint abnormalities occurring in children are caused by injuries, a painful or misshapen hip may be due to some congenital defect, a bone infection, or an acquired disorder such as juvenile rheumatoid arthritis (also known as Still's disease).

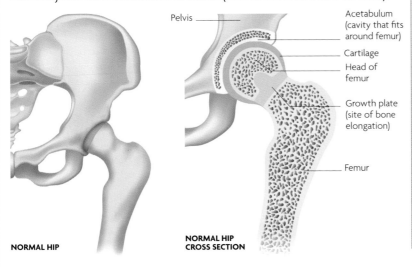

Pelvis

Acetabulum (cavity that fits around femur)

Cartilage

Head of femur

Growth plate (site of bone elongation)

Femur

NORMAL HIP

NORMAL HIP CROSS SECTION

CONGENITAL HIP DYSPLASIA

THIS CONDITION RESULTS FROM A FLATTENED OR MISPLACED SOCKET IN THE PELVIS FAILING TO HOLD THE FEMUR.

Also known as congenital dislocation of the hip, or CDH, this problem is usually detected during the postnatal check given to babies soon after birth. The condition may amount to mild looseness of the joint; occasional dislocation if manipulated; or complete displacement of the femoral head outside the socket in the hip bone and formation of a false joint (see right). If picked up at birth, congenital hip dysplasia may simply be monitored as the infant grows or treated with splints, a harness or a cast, or even surgery. However, the dysplasia may be missed if it is very slight. It can then come to light when the child begins to walk with a limp.

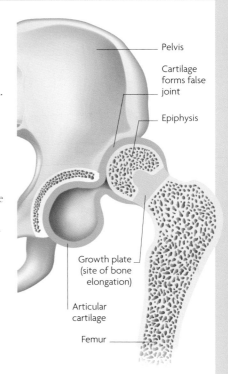

Pelvis

Cartilage forms false joint

Epiphysis

Growth plate (site of bone elongation)

Articular cartilage

Femur

PERTHES' DISEASE

THIS DISORDER IS THOUGHT TO BE DUE TO ABNORMAL BLOOD CIRCULATION IN THE HEAD OF THE FEMUR.

In Perthes' disease, the rounded head of the femur softens and becomes deformed, leading to pain in the thigh and groin, which may cause limping. The disease often affects only one hip. Perthes' disease is more common in boys than girls, and tends to occur around the ages of four to eight years. It is thought to be caused by abnormal blood circulation. Treatment is required, including rest, splinting, and perhaps traction and surgery, to help prevent osteoarthritis later in life.

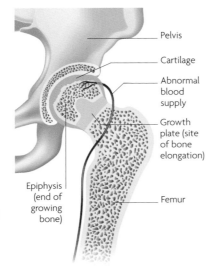

Pelvis

Cartilage

Abnormal blood supply

Growth plate (site of bone elongation)

Epiphysis (end of growing bone)

Femur

SLIPPED EPIPHYSIS

THE HEAD OF THE FEMUR, OR PROXIMAL EPIPHYSIS, MAY SLIP THROUGH INJURY OR GRADUALLY BECOME DISPLACED.

The bony ball-shaped head (epiphysis) of the femur is separated from its shaft by a soft, cartilaginous region, known as the growth plate, where bone growth occurs. This is the usual site of slippage. Whether the displacement is slow or sudden, it tends to happen during rapid growth phases, often at puberty, when growth hormone may cause the tissues to soften. Surgical repair is carried out to reposition the displaced bone, which may then be secured with metal pins.

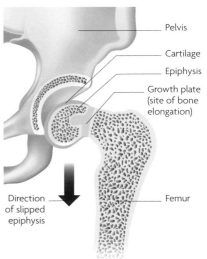

Pelvis

Cartilage

Epiphysis

Growth plate (site of bone elongation)

Direction of slipped epiphysis

Femur

ARTHRITIS

"Arthritis" is a collective term used to describe several different disorders that damage joints, causing pain, swelling, and restricted movement. The most common disorder in this group is osteoarthritis, which is widespread among older people. Rheumatoid arthritis can occur at any age, including during childhood, but usually begins after age 40.

OSTEOARTHRITIS

IN OSTEOARTHRITIS, THE CARTILAGE COVERING THE BONE ENDS (ARTICULAR CARTILAGE) INSIDE A JOINT BEGINS TO DEGENERATE, CAUSING PAIN AND SWELLING.

Osteoarthritis is often confused with rheumatoid arthritis (see opposite), but the two disorders have different causes and progressions. Osteoarthritis may affect only a single joint and can be triggered by localized "wear and tear", resulting in painful inflammation from time to time. Joint degeneration may be hastened by a congenital defect, injury, infection, or obesity. Because cartilage normally wears away as the body ages, a mild form of osteoarthritis affects many people after about the age of 60 years. Typical symptoms are pain and swelling in the joint that worsen with activity and fade with rest; stiffness for a short time after rest; restricted movement; crepitus (crackling noises) when moving the joint; and referred pain (in areas

remote from the site of damage but on the same nerve pathway as the affected joint). Symptomatic treatment and lifestyle changes are effective in many milder cases.

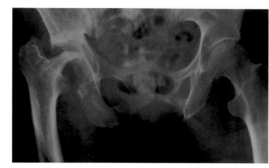

OSTEOARTHRITIS OF THE HIP
The right hip, on the left of this X-ray, is badly eroded by osteoarthritis. The head of the femur, which is normally round, is flattened.

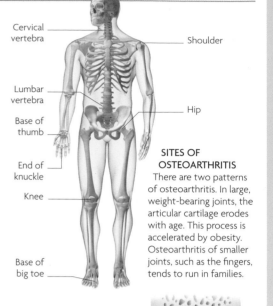

Cervical vertebra

Shoulder

Lumbar vertebra

Hip

Base of thumb

End of knuckle

Knee

Base of big toe

SITES OF OSTEOARTHRITIS
There are two patterns of osteoarthritis. In large, weight-bearing joints, the articular cartilage erodes with age. This process is accelerated by obesity. Osteoarthritis of smaller joints, such as the fingers, tends to run in families.

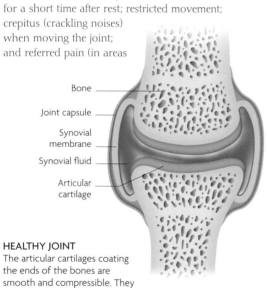

Bone

Joint capsule

Synovial membrane

Synovial fluid

Articular cartilage

HEALTHY JOINT
The articular cartilages coating the ends of the bones are smooth and compressible. They are lubricated by synovial fluid and slip past each other with minimal friction.

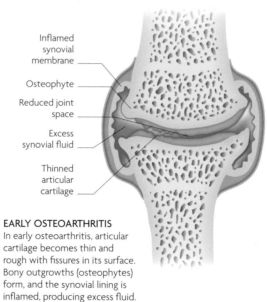

Inflamed synovial membrane

Osteophyte

Reduced joint space

Excess synovial fluid

Thinned articular cartilage

EARLY OSTEOARTHRITIS
In early osteoarthritis, articular cartilage becomes thin and rough with fissures in its surface. Bony outgrowths (osteophytes) form, and the synovial lining is inflamed, producing excess fluid.

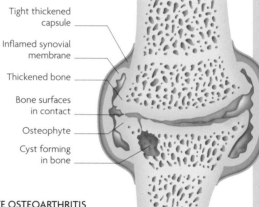

Tight thickened capsule

Inflamed synovial membrane

Thickened bone

Bone surfaces in contact

Osteophyte

Cyst forming in bone

LATE OSTEOARTHRITIS
In severe cases of osteoarthritis, cartilage and underlying bone crack and erode. The bones rub together, thicken, and overgrow, causing extreme discomfort. The joint capsule thickens.

JOINT REPLACEMENT

When the symptoms of an osteoarthritic hip cannot be controlled with drug treatment the hip may be replaced by an artificial joint, or prosthesis. Joint replacement may also be used to treat hip fractures. A hip prosthesis is made of metal, ceramic, or plastic, and comprises a shaft with a ball-shaped head, and a cup-like pelvic socket, cemented in place. Other joints that can be replaced by prostheses include the knee, shoulder, and small joints in the hand. After the operation the joint is no longer painful, but physiotherapy is needed to strengthen the muscles and restore full function.

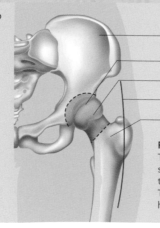

Pelvis

Area of pelvis hollowed out

Head of femur

Skin incision

Shaft of femur

PREPARING THE HIP
The hip joint is exposed by a skin incision and by moving the muscles and ligaments. The socket is cleared and the head of the femur removed.

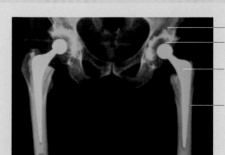

Pelvis

Pelvic socket

Hip prosthesis

Shaft of femur

DOUBLE HIP REPLACEMENT
This X-ray shows a hip prosthesis (light blue) in each leg. The ball-shaped head and an anchoring "spike" are clearly visible.

RHEUMATOID ARTHRITIS

IN THIS AUTOIMMUNE FORM OF ARTHRITIS, THE IMMUNE SYSTEM DAMAGES THE BODY'S OWN TISSUES, IN THIS CASE THE JOINTS. IT CAN AFFECT SEVERAL BODY SYSTEMS.

Rheumatoid arthritis develops when the immune system produces antibodies that attack its own body tissues – especially the synovial membranes inside joints. The joints become swollen and deformed, with painful and restricted movement. Early general symptoms include fever, pale skin, and weakness. Characteristically, many of the small joints are affected in a symmetrical pattern; for example, the hands and feet may become inflamed to the same degree on both sides. Painless small lumps or nodules (clusters of inflamed

tissue cells), form in areas of pressure, commonly on the forearms, and the skin over the joint is thin and fragile. Stiffness is often worse in the mornings but eases during the day. The condition may flare up then fade for a time. The diagnosis is supported if a blood test detects an antibody, rheumatoid factor (RhF), associated with rheumatoid arthritis. The disease can also affect the tissues of the eyes, skin, heart, nerves, and lungs. Anaemia may also develop.

Treatments range from simple anti-inflammatory drugs to stronger drugs that suppress the autoimmune process.

JOINT INFLAMMATION
In this X-ray, the middle knuckles of the hands are severely damaged by rheumatoid arthritis (red). Inflammation of the joints causes abnormal bending of the fingers.

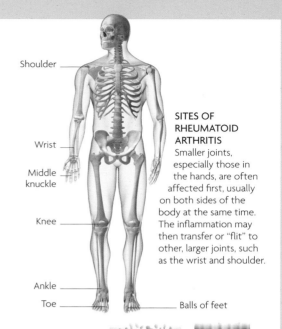

SITES OF RHEUMATOID ARTHRITIS
Smaller joints, especially those in the hands, are often affected first, usually on both sides of the body at the same time. The inflammation may then transfer or "flit" to other, larger joints, such as the wrist and shoulder.

Labels: Shoulder, Wrist, Middle knuckle, Knee, Ankle, Toe, Balls of feet

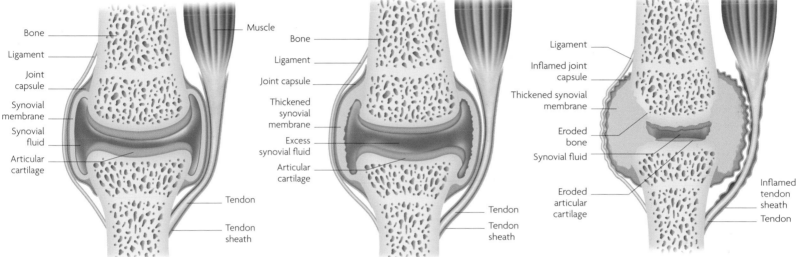

HEALTHY JOINT
Cartilage is smooth and intact in a healthy joint. Ligaments aid stability, and tendons slide in sheaths as muscles pull on them.
Labels: Bone, Ligament, Joint capsule, Synovial membrane, Synovial fluid, Articular cartilage, Muscle, Tendon, Tendon sheath

EARLY RHEUMATOID ARTHRITIS
The synovial membrane becomes inflamed and thickens, spreading across the joint. Excess synovial fluid accumulates.
Labels: Bone, Ligament, Joint capsule, Thickened synovial membrane, Excess synovial fluid, Articular cartilage, Tendon, Tendon sheath

LATE RHEUMATOID ARTHRITIS
As the synovial membrane thickens, the cartilage and bone ends are eroded. The joint capsule and tendon sheath become inflamed.
Labels: Ligament, Inflamed joint capsule, Thickened synovial membrane, Eroded bone, Synovial fluid, Eroded articular cartilage, Inflamed tendon sheath, Tendon

GOUT

IN GOUT, CRYSTALS OF URIC ACID FORM WITHIN A JOINT, CAUSING INTENSELY PAINFUL ARTHRITIS. IT CAN AFFECT ANY JOINT BUT COMMONLY OCCURS IN THE BIG TOE.

Gout is a type of crystal-induced arthritis that may cause sudden and severe pain, swelling, and redness in one or more joints. The problem is more common in men than in women, and when it occurs in women, it is usually after the menopause. Owing to a problem of metabolism, the cause of which is unclear but sometimes inherited, excess uric acid accumulates in the body. Normally, uric acid stays in dissolved form, is collected by the blood, and then excreted in urine. In gout, however, this uric acid comes out of solution in the synovial fluid of a joint, forming needle-like crystals. The affected joint becomes red, hot, swollen, and very painful. Gout can occur spontaneously or be linked with drinking alcohol, certain forms of surgery, or some medications such as diuretics or chemotherapy. Drug treatment can relieve the pain of an attack and help prevent recurrence.

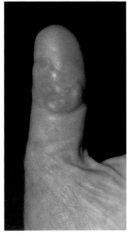

SWOLLEN THUMB
Here, uric acid crystals (pale yellow) have been deposited in the soft tissues of the thumb. They can eventually discharge through the skin as a chalky substance.

JOINT ASPIRATION

In this procedure, excess fluid is removed from a swollen joint by sucking it out with a needle and syringe, possibly under local anaesthetic. The procedure can be used for diagnosis, treatment, or both. For example, the fluid may be examined for characteristic contents, such as the uric acid crystals of gout, while removal of the fluid eases the joint's swelling and pain. A similar procedure is used to inject medication directly into the joint.

ASPIRATING THE KNEE
The patella is held still with the knee relaxed. A needle is inserted into the space under the patella to withdraw the fluid.

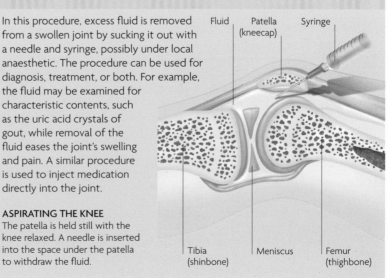
Labels: Fluid, Patella (kneecap), Syringe, Tibia (shinbone), Meniscus, Femur (thighbone)

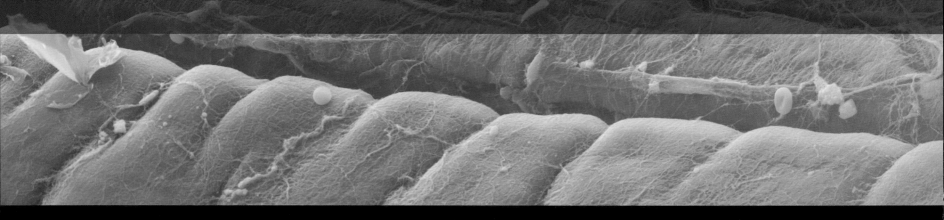

THE MUSCULAR SYSTEM PRODUCES AN ENDLESS VARIETY
OF ACTIONS BY USING MUSCLES AS COORDINATED TEAMS.
MUSCLE TISSUE CREATES BODILY MOVEMENTS AND IT ALSO
POWERS INTERNAL PROCESSES, FROM THE HEARTBEAT AND
THE MOVEMENT OF FOOD THROUGH THE INTESTINES TO
THE ADJUSTMENT OF ARTERY DIAMETER AND FOCUSING
THE EYE. THE MUSCULAR SYSTEM LEADS A VERY PHYSICAL
EXISTENCE, IN WHICH REGULAR USE PREVENTS WASTING,
AND INJURY IS MORE COMMON THAN DISEASE. HOWEVER,
MUSCLES ARE HELPLESS WITHOUT THE NERVOUS SYSTEM

MUSCULAR SYSTEM

● SEE DVD-ROM

MUSCLES OF THE BODY

MUSCLES ARE THE BODY'S "FLESH". THEY BULGE AND RIPPLE JUST UNDER THE SKIN, AND ARE ARRANGED IN CRISS-CROSSING LAYERS DOWN TO THE BONES. THEIR JOB IS TO CONTRACT AND PULL THE BONES TO WHICH THEY ARE ANCHORED. RARELY WORKING ALONE, THEY USUALLY CONTRACT IN GROUPS, MOVING BONES AT ACCURATE ANGLES AND BY PRECISE DISTANCES.

The typical male body contains approximately 640 muscles, which compose around two-fifths of its weight. The same number in a female body make up a slightly smaller proportion. A typical muscle spans a joint and tapers at each end into a fibrous tendon anchored to a bone. The more stable attachment of a muscle, usually nearer the centre of the body, is known as its origin. This end moves little (if at all) on contraction. The other end, the insertion, is towards the body's periphery and moves more. Some muscles divide to attach to different bones. The names of some muscles reflect their shape: the deltoid in the shoulder, for example, is triangular. Superficial muscles, those just under the skin, are pictured here on the left side of a male body. On the right of this body are the deeper layers – the intermediate muscles and deep muscles.

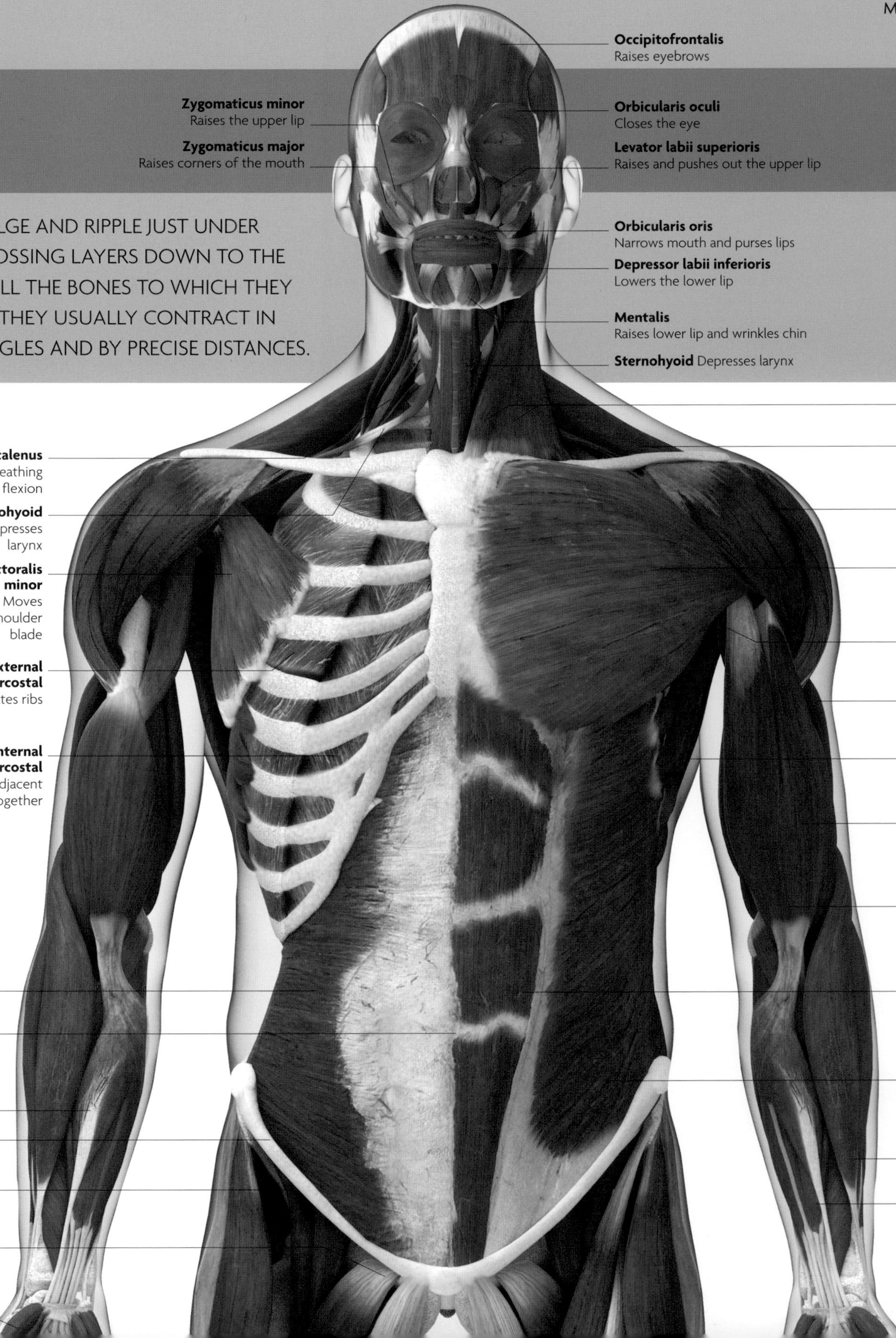

Occipitofrontalis
Raises eyebrows

Orbicularis oculi
Closes the eye

Levator labii superioris
Raises and pushes out the upper lip

Orbicularis oris
Narrows mouth and purses lips

Depressor labii inferioris
Lowers the lower lip

Mentalis
Raises lower lip and wrinkles chin

Sternohyoid Depresses larynx

Zygomaticus minor
Raises the upper lip

Zygomaticus major
Raises corners of the mouth

Sternocleidomastoid
Tilts and twists neck

Trapezius
Rotates and retracts shoulder blade

Deltoid
Raises arm away from body to front, side, and rear

Pectoralis major
Draws arm in towards body and rotates upper arm inward

Long head of triceps
Extends forearm at elbow and straightens arm

Brachialis
Brings forearm towards shoulder

Serratus anterior
Pulls shoulder blades away from spine

Biceps brachii
Flexes forearm at elbow and turns the palm upward

Medial head of triceps
Extends forearm at elbow and straightens arm

Rectus abdominis
Flexes spine and draws pelvis forward

External oblique abdominal
Flexes and rotates trunk

Brachioradialis
Flexes arm at elbow

Flexor digitorum superficialis
Flexes joints of hand and wrist

Scalenus
Aids breathing and neck flexion

Omohyoid
Depresses larynx

Pectoralis minor
Moves shoulder blade

External intercostal
Elevates ribs

Internal intercostal
Pulls adjacent ribs together

Internal oblique abdominal
Flexes and rotates trunk

Linea alba
Tendinous structure dividing left and right abdominal muscles

Flexor carpi radialis
Flexes hand at wrist

Inguinal ligament

Iliopsoas
Flexes thigh at hip

Pectineus
Flexes and draws thigh in towards body

Abductor pollicis brevis
Pulls thumb in towards palm

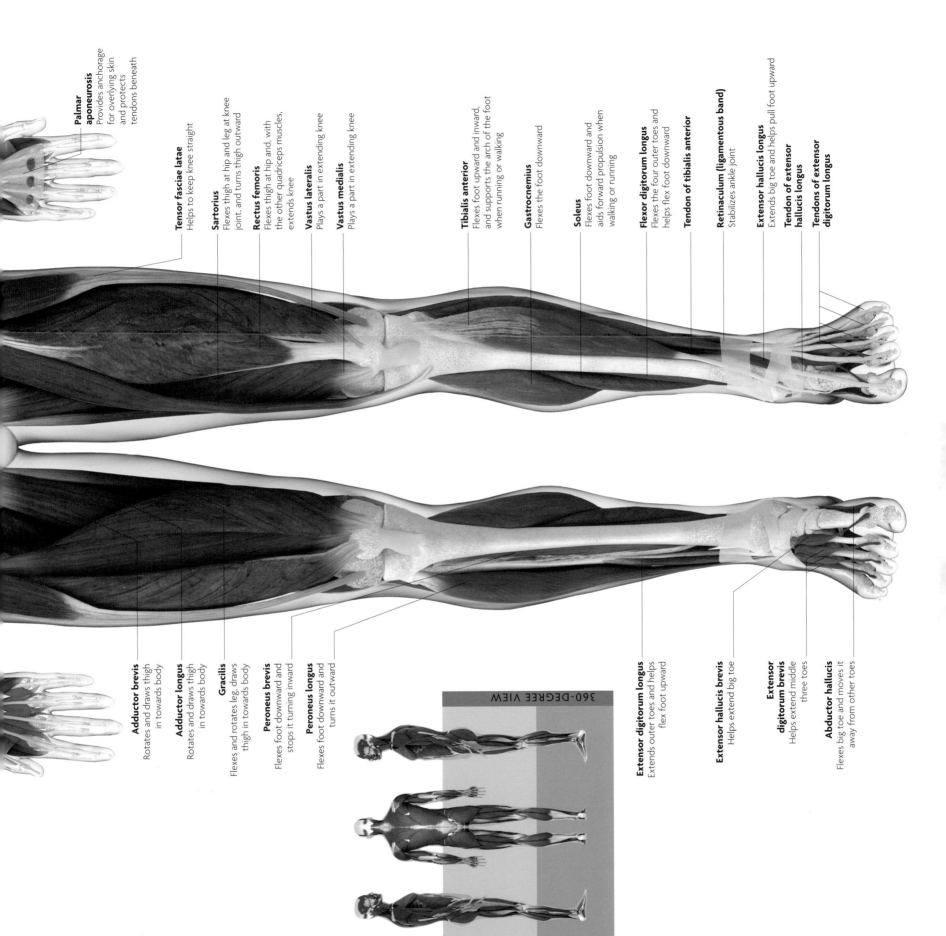

Palmar aponeurosis
Provides anchorage for overlying skin and protects tendons beneath

Tensor fasciae latae
Helps to keep knee straight

Sartorius
Flexes thigh at hip and leg at knee joint, and turns thigh outward

Rectus femoris
Flexes thigh at hip and, with the other quadriceps muscles, extends knee

Vastus lateralis
Plays a part in extending knee

Vastus medialis
Plays a part in extending knee

Tibialis anterior
Flexes foot upward and inward, and supports the arch of the foot when running or walking

Gastrocnemius
Flexes the foot downward

Soleus
Flexes foot downward and aids forward propulsion when walking or running

Flexor digitorum longus
Flexes the four outer toes and helps flex foot downward

Tendon of tibialis anterior

Retinaculum (ligamentous band)
Stabilizes ankle joint

Extensor hallucis longus
Extends big toe and helps pull foot upward

Tendon of extensor hallucis longus

Tendons of extensor digitorum longus

Adductor brevis
Rotates and draws thigh in towards body

Adductor longus
Rotates and draws thigh in towards body

Gracilis
Flexes and rotates leg, draws thigh in towards body

Peroneus brevis
Flexes foot downward and stops it turning inward

Peroneus longus
Flexes foot downward and turns it outward

Extensor digitorum longus
Extends outer toes and helps flex foot upward

Extensor hallucis brevis
Helps extend big toe

Extensor digitorum brevis
Helps extend middle three toes

Abductor hallucis
Flexes big toe and moves it away from other toes

360-DEGREE VIEW

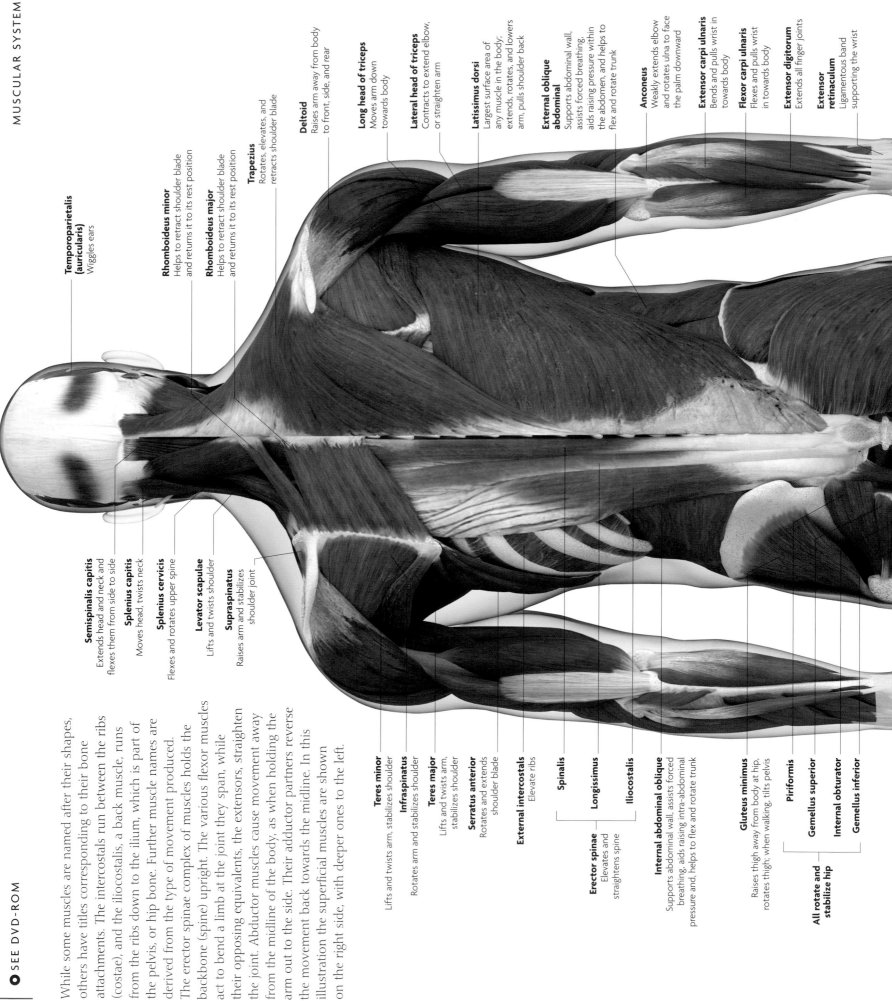

While some muscles are named after their shapes, others have titles corresponding to their bone attachments. The intercostals run between the ribs (costae), and the iliocostalis, a back muscle, runs from the ribs down to the ilium, or hip bone. Further muscle names are derived from the type of movement produced. The erector spinae complex of muscles holds the backbone (spine) upright. The various flexor muscles act to bend a limb at the joint they span, while their opposing equivalents, the extensors, straighten the joint. Abductor muscles cause movement away from the midline of the body, as when holding the arm out to the side. Their adductor partners reverse the movement back towards the midline. In this illustration the superficial muscles are shown on the right side, with deeper ones to the left.

Temporoparietalis (auricularis)
Wiggles ears

Rhomboideus minor
Helps to retract shoulder blade and returns it to its rest position

Rhomboideus major
Helps to retract shoulder blade and returns it to its rest position

Trapezius
Rotates, elevates, and retracts shoulder blade

Deltoid
Raises arm away from body to front, side, and rear

Long head of triceps
Moves arm down towards body

Lateral head of triceps
Contracts to extend elbow, or straighten arm

Latissimus dorsi
Largest surface area of any muscle in the body; extends, rotates, and lowers arm, pulls shoulder back

External oblique abdominal
Supports abdominal wall, assists forced breathing, aids raising pressure within the abdomen, and helps to flex and rotate trunk

Anconeus
Weakly extends elbow and rotates ulna to face the palm downward

Extensor carpi ulnaris
Bends and pulls wrist in towards body

Flexor carpi ulnaris
Flexes and pulls wrist in towards body

Extensor digitorum
Extends all finger joints

Extensor retinaculum
Ligamentous band supporting the wrist

Semispinalis capitis
Extends head and neck and flexes them from side to side

Splenius capitis
Moves head, twists neck

Splenius cervicis
Flexes and rotates upper spine

Levator scapulae
Lifts and twists shoulder

Supraspinatus
Raises arm and stabilizes shoulder joint

Teres minor
Lifts and twists arm, stabilizes shoulder

Infraspinatus
Rotates arm and stabilizes shoulder

Teres major
Lifts and twists arm, stabilizes shoulder

Serratus anterior
Rotates and extends shoulder blade

External intercostals
Elevate ribs

Spinalis

Longissimus

Iliocostalis

Erector spinae
Elevates and straightens spine

Internal abdominal oblique
Supports abdominal wall, assists forced breathing, aids raising intra-abdominal pressure and, helps to flex and rotate trunk

Gluteus minimus
Raises thigh away from body at hip, rotates thigh; when walking, tilts pelvis

Piriformis

Gemellus superior

Internal obturator

Gemellus inferior

All rotate and stabilize hip

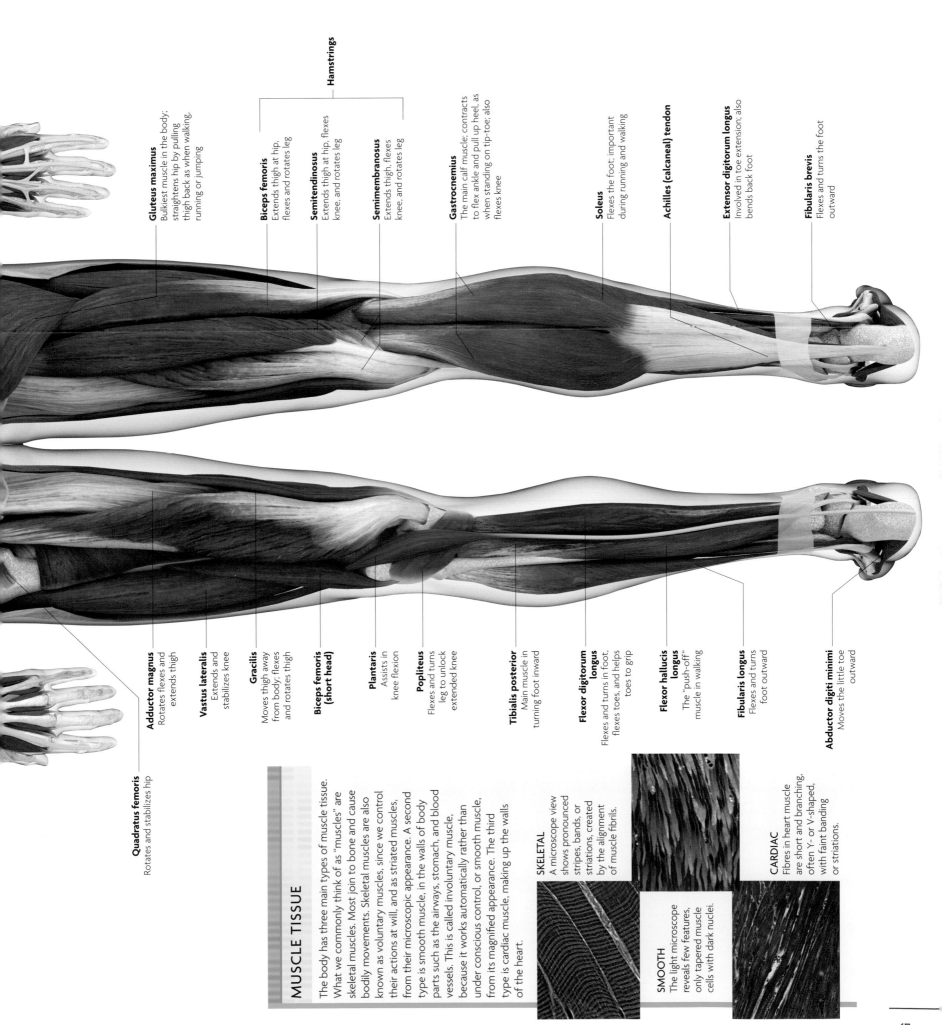

Quadratus femoris
Rotates and stabilizes hip

Gluteus maximus
Bulkiest muscle in the body; straightens hip by pulling thigh back as when walking, running or jumping

Adductor magnus
Rotates flexes and extends thigh

Vastus lateralis
Extends and stabilizes knee

Gracilis
Moves thigh away from body; flexes and rotates thigh

Biceps femoris (short head)

Hamstrings

Biceps femoris
Extends thigh at hip, flexes and rotates leg

Semitendinosus
Extends thigh at hip, flexes knee, and rotates leg

Plantaris
Assists in knee flexion

Semimembranosus
Extends thigh, flexes knee, and rotates leg

Popliteus
Flexes and turns leg to unlock extended knee

Gastrocnemius
The main calf muscle; contracts to flex ankle and pull up heel, as when standing on tip-toe; also flexes knee

Tibialis posterior
Main muscle in turning foot inward

Flexor digitorum longus
Flexes and turns in foot, flexes toes, and helps toes to grip

Soleus
Flexes the foot; important during running and walking

Flexor hallucis longus
The "push-off" muscle in walking

Achilles (calcaneal) tendon

Fibularis longus
Flexes and turns foot outward

Extensor digitorum longus
Involved in toe extension; also bends back foot

Fibularis brevis
Flexes and turns the foot outward

Abductor digiti minimi
Moves the little toe outward

MUSCLE TISSUE

The body has three main types of muscle tissue. What we commonly think of as "muscles" are skeletal muscles. Most join to bone and cause bodily movements. Skeletal muscles are also known as voluntary muscles, since we control their actions at will, and as striated muscles, from their microscopic appearance. A second type is smooth muscle, in the walls of body parts such as the airways, stomach, and blood vessels. This is called involuntary muscle, because it works automatically rather than under conscious control, or smooth muscle, from its magnified appearance. The third type is cardiac muscle, making up the walls of the heart.

SKELETAL
A microscope view shows pronounced stripes, bands, or striations, created by the alignment of muscle fibrils.

SMOOTH
The light microscope reveals few features, only tapered muscle cells with dark nuclei.

CARDIAC
Fibres in heart muscle are short and branching, often Y- or V-shaped, with faint banding or striations.

59

MUSCLES OF THE FACE, HEAD, AND NECK

TO STEADY AND MOVE THE HEAD AND TO MOVE FACIAL FEATURES SUCH AS THE EYEBROWS, EYELIDS, AND LIPS, THE MUSCLES OF THE FACE, HEAD AND NECK INTERACT. THE MUSCULATURE INVOLVED IS HIGHLY COMPLEX, ALLOWING FOR A HUGE RANGE OF FACIAL EXPRESSIONS.

FACIAL MUSCLES

Some facial muscles are anchored to bones. Others are joined to tendons or to dense, sheet-like clusters of fibrous connective tissue called aponeuroses. This means, that some facial muscles are joined to each other. Many of these muscles have their other end inserted into deeper layers of the skin. The advantage of this complex system is that even a slight degree of muscle contraction produces movement of the face's skin, which reveals itself as a show of expression or emotion. Almost all facial muscles are controlled by the facial nerve called cranial VII (see p.82). Damage or disease of this nerve results in loss of facial mobility and expression, reducing the ability to communicate.

NERVE-MUSCLE JUNCTION

In this microscope image a nerve cell (top left) joins a facial muscle fibre. At the point of contact is the motor end plate (centre), an area of highly excitable muscle fibre.

LAUGHTER LINES

Healthy young skin contains resilient fibres made of the protein elastin which help it return to its original position, for example, after smiling. With increasing age, the elastin degenerates and the skin's dermis (see pp.146–47) becomes more loosely attached to the muscle beneath. This causes wrinkles as the skin can no longer stretch or shrink easily. Initially "crow's feet" radiate from the corners of the eyes. These are followed by lines around the brow and mouth, in front of the ears, between the eyebrows, on the chin and bridge of the nose. Facial wrinkles are always at right angles to the muscle fibres so they reveal the pattern of facial muscles. Exposure to excessive sunlight and temperature hastens wrinkling.

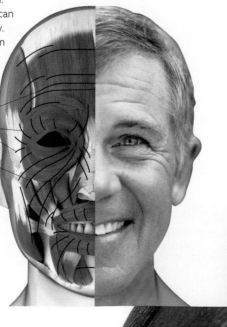

Forehead wrinkles

Crow's foot

Cheek crease

SIGNS OF AGEING

Wrinkles and furrows tend to appear around often-used muscles. For example, crow's feet are associated with the orbicularis oculi, forehead wrinkles with the frontalis, and creases in the cheeks with the levator labii superioris.

FACE AND NECK MUSCLES

Intermeshing muscles around the lips are involved in speech, non-verbal expression, eating, and drinking. Some facial muscles act as sphincters to open and close orifices, such as the eyelids, nostrils, and lips.

Occipitofrontalis
Raises eyebrows

Corrugator supercilii
Pulls eyebrows together and wrinkles lower forehead

Procerus
Pulls eyebrows down and together

Orbicularis oculi
Closes eyelid

Compressor naris
Closes nostrils

Levator labii superioris
Raises and pushes out the upper lip

Dilator naris
Opens and flares nostrils

Zygomaticus minor
Raises the upper lip

Zygomaticus major
Pulls corner of the mouth up and out

Risorius
Pulls corner of the mouth outwards

Orbicularis oris
Narrows mouth and purses lips

Depressor labii inferioris
Pulls down lower lip

Mentalis
Raises the lower lip and wrinkles chin

Depressor anguli oris
Lowers corner of the mouth

Sternohyoid
Depresses larynx

Platysma
Lowers mandible and corners of the mouth

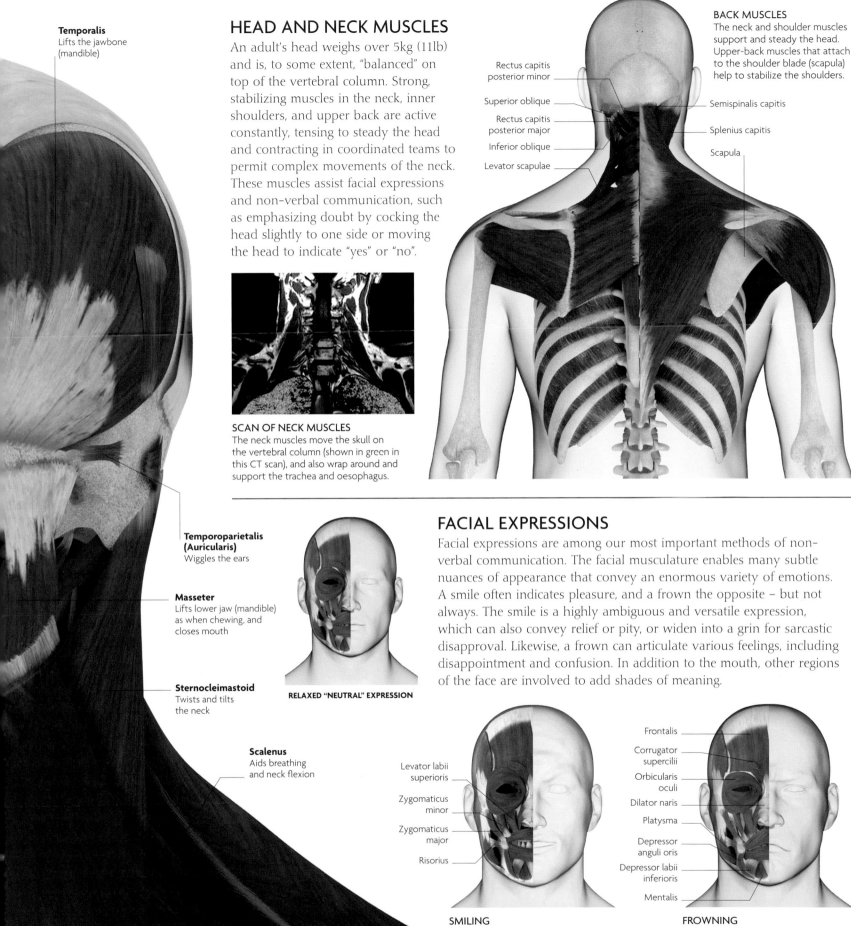

Temporalis
Lifts the jawbone (mandible)

HEAD AND NECK MUSCLES

An adult's head weighs over 5kg (11lb) and is, to some extent, "balanced" on top of the vertebral column. Strong, stabilizing muscles in the neck, inner shoulders, and upper back are active constantly, tensing to steady the head and contracting in coordinated teams to permit complex movements of the neck. These muscles assist facial expressions and non-verbal communication, such as emphasizing doubt by cocking the head slightly to one side or moving the head to indicate "yes" or "no".

SCAN OF NECK MUSCLES
The neck muscles move the skull on the vertebral column (shown in green in this CT scan), and also wrap around and support the trachea and oesophagus.

Rectus capitis posterior minor
Superior oblique
Rectus capitis posterior major
Inferior oblique
Levator scapulae

BACK MUSCLES
The neck and shoulder muscles support and steady the head. Upper-back muscles that attach to the shoulder blade (scapula) help to stabilize the shoulders.

Semispinalis capitis
Splenius capitis
Scapula

Temporoparietalis (Auricularis)
Wiggles the ears

Masseter
Lifts lower jaw (mandible) as when chewing, and closes mouth

Sternocleimastoid
Twists and tilts the neck

RELAXED "NEUTRAL" EXPRESSION

Scalenus
Aids breathing and neck flexion

FACIAL EXPRESSIONS

Facial expressions are among our most important methods of non-verbal communication. The facial musculature enables many subtle nuances of appearance that convey an enormous variety of emotions. A smile often indicates pleasure, and a frown the opposite – but not always. The smile is a highly ambiguous and versatile expression, which can also convey relief or pity, or widen into a grin for sarcastic disapproval. Likewise, a frown can articulate various feelings, including disappointment and confusion. In addition to the mouth, other regions of the face are involved to add shades of meaning.

Levator labii superioris
Zygomaticus minor
Zygomaticus major
Risorius

Frontalis
Corrugator supercilii
Orbicularis oculi
Dilator naris
Platysma
Depressor anguli oris
Depressor labii inferioris
Mentalis

SMILING
The levator labii superioris lifts the upper lip, while the zygomaticus major and minor and the risorius pull the angle of the mouth and the lip corners up and sideways.

FROWNING
The platysma and depressor muscles pull the mouth and corners of the lips down, and the mentalis wrinkles the chin. The corrugator supercilii furrows the brow, the dilator naris flares the nostrils, and the orbicularis oculi narrows the eyes.

MUSCLES AND TENDONS

MUSCLES CAN ONLY CONTRACT AND SHORTEN. TO RETURN
TO THEIR ORIGINAL SHAPE, THEY RELAX AND LENGTHEN
PASSIVELY AS OTHER MUSCLES CONTRACT.
CONTRACTION OF SKELETAL MUSCLES AND
TENDONS GENERATES BODY MOTION.

MUSCLE STRUCTURE

Skeletal (striated or voluntary) muscle consists
of densely packed groups of hugely elongated
cells known as myofibres. These are grouped
into bundles (fascicles). A typical myofibre is
2–3cm (¾–1⅓in) long and 0.05mm (¹⁄₅₀in)
in diameter and is composed of narrower
structures – myofibrils. These contain thick
and thin myofilaments made up mainly of
the proteins actin and myosin. Numerous
capillaries keep the muscle supplied with the
oxygen and glucose needed to fuel contraction.

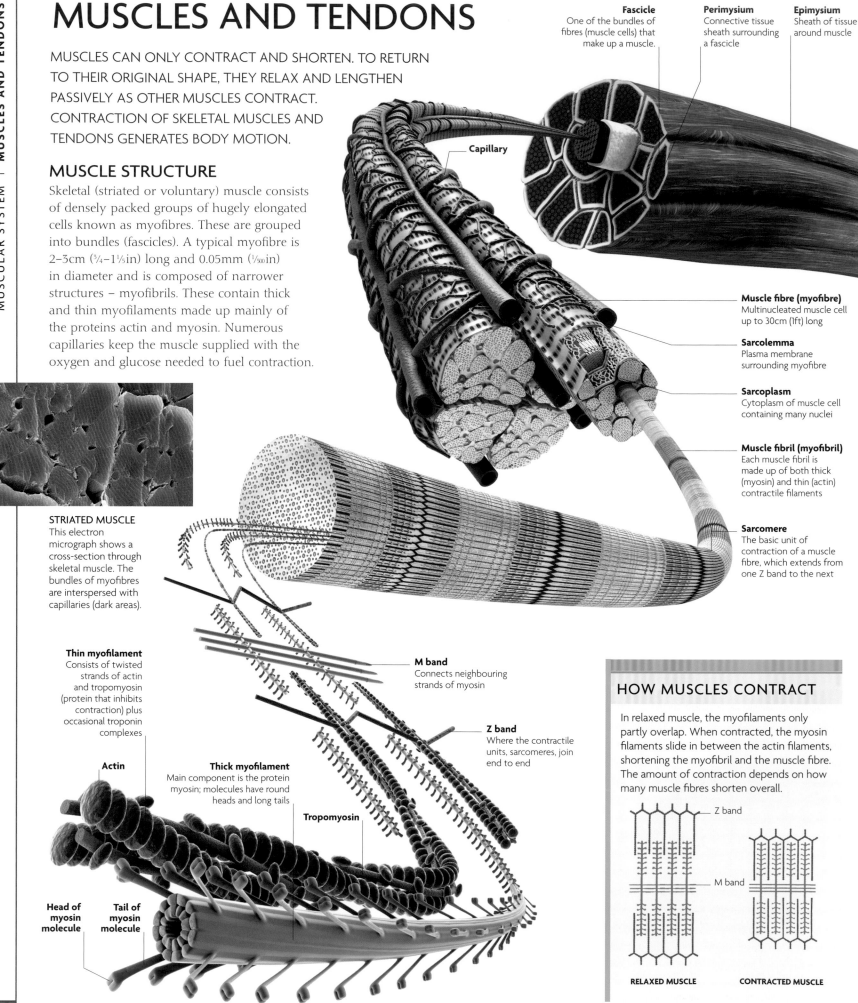

Fascicle
One of the bundles of
fibres (muscle cells) that
make up a muscle.

Perimysium
Connective tissue
sheath surrounding
a fascicle

Epimysium
Sheath of tissue
around muscle

Capillary

Muscle fibre (myofibre)
Multinucleated muscle cell
up to 30cm (1ft) long

Sarcolemma
Plasma membrane
surrounding myofibre

Sarcoplasm
Cytoplasm of muscle cell
containing many nuclei

Muscle fibril (myofibril)
Each muscle fibril is
made up of both thick
(myosin) and thin (actin)
contractile filaments

Sarcomere
The basic unit of
contraction of a muscle
fibre, which extends from
one Z band to the next

STRIATED MUSCLE
This electron
micrograph shows a
cross-section through
skeletal muscle. The
bundles of myofibres
are interspersed with
capillaries (dark areas).

Thin myofilament
Consists of twisted
strands of actin
and tropomyosin
(protein that inhibits
contraction) plus
occasional troponin
complexes

M band
Connects neighbouring
strands of myosin

Z band
Where the contractile
units, sarcomeres, join
end to end

Actin

Thick myofilament
Main component is the protein
myosin; molecules have round
heads and long tails

Tropomyosin

**Head of
myosin
molecule**

**Tail of
myosin
molecule**

HOW MUSCLES CONTRACT

In relaxed muscle, the myofilaments only
partly overlap. When contracted, the myosin
filaments slide in between the actin filaments,
shortening the myofibril and the muscle fibre.
The amount of contraction depends on how
many muscle fibres shorten overall.

Z band

M band

RELAXED MUSCLE   **CONTRACTED MUSCLE**

BODY PARTS AS LEVERS

Movements in the body, such as nodding and walking, employ the mechanical principles of applying a force to one part of a rigid lever, which tilts at a pivot point (fulcrum), to move a weight (load) elsewhere on the lever. The muscles apply force, the bones serve as levers, and the joints function as fulcrums. A whole range of lever systems exist in the body and between them they allow a wide range of movement as well as providing a means to lift and carry things.

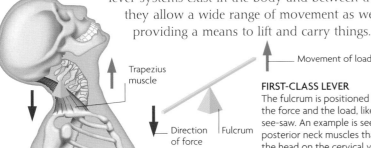

Trapezius muscle
Movement of load
Direction of force
Fulcrum

FIRST-CLASS LEVER
The fulcrum is positioned between the force and the load, like a see-saw. An example is seen in the posterior neck muscles that tilt back the head on the cervical vertebrae.

SECOND-CLASS LEVER
The load lies between the force and the fulcrum. Standing on tip-toe, the calf muscles provide the force, the heel and foot form the lever, and the toes provide the fulcrum.

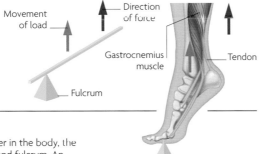

Movement of load
Direction of force
Gastrocnemius muscle
Tendon
Fulcrum

THIRD-CLASS LEVER
The most common type of lever in the body, the force is applied between load and fulcrum. An example is flexing the elbow joint (the fulcrum) by contracting the biceps brachii muscle.

Biceps brachii muscle
Tendon
Movement of load
Direction of force
Fulcrum

POSITIONAL SENSE

Muscles contain many tiny sensors, known as neuromuscular spindles. These are modified muscle fibres with a spindle-shaped sheath or capsule and several types of nerve supply. The sensory or afferent nerve fibres, which are wrapped around the modified muscle fibres, relay information to the brain about muscle length and tension as the muscle stretches. The motor neurons stimulate the opposite reaction, causing the muscle to contract and shorten, and restoring muscle tension to normal. Similar receptors are found in ligaments and tendons. Together they provide the body's innate sense of its own position and posture, called proprioception.

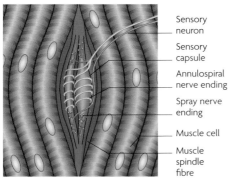

Sensory neuron
Sensory capsule
Annulospiral nerve ending
Spray nerve ending
Muscle cell
Muscle spindle fibre

NEUROMUSCULAR SPINDLE
The effect of motor signals sent to the spindle's muscle fibres is fed back by the sensory nerve fibres, allowing the brain to gauge the muscle's tension and elongation.

Tendons are tough, fibrous cords of connective tissue that link skeletal muscles to bones. Within them, Sharpey's fibres pass through the bone covering (periosteum) to embed in the bone. Tendons in the hands and feet are enclosed in self-lubricating sheaths to protect them from rubbing against the bones. From the hand bones, tendons extend upwards to muscles near the elbow.

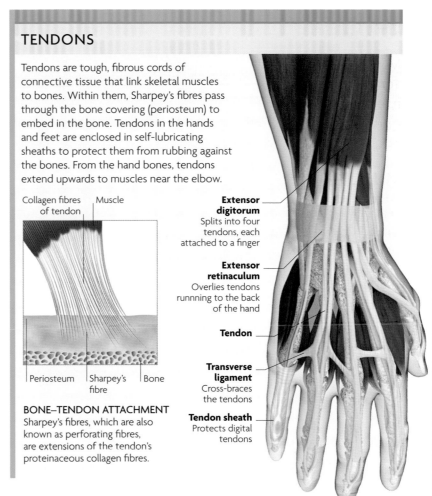

Collagen fibres of tendon
Muscle
Periosteum
Sharpey's fibre
Bone

Extensor digitorum
Splits into four tendons, each attached to a finger

Extensor retinaculum
Overlies tendons runnning to the back of the hand

Tendon

Transverse ligament
Cross-braces the tendons

Tendon sheath
Protects digital tendons

BONE–TENDON ATTACHMENT
Sharpey's fibres, which are also known as perforating fibres, are extensions of the tendon's proteinaceous collagen fibres.

HOW MUSCLES WORK TOGETHER

Muscles can only pull, not push, and so are arranged in pairs that act in opposition to one other. The movement produced by one muscle can be reversed by its opposing partner. When a muscle contracts to produce movement, it is called the agonist, while its opposite partner, the antagonist, relaxes and is passively stretched. In reality, few movements are achieved by a single muscle contraction. Usually, whole teams of muscles act as agonists to give the precisely required degree and direction of motion, while the antagonists tense to prevent the movement over-extending.

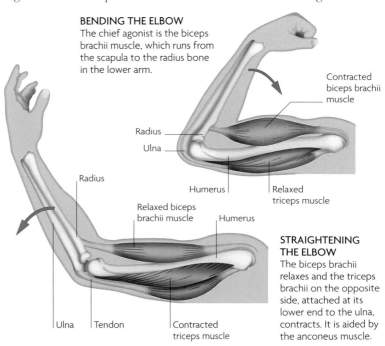

BENDING THE ELBOW
The chief agonist is the biceps brachii muscle, which runs from the scapula to the radius bone in the lower arm.

Contracted biceps brachii muscle
Radius
Ulna
Humerus
Relaxed triceps muscle
Radius
Relaxed biceps brachii muscle
Humerus
Ulna
Tendon
Contracted triceps muscle

STRAIGHTENING THE ELBOW
The biceps brachii relaxes and the triceps brachii on the opposite side, attached at its lower end to the ulna, contracts. It is aided by the anconeus muscle.

MUSCLE AND TENDON DISORDERS

INJURIES TO MUSCLES AND THEIR TENDON ATTACHMENTS ARE USUALLY THE RESULT OF PHYSICAL EXERTION DURING DAILY ACTIVITIES, OR DUE TO SUDDEN PULLING OR TWISTING MOVEMENTS, SUCH AS THOSE OCCURRING IN SPORT OR AN ACCIDENT. REPETITIVE ACTIONS, FOR EXAMPLE AS PART OF EMPLOYMENT, CAN ALSO DAMAGE MUSCLES AND TENDONS OVER TIME. A NUMBER OF RARE MUSCLE DISORDERS MAY BE RESPONSIBLE FOR MUSCLE WEAKNESS AND PROGRESSIVE DEGENERATION.

MUSCLE STRAINS AND TEARS

A MILD INJURY RESULTING FROM AN OVERSTRETCHED MUSCLE IS CALLED A STRAIN; MORE SEVERE DAMAGE IS A TEAR.

Muscle strain is the term used for a moderate amount of soft-tissue damage to muscle fibres, usually caused by sudden, strenuous movements. Limited bleeding inside the muscle causes tenderness and swelling, which may be accompanied by painful spasms or contractions. Visible bruising may follow. More serious damage, involving a larger number of torn or ruptured fibres, is called a muscle tear. A torn muscle causes severe pain and swelling. Following a medical check to gauge severity, the usual treatment is rest, anti-inflammatory medication, and perhaps physiotherapy. Rarely, surgery may be needed to repair a muscle that has been badly torn. The risk of muscle strains and tears can be reduced by warming-up adequately before exercise.

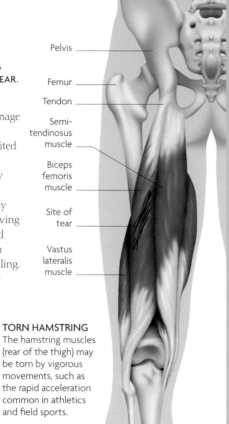

Pelvis
Femur
Tendon
Semi-tendinosus muscle
Biceps femoris muscle
Site of tear
Vastus lateralis muscle

TORN HAMSTRING
The hamstring muscles (rear of the thigh) may be torn by vigorous movements, such as the rapid acceleration common in athletics and field sports.

SOFT-TISSUE INFLAMMATION

THE BODY'S OWN DEFENCES CAUSE MUSCLE TISSUE TO BECOME INFLAMED AS THE HEALING PROCESS BEGINS.

Like any soft tissue, muscle reacts to damage – such as that from a physical blow – with inflammation (see pp.160–61). The affected area becomes hot, red, and swollen as blood and fluids accumulate from ruptured cells and capillaries. Blood vessels widen (dilate) as white blood cells congregate, attracted by the leaking debris from muscle fibres (cells) and other tissues. Moving the muscle causes discomfort or pain. Longer-term causes of muscle tissue inflammation are the group of disorders called repetitive strain injuries (RSIs). The basic cause is a particular movement or action repeated often over a long period. Movements that are rapid and forceful increase the risk. RSIs are linked to many and varied daily activities, from working on production lines or with computers, to sport or playing a musical instrument.

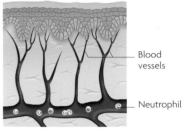

Blood vessels
Neutrophil

NORMAL TISSUE
Blood flows through undamaged vessels, where occasional white cells, such as neutrophils, scavenge debris and attack microorganisms that have managed to enter.

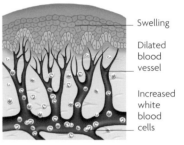

Swelling
Dilated blood vessel
Increased white blood cells

INFLAMED TISSUE
Blood vessels enlarge in diameter, bringing increased numbers of white blood cells, as fluid leaks from disrupted cells and tissues. Heat, pain, and redness result.

TENDINITIS AND TENOSYNOVITIS

INFLAMMATION CAN AFFECT THE TENDON ITSELF, AS TENDINITIS, OR THE LININGS OF THE TENDON SHEATHS THAT ENCLOSE THEM, AS TENOSYNOVITIS.

Tendinitis may occur when strong or repeated movement creates excessive friction between the tendon's outer surface and an adjacent bone. Tenosynovitis may be the result of overstretching or repeated movement causing inflammation of the lubricating sheaths that enclose some tendons. Both of these problems can occur together and may be part of the group of disorders known as repetitive strain injuries (RSIs), as described in soft-tissue inflammation, above. Areas affected include the shoulder, elbow, wrist, fingers, knee, and the back of the heel. Symptoms of both tendinitis and tenosynovitis are stiffness, swelling, and pain, with hot, reddened skin at the site.

Clavicle (collarbone)
Inflamed supraspinous tendon
Humerus

TENDINITIS
Repeated arm lifting, such as in racquet sports, may force the supraspinous tendon to rub against the shoulder blade's acromion process, causing tendinitis.

Acromion process of shoulder blade
Supraspinatus muscle

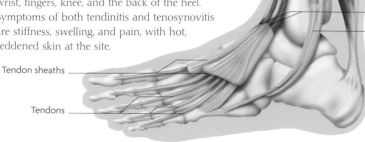

Tendon sheaths
Tendons
Inflammation
Tendon sheath

TENOSYNOVITIS
The complex, weight-bearing nature of the foot makes it susceptible to tendon damage. Activities that involve running or kicking, and awkward movements, such as dancing, may cause inflammation.

TENNIS ELBOW

TENNIS AND GOLFER'S ELBOW ARE COMMON NAMES FOR TENDON DAMAGE IN THE AREA WHERE THE ARM MUSCLES ATTACH TO BONES NEAR THE ELBOW JOINT.

Most cases of tennis elbow involve the common extensor tendon, which anchors several forearm muscles involved in wrist and hand movements to the lateral epicondyle, a knob-like projection on the upper arm bone (humerus). Golfer's elbow is a similar type of injury but the pain is at the site of the medial epicondyle on the elbow's inner side.

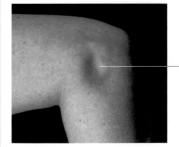

Area of lateral epicondyle damage

ELBOW INFLAMMATION
In tennis elbow, vigorous, repeated use of the forearm against resistance causes small tears in the tendon, leading to tenderness and pain on the outer side of the joint.

RUPTURED TENDON

A SUDDEN, POWERFUL MUSCLE CONTRACTION OR WRENCHING INJURY CAN COMPLETELY TEAR A TENDON.

Playing sport and unaccustomed lifting of heavy weights may result in torn, or ruptured, tendons. Examples are tearing of the tendons attached to the biceps brachii muscle in the upper arm, or of the quadriceps tendon at the front of the thigh that stretches over the knee. A sudden impact that bends a fingertip towards the palm may snap the extensor tendon on the back of the finger. In severe cases, the tendon

may even be torn away from the bone. Main symptoms include a snapping or twanging sensation, pain, swelling, and impaired movement. Some injuries, such as a ruptured Achilles tendon (at the back of the heel), may require immobilizaton of the affected area with a cast to prevent the tendon from stretching in the early stages of healing.

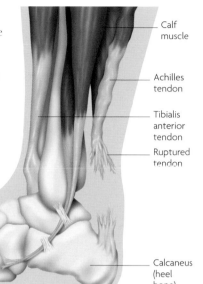

Calf muscle

Achilles tendon

Tibialis anterior tendon

Ruptured tendon

Calcaneus (heel bone)

TORN ACHILLES TENDON
The Achilles (long calcaneal) tendon attaches the calf muscle to the heel bone (calcaneus). It can snap after sudden exertion and may need to be treated by surgery and immobilization in a cast.

MYASTHENIA GRAVIS

THIS AUTOIMMUNE DISORDER CAUSES CHRONIC MUSCLE WEAKNESS; EYE AND FACIAL MUSCLES ARE AFFECTED MOST.

Myasthenia gravis is caused by antibodies that attack and gradually destroy the receptors in muscle fibres that receive nerve signals. As a result, muscles are not stimulated to contract, or respond only very weakly. Affected

muscles include those of the face, throat, and eyes, which can lead to problems with speech and vision. Arm, leg, and respiratory muscles are more rarely affected. A thymus disorder may trigger the disease, and so the thymus gland may be removed, along with immunosuppressant and other drugs given as treatment.

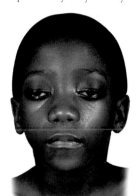
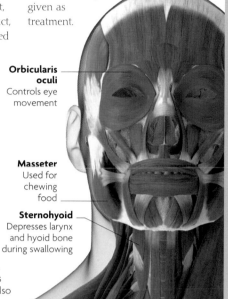

Orbicularis oculi
Controls eye movement

Masseter
Used for chewing food

Sternohyoid
Depresses larynx and hyoid bone during swallowing

EFFECTS OF MYASTHENIA GRAVIS
Early symptoms include drooping eyelids (above) as facial muscles weaken. Muscles involved in chewing and swallowing are also affected, so eating can become difficult.

MUSCULAR DYSTROPHY

MUSCULAR DYSTROPHIES ARE A GROUP OF INHERITED DISORDERS THAT CAUSE DEGENERATION OF MUSCLE, LEADING TO WEAK AND IMPAIRED MOVEMENTS.

Common symptoms of various types of muscular dystrophy (MD) are progressive wasting of muscles and loss of movement. There is no effective treatment to halt the underlying process. However, stretching exercises and surgery to release shortened muscles and tendons can benefit some sufferers by improving mobility. Among the well-known forms are Duchenne and Becker MD, in which the genetic abnormality is carried on the X chromosome; they almost always affect boys.

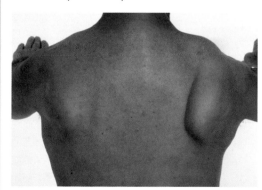

EFFECT OF MUSCULAR DYSTROPHY
In facioscapulohumeral muscular dystrophy (FSH), the muscles of the face, shoulder, and upper arm become weak. Holding the arm out forward causes "winging" of the shoulder blade (scapula), where the bone's inner edge protrudes rearward.

CARPAL TUNNEL SYNDROME

COMPRESSION OF A NERVE IN THE WRIST LEADS TO SYMPTOMS SUCH AS TINGLING AND PAIN IN THE HAND, WRIST, AND FOREARM, AND WEAKENED GRIP.

The carpal tunnel is a narrow passageway formed by the carpal ligament (flexor retinaculum), on the inside of the wrist, and the underlying wrist bones, the carpals. Long tendons run through the passage from the muscles in the forearm to the bones of the hand and fingers. The median nerve also passes through the carpal tunnel, to control hand muscles

and convey sensations from the fingers. In carpal tunnel syndrome (CTS) the median nerve is compressed by swelling of the tissues around it in the tunnel. Causes include diabetes mellitus, pregnancy, a wrist injury, rheumatoid arthritis, and repetitive movements; in some cases the cause is not clear. CTS tends to affect women aged 40–60 and can occur in both wrists. The nerve compression causes numbness and pain, especially in the thumb to middle fingers and one side of the ring finger. Anti-inflammatory drugs and perhaps surgery to loosen the ligament can bring relief.

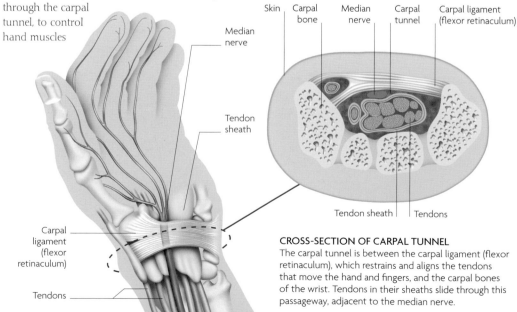

Median nerve

Tendon sheath

Carpal ligament (flexor retinaculum)

Tendons

Skin / Carpal bone / Median nerve / Carpal tunnel / Carpal ligament (flexor retinaculum)

Tendon sheath / Tendons

CROSS-SECTION OF CARPAL TUNNEL
The carpal tunnel is between the carpal ligament (flexor retinaculum), which restrains and aligns the tendons that move the hand and fingers, and the carpal bones of the wrist. Tendons in their sheaths slide through this passageway, adjacent to the median nerve.

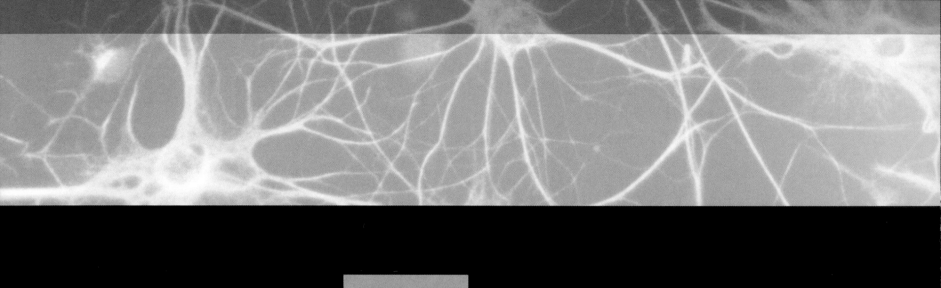

IN SOME WAYS, THE HUMAN BRAIN RESEMBLES A
COMPUTER. BUT IN ADDITION TO LOGICAL PROCESSING,
IT IS CAPABLE OF COMPLEX DEVELOPMENT, LEARNING,
SELF-AWARENESS, EMOTION, AND CREATIVITY. EVERY
SECOND, MILLIONS OF CHEMICAL AND ELECTRICAL
SIGNALS PASS AROUND THE BRAIN AND THE BODY'S
INTRICATE NERVE NETWORK. BUT NERVOUS TISSUE IS

NERVOUS SYSTEM

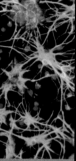

● SEE DVD-ROM

NERVOUS SYSTEM

CONSTANTLY ALIVE WITH ELECTRICITY, THE NERVOUS SYSTEM IS THE BODY'S PRIME COMMUNICATION AND COORDINATION NETWORK. IT IS SO VAST AND COMPLEX THAT, AT A CAUTIOUS ESTIMATE, ALL THE INDIVIDUAL NERVES FROM ONE BODY JOINED END TO END COULD REACH AROUND THE WORLD TWO AND A HALF TIMES.

The nervous system actually comprises three systems or components, defined by both anatomy and function. The central nervous system, CNS, is central to the body's structure and workings. It is composed of the brain and its chief nerve, the spinal cord, which runs along the inside of the backbone (spinal or vertebral column). From the CNS 43 pairs of nerves branch: 12 from the brain and 31 from the cord. As these divide, snake among organs and tissue, and infiltrate every tiny nook and cranny, they form the network of the peripheral nervous system, PNS. The CNS can be viewed as the coordinator and decision-maker, with the PNS sending information as sensory input, and receiving instructions as motor output to muscles and glands. The third component is the autonomic nervous system, ANS. This has some elements located in the CNS and shares some nerves with the PNS; it also has its own nerve chains alongside the spinal cord. Its work is primarily "automatic" in that it deals with activities such as blood pressure control and heart rate adjustment, of which we are rarely aware.

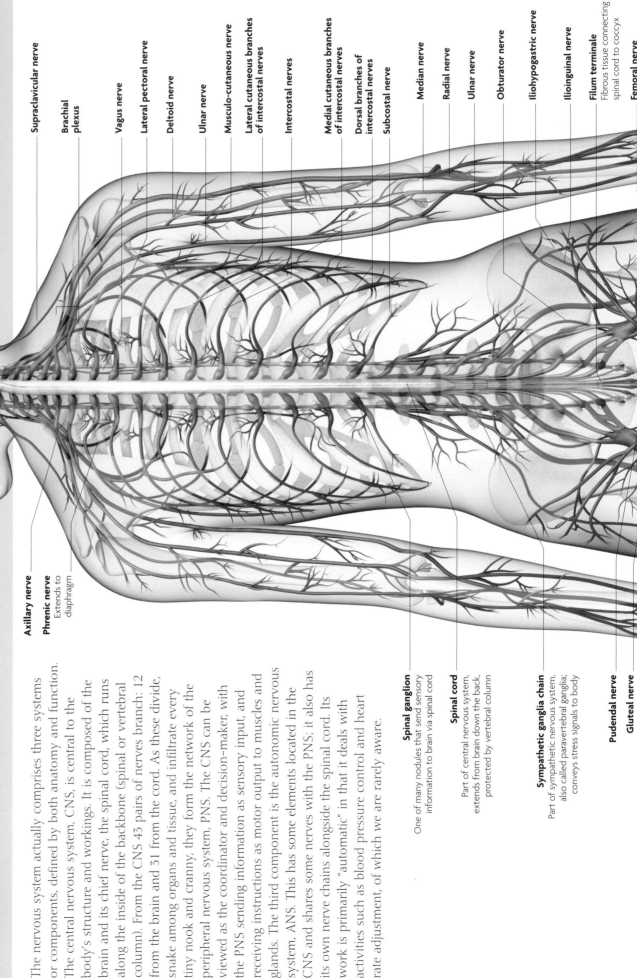

Brain

Auriculotemporal nerve

Facial nerve

Supraclavicular nerve

Brachial plexus

Vagus nerve

Lateral pectoral nerve

Deltoid nerve

Ulnar nerve

Musculo-cutaneous nerve

Lateral cutaneous branches of intercostal nerves

Intercostal nerves

Medial cutaneous branches of intercostal nerves

Dorsal branches of intercostal nerves

Subcostal nerve

Median nerve

Radial nerve

Ulnar nerve

Obturator nerve

Iliohypogastric nerve

Ilioinguinal nerve

Filum terminale
Fibrous tissue connecting spinal cord to coccyx

Femoral nerve

Axillary nerve

Phrenic nerve
Extends to diaphragm

Spinal ganglion
One of many nodules that send sensory information to brain via spinal cord

Spinal cord
Part of central nervous system, extends from brain down the back, protected by vertebral column

Sympathetic ganglia chain
Part of sympathetic nervous system, also called paravertebral ganglia; conveys stress signals to body

Pudendal nerve

Gluteal nerve

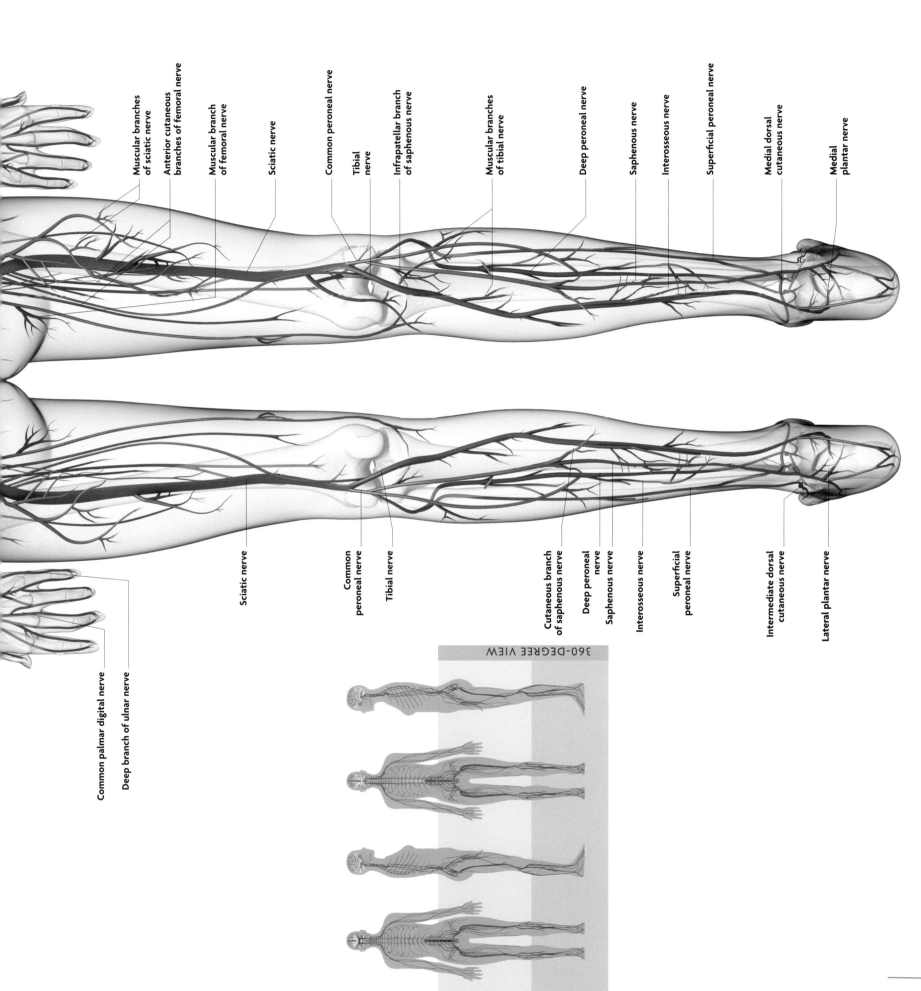

Muscular branches of sciatic nerve

Anterior cutaneous branches of femoral nerve

Muscular branch of femoral nerve

Sciatic nerve

Common peroneal nerve

Tibial nerve

Infrapatellar branch of saphenous nerve

Muscular branches of tibial nerve

Deep peroneal nerve

Saphenous nerve

Interosseous nerve

Superficial peroneal nerve

Medial dorsal cutaneous nerve

Medial plantar nerve

Common palmar digital nerve

Deep branch of ulnar nerve

Sciatic nerve

Common peroneal nerve

Tibial nerve

Cutaneous branch of saphenous nerve

Deep peroneal nerve

Saphenous nerve

Interosseous nerve

Superficial peroneal nerve

Intermediate dorsal cutaneous nerve

Lateral plantar nerve

360-DEGREE VIEW

NERVES AND NEURONS

THE BRAIN HAS OVER 100 BILLION NERVE CELLS, OR NEURONS, AND THE BODY CONTAINS MILLIONS MORE. BUNDLES OF NERVE FIBRES PROJECTING FROM NEURONS FORM A BODY-WIDE NETWORK OF NERVES. NEURONS ARE HIGHLY SPECIALIZED IN THEIR STRUCTURE, FUNCTION, AND THE WAY THEY LINK TOGETHER TO COMMUNICATE.

NEURON STRUCTURE

Like all other cells, a typical neuron has a main cell body with a nucleus. But a neuron also has long, wire-like processes that reach out to transmit messages to other neurons at junctions called synapses. These processes are of two main kinds. Dendrites receive messages from other neurons, or from nerve-like cells in sense organs, and conduct them towards the cell body of the neuron. Axons convey messages away from the cell body, to other neurons or to muscle or gland cells. Dendrites tend to be short and have many branches, while axons are usually longer and branch less along their length. Neurons in the brain and spinal cord are protected and nurtured by supporting nerve cells known as glial cells.

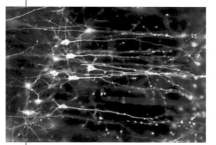

MICROSCOPE VIEW
Nerve cells under the microscope display their cell bodies with nuclei (left) and processes (right).

TYPES OF NEURON

The shapes and sizes of the bodies of neuron cells vary greatly, as do the type, number, and length of their projections. Neurons are classified according to the number of processes that extend from the cell body. Bipolar neurons are the "original" neuronal design in the embryo, but by adulthood, they are found in only a few locations, such as the eye's retina and the olfactory nerve in the nose. Most neurons in the brain and spinal cord are multipolar. Unipolar neurons are present mainly in the sensory nerves of the peripheral nervous system.

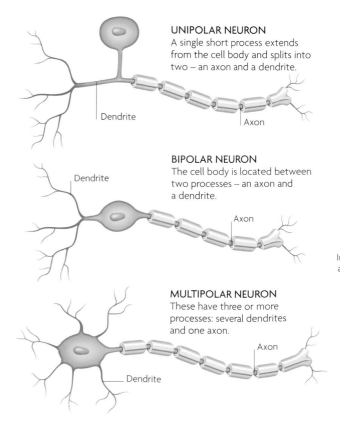

UNIPOLAR NEURON
A single short process extends from the cell body and splits into two – an axon and a dendrite.

Dendrite

Axon

BIPOLAR NEURON
The cell body is located between two processes – an axon and a dendrite.

Dendrite

Axon

MULTIPOLAR NEURON
These have three or more processes: several dendrites and one axon.

Axon

Dendrite

Axon terminal fibre

Schwann cell
Produces myelin

Schwann cell nucleus

NEURONAL NETWORK
The snaking dendrites and axons of a neural net, which are reaching out to communicate, are clearly visible in this image. These neurons are of the multipolar type, found especially in the cortex of the brain. A single neuron can correspond via its processes with tens of thousands of others.

Dendrite process
Receives messages from other neurons

Axon process
Transmits messages from the nerve cell body to other tissues

Mitochondrion
Involved in cell respiration and production of energy

Nucleus
Located towards the middle of the cell body

Cell body

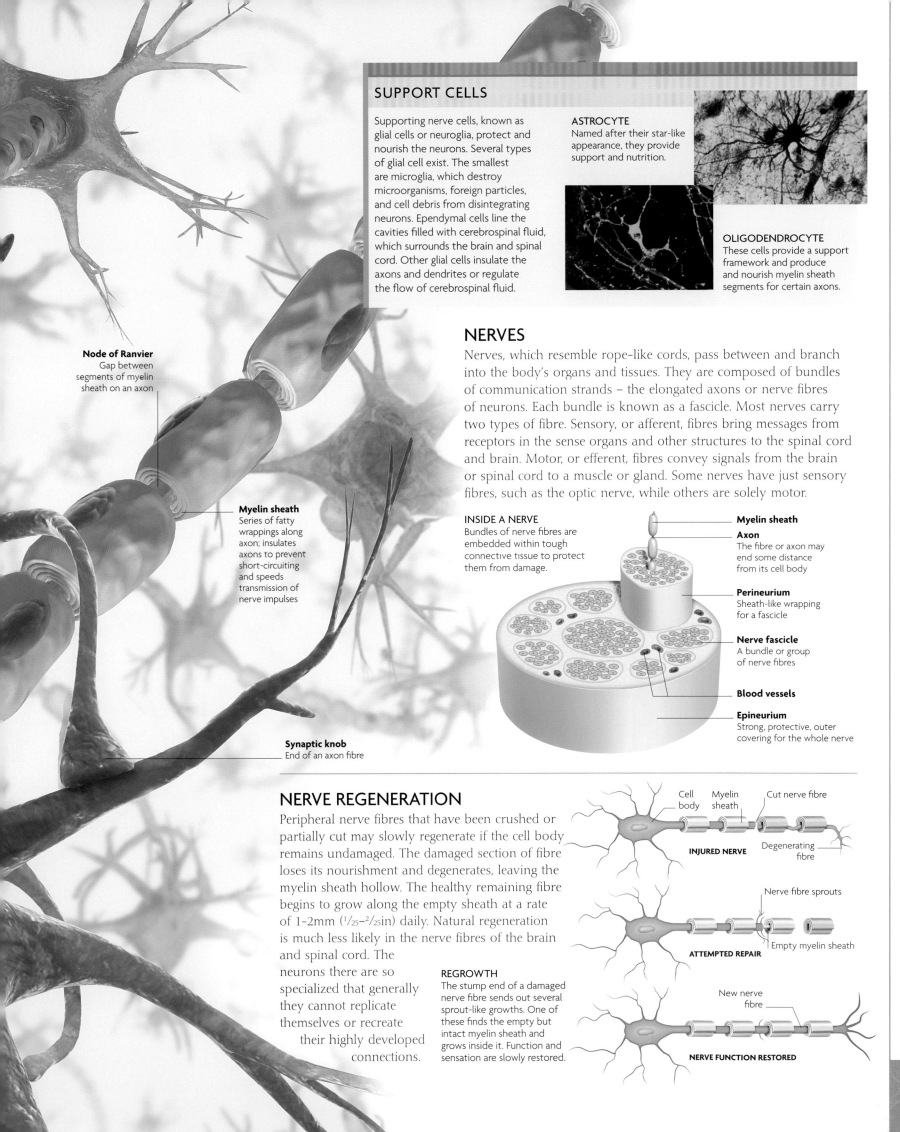

SUPPORT CELLS

Supporting nerve cells, known as glial cells or neuroglia, protect and nourish the neurons. Several types of glial cell exist. The smallest are microglia, which destroy microorganisms, foreign particles, and cell debris from disintegrating neurons. Ependymal cells line the cavities filled with cerebrospinal fluid, which surrounds the brain and spinal cord. Other glial cells insulate the axons and dendrites or regulate the flow of cerebrospinal fluid.

ASTROCYTE
Named after their star-like appearance, they provide support and nutrition.

OLIGODENDROCYTE
These cells provide a support framework and produce and nourish myelin sheath segments for certain axons.

Node of Ranvier
Gap between segments of myelin sheath on an axon

Myelin sheath
Series of fatty wrappings along axon; insulates axons to prevent short-circuiting and speeds transmission of nerve impulses

Synaptic knob
End of an axon fibre

NERVES

Nerves, which resemble rope-like cords, pass between and branch into the body's organs and tissues. They are composed of bundles of communication strands – the elongated axons or nerve fibres of neurons. Each bundle is known as a fascicle. Most nerves carry two types of fibre. Sensory, or afferent, fibres bring messages from receptors in the sense organs and other structures to the spinal cord and brain. Motor, or efferent, fibres convey signals from the brain or spinal cord to a muscle or gland. Some nerves have just sensory fibres, such as the optic nerve, while others are solely motor.

INSIDE A NERVE
Bundles of nerve fibres are embedded within tough connective tissue to protect them from damage.

Myelin sheath

Axon
The fibre or axon may end some distance from its cell body

Perineurium
Sheath-like wrapping for a fascicle

Nerve fascicle
A bundle or group of nerve fibres

Blood vessels

Epineurium
Strong, protective, outer covering for the whole nerve

NERVE REGENERATION

Peripheral nerve fibres that have been crushed or partially cut may slowly regenerate if the cell body remains undamaged. The damaged section of fibre loses its nourishment and degenerates, leaving the myelin sheath hollow. The healthy remaining fibre begins to grow along the empty sheath at a rate of 1-2mm ($^1/_{25}$–$^2/_{25}$in) daily. Natural regeneration is much less likely in the nerve fibres of the brain and spinal cord. The neurons there are so specialized that generally they cannot replicate themselves or recreate their highly developed connections.

REGROWTH
The stump end of a damaged nerve fibre sends out several sprout-like growths. One of these finds the empty but intact myelin sheath and grows inside it. Function and sensation are slowly restored.

Cell body | Myelin sheath | Cut nerve fibre
INJURED NERVE — Degenerating fibre

Nerve fibre sprouts
ATTEMPTED REPAIR — Empty myelin sheath

New nerve fibre
NERVE FUNCTION RESTORED

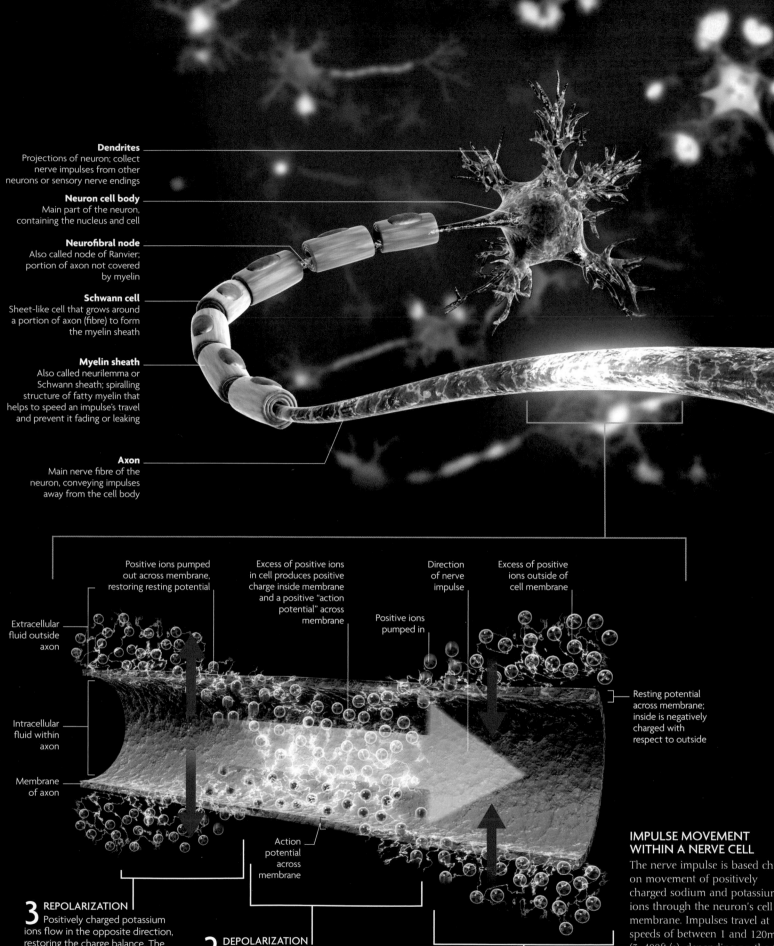

Dendrites
Projections of neuron; collect nerve impulses from other neurons or sensory nerve endings

Neuron cell body
Main part of the neuron, containing the nucleus and cell

Neurofibral node
Also called node of Ranvier; portion of axon not covered by myelin

Schwann cell
Sheet-like cell that grows around a portion of axon (fibre) to form the myelin sheath

Myelin sheath
Also called neurilemma or Schwann sheath; spiralling structure of fatty myelin that helps to speed an impulse's travel and prevent it fading or leaking

Axon
Main nerve fibre of the neuron, conveying impulses away from the cell body

Positive ions pumped out across membrane, restoring resting potential

Excess of positive ions in cell produces positive charge inside membrane and a positive "action potential" across membrane

Direction of nerve impulse

Excess of positive ions outside of cell membrane

Extracellular fluid outside axon

Positive ions pumped in

Resting potential across membrane; inside is negatively charged with respect to outside

Intracellular fluid within axon

Membrane of axon

Action potential across membrane

IMPULSE MOVEMENT WITHIN A NERVE CELL

The nerve impulse is based chiefly on movement of positively charged sodium and potassium ions through the neuron's cell membrane. Impulses travel at speeds of between 1 and 120m/s (3–400ft/s), depending on the type of nerve. Movement is much faster in sheathed (myelinated) axons, in which the action potential jumps along successive myelin-coated sections from one node to the next (see above).

3 REPOLARIZATION
Positively charged potassium ions flow in the opposite direction, restoring the charge balance. The change in electrical charge stimulates an adjacent area of membrane, and the next, and so on. The impulse moves along the membrane as a wave of depolarization and repolarization.

2 DEPOLARIZATION
During this phase (depolarization), positive sodium ions rush in through ion channels in a patch of neuron membrane. The membrane is first depolarized, then its polarity is reversed to become slightly positive, resulting in an "action potential" of +30 millivolts on the inside.

1 RESTING POTENTIAL
With no impulse, there are more positively charged ions, particularly sodium ions, outside the cell membrane and more negative ions inside. This produces an electrical "resting potential" of –70 millivolts. The membrane is polarized, with the inside negative.

NERVE IMPULSE

NERVE CELLS, OR NEURONS, ARE EXCITABLE. WHEN STIMULATED, THEY
UNDERGO CHEMICAL CHANGES THAT PRODUCE TINY TRAVELLING WAVES
OF ELECTRICITY – NERVE SIGNALS, OR IMPULSES. THESE PASS TO OTHER
NEURONS, ELICITING SIMILAR RESPONSES FROM THEM.

Throughout the nervous system, information is conveyed as tiny electrical signals called nerve impulses, or action potentials. These impulses are the same all over the body – about 100 millivolts (0.1 volts) in strength and lasting just 1 millisecond ($^1/_{1000}$ s). The information carried depends on their position in the nervous system, and their frequency – from one impulse every few seconds to several hundreds per second. Typically, when a neuron receives enough impulses from other neurons it fires one of its own, as wave-like movements of ions (electrically-charged particles). Impulses jump from one neuron to another at junctions known as synapses.

EXCITEMENT AND INHIBITION

When neurotransmitters land on their receptor sites, they can either excite or inhibit the receiving cell. Both responses are equally valuable in relaying messages through the nervous system. To excite a receiving cell, positive sodium ions flow into it, depolarizing the membrane in a similar way to a nerve impulse (see opposite). The depolarizing effect spreads through the membrane for a few milliseconds, fading as it does so. If further signals enter the cell, they may become strong enough to fire a new nerve impulse. To inhibit a cell, negatively charged chloride ions rush into a cell. The negative effect spreads through the cell membrane and prevents its excitement.

CROSSING THE GAP BETWEEN NEURONS

When an electrical impulse arrives at the junction (synapse), it triggers the release of chemicals called neurotransmitters. They cross the incredibly thin gap (synaptic cleft) between the membranes of the presynaptic (sending) and postsynaptic (receiving) neurons. They either trigger a new impulse in the receiving neuron or actively inhibit it from firing.

Microfilament
Thinnest element of the flexible, supporting scaffolding found in most cells

Mitochondrion
Standard cellular component that provides energy

Synaptic vesicle
Package of neurotransmitter molecules that fuses with the cell membrane when an impulse arrives, releasing the molecules

Neurotransmitter
Molecule that flows across the synaptic cleft in about 1 millisecond, passing on the nerve impulse in chemical form

Presynaptic membrane
Membrane of sending cell's axon

Postsynaptic membrane
Membrane of receiving cell's dendrite

Neurotubule
Specialized microtubule that works as a conveyor belt to bring synaptic vesicles from the cell body to the axon terminal

Positive ion

Synaptic knob
Enlarged end of axon terminal

Membrane channel protein
Complex protein embedded in cell membrane; when enough ions flood through the channel they cause a response in the receiving cell

Receptor
Site in membrane channel into which neurotransmitter molecules slot, altering the shape of the channel to admit charged ions

Synaptic cleft
Fluid-filled gap between the sending and receiving neuron, just 25 nanometres (25 billionths of a metre, $^1/_{1,000,000}$ in) wide

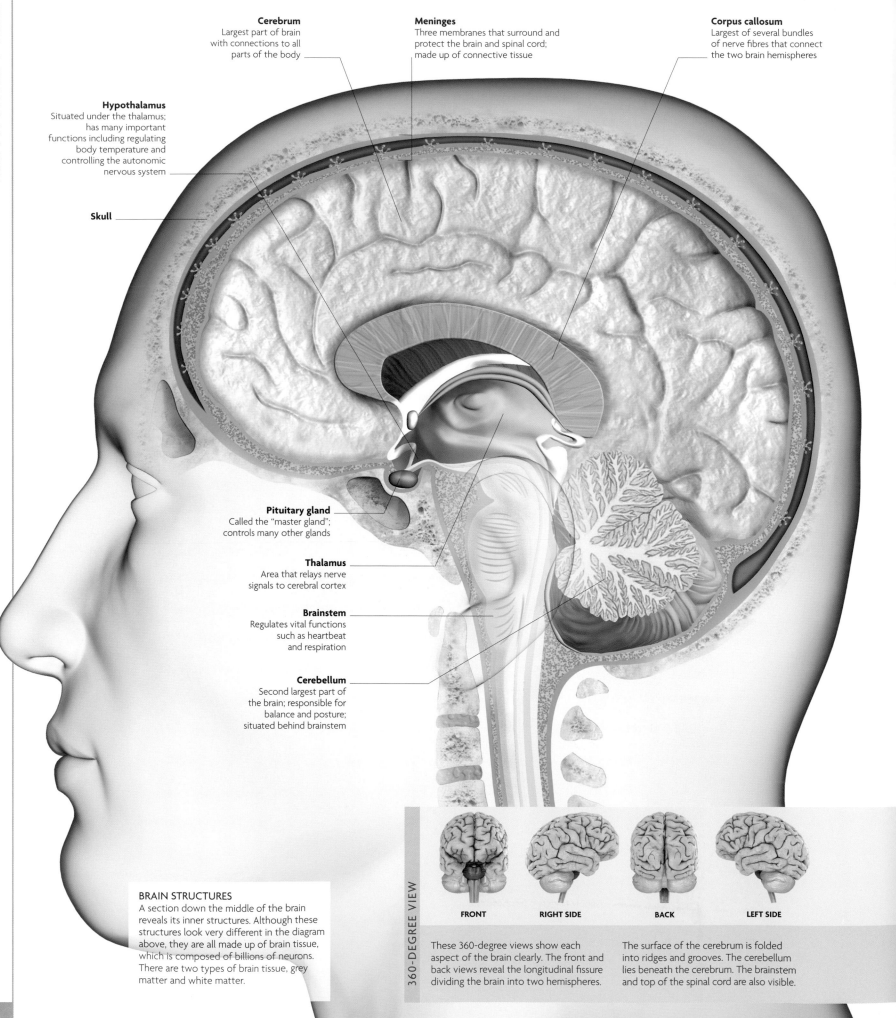

Cerebrum
Largest part of brain with connections to all parts of the body

Meninges
Three membranes that surround and protect the brain and spinal cord; made up of connective tissue

Corpus callosum
Largest of several bundles of nerve fibres that connect the two brain hemispheres

Hypothalamus
Situated under the thalamus; has many important functions including regulating body temperature and controlling the autonomic nervous system

Skull

Pituitary gland
Called the "master gland"; controls many other glands

Thalamus
Area that relays nerve signals to cerebral cortex

Brainstem
Regulates vital functions such as heartbeat and respiration

Cerebellum
Second largest part of the brain; responsible for balance and posture; situated behind brainstem

BRAIN STRUCTURES
A section down the middle of the brain reveals its inner structures. Although these structures look very different in the diagram above, they are all made up of brain tissue, which is composed of billions of neurons. There are two types of brain tissue, grey matter and white matter.

360-DEGREE VIEW

FRONT   **RIGHT SIDE**   **BACK**   **LEFT SIDE**

These 360-degree views show each aspect of the brain clearly. The front and back views reveal the longitudinal fissure dividing the brain into two hemispheres.

The surface of the cerebrum is folded into ridges and grooves. The cerebellum lies beneath the cerebrum. The brainstem and top of the spinal cord are also visible.

BRAIN

THE BRAIN, IN CONJUNCTION WITH THE SPINAL
CORD, REGULATES BOTH NON-CONSCIOUS PROCESSES
AND COORDINATES MOST VOLUNTARY MOVEMENT.
FURTHERMORE, THE BRAIN IS THE SITE OF CONSCIOUSNESS,
ALLOWING HUMANS TO THINK AND LEARN.

BRAIN STRUCTURE

The largest part of the brain is the cerebrum, which has a heavily
folded surface – the pattern of which is unique in each person.
The grooves are called sulci when shallow and fissures when deep.
Fissures and some of the large sulci outline four functional areas
called lobes: frontal, parietal,
occipital, and temporal (see
p.76). A ridge on the surface of
the brain is called a gyrus. The
centre of the brain contains
the thalamus, which acts as the
brain's information relay station.
Surrounding this is a group of
structures known as the limbic
system (see p.78), which is
involved in survival instincts,
behaviour, and emotions. Closely
linked with the limbic system
is the hypothalamus, which
receives sensory information.

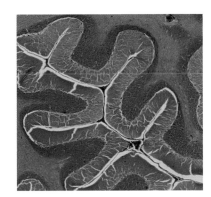

CEREBELLUM
The cerebellum (section shown above)
contains billions of neurons that link up
with other regions of the brain and spinal
cord to facilitate precise movement.

BLOOD SUPPLY TO THE BRAIN

The brain accounts for 2 per cent of total body weight, yet it
requires 20 per cent of the body's blood. Both oxygen and glucose
are transported by blood; without these essential elements, brain
function quickly deteriorates and dizziness, confusion, and loss
of consciousness may occur. Within only four to eight minutes of
oxygen depravation, brain damage, or death results. The brain has
an abundant supply of blood from a vast network of blood vessels
that stem from the carotid arteries,
which run up each side of the neck,
and from two vertebral arteries
that run alongside the spinal cord.

CIRCLE OF WILLIS
A ring of communicating arteries, known as the
Circle of Willis, encircle the base of the brain.
This arterial ring provides multiple pathways to
supply oxygenated blood to all parts of the brain.
If one pathway becomes blocked, blood can be
supplied from an alternative artery in the circle.

BLOOD SUPPLY
The brain has an extensive blood
supply from two front and two
rear arteries, as illustrated in
this colour, three-dimensional
magnetic resonance angiography
(MRA) scan. The blood vessels are
coloured in red; here they are seen
supplying oxygenated blood to
various parts of the brain, which
is shown as the blue area.

PROTECTION

The brain has several forms of protection. It is shielded by the three
protective membranes (meninges) that envelop it, and the ventricles
(chambers) in the brain produce a watery medium within the
skull known as cerebrospinal fluid (CSF, see below) that absorbs
and disperses excessive mechanical forces which might otherwise
cause serious injury. An
analysis of the chemical
constituents and flow
pressure of CSF has
offered vital clues in
the diagnosis of many
diseases and disorders
of the brain and spinal
cord, such as meningitis.

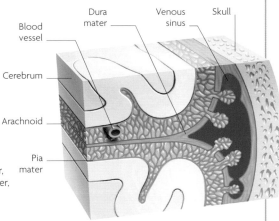

MENINGES
The outermost membrane, dura mater,
contains blood vessels; the middle layer,
arachnoid, consists of connective
tissue; and the innermost membrane,
pia mater, lies closest to the brain.

CEREBROSPINAL FLUID FLOW

The soft tissue of the brain floats in cerebrospinal fluid (CSF) within
the bony casing of the skull. CSF is a clear liquid, which is renewed four
to five times a day. It contains proteins and glucose that provide energy
for brain cell function as well as lymphocytes that guard against
infection. The CSF protects and nourishes both the brain and spinal
cord as it flows around them. The fluid is produced by the choroid
plexuses in the lateral ventricles, which drains into the third ventricle.
It then flows into the fourth ventricle, located in front of the cerebellum.
Circulation of the fluid is aided by pulsations of the cerebral arteries.

1 Site of fluid production (choroid plexuses)
The CSF found in the ventricles
in the brain is produced in
clusters of thin-walled capillaries,
known as choroid plexuses.
These capillaries line the walls
of the ventricles.

2 Direction of flow
Fluid moves from the brain's
lateral ventricles into the third
and fourth ventricles. The fluid
then flows up the back of the
brain, down around the spinal
cord, and up to the front
of the brain, as indicated
by the arrows.

4 Site of reabsorption (arachnoid granulations)
After circulating around the brain,
CSF is reabsorbed into the blood
via structures known as arachnoid
granulations, which are projections
of the arachnoid layer into the large
sagittal sinus, or cerebral vein.

3 Circulation around spinal cord
Aided by vertebral movement,
the CSF flows downward
along the back of the spinal
cord and in the central canal,
and then returns upward along
the front of the spinal cord.

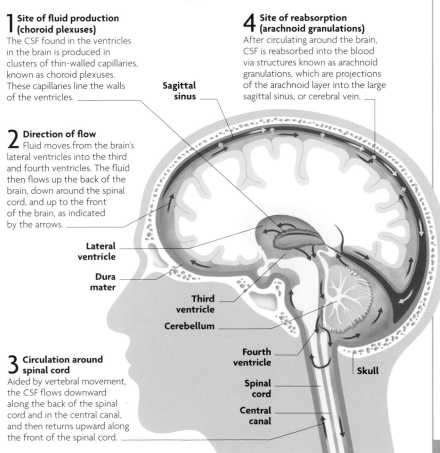

BRAIN STRUCTURES

THE BRAIN COMPRISES ABOUT ONE-FIFTIETH OF THE WEIGHT OF THE WHOLE
BODY, AVERAGING 1.4KG (3LB 2OZ) IN ADULTS. ANATOMICALLY, IT HAS FOUR
MAIN STRUCTURES: THE LARGE, DOMED CEREBRUM; THE DEEPER, INNER
DIENCEPHALON (CONSISTING OF THE THALAMUS AND NEARBY STRUCTURES);
THE CEREBELLUM TO THE LOWER REAR; AND THE BRAINSTEM AT THE BASE.

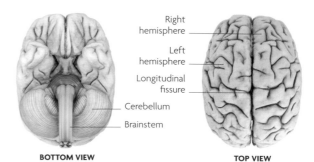

Right
hemisphere
Left
hemisphere
Longitudinal
fissure
Cerebellum
Brainstem

BOTTOM VIEW   **TOP VIEW**

EXTERNAL BRAIN FEATURES

The brain's most obvious feature is the cerebrum, which makes
up more than four-fifths of all its tissues. It has a grooved
appearance due to its heavily folded surface, which is called the
cerebral cortex. The cerebrum partly envelops the thalamus and
nearby structures (diencephalon) and the brainstem below this
(see opposite). The smaller cerebellum forms about one-tenth
of the brain's whole volume; it is mainly concerned with the
organization of motor information being sent to muscles
to make movements smooth and coordinated.

OUTER BRAIN STRUCTURES
The cerebrum is partly separated into two halves
(cerebral hemispheres) by the deep longitudinal fissure.
The cerebellum is the smaller bulbous structure
responsible for muscle control. Beneath the cerebellum
is the brainstem, which controls basic life processes.

BRAIN-PRINT
A scan reveals a unique "brain-
print" – the pattern of cerebral
grooves and bulges that is
different in each person.

Frontal lobe
Speech production,
movement initiation,
and aspects of
"personality" are
based in this lobe

Parietal lobe
Area in which bodily
sensations such as touch,
temperature, pressure,
and pain are perceived
and interpreted, in
the region called the
somatosensory cortex

Postcentral gyrus
A ridge, or bulge, on the
brain's surface is called a
gyrus; the postcentral
gyrus (just behind mid-point from
front to rear) is an important
anatomical landmark

Parietal occipital fissure
Fissure (deep groove)
that demarcates border
between parietal and
occipital lobes

Lateral sulcus
Groove running
along upper part of
temporal lobe

**Superior
temporal sulcus**
Upper of two
main sulci (shallow
grooves) that divide
chief gyri (bulges) of
temporal lobe

Temporal lobe
Recognition of sounds,
their tones and
loudness, takes place
in temporal lobes;
they also play a role in
storage of memory

Pons
Upper portion
of brainstem

Occipital lobe
This area is mainly
concerned with
analysing and
interpreting visual
information, from
sensory nerve signals
sent by the eyes

Inferior temporal sulcus
Lower of two main sulci (shallow
grooves) that divide gyri (bulges)
of temporal lobe

Brainstem
Lowest, mainly
"automatic" region
of brain
(see opposite)

Cerebellum
This "little brain" is involved with timing
and accuracy of skilled movements, and
controls balance and posture

LOBES OF THE BRAIN
Traditionally the cerebral surface is divided
into four major lobes, partly by patterns
of deeper grooves, or fissures, and partly
by functional significance – the roles each
fulfils. The names of some of the lobes
parallel the names of the skull bones that
overlie them (see p.42).

THE HOLLOW BRAIN

The brain is, in a sense, hollow: it contains four chambers known as ventricles, filled with cerebrospinal fluid, or CSF (see p.75). There are two lateral ventricles, one in each hemisphere, and the fluid is produced here. It then drains via the interventricular foramen into the third ventricle, which is situated close to the thalamus. From here it flows through the cerebral aqueduct and into the fourth ventricle, which extends down between the pons and cerebellum into the medulla. The total volume of CSF in the ventricles is about 25ml (⁹/₁₀ fl oz). Circulation is aided by head movements and pulsations of the cerebral arteries.

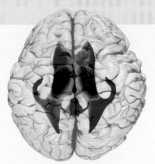

VIEW FROM ABOVE
The lateral ventricles have frontward-, backward-, and side-facing horns, or cornua. Seen between them in this view is the central third ventricle.

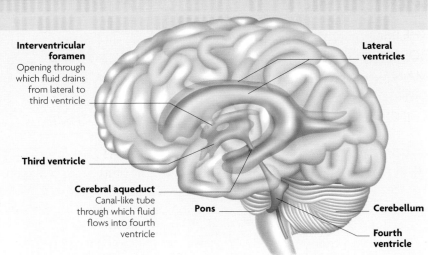

Interventricular foramen
Opening through which fluid drains from lateral to third ventricle

Third ventricle

Cerebral aqueduct
Canal-like tube through which fluid flows into fourth ventricle

Pons

Lateral ventricles

Cerebellum

Fourth ventricle

GREY AND WHITE MATTER

The bulk of the cerebrum has two main layers. The outer, pale-grey layer, often known as "grey matter", is the cerebral cortex. It follows the folds and bulges of the cerebrum to cover its entire surface. Its average thickness is 3–5mm (¹/₁₀–²/₁₀ in), and spread out flat, it would cover about the same area as a pillowcase. Deeper within the cerebrum are small islands of grey matter. These and the cerebral cortex are composed chiefly of the cell bodies and impulse-collecting projections (dendrites) of nerve cells (neurons). Beneath the cortex's grey matter is the paler "white matter", forming the bulk of the cerebrum's interior. It is composed mainly of nerve fibres.

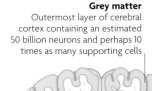

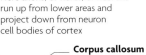

Grey matter
Outermost layer of cerebral cortex containing an estimated 50 billion neurons and perhaps 10 times as many supporting cells

White matter interior
Here axons, or fibres, of neurons run up from lower areas and project down from neuron cell bodies of cortex

Corpus callosum
Largest of several bundles of nerve fibres, called commissures, which connect specific areas of the two halves, or cerebral hemispheres, of the upper brain

Basal ganglia
"Islands" of grey matter deep in cerebrum

Motor nerve tracts
Large fibre bundles that carry instructions for movements down to the spinal cord, and that cross over in lower brainstem

Brainstem

VERTICAL SECTION
A vertical "slice" through the middle of the brain reveals the paired structures, outer grey layer, and inner white matter. The corpus callosum contains more than 100 million nerve fibres and is the main "bridge" between the two hemispheres.

BASAL GANGLIA
These structures include the lentiform nucleus (putamen and globus pallidus), caudate nucleus, subthalamic nucleus, and substantia nigra (the latter two not seen in this view). They are a complex interface between sensory inputs and motor skills, especially for semi-automatic movements, such as walking.

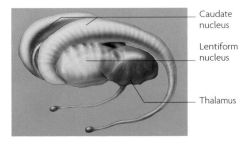

Caudate nucleus

Lentiform nucleus

Thalamus

VERTICAL LINKS

Sheathed (myelinated) nerve fibres, organized into bundles known as projection tracts, transmit impulses between the spinal cord and lower brain areas and the cerebral cortex above. These nerve tracts pass through a communication link called the internal capsule and also intersect the corpus callosum. In addition, similar bundles pass through the upper, outer zones of the white matter, from one area of the cerebral cortex to another. These association tracts convey nerve signals directly between different regions or centres of the cortex.

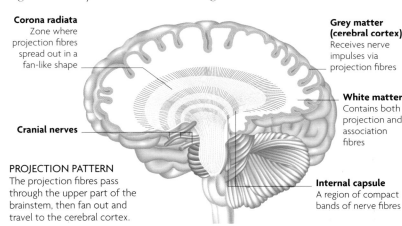

Corona radiata
Zone where projection fibres spread out in a fan-like shape

Cranial nerves

Grey matter (cerebral cortex)
Receives nerve impulses via projection fibres

White matter
Contains both projection and association fibres

Internal capsule
A region of compact bands of nerve fibres

PROJECTION PATTERN
The projection fibres pass through the upper part of the brainstem, then fan out and travel to the cerebral cortex.

THE THALAMUS AND BRAINSTEM

The thalamus sits on top of the brainstem and is shaped like two eggs side by side and lies almost at the "heart" of the brain. It is a major relay station that monitors and processes incoming information before this is sent to the upper regions of the brain. The brainstem contains centres that regulate several functions vital for survival: these include heartbeat, respiration, blood pressure, and some reflex actions, such as swallowing and vomiting.

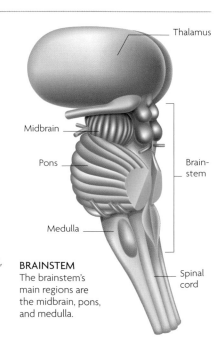

Thalamus

Midbrain

Pons

Medulla

Brainstem

Spinal cord

BRAINSTEM
The brainstem's main regions are the midbrain, pons, and medulla.

THE PRIMITIVE BRAIN

HUMAN BEHAVIOUR IS NOT ALWAYS RATIONAL. IN TIMES OF STRESS OR CRISIS, DEEP-SEATED INSTINCTS WELL UP FROM DEEP WITHIN AND TAKE OVER OUR AWARENESS. SUCH EVENTS INVOLVE THE "PRIMITIVE BRAIN", WHICH IS BASED MAINLY IN A SERIES OF PARTS KNOWN AS THE LIMBIC SYSTEM.

THE LIMBIC SYSTEM

The limbic system influences subconscious, instinctive behaviour, similar to animal responses that relate to survival and reproduction. In humans, many of these innate, early-evolved "primitive" behaviours are modified by conscious, thoughtful considerations based in upper regions of the brain, as we take into account moral, social, and cultural codes, and the results of our actions. However, primal urges sometimes prevail, and this is when the limbic system and associated structures take over. At other times they play lesser, but still complex and important, roles in the expression of instincts, drives, and emotions.

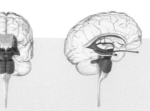 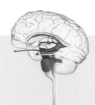

360-DEGREE VIEW

FRONT   **RIGHT SIDE**   **BACK**   **LEFT SIDE**

The limbic system involves parts situated between the "automatic" centres of the mid and lower brainstem, and the "thinking" regions associated with higher mental functions in the cortex. The limbic cortex is on the inner sides of the cortical lobes where they fold up against the midbrain (see the Back view).

LIMBIC STRUCTURES
The components of the ring-shaped limbic system, located in the lower centre of the brain, mediate the effects of innermost moods on external behaviour. They also influence changes in bodily functions, such as those involving digestion and urination. The association of emotions with sensory inputs is also influenced by this system.

Cingulate gyrus
With the parahippocampal gyrus and olfactory bulbs, comprises the limbic cortex, which modifies behaviour and emotions

Fornix
Pathway of nerve fibres that transmits information from hippocampus and other limbic areas to the mamillary bodies

Column of fornix

Mamillary body
Tiny lump of neurons that acts as a relay station, transmitting information mainly between fornix and thalamus; involved in memory processes

Olfactory bulbs
The brain's "smell processors"; they are "hard-wired" into the limbic system, which helps to explain why the sense of smell can evoke such strong memories and emotional responses

Pituitary gland

Pons
Part of the brainstem; not part of the limbic system

Midbrain
Uppermost part of brainstem; limbic areas in the midbrain connect to the cortex and to the thalamus, and also link to the clusters of nerve cell bodies known as basal ganglia

Hippocampus
Curved band of grey matter involved with learning, recognizing new experiences, and with memory, especially short-term memory and information relating to recent events

Amygdala
Double-almond-shaped structure that influences behaviour and activities so that they are directed towards the body's needs; also concerned with emotions such as anger and jealousy, and drives such as hunger, thirst, and sexual desire

Parahippocampal gyrus
Helps to modify expression of forceful emotions; also forms and recalls topographic memories of scenes and views (rather than objects, faces, or facts)

Mamillary bodies

Corpus callosum

Fornix

RINGED AND ARCHED
The limbic system encompasses parts in the cerebrum, diencephalon, and midbrain, and links (the meaning of "limbic") the cortical and midbrain areas with lower centres that control automatic functions.

THE HYPOTHALAMUS

The hypothalamus ("below the thalamus") is about the size of a sugar cube and contains numerous tiny clusters of neurons called nuclei. It is usually regarded as the vital integrating centre of the limbic system. A stalk below links it to the pituitary, the chief gland of the hormonal system. In addition to this major endocrine connection, the hypothalamus also has complex associations with the rest of the limbic system around it, and with the autonomic parts of the general nervous system. Hypothalamic functions include monitoring and regulating vital internal conditions such as body temperature, nutrient levels, water-salt balance, blood flow, the sleep-wake cycle, and the levels of hormones. The hypothalamus initiates feelings, actions, and emotions such as hunger, thirst, rage, and terror.

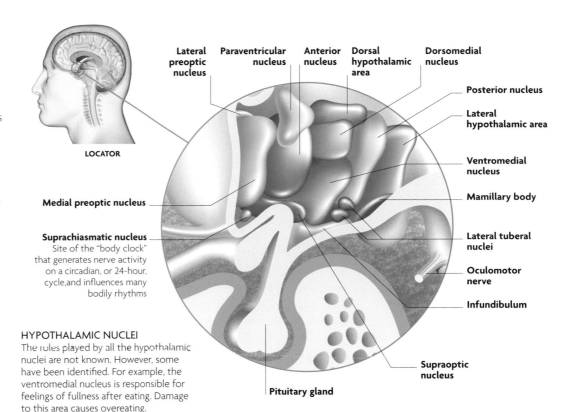

LOCATOR

Lateral preoptic nucleus
Paraventricular nucleus
Anterior nucleus
Dorsal hypothalamic area
Dorsomedial nucleus
Posterior nucleus
Lateral hypothalamic area
Ventromedial nucleus
Mamillary body
Lateral tuberal nuclei
Oculomotor nerve
Infundibulum
Supraoptic nucleus
Pituitary gland

Medial preoptic nucleus

Suprachiasmatic nucleus
Site of the "body clock" that generates nerve activity on a circadian, or 24-hour, cycle, and influences many bodily rhythms

HYPOTHALAMIC NUCLEI
The roles played by all the hypothalamic nuclei are not known. However, some have been identified. For example, the ventromedial nucleus is responsible for feelings of fullness after eating. Damage to this area causes overeating.

THE RETICULAR FORMATION

The reticular formation is a series of long, slim nerve tracts located in much of the length of the brainstem, with fibres extending to the cerebellum behind, the diencephalon above, and the spinal cord below. It comprises several distinct neural systems, each with its own neurotransmitter (the chemical that passes on nerve signals at the junctions, or synapses, between neurons). One of its functions is to operate an arousal system, known as the reticular activating system (RAS), that keeps the brain awake and alert. The recticular formation also includes the cardioregulatory and respiratory centres that control heart rate and breathing, and other essential centres.

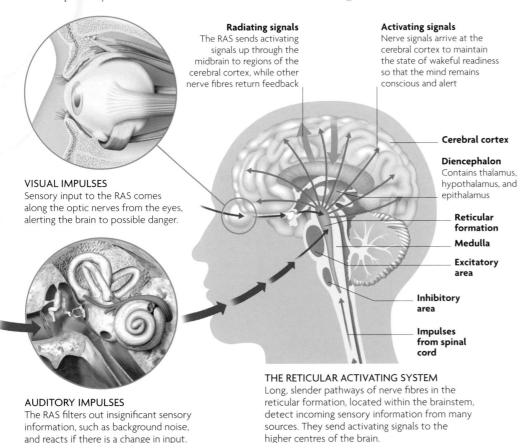

Radiating signals
The RAS sends activating signals up through the midbrain to regions of the cerebral cortex, while other nerve fibres return feedback

Activating signals
Nerve signals arrive at the cerebral cortex to maintain the state of wakeful readiness so that the mind remains conscious and alert

Cerebral cortex

Diencephalon
Contains thalamus, hypothalamus, and epithalamus

Reticular formation

Medulla

Excitatory area

Inhibitory area

Impulses from spinal cord

VISUAL IMPULSES
Sensory input to the RAS comes along the optic nerves from the eyes, alerting the brain to possible danger.

AUDITORY IMPULSES
The RAS filters out insignificant sensory information, such as background noise, and reacts if there is a change in input.

THE RETICULAR ACTIVATING SYSTEM
Long, slender pathways of nerve fibres in the reticular formation, located within the brainstem, detect incoming sensory information from many sources. They send activating signals to the higher centres of the brain.

SLEEP CYCLES

During sleep, much of the body rests, but not the brain. Its billions of neurons continue to send signals, as shown by EEG traces. Sleep occurs in cycles, made up of lengthening phases of REM (rapid eye movement) sleep, when dreaming occurs, and four stages of NREM (non-rapid eye movement sleep), which is dreamless. In stage 1, sleep is light: people wake relatively easily and brain waves are active. In stage 2, brain waves begin to slow down. In stage 3, fast and slow waves are interspersed and finally in stage 4, the deepest stage, there are slow waves only.

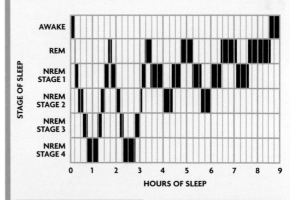

STAGE OF SLEEP

AWAKE
REM
NREM STAGE 1
NREM STAGE 2
NREM STAGE 3
NREM STAGE 4

0 1 2 3 4 5 6 7 8 9
HOURS OF SLEEP

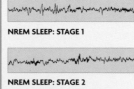

NREM SLEEP: STAGE 1

REM SLEEP

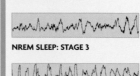

NREM SLEEP: STAGE 2

NREM SLEEP: STAGE 3

NREM SLEEP: STAGE 4

SLEEP STAGES
EEG traces show different waveforms of brain activity for each sleep stage. As the body reaches the later stages, body temperature, heartbeat rate, breathing rate, and blood pressure all reduce. During REM sleep these functions rise slightly and dreams usually occur.

SPINAL CORD

THE NERVE FIBRES OF THE SPINAL CORD LINK THE BRAIN WITH THE TORSO, ARMS, AND LEGS. THE BRAIN IS DIRECTLY CONNECTED TO THE SENSE ORGANS IN THE HEAD BY THE CRANIAL NERVES (SEE P.82) BUT NEEDS THE SPINAL CORD TO CARRY INFORMATION TO AND FROM THE REST OF THE BODY. THE CORD IS MORE THAN A PASSIVE CONDUIT FOR NERVE SIGNALS – WHEN NECESSARY IT CAN BYPASS THE BRAIN, FOR EXAMPLE IN REFLEX ACTIONS.

SPINAL CORD ANATOMY

The spinal cord is a complex bundle of nerve fibres (axons) that is about 40–45cm (16–18in) long. It extends from the base of the brain, down to the lower (lumbosacral) part of the spinal column. It is shaped like a flattened cylinder and is only slightly wider than a pencil for most of its length, tapering to a thread-like tail at the base. Branching out from the spinal cord are 31 pairs of spinal nerves, which connect it to the skin, muscles, and other parts of the limbs, chest, and abdomen. The nerves carry sensory information to the cord about conditions within the body and transmit the sense of touch from the skin. They also convey motor information to muscles throughout the body and to glands within the chest and abdomen.

NERVE CROSSOVER

Bundles of nerve fibres (axons) in the left and right sides of the spinal cord do not all pass straight up into the left and right sides of the brain. In the uppermost portion of the cord and the lower brainstem (medulla), many of the fibres cross over, or decussate, to the other side – left to right, and right to left. This means nerve signals about, for example, touch sensations on the left side of the body reach the touch centre (somatosensory cortex) on the right side of the brain. Likewise, motor signals from the right motor cortex and right side of the cerebellum travel to the muscles on the left side of the body. Different major bundles, or tracts, of fibres decussate at slightly different levels. About one-tenth of those that cross over do so in the upper spinal cord, and the remainder cross over in the medulla.

SPINAL GREY MATTER
This microscope view of a cross-section through the spinal cord shows one brown-stained "wing" of the butterfly-shaped grey matter, which lies at the cord's centre.

Spinal cord

Spinal nerve

Spinal nerve root

Vertebra

Intervertebral disc

REAR OF BODY

HOW SPINAL NERVES ATTACH
The spinal nerves reach the cord through gaps between vertebrae, which are held apart by pads of cartilage, known as intervertebral discs. The nerves divide and enter the back and front of the spinal cord as spinal nerve roots, each composed of many rootlets.

Nerve fibre tract
Bundle of nerve fibres (axons) that carries signals to and from spinal cord and specific areas of brain

Central canal
Cerebrospinal fluid fills the narrow central canal and provides nourishment and waste collection for neurons and tissues around it

White matter

Grey matter

Sensory nerve rootlets (dorsal)
Bundles of fibres that enter spinal cord at rear (dorsal side); carry impulses of incoming information about touch sensations on skin, and conditions within the body

Spinal nerve
Sensory and motor nerve rootlets merge to form spinal nerve

Motor nerve rootlets (ventral)
Bundles of fibres that emerge from front (ventral side) of spinal cord; carry signals to voluntary skeletal muscles and involuntary smooth muscles

Sensory root ganglion
Cluster of nerve cell bodies on each spinal nerve; partially processes incoming information

Anterior fissure
Deep groove along front of spinal cord; almost reaches grey matter and central canal

Subarachnoid space

Pia mater

Arachnoid

Dura mater

SPINAL CORD
The inner organization of the spinal cord resembles an "inside out" brain. The brain has grey matter outside and white within. The cord has an inner, butterfly-shaped core of grey matter. This is made up of neuron cell bodies and nonsheathed (unmyelinated) nerve fibres. Around this is the outer later of white matter, composed mainly of myelinated nerve fibre tracts that carry nerve impulses up and down the cord, between the brain and body.

Meninges
Three layers of connective tissues that protect spinal cord; cerebrospinal fluid fills space under middle layer

FRONT OF BODY

PROTECTION OF SPINAL CORD

The spinal cord is located inside the spinal canal – a long tunnel within the aligned column of backbones (vertebrae). The vertebral column, along with its strengthening ligaments and muscles, bends and flexes the cord, but also guards it from direct knocks and blows. Within the spinal canal the circulating cerebrospinal fluid acts as a shock-absorber and the epidural space provides a cushioning layer of fat and connective tissue. The epidural tissues lie between the periosteum (the membrane that lines the bone of the spinal canal) and the dura mater, the outer layer of the meninges.

INSIDE THE SPINAL CANAL

A cross-section of the vertebral column in the neck (cervical) region shows how the spinal cord nestles in the well-padded bony cavity. Although the vertebrae shift position as the trunk of the body moves, the spinal cord remains well supported and protected.

EXTENT OF SPINAL CORD

During growth, the spinal cord does not continue to lengthen the way that the spinal bones do. By adulthood, it extends from the brain down to the first lumbar vertebra (L1) in the lower back. Here, it forms a cone-like ending that tapers to a slender, tail-like filament, known as the filum terminale. This extends down through the lumbar and sacral vertebrae to the coccyx.

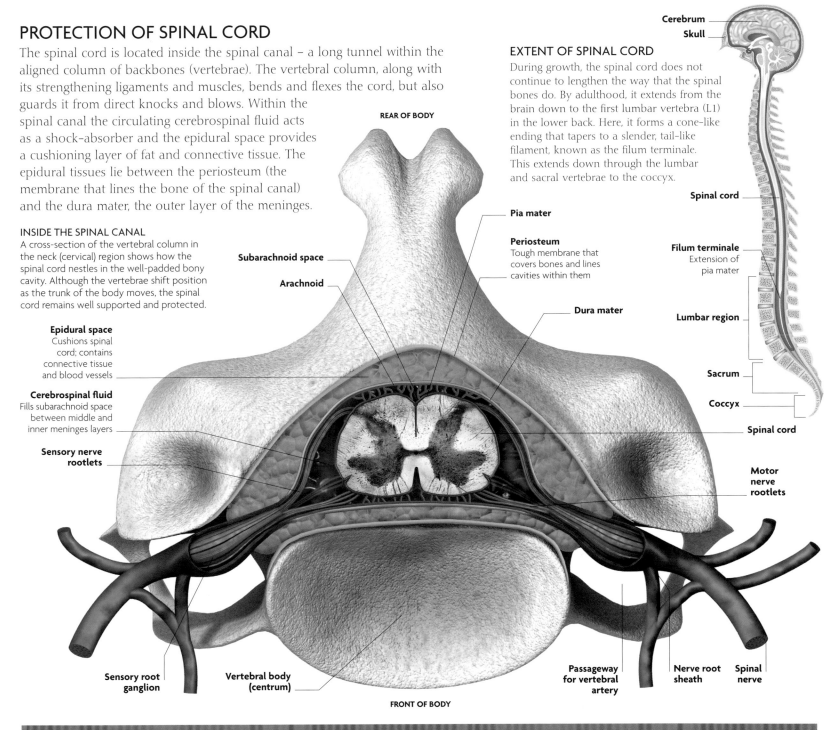

REAR OF BODY

Epidural space
Cushions spinal cord; contains connective tissue and blood vessels

Cerebrospinal fluid
Fills subarachnoid space between middle and inner meninges layers

Sensory nerve rootlets

Subarachnoid space

Arachnoid

Pia mater

Periosteum
Tough membrane that covers bones and lines cavities within them

Dura mater

Motor nerve rootlets

Sensory root ganglion

Vertebral body (centrum)

Passageway for vertebral artery

Nerve root sheath

Spinal nerve

FRONT OF BODY

Cerebrum
Skull

Spinal cord

Filum terminale
Extension of pia mater

Lumbar region

Sacrum

Coccyx

Spinal cord

NERVE TRACTS OF SPINAL CORD

In the white matter of the spinal cord, nerve fibres are grouped into main bundles, or tracts, according to the direction of the nerve signals they carry and the type of signals they transmit and respond to, such as pain or temperature. Some of these tracts connect and relay impulses between a few local pairs of spinal nerves, without sending fibres up to the brain. The central grey matter of the cord is organized into horns, or columns.

ASCENDING TRACTS
These bundles of nerve fibres relay impulses about bodily sensations and inner sensors like pain up the spinal cord to the brain.

DESCENDING TRACTS
These convey motor signals from the brain to skeletal muscles of the torso and limbs in order to bring about voluntary movements.

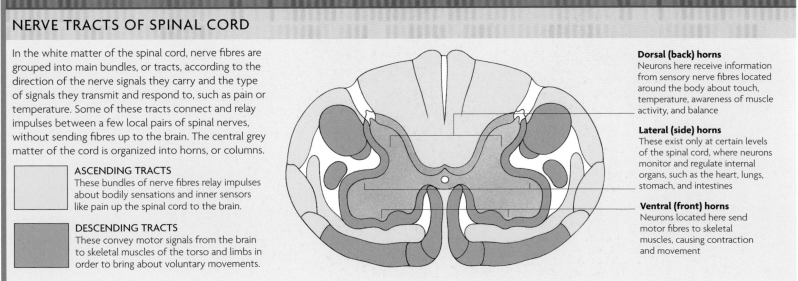

Dorsal (back) horns
Neurons here receive information from sensory nerve fibres located around the body about touch, temperature, awareness of muscle activity, and balance

Lateral (side) horns
These exist only at certain levels of the spinal cord, where neurons monitor and regulate internal organs, such as the heart, lungs, stomach, and intestines

Ventral (front) horns
Neurons located here send motor fibres to skeletal muscles, causing contraction and movement

PERIPHERAL NERVES

THE BODY'S NETWORK OF PERIPHERAL NERVES CONVEYS INFORMATION TO AND FROM THE BRAIN AND SPINAL CORD. SENSORY FIBRES IN THE NERVES CARRY MESSAGES FROM THE SENSE ORGANS, SUCH AS THE EYES, EARS, AND SKIN, AND FROM INTERNAL ORGANS. MOTOR FIBRES CONTROL MUSCLE MOVEMENT AND GLAND ACTIVITY.

CRANIAL NERVES

The 12 pairs of cranial nerves connect directly to the brain, rather than via the spinal cord. Some nerves perform sensory functions for organs and tissues in the head and neck, while others provide motor functions. The nerves with predominantly motor fibres also contain some sensory fibres that convey information to the brain about the amount of stretch and tension in the muscles they serve, as part of the proprioceptive sense (see p.63). Most of the cranial nerves are named according to the body parts they serve, such as the optic nerves (eyes). By convention, the nerves are also identified by Roman numerals, so the trigeminal nerve, for example, is cranial V (five).

Olfactory nerve (I, sensory)
Relays information about smells from the olfactory epithelium inside the nose, just above the nasal chamber, via the olfactory bulbs and the olfactory tracts to the brain's limbic centres.

Trigeminal nerve (V, two sensory and one mixed branch)
Ophthalmic and maxillary branches gather signals from the eye, face, and teeth; mandibular motor fibres control chewing muscles, and sensory fibres bring signals from the lower jaw.

Facial nerve (VII, mixed)
Sensory branches come from the taste buds of the front two-thirds of the tongue; motor fibres run to the muscles of facial expression and to the salivary and lacrimal glands.

Optic nerve (II, sensory)
The optic nerve brings visual information from the rod and cone cells in the retina to the visual cortex in the brain; parts of the two nerves cross at the optic chiasm (see p.93) where they form bands of nerve fibres, called optic tracts. Each nerve consists of a bundle of about one million sensory fibres – it carries the most information of any cranial nerve.

Oculomotor, trochlear, and abducens nerves (III, IV, VI, mainly motor)
These three nerves regulate voluntary movements of the eye muscles, to move the eyeball and eyelids; the oculomotor also controls pupil constriction by the iris muscles and focusing changes in the lens by the ciliary muscles.

Vestibulocochlear nerve (VIII, sensory)
The vestibular branch collects nerve signals from the inner ear about head orientation and balance; the cochlear branch brings signals from the ear concerning sound and hearing.

Glossopharyngeal and hypoglossal nerves (IX, XII, both mixed)
Motor fibres of these nerves are involved in tongue movement and swallowing, while sensory fibres relay information about taste, touch, and temperature from the tongue and pharynx.

Spinal accessory nerve (XI, mainly motor)
This nerve controls muscles and movements in the head, neck, and shoulders. It also stimulates the muscles of the pharynx and larynx, which are involved in swallowing.

Vagus nerve (X, mixed)
The longest and most branched cranial nerve, the vagus (meaning "wanderer") has sensory, motor, and autonomic fibres that pass to the lower head, throat, neck, chest, and abdomen; these are involved in many vital bodily functions, including swallowing, breathing, heartbeat, and the formation of stomach acid.

VIEW FROM BELOW
In this view of the brain's underside, the cranial nerves are seen joining mainly to the lower regions of the brain. Some of these nerves are sensory, taking impulses to the brain. Others are motor, bringing nerve signals from the brain to muscles and glands. Some are mixed, with both sensory and motor nerve fibres.

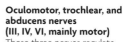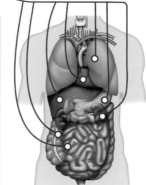

SPINAL REFLEXES

A reflex is a rapid, involuntary, predictable response to a stimulus. Most reflexes are concerned with survival and defending the body against damage and harm, such as coughing to remove irritants from the lower airways and sneezing to clear the nasal airways. In general, a reflex occurs in a complete neural circuit that does not involve the higher regions of the brain, where consciousness and awareness occur; the mind usually becomes aware of the reflex response just after it has occurred, when it is too late to prevent. Spinal reflexes involve circuits of sensory nerve fibres that feed information to the spinal cord and then connect directly, or via an intermediate neuron, to motor nerve fibres, so that the resulting instructions for movement go directly out from the cord to the relevant muscles.

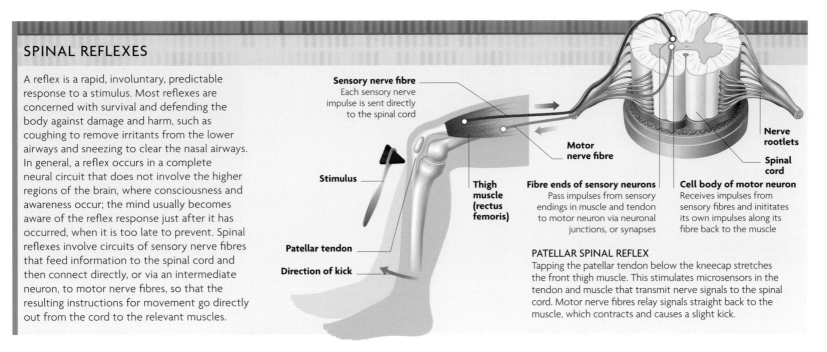

Sensory nerve fibre Each sensory nerve impulse is sent directly to the spinal cord

Stimulus

Thigh muscle (rectus femoris)

Patellar tendon

Direction of kick

Motor nerve fibre

Nerve rootlets

Spinal cord

Fibre ends of sensory neurons Pass impulses from sensory endings in muscle and tendon to motor neuron via neuronal junctions, or synapses

Cell body of motor neuron Receives impulses from sensory fibres and inititates its own impulses along its fibre back to the muscle

PATELLAR SPINAL REFLEX
Tapping the patellar tendon below the kneecap stretches the front thigh muscle. This stimulates microsensors in the tendon and muscle that transmit nerve signals to the spinal cord. Motor nerve fibres relay signals straight back to the muscle, which contracts and causes a slight kick.

SPINAL NERVES

The 31 pairs of peripheral spinal nerves emerge from the spinal cord through spaces between the vertebrae. Each nerve divides and subdivides into a number of branches; the dorsal branches serve the rear portion of the body, while the ventral serve the front and sides. The branches of one spinal nerve may join with other nerves to form meshes called plexuses where information is shared. The plexuses send signals along secondary nerve branches to areas of complex function or movement.

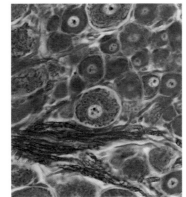

SPINAL NERVE GANGLION
This microscope image shows a section through a cluster of spinal nerve cells (ganglion), where nerve impulses are coordinated. Each neuron (purple) is surrounded by support cells (light blue).

Cervical region (C1–C8)
Eight pairs of cervical spinal nerves form two networks, the cervical (C1–C4) and brachial plexuses (C5–C8/T1). These run to the chest, head, neck, shoulders, arms, and hands, and to the diaphragm.

Thoracic region (T1–T12)
Apart from T1, which is considered part of the brachial plexus, thoracic spinal nerves are connected to the intercostal muscles between the ribs, the deep back muscles, and the abdominal muscles.

Lumbar region (L1–L5)
Four of the five pairs of lumbar spinal nerves (L1–L4) form the lumbar plexus, which supplies the lower abdominal wall and parts of the thighs and legs. L4 and L5 interconnect with the first four sacral nerves (S1–S4).

Sacral region (S1–S5)
Two nerve networks, the sacral plexus (L5–S3) and the coccygeal plexus (S4/S5/Co 1), send branches to the thighs, buttocks, muscles and skin of the legs and feet, and anal and genital areas.

SPINAL REGIONS
The organization and naming of the four main spinal nerve regions reflect the regions of the spine itself – cervical or neck, thoracic or chest, lumbar or lower back, and sacral or base of spine.

DERMATOMES

A dermatome is a region or zone of skin supplied by the dorsal (rear, sensory) nerve roots of one pair of spinal nerves. The nerve branches carry sensory information about touch, pressure, heat, cold, and pain from the skin microsensors within the zone, along the sensory nerve fibres of the branches of the spinal nerve, to the spinal nerve root and then into the spinal cord. A "skin map" delineates these skin zones, or dermatomes. In real life, the distribution of nerve roots, and so of sensations, overlaps slightly.

DERMATOME MAP
Spinal nerve C1 lacks sensory fibres from the skin and so is missing; the face and forehead send signals via the three branches of the trigeminal cranial (V) nerve, coded here as V1–V3.

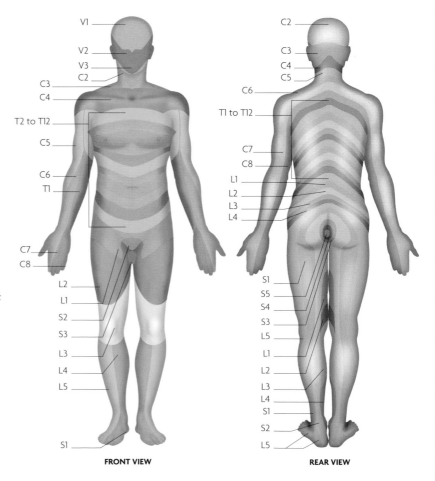

FRONT VIEW

REAR VIEW

AUTONOMIC NERVOUS SYSTEM

THE AUTONOMIC NERVOUS SYSTEM (ANS) HAS THE KEY TASK OF MAINTAINING CONSTANT CONDITIONS WITHIN THE BODY, A PROCESS KNOWN AS HOMEOSTASIS. MOST OF THE ACTIVITY IN THE ANS IS INDEPENDENT (AUTONOMIC) OF THE CONSCIOUS MIND, SO WE ARE RARELY AWARE OF ITS WORKINGS.

AUTOMATIC FUNCTIONS

The ANS is one of the three main components of the nervous system. The central and peripheral nervous systems share some nerve structures with the ANS, and it also has chains of ganglia (clusters of nerve cells where axons communicate) along each side of the spinal cord. The ANS works largely "automatically" to provide involuntary responses, both immediate and longer-term. Sensory nerve fibres send information about the organs and internal activities, such as heart rate. This information is integrated in the hypothalamus, brainstem, or spinal cord. The ANS then sends commands, as motor nerve signals, to three main destinations: the involuntary smooth muscles of many organs and blood vessels; cardiac muscle; and certain glands.

TWO DIVISIONS
The ANS has two divisions: sympathetic and parasympathetic. The ganglia of the sympathetic division are arranged into two ganglion chains, one either side of the spinal column (only one shown here). The ganglia of the parasympathetic ANS are inside organs (see diagram). Only skin and blood vessels receive nerve messages from all positions on the cord.

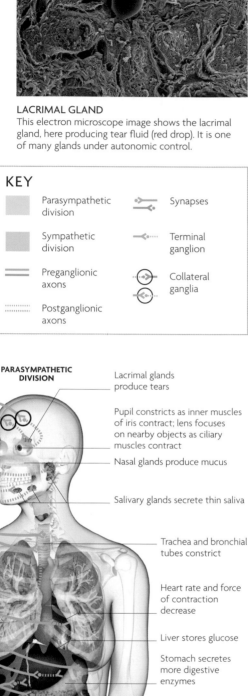

LACRIMAL GLAND
This electron microscope image shows the lacrimal gland, here producing tear fluid (red drop). It is one of many glands under autonomic control.

KEY

▢ Parasympathetic division	⊶ Synapses
▢ Sympathetic division	⊷ Terminal ganglion
═ Preganglionic axons	⊛ Collateral ganglia
⋯ Postganglionic axons	

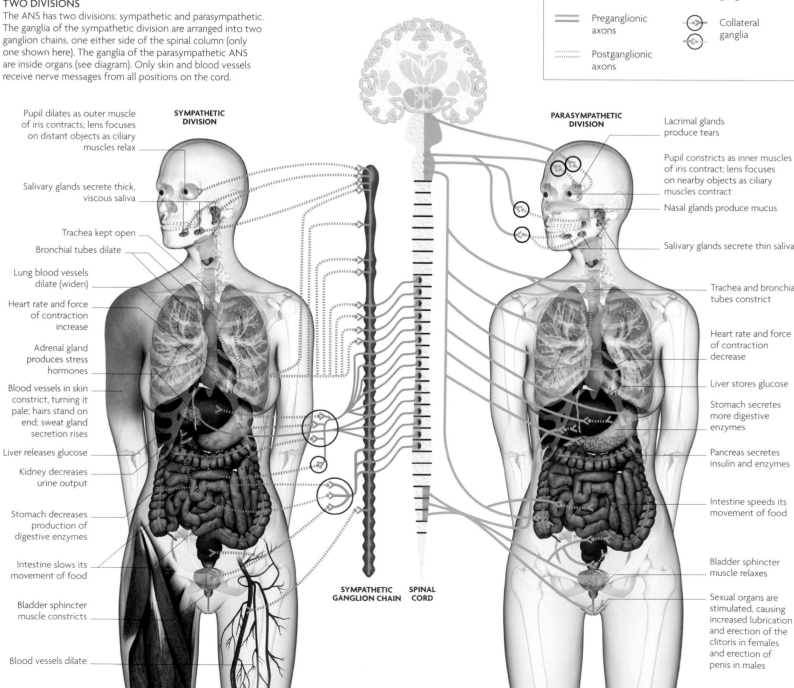

SYMPATHETIC DIVISION

Pupil dilates as outer muscle of iris contracts; lens focuses on distant objects as ciliary muscles relax

Salivary glands secrete thick, viscous saliva

Trachea kept open

Bronchial tubes dilate

Lung blood vessels dilate (widen)

Heart rate and force of contraction increase

Adrenal gland produces stress hormones

Blood vessels in skin constrict, turning it pale; hairs stand on end; sweat gland secretion rises

Liver releases glucose

Kidney decreases urine output

Stomach decreases production of digestive enzymes

Intestine slows its movement of food

Bladder sphincter muscle constricts

Blood vessels dilate

SYMPATHETIC GANGLION CHAIN   **SPINAL CORD**

PARASYMPATHETIC DIVISION

Lacrimal glands produce tears

Pupil constricts as inner muscles of iris contract; lens focuses on nearby objects as ciliary muscles contract

Nasal glands produce mucus

Salivary glands secrete thin saliva

Trachea and bronchial tubes constrict

Heart rate and force of contraction decrease

Liver stores glucose

Stomach secretes more digestive enzymes

Pancreas secretes insulin and enzymes

Intestine speeds its movement of food

Bladder sphincter muscle relaxes

Sexual organs are stimulated, causing increased lubrication and erection of the clitoris in females and erection of penis in males

SYMPATHETIC AND PARASYMPATHETIC FUNCTIONS

The sympathetic and parasympathetic division nerves produce contrasting responses. The sympathetic division prepares the body for action and stress. The parasympathetic division restores normal function to conserve energy.

AFFECTED ORGAN	SYMPATHETIC RESPONSE	PARASYMPATHETIC RESPONSE
EYES	Pupils dilate	Pupils constrict
LUNG	Bronchial tubes dilate (widen)	Bronchial tubes constrict
HEART	Rate and strength of heartbeat increase	Rate and strength of heartbeat decrease
STOMACH	Enzymes decrease	Enzymes increase

BALANCED COORDINATION

The ANS divisions primarily send out signals to muscles, creating a "push-pull" relationship between them. These opposing effects interact and balance. For example, involuntary changes in eye pupil size occur constantly. Smooth muscle fibres in the iris are arranged as a circular inner band and radial outer band. Sensory receptors in the eyes respond to light and send nerve signals to the brain, which sends messages to one or the other muscle band to adjust pupil size.

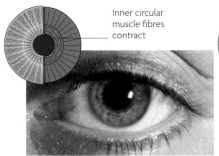

Inner circular muscle fibres contract

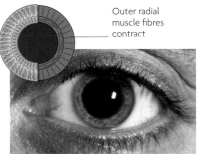

Outer radial muscle fibres contract

CONSTRICTED PUPIL
In bright light or to view nearby objects, the pupil constricts as parasympathetic influence stimulates muscle contraction.

DILATED PUPIL
Widening of the pupil signals the body's heightened awareness as sympathetic nerve messages signal muscle fibres to shorten.

INVOLUNTARY RESPONSES

There are two main categories of involuntary, or automatic, responses, which do not usually involve conscious awareness. One category involves reflex actions (see p.83). Reflexes mainly affect muscles normally under voluntary control. The other type of response includes autonomic motor actions. The initial nerve pathways for these responses run along spinal nerves into the spinal cord, then up ascending nerve tracts to the lower autonomic regions of the brain, particularly the hypothalamus and parts of the limbic system. These regions analyse and process the information received and then use the autonomic pathways to send out motor impulses, as instructions for the involuntary muscles and the glands. Parasympathetic and sympathetic response signals have separate pathways.

RESPONSES UNDER VOLUNTARY CONTROL

Nervous responses under voluntary control are the opposite of reactions controlled by the ANS. Stimulated by incoming sensory nerve messages, or by conscious thought and intention, the brain's cerebral cortex (outer layer) formulates a central motor plan for a particular movement, and sends out instructions as motor nerve signals to voluntary muscles. As the movement progresses, it is monitored by sensory endings in the muscles, tendons, and joints. The sensory endings update the cerebellum, so that the cerebral cortex can send corrective nerve signals back to the muscles, to keep the movement coordinated and on course.

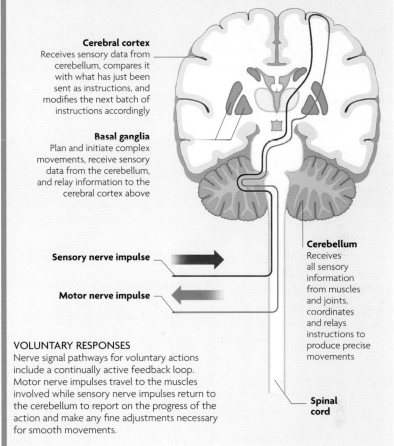

Cerebral cortex
Receives sensory data from cerebellum, compares it with what has just been sent as instructions, and modifies the next batch of instructions accordingly

Basal ganglia
Plan and initiate complex movements, receive sensory data from the cerebellum, and relay information to the cerebral cortex above

Sensory nerve impulse

Motor nerve impulse

Cerebellum
Receives all sensory information from muscles and joints, coordinates and relays instructions to produce precise movements

Spinal cord

VOLUNTARY RESPONSES
Nerve signal pathways for voluntary actions include a continually active feedback loop. Motor nerve impulses travel to the muscles involved while sensory nerve impulses return to the cerebellum to report on the progress of the action and make any fine adjustments necessary for smooth movements.

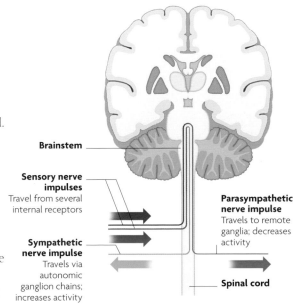

Brainstem

Sensory nerve impulses
Travel from several internal receptors

Sympathetic nerve impulse
Travels via autonomic ganglion chains; increases activity

Parasympathetic nerve impulse
Travels to remote ganglia; decreases activity

Spinal cord

AUTONOMIC RESPONSES
Nerve signals pass along spinal nerves and up the spinal cord to the lower autonomic regions of the brain, which output motor impulses in response.

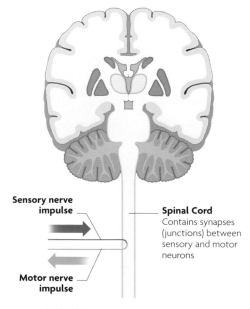

Sensory nerve impulse

Motor nerve impulse

Spinal Cord
Contains synapses (junctions) between sensory and motor neurons

REFLEXES
Sensory signals arrive, and motor signals depart, wholly within the spinal cord, and without brain involvement – although the brain becomes aware soon after.

MEMORIES, THOUGHTS, AND EMOTIONS

THE BRAIN IS ENORMOUSLY COMPLEX AND INTEGRATED, AND MANY OF ITS MENTAL FACULTIES ARE NOT CONTROLLED BY ONE AREA. FOR EXAMPLE, THERE IS NO SINGLE "MEMORY CENTRE". THOUGHTS, FEELINGS, AWARENESS, EMOTIONS, AND MEMORY INVOLVE MANY PARTS OF THE BRAIN.

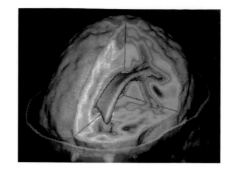

BRAIN ACTION IN SPEECH
This PET scan (see opposite) provides a "snapshot" of a brain taken while the person is talking. Red patches indicate areas of high activity. Here, they show Broca's area, which controls speech (bottom), and Wernicke's area, where language is analysed (rear). In most people, speech and language comprehension centres are on the left side of the brain.

MAP OF THE CORTEX

Certain regions of the brain's cortex are called primary sensory areas. Each of these receives sensory information from a specific sense. The primary visual cortex, for instance, analyses data from the eyes. Around each region are association areas, where data from the specific sense is integrated with data from other senses, compared with memories and knowledge, and associated with feelings and emotions. In this way, seeing a particular scene allows us to recognize, identify, and name the objects in it, remember where we saw them previously, recall related sensory data, such as a certain smell, and re-experience associated emotions.

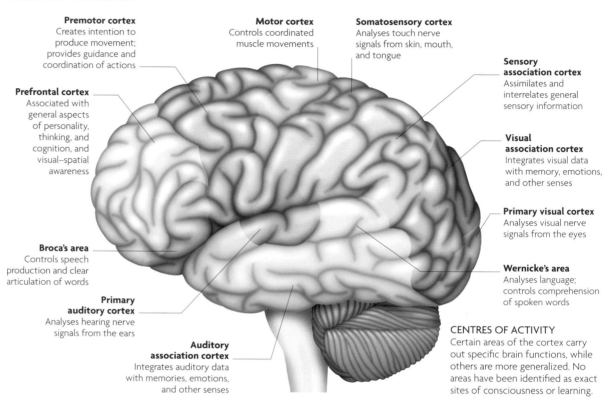

Premotor cortex
Creates intention to produce movement; provides guidance and coordination of actions

Prefrontal cortex
Associated with general aspects of personality, thinking, and cognition, and visual–spatial awareness

Broca's area
Controls speech production and clear articulation of words

Primary auditory cortex
Analyses hearing nerve signals from the ears

Auditory association cortex
Integrates auditory data with memories, emotions, and other senses

Motor cortex
Controls coordinated muscle movements

Somatosensory cortex
Analyses touch nerve signals from skin, mouth, and tongue

Sensory association cortex
Assimilates and interrelates general sensory information

Visual association cortex
Integrates visual data with memory, emotions, and other senses

Primary visual cortex
Analyses visual nerve signals from the eyes

Wernicke's area
Analyses language; controls comprehension of spoken words

CENTRES OF ACTIVITY
Certain areas of the cortex carry out specific brain functions, while others are more generalized. No areas have been identified as exact sites of consciousness or learning.

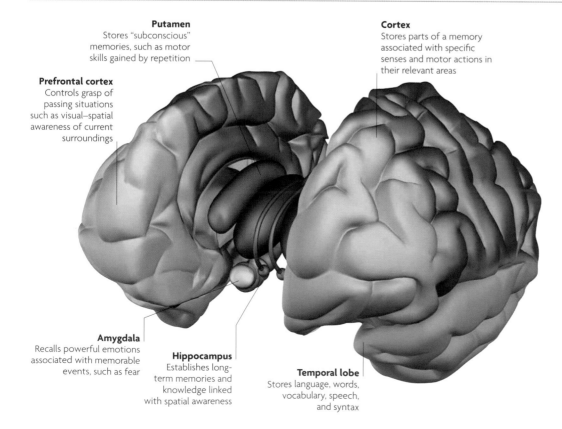

Putamen
Stores "subconscious" memories, such as motor skills gained by repetition

Prefrontal cortex
Controls grasp of passing situations such as visual–spatial awareness of current surroundings

Amygdala
Recalls powerful emotions associated with memorable events, such as fear

Hippocampus
Establishes long-term memories and knowledge linked with spatial awareness

Cortex
Stores parts of a memory associated with specific senses and motor actions in their relevant areas

Temporal lobe
Stores language, words, vocabulary, speech, and syntax

MEMORY AND RECALL

Memories are the brain's information storehouse. They include not only formally learned facts and data, but also informal information, such as likes and dislikes, and experiences encountered during emotionally significant events. No single region of the brain processes memories as they are being established, or acts as a storage site for all memories. These processes depend on several factors: the significance and time span of the memory, its depth of emotional impact, and its association with specific senses such as eyesight. For example, musical recall comes partially from the areas in the cortex that deal with auditory information.

AREAS INVOLVED IN MEMORY STORAGE
The outer grey layer of the cortex is heavily involved in memory. The hippocampus takes part in the transfer of immediate thoughts and sensory information into short- and long-term memory stores. If it is damaged, a person can recall events from long ago, before the damage, but not what happened a few hours, or even minutes, previously.

FORMING MEMORIES

To create memories, neurons (nerve cells) are thought to form new projections (axons) and interconnections. Information is constantly monitored for its significance by parts of the brain such as the thalamus and cortex. Certain facts, feelings, and sensory data, such as a smell, are selected for inclusion in the initial stages of memory formation by parts such as the amygdala and hippocampus. Various aspects of the memory are assigned to their relevant areas. Nerve cells form new links, or synapses, that create a new circuit, called a memory trace, or engram, for that particular aspect of the memory.

Input — Dendrite
Existing synapse
Increasing activity
New synapse

1 INPUT
A neuron receives a memory-associated input as nerve impulses collected by its dendrites. It outputs a corresponding series of impulses to a second neuron.

2 CIRCUIT FORMATION
The second neuron forms new links with a third, as does the first. The new synapses are established by growth of the axon terminals and dendrites.

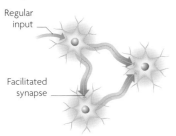

Regular input
Facilitated synapse

3 INCREASING ACTIVITY
Further activity creates more synapses, which gradually become established (facilitated). Recalling the memory "refreshes" the circuit to prolong retention.

4 INTEGRATION
Through continued activation, the memory circuit is assimilated into a network of surrounding neurons. The full web represents a single memory.

LONG- OR SHORT-TERM?

There are several systems for classifying memories and the processes by which they form. One is "durational" (based on time) and involves three basic stages. Sensory memory, such as the brief recognition of a sound, is fleeting and generally stored for up to half a second only. If consciously retained and interpreted, this sensory input may become short-term memory for a few minutes. The transfer of short-term to long-term memory is known as consolidation and requires attention, repetition, and associative ideas. How easily the information is recalled depends on how it was consolidated.

FROM INPUT TO MEMORY
Sensory input is monitored for significant information, which is then either retained briefly or, if focused upon, is consolidated and stored.

INPUT FROM SENSES
↓
SENSORY MEMORY → ATTENTION NOT PAID
↓
ATTENTION PAID → INFORMATION LOST
↓
SHORT-TERM MEMORY → MEMORIES NOT CONSOLIDATED
↓
MEMORIES CONSOLIDATED
↓
LONG-TERM MEMORY

THOUGHT IN ACTION

The advent of real-time scanning methods such as fMRI (functional magnetic resonance imaging) allows researchers to monitor activity levels in different parts of the brain. The fMRI scans reveal tiny localized increases in blood flow (haemodynamic activity). Scans showing haemodynamic activity form instantaneous "maps" that reveal which areas of the brain are busy during well-defined mental activities, such as studying the visual details of an image, listening to and understanding speech, or performing a particular set of movements. For many mental functions, several areas of the brain "light up" simultaneously, showing the complexity of the regional interactions that take place during thought.

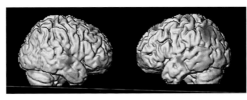

RIGHT SIDE OF BRAIN   LEFT SIDE OF BRAIN

PLANNING A MOVEMENT
The subject of this fMRI scan was asked to think about performing a task during the scan. The image shows activity in the left and right prefrontal areas and also in the left and right auditory cortex.

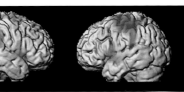

RIGHT SIDE OF BRAIN   LEFT SIDE OF BRAIN

MAKING THAT MOVEMENT
When actually performing the task, large parts of the premotor and motor cortex show up on the brain's left side. The cerebellum (at the base of the brain) helps control precise muscle coordination.

EMOTIONAL MEMORY

Many memories include powerful emotions linked with an event, such as grief at the loss of a loved one, or great joy at hearing good news. Also, experiencing an associated situation can cause emotional recall. For example, a person witnessing a road traffic accident may be reminded of an accident he or she personally experienced previously, and the strong feelings of fear and pain felt at the time may recur. One chief correlating structure in the storage and recall of such strong emotions is the amygdala, located within the temporal lobe on each side of the brain. Normally, the powerful emotional responses it can elicit are kept in check by other brain areas, especially the prefrontal cortex and thalamus.

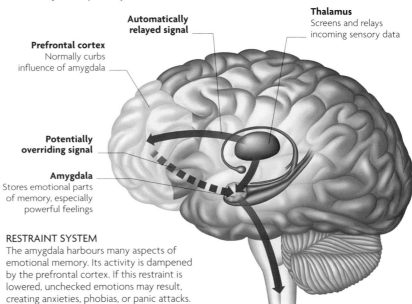

Automatically relayed signal
Thalamus
Screens and relays incoming sensory data
Prefrontal cortex
Normally curbs influence of amygdala
Potentially overriding signal
Amygdala
Stores emotional parts of memory, especially powerful feelings

RESTRAINT SYSTEM
The amygdala harbours many aspects of emotional memory. Its activity is dampened by the prefrontal cortex. If this restraint is lowered, unchecked emotions may result, creating anxieties, phobias, or panic attacks.

TOUCH, TASTE, AND SMELL

RECEPTORS THAT SENSE PRESSURE, PAIN, AND TEMPERATURE ARE WIDESPREAD IN THE BODY. TASTE AND SMELL, IN CONTRAST, ARE "SPECIAL SENSES" BECAUSE THEIR RECEPTORS ARE COMPLEX, LOCALIZED, AND DETECT SPECIFIC STIMULI.

SMELL

Smell (along with taste) is a chemosense – a sense that can detect chemical substances. The sense of smell detects molecules, or tiny particles, known as odorants floating in the air. In humans, smell is much more sensitive than taste and is able to distinguish over 10,000 odours. Specialized epithelial tissue provides a smelling zone, known as the olfactory epithelium, on the roof of the nasal chamber. In addition to warning of dangers, such as smoke and poisonous gas, smell makes an important contribution to the appreciation of food and drink. The sense of smell tends to deteriorate with age, so children and young adults are able to distinguish a wider range of odours and experience them more vividly than older people.

NASAL LINING
Epithelial cells lining the nasal chamber have tufts of hair-like cilia, which wave germ- and odorant-trapping mucus towards the back of the chamber to be swallowed.

HOW WE SMELL

Incoming odour molecules dissolve in the mucus lining the nasal chamber. In the roof of the chamber, they touch the cilia (microscopic hair-like endings of olfactory receptor cells). If the correct odour molecule slots into the same-shaped receptor on the cilial membrane, like a key in a lock, a nerve impulse is generated. The impulses are partly processed by intermediate neurons called glomeruli in the olfactory bulb.

LOCATION

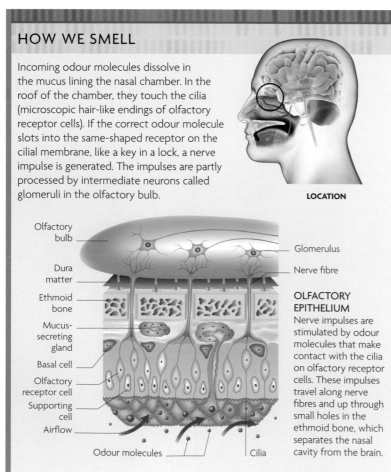

Olfactory bulb
Dura matter
Ethmoid bone
Mucus-secreting gland
Basal cell
Olfactory receptor cell
Supporting cell
Airflow
Odour molecules
Glomerulus
Nerve fibre
Cilia

OLFACTORY EPITHELIUM
Nerve impulses are stimulated by odour molecules that make contact with the cilia on olfactory receptor cells. These impulses travel along nerve fibres and up through small holes in the ethmoid bone, which separates the nasal cavity from the brain.

TOUCH

The sense of touch is provided by microscopic sensory receptors (which are specialized endings of nerve cells) in the skin or in deeper tissues (see p.148). Some receptors are enclosed in capsules of connective tissue, while others remain uncovered. Different shapes and sizes of receptor detect a range of stimuli, such as light touch, heat, cold, pressure, and pain. These receptors relay their signals via the spinal cord and lower brain to a strip curving around the cerebral cortex, known as the somatosensory cortex, or "touch centre".

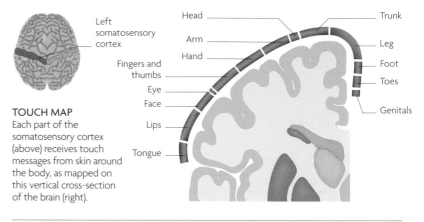

Left somatosensory cortex
Head
Arm
Hand
Fingers and thumbs
Eye
Face
Lips
Tongue
Trunk
Leg
Foot
Toes
Genitals

TOUCH MAP
Each part of the somatosensory cortex (above) receives touch messages from skin around the body, as mapped on this vertical cross-section of the brain (right).

TASTE

Taste works in a similar way to smell. Its gustatory cell (taste) receptors detect specific chemicals dissolved in saliva by a "lock-and-key" method (see box, left). Groups of receptor cells are known as taste buds. A child has about 10,000 taste buds, but with age, their numbers may fall to fewer than 5,000. They are located mainly on and between the pimple-like protuberances (papillae) that dot certain regions of the tongue's upper surface. There are also some taste buds on the palate (roof of the mouth), throat, and epiglottis.

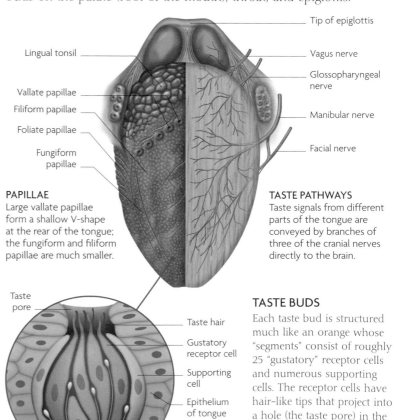

Lingual tonsil
Vallate papillae
Filiform papillae
Foliate papillae
Fungiform papillae
Tip of epiglottis
Vagus nerve
Glossopharyngeal nerve
Manibular nerve
Facial nerve
Taste pore
Taste hair
Gustatory receptor cell
Supporting cell
Epithelium of tongue
Nerve fibre

PAPILLAE
Large vallate papillae form a shallow V-shape at the rear of the tongue; the fungiform and filiform papillae are much smaller.

TASTE PATHWAYS
Taste signals from different parts of the tongue are conveyed by branches of three of the cranial nerves directly to the brain.

TASTE BUDS
Each taste bud is structured much like an orange whose "segments" consist of roughly 25 "gustatory" receptor cells and numerous supporting cells. The receptor cells have hair-like tips that project into a hole (the taste pore) in the tongue's surface. Their nerve fibres gather at the bud base.

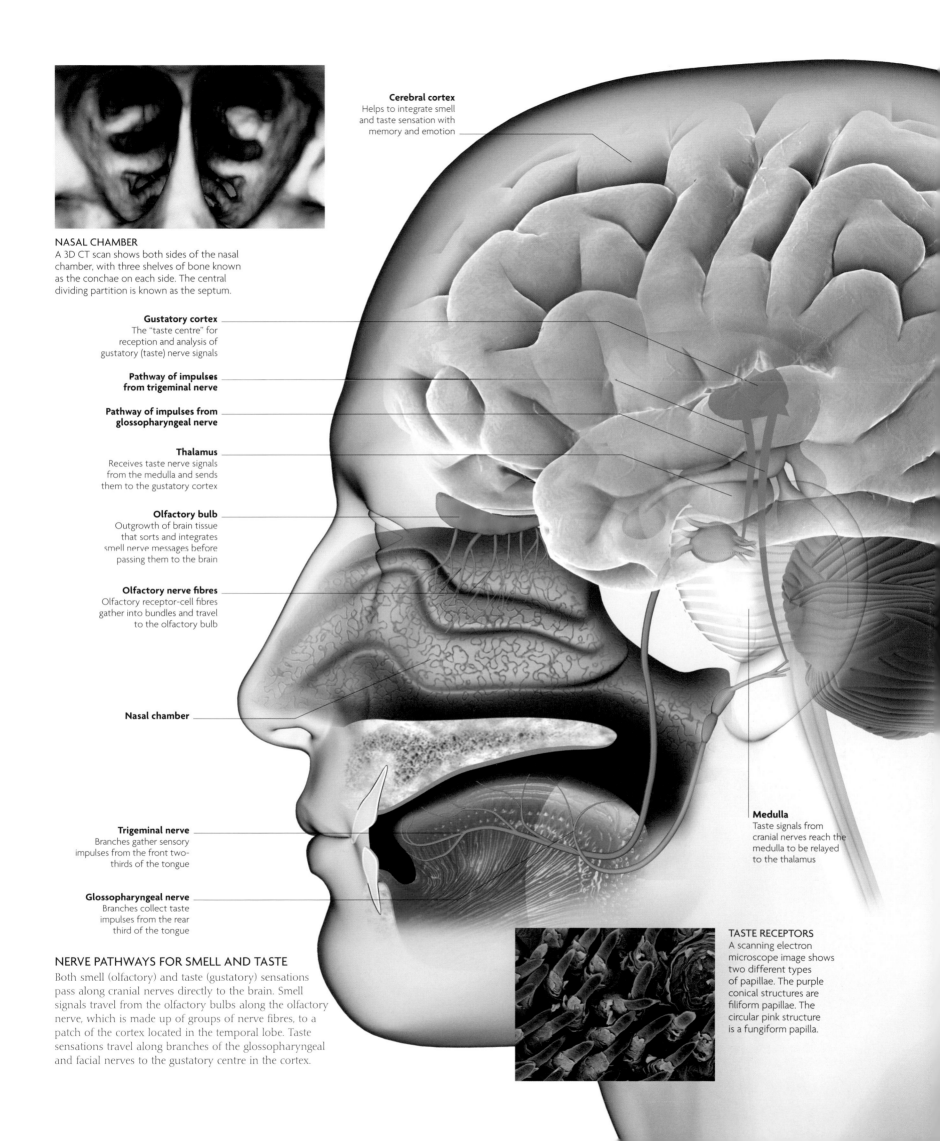

NASAL CHAMBER
A 3D CT scan shows both sides of the nasal chamber, with three shelves of bone known as the conchae on each side. The central dividing partition is known as the septum.

Cerebral cortex
Helps to integrate smell and taste sensation with memory and emotion

Gustatory cortex
The "taste centre" for reception and analysis of gustatory (taste) nerve signals

Pathway of impulses from trigeminal nerve

Pathway of impulses from glossopharyngeal nerve

Thalamus
Receives taste nerve signals from the medulla and sends them to the gustatory cortex

Olfactory bulb
Outgrowth of brain tissue that sorts and integrates smell nerve messages before passing them to the brain

Olfactory nerve fibres
Olfactory receptor-cell fibres gather into bundles and travel to the olfactory bulb

Nasal chamber

Trigeminal nerve
Branches gather sensory impulses from the front two-thirds of the tongue

Glossopharyngeal nerve
Branches collect taste impulses from the rear third of the tongue

Medulla
Taste signals from cranial nerves reach the medulla to be relayed to the thalamus

NERVE PATHWAYS FOR SMELL AND TASTE

Both smell (olfactory) and taste (gustatory) sensations pass along cranial nerves directly to the brain. Smell signals travel from the olfactory bulbs along the olfactory nerve, which is made up of groups of nerve fibres, to a patch of the cortex located in the temporal lobe. Taste sensations travel along branches of the glossopharyngeal and facial nerves to the gustatory centre in the cortex.

TASTE RECEPTORS
A scanning electron microscope image shows two different types of papillae. The purple conical structures are filiform papillae. The circular pink structure is a fungiform papilla.

EARS, HEARING, AND BALANCE

THE EARS PROVIDE THE SENSE OF HEARING. THEY ALSO DETECT HEAD POSITION AND MOTION, SO ARE ESSENTIAL TO BALANCE. THE PARTS CONCERNED WITH HEARING AND BALANCE ARE LOCATED IN DIFFERENT AREAS OF THE EAR, BUT THE FUNCTION OF BOTH IS BASED ON "HAIR CELL" RECEPTORS.

INSIDE THE EAR

The ear is divided into three parts. The outer ear comprises the ear flap (pinna) and the slightly S-shaped outer ear canal (external acoustic meatus). The ear canals guides sound waves to the second region, the middle ear. The elements of the middle ear amplify the sound waves and transfer them from the air into the fluid of the inner ear. They include the eardrum (tympanic membrane) and the three smallest bones in the body, the auditory ossicles, which span the air-filled middle-ear cavity (tympanic chamber). The fluid-filled inner ear changes sound waves to nerve signals inside the snail-shaped cochlea. The middle ear cavity connects to the throat by means of the Eustachian tube, and so to the air outside. This connection allows atmospheric pressure to transfer to the cavity, equalizing the air pressure on either side of the eardrum and preventing it from bulging as the outside pressure changes.

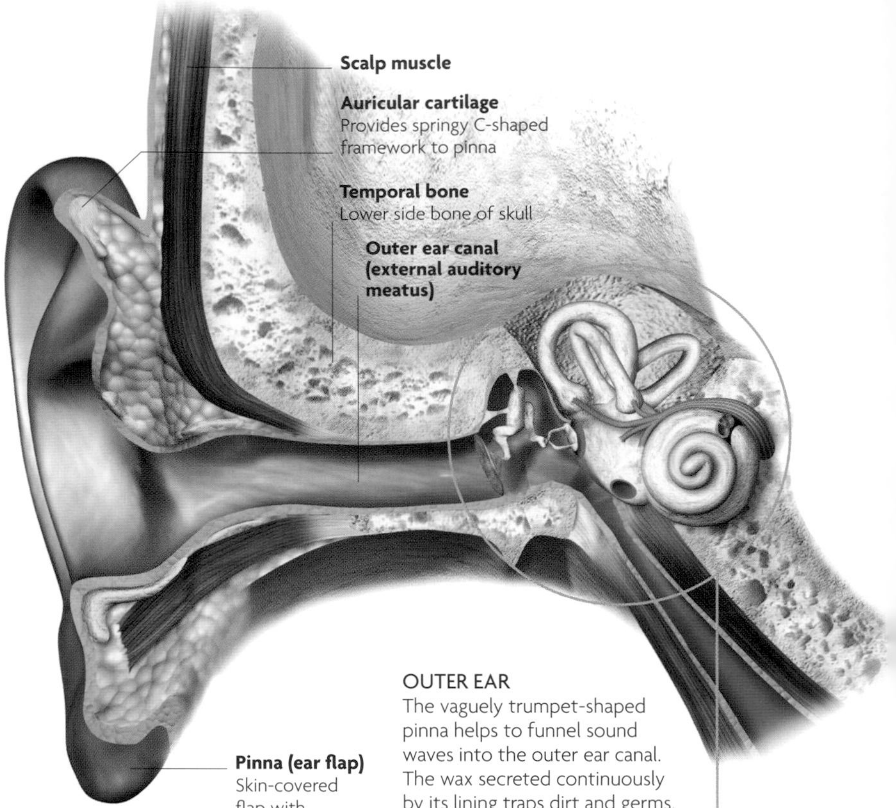

Scalp muscle

Auricular cartilage
Provides springy C-shaped framework to pinna

Temporal bone
Lower side bone of skull

Outer ear canal (external auditory meatus)

Pinna (ear flap)
Skin-covered flap with subcutaneous fat, cartilage, and connective tissue

OUTER EAR
The vaguely trumpet-shaped pinna helps to funnel sound waves into the outer ear canal. The wax secreted continuously by its lining traps dirt and germs, and slowly flakes off to work its way out by jaw movements when chewing and talking.

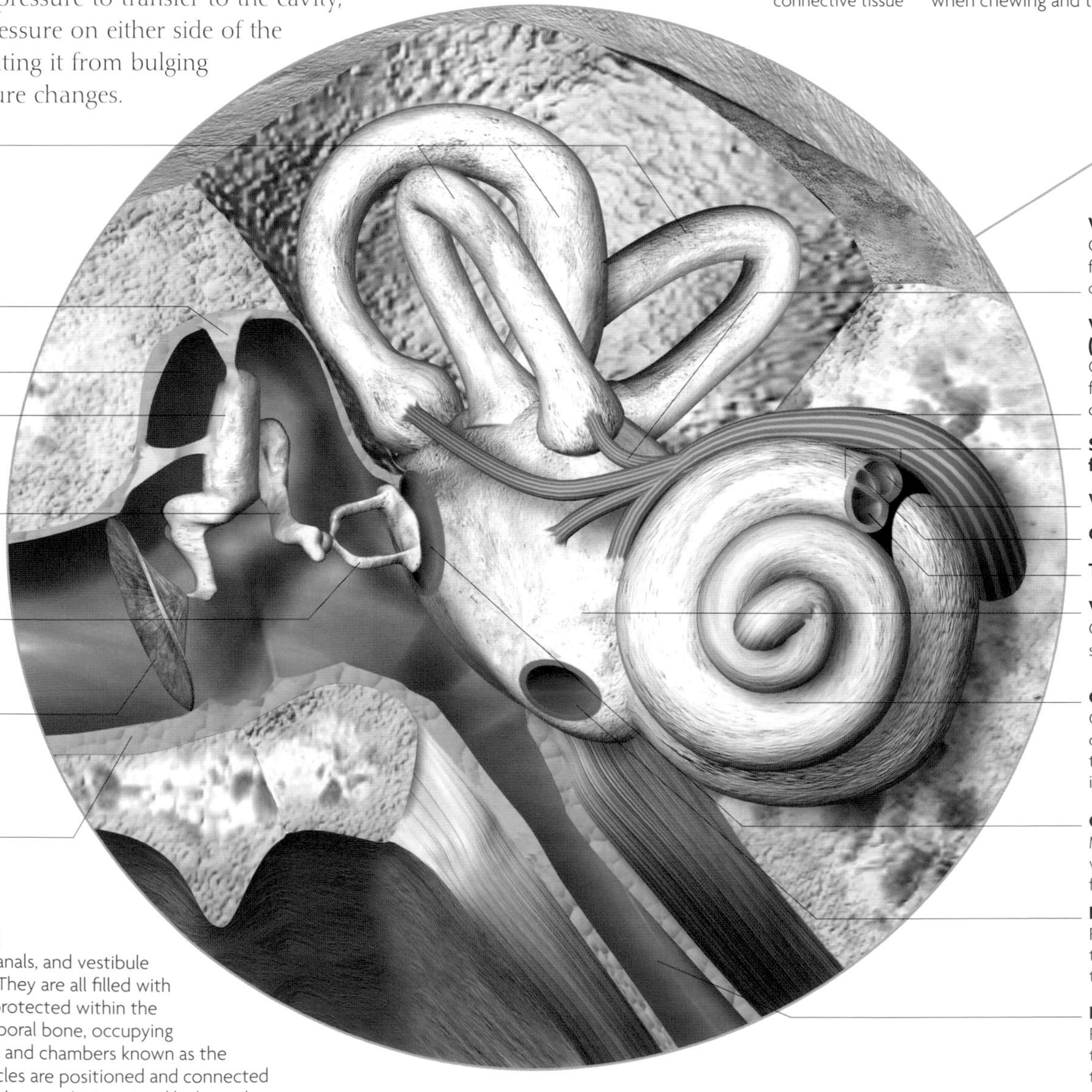

Semicircular canals
Contain sense organs functioning in balance

Suspensory ligament
Ossicle ligaments keep the bones in position but free to vibrate

Tympanic chamber (middle-ear cavity)

Malleus (hammer)

Ear ossicles

Incus (anvil)

Stapes (stirrup)

Tympanum, or tympanic membrane (eardrum)
About the size of the owner's little fingernail; resembles thin skin

Canal lining
Secretes wax, which traps unwanted debris

Vestibular nerve
Carries nerve signals from the balance organs to the brain

Vestibulocochlear (auditory) nerve
Conveys nerve signals from the vestibule and cochlea to the brain

Section cut from cochlea

Vestibular canal

Cochlear duct

Tympanic canal

Vestibule
Contains the utricle and saccule, organs of balance

Cochlea
Containins the organ of hearing; hardly larger than the little finger's tip, it spirals for 2¾ turns

Oval window
Membrane in the cochlea wall receiving vibrations from the stapes

Round window
Pressure relief membrane that allows cochlear fluid to bulge with vibrations

Eustachian tube
Runs to an opening in the side of the upper throat, level with the soft palate

MIDDLE AND INNER EAR
The cochlea, semicircular canals, and vestibule of the inner ear are linked. They are all filled with fluid and are encased and protected within the thickness of the skull's temporal bone, occupying a complex series of tunnels and chambers known as the osseous labyrinth. The ossicles are positioned and connected by miniature ligaments, tendons, and joints, just like larger bones.

HOW WE HEAR

Ears act as energy converters, changing pressure differences in air, known as sound waves, into electrochemical nerve impulses. Sound waves, which usually occur as a complex pattern of frequencies, set the eardrum vibrating in the same pattern. The vibrations are conducted along the ossicle chain, which rocks like a bent lever and forces the footplate of the stapes to act like a piston, pushing and pulling at the flexible oval window of the cochlea. The motions set off waves through the perilymph fluid inside the cochlea. These in turn transfer their vibrational energy to the tube-shaped organ of Corti (spiral organ), which coils within the cochlea.

HAIR CELLS
Within the organ of Corti, with the tectorial membrane removed on the right, each hair cell is seen to have 40–100 hairs arranged in a curve. Nerve fibres run from the cell bases.

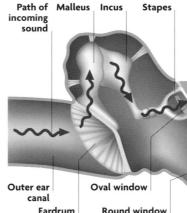

Hair cell · Hairs of hair cell

Organ of Corti
Central spiral element of the cochlea, composed of tectorial and basilar membranes linked by sensitive hair cells

Hair cells
Generate nerve signals in response to motion of basilar and tectorial membranes

Cochlear nerve
Carries nerve signals to brain

Path of incoming sound · **Malleus** · **Incus** · **Stapes**

Vestibular canal
Transmits vibrations to basilar membrane

Outer ear canal · **Eardrum**

Oval window · **Round window**

Eustachian tube

Tympanic canal
Conveys residual vibrations returning to round window

Nerve fibre

Nerve signal

Tectorial membrane
Tips of hairs from hair cells embed in this

Basilar membrane
Supports the bases of hair cells and their nerve fibres

Frequency response
Organ of Corti "shakes" at a particular point along its length, according to frequency of vibration

HEARING RANGE

Human ears respond to a range of sound frequencies (pitches) from about 20Hz (vibrations per second) to over 16,000Hz. Pressure waves beyond this range (infrasound and ultrasound) cannot be heard. Hearing range varies among individuals and reduces with age, especially at the upper end.

AUDIOGRAM
A graph plotting the lowest audible pressure of sound waves (the hearing threshold) is called an audiogram, and it reveals that the human ear is most sensitive to sounds of medium frequency.

"Middle C" is at 262Hz

Top of hearing range; above this is ultrasound

Bottom of hearing range; below this is infrasound

THRESHOLD OF HEARING (dB): 80, 70, 60, 50, 40, 30, 20, 10, 0, -10, -20

FREQUENCY (Hz): 7.8, 15.6, 31.2, 62.5, 125, 250, 500, 1000, 2000, 4000, 8000, 16,000

VIBRATION TRANSFER
Vibrations travel from the oval window, through the cochlea's fluid in the vestibular canal, and transfer to the organ of Corti. Here, hair cells on the basilar membrane have their microhair tips embedded in the jelly-like tectorial membrane above. As this structure vibrates, various forces pull the hairs, stimulating their cells to produce nerve impulses. These travel via the cochlear nerve to the auditory cortex for interpretation. Residual vibrations from the vestibular canal pass down the tympanic canal to the round window.

THE PROCESS OF BALANCE

Balance is not a single sense, but a process involving a range of sensory inputs, analysis in the brain, and motor outputs. Inputs arrive from the eyes (see p.92), microreceptors in muscles and tendons (see p.63), and skin pressure sensors (see p.148), as in the soles of the feet. The inner ear's fluid-filled vestibule and semicircular canals also play a key role. They incorporate sensitive hair cells similar to the cochlea's (see above). The vestibule responds mainly to the head's position relative to gravity (static equilibrium), while the canals react chiefly to the speed and direction of head movements (dynamic equilibrium). In practise, both respond to most head positions and movements.

VESTIBULE
The vestibule's two parts, the utricle and saccule, each have a patch, the macula, containing hair cells. The tips of the cells extend into a membrane covered in heavy mineral crystals (otoliths). With head level, the saccule's macula is vertical and the utricle's horizontal. As the head bends forward, the hair cells monitor the head's position in relation to the ground.

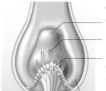

MACULA ACTION

Mineral crystals (otolithis) cover membrane

Otolithic membrane

Hair of hair cell

Hair cell

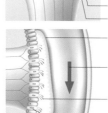

Utricular macula rotated to vertical

Gravity pulls membrane

Hairs deflected

Hair cell stimulated

CANALS
Each semicircular canal has a bulge near one end called the ampulla. This houses a low mound of hair cells, their hair ends set into a taller jelly-like mound, the cupula. As the head moves, fluid in the canal lags behind, swirls past the cupula and bends it. This pulls the hairs and triggers their cells to fire nerve signals.

AMPULLA ACTION

Cupula

Hairs of hair cells

Mound of hair cells (crista ampullaris)

Ampulla

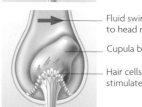

Fluid swirls due to head motion

Cupula bends

Hair cells stimulated

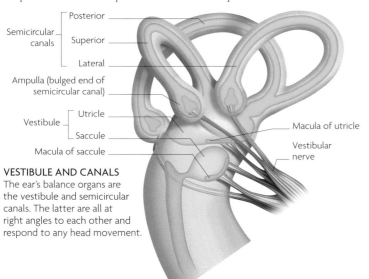

Posterior

Semicircular canals · Superior

Lateral

Ampulla (bulged end of semicircular canal)

Vestibule · Utricle

Saccule

Macula of saccule

Macula of utricle

Vestibular nerve

VESTIBULE AND CANALS
The ear's balance organs are the vestibule and semicircular canals. The latter are all at right angles to each other and respond to any head movement.

EYES AND VISION

EYESIGHT PROVIDES THE BRAIN WITH MORE INPUT THAN ALL OTHER SENSES COMBINED. EACH OPTIC NERVE CONTAINS ONE MILLION NERVE FIBRES, AND IT IS ESTIMATED THAT MORE THAN HALF THE INFORMATION IN THE CONSCIOUS MIND ENTERS THROUGH THE EYES.

THE SEQUENCE OF VISION

Rays of light enter the eye through the clear, domed front of the eyeball, the cornea, where they are partly bent (refracted). The rays then pass through the transparent lens, which changes shape to fine-focus the image, a mechanism known as accommodation. The light carries on through the fluid, or vitreous humour, within the eyeball and shines an upside-down image onto the retina lining. The retina contains over 120 million cone cells and about 7 million rod cells. These convert the light energy falling onto them into nerve signals. Rods are scattered through the retina and respond to low levels of light, but do not differentiate colours. Cones are concentrated in the fovea, need brighter conditions to function, and distinguish colours and fine details. Nerve fibres from the rods and cones connect via intermediate retinal cells to the fibres that form the optic nerve. Through this, the image is transmitted to the visual cortex in the brain where it is turned upright.

BLOOD SUPPLY
The choroid layer of the eye has a dense network of tiny blood vessels which provide the eyeball's other layers with oxygen and nourishment.

Sclera Tough white protective outer sheath of eyeball

Choroid Blood-rich layer that supplies retina and sclera

Retina Thin layer of light-sensitive rod and cone cells

Fovea Region of retina with dense concentration of cone cells, enabling precise vision

Optic nerve Conveys nerve signals to brain

Optic disc Point at which nerve fibres leave the eye; contains no light-sensitive cells

Lateral rectus Small muscle that swivels the eye to look out to the side

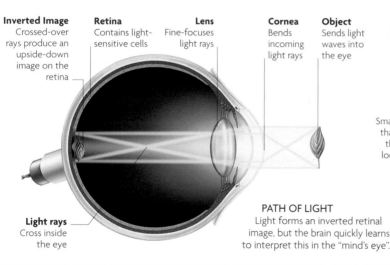

Inverted Image Crossed-over rays produce an upside-down image on the retina

Retina Contains light-sensitive cells

Lens Fine-focuses light rays

Cornea Bends incoming light rays

Object Sends light waves into the eye

Light rays Cross inside the eye

PATH OF LIGHT
Light forms an inverted retinal image, but the brain quickly learns to interpret this in the "mind's eye".

ACCOMMODATION

The cornea provides most of the eye's focusing power, bending light waves so that they converge, which allows for sharper focus on the retina. Fine adjustment is carried out by the lens, which is altered in shape by the ring-like ciliary muscle around it. When the muscle contracts, the elastic lens bulges and thickens, providing greater focusing power to converge light waves from nearby objects. As the ciliary muscle relaxes, the lens becomes flatter and thinner, which allows the eyes to focus on more distant objects.

NEAR VISION
Light waves from close objects diverge more and so need the extra focusing power of a fatter lens to bend the light waves so that they converge.

DISTANT VISION
Light waves from distant objects are almost parallel and require less refracting power to focus, so the ciliary muscle relaxes to make the lens bulge less.

Point of focus

Rounder lens bends light more

Ciliary muscle

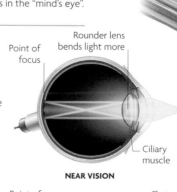

NEAR VISION

Point of focus

Flatter lens bends light less

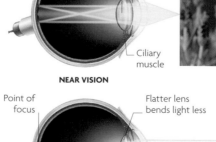

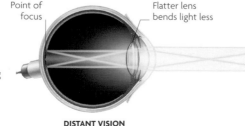

DISTANT VISION

VISUAL PATHWAYS

Nerve signals from the left and right optic nerves converge at the base of the brain at a crossover junction, called the optic chiasm, before travelling to the visual cortex or "sight centres" at the rear of the brain. At the optic chiasm fibres carrying signals from the left side of each retina join and proceed as the left optic tract to the left visual cortex. Likewise fibres from the right sides of both retinas come together as the right optic tract and go to the right visual cortex. Because the two eyes are set apart, each sees a slightly different view of an object. The nearer the object, the more different these views. In the visual centres of the brain, the views are compared to help judge the object's distance. The combination of the views of both eyes into a single image is called binocular vision.

BINOCULAR VISION
The total field of vision for both eyes is 180–200° wide. Each eye has a visual field of 140–150°. The fields of the two eyes overlap by about 100° directly in front and only objects in this area form an image in each eye, allowing the visual cortex to compare them when assessing distance and depth.

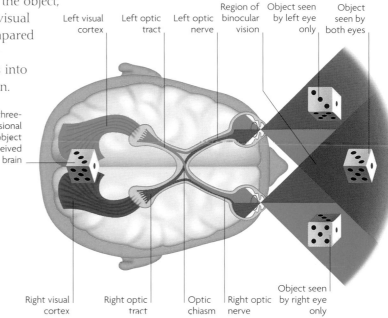

INSIDE THE EYE
An average eyeball is 25mm (1in) in diameter and has three main outer layers: the sclera, choroid, and retina. Near the front, the sclera can be seen as the white of the eye, and at the front it becomes the clear cornea. The main bulk of the eye, between the lens and retina, is filled with a clear, jelly-like fluid known as vitreous humour. This maintains the eyeball's spherical shape.

Superior rectus Small muscle that swivels eye to look up

Suspensory ligaments Hold lens within the ring of ciliary muscle

Posterior chamber Fluid-filled cavity behind the iris

Iris Ring of muscle that changes size of pupil to regulate amount of light entering the eye

Anterior chamber Between cornea and iris, filled with aqueous humour fluid

Pupil Hole in iris that becomes wider in dim light

Cornea Domed transparent "window" at front of eye

Conjunctiva Delicate, sensitive covering of cornea and eyelid lining

Ciliary muscle Ring of muscle that alters lens shape

Lens Transparent disc of tissue that changes shape for near or far vision

Lacrimal canals Collect tears draining through small holes in the corner of the eye

Lacrimal sac Channels tears towards nose

Nasolacrimal duct Opens into nasal cavity

AROUND THE EYE

The accessory structures around the eye are not involved directly in vision but help the eye to function and remain healthy. The skin folds of the eyelids contain a ring-like (sphincter) muscle known as the palpebral orbicularis oculi. When this contracts it narrows the gap in its centre to shut the eyelids. This protects the eye and also smears lacrimal, or tear, fluid over the conjunctiva. The fluid flows from the lacrimal gland to wash dirt and dust off the surface and provides anti-microbial protection. Additionally, there are six small, strap-like muscles attaching the eyeball to the rear of the eye socket (orbit) in the skull bone. Known as extraocular or extrinsic eye muscles, they swivel, or roll, the eyeball in its socket to look up or down, inward or out. These muscles are very fast-acting and are controlled by branches of the oculomotor, trochlear, and abducens nerves, which are cranial nerves (see p.82).

Lacrimal gland Secretes tears to keep eye clean and moist

Lacrimal ducts 5–10 ducts convey fluid to eye surface

TEAR APPARATUS The tear (lacrimal) gland is under the soft tissues of the upper eyelid's outer part. It produces 1–2ml (⅓–⅔fl oz) of fluid daily.

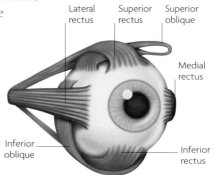

EYE MUSCLES OF RIGHT EYE The six extrinsic eye muscles are 30–35mm (1⅕–1⅖in) long. They contract or relax in close coordination to move the eyeball within its socket.

CEREBROVASCULAR DISORDERS

THE TERM CEREBROVASCULAR DISORDERS COVERS ANY PROBLEM THAT AFFECTS THE BLOOD VESSELS SUPPLYING THE BRAIN. STROKE IS ONE OF THE MOST SERIOUS OF SUCH DISORDERS, WITH ONE IN FIVE VICTIMS DYING. ALSO SERIOUS IS BLEEDING INSIDE THE SKULL, WHICH MAY OCCUR SPONTANEOUSLY DUE TO A DEFECT PRESENT FROM BIRTH OR AS A RESULT OF HEAD INJURY. MIGRAINE INVOLVES BLOOD VESSELS IN THE SCALP AND BRAIN BUT DOES NOT CAUSE ANY PERMANENT LOSS OF FUNCTION.

STROKE

DAMAGE TO THE BRAIN OCCURS IF ITS BLOOD SUPPLY IS INTERRUPTED AS A RESULT OF A BLOCKAGE OR BLEEDING FROM ONE OF THE ARTERIES SUPPLYING THE BRAIN.

Any disruption of blood supply to the brain starves some of the nerve cells of oxygen and nutrients. These affected cells are unable to communicate with parts of the body they serve, which results in a temporary or permanent loss of function. In most people, symptoms of stroke develop rapidly over seconds or minutes and may include weakness or numbness on one side of the body, visual disturbances, slurred speech, and difficulty maintaining balance. Immediate admission to hospital is essential if there is to be a chance of preventing brain damage, and close monitoring is required. In some types of stroke, drugs may be given to dissolve a blood clot. Long-term treatment to reduce the risk of further strokes depends on the cause of the stroke but usually consists of drug treatment and sometimes surgery; rehabilitative treatments, such as physiotherapy and speech therapy are often needed. The after-effects of a stroke are variable and range from mild, temporary symptoms, such as slurred speech, to lifelong disability or death.

BLEEDING WITHIN THE BRAIN
An intracerebral haemorrhage, bleeding within brain tissue, is a main cause of stroke in older people who have hypertension. High blood presssure may put extra strain on small arteries in the brain, which causes them to rupture.

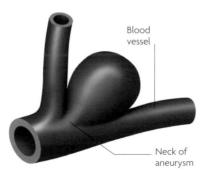

Haemorrhage   Blood vessel

Blockage of tiny vessels
Prolonged high blood pressure or diabetes may damage tiny blood vessels within the brain; this may lead to localized blockages known as lacunar strokes that sometimes result in a form of dementia

Branches of anterior cerebral artery

Thrombus
Build-up of fatty deposits within artery walls, called atherosclerosis, narrows blood vessels and may encourage formation of a blood clot, or thrombus; if thrombus blocks off an artery to the brain, a stroke follows

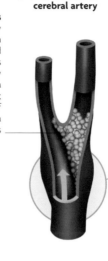

Common cartoid artery

Embolus
Blockage of a cerebral artery, resulting in a stroke, can be caused by a fragment of material, called an embolus, that has travelled through the bloodstream and lodged in the vessel

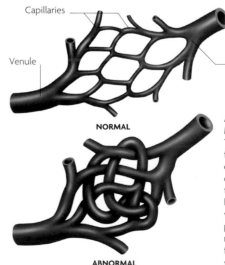

Posterior ceberal artery

Basilar artery

External carotid artery

Internal carotid artery

Vertebral artery

BLOCKED BLOOD VESSELS
Blocked arteries that cause a stroke can occur for several reasons, ranging from localized blockages in tiny blood vessels deep within the brain to a blockage caused by a fragment of material that has travelled to the brain from elsewhere.

SUBARACHNOID HAEMORRHAGE

RARELY, AN ARTERY NEAR THE BRAIN RUPTURES SPONTANEOUSLY AND LEAKS BLOOD INTO THE SUBARACHNOID SPACE BETWEEN THE MIDDLE AND INNERMOST OF THE MEMBRANES COVERING THE BRAIN.

The most common cause of subarachnoid haemorrhage is rupture of a berry aneurysm, an abnormal, berry-like swelling in a cerebral artery. Another major cause is rupture of an arteriovenous malformation, an abnormal tangle of blood vessels. Subarachnoid haemorrhage is life-threatening and needs emergency medical treatment. To stop bleeding from a berry aneurysm, a clip is applied around the neck. Distended or knotted vessels can sometimes be made safe without major surgery either by insertion of wire coils using a catheter, or by radiotherapy.

Blood vessel

Neck of aneurysm

BERRY ANEURYSM
A berry aneurysm usually forms at an arterial bifurcation, often on a blood vessel at the base of the brain (the circle of Willis). Berry aneurysms are thought to be present from birth, and there may be one or several.

Capillaries

Venule

Arteriole

NORMAL

ABNORMAL

ARTERIOVENOUS MALFORMATION
This defect, present from birth, is a tangle of blood vessels. Fewer capillary connections than normal exist between arterioles and venules. An increase in pressure results, which may cause blood to leak from the vessels into the subarachnoid space.

TRANSIENT ISCHAEMIC ATTACK

PART OF THE BRAIN SUDDENLY AND BRIEFLY FAILS TO FUNCTION DUE TO BLOCKAGE OF ITS BLOOD SUPPLY.

A transient ischaemic attack (TIA) produces temporary stroke-like symptoms usually lasting anything from a few minutes to a few hours and has no after-effects. If the symptoms persist for longer than 24 hours, the attack is classifed as a stroke (see opposite). Blockage of a blood vessel may be due to an embolus or a thrombus (see below) and these may have many different underlying causes, including atherosclerosis (fatty deposits in artery walls), a previous heart attack, irregular heartbeat, and diabetes mellitus. Of people who have a TIA, about 1 in 5 will have a stroke within a year. The more frequently TIAs occur, the higher the risk of having a stroke in the future. The risk of TIAs is reduced by treating underlying causes; lifestyle changes such as a low-fat diet and giving up smoking are often helpful.

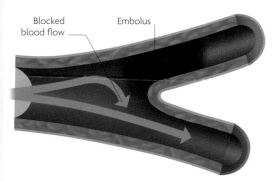

BLOCKAGE
An artery supplying the brain may become blocked if a fragment from a blood clot, called an embolus, detaches itself from elsewhere in the body and travels in the blood to block an artery. A blood clot, called a thrombus, may also develop in a cerebral artery itself, usually as a result of atherosclerosis (see p.122).

DISPERSAL
As normal blood flow breaks up and disperses the blood clot, oxygenated blood again reaches the area of the brain that has been starved of oxygen due to disruption of its blood supply. Although clots usually disperse and symptoms then disappear attacks tend to recur. People may have a number of attacks over one or several days. Sometimes several years elapse between attacks.

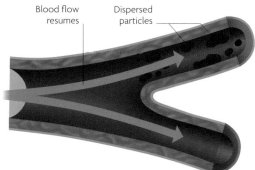

SUBDURAL HAEMORRHAGE

A TORN VEIN CAUSES BLEEDING INSIDE THE SKULL BETWEEN THE TWO OUTER MEMBRANES SURROUNDING THE BRAIN.

Bleeding may occur suddenly (acute subdural haemorrhage) following a severe blow to the head or blood may build up slowly over days or weeks (chronic subdural haemorrhage), often following an apparently trivial head injury. Symptoms such as headache, confusion, and drowsiness may come on within minutes or over months depending on the type. The symptoms are caused by the formation of a blood clot, which enlarges and compresses the surrounding brain tissue. Surgery to drain the blood may be required. The outlook depends on the size and location of the clot. Many people recover quickly, but if the haemorrhage has affected a large area of the brain, the condition may be fatal.

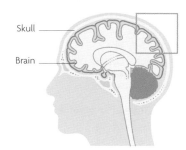

LOCATION

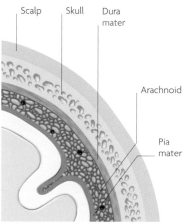

NORMAL
Three membranes, the meninges, cover the brain. The outermost membrane is the dura mater, which contains veins and arteries that nourish cranial bones. Next is the arachnoid, consisting of elastic tissue, and nearest the brain is the pia mater.

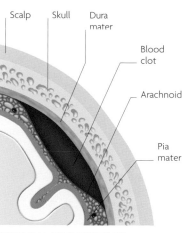

SUBDURAL HAEMORRHAGE
If a vein in the dura mater is torn, bleeding (haemorrhage) leaks into the subdural space, between the dura mater and the arachnoid. The blood accumulates and forms a clot, which can compress surrounding brain tissue.

MIGRAINE

ABOUT 1 IN 10 PEOPLE ARE MIGRAINE SUFFERERS. THEY HAVE EPISODES OF SEVERE HEADACHE OFTEN ASSOCIATED WITH VISUAL DISTURBANCES, NAUSEA, AND VOMITING.

The underlying cause of a migraine is unknown but changes in the diameter of the blood vessels in the scalp and brain are known to occur. Current research indicates that a disturbance in the activity of the brain chemical (neurotransmitter) serotonin plays a role. Triggers for a migraine attack include stress, missed meals, lack of sleep, and certain foods, such as cheese or chocolate. In many women, migraines are associated with menstruation.

TEMPERATURE CHANGES
This thermogram shows the head of a person during a severe migraine. The colours show temperatures that range from black (cold) through green (normal) to red, yellow, and white (hot).

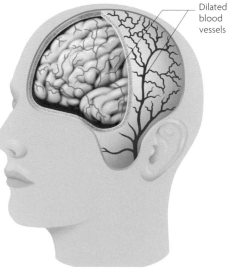

HEADACHE PHASE
During migraine, severe, throbbing pain may affect half or all of the head as blood vessels in the scalp and brain widen (dilate). The neurotransmitter serotonin controls the diameter of blood vessels.

SYMPTOMS OF MIGRAINE

The two major types of migraine are migraine with aura and migraine without aura. In either type, the main symptoms are sometimes preceded by what is known as a prodrome, which includes anxiety or mood changes; an altered sense of taste and smell; and either an excess or a lack of energy. People who have a migraine with aura experience a number of further symptoms before the migraine, including: visual disturbances, such as blurred vision and bright flashes; and pins and needles, numbness, or a sensation of weakness on the face or on one side of the body. The main symptoms, common to both types of migraine, then develop. These symptoms include: headache that is severe, throbbing, made worse by movement, and usually felt on one side of the head, over one eye, or around one temple; nausea or vomiting; and dislike of bright light or loud noises. A migraine may last for anything from a few hours to a few days.

BRAIN AND SPINAL CORD DISORDERS

STRUCTURAL, BIOCHEMICAL, OR ELECTRICAL CHANGES IN THE BRAIN AND SPINAL CORD, OR IN THE NERVES LEADING TO OR FROM THEM, MAY CAUSE DISORDERS THAT RESULT IN PARALYSIS, WEAKNESS, POOR COORDINATION, SEIZURES, OR LOSS OF SENSATION. ALTHOUGH INCREASED UNDERSTANDING OF BRAIN FUNCTION HAS GENERATED IMPROVEMENTS IN TREATMENT, SOME COMMON CONDITIONS ARE DIFFICULT TO REVERSE. ALL THAT CAN BE OFFERED TO THOSE AFFECTED IS RELIEF OF SYMPTOMS.

EPILEPSY

RECURRENT SEIZURES OR BRIEF EPISODES OF ALTERED CONSCIOUSNESS ARE CAUSED BY ABNORMAL ELECTRICAL ACTIVITY IN THE BRAIN.

Often the cause of epilepsy is unknown, but in some cases it may be due to a brain condition such as a tumour or abscess, a head injury, stroke, or a chemical imbalance. Epileptic seizures may be generalized or partial, depending on how much of the brain is affected by abnormal electrical activity. There are two types of generalized seizure. In a tonic-clonic seizure, the body stiffens before uncontrolled movements of the limbs and trunk begin, lasting for as long as several minutes. In absence (petit mal) seizures, which affect mainly children, the victim may be briefly unaware of the outside world but does not lose consciousness. There are also two types of partial seizure. In a simple partial seizure, the affected person remains conscious. The head and eyes may turn to one side, and the hand, arm, and one side of the face may twitch or feel tingly. A complex partial seizure affects consciousness, and most often takes place in one of the two temporal lobes (see far right).

NORMAL EEG

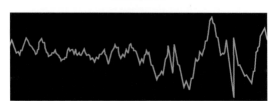
EEG DURING A SIMPLE PARTIAL SEIZURE

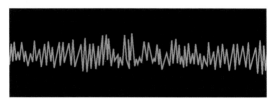
EEG DURING A GENERALIZED SEIZURE

ELECTRICAL ACTIVITY IN THE BRAIN
Normal electrical impulses in the brain show a regular pattern on an EEG recording. In a partial seizure, activity is irregular, and in a generalized seizure, the pattern is chaotic.

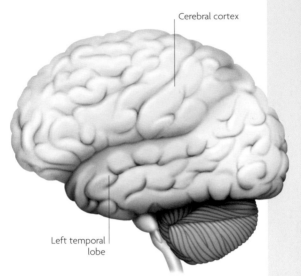
Cerebral cortex
Left temporal lobe

TEMPORAL LOBE EPILEPSY
In this condition, a seizure occurs in one of the temporal lobes. Before the attack, the victim may experience smells or sounds that others cannot detect. During the attack, there may be involuntary movements, especially chewing and sucking, and a partial loss of consciousness. The attack may also cause irrational feelings of fear or anger.

PARKINSON'S DISEASE

DEGENERATION OF CELLS IN A PART OF THE BRAIN CALLED THE SUBSTANTIA NIGRA CAUSES SHAKING AND PROBLEMS WITH MOVEMENT THAT BECOME PROGRESSIVELY WORSE.

Normally, the cells in the substantia nigra produce a neurotransmitter called dopamine, which acts with acetylcholine, another neurotransmitter, to fine-tune muscle control. In Parkinson's disease, the level of dopamine relative to acetylcholine is reduced, adversely affecting muscle control. Treatment consists of drugs that increase dopamine activity or decrease acetylcholine activity. The drugs help relieve symptoms, but none can reverse disease progress. In some cases, surgery may be appropriate if the disease does not respond to drugs. Deep brain stimulation with electrical impulses may be effective in carefully selected cases.

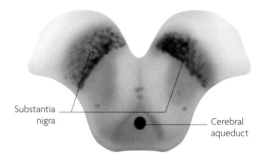
Substantia nigra
Cerebral aqueduct
HEALTHY BRAIN
The substantia nigra consist of large pigmented nerve cells that produce dopamine, a neurotransmitter (brain chemical) needed for control of movement.

Location of substantia nigra
LOCATION OF SUBSTANTIA NIGRA
This false-colour MRI scan of a horizontal section through a human head shows the location of the substantia nigra deep within the brain. The front of the head is at the top.

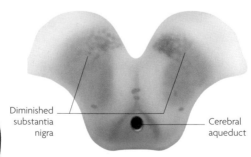
Diminished substantia nigra
Cerebral aqueduct
DISEASED BRAIN
In Parkinson's disease, the substantia nigra degenerate so that reduced amounts of dopamine are produced. As a result, problems with movement occur.

CREUTZFELDT–JAKOB DISEASE

BRAIN TISSUE IS PROGRESSIVELY DESTROYED BY AN INFECTIOUS AGENT CALLED A PRION, WHICH REPLICATES IN THE BRAIN, CAUSING BRAIN DAMAGE.

Creutzfeldt–Jakob disease (CJD) leads to a general decline in all areas of mental and physical ability and ultimately to death. Usually the source of infection is unknown, but a rare variant called vCJD is believed to be linked with eating contaminated meat from cattle with bovine spongiform encephalopathy (BSE). There is no cure for CJD but drugs can relieve some symptoms. However, the disorder is usually fatal within 3 years of symptoms first appearing.

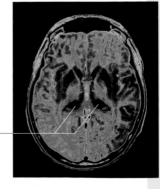
Areas of damaged brain tissue
BRAIN IN CJD
This colour-enhanced MRI scan shows a brain affected by CJD. The two red areas are parts of the thalamus diseased with CJD. The thalamus relays incoming sensory information to the cerebral cortex (outer layer of brain).

MULTIPLE SCLEROSIS

PROGRESSIVE DAMAGE TO NERVES IN THE BRAIN AND SPINAL CORD CAUSES WEAKNESS AND PROBLEMS WITH SENSATION AND VISION.

Multiple sclerosis (MS) is due to immune system damage to the myelin sheaths that protect nerve fibres, so that impulses are no longer conducted normally along the nerves. The condition causes a wide range of symptoms that affect sensation, movement, body functions, and balance. For example, damage to the spinal cord nerves may affect balance. In some people, symptoms may last for days or weeks and then clear up for months or even years. In others, there is a gradual worsening of symptoms. MS cannot be cured but interferon beta drugs may help to lengthen remission periods and shorten attacks. In addition, many symptoms can be relieved by drugs.

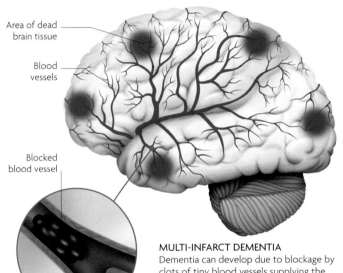

EARLY STAGE
In MS, the insulating myelin sheaths of nerve fibres are damaged. Macrophages, a type of scavenging cell, remove the damaged areas, exposing the fibres and impairing nerve conduction. In the early stages, there are only small patches of damage.

LATE STAGE
As MS progresses, the amount of damage to the myelin sheaths gradually increases, impairing nerve conduction further and sometimes completely preventing it. In addition, more and more nerve fibres are damaged. As damage worsens and becomes more widespread, symptoms become progressively worse.

DEMENTIA

A DECLINE IN THE NUMBER OF BRAIN CELLS RESULTS IN SHRINKAGE OF BRAIN TISSUE AND CONSEQUENT DETERIORATION IN MENTAL ABILITY.

Dementia is a combination of memory loss, confusion, and general intellectual decline. The disorder mainly occurs in people over the age of 65, but young people are sometimes affected. In the early stages of dementia, a person is prone to becoming anxious or depressed due to awareness of the memory loss. As the dementia worsens, the person may become more dependent on others and may eventually need full-time care in a nursing home. Carers may also need support.

ALZHEIMER'S DISEASE

The most common form of dementia is Alzheimer's disease. Brain damage occurs due to the abnormal production of the protein amyloid, which builds up in the brain. No cure has been found, but drugs slow the progress of the disease in some people.

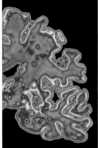
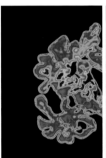

MULTI-INFARCT DEMENTIA
Dementia can develop due to blockage by clots of tiny blood vessels supplying the brain. Each clot prevents oxygen reaching a small part of the brain, causing tissue death (infarct) in the affected part.

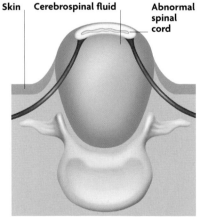

ALZHEIMER'S DISEASE   HEALTHY BRAIN

BRAIN IN ALZHEIMER'S DISEASE
This computer graphic shows a slice through the brain of a person affected by Alzheimer's disease compared to that of a healthy brain. The Alzheimer's disease brain is considerably shrunken due to the degeneration and death of nerve cells. Apart from a decrease in brain volume, the surface of a brain affected by Alzheimer's disease may be more deeply folded.

SPINA BIFIDA

ABNORMAL DEVELOPMENT OF THE EMBRYO IN EARLY PREGNANCY RESULTS IN FAILURE OF THE SPINE TO CLOSE COMPLETELY.

There are three main forms of spina bifida: spina bifida occulta, meningocele, and myelomeningocele. Spina bifida occulta may require surgery to avoid serious neurological complications later in life. Meningoceles usually have a good prognosis after surgery. Myelomeningocele has effects that may include paralysis or weakness in the legs, and lack of bladder and bowel control. Children with this form are permanently disabled and require lifelong care. Folic acid helps prevent spina bifida, and women are advised to take supplements when planning to conceive and during the first 12 weeks of pregnancy.

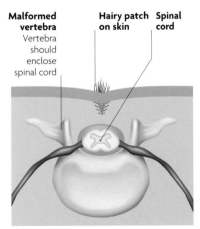

SPINA BIFIDA OCCULTA
In the mildest form of spina bifida, one or more vertebrae are malformed. There is no damage to the spinal cord, and the external effects may be dimpling or a tuft of hair at the base of the spine, a birthmark, or a fatty lump (lipoma) on the skin.

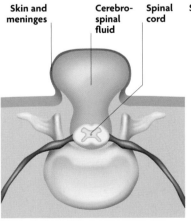

MENINGOCELE
The protective coverings around the spinal cord (meninges) protrude through a malformed vertebra. They form a visible sac called a meningocele that is filled with cerebrospinal fluid. The spinal cord remains intact and the defect can be repaired.

MYELOMENINGOCELE
A portion of the spinal cord itself, contained within a sac of cerebrospinal fluid, protrudes through a defect in the skin, forming a large outward bulge. This is the most severe form of spina bifida and affected children require lifelong care.

BRAIN INFECTIONS, INJURIES, AND TUMOURS

INJURIES AND DISORDERS AFFECTING THE BRAIN AND NERVOUS SYSTEM CAN RESULT IN A WIDE RANGE OF BOTH PHYSICAL AND MENTAL DISABILITIES. THE SKULL IS A CLOSED BOX, SO ANY SWELLING WITHIN THE BRAIN RAISES PRESSURE AND CAN COMPRESS STRUCTURES. THIS CAN CAUSE DAMAGE TO VITAL NERVE TISSUE, WITH SOME LOSS OF BODY CONTROL AND FUNCTION. SPINAL INJURIES CAN CAUSE HARM TO NERVE TRACTS, WHICH MAY RESULT IN SENSORY LOSS OR PARALYSIS.

BRAIN INFECTIONS

INFECTION OF BRAIN TISSUE OR OF ITS PROTECTIVE COVERINGS CAN BE CAUSED BY A WIDE VARIETY OF VIRUSES, BACTERIA, AND TROPICAL PARASITES.

Infection of the brain, or encephalitis, can be a rare complication of a viral infection, such as mumps or measles. The condition can occasionally be fatal, and babies and elderly people are most at risk.

MENINGITIS

Inflammation of the meninges (membranes) is termed meningitis and is usually caused by either viral or bacterial infection. Initially, meningitis may cause vague flu-like symptoms. More pronounced symptoms may also develop, such as headache, fever, nausea and vomiting, stiff neck, and a dislike of bright light. In young children, the symptoms may be less obvious. They may include fever and other signs of being unwell such as crying, vomiting, diarrhoea, reluctance to feed, and drowsiness. In meningitis due to *Meningococcus* bacteria, there is a distinctive reddish-purple rash. If meningitis is suspected, immediate admission to hospital is necessary. A lumbar puncture is performed to test for infection and then intravenous antibiotics are commenced. If bacterial meningitis is confirmed, treatment in intensive care is often required. It may take weeks or months to make a complete recovery from bacterial meningitis. Occasionally, there may be persistent problems such as memory impairment. Bacterial meningitis can be fatal despite treatment. Recovery from viral meningitis usually takes up to two weeks. No specific treatment is needed.

BRAIN ABSCESS

An abscess is a collection of pus. Brain abscesses are rare and are usually caused by a bacterial infection that has spread to the brain from an infection in nearby tissues in the skull. Treatment consists of high doses of antibiotics and possibly corticosteroids to control swelling of the brain. Surgery may be needed to drain pus through a hole drilled in the skull. If given early treatment, many people with a brain abscess recover. However, some have persistent problems, such as seizures, slurred speech, or weakness of a limb.

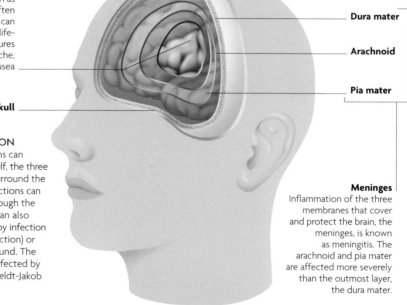

Brain tissue Infection of brain tissue, known as encephalitis, is often often mild, but can occasionally be life-threatening; features include headache, fever, and nausea

Skull

Dura mater

Arachnoid

Pia mater

SITES OF INFECTION Infectious organisms can affect the brain itself, the three membranes that surround the brain, or both. Infections can reach the brain through the bloodstream but can also spread from a nearby infection (such as an ear infection) or through a skull wound. The brain can also be infected by prions (see Creutzfeldt-Jakob disease, p.96).

Meninges Inflammation of the three membranes that cover and protect the brain, the meninges, is known as meningitis. The arachnoid and pia mater are affected more severely than the outmost layer, the dura mater.

LUMBAR PUNCTURE

A lumbar puncture, also known as a spinal tap, may be performed to look for evidence of meningitis. The procedure is carried out under local anaesthesia and takes about 15 minutes. The patient lies on his or her side while a hollow needle is inserted into the spine and a sample of cerebrospinal fluid is withdrawn. The sample is analysed in a laboratory for evidence of infection and to determine the type of infectious organism. After the procedure, the patient is advised to remain lying down and rest for an hour to prevent a severe headache.

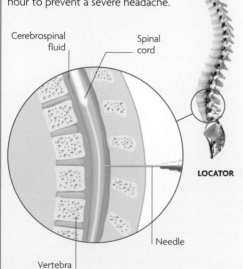

Cerebrospinal fluid

Spinal cord

LOCATOR

Needle

Vertebra

THE PROCEDURE A small, hollow needle is inserted between two vertebrae in the lower spine, usually the third and fourth lumbar vertebrae, below the point where the spinal cord ends. The tip of the needle is pushed carefully into the space surrounding the spinal cord and a sample of cerebrospinal fluid is withdrawn into a syringe.

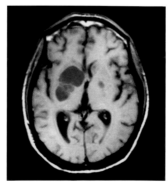

BRAIN ABSCESS This MRI scan of the brain shows an abscess (blue area) due to a fungal infection in a person affected by AIDS. People with AIDS are at increased risk of developing a brain abscess.

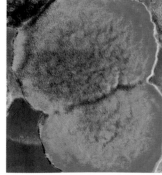

MENINGITIS BACTERIUM This scanning electron microscope image shows the bacterium *Neisseria meningitidis*. Protection against some forms of meningitis is available through immunization programmes.

TESTING A MENINGITIS RASH In meningococcal meningitis, bacteria in the blood may cause dark-red or purple spots that develop into blotches. The rash does not fade when pressed with a glass.

CEREBRAL PALSY

ABNORMALITIES OF MOVEMENT AND POSTURE ARE CAUSED BY DAMAGE TO THE IMMATURE BRAIN.

Cerebral palsy is not a specific disease but a group of disorders that result from damage to the developing brain either before or during birth or during a child's early years. Children with cerebral palsy lack normal control of limbs and posture, and may also have difficulty in swallowing, speech problems, and chronic constipation; however, intellect is often unaffected. Damage to the brain does not progress, but the disabilities it causes change as a child grows. Children with mild physical disabilities usually lead active, full, and long lives and often live independently as adults. Severely disabled children require long-term specialist support. Some, especially those with swallowing difficulties, who are more susceptible to serious chest infections, have a shorter life expectancy.

BRAIN TUMOURS

CANCEROUS OR NONCANCEROUS GROWTHS CAN DEVELOP IN BRAIN TISSUE OR THE COVERINGS OF THE BRAIN.

Tumours that first develop in brain tissue or their membrane coverings are called primary and may be either cancerous or noncancerous. Secondary brain tumours (metastases) are much more common than primary tumours and are always cancerous, having developed from cells carried in the bloodstream from cancerous tumours in areas such as the breast or lungs. The general outlook for brain tumours depends on their location, size, and rate of growth. The outcome is usually better for noncancerous tumours that are slow-growing; many people with this type are cured by surgery. Most people with brain metastases do not live longer than six months.

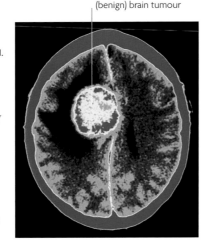

Large, noncancerous (benign) brain tumour

BRAIN TUMOUR
This colour-enhanced CT scan shows a meningioma, which is a noncancerous, slow-growing tumour that develops from the arachnoid, one of the membranes (meninges) that cover the brain. It may be possible to remove the tumour surgically.

HEAD INJURIES

DAMAGE TO THE SCALP, SKULL, OR BRAIN CAN VARY IN SEVERITY FROM MINOR TO LIFE-THREATENING.

Minor bumps to the head or injury to the scalp alone are not usually serious and have no long-term consequences. However, any injury in which the brain is injured is potentially extremely serious. Direct damage to the brain may occur if both the scalp and skull are penetrated. Indirect damage occurs as a result of a blow to the head that does not damage the skull (see below). These injuries can still be serious, particularly if there is bleeding inside the skull (see Subdural haemorrhage, p.95). Anyone with a serious head injury is admitted to hospital; treatment may consist of antibiotics, surgery, or both. About 50 per cent of people survive a serious injury, but some impairment may remain.

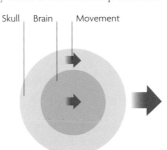

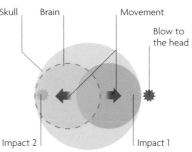

1 RAPIDLY MOVING PERSON
The skull and brain within it travel at the same speed. If movement suddenly stops, as in a fall, the brain may be injured.

2 SUDDEN DECELERATION
The brain may be injured as it smashes against the skull's hard inner surface, and sustain further injury as it rebounds.

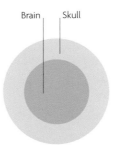

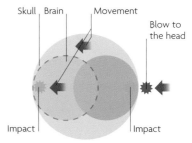

1 STATIONARY HEAD
Both the skull and the brain are motionless. If the head is suddenly struck, as in boxing, injury to the brain can occur.

2 SUDDEN ACCELERATION
The brain may be compressed against the inside of the skull and then bounces off the opposite inner surface of the skull.

PARALYSIS

LOSS OF MUSCLE FUNCTION DUE TO BRAIN OR MUSCLE DAMAGE MAY BE TEMPORARY OR PERMANENT.

Paralysis can affect anything from a small facial muscle to many of the major muscles of the body. Voluntary muscle activity as well as automatic functions, such as breathing, may be affected, and there may be loss of sensation. Paralysis results from damage to motor areas of the brain or nerve pathways of the spinal cord. It can also be caused by a muscle disorder. The underlying cause of paralysis is treated if possible. Physiotherapy is used to prevent joints becoming locked and can also help retrain muscles if paralysis is temporary. Paralysed people confined to a wheelchair require nursing care to avoid complications of immobility.

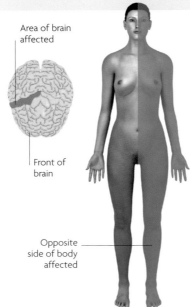

Area of brain affected

Front of brain

Opposite side of body affected

HEMIPLEGIA
Damage to the motor areas on one side of the brain can lead to paralysis of the opposite side of the body. This type of one-sided paralysis is known as hemiplegia.

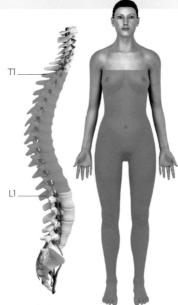

T1

L1

PARAPLEGIA
Damage to the middle or lower area of the spinal cord can cause paralysis of both legs and possibly part of the trunk. Bladder and bowel control may also be affected.

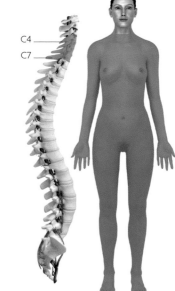

C4

C7

QUADRIPLEGIA
Damage to the spinal cord in the lower neck can cause paralysis of the whole trunk plus arms and legs. If damage is between C1 and C2 or higher, survival is unlikely.

EAR AND EYE DISORDERS

THE EARS AND EYES ARE VULNERABLE TO MANY DISORDERS, RANGING FROM DAMAGE CAUSED BY
AN EXCESS OF SOUND AND LIGHT TO THE NATURAL DEGENERATION OF THE SENSES DUE TO AGE.
HEARING AND VISION ARE MUTUALLY SUPPORTIVE, SO THAT WHEN ONE OF THEM SUFFERS REDUCED
PERFORMANCE, THE OTHER MAY BECOME MORE ACUTE AS A WAY OF COMPENSATING.

DEAFNESS

HEARING IMPAIRMENT MAY RESULT FROM DISEASE OR INJURY
OR MAY BE PRESENT FROM BIRTH; MOST PEOPLE EXPERIENCE
DETERIORATION OF HEARING WITH AGE.

There are two types of hearing loss: conductive and
sensorineural. Conductive hearing loss results from
impaired transmission of sound waves to the inner ear,
and is often temporary. In children, the most common
cause is glue ear (see below). In adults, it is most commonly
due to blockage by earwax. Other causes include damage
to the eardrum or, rarely, stiffening of a bone in the middle
ear so that it cannot transmit sound. Sensorineural hearing
loss is most commonly due to deterioration of the cochlea
with age. It may also result from damage to the cochlea
by excessive noise or by Ménière's disease (see opposite).
Rarely, hearing loss is caused by an acoustic neuroma
or by certain drugs. Simple measures can be effective for
treatment of conductive deafness, such as syringing the ear
for removing earwax. Surgery may be required for glue
ear or otosclerosis. Sensorineural deafness usually cannot
be cured, but hearing aids can help. A cochlear implant, in
which electrodes are surgically implanted in the cochlea,
may help in profound deafness.

GLUE EAR TREATMENT

In this condition, the middle ear becomes
filled with a thick, sticky, glue-like fluid,
impairing hearing. If glue ear does not
clear up, a small plastic tube called a
grommet may be surgically inserted into
the eardrum. The tube allows fluid to
drain away and ventilates the middle ear.
Grommets usually fall out 6–12 months
later, and the hole in the eardrum closes.

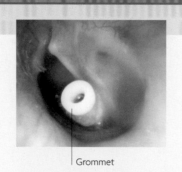

Grommet

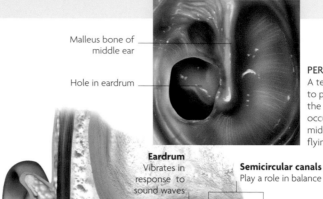

Malleus bone of
middle ear

Hole in eardrum

PERFORATED EARDRUM
A tear or hole in the eardrum may occur due
to pressure from build-up of pus or fluid in
the middle ear during an infection. It may also
occur due to unequal pressures between the
middle and outer ear, as may happen when
flying. Healing usually takes about a month.

Eardrum
Vibrates in
response to
sound waves

Semicircular canals
Play a role in balance

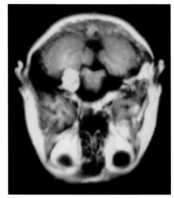

ACOUSTIC NEUROMA
This MRI scan shows a noncancerous,
tumour (red area) called an acoustic
neuroma. It grows around and presses
on the vestibulocochlear nerve, causing
progressive hearing loss.

HEALTHY EAR

Outer ear canal
Conducts sound
waves to eardrum

**Eustachian
tube**

Bones of
middle ear
(ossicles)

Auditory nerve

Cochlea

GLUE EAR
A persistent collection of fluid in the middle
ear, which occurs more commonly in children,
can cause difficulty hearing. Fluid build-up is
caused by blockage of the eustachian tube, which
ventilates the middle ear, often as a result of infection.

Glue-like
fluid

VERTIGO

A FALSE SENSATION OF MOVEMENT AND A SPINNING
SENSATION ARE OFTEN ASSOCIATED WITH NAUSEA
AND SOMETIMES SEVERE VOMITING.

Vertigo may result from disturbance affecting the
organs of balance in the inner ear, the nerve that
connects the inner ear to the brain, or areas of the
brain concerned with balance. Rarely, it is a sign
of a serious underlying condition. Vertigo often
develops suddenly and may last from a few seconds
to several days, occurring either intermittently or
constantly. The condition can be very distressing
and, in severe cases, may make it impossible to walk
or stand. Usually, vertigo disappears on its own or
following treatment of the underlying disorder.

MOTION SICKNESS

NAUSEA AND OTHER SYMPTOMS OCCUR DURING
TRAVEL WHEN VISUAL INFORMATION TO THE BRAIN
CONFLICTS WITH THAT ABOUT BALANCE.

The initial symptoms of motion sickness usually
include nausea; headache and dizziness; and
lethargy and tiredness. If the motion continues,
the initial symptoms get worse and others
develop, such as pale skin, excessive sweating,
hyperventilation, and vomiting. To avoid motion
sickness, it helps to look at the horizon or a
distant object in the direction of travel. Effective
medications for preventing or treating motion
sickness are available. To prevent symptoms,
medications should be taken before travelling.

TINNITUS

THE SENSATION OF SOUNDS THAT ORIGINATE WITHIN
THE EAR ITSELF MAY INCLUDE RINGING, BUZZING,
WHISTLING, ROARING, OR HISSING NOISES.

Tinnitus may occur in brief episodes, but for
many people it is long-term. The condition is
often associated with hearing loss, and exposure
to loud noise increases the risk of developing it.
Tinnitus may occur for no apparent reason but is
often associated with certain ear disorders, such
as Ménière's disease (see opposite). Tinnitus may
improve if an underlying cause is found and treated
successfully. If it persists, a device called a masker,
worn in or behind the ear like a hearing aid, may
help by producing distracting sounds.

MÉNIÈRE'S DISEASE

SUDDEN EPISODES OF SEVERE DIZZINESS, COMBINED WITH HEARING LOSS, TINNITUS, AND A FEELING OF PRESSURE IN THE EARS MAY LAST A FEW MINUTES OR SEVERAL DAYS.

The precise cause of Ménière's disease is unknown, but it is a problem with the fluid balance regulating system in the inner ear (see right) that results in an increase in fluid in the inner ear,. Attacks occur suddenly and may last from a few minutes to several days, and the length of time between attacks may range from days to years. With repeated attacks, hearing often deteriorates progressively. There is no cure for the disease, but medications may help relieve symptoms and reduce frequency of attacks. In cases of severe vertigo, surgical options include severing the vestibular nerve or destroying the labyrinthine structure in the ear.

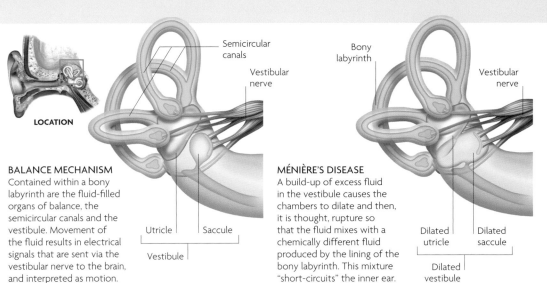

LOCATION

Semicircular canals

Vestibular nerve

Bony labyrinth

Vestibular nerve

Utricle | Saccule

Vestibule

Dilated utricle | Dilated saccule

Dilated vestibule

BALANCE MECHANISM
Contained within a bony labyrinth are the fluid-filled organs of balance, the semicircular canals and the vestibule. Movement of the fluid results in electrical signals that are sent via the vestibular nerve to the brain, and interpreted as motion.

MÉNIÈRE'S DISEASE
A build-up of excess fluid in the vestibule causes the chambers to dilate and then, it is thought, rupture so that the fluid mixes with a chemically different fluid produced by the lining of the bony labyrinth. This mixture "short-circuits" the inner ear.

FOCUSING PROBLEMS

ALSO KNOWN AS REFRACTIVE ERRORS, THE MOST COMMON DISORDERS OF VISION ARE PROBLEMS WITH FOCUSING.

Problems with focusing for near vision (longsightedness or hypermetropia) or far vision (shortsightedness or myopia) result from the eyeball being either too short or too long so that light rays are focused either behind or in front of the retina rather than on it (see below). In astigmatism, vision is blurred because the cornea is irregularly curved, and the lens of the eye is unable to bring all light rays from an object into focus on the retina. Normal ageing often brings on difficulty with near vision, as the lens gradually loses its elasticity and cannot easily adjust its shape; this condition is called presbyopia. Refractive errors can usually be corrected by glasses or contact lenses. Surgery can also be used to correct some refractive errors (except presbyopia) permanently. The main techniques are laser-assisted in-situ keratomileusis (LASIK) and photorefractive keratectomy (PRK). In LASIK, the middle layers of the cornea are reshaped by a laser, while in PRK, areas of the cornea's surface are shaved away by a laser to alter its shape.

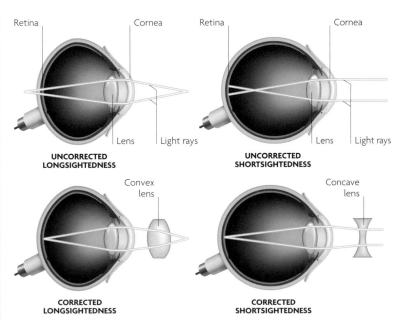

Retina | Cornea

Lens | Light rays

UNCORRECTED LONGSIGHTEDNESS

Retina | Cornea

Lens | Light rays

UNCORRECTED SHORTSIGHTEDNESS

Convex lens

CORRECTED LONGSIGHTEDNESS

Concave lens

CORRECTED SHORTSIGHTEDNESS

LONGSIGHTEDNESS
In longsightedness, the eyeball is too short relative to the focusing power of the cornea and lens. Light rays are focused behind the retina, and the image is blurred. Convex lenses make the light rays bend together (converge) so that they are focused on the retina, correcting vision.

SHORTSIGHTEDNESS
In shortsightedness, the eyeball is too long relative to the focusing power of the cornea and lens. Light rays are focused in front of the retina, and the image is blurred. Concave lenses are required, which make the light rays bend apart (diverge) so that they are focused on the retina.

CAUSES OF BLINDNESS

SEVERE TO TOTAL LOSS OF VISION THAT CANNOT BE RECTIFIED BY CORRECTIVE LENSES HAS MANY DIFFERENT CAUSES.

The risk of blindness increases with age; rarely, it is present from birth. Causes include damage to the retina due to cataracts, glaucoma (which is rare before age 40), and diabetes mellitus or hypertension, both of which are more common in older people. People over 60 may be affected by macular degeneration – damage to the area of the retina responsible for detailed vision.

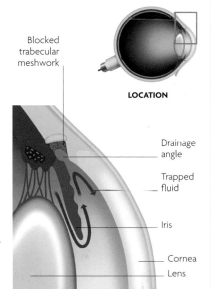

Blocked trabecular meshwork

LOCATION

Drainage angle

Trapped fluid

Iris

Cornea

Lens

Glaucoma

Glaucoma is abnormally high pressure inside the eye due to build-up of fluid. The pressure may permanently damage nerve fibres in the retina or the optic nerve. The condition may be acute, developing suddenly with severe pain, or chronic (see right), coming on slowly and painlessly over many years.

CHRONIC GLAUCOMA
Fluid continually moves into and out of the eye to nourish its tissues and maintain the shape of the eye. Normally, the fluid flows out through the pupil and drains out of the trabecular meshwork within the drainage angle. In chronic glaucoma, the meshwork is blocked, and pressure builds up.

Cataracts

In a cataract, the normally transparent lens of the eye is cloudy as a result of changes in the protein fibres in the lens. The clouding affects the transmission and focusing of light entering the eye, reducing the clarity of vision. The most common cause of cataracts seems to be the general ageing process, and most people over 75 have some cataract formation. Cataracts are sometimes present from birth, which may be caused when a woman is infected with rubella during early pregnancy. Diabetes mellitus and exposure to sunlight are other possible causes. Cataracts can be treated by surgically implanting an artificial lens.

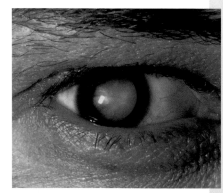

SEVERE CATARACT
This cataract, seen as a cloudy area behind the pupil, affects a large part of the lens. Such a cataract can cause total loss of clarity and detail of vision. However, the eye will still be able to detect light and shade.

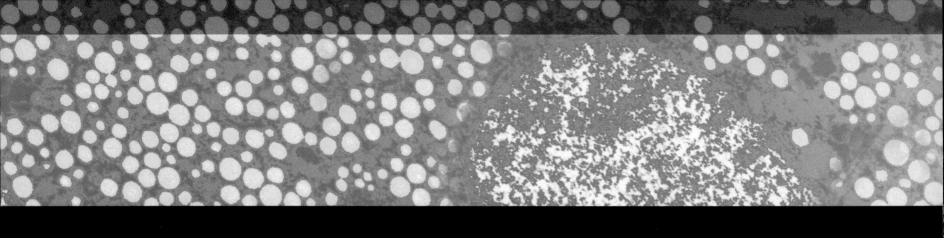

ALTHOUGH OFTEN OVERSHADOWED BY THE BRAIN AND
NERVES, THE ENDOCRINE SYSTEM IS ALSO INVOLVED
IN THE INFORMATION BUSINESS. HORMONES CARRY
ESSENTIAL MESSAGES THAT HAVE FAR-REACHING EFFECTS.
THEY CONTROL PROCESSES AT EVERY LEVEL, FROM
ENERGY UPTAKE OF A SINGLE CELL TO THE WHOLE
BODY'S RATE OF GROWTH AND DEVELOPMENT. TODAY,

ENDOCRINE SYSTEM

ENDOCRINE ANATOMY

THE BODY'S CHEMICAL MESSENGERS (HORMONES) ARE MADE BY ENDOCRINE GLANDS. THESE GLANDS HAVE NO DUCTS BUT SECRETE THEIR HORMONES DIRECTLY INTO THE BLOOD, BY WHICH MEANS THEY REACH EVERY CELL IN THE BODY. HORMONES AFFECT CERTAIN TARGET TISSUES OR ORGANS AND REGULATE THEIR ACTIVITIES.

The endocrine system is composed of bodies of glandular tissue, such as the thyroid, but also consists of glands within certain organs, such as the testis, ovary, and heart. The system uses hormones to control and coordinate body functions in much the same way as the nervous system uses tiny electrical signals. The two systems integrate in the brain and complement each other, but they tend to work at different speeds. Nerves respond within split seconds but their action soon fades; some hormones have longer lasting effects and act over hours, weeks, and years. Hormones regulate processes such as the breakdown of chemical substances in metabolism, fluid balance and urine production, the body's growth and development, and sexual reproduction. Hormone output from a gland can be influenced by several factors, including levels of substances in the blood and input from the nervous system. Since hormones travel in the blood, each hormone reaches every body part. However, the specific molecular shape of each hormone slots only into receptors on its target tissues or organs.

Pineal gland (pineal body)
Pea-sized gland in middle of brain; makes melatonin, a hormone important in body rhythms such as the sleep–wake cycle; also influences sexual development

Hypothalamus
Cluster of nerve cells that serves as the main link between nerves and hormones; produces "releasing factors" (regulatory hormones) that travel to pituitary gland

Pituitary gland
Called the "master gland"; controls many other endocrine glands

Thyroid gland
Controls rate of metabolism, including maintenance of body weight, rate of energy use, and heart rate; unlike other endocrine glands, it can store its hormones

Thymus gland
Produces three hormones involved in development of white blood cells called T-cells, which function in the immune system

360-DEGREE VIEW

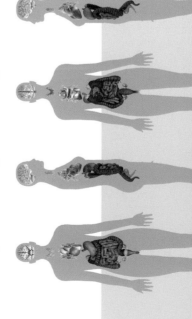

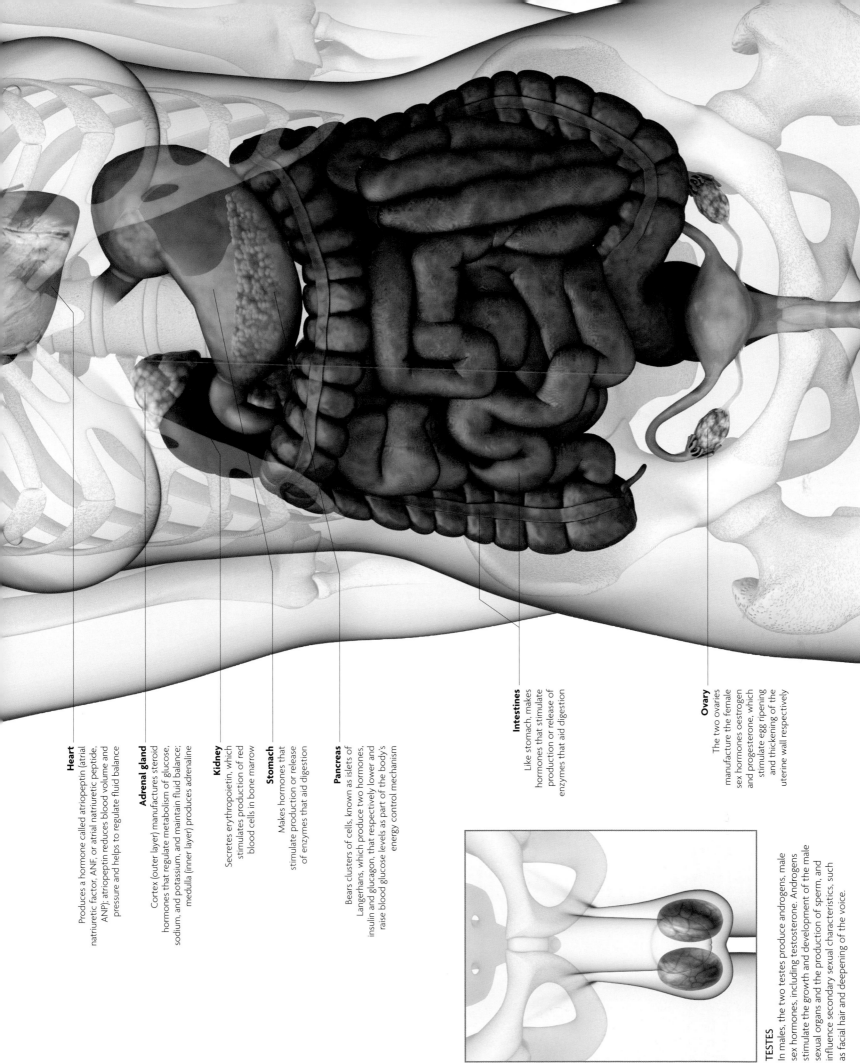

Heart
Produces a hormone called atriopeptin (atrial natriuretic factor, ANF, or atrial natriuretic peptide, ANP); atriopeptin reduces blood volume and pressure and helps to regulate fluid balance

Adrenal gland
Cortex (outer layer) manufactures steroid hormones that regulate metabolism of glucose, sodium, and potassium, and maintain fluid balance; medulla (inner layer) produces adrenaline

Kidney
Secretes erythropoietin, which stimulates production of red blood cells in bone marrow

Stomach
Makes hormones that stimulate production or release of enzymes that aid digestion

Pancreas
Bears clusters of cells, known as islets of Langerhans, which produce two hormones, insulin and glucagon, that respectively lower and raise blood glucose levels as part of the body's energy control mechanism

Intestines
Like stomach, makes hormones that stimulate production or release of enzymes that aid digestion

Ovary
The two ovaries manufacture the female sex hormones oestrogen and progesterone, which stimulate egg ripening and thickening of the uterine wall respectively

TESTES
In males, the two testes produce androgens, male sex hormones, including testosterone. Androgens stimulate the growth and development of the male sexual organs and the production of sperm, and influence secondary sexual characteristics, such as facial hair and deepening of the voice.

HORMONE PRODUCERS

HORMONES CARRY THE CHEMICAL DATA THAT CONTROL
THE RATE AT WHICH GLANDS AND OTHER ORGANS WORK.
HORMONE-PRODUCING CELLS ARE FOUND ALL AROUND
THE BODY. MANY ARE GROUPED IN GLANDS, THAT HAVE
SPECIALIZED FUNCTIONS SUCH AS THE THYROID.

MASTER GLAND

The pituitary, or hypophysis is the most influential gland in the
endocrine system. It is actually two distinct glands in one. Its front,
or anterior lobe also known as the adenohypophysis, makes up the
majority of its bulk. Behind is the posterior lobe, or neurohypophysis.
The anterior pituitary manufactures its eight major hormones on site
and releases them into the bloodstream. The posterior pituitary receives
its two main hormones from the hypothalamus, which lies
above it, where they are manufactured by neurosecretory
cells. Other neurosecretory cells make regulatory
hormones, which travel via capillaries to the anterior
lobe and control the release of hormones there.

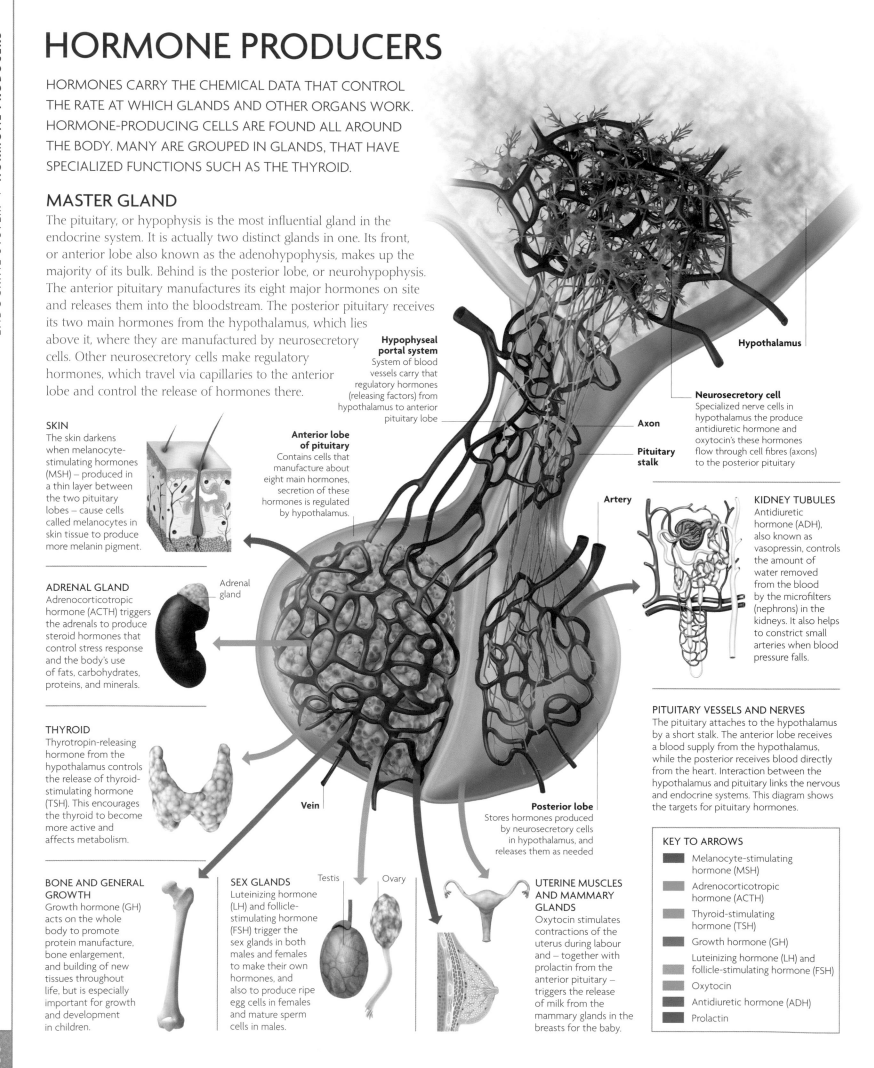

Hypophyseal portal system
System of blood vessels carry that regulatory hormones (releasing factors) from hypothalamus to anterior pituitary lobe

Hypothalamus

Neurosecretory cell
Specialized nerve cells in hypothalamus the produce antidiuretic hormone and oxytocin's these hormones flow through cell fibres (axons) to the posterior pituitary

Axon

Pituitary stalk

Anterior lobe of pituitary
Contains cells that manufacture about eight main hormones, secretion of these hormones is regulated by hypothalamus.

Artery

KIDNEY TUBULES
Antidiuretic hormone (ADH), also known as vasopressin, controls the amount of water removed from the blood by the microfilters (nephrons) in the kidneys. It also helps to constrict small arteries when blood pressure falls.

SKIN
The skin darkens when melanocyte-stimulating hormones (MSH) – produced in a thin layer between the two pituitary lobes – cause cells called melanocytes in skin tissue to produce more melanin pigment.

ADRENAL GLAND
Adrenocorticotropic hormone (ACTH) triggers the adrenals to produce steroid hormones that control stress response and the body's use of fats, carbohydrates, proteins, and minerals.

Adrenal gland

THYROID
Thyrotropin-releasing hormone from the hypothalamus controls the release of thyroid-stimulating hormone (TSH). This encourages the thyroid to become more active and affects metabolism.

Vein

Posterior lobe
Stores hormones produced by neurosecretory cells in hypothalamus, and releases them as needed

PITUITARY VESSELS AND NERVES
The pituitary attaches to the hypothalamus by a short stalk. The anterior lobe receives a blood supply from the hypothalamus, while the posterior receives blood directly from the heart. Interaction between the hypothalamus and pituitary links the nervous and endocrine systems. This diagram shows the targets for pituitary hormones.

BONE AND GENERAL GROWTH
Growth hormone (GH) acts on the whole body to promote protein manufacture, bone enlargement, and building of new tissues throughout life, but is especially important for growth and development in children.

SEX GLANDS
Luteinizing hormone (LH) and follicle-stimulating hormone (FSH) trigger the sex glands in both males and females to make their own hormones, and also to produce ripe egg cells in females and mature sperm cells in males.

Testis   Ovary

UTERINE MUSCLES AND MAMMARY GLANDS
Oxytocin stimulates contractions of the uterus during labour and – together with prolactin from the anterior pituitary – triggers the release of milk from the mammary glands in the breasts for the baby.

KEY TO ARROWS
- Melanocyte-stimulating hormone (MSH)
- Adrenocorticotropic hormone (ACTH)
- Thyroid-stimulating hormone (TSH)
- Growth hormone (GH)
- Luteinizing hormone (LH) and follicle-stimulating hormone (FSH)
- Oxytocin
- Antidiuretic hormone (ADH)
- Prolactin

PANCREAS

The pancreas is a dual-purpose gland. It produces digestive enzymes in cells called acini, but also has an endocrine function. Within the acinar tissues are about one million cell clusters called islets of Langerhans. These contain cells that produce hormones involved in controlling glucose (blood sugar), the body's main energy source. Beta cells make the hormone insulin, which promotes glucose uptake by cells and speeds conversion of glucose into glycogen for storage in the liver. In this way, insulin lowers blood glucose levels. Another hormone, glucagon, is produced by alpha cells and has opposing actions, raising blood glucose levels. Delta cells make somatostatin, which regulates the alpha and beta cells.

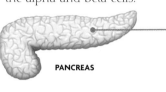

PANCREAS

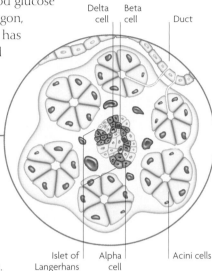

Delta cell · Beta cell · Duct

Islet of Langerhans · Alpha cell · Acini cells

PANCREATIC ISLETS
Surrounded by enzyme-producing acini cells, the tiny pancreatic islets contain three types of cells: alpha, beta, and delta. The secretions of the latter help regulate insulin and glucagon production.

THYROID AND PARATHYROID GLANDS

The thyroid is located in the front of the neck, with the four tiny parathyroid glands embedded in its rearmost "wings". The hormones it produces have wide-ranging effects on body chemistry, including the maintenance of body weight, the rate of energy use from blood glucose, and heart rate. Unlike other glands, it can store the hormones it produces. The parathyroids produce parathormone (PTH), which increases the levels of calcium in the blood. PTH acts on bones to release their stored calcium, on the intestines to increase calcium absorption, and on the kidneys to prevent calcium loss.

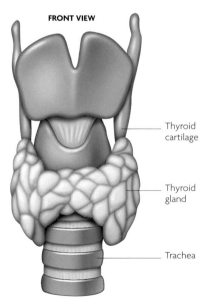

FRONT VIEW

Thyroid cartilage

Thyroid gland

Trachea

BACK VIEW

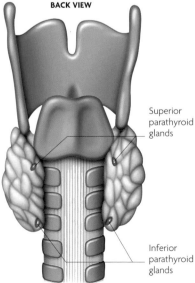

Superior parathyroid glands

Inferior parathyroid glands

THYROID
The bow-tie-like thyroid straddles the upper windpipe (trachea). Its ball-shaped groups of follicular cells produce thyroxine (T_4 and T_3) which regulate the body's metabolism.

PARATHYROIDS
The small parathyroid glands are set into the rear corners of the thyroid's lobes, at the back of the trachea. There are usually four, but their number and exact locations vary.

ADRENAL GLANDS

The inner medulla and outer cortex of the adrenal gland each secretes different hormones. The cortical hormones are steroids (see p.108) and include glucocorticoids, such as cortisol, which affect metabolism; mineralocorticoids, such as aldosterone, which influence salt and mineral balance; and gonadocorticoids, which act on the ovaries and testes. The inner medulla functions as a separate gland. Its nerve fibres link to the sympathetic nervous system, and it makes the fight-or-flight hormones, such as adrenaline.

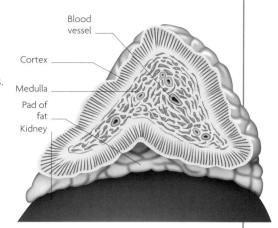

Blood vessel

Cortex

Medulla

Pad of fat

Kidney

ADRENAL ANATOMY
Each adrenal gland is shaped like a low cone or pyramid located on top of the kidney, cushioned by a pad of fat. The glands consist of two parts: the cortex, which forms about nine-tenths of the gland's bulk and has three layers, and the medulla, containing nerve fibres and blood vessels.

ADRENAL HORMONES

Adrenal cortical hormones have life-sustaining actions in helping to coordinate and maintain internal conditions (homeostasis), while the medullary hormones are involved in the body's response to stress.

ALDOSTERONE	Secreted by the outer zone of the cortex, this hormone inhibits the level of sodium excreted in urine and promotes potassium loss, maintaining blood volume and pressure.
CORTISOL	The middle layer of the cortex produces this hormone, which controls how the body uses fat, protein, carbohydrates, and minerals, and helps to reduce inflammation.
GONADOCORTICOIDS	Produced by the inner cortex layer, these sex hormones affect sperm production in males and the distribution of body hair in females, working in conjunction with ACTH.
ADRENALINE AND NORADRENALINE	These medullary hormones work with the sympathetic nervous system to raise heart rate and blood pressure, trigger carbohydrate metabolism, and prime the body for action.

SEX GLANDS AND HORMONES

The main sex glands are the ovaries in females and testes in males. The sex hormones they produce stimulate the production of eggs and sperm respectively, and influence the early development of the embryo into a boy or girl. After birth, the circulating levels remain low until puberty. Then, in males, the testes increase their output of androgens (male sex hormones), such as testosterone. In females, the ovaries produce more oestrogens and progesterone.

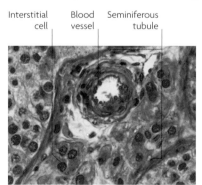

Interstitial cell · Blood vessel · Seminiferous tubule

TESTOSTERONE PRODUCERS
Interstitial cells in the testis shown in pink in this microscopic image, secrete testosterone. They are found in the connective tissue between seminiferous tubules.

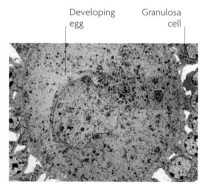

Developing egg · Granulosa cell

OESTROGEN PRODUCERS
This electron microscope shows a developing egg (pink) in an ovary surrounded by granulosa cells (blue and green). These cells secrete oestrogen.

HORMONAL ACTION

HORMONES WORK BY ALTERING THE CHEMISTRY OF THEIR
TARGET CELLS. A HORMONE DOES NOT INITIATE A CELL'S
BIOCHEMICAL REACTIONS, BUT ADJUSTS THE RATE AT
WHICH THEY OCCUR. DIFFERENT HORMONES ARE RELEASED
ACCORDING TO DIFFERENT TRIGGER MECHANISMS.

HORMONAL TRIGGERS

The stimuli that cause an endocrine gland to release more of its
hormone vary. In some cases, the gland responds directly to the
level of a certain substance in the blood, using a feedback loop
(see below). In other cases, there is an intermediate mechanism in
the feedback system, such as the hypothalamus–pituitary complex.
The adrenal gland has a dual trigger. Its outer part, the cortex,
is controlled by circulating adrenocorticotropic hormone (ACTH),
released by the pituitary on cue from the hypothalamus. The inner
medulla is stimulated by nerve impulses direct from the hypothalamus.

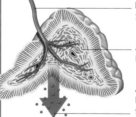

Blood vessel
Blood calcium
level detected

Thyroid
Calcitonin lowers
blood calcium

Parathyroid
Parathormone raises
blood calcium

Hormone release

BLOOD LEVEL STIMULATION
Falling calcium levels in the blood inhibit
the release of calcitonin from the thyroid
and stimulate the parathyroids to release
parathormone; calcium levels are raised.

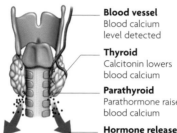

Nerve
Stimulates medulla

Adrenal medulla
Produces adrenaline

Adrenaline release
Prepares body
for action

DIRECT INNERVATION
The adrenal medulla receives nerve fibres
(is innervated) from the hypothalamus
via the sympathetic nervous system.

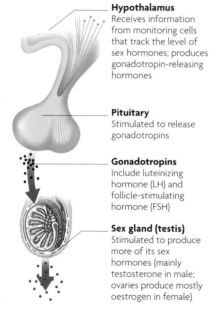

Hypothalamus
Receives information
from monitoring cells
that track the level of
sex hormones; produces
gonadotropin-releasing
hormones

Pituitary
Stimulated to release
gonadotropins

Gonadotropins
Include luteinizing
hormone (LH) and
follicle-stimulating
hormone (FSH)

Sex gland (testis)
Stimulated to produce
more of its sex
hormones (mainly
testosterone in male;
ovaries produce mostly
oestrogen in female)

HYPOTHALMIC–PITUITARY CONTROL
As sex hormone levels fall, gonadotropin-
releasing hormones (GnRH) are sent from
the hypothalamus to the pituitary, which
in turn releases gonadotropic hormones.
These increase sex gland activity.

HORMONE CONTROL MECHANISMS

Chemically, there are two main types of hormones, those
consisting of protein and amine molecules, and those made of
steroid molecules. These two groups work in a similar way overall.
They act biochemically to alter the rate of production of a certain
substance, usually by either increasing or decreasing production
of the enzyme that speeds up the manufacture of that substance.
At cellular level, the two hormone groups have different
mechanisms of action. Protein and amine hormones have their
effect on fixed receptor sites at the cell's surface, while steroid
hormones act on mobile receptors inside the cell.

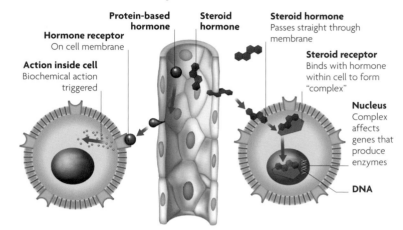

Protein-based hormone

Hormone receptor
On cell membrane

Action inside cell
Biochemical action
triggered

Steroid hormone

Steroid hormone
Passes straight through
membrane

Steroid receptor
Binds with hormone
within cell to form
"complex"

Nucleus
Complex
affects
genes that
produce
enzymes

DNA

PROTEIN-BASED HORMONES
Protein-derived hormones are water
soluble and cannot pass through the fatty
cell membrane. They bind to receptor sites
on the membrane, activating an enzyme
that controls the cell's biochemical action.

STEROID-BASED HORMONES
Steroids are fat soluble and pass through
the cell membrane into the cytoplasm.
The hormone binds to a receptor and enters
the nucleus. It triggers genes to produce
enzymes that prompt biochemical action.

FEEDBACK MECHANISMS

The level of hormones within the blood is controlled by
feedback mechanisms, or loops. These mechanisms work much
as a thermostat controls a central heating system. The amount
of a particular hormone circulating or being secreted into the
bloodstream is detected and passed on to a control unit. For many
hormones, the control unit is the hypothalamus–pituitary complex
in the brain, as in the case of the thyroid hormones below. If the
level of a particular hormone increases beyond a normal level, the
control unit responds by reducing hormone production. Likewise, if
the hormone level decreases, the control unit acts again, stimulating
production to raise the amount of hormone to the required level.

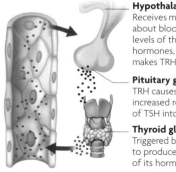

Hypothalamus
Receives messages
about blood
levels of thyroid
hormones,
makes TRH

Pituitary gland
TRH causes
increased release
of TSH into blood

Thyroid gland
Triggered by TSH
to produce more
of its hormones

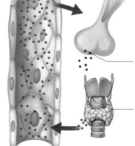

Hypothalamus
Detects rising
blood levels of
thyroid hormones;
produces less TRH
for pituitary

Pituitary gland
Releases less TSH
into blood

Thyroid gland
Reduced
hormone
production

INCREASING LEVELS
For low levels of thyroid hormones, the
hypothalamus makes thyrotropin-releasing
hormone (TRH). This triggers the pituitary to
secrete thyroid-stimulating hormone (TSH).

DECREASING LEVELS
High thyroid hormone levels prompt
negative feedback, so the hypothalamus
produces less TRH. This reduces TSH levels
and the thyroid produces fewer hormones.

PINEAL GLAND TRIGGER

The pea-sized pineal gland is near
the centre of the brain, just behind
the thalamus. It is closely involved
in the body's sleep–wake cycle
and diurnal (24-hour) rhythms, and
is triggered by darkness. Pineal
activity is inhibited by light, which
is detected by the eye's retina,
and sent by a series of nerve
connections to the gland (see
pp.18–19). Darkness removes this
inhibition, and the pineal releases
its sleep hormone, melatonin.

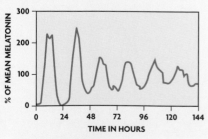

MELATONIN LEVELS
The amount of circulating melatonin rises
at night or in dark conditions, creating a daily
rhythm of rising and falling hormone levels.

HORMONAL DISORDERS

SOME HORMONES HAVE WIDESPREAD EFFECTS, SO HORMONAL DISORDERS CAUSE EXTENSIVE PROBLEMS AROUND THE BODY. "HYPER-" IMPLIES AN EXCESS OF HORMONE, MAKING ITS TARGETS TOO ACTIVE. "HYPO-" IMPLIES REDUCED HORMONE ACTION. DISORDERS ARE OFTEN DUE TO DAMAGE TO A GLAND, WHICH MAY BE THE RESULT OF AN AUTOIMMUNE CONDITION OR DAMAGE TO THE BLOOD SUPPLY.

PITUITARY TUMOURS

THE PITUITARY CONTROLS MANY OTHER ENDOCRINE GLANDS, AS WELL AS MAKING ITS OWN HORMONES, SO ITS DISORDERS CAN HAVE WIDE-RANGING EFFECTS.

The central role of the pituitary in the endocrine system is reflected in the problems caused by a pituitary tumour, which may grow in any part of the gland; those in the anterior lobe are more likely to be benign (noncancerous). One result may be excess growth hormone, which causes enlargement of certain bones, such as those in the face, hands and feet, and of some tissues, such as the tongue, as well as the appearance of coarse body hair and deepening of the voice. This condition is known as acromegaly. Some tumours cause excessive prolactin secretion or overstimulate the adrenal cortex (see right, far right).

PROLACTINOMAS

About 40 per cent of pituitary tumours are prolactinomas – slow-growing, non-cancerous tumours that cause the anterior lobe to secrete excessive prolactin. Normally this hormone promotes breast development and milk production in pregnancy. Symptoms include irregular periods and lowered fertility in women; breast enlargement and impotence in men; and fluid leakage from the nipples along with reduced sexual desire. In most cases, drug medication helps to shrink the tumour and reduce prolactin output, otherwise surgery or radiotherapy may be necessary.

PITUITARY TUMOUR
An enlarging tumour may press on the optic nerves that pass just above it, causing headache and visual disturbances, such as losing part of the visual field.

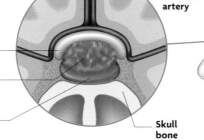
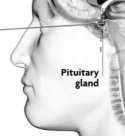

Anterior cerebral artery

Compressed optic nerve

Pituitary tumour
Tumour presses on optic nerve above

Pituitary gland
May fail to functiion normally

Skull bone

Pituitary gland

CUSHING SYNDROME

THIS CHARACTERISTIC GROUP OF SYMPTOMS IS DUE TO OVERACTIVITY OF THE CORTICOSTEROID HORMONES PRODUCED BY THE ADRENALS.

Corticosteroids help to regulate metabolic rate, salt and water balance, and blood pressure. The effects of this syndrome are linked to disrupted regulation: rounded, reddened face, weight gain, more noticeable body hair, irregular or absent periods, muscle weakness, and depression. The main cause is long-term oral corticosteroid drug treatment, which enhances the effects of the adrenals' natural corticosteroids. Less common are an adrenal tumour elevating production of corticosteroids, or a pituitary tumour overstimulating the adrenal.

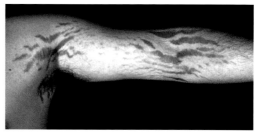

STRETCH MARKS
Characteristic of Cushing's syndrome are easily bruised skin and reddish or red-purple stretch marks, especially on the abdomen and also the thighs and arms.

HYPERTHYROIDISM

THYROID HORMONES AFFECT THE RATE OF METABOLISM AND ENERGY USE. AN EXCESS MAKES THE BODY "SPEED UP".

Three-quarters of overstimulated thyroid cases are due to Grave's disease, an autoimmune disorder in which antibodies attack the thyroid, causing excessive hormone production. It is one of the commonest hormonal disorders, especially in women aged 20–50. A less common cause is small lumps (nodules) in the gland. Raised hormone levels push up metabolic rate, with weight loss due to increased energy usage, rapid irregular heartbeat, trembling, sweating, anxiety, insomnia, weakness, and more bowel movements; the enlarged thyroid may show as a swelling in the neck (goitre). Drugs can usually control the condition.

GRAVE'S DISEASE
Hyperthyroidism due to Grave's disease can cause bulging eyes, giving a staring appearance and possibly blurred vision.

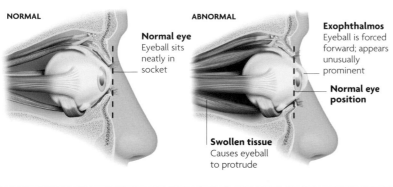

NORMAL

Normal eye
Eyeball sits neatly in socket

ABNORMAL

Exophthalmos
Eyeball is forced forward; appears unusually prominent

Normal eye position

Swollen tissue
Causes eyeball to protrude

HYPOTHRYOIDISM

THIS CONDITION INVOLVES DECREASED OUTPUT OF THYROID HORMONES, SO THE BODY GRADUALLY SLOWS DOWN.

In hypothyroidism, the thyroid hormones, tri-iodothyronine and thyroxine, are underproduced. As these govern the speed of many metabolic processes, a lack of them leads to a slowing down of bodily functions. Symptoms include fatigue, weight gain, slow bowel activity and constipation, swollen face, puffy eyes, thickened skin, thinned hair, hoarse voice, and inability to cope with cold. The usual cause is inflammation of the thyroid gland due to an autoimmune condition called Hashimoto's thyroiditis, in which antibodies mistakenly damage the gland. Hashimoto's thyroiditis runs in families and is more common in older women. The thyroid gland may swell considerably as a lump, or goitre, in the neck. A less common cause of hypothyroidism, especially in under-developed regions, is a lack of the mineral iodine – needed to make the thyroid hormones – in the diet. A rarer possibility is damage to the pituitary gland by a tumour. Treatment of all cases of hypothyroidism is with synthetic thyroid hormones.

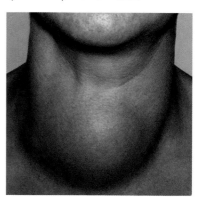

GOITRE
A swollen thyroid (goitre) may be due to thyroiditis, hyper- or hypothyroidism, thyroid nodules, or cancer of the thyroid gland.

DIABETES MELLITUS

The main energy source for body cells is glucose, which they absorb from the blood with the help of a hormone called insulin. In diabetes mellitus, this process does not work properly, so cells cannot take up enough glucose and too much remains in the blood. There are two main types of diabetes mellitus, type 1 and type 2; a third form, gestational diabetes, develops in pregnancy.

BLOOD SUGAR REGULATION

THE BODY NEEDS TO REGULATE BLOOD GLUCOSE LEVELS AT ALL TIMES, SO THAT CELLS RECEIVE ENOUGH ENERGY TO MEET THEIR NEEDS EXACTLY.

During digestion, the body breaks down nutrients from food and drink to make substances that cells use to fuel and repair themselves. The main source of fuel is glucose (blood sugar), which is carried in the bloodstream to cells. Any excess is stored in the liver, muscle cells, and fat cells, to be released later if needed. The body has to adjust blood glucose levels to keep them steady. If the levels fall too low, the cells will not have enough energy, but excess blood glucose can cause autoimmune disease and pancreatitis. Regulation is carried out by two groups of hormone-secreting cells in the pancreas, in structures called the islets of Langerhans. Beta cells secrete insulin, which reduces high levels, and alpha cells secrete glucagon, which increases blood sugar if levels are low.

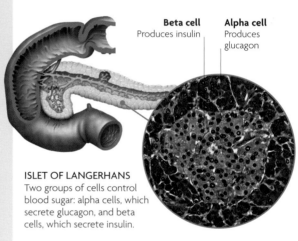

Beta cell
Produces insulin

Alpha cell
Produces glucagon

ISLET OF LANGERHANS
Two groups of cells control blood sugar: alpha cells, which secrete glucagon, and beta cells, which secrete insulin.

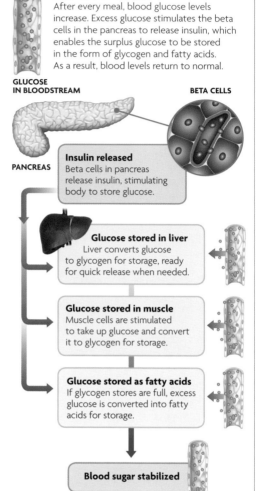

HIGH BLOOD SUGAR
After every meal, blood glucose levels increase. Excess glucose stimulates the beta cells in the pancreas to release insulin, which enables the surplus glucose to be stored in the form of glycogen and fatty acids. As a result, blood levels return to normal.

GLUCOSE IN BLOODSTREAM

BETA CELLS

PANCREAS

Insulin released
Beta cells in pancreas release insulin, stimulating body to store glucose.

Glucose stored in liver
Liver converts glucose to glycogen for storage, ready for quick release when needed.

Glucose stored in muscle
Muscle cells are stimulated to take up glucose and convert it to glycogen for storage.

Glucose stored as fatty acids
If glycogen stores are full, excess glucose is converted into fatty acids for storage.

Blood sugar stabilized

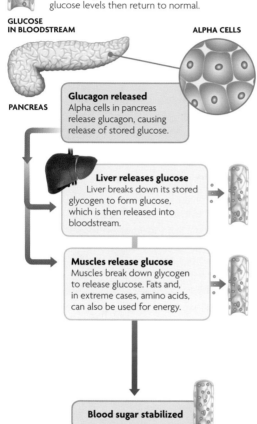

LOW BLOOD SUGAR
If the body is not fed for several hours, blood glucose levels drop. This decrease stimulates alpha cells in the pancreas to secrete glucagon, which enables the body to release glucose from its stores. Blood glucose levels then return to normal.

GLUCOSE IN BLOODSTREAM

ALPHA CELLS

PANCREAS

Glucagon released
Alpha cells in pancreas release glucagon, causing release of stored glucose.

Liver releases glucose
Liver breaks down its stored glycogen to form glucose, which is then released into bloodstream.

Muscles release glucose
Muscles break down glycogen to release glucose. Fats and, in extreme cases, amino acids, can also be used for energy.

Blood sugar stabilized

TYPE 1 DIABETES

THIS FORM OF DIABETES OCCURS WHEN BETA CELLS IN THE PANCREAS ARE DESTROYED, SO THE PANCREAS PRODUCES TOO LITTLE INSULIN OR NONE AT ALL.

Type 1 diabetes mellitus is an autoimmune disorder (see pp.168–69). It occurs when the immune system misidentifies the beta cells as foreign and destroys them. The cause is unknown, but the disease may be triggered by a viral infection or by inflammation in the pancreas. It usually develops rapidly in childhood or adolescence. Symptoms include thirst, dry mouth, hunger, frequent urination, fatigue, blurred vision, and weight loss. If untreated, the disorder can cause ketoacidosis, in which toxic chemicals called ketones build up in the blood. Affected people need urgent medical attention; otherwise they can fall into a coma. There can also be long-term complications (see Type 2 diabetes, opposite). Treatment involves frequent insulin injections. There is no cure; a kidney and pancreas transplant can relieve the disorder, but drugs are needed for life so the body will not reject the organs.

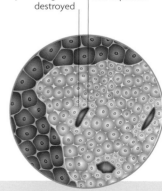

Beta cells
Insulin-producing cells

Insulin
Insulin secreted into capillaries

Damaged beta cells
Insulin-producing cells destroyed

Capillary
No insulin is secreted into capillaries

DAMAGED BETA CELLS
If the beta cells are damaged, they cannot release insulin. As a result, body cells cannot take up glucose, and blood glucose levels rise too high. The body registers the lack of glucose in cells and stimulates glucagon production, which raises blood glucose levels still further.

NORMAL BETA-CELL FUNCTION
As food and drink are digested, the presence of glucose, amino acids, and fatty acids in the intestine stimulates beta cells to release insulin into the bloodstream via tiny blood vessels called capillaries, which run through the islets of Langerhans.

INSULIN THERAPY

Injections of insulin are given to make up for the insulin that the body fails to produce. Treatment follows natural patterns of insulin production. Short-acting insulins are given before meals, creating high levels to cope with the glucose that comes into the body. Longer-acting insulins are taken once or twice a day to maintain a constant background level of the hormone.

TYPE 2 DIABETES

THE MOST COMMON FORM OF DIABETES MELLITUS, TYPE 2 DIABETES DEVELOPS WHEN BODY CELLS BECOME RESISTANT TO THE EFFECTS OF INSULIN.

In type 2 diabetes, the pancreas secretes insulin, but the body cells are unable to respond to it. The cause is unknown, but some people may be predisposed to developing it. This form of diabetes is often associated with obesity and is a growing problem in affluent societies. The disorder develops slowly. There may be initial symptoms such as thirst, fatigue, and frequent urination, but in some cases, the diabetes goes unnoticed for several years. As a result, complications may arise. Persistent high glucose levels can cause damage to small blood vessels around the body. People with type 2 diabetes are also more prone to high cholesterol levels, atherosclerosis (see p.122), and high blood pressure. The condition can be controlled with a healthy diet, regular exercise, and daily monitoring of blood glucose. However, in some cases, drugs are needed to boost insulin production or help the cells absorb glucose.

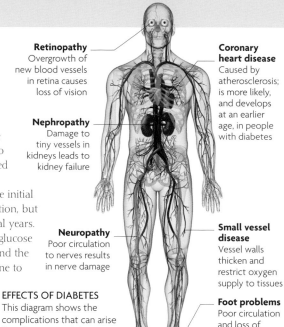

Retinopathy
Overgrowth of new blood vessels in retina causes loss of vision

Nephropathy
Damage to tiny vessels in kidneys leads to kidney failure

Neuropathy
Poor circulation to nerves results in nerve damage

Coronary heart disease
Caused by atherosclerosis; is more likely, and develops at an earlier age, in people with diabetes

Small vessel disease
Vessel walls thicken and restrict oxygen supply to tissues

Foot problems
Poor circulation and loss of feeling leads to skin ulcers and gangrene

EFFECTS OF DIABETES
This diagram shows the complications that can arise from long-term diabetes, usually if the problem is poorly controlled.

GESTATIONAL DIABETES

This form of diabetes mellitus develops in about 1 in 50 women during pregnancy; it is more common in overweight women, those over the age of 30, and those with a family history of diabetes. Some of the hormones that the placenta produces during pregnancy have an anti-insulin effect. If the body cannot produce enough insulin to counter this effect, blood glucose levels rise too high and gestational diabetes develops. The symptoms include fatigue, thirst, increased urination, and possibly yeast infections or bladder infections. If the diabetes is not controlled, the fetus may grow too large and birth may be difficult. The condition is diagnosed with blood and urine tests to detect glucose. It can be controlled with a low-sugar diet and usually disappears after the birth. However, some women who have had gestational diabetes go on to develop type 2 diabetes a few years later.

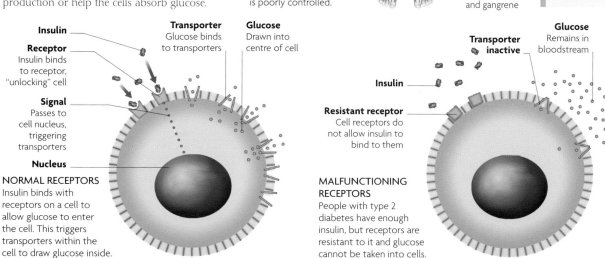

Insulin

Receptor
Insulin binds to receptor, "unlocking" cell

Signal
Passes to cell nucleus, triggering transporters

Nucleus

Transporter
Glucose binds to transporters

Glucose
Drawn into centre of cell

NORMAL RECEPTORS
Insulin binds with receptors on a cell to allow glucose to enter the cell. This triggers transporters within the cell to draw glucose inside.

Insulin

Resistant receptor
Cell receptors do not allow insulin to bind to them

Transporter inactive

Glucose
Remains in bloodstream

MALFUNCTIONING RECEPTORS
People with type 2 diabetes have enough insulin, but receptors are resistant to it and glucose cannot be taken into cells.

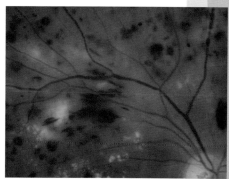

DIABETIC RETINOPATHY
This image shows damaged blood vessels of the retina (diabetic retinopathy). The blotches are aneurysms and haemorrhages, where blood vessels have leaked.

OBESITY

An excessive level of body fat is called obesity. The condition is usually caused by overeating and lack of exercise. Obesity is a major problem in rich countries but, is increasingly common across the world. Obese people are at higher risk of developing serious disorders. Major threats include coronary heart disease (see p.122) and stroke (see p.94), due to the build-up of fatty deposits in arteries, and type 2 diabetes (see above); these are particular risks for people with excess fat around the abdomen. Other problems include certain cancers, such as breast cancer and colon cancer. Excess weight puts strain on muscles and joints, and fat around the face and neck can interfere with breathing during sleep.

One measure of obesity is the body mass index (see right), by which people are defined as obese if they are more than 20 per cent above the maximum healthy weight for their body size. However, this index does not take account of skeletal size and muscle mass; some muscular people may actually be classed as "overweight". Another helpful guide is waist measurement. A figure above 102cm (40in) for men or 89cm (35in) for women may indicate excess abdominal fat.

EXCESS BODY FAT
Body fat may be laid down just under the skin (subcutaneous fat) and can also collect in the abdominal cavity (central or visceral fat). Fat distribution partly depends on sex; males are more likely to have excess fat concentrated around and inside the abdomen, whereas females tend to accumulate surplus fat on the hips, thighs, and buttocks.

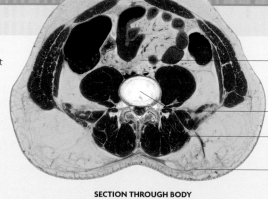

SECTION THROUGH BODY

Central or visceral fat
Collects in abdominal cavity and around organs

Spinal column

Back muscles

Subcutaneous fat
Accumulates in layer beneath skin

BODY MASS INDEX
The body mass index (BMI) is used to determine whether a person is a healthy weight for his or her size. BMI is usually expressed as a number. The ideal range is between 20 and 25 (shown here by the red band). Anyone over 25 is overweight, and anyone over 30 is obese. A person with a BMI under 20 is underweight.

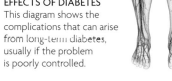

Overweight
BMI over 25

Ideal range
BMI between 20 and 25

Underweight
BMI less than 20

WEIGHT IN KG — 0, 25, 50, 75, 100

HEIGHT IN CM — 140, 150, 160, 170, 180, 190, 200

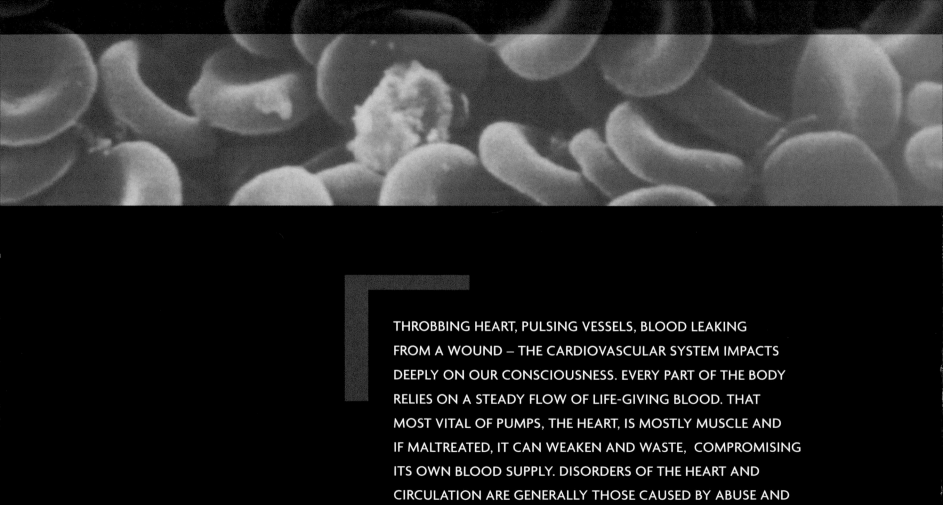

THROBBING HEART, PULSING VESSELS, BLOOD LEAKING
FROM A WOUND – THE CARDIOVASCULAR SYSTEM IMPACTS
DEEPLY ON OUR CONSCIOUSNESS. EVERY PART OF THE BODY
RELIES ON A STEADY FLOW OF LIFE-GIVING BLOOD. THAT
MOST VITAL OF PUMPS, THE HEART, IS MOSTLY MUSCLE AND
IF MALTREATED, IT CAN WEAKEN AND WASTE, COMPROMISING
ITS OWN BLOOD SUPPLY. DISORDERS OF THE HEART AND
CIRCULATION ARE GENERALLY THOSE CAUSED BY ABUSE AND
EXCESS: SMOKING TOBACCO, TOO MUCH FOOD LEADING TO

CARDIOVASCULAR SYSTEM

● SEE DVD-ROM

CARDIOVASCULAR ANATOMY

THE CIRCULATORY SYSTEM (OR CARDIOVASCULAR SYSTEM) IS RESPONSIBLE FOR DELIVERING OXYGEN AND OTHER NUTRIENTS TO VIRTUALLY ALL BODY CELLS AND REMOVING CARBON DIOXIDE AND OTHER WASTE PRODUCTS FROM THEM. IN COMMON WITH THE NERVOUS AND LYMPHATIC SYSTEMS, THIS COMPLEX NETWORK EXTENDS INTO EVERY CREVICE OF THE BODY.

The circulatory system is composed of the heart, blood vessels, and blood. Although the heart is linked to emotions and virtues, such as love and courage, it is simply a muscular pump. Its regular beats send blood into tough, elastic tubes called arteries, which branch into smaller vessels and convey oxygen-rich blood through the body. The arteries eventually divide into tiny capillaries, the walls of which are so thin that oxygen, nutrients, minerals, and other substances pass through to surrounding cells and tissues. Waste substances flow from the tissues and cells into the blood for disposal. The capillaries join and enlarge to create tubes that eventually become veins, which take blood back to the heart. Vessels carrying oxygenated blood (usually arteries) are shown in red and those carrying deoxygenated blood (usually veins) are blue. The intricate network has a length of some 150,000km (90,000 miles) – equivalent to almost four times around the Earth.

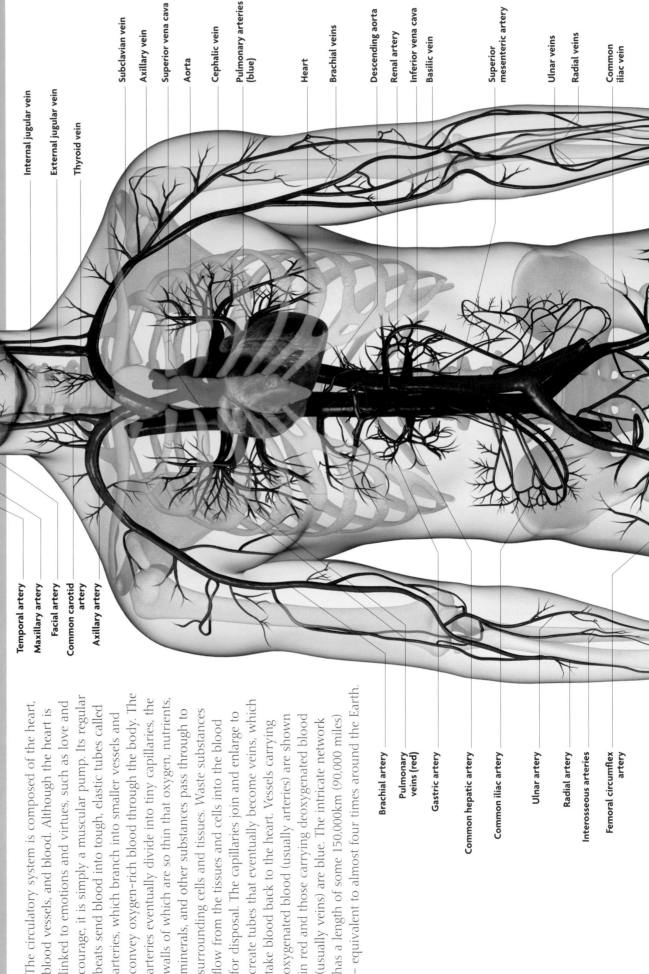

Cerebral vein, or sagittal sinus

Superficial temporal vein

Angular vein

Facial vein

Internal jugular vein

External jugular vein

Thyroid vein

Subclavian vein

Axillary vein

Superior vena cava

Aorta

Cephalic vein

Pulmonary arteries (blue)

Heart

Brachial veins

Descending aorta

Renal artery

Inferior vena cava

Basilic vein

Superior mesenteric artery

Ulnar veins

Radial veins

Common iliac vein

Temporal artery

Maxillary artery

Facial artery

Common carotid artery

Axillary artery

Brachial artery

Pulmonary veins (red)

Gastric artery

Common hepatic artery

Common iliac artery

Ulnar artery

Radial artery

Interosseous arteries

Femoral circumflex artery

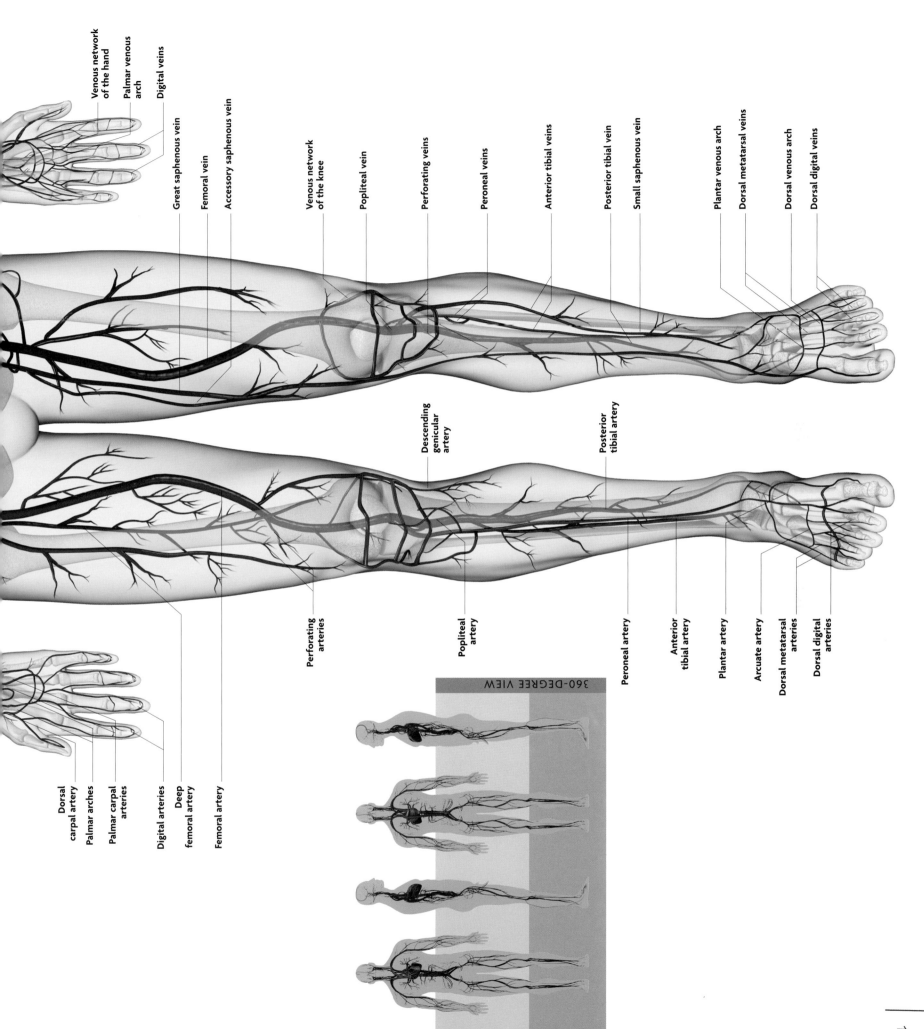

Venous network of the hand

Palmar venous arch

Digital veins

Great saphenous vein

Femoral vein

Accessory saphenous vein

Venous network of the knee

Popliteal vein

Perforating veins

Peroneal veins

Anterior tibial veins

Posterior tibial vein

Small saphenous vein

Plantar venous arch

Dorsal metatarsal veins

Dorsal venous arch

Dorsal digital veins

Descending genicular artery

Posterior tibial artery

Dorsal carpal artery

Palmar arches

Palmar carpal arteries

Digital arteries

Deep femoral artery

Femoral artery

Perforating arteries

Popliteal artery

Peroneal artery

Anterior tibial artery

Plantar artery

Arcuate artery

Dorsal metatarsal arteries

Dorsal digital arteries

360-DEGREE VIEW

115

BLOOD AND BLOOD VESSELS

BLOOD IS A COLLECTION OF SPECIALIZED CELLS SUSPENDED IN A STRAW-COLOURED LIQUID CALLED PLASMA. BLOOD DELIVERS OXYGEN AND NUTRIENTS TO BODY CELLS, COLLECTS WASTE, DISTRIBUTES HORMONES, SPREADS HEAT AROUND THE BODY TO CONTROL TEMPERATURE, AND PLAYS A PART IN FIGHTING INFECTION AND HEALING INJURIES.

WHAT IS BLOOD?

Blood forms about one-twelfth of the body weight of an adult, amounting to about 5 litres (11 pints) in volume. Roughly 50–55 per cent of blood is plasma, the liquid-only portion in which cellular components are distributed. Plasma is 90 per cent water containing dissolved substances such as glucose (blood sugar), hormones, enzymes, and also waste products such as urea and lactic acid. Plasma also contains proteins such as albumins, fibrinogen (important in clotting), and globular proteins or globulins. Alpha and beta globulins help to transport lipids, which are fatty substances such as cholesterol. Gamma globulins are mostly the disease-fighting substances known as antibodies. The remaining 45–50 per cent of blood is made up of three types of specialized cells. Red cells or erythrocytes carry oxygen; various white cells, known as leucocytes, are part of the defence system; and cellular fragments (platelets or thrombocytes) are involved in the process of clotting.

PARTS OF BLOOD
Blood is made up of a liquid portion (plasma), red blood cells, and a small band of platelets and white blood cells.

Plasma (about 50–55%)

White blood cells and platelets (1–2%)

Red blood cells (about 45–50%)

RED BLOOD CELL STRUCTURE
A biconcave disc with no nucleus or discernible inner structure, each red blood cell contains 300 million haemoglobin molecules.

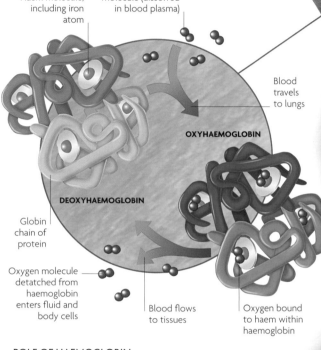

Cytoplasm

Cell membrane

Haem molecule, including iron atom

Free oxygen molecule (dissolved in blood plasma)

Blood travels to lungs

OXYHAEMOGLOBIN

DEOXYHAEMOGLOBIN

Globin chain of protein

Oxygen molecule detached from haemoglobin enters fluid and body cells

Blood flows to tissues

Oxygen bound to haem within haemoglobin

ROLE OF HAEMOGLOBIN
Haemoglobin is composed of haem, an iron-rich pigment, and globin, ribbon-like protein chains. Oxygen in the lungs latches onto haem to make oxyhaemoglobin. In this conjoined form, oxygen travels through the bloodstream to all parts of the body.

BLOOD GROUPS

Every individual belongs to on of four blood groups, which are determined by markers on red blood cells known as antigens (agglutinogens). The antigens may be either A, B, both (AB), or neither (O) and blood groups are named correspondingly. Plasma contains different antibodies (isohaemagglutinins). For example, a person with blood group A has plasma containing B antibodies. If mixed with type B blood (with A antibodies in its plasma), A antibodies clump (or agglutinate) with A antigens. This is the reason why blood types must be matched to transfuse blood safely from donor to recipient.

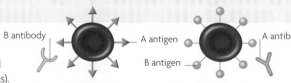

B antibody

A antigen

A antigen

A antibody

B antigen

BLOOD GROUP A
Red blood cells have A antigens with B antibodies contained in the plasma.

BLOOD GROUP B
Red blood cells have B antigens and the plasma contains A antibodies.

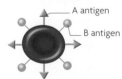

A antigen

B antigen

BLOOD GROUP AB
Red blood cells have A and B antigens, with neither A nor B in plasma.

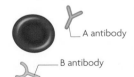

A antibody

B antibody

BLOOD GROUP O
This lacks A and B antigens, but the plasma contains both A and B antibodies.

ARTERIES

Arteries carry blood away from the heart towards organs and tissues. Apart from the pulmonary arteries, all arteries carry oxygenated blood. Their thick walls and muscular and elastic layers can withstand the high pressure that occurs when the heart contracts. An artery narrows when the heart relaxes, helping to push blood onwards. The largest artery is the aorta, with a diameter of 25mm (1in); it conveys blood from the heart at up to 40cm (16in) per second. Most other arteries have a diameter of 4–7mm ($^1/_6$–$^1/_4$ in) and walls 1mm ($^1/_{25}$ in) thick.

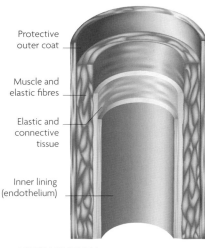

Protective outer coat

Muscle and elastic fibres

Elastic and connective tissue

Inner lining (endothelium)

ARTERY SECTION
Four distinct layers are found in an artery, with the blood-carrying space, called the lumen, in the centre.

VEINS

A vein is more flexible than an artery and its walls are considerably thinner. The blood inside a vein is under relatively low pressure and, as a result, it flows slowly and smoothly. Many larger veins, particularly the long veins in the legs, contain valves that are formed from pouch-like pockets of single-cell lining tissue (endothelium). These prevent blood flowing back down the legs, a job helped by muscles around the veins that contract during movement. The two main veins returning blood from the upper and lower halves of the body are known as the superior and inferior venae cavae.

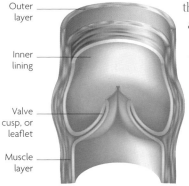

Outer layer

Inner lining

Valve cusp, or leaflet

Muscle layer

VEIN SECTION
The muscle layer of a vein is thin and enclosed by two layers; the innermost layer of some veins has valves at regular intervals.

White blood cell
Also called leucocytes, white blood cells are a vital part of the body's defence system.

Platelet
Tiny, short-lived cell fragment that has an important role in the clotting of blood.

Red blood cell
Red blood cells (erythrocytes) have a lifespan of around 3 months.

Blood vessel wall
The thickness of the wall is dependent on the pressure of the blood flowing through it.

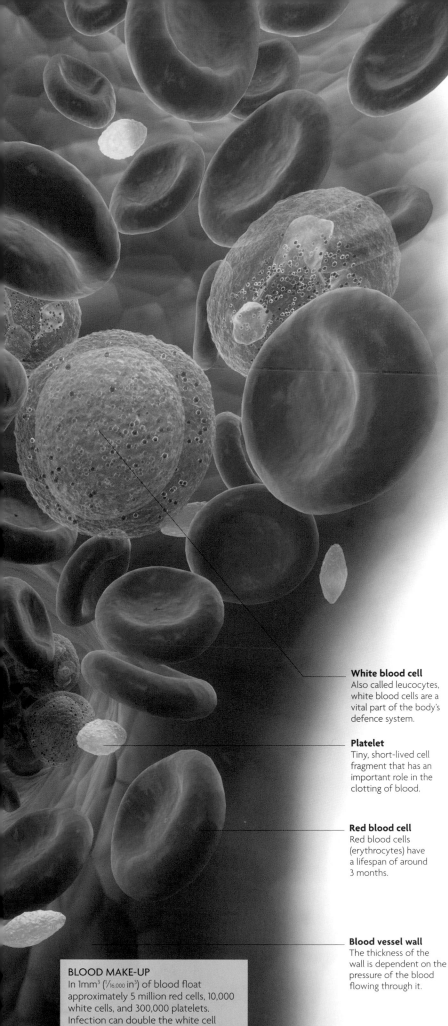

BLOOD MAKE-UP
In 1mm³ ($^1/_{16,000}$ in³) of blood float approximately 5 million red cells, 10,000 white cells, and 300,000 platelets. Infection can double the white cell count within hours. In capillaries, the cells may have to move in single file.

CAPILLARIES

The smallest and most numerous of the blood vessels, capillaries convey blood between arteries and veins. A typical capillary is 1mm ($^1/_{25}$ in) or less in length, about 0.01mm ($^1/_{2,500}$ in) in diameter, and only slightly wider than a red blood cell, which is 0.007mm ($^1/_{3,500}$ in) across. Many capillaries enter tissue to form a capillary bed – the area where oxygen and other nutrients are released, and where waste matter passes into the blood. At any moment, only 5 per cent of the body's blood is travelling in capillaries, with 20 per cent in arteries, and 75 per cent in veins.

CAPILLARY BED
Capillaries connect small arteries (arterioles) to veins (venules)

Arteriole
Carries red blood rich in oxygen and nutrients

Capillary

Venule
Contains dark reddish-blue blood low in oxygen

Capillary wall
Made up of a single layer of curved cells.

Cell nucleus

CAPILLARY SECTION
The thinness of the capillary wall allows smooth, effortless movement of substances between surrounding tissues

HEART STRUCTURE

THE HEART IS A POWERFUL ORGAN ABOUT THE SIZE OF A CLENCHED FIST. LOCATED JUST TO THE LEFT OF CENTRE IN BETWEEN THE LUNGS, IT OPERATES AS TWO COORDINATED PUMPS THAT SEND BLOOD AROUND THE BODY.

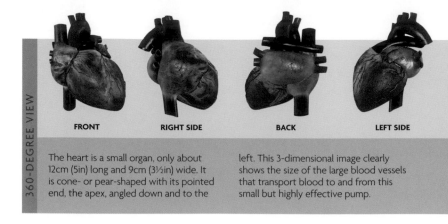

FRONT   **RIGHT SIDE**   **BACK**   **LEFT SIDE**

360-DEGREE VIEW

The heart is a small organ, only about 12cm (5in) long and 9cm (3½in) wide. It is cone- or pear-shaped with its pointed end, the apex, angled down and to the left. This 3-dimensional image clearly shows the size of the large blood vessels that transport blood to and from this small but highly effective pump.

THE HEART'S BLOOD SUPPLY

The muscular wall, or myocardium, of the heart is constantly active and needs a generous supply of oxygen and energy from blood. To provide this, the heart muscle has its own network of blood vessels known as the coronary arteries. These two arteries – the right and the left – branch from the main artery, the aorta, just after it leaves the heart, divide over the heart's surface, and send smaller blood vessels into the heart muscle. The pattern of the coronary veins, which collect wastes from the muscle tissue, is similar. Most of the blood in these veins is collected by the coronary sinus, a large vein at the back of the heart, which empties into the right atrium.

Right coronary artery

Aorta

Left coronary artery

Coronary vein

Main branch of left coronary artery

Coronary sinus

Small connecting blood vessels

CORONARY VESSELS
There are many connecting vessels between the coronary arteries. If an artery becomes blocked, these can provide an alternative route for the blood flow.

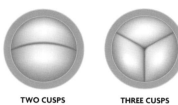

TWO CUSPS   **THREE CUSPS**

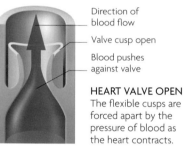

PULMONARY SEMILUNAR VALVE
This valve lies between the right ventricle of the heart and the pulmonary artery. It opens as the right ventricle contracts and forces blood out of the heart towards the lungs.

HEART VALVES

The heart has four valves to control blood flow. Each has the same basic structure, although they differ in certain details. The two atrioventricular valves lie between the atria and ventricles. The mitral valve on the left side has two cusps, while its right counterpart, the tricuspid valve, has three. The two semilunar valves are at the exits from the ventricles: the pulmonary valve between the right ventricle and the pulmonary artery, and the aortic valve between the left ventricle and the aorta.

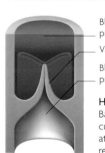

Direction of blood flow

Valve cusp open

Blood pushes against valve

HEART VALVE OPEN
The flexible cusps are forced apart by the pressure of blood as the heart contracts.

Blood at high pressure

Valve cusp shut

Blood at low pressure

HEART VALVE CLOSED
Back pressure causes the cusps to close and seal at their edges, to stop reverse blood flow.

DOUBLE CIRCULATION

The right side of the heart pumps blood to the lungs to be oxygenated and then back to the left side of the heart (pulmonary circulation). The left side of the heart pumps oxygen-rich blood to all the body's tissues and oxygen, depleted blood back to the right side of the heart (systemic circulation).

Vessels in upper body

Aorta
Carries oxygen-rich blood from the heart to the tissues

Pulmonary veins
Take oxygen-rich blood from the lungs to the heart

Network of vessels in right lung
Gas exchange takes place in the lungs' capillarynetwork; oxygen passes into the blood, and carbon dioxide passes out

Network of vessels in left lung

Superior vena cava
Collects oxygen-depleted blood from the upper parts of the body and arms

Pulmonary artery
Carries oxygen-depleted blood from the heart to the lungs

Inferior vena cava
Collects oxygen-depleted blood from the lower parts of the body and legs

Portal vein
Conveys nutrient-rich blood from intestines to liver

Blood vessels in liver   **Vessels in lower body**   **Blood vessels in digestive system**

CARDIAC SKELETON

A set of four fibrous, cuff-like rings known as the cardiac skeleton is built into the upper heart. The rings provide rigid points of attachment for the four heart valves and for the various sections of heart muscle. The wrap-around arrangement of the muscle fibres in ventricle walls, and the timing of their contractions, means the ventricles squirt blood from the apex (lower pointed end) upwards, and out through the pulmonary and aortic valves, rather than squeezing blood down so it pools into the apex region.

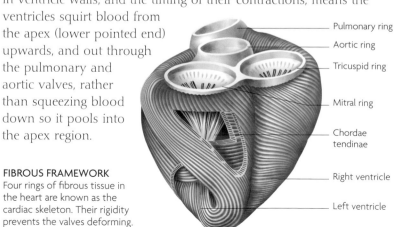

Pulmonary ring

Aortic ring

Tricuspid ring

Mitral ring

Chordae tendinae

Right ventricle

Left ventricle

FIBROUS FRAMEWORK
Four rings of fibrous tissue in the heart are known as the cardiac skeleton. Their rigidity prevents the valves deforming.

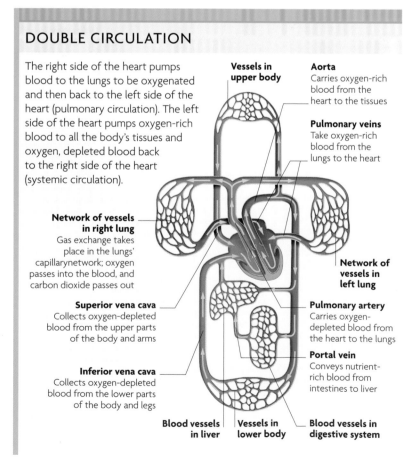

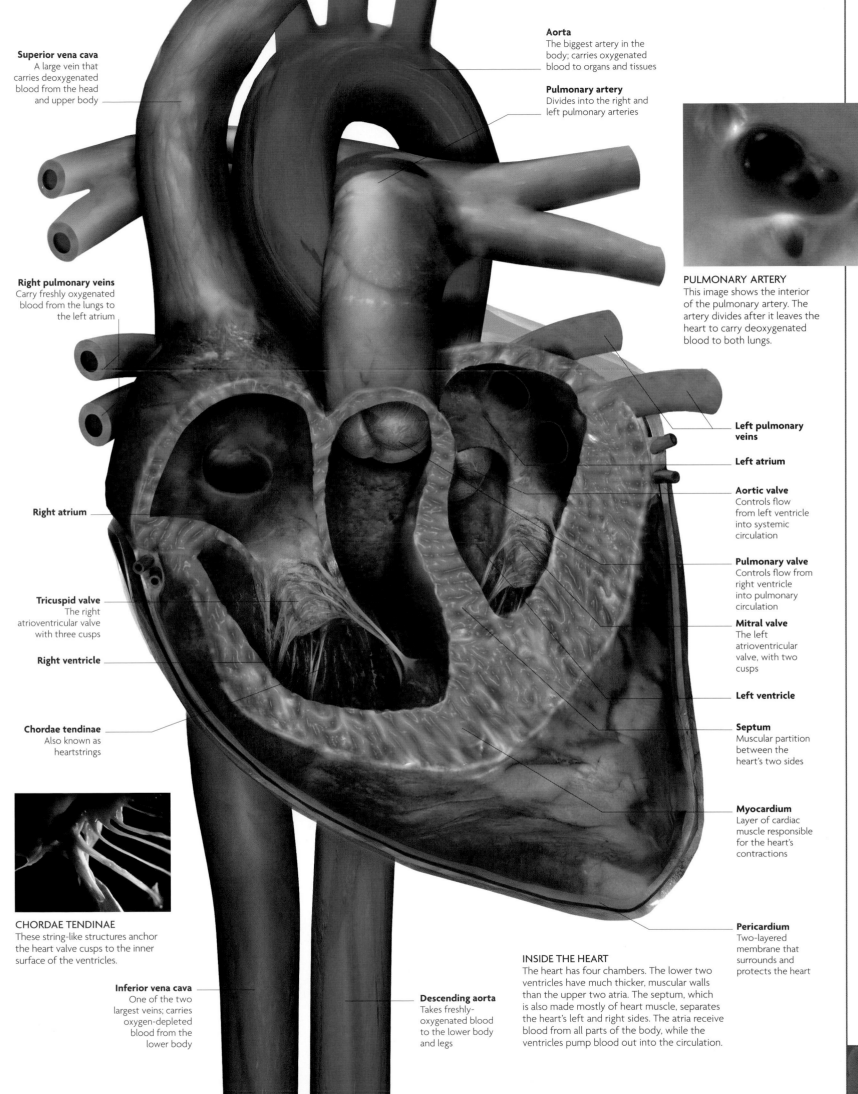

Superior vena cava
A large vein that carries deoxygenated blood from the head and upper body

Aorta
The biggest artery in the body; carries oxygenated blood to organs and tissues

Pulmonary artery
Divides into the right and left pulmonary arteries

Right pulmonary veins
Carry freshly oxygenated blood from the lungs to the left atrium

Right atrium

Tricuspid valve
The right atrioventricular valve with three cusps

Right ventricle

Chordae tendinae
Also known as heartstrings

PULMONARY ARTERY
This image shows the interior of the pulmonary artery. The artery divides after it leaves the heart to carry deoxygenated blood to both lungs.

Left pulmonary veins

Left atrium

Aortic valve
Controls flow from left ventricle into systemic circulation

Pulmonary valve
Controls flow from right ventricle into pulmonary circulation

Mitral valve
The left atrioventricular valve, with two cusps

Left ventricle

Septum
Muscular partition between the heart's two sides

Myocardium
Layer of cardiac muscle responsible for the heart's contractions

CHORDAE TENDINAE
These string-like structures anchor the heart valve cusps to the inner surface of the ventricles.

Inferior vena cava
One of the two largest veins; carries oxygen-depleted blood from the lower body

Descending aorta
Takes freshly-oxygenated blood to the lower body and legs

INSIDE THE HEART
The heart has four chambers. The lower two ventricles have much thicker, muscular walls than the upper two atria. The septum, which is also made mostly of heart muscle, separates the heart's left and right sides. The atria receive blood from all parts of the body, while the ventricles pump blood out into the circulation.

Pericardium
Two-layered membrane that surrounds and protects the heart

HOW THE HEART BEATS

THE HEART IS A DYNAMIC, UNTIRING, PRECISELY ADJUSTABLE DOUBLE-PUMP THAT FORCES BLOOD AROUND THE BODY'S IMMENSE NETWORK OF BLOOD VESSELS – PERHAPS MORE THAN THREE BILLION TIMES DURING A LIFETIME.

The heart's power comes from its two lower chambers (ventricles), which have thick muscular walls that contract to squeeze blood out into the arteries. The upper chambers (atria) have thinner walls and function partly as passive reservoirs for blood oozing in from the main veins. Each heartbeat has two main phases:

in the first phase (diastole), the heart relaxes and refills with blood; during the second stage (systole), it contracts, forcing the blood out. The whole cycle takes, on average, less than a second. During vigorous activity or stress, both the beating rate and the volume of blood pumped out of the heart increase greatly.

CONDUCTING FIBRES
The heart's conducting fibres are specialized long, thin cardiac muscle cells known as conducting myofibres or Purkinje fibres. These cells convey electrical impulses through the heart.

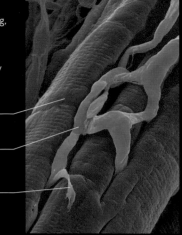

Cardiac muscle fibre

Capillary

Cardiac conducting myofibre

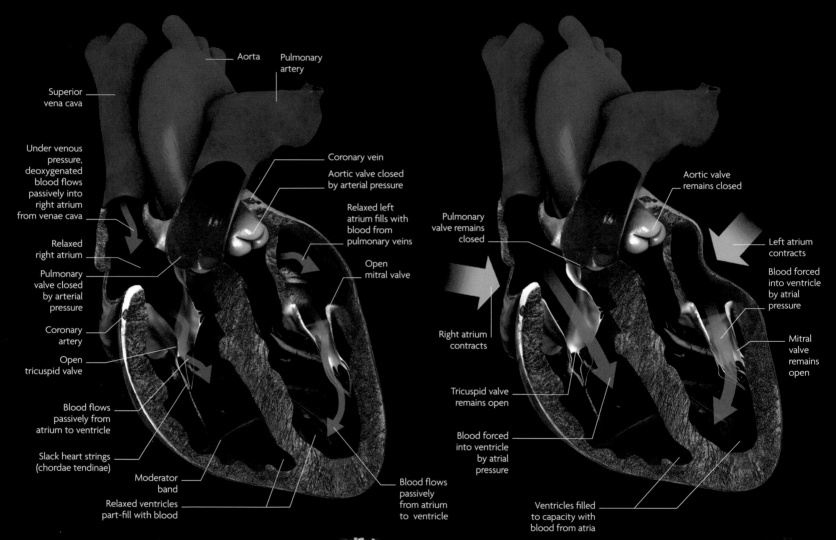

Aorta

Pulmonary artery

Superior vena cava

Under venous pressure, deoxygenated blood flows passively into right atrium from venae cava

Relaxed right atrium

Pulmonary valve closed by arterial pressure

Coronary artery

Open tricuspid valve

Blood flows passively from atrium to ventricle

Slack heart strings (chordae tendinae)

Moderator band

Relaxed ventricles part-fill with blood

Coronary vein

Aortic valve closed by arterial pressure

Relaxed left atrium fills with blood from pulmonary veins

Open mitral valve

Blood flows passively from atrium to ventricle

Aortic valve remains closed

Pulmonary valve remains closed

Right atrium contracts

Tricuspid valve remains open

Blood forced into ventricle by atrial pressure

Ventricles filled to capacity with blood from atria

Left atrium contracts

Blood forced into ventricle by atrial pressure

Mitral valve remains open

1 RELAXATION (LATE DIASTOLE)
During this phase of the heartbeat sequence, the muscular walls of the heart relax. The atrial chambers balloon slightly as they fill with blood coming in under quite low pressure from the main veins. Deoxygenated blood from the body enters the right atrium, while oxygenated blood from the lungs enters the left atrium. Some of the blood in the atria flows down into the ventricles. By the end of this phase, the ventricles are filled to about 80 per cent of capacity.

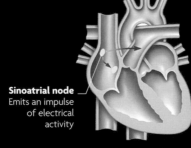

Sinoatrial node
Emits an impulse of electrical activity

PACEMAKER (SINOATRIAL NODE)
The sinoatrial node is inactive during most of diastole. As systole approaches, it begins to send out a wave of electrical impulses which will coordinate the heartbeat.

2 CONTRACTION OF THE ATRIA (ATRIAL SYSTOLE)
The heart's natural pacemaker, known as the sinoatrial node, is located in the upper part of the right atrium. It "fires" electrical impulses, much like those generated by nerves, which set off the contraction phase. Some impulses spread through the atrial walls and stimulate their cardiac muscle to contract. This squeezes blood inside the atria through the atrioventricular (tricuspid and mitral) valves into the ventricles, whose walls remain relaxed.

Electrical impulse
Spreads over surface of both atria, simulating them to contract

Atrioventricular node

ELECTRICAL IMPULSES SPREAD
Impulses travelling through atrial muscles make them contract within 0.1 seconds. Some signals pass faster along conducting fibres to the atrioventricular node.

CONTROL OF THE HEART RATE

Without control, the heart would beat at its natural, intrinsic rate of about 100 times per minute. However, a region known as the cardioregulatory centre in the medulla of the brainstem sends electrical impulses along nerves (especially the cranial vagus nerve) to set an average resting rate of about 70 beats per minute. During activity or stress, the sympathetic cardiac nerve signals, controlled by the hypothalamus, convey overriding signals to speed up the heart rate. The rate is also influenced by hormones such as adrenaline.

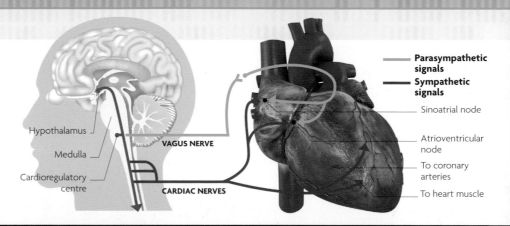

THE BRAIN'S INFLUENCE
The heart controls its own rhythm, but its rate is controlled by the central nervous system.

Parasympathetic signals
Sympathetic signals

Hypothalamus
Medulla
Cardioregulatory centre
VAGUS NERVE
CARDIAC NERVES

Sinoatrial node
Atrioventricular node
To coronary arteries
To heart muscle

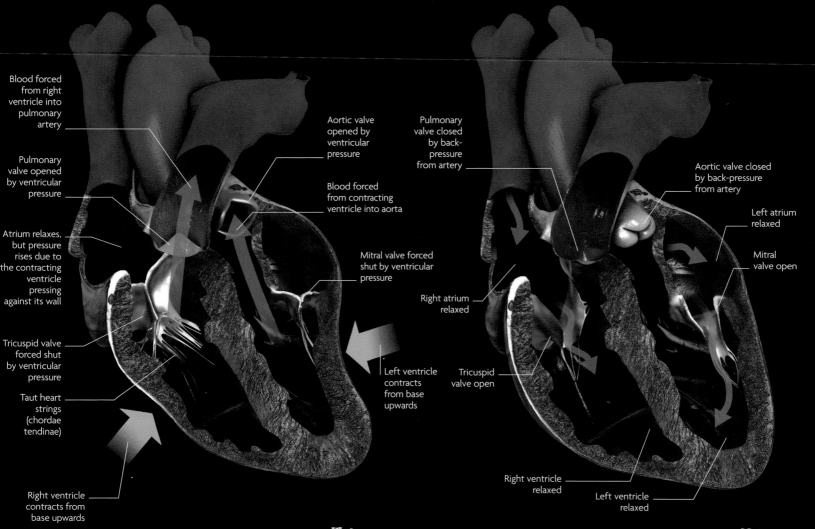

Blood forced from right ventricle into pulmonary artery

Pulmonary valve opened by ventricular pressure

Atrium relaxes, but pressure rises due to the contracting ventricle pressing against its wall

Tricuspid valve forced shut by ventricular pressure

Taut heart strings (chordae tendinae)

Right ventricle contracts from base upwards

Aortic valve opened by ventricular pressure

Blood forced from contracting ventricle into aorta

Mitral valve forced shut by ventricular pressure

Left ventricle contracts from base upwards

Pulmonary valve closed by back-pressure from artery

Aortic valve closed by back-pressure from artery

Left atrium relaxed

Mitral valve open

Right atrium relaxed

Tricuspid valve open

Right ventricle relaxed

Left ventricle relaxed

3 CONTRACTION OF THE VENTRICLES (VENTRICULAR SYSTOLE)

During this most active and powerful stage of the heartbeat, the thick cardiac muscle in the ventricle walls contracts, stimulated by electrical impulses relayed by the atrioventricular node. This causes a rise in ventricular pressure, which opens the aortic and pulmonary valves at the exits of the ventricles. Blood is forced out into the main arteries, making the atrioventricular valves snap shut.

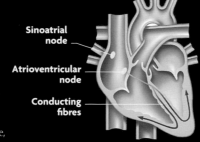

Sinoatrial node
Atrioventricular node
Conducting fibres

ATRIOVENTRICULAR SIGNALS FIRE
The atrioventricular node "fast-tracks" impulses along conducting fibres within the septum (dividing wall) to the lower ventricles and up through ventricle muscle.

4 RELAXATION (EARLY DIASTOLE)

The walls of the ventricles begin to relax, causing ventricular pressure to reduce. The pressure of the recently ejected blood in the main arteries is now high, so both the aortic and pulmonary valves close. This prevents back-flow into the ventricles. As ventricular pressure on the atrioventricular valves relaxes, the valves open. This reduces pressure in the atria, allowing blood to enter once again from the main veins.

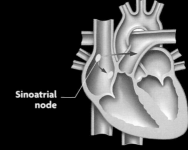

Sinoatrial node

ELECTRICAL IMPULSES FADE
Impulses spread through the ventricular walls back towards the atria within 0.2 seconds of leaving the sinoatrial node, which then fires again to continue the cycle.

SEE DVD-ROM ●

CORONARY HEART DISEASE

THE CARDIAC MUSCLE, OR MYOCARDIUM, OF THE HEART WALL DEPENDS ON A CONSTANT FLOW OF BLOOD SUPPLIED BY THE CORONARY ARTERIES. IF THIS SUPPLY IS RESTRICTED, THEN OXYGEN AND NUTRIENTS CANNOT REACH THE MUSCLE AND THE RESULT COULD BE A FORM OF CORONARY HEART DISEASE (CHD). THE EXTENT OF THE SYMPTOMS OF CHD DEPENDS ON THE LOCATION, SEVERITY, AND SPEED OF ONSET OF THE RESTRICTED BLOOD SUPPLY.

ATHEROSCLEROSIS

ATHEROSCLEROSIS IS CAUSED BY THE NARROWING AND STIFFENING OF THE ARTERIES DUE TO FATTY DEPOSITS, KNOWN AS ATHEROMA, ACCUMULATING IN THEIR WALLS.

The process that leads to atherosclerosis begins with abnormally high levels of excess fats and cholesterol in the blood. These substances infiltrate the lining of arteries at sites of microscopic damage, forming deposits known as atheroma. This can happen in any of the body's arteries, including those supplying the brain with blood, when the result may be a stroke. The atheromatous deposits gradually form raised patches known as plaques. These consist of fatty cores within the arterial wall, covered by fibrous caps. The plaques narrow the space, or lumen, within the artery and this restricts the overall flow of blood to tissues beyond the site. It also causes turbulence that disrupts the smooth flow of blood and the eddies over the plaque surface mean that blood is more likely to clot. The major risk factors for atherosclerosis include smoking, a diet high in saturated fats, lack of exercise, and excess weight.

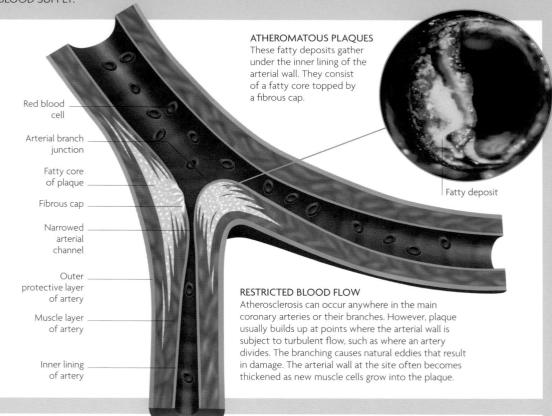

Red blood cell

Arterial branch junction

Fatty core of plaque

Fibrous cap

Narrowed arterial channel

Outer protective layer of artery

Muscle layer of artery

Inner lining of artery

ATHEROMATOUS PLAQUES
These fatty deposits gather under the inner lining of the arterial wall. They consist of a fatty core topped by a fibrous cap.

Fatty deposit

RESTRICTED BLOOD FLOW
Atherosclerosis can occur anywhere in the main coronary arteries or their branches. However, plaque usually builds up at points where the arterial wall is subject to turbulent flow, such as where an artery divides. The branching causes natural eddies that result in damage. The arterial wall at the site often becomes thickened as new muscle cells grow into the plaque.

ANGINA

ANGINA, CHEST PAINS THAT COME ON WITH EXERTION AND ARE RELIEVED BY REST, IS A SIGN THAT THE HEART MUSCLE IS NOT RECEIVING AN ADEQUATE SUPPLY OF BLOOD.

Angina is caused by a temporarily inadequate supply of blood to the heart muscle, usually because of arterial narrowing due to atherosclerosis. The pain most often occurs when the heart's workload is increased, for example with exercise, and fades with rest. Other triggers for angina are stress, cold weather, or a large meal. An angina attack typically begins with a heavy, constricting pain behind the breastbone. This can spread into the throat and jaw, and down into the arms, especially the left one. The pain usually subsides within 10–15 minutes. People with angina often take medication that relieves the pain by causing the coronary arteries to widen (dilate).

DAMAGED HEART MUSCLE
During angina, areas of heart muscle downstream from a narrowed artery suffer from lack of oxygen. After the attack, the muscle recovers.

WHY ANGINA OCCURS
Atherosclerosis of a coronary artery causes narrowing in the vessel and a reduction in blood flow. During exertion the heart beats faster and the muscle's demand for oxygen increases. However, extra blood cannot pass through the narrowed artery and the muscle "cramps".

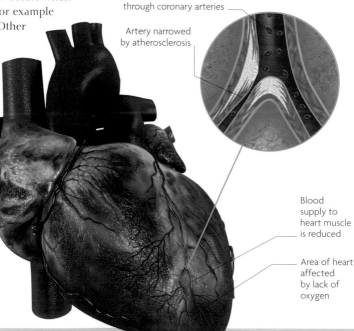

Blood enters heart through coronary arteries

Artery narrowed by atherosclerosis

Blood supply to heart muscle is reduced

Area of heart affected by lack of oxygen

ANGIOGRAPHY

The diagnostic procedure known as angiography shows the outline of blood vessels on a specialized X-ray image (called an angiogram). A fine catheter (hollow tube) is passed into an artery, usually in the leg, and then threaded up towards the heart via the aorta. A contrast medium, or radio-opaque dye, is injected into the catheter and X-ray images are viewed on a monitor. These show the dye flowing through the coronary artery network and reveal any narrowing or blockage.

X-RAY IMAGE
The pattern of coronary arteries is similar in most hearts. This coronary angiogram reveals a narrowing that restricts blood flow to a region of cardiac muscle.

Narrowed coronary artery

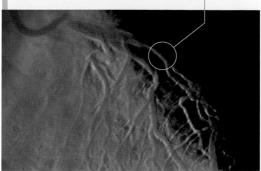

HEART ATTACK

A HEART ATTACK OCCURS WHEN AN AREA OF CARDIAC MUSCLE IS DEPRIVED OF BLOOD, AND THEREFORE OXYGEN, DUE TO A BLOCKAGE IN AN ARTERY.

A heart attack (myocardial infarction) is the result of coronary heart disease due to atherosclerosis, and the subsequent formation of a blood clot, or thrombus. Once formed, the clot can completely block blood flow to an area of heart muscle, starving it of blood and eventually causing tissue death. If possible, the blood flow must be restored to the damaged cells as quickly as possible. A heart attack usually occurs suddenly, with little or no warning. The chest pain may resemble that of angina, but it is more severe, is not necessarily brought on by exertion, and persists despite resting. A heart attack can also cause sweating, shortness of breath, nausea, and loss of consciousness.

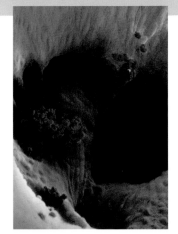

CLOTTED ARTERY
The healthy lining of a blood vessel allows blood to slip over it smoothly. Blood tends to clot where this smooth flow is disturbed by projections from the vessel wall, seen, for example, on the left of this image.

THROMBOLYTICS

The key to heart attack treatment is speed. The sooner the arterial blockage can be removed, then the sooner blood flow is restored to the damaged area and it may be able to recover. Thrombolytic drugs are often introduced directly into the blood stream after a heart attack. These help to dissolve the clot that is blocking the coronary artery by increasing levels of a substance called plasminogen in the blood. Plasminogen breaks down the strands of fibrin that bind the clot together and the clot dissolves. Antiplatelet drugs are routinely given for some time after discharge from hospital, as these thin the blood and prevent further clot formation.

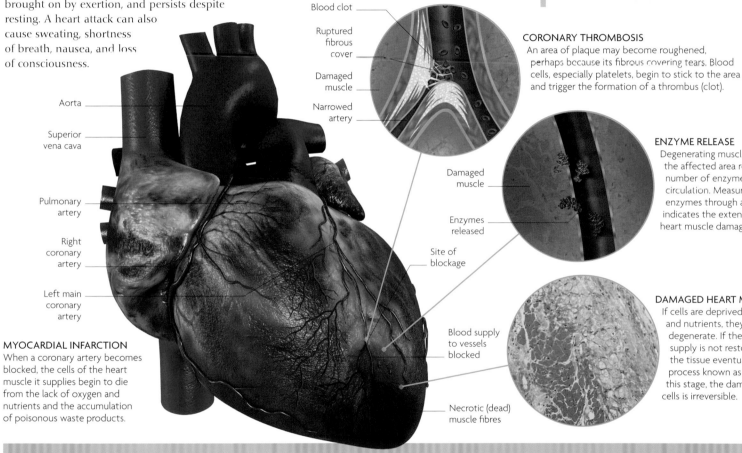

Aorta

Superior vena cava

Pulmonary artery

Right coronary artery

Left main coronary artery

MYOCARDIAL INFARCTION
When a coronary artery becomes blocked, the cells of the heart muscle it supplies begin to die from the lack of oxygen and nutrients and the accumulation of poisonous waste products.

Blood clot

Ruptured fibrous cover

Damaged muscle

Narrowed artery

CORONARY THROMBOSIS
An area of plaque may become roughened, perhaps because its fibrous covering tears. Blood cells, especially platelets, begin to stick to the area and trigger the formation of a thrombus (clot).

Damaged muscle

Enzymes released

ENZYME RELEASE
Degenerating muscle fibres in the affected area release a number of enzymes into the circulation. Measuring these enzymes through a blood test indicates the extent of the heart muscle damage.

Site of blockage

Blood supply to vessels blocked

Necrotic (dead) muscle fibres

DAMAGED HEART MUSCLE
If cells are deprived of oxygen and nutrients, they quickly degenerate. If the blood supply is not restored quickly, the tissue eventually dies, a process known as necrosis. At this stage, the damage to the cells is irreversible.

ANGIOPLASTY

This procedure is used to widen a section of coronary artery that has been narrowed or blocked by atheroma. It is often carried out to treat severe angina or after a heart attack. Angioplasty may be part of the same procedure as angiography, which visualizes the coronary arteries on an X-ray (see opposite page). Under local anaesthetic, a fine catheter (hollow tube) is inserted into the femoral artery in the groin (or sometimes the arm), and passed up the aorta and into the coronary artery network. When the affected site is reached, a tiny balloon at the end of the catheter is inflated to widen the narrowed area. An expandable stainless steel mesh stent is often left permanently in place after withdrawal of the balloon catheter. This prevents the artery from narrowing again.

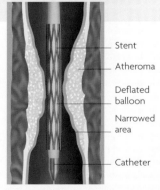

Stent

Atheroma

Deflated balloon

Narrowed area

Catheter

1 CATHETER INSERTED
The catheter is equipped with a small inflatable balloon near its end and, in this case, a metal mesh self-expanding tube called a stent.

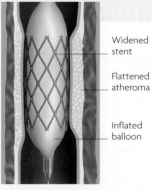

Widened stent

Flattened atheroma

Inflated balloon

2 BALLOON INFLATED
When the balloon is positioned within the narrowed area, it is inflated with gas or liquid to stretch the artery and widen the stent.

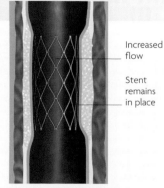

Increased flow

Stent remains in place

3 CATHETER REMOVED
The balloon is deflated and withdrawn, leaving the stent in place in its expanded form. In a few weeks, a thin layer of cells grows over the stent.

HEART MUSCLE DISORDERS

THE HEART IS COMPOSED MOSTLY OF SPECIALIZED MUSCLE, KNOWN AS THE CARDIAC MUSCLE, OR MYOCARDIUM. SOME HEART DISORDERS ARE CAUSED BY PROBLEMS WITH THIS MUSCLE OR WITH THE SAC-LIKE PERICARDIUM SURROUNDING THE HEART. LONG-STANDING OR SEVERE HEART MUSCLE PROBLEMS CAN LEAD TO HEART FAILURE, WHEN THE HEART'S PUMPING POWER IS REDUCED.

HEART MUSCLE DISEASE

INFLAMMATION OF THE HEART MUSCLE IS KNOWN AS MYOCARDITIS; NON-INFLAMMATORY HEART MUSCLE DISEASE IS CALLED CARDIOMYOPATHY.

Many cases of myocarditis are due to infection, often with a virus such as coxsackie. The problem may go unnoticed but, if severe, can lead to chest pain and long-term heart failure. Other causes of myocarditis include rheumatic fever, exposure to radiation or certain drugs or chemicals, or an autoimmune condition such as systemic lupus erythematosus (see p.168). Cardiomyopathy is non-inflammatory heart muscle disease in which the muscle becomes weakened, damaged, and stretched. This condition takes several forms with various causes, as illustrated below.

NORMAL HEART
The muscular walls of a normal heart, especially the ventricles, are substantial. They are also flexible and bend as they contract and squeeze out blood. The pumping rate and volume adjust to cope with the body's demands for oxygenated blood.

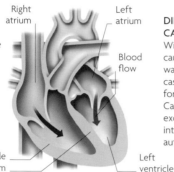

Right atrium / Left atrium / Blood flow / Right ventricle / Septum / Left ventricle

DILATED CARDIOMYOPATHY
Widening (dilation) causes the ventricle walls to thin. In some cases, blood clots form on the linings. Causes include excessive alcohol intake, viral illness, or an autoimmune disorder.

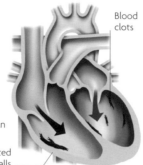

Blood clots / Dilated ventricle walls

HYPERTROPHIC CARDIOMYOPATHY
This condition causes the heart muscle to thicken, especially in the left ventricle and septum, so the heart cannot fill with blood properly. It is usually an inherited problem and a cause of sudden death in apparently healthy young people.

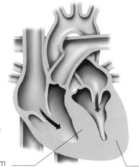

Thickened septum / Thickened wall of left ventricle

RESTRICTIVE CARDIOMYOPATHY
The walls of the ventricles become rigid, which restricts their ability to stretch when filled with blood, and also to flex on contraction to expel it. This problem is caused by scar tissue or by deposits of iron or abnormal protein.

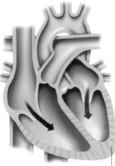

Rigid ventricular walls

PERICARDITIS

INFLAMMATION OF THE PERICARDIUM – THE TWO-LAYERED MEMBRANOUS SAC THAT SURROUNDS THE HEART – IS OFTEN DUE TO A VIRAL INFECTION OR A HEART ATTACK.

The most common cause of pericarditis is a viral infection that inflames the pericardium. Other causes include bacterial pneumonia, tuberculosis, the spread of a cancerous tumour to the pericardium, an autoimmune disorder such as rheumatoid arthritis, kidney failure, a heart attack, or a penetrating wound to the area. Any inflamed pericardium cannot lubricate the heart's beating motions normally, so it rubs and scrapes. Symptoms include pain in the centre of the chest, which is relieved by leaning forward but worsened by a deep breath, breathlessness, or fever.

PERICARDIAL EFFUSION
The outer (fibrous) layer of the pericardium is tough and elastic. The inner (serous) membrane forms a double layer around the heart, separated by a thin film of lubricating fluid. Pericardial effusion is an excess of fluid, caused by inflammation of the serous membrane, and can interfere with the heart's pumping.

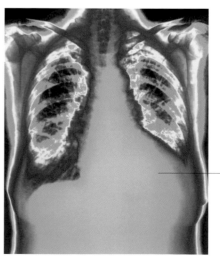

Outer fibrous layer of pericardium / Pericardial fluid / Inner serous layer of pericardium / Pericardial effusion / Heart muscle

HEART FAILURE

THE HEART'S INABILITY TO PUMP BLOOD EFFECTIVELY TO THE LUNGS AND BODY TISSUES CAN BE ACUTE (COMING ON SUDDENLY) OR CHRONIC (DEVELOPING OVER TIME).

Acute heart failure develops as a result of trauma to the heart, such as a heart attack or valve damage. Heart failure of the left side of the heart causes rapid accumulation of fluid in the lungs. This results in wheezing and breathlessness, sweaty pale skin, and a cough that brings up blood-stained sputum. Acute heart failure usually occurs in both sides of the heart.

Chronic heart failure is a long-term problem with many causes. These include coronary heart disease, persistent high blood pressure, cardiomyopathy, a heart valve or rhythm disorder, or chronic obstructive pulmonary disease (see pp.142–143). In left-sided chronic heart failure, the heart's left ventricle fails to pump blood out to the body as fast as it enters from the lungs. As a result, blood backs up in the pulmonary veins and lungs, causing congestion. The pressure in the lungs causes fluid to collect there (a condition known as pulmonary oedema) and oxygen is absorbed less efficiently, producing symptoms such as breathlessness, coughing, and fatigue. In right-sided chronic heart failure, the right ventricle cannot pump blood out to the lungs as fast as it comes in from body tissues. Blood backs up in the main veins, again causing congestion. Increased venous pressure forces fluid out of the capillaries into the tissues with noticeable swelling (oedema) in the ankles and lower back. Other symptoms include breathlessness, fatigue, and nausea.

Indentation

FLUID RETENTION
Fluid accumulation due to chronic heart failure makes the tissues swollen and soggy. An indentation caused by pressing tends to stay after the pressure is removed.

Enlarged heart due to heart failure

ENLARGED HEART
In heart failure, the heart becomes grossly enlarged over time as it struggles to pump blood through the body's circulation.

STRUCTURAL DISORDERS

STRUCTURAL HEART DISORDERS CAN AFFECT PEOPLE OF ANY AGE; CONGENITAL HEART DEFECTS ARE PRESENT AT BIRTH, WHILE VALVE DISORDERS GENERALLY ARISE LATER IN LIFE. MEDICAL ADVANCES MEAN THAT SOME DEFECTS IN THE HEART ARE EFFECTIVELY TREATED WITH SURGICAL TECHNIQUES. EQUALLY, DISEASED VALVES CAN BE SURGICALLY WIDENED OR REPLACED.

CONGENITAL HEART DEFECTS

HEART DEFECTS PRESENT FROM BIRTH (CONGENITAL) MAY BE DUE TO A FAULT IN DEVELOPMENT DURING EARLY EMBRYO DEVELOPMENT.

Some types of congenital heart defect (CHD) run in families, suggesting there is a genetic influence, although usually there is no obvious cause. However, in some cases there is a link with the mother catching an infection such as rubella during pregnancy or being exposed to certain drugs including alcohol. Symptoms of CHD include breathlessness (which can affect feeding) and slow weight gain. Ultrasound scans can help to reveal some types of CHD so that medical staff can plan ahead for treatment.

HEART DEVELOPMENT

In the embryo, the heart develops as a section of blood vessel that thickens its walls and begins to twist and loop, creating atrial and ventricular chambers. Complex connections of arteries and veins begin to take shape. Many congenital heart defects arise from a problem during this initial stage of development. Here, deoxygenated blood is blue; red is oxygenated blood.

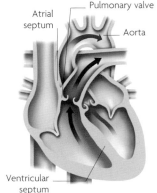

Atrial septum · Pulmonary valve · Aorta · Ventricular septum

COARCTATION OF AORTA

A short section of the aorta is narrowed, usually at a point where the main arteries branch off for the head, brain, arms, and upper body. This results in restricted blood flow to the lower body and legs. The heart works harder to compensate and so blood pressure in the upper body is elevated. A sufferer is usually pale and finds it difficult to breathe or eat. Urgent corrective surgery may be needed.

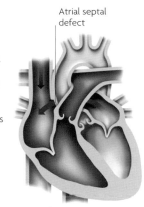

Aortic narrowing · Reduced blood flow

VENTRICULAR SEPTAL DEFECT

This is a hole in the wall between the two ventricles (ventricular septum), causing the blood to mix (purple colour). Oxygenated blood from the left ventricle flows through the hole so that too much blood is pumped by the right ventricle into the lungs. A small hole may close as the child grows, but a larger one will need surgical repair.

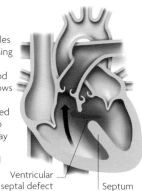

Ventricular septal defect · Septum

ATRIAL SEPTAL DEFECT

This is an abnormal opening in the wall (atrial septum) between the two upper chambers (atria). As a result, blood shunts from the high-pressure left side of the heart into the right side (purple area). The blood flow to the lungs increases in consequence and less is pumped around the body. Both atrial and ventricular septal defects are common in children with Down Syndrome.

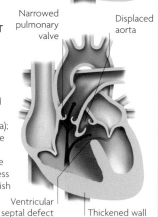

Atrial septal defect

TETRALOGY OF FALLOT

A combination of four structural defects: a ventricular septal defect; an aorta that is displaced towards the right side so that deoxygenated blood can flow into it from the right ventricle (purple area); narrowed pulmonary valve (pulmonary stenosis); and a thickened right ventricle wall. A sufferer is breathless and has a distinctive blueish skin colour (cyanosis).

Narrowed pulmonary valve · Displaced aorta · Ventricular septal defect · Thickened wall

VALVE DISORDERS

THERE ARE SEVERAL CONDITIONS THAT CAN AFFECT THE EFFICIENT FUNCTIONING OF ANY OF THE HEART'S FOUR VALVES.

There are two main types of valve disorder. In stenosis, the valve outlet is too narrow and so restricts blood flow. It may be congenital or due to an infection such as rheumatic fever. Stenosis is also part of the ageing process. In incompetence, the valve does not close fully, allowing backflow of blood. This problem can occur as a result of a heart attack or an infection of the valve.

MITRAL VALVE

This image of a healthy human heart valve shows the heart strings (chordae tendinae) and cusps. The mitral valve lies between the left atrium and the left ventricle.

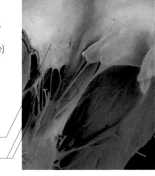

Cusp · Chordae tendinae

NORMAL VALVE OPEN

As a heart chamber contracts, the high pressure pushes against the cusps of the valve, forcing it open and allowing blood to flow past.

Normal blood flow · Valve open · Cusp

NORMAL VALVE CLOSED

The pressure on the other side of the valve increases and the valve cusps snap shut so that blood cannot flow backward.

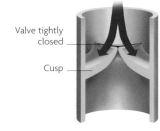

Valve tightly closed · Cusp

STENOSIS

The valve tissue is stiffened and cannot open fully. Blood passing through it is restricted so the heart beats harder to maintain flow.

Restricted blood flow · Valve partially open · Abnormal cusp

INCOMPETENCE

The valve cusps do not close properly and allow blood to leak backward. As a result, the heart has to work harder to circulate blood.

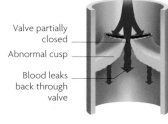

Valve partially closed · Abnormal cusp · Blood leaks back through valve

HEART MURMURS

UNUSUAL HEART SOUNDS PRODUCED BY TURBULENT BLOOD FLOW MAY BE DUE TO A HEART VALVE DEFECT.

The "lub–dub" sound of the heartbeat is made by healthy valves snapping shut. Some types of unusual sounds are known as "murmurs" and may indicate an abnormality. However, many murmurs, particularly in children, do not indicate valve abnormalities.

ABNORMAL FLOW

Murmurs can be produced by turbulent flow as blood rushes around the cusps of a stenosed valve or leaks back through an incompetent valve and collides with oncoming blood.

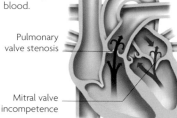

Pulmonary valve stenosis · Mitral valve incompetence

CIRCULATORY AND HEART-RATE DISORDERS

A CONSTANT AND ADEQUATE BLOOD SUPPLY IS ESSENTIAL FOR HEALTHY TISSUES. SHOULD A BLOCKAGE OCCUR IN A BLOOD VESSEL, THE TISSUES BEYOND IT MAY BE STARVED OF OXYGEN, CAUSING TISSUE DAMAGE OR, IN MORE SEVERE CASES, TISSUE DEATH. THE HEART MAY ALSO BE AFFECTED IF THE ELECTRICAL SYSTEM, WHICH MAINTAINS HEART RATE AND RHYTHM, IS DISTURBED.

EMBOLISM

AN EMBOLUS – A FRAGMENT OF MATERIAL THAT BREAKS AWAY FROM ITS ORIGINAL SITE – CAN CAUSE THE PARTIAL OR TOTAL BLOCKAGE OF A BLOOD VESSEL.

Most emboli are fragments of a blood clot (thrombus), or even a whole clot, that has detached from its original site and travelled in the bloodstream to lodge in a blood vessel. An embolus may also be made of fatty material from an atheromatous plaque (see p.122) in an arterial wall, crystals of cholesterol, fatty bone marrow that has entered the circulation following a bone fracture, or an air bubble or amniotic fluid. In a pulmonary embolism, a clot originating elsewhere in the body travels to the lungs in veins. Clots that form in the heart or arteries can block circulation anywhere in the body. An embolus is most likely to block a blood vessel where it narrows or branches, depriving tissues beyond of vital oxygen. Symptoms depend on the site affected; for example an embolus blocking an artery supplying the brain may lead to a stroke. If the embolus is a fragment of a clot, it can be treated with thrombolytic, or "clot-busting", drugs.

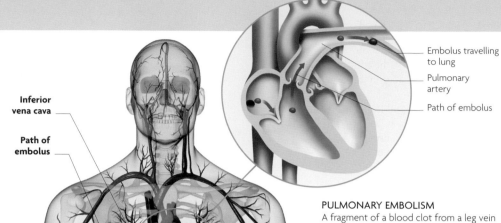

Inferior vena cava

Path of embolus

Embolus travelling to lung

Pulmonary artery

Path of embolus

PULMONARY EMBOLISM
A fragment of a blood clot from a leg vein may travel through the venous system to the heart's right side, then out along the pulmonary arteries to a lung. It may lodge here, depriving lung tissue of vital oxygen and reducing oxygen uptake by the pulmonary circulation.

Thrombotic embolus
A fragment (embolus) composed of blood clot (thrombotic) material; may arise anywhere in body, but veins of the legs and pelvis are common sites

THROMBOSIS

THE PARTIAL OR TOTAL BLOCKAGE OF AN ARTERY, VEIN, OR EVEN THE HEART CAN OCCUR WHEN A BLOOD CLOT (THROMBUS) FORMS DUE TO A CIRCULATORY PROBLEM.

Thrombosis is most likely to occur where the normal smooth flow of blood is disrupted and either slows down or becomes turbulent. This disruption may be caused by plaques of fatty atheromatous tissue in the walls of an artery or by inflammation of the blood vessel. The clot eventually narrows or blocks the passage for blood so that tissues downstream are deprived of oxygen and nutrients. The effects depend on the site of the thrombosis.

THROMBUS FORMATION
Thrombosis can occur in arteries and veins, but commonly happens at a site of atherosclerosis in an artery wall, which disrupts normal blood flow.

Fibrin strands

Thrombus blocking artery; thrombi can also form in veins

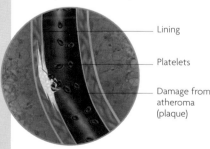

Lining

Platelets

Damage from atheroma (plaque)

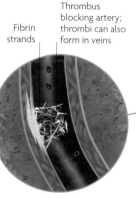

1 INTERNAL DAMAGE
When an artery lining is damaged by plaque, platelets in the area clump together, stick to the wall and release chemicals that begin the clotting or coagulating process.

2 CLOT FORMATION
The chemicals help convert fibrinogen into insoluble fibrin strands. These trap platelets and other blood cells, and clot formation escalates.

DEEP VEIN THROMBOSIS

Blood that flows slowly is more likely to thrombose, or clot. This can happen in the deep veins of the legs and lower body, which rely to some extent on contracting muscles to assist blood flow. Deep vein thrombosis (DVT) tends to occur during periods of immobility, particularly during long journeys, when muscles are relaxed and blood pools in the veins. To help prevent clots forming, keep moving and drink non-alcoholic beverages. Symptoms of DVT include tenderness, pain, and swelling in the leg, and visibly engorged veins. Treatment with anticoagulant drugs reduces the risk that part of the clot will break off and travel to the lung (see above).

X-RAY DIAGNOSIS
A deep-vein thrombosis in the calf is revealed here by injecting a radio-opaque dye into the circulation and taking an X-ray.

Visible clot

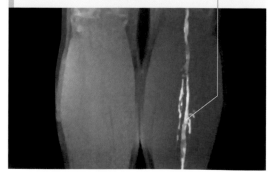

ANEURYSM

ABNORMAL SWELLING OF A WEAKENED ARTERIAL WALL MAKE THE WALL BULGE OUT LIKE A BALLOON.

This defect in an arterial wall may be due to disease or injury, or it can be congenital. Although aneurysms may occur in arteries anywhere in the body, they most often affect the main artery from the heart, the aorta. Most aortic aneurysms occur in the abdominal section below the kidneys, rather than in the chest, and this type of aneurysm tends to run in families. Small aortic aneurysms are usually symptomless, although large ones may cause localized pain. Aneurysms may be treated by surgery, the aim of which is to repair the artery before the aneurysm dissects, or ruptures (see right). Berry aneurysms occur in the small arteries at the base of the brain. There may be one or several of them, and they are thought to be present from birth. If a berry aneurysm ruptures, it causes a subarachnoid haemorrhage (see p.94) and results in an intensely painful headache.

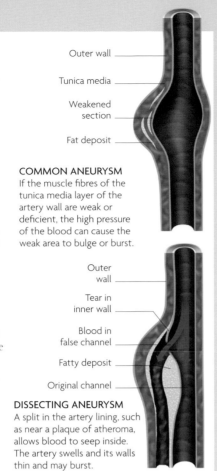

COMMON ANEURYSM
If the muscle fibres of the tunica media layer of the artery wall are weak or deficient, the high pressure of the blood can cause the weak area to bulge or burst.

Outer wall
Tunica media
Weakened section
Fat deposit

Outer wall
Tear in inner wall
Blood in false channel
Fatty deposit
Original channel

DISSECTING ANEURYSM
A split in the artery lining, such as near a plaque of atheroma, allows blood to seep inside. The artery swells and its walls thin and may burst.

HYPERTENSION

PERSISTENT, HIGHER-THAN-NORMAL, BLOOD PRESSURE CAN DAMAGE INTERNAL ORGANS IF UNTREATED.

Normally, blood is under pressure as the heart forces it around the circulation. In hypertension, this pressure is above normal limits. There are no symptoms at first, but despite this, over time it increases the risk of many serious disorders, such as stroke, heart disease, and kidney failure. There is no obvious cause for hypertension; however, lifestyle and genetic factors may contribute as do being overweight, drinking excessive amounts of alcohol, smoking, and having a high-salt diet. Hypertension is most common in middle-aged and elderly people. A stressful lifestyle may aggravate the condition. Hypertension cannot be cured, but it can be controlled. A change of diet and lifestyle may be all that is necessary, but more severe cases may be treated with antihypertensive drugs.

BLOOD PRESSURE GRAPH
Normal blood pressure varies according to activity levels. This graph shows that during sleep, both the systolic and diastolic pressures (see pp.120–121) are much lower.

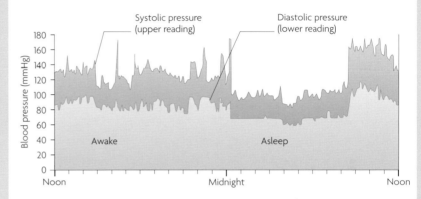

Systolic pressure (upper reading)
Diastolic pressure (lower reading)
Blood pressure (mmHg)
180 160 140 120 100 80 60 40 20 0
Awake *Asleep*
Noon *Midnight* *Noon*

ARRHYTHMIA

AN ABNORMAL HEART RATE OR RHYTHM IS CAUSED BY A DISTURBANCE IN THE ELECTRICAL SYSTEM THAT CONTROLS THE WAY HEART MUSCLE CONTRACTS.

An arrhythmia is a heart rate that is unusually slow or fast, or erratic. A normal heartbeat is initiated by specialized cells in the natural "pacemaker", the sinoatrial (SA) node, at the top of the right atrium. They send electrical signals resembling nerve impulses out through the atrial muscle tissue, stimulating it to contract. These signals are relayed by the atrioventricular (AV) node along nerve-like fibres through the septum (central dividing wall) and into the thick muscle tissue of the ventricle walls. A fault in the system can lead to the arrhythmias described here.

SINUS TACHYCARDIA
In sinus tachycardia there is a regular but rapid heart rate, usually more than 100 beats per minute. This can occur during fever, exercise, great stress, or as a response to stimulants, such as caffeine.

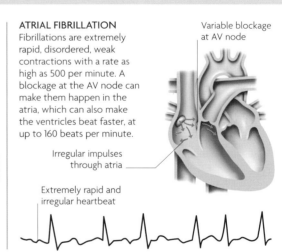

SA node *AV node*
Very fast heartbeat
Atrium
Ventricle

ATRIAL FIBRILLATION
Fibrillations are extremely rapid, disordered, weak contractions with a rate as high as 500 per minute. A blockage at the AV node can make them happen in the atria, which can also make the ventricles beat faster, at up to 160 beats per minute.

Variable blockage at AV node
Irregular impulses through atria
Extremely rapid and irregular heartbeat

TREATMENTS

Often, heart arrhythmias can be treated with drugs. Another solution is to implant an artificial pacemaker into the chest wall. The pacemaker is connected to the heart by wires and takes over the role of supplying electrical signals to the heart muscle. In some cases, cardioversion (sometimes known as defibrillation) is also possible using an implant. A cardiac defibrillator (ICD), about the size of a pager, can be implanted just below the collarbone. It monitors heart rate and can detect life threatening arrhythmias. The ICD reacts by shocking the heart with a jolt of electricity, which restores its normal rhythm.

BUNDLE-BRANCH BLOCK
Damage to a branch of the nerve-like fibre bundles that carry the electrical signals impedes their flow. Some signals may "leak" across from the other, healthy side. If both right and left bundles are affected, the heart rate slows to a very low rate.

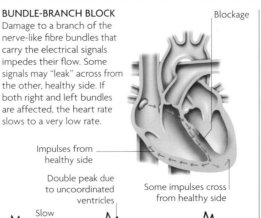

Blockage
Impulses from healthy side
Double peak due to uncoordinated ventricles
Some impulses cross from healthy side
Slow heartbeat

VENTRICULAR TACHYCARDIA
Very fast contractions of the ventricles may be caused by damaged heart muscle, for example due to heart disease or a heart attack. Electrical impulses have difficulty passing through the scarred heart muscle and so recirculate.

Circular impulses
Slowed conduction through damaged area
Damaged heart muscle
Rapid heartbeat

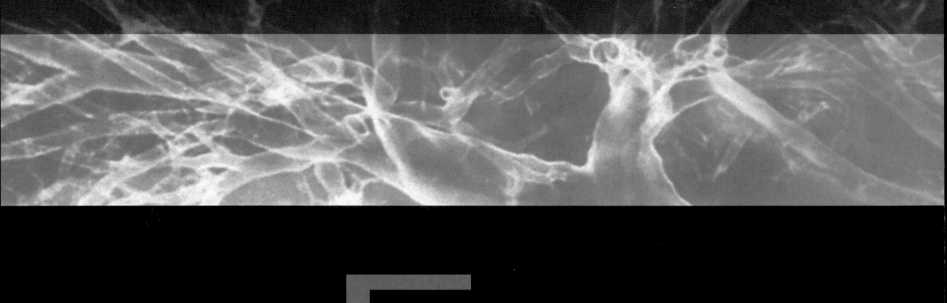

OXYGEN IS VITAL FOR LIFE. THE RESPIRATORY SYSTEM
TRANSFERS OXYGEN FROM AIR TO BLOOD, SO THE
CARDIOVASCULAR SYSTEM CAN DISTRIBUTE IT, WHILE THE
MUSCULAR AND SKELETAL SYSTEMS DRIVE THE MOVEMENTS
OF BREATHING. THE AIR IS OFTEN CONTAMINATED WITH
DUST PARTICLES, HARMFUL MICROBES, ALLERGENS, AND
HAZARDOUS, IRRITANT, AND CANCER-CAUSING CHEMICALS;

RESPIRATORY SYSTEM

RESPIRATORY ANATOMY

THE RESPIRATORY SYSTEM, IN CLOSE CONJUNCTION WITH THE CIRCULATORY SYSTEM, IS RESPONSIBLE FOR SUPPLYING ALL BODY CELLS WITH ESSENTIAL OXYGEN AND REMOVING POTENTIALLY HARMFUL CARBON DIOXIDE FROM THE BODY. THE MOUTH AND NOSE CHANNEL AIR FROM OUTSIDE THE BODY THROUGH A SYSTEM OF TUBES OF DIMINISHING SIZE THAT EVENTUALLY REACH THE TWO LUNGS SITUATED ON EITHER SIDE OF THE HEART WITHIN THE CHEST CAVITY.

Air enters the body mainly through the nostrils (but sometimes through the mouth). The nostrils lead into the nasal cavity, which opens up within the skull and joins with the pharynx (part of the throat) towards the rear. The pharynx is a short funnel-shaped tube that extends partway down the neck. The first part of the pharynx conveys only air, but lower down, food and liquids also travel through. The larynx, home to the vocal cords, joins the pharynx to the windpipe (trachea). A loose flap of cartilage, the epiglottis, lies just above the larynx and blocks it off during swallowing to prevent food and liquids entering the trachea. The trachea splits into two airways called primary bronchi, one of which enters the right lung and the other the left lung. Each bronchus divides further into secondary and tertiary bronchi, and eventually into tiny bronchioles. This continuous branching is referred to as the bronchial tree. Deep within the paired, cone-shaped lungs, exchange of gases takes place.

360-DEGREE VIEW

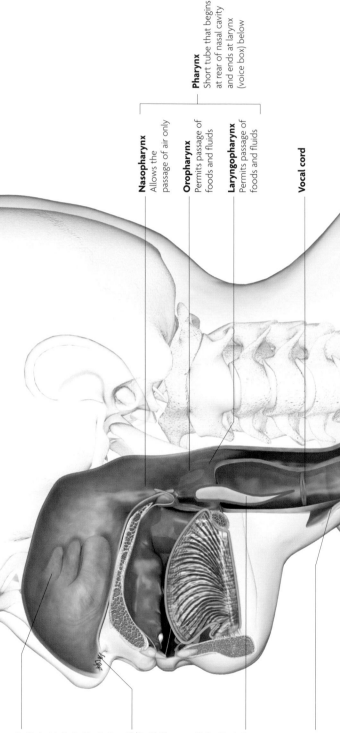

Nasopharynx
Allows the passage of air only

Oropharynx
Permits passage of foods and fluids

Laryngopharynx
Permits passage of foods and fluids

Pharynx
Short tube that begins at rear of nasal cavity and ends at larynx (voice box) below

Vocal cord

Nasal cavity
Main route for air to and from the lungs; lined with a sticky, mucus-covered membrane that traps dust particles and germs; divided into two by central plate of cartilage (nasal septum); fuzzy-looking patches (olfactory epithelia) in roof of cavity, are the sensory organs of smell

Nose hairs
Situated inside entrance of nostrils; help to filter large particles of dust and debris

Epiglottis
Cartilage flap that tilts over entrance to larynx when swallowing, to prevent food, drink, and saliva entering trachea

Larynx
Short, cartilaginous tube joining pharynx with trachea; together with vocal cords within the larynx, it has a vital role in speech production

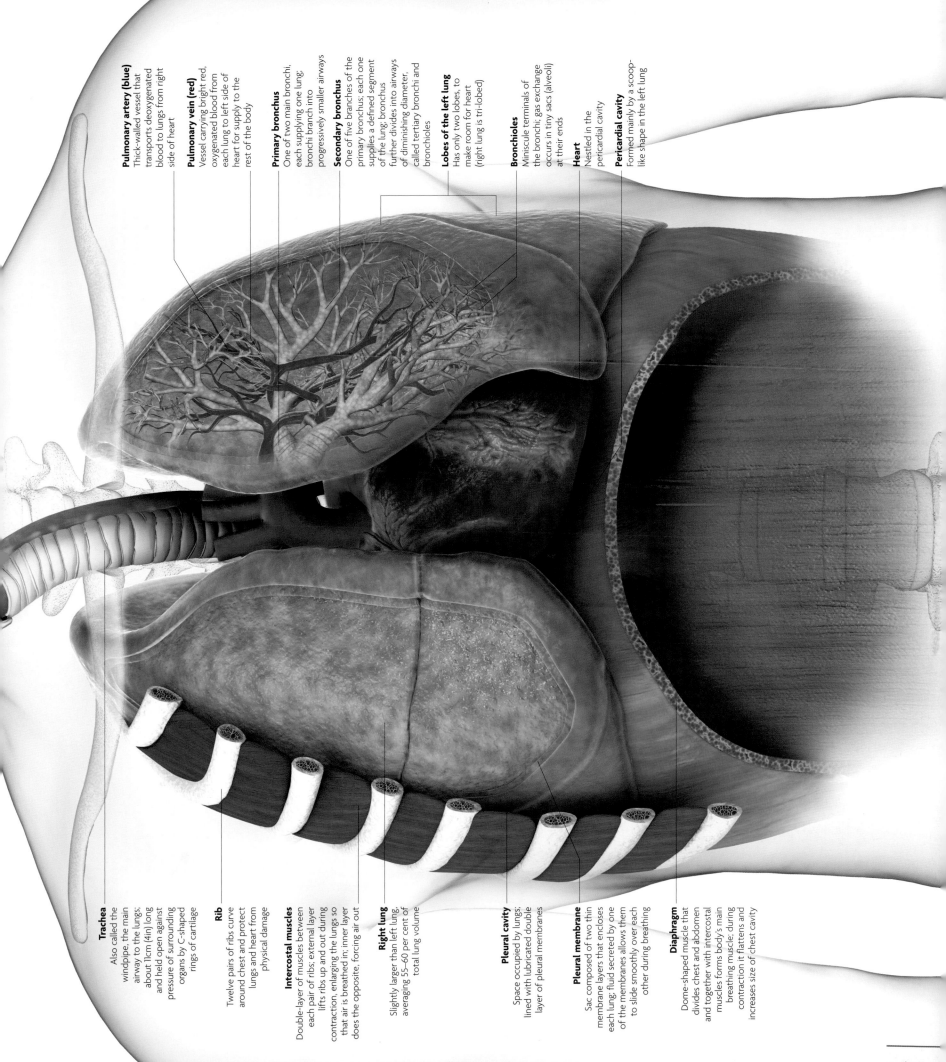

Pulmonary artery (blue)
Thick-walled vessel that transports deoxygenated blood to lungs from right side of heart

Pulmonary vein (red)
Vessel carrying bright red, oxygenated blood from each lung to left side of heart for supply to the rest of the body

Primary bronchus
One of two main bronchi, each supplying one lung; bronchi branch into progressively smaller airways

Secondary bronchus
One of five branches of the primary bronchus; each one supplies a defined segment of the lung; bronchus further divides into airways of diminishing diameter, called tertiary bronchi and bronchioles

Lobes of the left lung
Has only two lobes, to make room for heart (right lung is tri-lobed)

Bronchioles
Miniscule terminals of the bronchi; gas exchange occurs in tiny sacs (alveoli) at their ends

Heart
Nestled in the pericardial cavity

Pericardial cavity
Formed mainly by a scoop-like shape in the left lung

Trachea
Also called the windpipe, the main airway to the lungs; about 11cm (4in) long and held open against pressure of surrounding organs by C-shaped rings of cartilage

Rib
Twelve pairs of ribs curve around chest and protect lungs and heart from physical damage

Intercostal muscles
Double-layer of muscles between each pair of ribs; external layer lifts ribs up and out during contraction, enlarging the lungs so that air is breathed in; inner layer does the opposite, forcing air out

Right lung
Slightly larger than left lung, averaging 55–60 per cent of total lung volume

Pleural cavity
Space occupied by lungs; lined with lubricated double layer of pleural membranes

Pleural membrane
Sac composed of two thin membrane layers that encloses each lung; fluid secreted by one of the membranes allows them to slide smoothly over each other during breathing

Diaphragm
Dome-shaped muscle that divides chest and abdomen and together with intercostal muscles forms body's main breathing muscle; during contraction it flattens and increases size of chest cavity

LUNGS

THE TWO SPONGE-LIKE LUNGS FILL MOST OF THE CHEST CAVITY AND ARE PROTECTED BY THE FLEXIBLE RIBCAGE. TOGETHER THEY FORM ONE OF THE BODY'S LARGEST ORGANS. THEIR ESSENTIAL FUNCTION IS GAS EXCHANGE – TAKING IN VITAL OXYGEN FROM THE AIR AND EXPELLING WASTE CARBON DIOXIDE TO THE AIR.

LUNG STRUCTURE

Air enters the lungs from the trachea, which branches at its base into two main airways, the primary bronchi. Each primary bronchus enters its lung at a site called the hilum, which is also where the main blood vessels pass in and out of the lung. The primary bronchus divides into secondary bronchi, and these subdivide into tertiary bronchi, all the time decreasing in diameter. Many subsequent divisions form the narrowest airways: the terminal and then respiratory bronchioles, which distribute air to the alveoli. This intricate network of air passages resembles an inverted tree, with the trachea as the trunk, and is known as the bronchial tree. There are corresponding trees for the pulmonary arteries and arterioles, bringing low-oxygen blood from the heart's right side, and the pulmonary venules and veins, returning high-oxygen blood to the heart's left side.

KEEPING CLEAN
The airway linings have millions of cilia (microhairs). These beat with a wave-like motion to propel mucus, microbes, and dust up the trachea, to be coughed up.

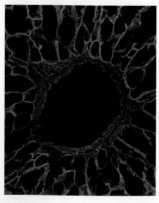

Area occupied by left lung
Descending aorta
Heart
Area occupied by right lung
Vertebra
Rib

CHEST SECTION
This CT scan shows a horizontal slice through the chest. The heart nestles in the left side of the chest cavity.

Right secondary bronchus
Right primary bronchus
Trachea
Left tertiary bronchus
Terminal bronchiole

BRONCHIAL CAST
By filling a lung's airways with a resin that hardens, a cast such as this can be made of the bronchial tree. Each colour indicates an individual bronchopulmonary segment aerated by a tertiary, or segmental, bronchus.

Right lung
Like the left lung has ten bronchopulmonary segments

Superior lobe
Contains three bronchopulmonary segments

Horizontal fissure
Between superior and middle lobes of right lung

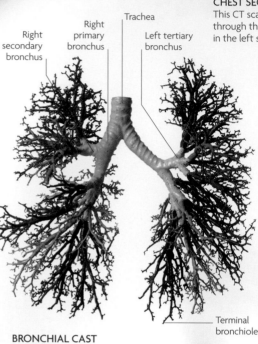

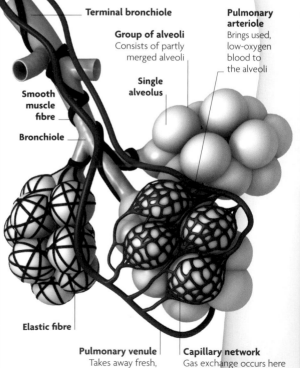

Terminal bronchiole

Group of alveoli
Consists of partly merged alveoli

Single alveolus

Smooth muscle fibre

Bronchiole

Pulmonary arteriole
Brings used, low-oxygen blood to the alveoli

Elastic fibre

Pulmonary venule
Takes away fresh, high-oxygen blood

Capillary network
Gas exchange occurs here

ALVEOLI

The lungs' microscopic air sacs, alveoli, are elastic, thin-walled structures arranged in clumps at the ends of respiratory bronchioles. They resemble bunches of grapes, although the alveoli are partly merged with each other. White blood cells known as macrophages are always present on their inner surfaces, where they ingest and destroy airborne irritants such as bacteria, chemicals, and dust. Around the alveoli are networks of capillaries. Oxygen passes from the air in the alveoli into the blood by diffusion through the alveolar and capillary walls (see p.134). Carbon dioxide diffuses from blood into the alveoli. There are more than 300 million alveoli in both lungs, providing a huge surface area for gas exchange – about 40 times greater than the body's outer surface.

BRONCHIOLE AND ALVEOLI
This microview shows a cross-sectioned bronchiole (red) surrounded by alveoli that have been cut through, so that they resemble air bubbles in a sponge.

Inferior lobe
Contains five bronchopulmonary segments

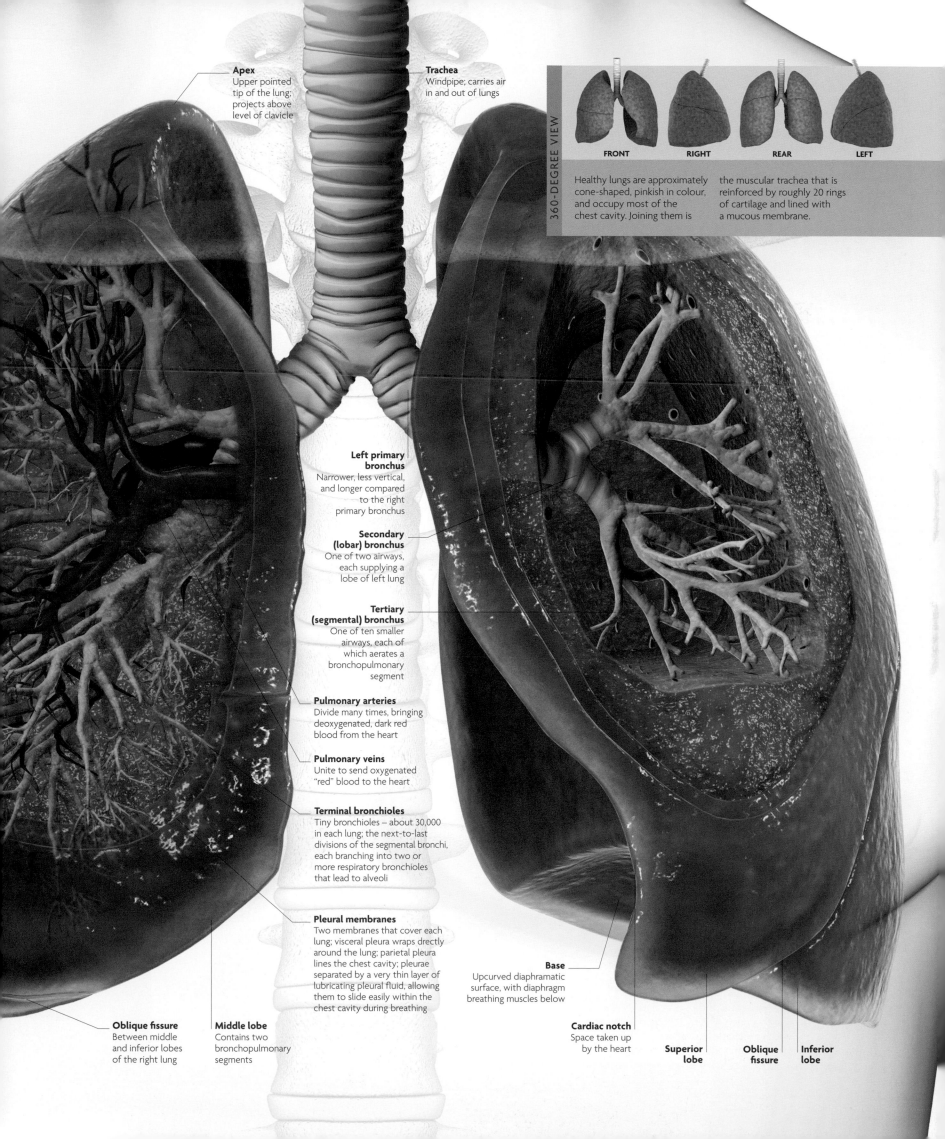

Apex
Upper pointed tip of the lung; projects above level of clavicle

Trachea
Windpipe; carries air in and out of lungs

FRONT   RIGHT   REAR   LEFT

Healthy lungs are approximately cone-shaped, pinkish in colour, and occupy most of the chest cavity. Joining them is the muscular trachea that is reinforced by roughly 20 rings of cartilage and lined with a mucous membrane.

Left primary bronchus
Narrower, less vertical, and longer compared to the right primary bronchus

Secondary (lobar) bronchus
One of two airways, each supplying a lobe of left lung

Tertiary (segmental) bronchus
One of ten smaller airways, each of which aerates a bronchopulmonary segment

Pulmonary arteries
Divide many times, bringing deoxygenated, dark red blood from the heart

Pulmonary veins
Unite to send oxygenated "red" blood to the heart

Terminal bronchioles
Tiny bronchioles – about 30,000 in each lung; the next-to-last divisions of the segmental bronchi, each branching into two or more respiratory bronchioles that lead to alveoli

Pleural membranes
Two membranes that cover each lung; visceral pleura wraps dirctly around the lung; parietal pleura lines the chest cavity; pleurae separated by a very thin layer of lubricating pleural fluid, allowing them to slide easily within the chest cavity during breathing

Base
Upcurved diaphramatic surface, with diaphragm breathing muscles below

Oblique fissure
Between middle and inferior lobes of the right lung

Middle lobe
Contains two bronchopulmonary segments

Cardiac notch
Space taken up by the heart

Superior lobe

Oblique fissure

Inferior lobe

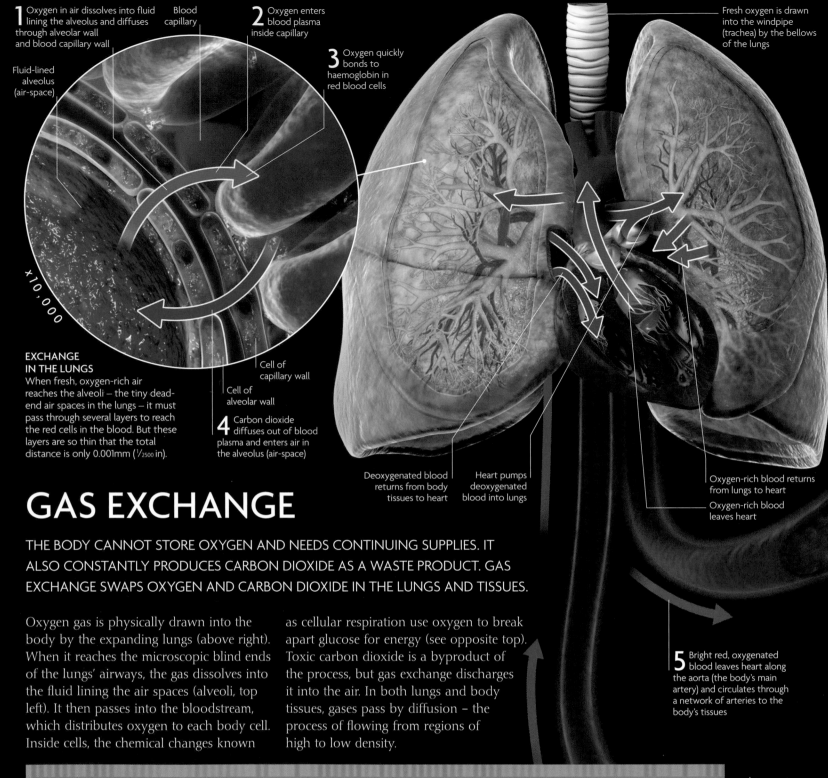

1 Oxygen in air dissolves into fluid lining the alveolus and diffuses through alveolar wall and blood capillary wall

Blood capillary

2 Oxygen enters blood plasma inside capillary

3 Oxygen quickly bonds to haemoglobin in red blood cells

Fresh oxygen is drawn into the windpipe (trachea) by the bellows of the lungs

Fluid-lined alveolus (air-space)

×10,000

EXCHANGE IN THE LUNGS

When fresh, oxygen-rich air reaches the alveoli – the tiny dead-end air spaces in the lungs – it must pass through several layers to reach the red cells in the blood. But these layers are so thin that the total distance is only 0.001mm ($^1/_{2500}$ in).

Cell of capillary wall

Cell of alveolar wall

4 Carbon dioxide diffuses out of blood plasma and enters air in the alveolus (air-space)

Deoxygenated blood returns from body tissues to heart

Heart pumps deoxygenated blood into lungs

Oxygen-rich blood returns from lungs to heart

Oxygen-rich blood leaves heart

GAS EXCHANGE

THE BODY CANNOT STORE OXYGEN AND NEEDS CONTINUING SUPPLIES. IT ALSO CONSTANTLY PRODUCES CARBON DIOXIDE AS A WASTE PRODUCT. GAS EXCHANGE SWAPS OXYGEN AND CARBON DIOXIDE IN THE LUNGS AND TISSUES.

Oxygen gas is physically drawn into the body by the expanding lungs (above right). When it reaches the microscopic blind ends of the lungs' airways, the gas dissolves into the fluid lining the air spaces (alveoli, top left). It then passes into the bloodstream, which distributes oxygen to each body cell. Inside cells, the chemical changes known as cellular respiration use oxygen to break apart glucose for energy (see opposite top). Toxic carbon dioxide is a byproduct of the process, but gas exchange discharges it into the air. In both lungs and body tissues, gases pass by diffusion – the process of flowing from regions of high to low density.

5 Bright red, oxygenated blood leaves heart along the aorta (the body's main artery) and circulates through a network of arteries to the body's tissues

Lower vena cava (one of the body's two main veins) returns deoxygenated blood from lower body to heart

SUPPORTING THE ALVEOLI

Alveoli are only 0.2mm ($^1/_{125}$ in) across when fully inflated. They should collapse inwards like deflated balloons due to powerful surface tension in their fluid lining. Their collapse is prevented by a natural substance with detergent-like properties called surfactant. It is produced by alveolar cells and consists mainly of fatty substances, such as cholesterol and phospholipids, and proteins. Besides keeping alveoli inflated, it plays a role in disabling bacteria, preventing certain lung infections.

Alveolar wall

Air

Fluid layer

ALVEOLUS (AIR SPACE)

Cohesive force

Forces collapsing alveolar wall

Fluid molecule

WITHOUT SURFACTANT
Molecules in the watery fluid lining attract and cohere to each other, making the alveolar wall pull inwards and collapse.

Stable alveolar wall

Surfactant molecules

Weakened forces between fluid molecules

WITH SURFACTANT
Molecules of surfactant flow between the fluid molecules and reduce their cohesive forces, allowing the alveoli to stay inflated.

CELLULAR RESPIRATION

Glucose (blood sugar) is the body's main energy source. Cellular respiration occurs in every body cell when oxygen reacts with glucose to free its energy in chemical form. The end products are carbon dioxide and water, which is known as metabolic water and amounts to about 300ml (10fl oz) daily throughout the body. The whole process is called aerobic (oxygen-requiring) cellular, or internal, respiration.

Six water molecules

Six carbon dioxide molecules

Carbon dioxide diffuses into blood

Glucose molecule

Oxygen combines with glucose

Tissue cell

Oxygen diffuses out of blood

Capillary wall

Six oxygen molecules

Blood plasma

RESPIRATION REACTION
Cells take up oxygen to drive the key respiration reaction that releases energy from glucose.

Capillary

Red blood cell

6 Oxygenated blood is carried through tissues in capillaries thinner than hair

EXCHANGE IN THE BODY TISSUES
Oxygen levels are higher in the blood than in surrounding tissues. The difference in levels forces oxygen to break its bonds to the haemoglobin in red blood cells and diffuse out of the blood into the adjacent cells. The reverse applies to carbon dioxide, which diffuses from the tissue into the blood plasma.

9 Carbon dioxide diffuses out of tissue cell, across wall of blood capillary, and into blood plasma

7 Arriving red blood cells are rich in oxygen, which is bound to haemoglobin in the body of each cell

8 Oxygen leaves the haemoglobin within the red blood cells, diffuses across the blood capillary walls, and into tissue cells

x10,000

Capillary bed running through tissue

BREATHING AND VOCALIZATION

THE MOVEMENTS OF BREATHING, ALSO KNOWN AS BODILY RESPIRATION, BRING FRESH AIR CONTAINING OXYGEN DEEP INTO THE LUNGS AND THEN REMOVE STALE AIR CONTAINING THE WASTE PRODUCT CARBON DIOXIDE.

BREATHING

The physical movement of air into and out of the lungs is generated by differences in pressure within the lungs compared to the surrounding atmospheric pressure. The pressure differences are produced by forcefully expanding the chest and lungs by muscular action, and then passively allowing them to return to their former size. The rate and depth of breathing can be consciously modified. However, the underlying need to breathe is controlled by areas within the brain stem, where responses to regulate the breathing muscles (of which we are usually not aware) occur according to the levels of carbon dioxide and oxygen in the blood.

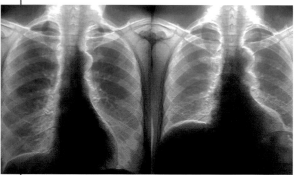

DIAPHRAGM MOVEMENT
The abdominal contents (dark area at the bottom of this X-ray) are flattened by the diaphragm muscle during inhalation (left) and then rise up during exhalation (right).

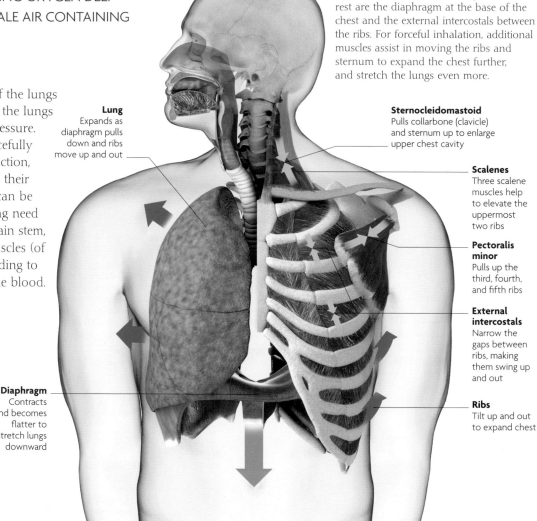

Lung
Expands as diaphragm pulls down and ribs move up and out

Diaphragm
Contracts and becomes flatter to stretch lungs downward

INHALATION
The chief muscles used in respiration at rest are the diaphragm at the base of the chest and the external intercostals between the ribs. For forceful inhalation, additional muscles assist in moving the ribs and sternum to expand the chest further, and stretch the lungs even more.

Sternocleidomastoid
Pulls collarbone (clavicle) and sternum up to enlarge upper chest cavity

Scalenes
Three scalene muscles help to elevate the uppermost two ribs

Pectoralis minor
Pulls up the third, fourth, and fifth ribs

External intercostals
Narrow the gaps between ribs, making them swing up and out

Ribs
Tilt up and out to expand chest

VOLUME AND PRESSURE

Breathing alters the volume of the chest (thoracic cavity). The lungs "suck" onto the inner chest wall, so that as the cavity expands, they also become larger. The main expanding forces are provided by the diaphragm and intercostal muscles. At rest, the diaphragm carries out most of the work, as 0.5 litres (17fl oz) of air – the tidal volume – shifts in and out with each breath (12 to 17 times every minute). Rate and volume increase automatically if the body needs more oxygen, as during exercise. Then forced inspiration can suck in an extra 2 litres (70fl oz), and forced expiration expels almost as much, leading to a total air shift, or vital capacity, of more than 4.5 litres (150fl oz) in a large, healthy adult. The breathing rate can triple, producing a total air exchange more than 20 times greater than at rest.

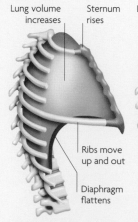

Lung volume increases
Sternum rises
Ribs move up and out
Diaphragm flattens

BREATHING IN
The diaphragm contracts to become less dome-like, while the ribs swing upward and outward with a "bucket handle" action to raise the sternum.

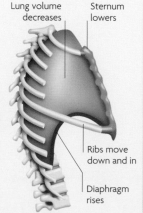

Lung volume decreases
Sternum lowers
Ribs move down and in
Diaphragm rises

BREATHING OUT
The diaphragm relaxes, and the elastic, stretched lungs recoil to become smaller again, allowing the sternum and ribs to move down and inward.

NEGATIVE PRESSURE
As lung volume increases, air pressure within decreases. Atmospheric pressure outside the body is now higher and air is drawn down the airways and into the lungs – in effect, air is "sucked" in.

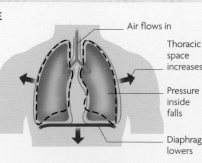

Air flows in
Thoracic space increases
Pressure inside falls
Diaphragm lowers

POSITIVE PRESSURE
As the lung volume diminishes when exhaling, the air is compressed, raising its pressure within the lungs. So the air is pushed back along the airways, and out of the nose and mouth.

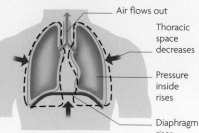

Air flows out
Thoracic space decreases
Pressure inside rises
Diaphragm rises

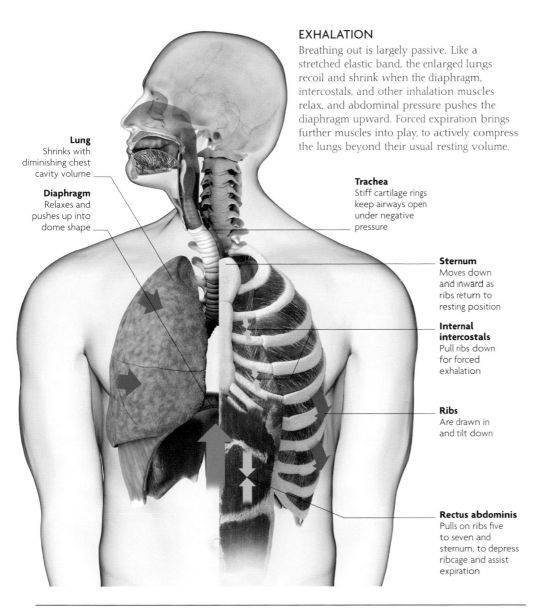

EXHALATION

Breathing out is largely passive. Like a stretched elastic band, the enlarged lungs recoil and shrink when the diaphragm, intercostals, and other inhalation muscles relax, and abdominal pressure pushes the diaphragm upward. Forced expiration brings further muscles into play, to actively compress the lungs beyond their usual resting volume.

Lung
Shrinks with diminishing chest cavity volume

Diaphragm
Relaxes and pushes up into dome shape

Trachea
Stiff cartilage rings keep airways open under negative pressure

Sternum
Moves down and inward as ribs return to resting position

Internal intercostals
Pull ribs down for forced exhalation

Ribs
Are drawn in and tilt down

Rectus abdominis
Pulls on ribs five to seven and sternum, to depress ribcage and assist expiration

THE LARYNX

The larynx is sited between the pharynx and the trachea. It has a framework of nine cartilages, being the paired arytenoids, cuneiforms, and corniculates, and the unpaired epiglottic, thyroid, and cricoid. The thyroid cartilage forms a prominent mound under the skin of the neck, called the "Adam's apple", which is larger and more pronounced in adult males. The cartilages are held in position by numerous muscles and ligaments, and the larynx is also associated with the hyoid bone just above it, which anchors some of these muscles.

INTERNAL STRUCTURE

The larynx forms a hollow chamber through which air flows silently during normal breathing, and which can tilt its cartilages to bring the vocal cords together for speech.

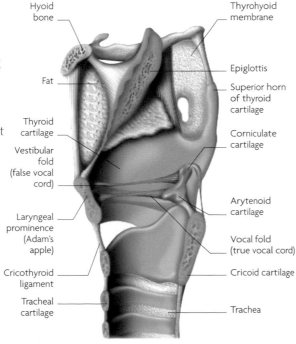

Hyoid bone

Thyrohyoid membrane

Fat

Epiglottis

Superior horn of thyroid cartilage

Thyroid cartilage

Corniculate cartilage

Vestibular fold (false vocal cord)

Arytenoid cartilage

Laryngeal prominence (Adam's apple)

Vocal fold (true vocal cord)

Cricothyroid ligament

Cricoid cartilage

Tracheal cartilage

Trachea

VOCALIZATION

The vocal cords (vocal folds) are paired bands of fibrous tissue near the base of the larynx. In normal breathing there is a V-shaped gap between them, called the glottis. Sound is produced when the cords close together, tighten by muscle action, and vibrate as air from the lungs passes between them. The greater the tension in the cords, the higher the pitch (frequency). Above are the false vocal cords (vestibular folds). These do not produce sound but help to close off the larynx when swallowing.

Vocal cords

Corniculate cartilage

Vocal cords

False vocal cord

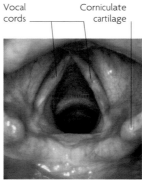

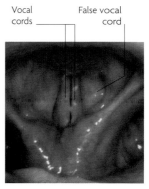

CORDS APART
A laryngoscope view shows the vocal cords angled apart during normal breathing, when air passes through the gap between them.

CORDS ADJACENT
Laryngeal muscles swing the arytenoid cartilages, to which the vocal cords are attached, and bring them together.

RESPIRATORY REFLEXES

The two important respiratory reflexes are coughing and sneezing. Both aim to blow out excess mucus, dust, irritants, and obstructions – coughing from the lower pharynx, larynx, trachea, and lung airways, and sneezing from the nasal chambers and nasopharynx. In both cases, a deep inhalation is followed by sudden contraction of the muscles involved in forceful exhalation (see above left). For a cough, the lower pharynx, epiglottis, and larynx close so that air pressure builds up in the lungs, and is released explosively, rattling the vocal cords. In a sneeze, the tongue closes off the mouth, to force air up and out through the nose.

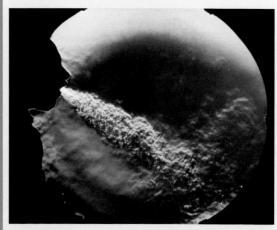

MUCUS SPRAY
Both coughs and sneezes propel a spray of tiny mucus droplets from the respiratory airways for distances of up to 3m (10ft). This image shows spray from a cough.

RESPIRATORY DISORDERS

MILLIONS OF MICROBES FLOAT IN EVEN THE CLEANEST OF AIR AND EACH BREATH BRINGS THOSE PARTICLES INTO THE RESPIRATORY TRACT. DESPITE DEFENCE SYSTEMS, SUCH AS MUCUS AND CILIA, THESE MICROBES HEIGHTEN THE RISK OF A RESPIRATORY INFECTION. IF THE NOSE, THROAT, OR LARYNX IS INVOLVED, THIS IS KNOWN AS AN UPPER RESPIRATORY TRACT INFECTION (URTI).

COMMON COLD

THIS VIRAL INFECTION IS VERY COMMON, AFFECTING SOME PEOPLE EVERY TWO OR THREE YEARS, BUT OTHERS TWO OR THREE TIMES A YEAR, ESPECIALLY IN CHILDHOOD.

The common cold is one of the most frequently experienced illnesses but also generally one of the less serious. At least 200 different and highly contagious types of virus can cause the problem. They spread in fluid that floats through air, in tiny droplets of mucus coughed or sneezed out by sufferers, and also in films of moisture transferred from person to person by close contact, such as shaking hands, or via shared objects, such as cups. Symptoms involve frequent sneezing, a runny nose, which at first runs with a clear, thin discharge that may later become thicker and greenish-yellow, a headache, slightly raised temperature, and perhaps an accompanying sore throat, cough, and sore, reddened eyes. Antibiotic drugs are ineffective as they do not work against viruses. Cold viruses change (mutate) their surface coatings so rapidly that even if antiviral drugs could be made to tackle existing strains, they would be ineffective against the new ones. Most cold remedies, such as decongestants or inhalants to relieve nasal stuffiness, treat the symptoms while the body's immune system attacks the invading microbes.

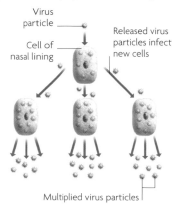
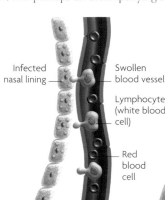
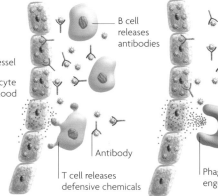
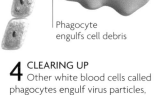

SPREADING INFECTION
Coughs and sneezes spread diseases – especially common cold viruses, which can be sprayed more than 3m (9½ft) in mucous droplets.

1 VIRUS INVADES CELLS
Virus particles in air land on and invade the cells lining the nose and throat. They rapidly replicate, killing their host cells.

2 WHITE CELLS ARRIVE
Defensive white blood cells squeeze from capillaries towards the infected lining cells, which are creating thin mucus.

3 ANTIBODY PRODUCTION
White blood cells called B cells produce antibodies, which immobilize the virus; other white blood cells destroy infected cells.

4 CLEARING UP
Other white blood cells called phagocytes engulf virus particles, damaged nasal lining cells, and other debris. The cold subsides.

INFLUENZA

USUALLY CALLED FLU, THIS INFECTION CAUSES SYMPTOMS INCLUDING FEVER, CHILLS, SNEEZING, SORE THROAT, HEADACHE, MUSCLE ACHES, AND FATIGUE.

Influenza is primarily an upper respiratory tract infection, but it also has body-wide symptoms: raised temperature, sensations of being hot and sweaty and then cold with shivers, muscle aches, and exhaustion. Even after the main infection has cleared up there may be lingering depression and fatigue. The influenza viruses are coded A, B, and C and are very contagious. Influenza A tends to produce regular outbreaks and can also affect domestic animals such as pigs, horses, and fowl. Influenza B usually causes more sporadic outbreaks in places where many people gather and interact. Influenza C is less likely to produce serious symptoms. The type A virus is most likely to change or mutate. People at risk of complications, such as those with existing illnesses, can be vaccinated before the main risk time of the winter season. Because the virus can mutate, new vaccines are prepared annually. Complications include respiratory tract infections, such as pneumonia and acute bronchitis. Influenza can be life-threatening to very young and elderly people; some epidemics kill people of all ages.

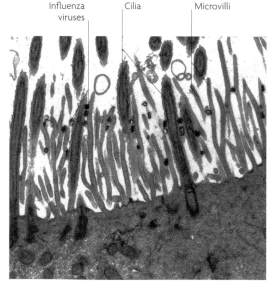

VIRAL INVASION
Influenza viruses (blue) attach themselves to hair-like microvilli and cilia on the surface of cells that line the upper respiratory tract. They then enter the cells and start to proliferate, eventually causing the cells to die and the symptoms of influenza to become apparent.

BIRD FLU

The influenza A virus (technically from a group of viruses known as the Orthomyxoviridae) had its origins in birds, causing the types of illness generally known as avian, or bird, flu. It has relatively recently "crossed over" into mammals, including humans. Virus subtype H5N1 infects several types of birds, including chickens. This strain can infect humans, causing a serious form of influenza with respiratory complications, which is fatal in up to half of sufferers. However, it is only contracted after close contact with infected birds. There is no clear evidence of human-to-human spread as in the other types.

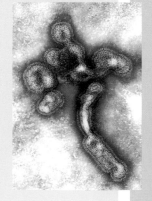

H5N1 VIRUS
A transmission electron micrograph of H5N1. Within the lipid envelope (green) are the proteins haemagglutinin (H) and neuraminidase (N).

UPPER AIRWAY INFECTION

MANY BACTERIA AND VIRUSES CAUSE UPPER RESPIRATORY TRACT INFECTIONS (URTI), WITH THE NAME OF THE INFECTION DEPENDING ON THE PART MOST AFFECTED.

The upper airway are is exposed to a continual intake of microbes with each breath. Harmful microbes may manage to break through the mucous lining and other defences at various places, and set up an infection zone there. Apart from the nasal chambers, which suffer most during a common cold, other sites at risk include the sinuses, the pharynx, or throat, and the larynx, or voicebox. The sinuses are air-filled cavities that branch from the nasal airways into the facial skull bones. There are also lumps of lymphoid tissue in the upper airways, which may swell markedly with infection. They include the pharyngeal tonsils, or adenoids, in the upper pharynx (nasopharynx), at the rear of the nasal chamber, and the palatine tonsils, or "the tonsils", on either side of the mid-pharynx, near the rear of the soft palate. Each area of infection causes specific symptoms. Inflammation and soreness in various combinations of the pharynx, palatine tonsils, and larynx are often known by the general name of "sore throat". The usual causes are viruses, which may be associated with infection spreading from a common cold. The adenoids and tonsils tend to be larger during childhood as this age group catches more infectious diseases because their immunity is still in the process of developing.

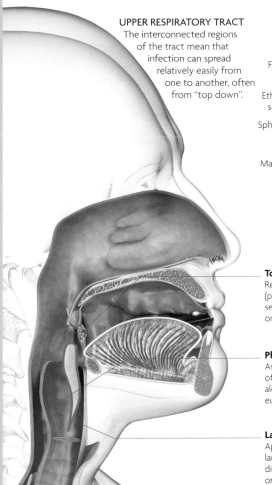

UPPER RESPIRATORY TRACT
The interconnected regions of the tract mean that infection can spread relatively easily from one to another, often from "top down".

Tonsillitis
Red, inflamed, swollen tonsils (palatine tonsils) can cause a severe sore throat and pain on swallowing.

Pharyngitis
As with other URTIs, the pain of pharyngitis may spread along the airway called the eustachian tube to the ear.

Laryngitis
Apart from a sore throat, laryngitis may produce discomfort when speaking, or even total voice loss.

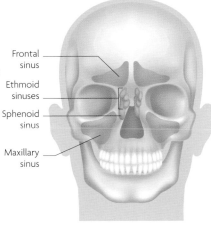

Frontal sinus

Ethmoid sinuses

Sphenoid sinus

Maxillary sinus

FRONT VIEW

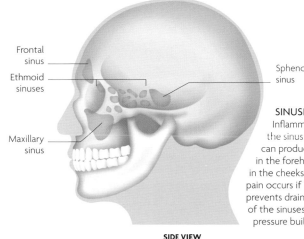

Frontal sinus

Ethmoid sinuses

Maxillary sinus

Sphenoid sinus

SIDE VIEW

SINUSITIS
Inflammation of the sinus linings can produce pain in the forehead or in the cheeks. Severe pain occurs if swelling prevents drainage of the sinuses and pressure builds up.

Infected tonsils

Infected larynx

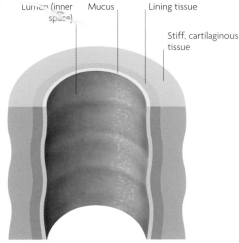

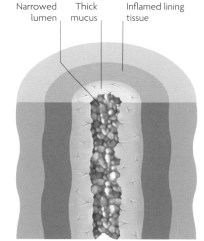

TONSILLITIS
A view into the throat shows the tonsils on either side as enlarged, reddened, and inflamed, or "angry". The white coating is commonly associated with this infection.

LARYNGITIS
The vocal cords (vocal folds) and laryngeal tissues are swollen and sore. The swelling prevents the cords from vibrating and the voice becomes husky or is lost entirely.

ACUTE BRONCHITIS

BRONCHITIS IS INFLAMMATION OF THE BRONCHI, WHICH ARE THE LARGER AIRWAYS THAT BRANCH FROM THE BASE OF THE TRACHEA, OR WINDPIPE, INTO THE LUNGS.

Acute bronchitis develops suddenly, within 24 to 48 hours. Its symptoms include a persistent and irritating cough yielding clear sputum (phlegm), a tight chest, wheezing and perhaps breathlessness, pain with the cough, and often a slightly raised temperature. This disorder may be a complication of an infection elsewhere in the upper respiratory tract, for example tonsillitis. Usually only the larger and medium-sized bronchi are affected, and they become inflamed and narrowed. Healthy adults usually manage to shake off the infection after a few days, without any need for medical intervention. However, in older people, or those with other respiratory problems, the condition may spread deeper into the lungs, causing a secondary infection, such as bacterial pneumonia.

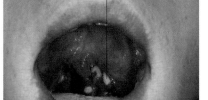

Lumen (inner space)

Mucus

Lining tissue

Stiff, cartilaginous tissue

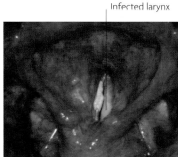

Narrowed lumen

Thick mucus

Inflamed lining tissue

NORMAL BRONCHUS
The airway lining secretes a thin but adequate layer of its protective mucus. This leaves a wide passageway, or lumen, for air to flow in and out of the lung tissues.

INFLAMED BRONCHUS
The lining tissue swells and produces excessive mucus, some of which will be coughed up. Any mucus remaining increases the risk of infection spreading deeper into the lungs.

PNEUMONIA

INFLAMMATION OF THE LUNG'S MICROSCOPIC AIR
SACS, THE ALVEOLI, AND THE SMALLEST AIRWAYS,
THE BRONCHIOLES, IS KNOWN AS PNEUMONIA.

Pneumonia can develop in different areas of the lung.
Lobar pneumonia affects one lobe (large division)
of the lung. Bronchopneumonia affects patches
of tissue in one or both lungs. The usual cause is
bacterial infection, commonly *Streptococcus pneumoniae*.
Pneumonia can be triggered as a secondary problem
by an upper respiratory tract viral infection, such
as a common cold. Causes also include a range of
other bacteria, as well as viruses such as those for
influenza and chickenpox, and more rarely, other
microorganisms such as protists (protozoa), and
fungi. The main symptoms are a cough that brings up
blood-stained, sputum (phlegm), breathlessness, chest
pain, and a high fever with confusion. If the cause of
the infection is bacterial, treatment is with antibiotics.

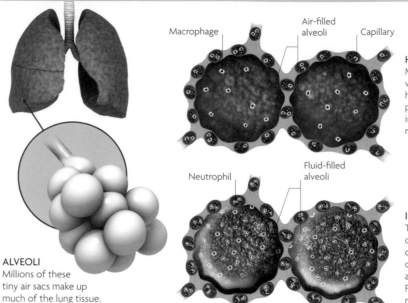

ALVEOLI
Millions of these
tiny air sacs make up
much of the lung tissue.

Macrophage · Air-filled alveoli · Capillary

HEALTHY ALVEOLI
Macrophages, a type of
white blood cell, scavenge in
healthy alveoli. They ingest
particles of dust and other
inert, inhaled irritants but
respond slowly to bacteria.

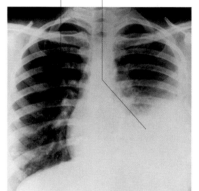

Neutrophil · Fluid-filled alveoli

INFLAMED ALVEOLI
The infective process triggers
capillary wall changes, and
other types of white blood
cell, including neutrophils,
arrive to attack the bacteria.
Fluid accumulates, which
reduces oxygen absorption.

LEGIONNAIRES' DISEASE

THIS FORM OF PNEUMONIA-LIKE LUNG
INFECTION IS DUE TO THE BACTERIUM
LEGIONELLA PNEUMOPHILIA.

Legionnaire's disease was first
described in 1976 after an outbreak
of a severe pneumonia-like illness
among war veterans at an American
Legion convention. It affects men
more often than women. Symptoms
resemble those of other pneumonias, in
particular, respiratory problems, but in
addition sufferers may have diarrhoea,
abdominal pain, or jaundice. It occurs
most often in middle-aged and older
people, and the disease may become
very serious or even fatal in people
with a weakened immune system.

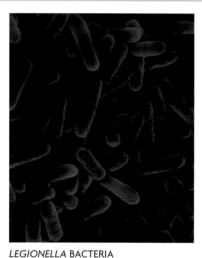

***LEGIONELLA* BACTERIA**
Rod-shaped *Legionella* bacteria are present
in most water supplies. They multiply rapidly
in water-cooled air-conditioning systems
and in plumbing where water can stagnate.

PLEURAL EFFUSION

EXCESS FLUID IN THE TWO-LAYERED
MEMBRANE SURROUNDING THE LUNG
IS KNOWN AS PLEURAL EFFUSION.

The two layers of membrane, or pleura,
are lubricated by a small amount of
fluid and allow the lungs to expand
and contract smoothly within the chest
wall. Infections such as pneumonia and
tuberculosis, heart failure, and some
cancers can lead to an accumulation of
fluid between the pleura, up to 3 litres
(6pt) in volume, which presses on the
lungs, causing breathlessness and chest
pain. Treatment may initially involve
removal of the fluid using a hollow
needle, or by inserting a tube (chest
drain) through the chest wall.

Normal air-filled lung · Fluid in pleural space

PLEURAL EFFUSION
In this X-ray, the white area over the lower
left lung (on the right of the image) is a
pleural effusion, which partly obscures the
normal dark lung tissues.

TUBERCULOSIS (TB)

THIS INFECTIOUS DISEASE, MAINLY AFFECTING
THE LUNG TISSUE, IS CAUSED BY THE BACTERIUM
MYCOBACTERIUM TUBERCULOSIS.

Many people harbour the TB microbe,
but it causes the disease in only a small
proportion, usually if an individual's
immunity or resistance is lowered.
Symptoms include fever and a
persistent cough, loss of appetite, and
general weakness. Oral antibiotics
have been very successful against TB,
but the number of people affected
by the disease has increased since
the 1980s. This is due partly to the
emergence of new antibiotic-resistant
strains of the bacteria, and partly
because of the spread of HIV/AIDS,
which lowers a person's immunity.

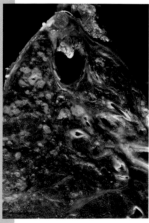

DAMAGED TISSUE
In advanced TB, the lung
tissue becomes riddled with
tubercles, which are small,
firm lumps formed to seal
off the centres of infection.

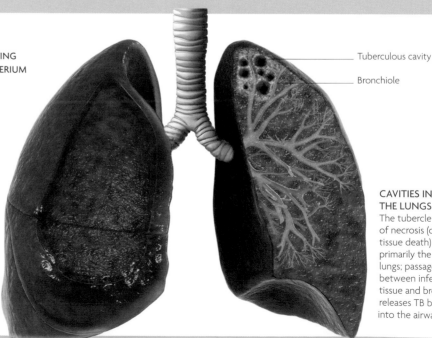

Tuberculous cavity · Bronchiole

CAVITIES IN THE LUNGS
The tubercle areas
of necrosis (cell and
tissue death) affect
primarily the upper
lungs; passage of air
between infected
tissue and bronchi
releases TB bacteria
into the airways.

PNEUMOTHORAX

PNEUMOTHORAX OCCURS WHEN ONE OR BOTH OF THE PLEURAL MEMBRANES IS BREACHED AND AIR ENTERS THE PLEURAL SPACE, CAUSING THE LUNG TO COLLAPSE.

The pleural membranes are separated by a very thin layer of pleural fluid that lubricates their movements. The balance of pressures between the chest wall, pleural layers, and lung tissue makes the lungs "suck" onto the inside of the chest wall. In a pneumothorax, air is allowed into the pleural space. The pressure balance changes, and the lung collapses. This leads to chest tightness, pain, and breathlessness. If more air enters the space but cannot escape (tension pneumothorax), the pressure around the lung compresses it even further, which can be life-threatening. A spontaneous pneumothorax may be due to rupture of an abnormally enlarged alveolus on the lung surface, or to a lung condition such as asthma. Traumatic causes are rib fracture and chest wounds.

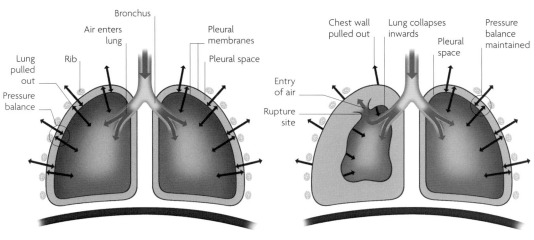

NORMAL BREATHING
The lungs inflate by being pulled out as they "suck" onto the chest wall. Pressure is maintained within the fluid-filled pleural space.

COLLAPSED (RIGHT) LUNG
Air from the right lung enters the surrounding pleural space and changes the pressure balance. The lung shrinks away from the chest wall

ASTHMA

ASTHMA IS AN INFLAMMATORY LUNG DISEASE THAT CAUSES RECURRENT ATTACKS OF BREATHLESSNESS AND WHEEZING, DUE TO NARROWED AIRWAYS IN THE LUNGS.

Asthma is one of the commonest and most variable of lung conditions, affecting as many as one in four children in some regions. Some people have the occasional slight episode; others are prone to severe breathlessness that can threaten life; and some have attacks that are variable and unpredictable from one day to the next. The muscle in the walls of the airways contracts spasmodically, causing the airways to be constricted, and bringing on an attack of breathlessness. The narrowing is worsened by the secretion of excess mucus. Most cases develop in childhood and may be linked to allergy-based problems such as eczema, with both having an inherited component. In many children, the trigger for an attack is an allergic reaction to a foreign substance, or allergen, which can include tiny inhaled particles such as pollen, mould from the droppings of house dust mites, and particles from animal hair or feathers. Other cases are due to food or drink allergies, certain drugs, anxiety, stress, respiratory infection, and vigorous activity in cold weather.

AFFECTED AIRWAYS
Asthma tends to affect, not the larger bronchi, but the more slender airways (red). These are the tertiary bronchi and the bronchioles that lead to the alveoli.

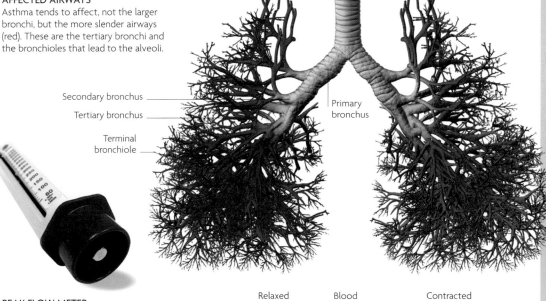

Secondary bronchus
Tertiary bronchus
Terminal bronchiole
Primary bronchus

PEAK FLOW METER
Asthma's severity can be monitored by blowing into a peak flow meter, which measures the rate of air flow.

ASTHMA TREATMENT

There are two main approaches to treatment, which are usually combined. Corticosteroid drugs (known as preventers) suppress the inflammatory reaction and should be taken regularly as prophylactics. Bronchodilator drugs (known as relievers) are used for quick relief to treat early symptoms of an attack; they work rapidly but last only a few hours. Reduced exposure to allergens may minimize the frequency and severity of asthma attacks.

INHALER
Inhaling a spray of anti-asthma medication gets the drug directly to the site of the problem in the lungs' small airways.

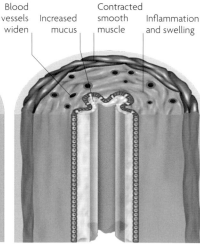

Blood vessel
Mucus
Relaxed smooth muscle
Blood vessels widen
Increased mucus
Contracted smooth muscle
Inflammation and swelling

HEALTHY AIRWAY
A normal bronchiole has relaxed smooth muscle in its walls and an adequate but thin coating of protective mucus covering the lining. The passageway for air, or lumen, is wide enough for sufficient oxygen-containing air to reach the alveoli.

ASTHMATIC AIRWAY
During an asthma attack, the smooth muscle contracts. Inflammation due to an allergic response causes the blood vessels to widen and the tissues in the airway wall to swell. The mucous layer also thickens. This results in narrowing of the lumen.

CHRONIC OBSTRUCTIVE PULMONARY DISEASE

Chronic obstructive pulmonary disease (COPD) consists primarily of chronic bronchitis and emphysema, two conditions that usually occur together in the same person. It is a long-term disorder in which there is progressive damage to lung tissue with increasing shortness of breath. Air flow into and out of the lungs is restricted and the lungs' ability to take in oxygen for the normal body processes diminishes. By far the most important contributory factor for COPD is smoking tobacco.

CHRONIC BRONCHITIS

CHRONIC INFLAMMATION OF THE LUNGS' AIRWAYS IS USUALLY CAUSED BY SMOKING. RARELY, RECURRENT ACUTE INFECTIONS LEAD TO CHRONIC BRONCHITIS.

In chronic bronchitis the main airways leading to the lungs, the bronchi, become inflamed, congested, and narrowed due to irritation caused by tobacco smoke, frequent infections, or prolonged exposure to pollutants. The inflamed airways begin to produce too much mucus (sputum), resulting in a typical cough that at first is troublesome mostly in damp, cold months but then persists throughout the year. Symptoms such as hoarseness, wheezing, and breathlessness also develop. Eventually a person becomes short of breath even at rest. If a secondary respiratory infection develops, the sputum may change appearance from clear or white to yellow or green.

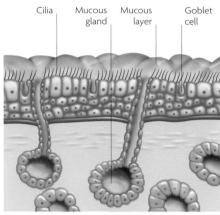

Cilia — Mucous gland — Mucous layer — Goblet cell

NORMAL AIRWAY LINING
Glands produce mucus that traps inhaled dust and germs. Tiny surface hairs (cilia) propel the mucus up into the throat where it is coughed up or swallowed.

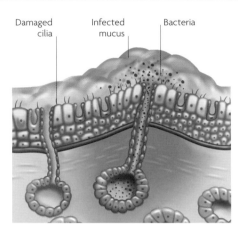

Damaged cilia — Infected mucus — Bacteria

AIRWAY IN CHRONIC BRONCHITIS
Inhaled irritants cause glands to produce more mucus. Damaged cilia cannot propel mucus along, so it becomes a bacterial breeding ground.

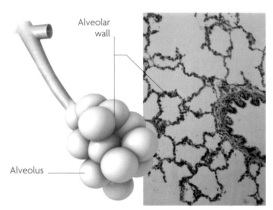

Alveolar wall — Alveolus

HEALTHY TISSUE
The alveoli are grouped, like grapes, and each tiny sac is partly separate from the others. The walls are thin and elastic so they can stretch.

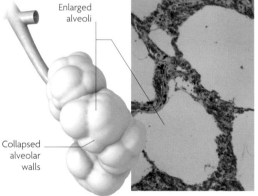

Enlarged alveoli — Collapsed alveolar walls

DAMAGED TISSUE
Smoke or other pollutants stimulate chemicals that cause the alveolar walls to break down and merge, reducing the area for gas exchange.

EMPHYSEMA

IN EMPHYSEMA, THE AIR SACS (ALVEOLI) BECOME OVERSTRETCHED. THEY ALSO RUPTURE AND MERGE SO THAT THEIR OXYGEN-ABSORBING SURFACES ARE REDUCED.

The alveoli not only lose their functional gas exchange area, but air also becomes trapped inside them due to their decreased wall elasticity. As a result, the lungs over-inflate, the volume of air moving in and out of the lungs is reduced, and less oxygen is absorbed into the bloodstream. Most people affected by emphysema are long-term heavy smokers, although a rare inherited condition called alpha1-antitrypsin deficiency can also cause the condition. Although the damage caused by emphysema is usually irreversible, giving up smoking can sometimes slow down the progression of the disease and allow the cilia (see above) to recover.

OCCUPATIONAL DISEASES

ASBESTOSIS, SILICOSIS, AND PNEUMOCONIOSIS ARE DUE TO INHALING PARTICLES THAT IRRITATE AND INFLAME THE LUNG TISSUE, LEADING TO FIBROSIS.

The people most at risk from occupational lung diseases, such as those listed above, are those whose work exposes them to harmful particles over many years – for example, miners, quarry workers, and stone masons. In occupational lung disease, there is gradual thickening (fibrosis) of the lung tissue, which eventually leads to irreversible scarring. Symptoms such as breathlessness and a cough may develop only slowly, but worsen for years after the exposure has ceased. In developed countries, the diseases are becoming less common as many workers wear protective clothing and masks in risky environments, but regulations are often lax in developing countries.

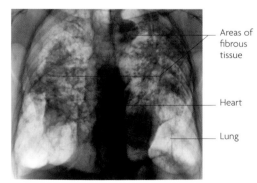

Areas of fibrous tissue — Heart — Lung

SILICOSIS
The orange patches on the lungs in this chest X-ray are areas of fibrosis caused by silicosis. Inhaled silica particles are ingested by scavenging white blood cells (macrophages). These burst, releasing the silica and other chemicals, which damage the lung tissue.

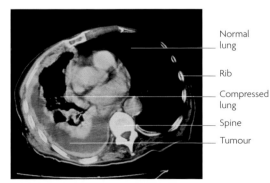

Normal lung — Rib — Compressed lung — Spine — Tumour

ASBESTOSIS
Asbestos is a substance that can cause serious lung damage if inhaled. In some cases of asbestosis, a form of lung cancer develops. This CT scan shows a malignant tumour, or mesothelioma, on the pleura, the thin membrane that surrounds the lung.

LUNG CANCER

A MALIGNANT TUMOUR IN THE LUNG, LUNG CANCER IS THE MOST COMMON CANCER WORLDWIDE WITH OVER A MILLION NEW CASES DIAGNOSED EACH YEAR.

The most common cause of lung cancer – responsible for almost 90 per cent of all cases – is tobacco smoke. In the past, lung cancer was far more common in men than women, because more men than women smoked. However, the incidence of the disease in women rose rapidly in the final decades of the 20th century. The disease is also becoming increasingly common in developing countries with the spread of tobacco smoking and growing urban populations. Many inhaled irritants trigger the growth of abnormal cells in the lungs, but cigarette smoke contains thousands of known carcinogenic (cancer-causing) substances. In rare cases, lung cancer is caused by asbestos, toxic chemicals, or the radioactive gas radon.

Symptoms of lung cancer

A persistent cough is usually the earliest symptom. Because most people who develop lung cancer are smokers, this is often dismissed as a "smoker's cough". Other symptoms include coughing up blood, wheezing, weight loss, persistent hoarseness, and chest pain. If tests confirm the presence of lung cancer, a lobectomy (removal of a lung lobe) or pneumonectomy (removal of a whole lung) may be performed. This is usually advised only if the tumour is small and has not spread. Chemotherapy and radiotherapy can be given to relieve symptoms, rather than with the aim of curing the disease.

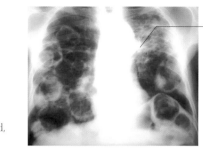
Tumour growing on hilum

TUMOUR
Several tumours (white patches) are visible in the lungs. One tumour is growing on the hilum, where the main airway enters the lung.

THE SPREAD OF LUNG CANCER
Lung cancer can spread (metastasize) to other parts of the body. Metastases in bones can cause pain and fractures; in the brain, headaches and confusion; and in the liver, weight loss and jaundice.

Brain metastasis
Lymph node metastasis
Primary tumour
Bone metastasis
Adrenal gland metastasis
Liver metastasis

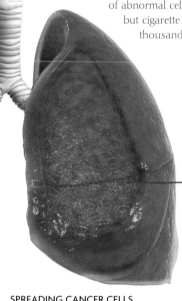

SPREADING CANCER CELLS
Tiny airborne carcinogenic particles lodge in the airways and contribute to the development of cancerous cells. Some of these cells may break away and travel in the blood or lymph to trigger secondary tumours.

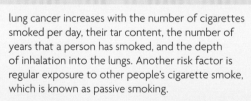
White blood cell

Carcinogens   Alveolus   Capillary

SMOKING AND LUNG CANCER

Tobacco smoke is a complex mixture of more than 3,000 different substances, including the addictive stimulant nicotine, benzene, ammonia, hydrogen cyanide, carbon monoxide, and tar. The burning tar elements in the smoke are known to be strongly cancer-causing (carcinogenic). The risk of developing lung cancer increases with the number of cigarettes smoked per day, their tar content, the number of years that a person has smoked, and the depth of inhalation into the lungs. Another risk factor is regular exposure to other people's cigarette smoke, which is known as passive smoking.

SMOKER'S LUNG
Tar is just one of thousands of chemicals in tobacco smoke. In smokers, healthy lung tissue becomes dotted with deposits of tar, visible here to the naked eye.

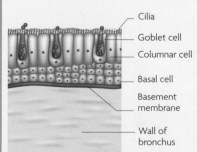

Cilia
Goblet cell
Columnar cell
Basal cell
Basement membrane
Wall of bronchus

1 HEALTHY AIRWAY LINING
Columnar cells topped by tiny, hair-like cilia line healthy airways (bronchi). Basal cells constantly divide to replace naturally damaged columnar cells.

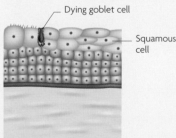

Dying goblet cell
Squamous cell

2 INITIAL DAMAGE
Over time, columnar cells damaged by smoking become squamous cells, which gradually lose their cilia. The mucus-secreting goblet cells die.

Basal cells become cancerous

3 CANCER BEGINS
To replace the damaged cells, basal cells start to multiply at an increased rate. Some of these new basal cells develop into cancerous cells.

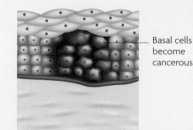

Multiplying cancer cells break through basement membrane

4 CANCER SPREADS
The cancerous cells replace healthy cells. If these cells break through the basement membrane, they can enter blood vessels to travel elsewhere.

FEW BODY PARTS RENEW AS RAPIDLY AS THE SKIN. EVERY
MONTH THE OUTER LAYER OF EPIDERMIS IS COMPLETELY
REPLACED, AT A RATE OF 30,000 FLAKE-LIKE DEAD CELLS
EVERY MINUTE. THE HAIR AND NAILS ARE LIKEWISE
SELF-REINSTATING AND SELF-REPAIRING. SKIN REFLECTS
ASPECTS OF GENERAL HEALTH, ESPECIALLY DIET AND

SKIN, HAIR, AND NAILS

SKIN, HAIR, AND NAIL STRUCTURE

TOGETHER, SKIN, HAIR, AND NAILS ARE KNOWN AS THE INTEGUMENTARY
SYSTEM. THE SKIN IS ONE OF THE LARGEST ORGANS IN THE BODY, WEIGHING
3–4KG (6–9LB) AND WITH A SURFACE AREA OF ALMOST 2M² (21SQ FT). IT IS A
COMPLEX ORGAN FORMED OF TWO MAIN LAYERS, WHICH CONTAIN MANY
DIFFERENT TYPES OF CELL, SOME OF WHICH PRODUCE HAIR AND NAIL TISSUE.

SKIN STRUCTURE

The skin is not simply a thin, waterproof covering for the human
body, but is a complex organ consisting of a number of specialized
cells. Its thickness varies from about 0.5mm (¹/₅₀ in) on delicate
areas such as the eyelids, to 5mm (¹/₅ in) or more on areas of wear
and tear. such as the soles of the feet. Skin has two main structural
layers. The outer epidermis is chiefly protective, and the underlying
dermis contains many different
tissues with varied functions.
The dermis contains thousands
of microsensors that enable the
sense of touch, as well as sweat
glands and adjustable blood
vessels that contribute to body
temperature regulation. Under
the dermis is a layer, sometimes
regarded as part of the skin,
called subcutaneous fat. It acts
as a buffer and provides extra
thermal insulation against
extreme heat and cold.

SKIN SECTION
This micrograph shows three hair follicles
and globules of sebum in the dermis (blue)
with the thin epidermis (pink) on top.

SKIN RENEWAL

The outer epidermis continually renews and replaces itself by cell
division. The basal layer consists of box-like cells that multiply
quickly and gradually move up to the surface, pushed by new cells
from below. As the cells travel upwards, they develop tiny spines or
prickles, which bind them together tightly. They then begin to flatten
and fill with a waterproofing
protein known as keratin.
Finally, the cells die and reach
the surface fully keratinized,
resembling untidy, scale-like,
interlocking tiles on a roof.
As they flake away with daily
wear and tear, more cells arrive
from below to replace them.
The journey from epidermal
base to surface takes about
four weeks, and a typical
person sheds more than
0.5kg (1lb) of skin every year.

EPIDERMAL LAYERS
The procession of skin cells from base to
surface creates four layers (five in areas
of great friction, such as the palms and
soles) in the epidermis. As they move
upwards, the cytoplasm and nucleus in
each cell is replaced by keratin.

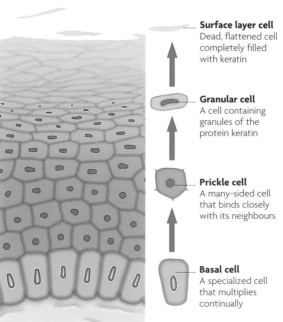

Surface layer cell
Dead, flattened cell
completely filled
with keratin

Granular cell
A cell containing
granules of the
protein keratin

Prickle cell
A many-sided cell
that binds closely
with its neighbours

Basal cell
A specialized cell
that multiplies
continually

SKIN STRUCTURE
A patch of skin about the size of a fingernail
contains 5 million microscopic cells of at
least a dozen main kinds, 100 sweat
glands and their pores, 1,000 touch
sensors, 100-plus hairs with their
sebaceous glands, up to 1m
(3¹/₃ft) of tiny blood vessels
and about 0.5m (1²/₃ft)
of nerve fibres.

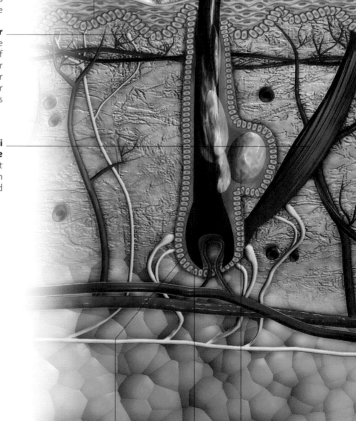

Hair shaft
Part of hair that
projects above
skin surface

Epidermal surface
Cornified layer of
flat, dead, flake-like
skin cells

**Basal epidermal
layer**
Layer in which fast
cell division renews
epidermis above

Touch sensor
Specialized nerve
ending at edge of
epidermis; other
touch sensor
types lie at greater
depths in dermis

**Erector pili
muscle**
Tiny muscle that
pulls hair up when
body is cold

Hair bulb
Lowest part of the hair,
where growth occurs

Hair follicle
Pouch of
epidermis at
root of hair

Sebaceous gland
Produces sebum
that protects hair
and lubricates skin

SKIN REPAIR

Owing to its location, skin suffers more physical damage than any other body organ. However, it has fast-acting repair mechanisms for mending small wounds. If the skin surface is breached, contents leak from damaged cells and stimulate the repair process. Platelets in the blood, and the blood-clotting protein fibrinogen, work together to form a meshwork of fibres that traps red cells as the beginning of a clot. Meanwhile, tissue-forming fibroblast cells collect in the area, as do white cells called neutrophils, which ingest cell debris and foreign matter such as dirt and germs. The clot gradually hardens and expels fluid to become a scab, as the tissues heal beneath.

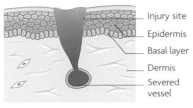

Injury site
Epidermis
Basal layer
Dermis
Severed vessel

1 INJURY
The wound breaks open cells and releases their contents. These components attract various defence and repair cells.

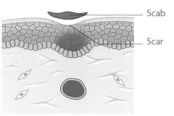

Blood clot
Fibroblast

2 CLOTTING
Blood seeps from the vessel and forms a clot. Fibroblasts multiply and migrate to the damaged area.

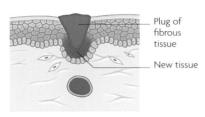

Plug of fibrous tissue
New tissue

3 PLUGGING
Fibroblasts produce a plug of fibrous tissue within the clot, which contracts and shrinks. New tissue begins to form beneath.

Scab
Scar

4 SCABBING
The plug hardens and dries into a scab, which eventually detaches. A scar may remain but usually fades with time.

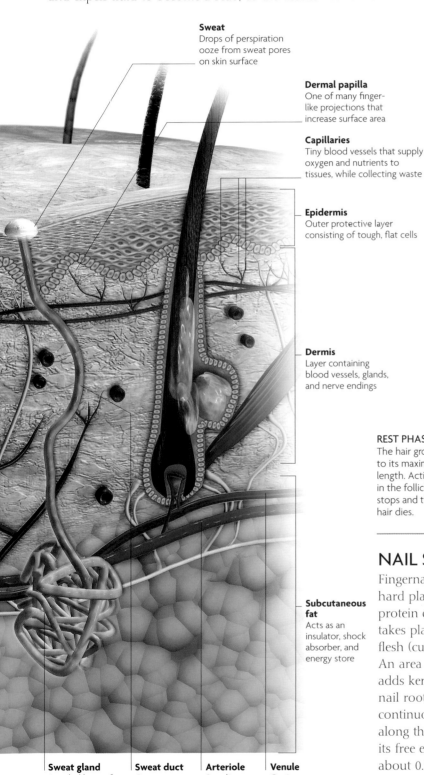

Sweat
Drops of perspiration ooze from sweat pores on skin surface

Dermal papilla
One of many finger-like projections that increase surface area

Capillaries
Tiny blood vessels that supply oxygen and nutrients to tissues, while collecting waste

Epidermis
Outer protective layer consisting of tough, flat cells

Dermis
Layer containing blood vessels, glands, and nerve endings

Subcutaneous fat
Acts as an insulator, shock absorber, and energy store

Sweat gland
A coiled knot of tubes secreting watery sweat

Sweat duct
Conveys sweat to skin surface

Arteriole
Supplies oxygenated blood

Venule
Carries away waste

HAIR GROWTH

Hairs are rods of dead, flattened cells filled with keratin and have a mainly protective role. The hair's root, or bulb, is buried in a pit, the follicle. As extra cells add to the root, the hair lengthens from its base. Different kinds of hairs grow at varying rates, with scalp hairs lengthening about 0.3mm ($^1/_{100}$ in) each day. However, hair does not grow continuously. After three to four years, the follicle goes into a rest phase and the hair may detach at its base. Three to six months later, the follicle activates again and begins to produce a new hair.

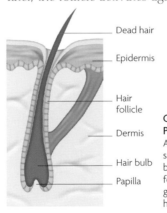

Dead hair
Epidermis
Hair follicle
Dermis
Hair bulb
Papilla

REST PHASE
The hair grows to its maximum length. Activity in the follicle stops and the hair dies.

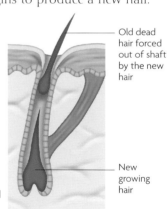

Old dead hair forced out of shaft by the new hair

New growing hair

GROWTH PHASE
A new hair sprouts at the base of the follicle. As it grows, the dead hair is shed.

NAIL STRUCTURE

Fingernails and toenails are hard plates made of a tough protein called keratin. Growth takes place under a fold of flesh (cuticle) at the nail base. An area called the nail matrix adds keratinized cells to the nail root, and the whole nail is continuously pushed forward along the nail bed towards its free edge. Most nails grow about 0.5mm ($^1/_{50}$ in) each week, with fingernails lengthening faster than toenails.

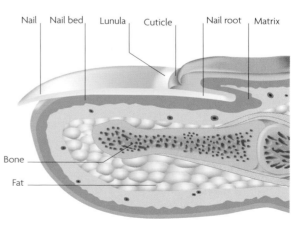

Nail | Nail bed | Lunula | Cuticle | Nail root | Matrix
Bone
Fat

CROSS-SECTION THROUGH NAIL AND FINGER

SKIN AND EPITHELIAL TISSUES

SKIN PLAYS A VITAL ROLE IN ENCLOSING AND PROTECTING THE DELICATE UNDERLYING TISSUES; IT IS ALSO IMPORTANT IN PROVIDING THE SENSE OF TOUCH. AS AN OUTER LAYER, SKIN IS A SPECIALIZED TYPE OF EPITHELIUM. EPITHELIAL TISSUES ARE WIDESPREAD IN THE BODY, PROVIDING COVERINGS AND LININGS FOR ALMOST ALL MAJOR BODY PARTS AND ORGANS.

COMPLEXITIES OF TOUCH

The sense of touch is based in the lower of the two skin layers, the dermis. Touch operates by means of microsensors – the endings of tiny nerve cells, which act as receptors for various kinds of physical change, from the lightest contact to heavy, painful pressure. There is a wide array of microsensors, the number and density of which vary from one location to another on the body. On average, a skin patch approximately the size of a fingernail contains about 1,000 receptors of various kinds. However, the skin on the fingertips has more than 3,000 receptors that detect light touch for precise feeling. There are also receptor fibres wrapped around the bases of hairs, in their follicles (pits) within the dermis. Different types of receptor respond more readily to certain types of stimulation, but almost all respond to most stimuli. It is thought that the brain runs through what looks like random incoming nerve signals but recognizes, then picks out, repeating patterns to determine if an object touched is hard or soft, hot or cold, rough or smooth, wet or dry, or static or moving.

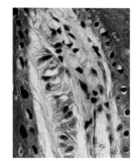

LIGHT-TOUCH SENSOR
This microscope view shows a Meissner's corpuscle (green) in a fingertip. It is important for light discriminatory touch.

TYPES OF SENSOR

Each type of microsensor is set at a particular depth in the dermis that best suits its function. The largest receptors, Pacinian corpuscles, are located at the deepest level, near the base of the dermis. Sensors for light touch are located near or just in the epidermal layer.

Free nerve endings
Branching, usually unsheathed sensors of temperature, light touch, pressure, and pain. They are found all over the body and in all types of connective tissue.

Meissner's corpuscle
Encapsulated nerve ending in the skin's upper dermis, especially on the palms, soles, lips, eyelids, external genitals, and nipples. Respond to light pressure.

Merkels's disc
Naked (unencapsulated) receptors, usually in the upper dermis or lower epidermis, especially in non-hairy areas. They sense faint touch and light pressure.

Ruffini corpuscle
Encapsulated receptor in the skin and deeper tissue that reacts to continuous touch and pressure. In joint capsules, it responds to rotational movement.

Pacinian corpuscle
Large, covered receptor located deep in the dermis, as well as in the bladder wall, and near joints and muscles. It senses stronger, more sustained pressure.

Superficial nerve ending
Penetrates the epidermis; occur everywhere in the skin and include free nerve endings

Meissner's corpuscle
Upper dermal nerve ending; mostly located just below the base of the epidermis

Merkels's disc receptor
Junction nerve ending; sited just above or below the boundary between epidermis and dermis

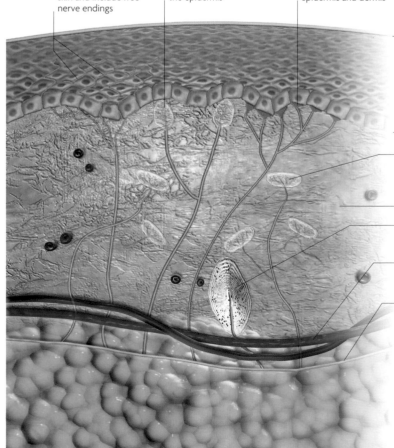

Epidermis
Layer of constantly renewing cells; multiply at base; harden and die as they move outward

Ruffini corpuscle
Mid-dermal nerve ending; mostly scattered through the middle or lower layers of the dermis

Dermis
Mix of collagen, elastin, and other connective tissue; houses most of the touch receptors

Pacinian corpuscle
Located deep in the dermis

Blood vessel
Brings nourishment to the skin layers and touch receptors

Nerve fibre
Receptors' nerve fibres gather into bundles; convey signals to the main nerves

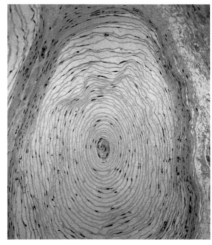

DEEP-PRESSURE SENSOR
Pacinian corpuscles have a multi-layered structure and are the largest of the skin receptors, in some areas being more than 1mm ($\frac{1}{25}$ in) long.

SKIN MICRORECEPTORS

Deformation of the layers within a receptor, and expansion or contraction due to temperature changes, will generate nerve impulses. The impulses travel along the receptor's nerve fibre, whichs join with bundles of other fibres in the deep dermis or below. Most receptors "fire" nerve signals infrequently and irregularly when not stimulated, increasing their firing rate as the skin is touched.

TEMPERATURE REGULATION

One of the skin's functions is to contribute to thermoregulation – maintenance of a constant body temperature. It does this in three main ways: widening and narrowing of blood vessels, sweating, and hair adjustment. If the body becomes hot, blood vessels in the dermis widen (vasodilate) to allow extra blood flow so more warmth can be lost from the surface. The skin may look flushed, and sweat oozes from sweat glands and evaporates, drawing away body heat. If the body is cold, the peripheral blood vessels narrow (vasoconstrict) to minimize heat loss, and sweating is reduced. Tiny body hairs are pulled upright by the erector pili muscles to trap air as an insulting layer.

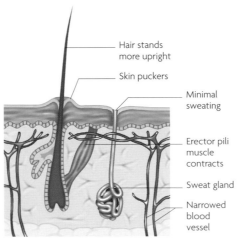

Hair stands more upright
Skin puckers
Minimal sweating
Erector pili muscle contracts
Sweat gland
Narrowed blood vessel

Hair lies flatter
Increased sweating
Erector pili muscle relaxes
Widened blood vessel

FEELING COLD
Tiny body hairs, raised by contraction of the erector pili muscles, create small mounds known as goose pimples at their bases. The peripheral blood vessels constrict, and sweat glands reduce their activity.

FEELING HOT
Tiny body hairs lie flatter as the erector pili muscles relax, and the small mounds at their bases disappear. Dermal blood vessels dilate, increasing blood flow, and the sweat glands raise their output of sweat.

EPITHELIUM

Epithelial tissue, also called epithelium, is an important structural element that acts as a lining or covering for other body tissues. Epithelium can be classified according to the shape and layout pattern of individual cells (see below), and also the arrangement of cells into one or more layers. Most epithelial tissues form membranes and are specialized for protection, absorption, or secretion. They do not contain blood vessels, and their cells are usually anchored to, and stabilized by, a basement membrane. There may be other cell types present, such as goblet cells that secrete blobs of mucus for release onto the surface.

PSEUDOSTRATIFIED EPITHELIUM

This type of columnar epithelium seems to be arranged in vertical layers. However, it actually consists of a single layer of cells of varying shapes and heights. The nuclei (control centres) of the different cell types are also at different levels, creating a layered (stratified) effect. Taller cells may be specialized into mucus-making goblet cells or ciliated cells that trap foreign particles. This type of epithelium occurs in the airway linings, and the excretory and male reproductive passages and ducts.

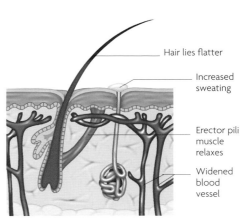

Cilia
Surface of goblet cell

TRACHEAL LINING
The electron micrograph shows cilia (green strands) projecting from the epithelial cells of the throat (trachea). Mucus-secreting goblet cells between the cilia possess tiny microvilli (yellow-brown).

TYPES OF EPITHELIAL CELL

The cells that make up the epithelial layers are usually classified according to their shape. Since most epithelia, as a consequence of their locations, are subject to friction, compression, and similar physical wear, they divide rapidly to replace themselves.

Squamous
Plate-like or flattened cells, wider than deep, resembling paving slabs or crazy-paving; flattened nuclei.

Features: Cells allow selective diffusion, or permeability, allowing certain substances to pass, owing to thinness of layer.

Cuboidal
Cube- or box-shaped cells, occasionally hexagonal or polygonal; nucleus usually in cell centre.

Features: Substances absorbed from one side of the layer can be altered as they pass through the cytoplasm of the cuboidal cells, before leaving.

Columnar
Tall, slim cells, often square, rectangular, or polygonal; large, oval nucleus near cell base.

Features: Cells protect and separate other tissues; may be topped with cilia for movement of fluid outside the cell or microvilli for absorption.

Glandular
Epithelial cells modified for secretion, usually cuboidal or columnar with secretory granules or vacuoles.

Features: Layers of these cells may be infolded to form pits, pockets, grooves, or ducts, as in sweat glands.

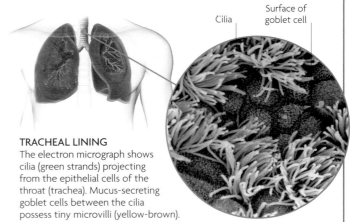

BLADDER LINING
The electron micrograph shows the tightly packed epithelial cells of the bladder lining. They are soft and pliable, enabling them to stretch as the bladder fills with urine.

Rounded epithelial cell

SIMPLE AND LAYERED EPITHELIUM

Simple epithelium is composed of a single layer of cells. It is often found in areas where substances need to pass through easily, a single-cell thickness offering minimal resistance. Layered (stratified) epithelium has two or more layers and is better for protection. Some complex epithelia have more than five layers, but two or three is more usual. The cells may be different shapes in the different layers.

EPITHELIUM IN THE EYE
The eye contains two types of epithelium: simple epithelium in the pigmented layer of the retina, and stratified squamous epithelium in the domed front "window" of the cornea.

TRANSITIONAL EPITHELIUM

This epithelial tissue is similar to layered (stratified) epithelium but has the ability to stretch without tearing. There are usually columnar cells in the basal layer, which become gradually more rounded in the upper layers. As these layers stretch, the cells flatten, or become more squamous. Transitional epithelium is well suited to the urinary system, where it lines areas within the kidney, ureters, bladder, and urethra. It allows these tubes to bulge as urine flows through at pressure. The epithelium also secretes mucus that protects it from acidic urine.

CORNEA STRUCTURE
The epithelium covering the cornea is transparent and about five layers thick. It permits light rays to enter the eye.

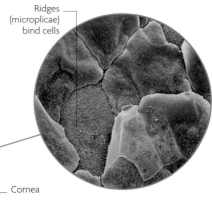

Ridges (microplicae) bind cells

Retina

Cornea

SKIN AND HAIR DEFENSIVE FUNCTIONS

Skin is the body's first line of defence against potential harm. As such, it is well equipped to prevent physical damage due to its supple, cushioned qualities. The epidermal cells that form skin's outermost layers are tightly knit together, but allow a certain amount of pliability. The cells are almost entirely full of the tough protein keratin, which resists attack by many kinds of chemicals. The natural secretion of sebum from the millions of sebaceous glands, each associated with a hair follicle, is slightly oily at body temperature and spreads easily. It furnishes the skin with partially water-repellent and antibiotic qualities, inhibiting the growth of certain microorganisms, and prevents hairs from becoming too brittle.

ULTRAVIOLET DEFENCES

The Sun's rays include a spectrum of colour wavelengths, including infrared or IR rays (the warming component) and ultraviolet, UV, rays. Both UV-A and UV-B wavelengths are invisible to human eyes, but exposure to the latter, in particular, is linked to forms of skin cancer (see opposite). Skin's self-defence is its dark colouring substance, or pigment, melanin. This forms a screen in the upper epidermis that shields the actively multiplying cells in the base of the epidermis.

MELANIN PRODUCTION
Melanocytes are melanin-producing cells in the base of the epidermis. They make parcels of melanin granules, melanosomes, which pass into surrounding cells.

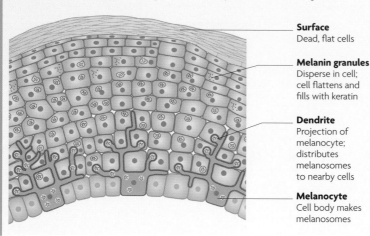

Surface
Dead, flat cells

Melanin granules
Disperse in cell; cell flattens and fills with keratin

Dendrite
Projection of melanocyte; distributes melanosomes to nearby cells

Melanocyte
Cell body makes melanosomes

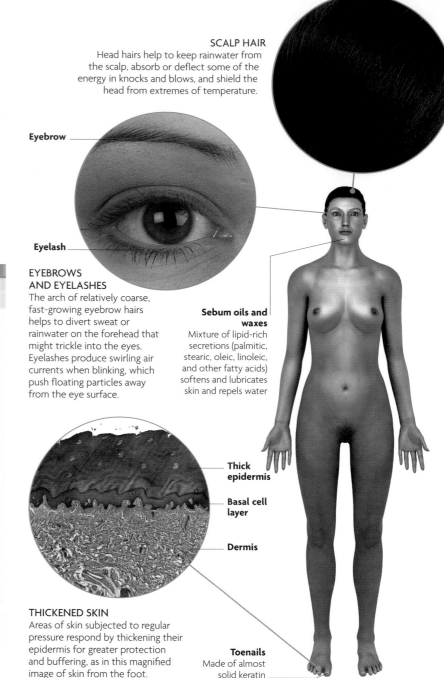

SCALP HAIR
Head hairs help to keep rainwater from the scalp, absorb or deflect some of the energy in knocks and blows, and shield the head from extremes of temperature.

Eyebrow

Eyelash

EYEBROWS AND EYELASHES
The arch of relatively coarse, fast-growing eyebrow hairs helps to divert sweat or rainwater on the forehead that might trickle into the eyes. Eyelashes produce swirling air currents when blinking, which push floating particles away from the eye surface.

Sebum oils and waxes
Mixture of lipid-rich secretions (palmitic, stearic, oleic, linoleic, and other fatty acids) softens and lubricates skin and repels water

Thick epidermis

Basal cell layer

Dermis

Toenails
Made of almost solid keratin

THICKENED SKIN
Areas of skin subjected to regular pressure respond by thickening their epidermis for greater protection and buffering, as in this magnified image of skin from the foot.

SKIN PIGMENTATION

Skin colour depends on the type and quantity of two main melanin pigments – reddish pheomelanin and brown-black eumelanin – in the epidermis, and on the way the pigment granules are distributed. Each melanocyte has finger-like dendrites that contact 30–40 surrounding cells (basal keratinocytes). The melanocyte produces its pigments as granules within membrane-bound organelles called melanosomes. These move along the dendrites and are "nipped off" into the cells. Darker skin has larger melanocytes with more melanosomes, which break down to give even pigmentation through skin cells. Lighter skin has smaller melanocytes and grouped melanosomes. Exposure to UV light stimulates melanocytes so the skin becomes darker, or tanned.

COLOUR VARIATION
Darker skin tends to have larger melanin-making cells that produce more, larger, denser melanosomes, in comparison to lighter skin. The former release their pigment granules while the latter's granules stay clumped.

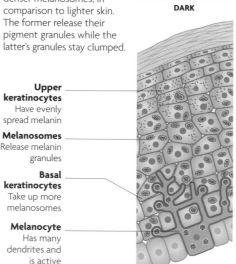

DARK | **INTERMEDIATE** | **LIGHT**

Upper keratinocytes
Have evenly spread melanin

Melanosomes
Release melanin granules

Basal keratinocytes
Take up more melanosomes

Melanocyte
Has many dendrites and is active

Surface
Tile-like cells

Upper keratinocytes
Contain little spread-out melanin

Melanosomes
Stay intact

Basal keratinocytes
Take up fewer, lighter melanosomes

Melanocyte
Has few dendrites; not very active

SKIN INJURY AND DISORDERS

SKIN CONTAINS SOME OF THE FASTEST-MULTIPLYING CELLS IN THE BODY. SEVERAL OF ITS DISORDERS RESULT FROM PROBLEMS IN THIS SELF-RENEWAL SYSTEM, INCLUDING VARIOUS GROWTHS AND TUMOURS. AS THE BODY'S FIRST LINE OF DEFENCE, SKIN IS SUSCEPTIBLE TO INJURY, ALLERGIC REACTION IN THE FORM OF RASHES, AND INFECTION BY BACTERIA, FUNGI, OR OTHER MICROORGANISMS.

SKIN CANCERS

SEVERAL TYPES OF MALIGNANCIES, OF VARYING SEVERITY, AFFECT SKIN. MOST ARE ASSOCIATED WITH PROLONGED EXPOSURE TO THE HARMFUL RADIATION IN SUNLIGHT.

Basal cell carcinoma usually develops slowly and is unlikely to spread to other body parts (metastasize). Typically it starts as a small, smooth, painless lump, pink or brownish-grey, with a pearly or wax-like border. As it widens it may form a central depression with rolled edges. Squamous cell carcinoma can be due to prolonged exposure to ultraviolet (UV) rays or carcinogens such as tar and oil chemicals. It begins as a red or red-brown lump with an irregular edge that is hard and painless, it may then weep and become ulcer-like. Malignant melanoma can develop from an existing mole, or as a fast-growing, dark-coloured, asymmetrical spot. Features include increasing size, an irregular border, itching, bleeding, and crusting. All of these types of skin cancer need prompt medical attention.

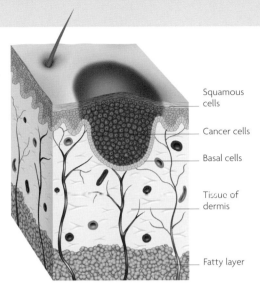

Squamous cells
Cancer cells
Basal cells
Tissue of dermis
Fatty layer

BASAL CELL CARCINOMA
Fast-dividing cells in the base of the epidermis are damaged by UV exposure and begin to multiply out of control, forming a mound of flattened, or squamous, cells. The growth remains localized within the epidermis.

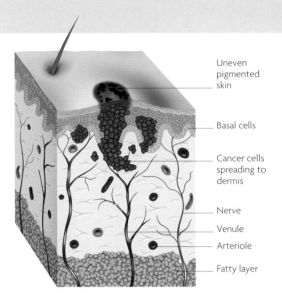

Uneven pigmented skin
Basal cells
Cancer cells spreading to dermis
Nerve
Venule
Arteriole
Fatty layer

MALIGNANT MELANOMA
Radiation damage to pigment-producing cells, called melanocytes, causes them to proliferate uncontrollably. A dark, irregular mass forms, while some cancer cells break into the dermis and may travel in the blood to other sites.

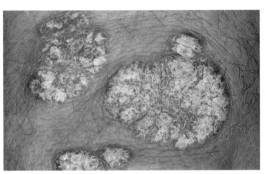

PSORASIS
There are several types of psoriasis, mostly characterized by intermittently itchy patches of red, thickened, scaly skin, as dead epidermal cells accumulate. Common sites are the knees, elbows, lower back, scalp, and behind the ears.

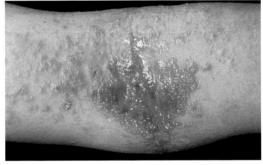

ECZEMA
A typical eczema rash is red, inflamed, and itchy, with small fluid-filled blisters or episodes of dry, scaly, thickened, and cracked skin. Common sites are the hands and creased areas of skin, such as the wrists, elbows, and knees.

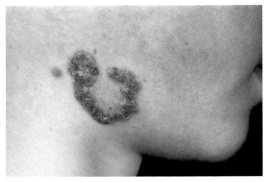

IMPETIGO
This bacterial infection is common on the face, most often around the nose and mouth. The skin reddens and develops fluid-filled blisters, which burst. This is followed by redness, weeping, and crusting that may itch.

VITILIGO
Depigmented patches of skin develop over months or years, especially on the face and hands, and usually before the age of 20. The areas are more distinct in people with dark skin. They do not carry any medical risks to health.

RASHES

MOST RASHES ARE AREAS OF SKIN INFLAMMATION. SOME ARE CONDITIONS OF THE SKIN ITSELF, OTHERS ARE PART GENERALIZED DISORDERS AFFECTING INTERNAL ORGANS.

Some skin rashes may be localized while others are more widespread. Localized rashes can occur on parts of the body exposed to, for example, sunlight, friction, or an irritant chemical. Some of these rashes have a strong inherited component, but often the actual cause or mechanism of rash formation is not clear. The condition may not pose a threat to survival, but it can be unsightly, affect quality of life, and require long-term control with self-help preventative measures and ongoing medications. Psoriasis is a common and widespread condition in which a patchy rash flares up now and again. Episodes may be triggered by infection, injury, stress, or as a side-effect of drug treatment. Eczema (a term that is mostly interchangeable with dermatitis) is one of the commonest skin conditions, especially in babies and children, although many people grow out of it. It is often linked to allergic tendencies such as asthma and perennial, or seasonal, rhinitis (hay fever), and may flare up during adolescence and adulthood. Impetigo is a blistering of the skin caused by bacterial infection, typically through a surface breach such as a cut, cold sore (*Herpes simplex* virus), or scratched, weeping eczema. Vitiligo has an autoimmune basis, where the body makes antibodies that attack the skin's pigment-making cells, melanocytes. It occurs in patchy areas, often symmetrically, over the body; in about one-third of cases, the pigmentation spontaneously returns.

SKIN MARKS AND BLEMISHES

Marks, swellings, and blemishes on the skin include small, pus-filled spots known as pustules, larger ones called boils, and acne, which usually occurs in the teenage years. Other marks or enlargements may be caused by a local increase in cell numbers, as in warts and moles. Swellings may also be due to different types of cyst. Some blemishes are caused by external factors, such as pressure and exposure to sunlight, or they can result from viral infection.

ACNE

A RASH OF SPOTS THAT APPEAR, USUALLY ON THE FACE, DUE TO BLOCKAGE AND INFLAMMATION OF GLANDS IN THE SKIN.

In acne vulgaris, the sebaceous glands produce an excessive amount of the oily-waxy secretion, sebum. This reacts in contact with air and forms a plug in the skin pore, which may be dark with pigmentation (not dirt), as a blackhead or comedone, or pale, as a whitehead. A combination of trapped sebum, dead cells, and bacterial infection inflame the area, causing a pustule. Acne is a common problem at puberty due to hormone surges.

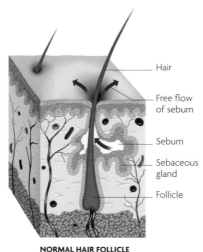
Hair
Free flow of sebum
Sebum
Sebaceous gland
Follicle
NORMAL HAIR FOLLICLE

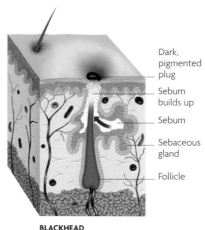
Dark, pigmented plug
Sebum builds up
Sebum
Sebaceous gland
Follicle
BLACKHEAD

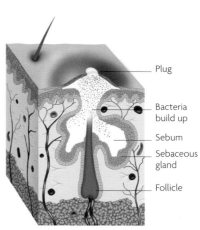
Plug
Bacteria build up
Sebum
Sebaceous gland
Follicle
INFECTED FOLLICLE

MOLE

A MOLE IS A FLAT OR RAISED MARK THAT VARIES IN SHAPE, COLOUR, AND TEXTURE, AND MAY BE SINGLE OR NUMEROUS.

A mole, or naevus, is a localized overproduction and aggregation of the skin's pigment cells (melanocytes), with increased amounts of melanin pigment. Moles are very common – most adults have 10–20 moles by the age of 30 years. They can occur almost anywhere on the body and are variable in size, but usually less than 1cm (⅖in) across. Rarely, moles become malignant, and any change in size or appearance, itching, or bleeding, should be discussed with a doctor.

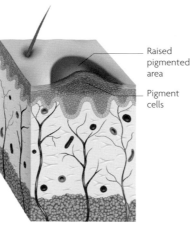
Raised pigmented area
Pigment cells
CROSS-SECTION OF A MOLE
Although raised to the exterior, the area of pigmentation in this mole does not extend to cells beneath the epidermis.

CYST

A HARMLESS, SAC-LIKE SWELLING UNDER THE SKIN THAT CONTAINS FLUID OR SEMI-SOLID MATERIALS IS CALLED A CYST.

The most common type of cyst is a sebaceous cyst, or wen, that forms in a hair follicle. A cyst contains sebaceous secretions and dead cells, which are restrained in a strong bag-like capsule. Its surface mound is usually smooth, and some cysts have a paler or darker central region. Common sites include the scalp, face, trunk, and genitals, although they can occur just about anywhere on the body. Treatment may be needed if the cyst becomes enlarged, unsightly, painful, or infected.

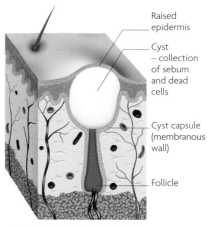
Raised epidermis
Cyst – collection of sebum and dead cells
Cyst capsule (membranous wall)
Follicle
CROSS-SECTION OF A CYST
The epidermis is stretched and raised into a dome-like lump where this sebaceous cyst protrudes from the dermis.

BOIL

FOUND ON THE SKIN, A BOIL IS A RED, INFLAMED, PUS-FILLED, TENDER AREA CAUSED BY A BACTERIAL INFECTION.

A boil is a collection of pus inside a hair follicle or a sebaceous gland; it may extend to both. Usually a result of bacterial infection, especially from various types of *Staphylococcus*, a boil starts as a small red lump. The bacteria multiply within the follicle or gland and the area becomes tender and swells as pus accumulates and "gathers" into a white or yellow head at the boil's centre. A cluster of boils may link to form a carbuncle. Recurrent boils may signify an underlying disorder.

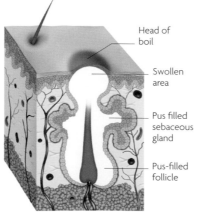
Head of boil
Swollen area
Pus filled sebaceous gland
Pus-filled follicle
CROSS-SECTION OF A BOIL
Both the hair follicle and the sebaceous gland are filled with pus causing a red and tender swelling in the overlying skin.

WART

A WART IS SMALL GROWTH CAUSED BY A VIRAL INFECTION; IT MAY BE FLAT OR RAISED AND SMOOTH OR ROUGH.

Warts are due to infection of the skin by the human papilloma virus (HPV). The virus invades the skin and causes a localized overgrowth of epidermal cells. Excess cells are pushed upward and outward to form a lump on the skin's surface. Warts may be described as common or flat and may occur in groups called crops. Warts on the sole are known as plantar warts and are flattened into the skin, causing pain. Warts often disappear of their own accord, but this may take some time.

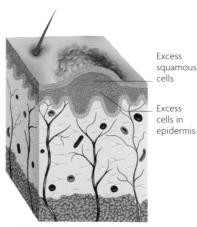
Excess squamous cells
Excess cells in epidermis
CROSS-SECTION OF A WART
Over-proliferation of epidermal cells causes this typical appearance of a common wart on the surface of the skin.

WOUNDS

WHEN THE SKIN'S SURFACE IS DAMAGED BY WOUNDING, HEALING CAN PROCEED ON ITS OWN OR WITH MEDICAL HELP.

Wounds may occur by accident, or as incisions during surgery. How well a wound heals depends on its extent and depth, the condition and alignment of the edges, the age and health of the sufferer, and the prevention of infection. A well-closed, clean wound usually heals in a few weeks and leaves hardly a blemish. An open, jagged-edged wound takes longer to heal and may leave a puckered scar. The healing process can be aided by stitching (suturing) or adhesive closures.

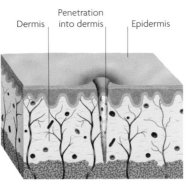

PUNCTURE WOUND
Punctures are small in area but deep in penetration. Healing is usually quick but infection is a risk, from microbes entering deep tissue – especially the tetanus bacterium (*Clostridium tetani*) found in soil.

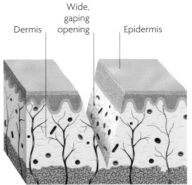

CUT
Neat-edged cuts usually heal with only minimal scarring if they are properly cleaned, closed to promote skin-edge healing, and covered to keep out infection. Deeper cuts may need stitches (sutures) to avoid scars.

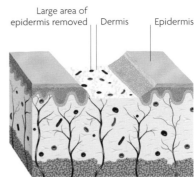

ABRASION
Grazes, or abrasions, may scrape a wide area of skin, damaging many nerve endings and causing considerable pain. Abrasions of the epidermis usually heal with no scar. Deeper abrasions are more likely to leave a scar.

BURNS, BRUISES, BLISTERS, AND SUNBURN

VARIOUS TYPES OF TRAUMA AND HEAT CAN HARM THE SKIN AND CAUSE PROBLEMS, SUCH AS BLISTERS FROM EXCESSIVE FRICTION OR PRESSURE, AND BURNS.

Burns may be caused by heat, electricity, radioactivity, or chemicals, and can cause extensive and, sometimes, life-threatening cell damage. A contusion, or bruise, is a discoloured area of skin caused by bleeding into underlying tissues, usually due to physical impact. Bruising around the eye is called a "black eye". Local physical trauma, such as rubbing and pressure, may lead to a raised, fluid-filled area called a blister. Blisters can also be caused by heat, including the sun's ultraviolet (UV) rays. Sunburn is skin damage as a result of acute or prolonged overexposure to the sun's UV rays. The skin firstly gets red, hot, swollen, and painful, followed by peeling. Excessive sun exposure, without adequate protection, can lead to skin cancer.

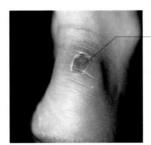

Red, inflamed skin

BURN
The skin is reddened (left) and the epidermis damaged in the region of a burn. If the dermis beneath is also affected, blisters soon form.

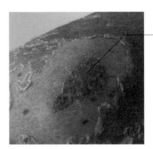

Bruise undergoes colour changes

BRUISE
Leaked blood cells break down causing the bruise to change colour from blue to brown yellow. Bruising for no apparent reason needs medical advice.

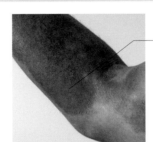

Burst blister requires covering

BLISTER
Fluid leaks from damaged vessels and collects under the skin's surface. New skin grows under the blister, and when it bursts, the old skin dries and peels away.

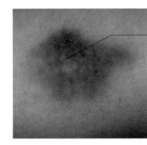

Dry skin peels or flakes

SUNBURN
After overexposure to the sun's UV rays, skin becomes hot, red, sore, and swollen; later it dries and peels. In severe cases, blisters may develop.

DANDRUFF AND ALOPECIA

DANDRUFF IS EXCESSIVE SHEDDING OF SKIN FLAKES FROM THE SCALP; ALOPECIA IS HAIR LOSS, SOMETIMES PERMANENT.

Dandruff is a harmless but unsightly and embarrassing condition, in which the normal shedding of skin cells from the scalp accelerates. The pale flakes show on the scalp and in the hair, and there may be itching. The condition is most common in young adults and may be linked to a yeast organism, *Pityrosporum ovale*. Alopecia is hair loss, which can be local or general, and temporary or permanent; it is most noticeable on the scalp. Various possible causes include sensitivity to testosterone, leading to male-pattern baldness, chemotherapy, and an autoimmune disorder – alopecia areata.

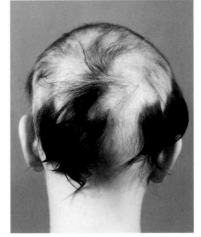

ALOPECIA AREATA
In this condition, hair is lost in patches over the scalp, leading to bald areas surrounded by shorter, broken hairs. The hair usually grows again over a few months. In rare cases, the disease can cause hair loss through the whole body and be permanent.

INGROWN NAIL

THE NAIL CURVES IN ALONG ONE OR BOTH SIDE EDGES, FORCING ITS WAY INTO THE FLESH OF A FINGER OR TOE.

An ingrowing nail penetrates into the tissue along its sides, causing inflammation, discomfort, pain, and a risk of infection. The big toe is most commonly affected, and often in young males. It may be triggered by ill-fitting footwear that presses on the nail and toe, along with incorrect trimming of the free nail edge, which should be cut straight across rather than around the curve. A toe injury is another possible cause. Poor foot hygiene increases the risk of infection and worsens the problem. Minor surgery can be carried out to remove the ingrowing part of the nail and to destroy its nail bed to prevent regrowth.

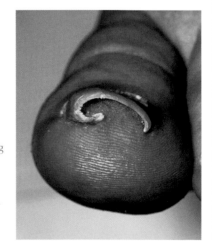

INGROWN TOENAIL
The nail of the big toe in this example clearly curves inward and cuts into the flesh. This produces redness, swelling, and broken skin, which may break and ooze pus, clear fluid, or even blood. The skin may react by overgrowing and enveloping the nail.

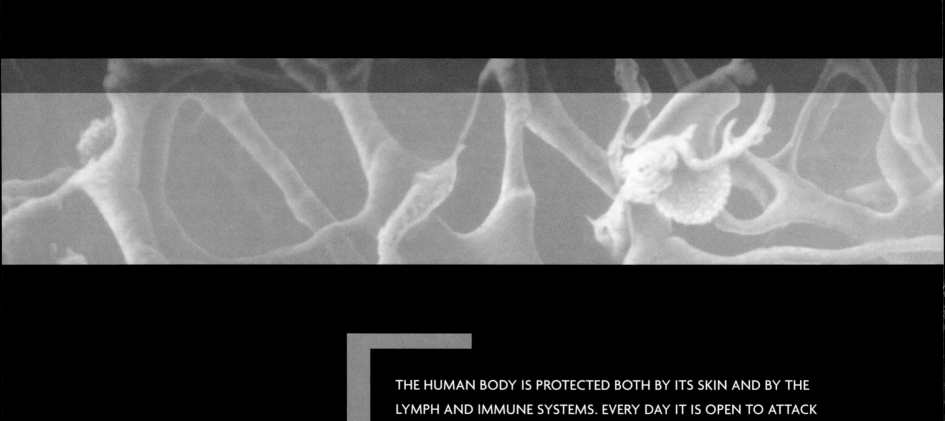

THE HUMAN BODY IS PROTECTED BOTH BY ITS SKIN AND BY THE
LYMPH AND IMMUNE SYSTEMS. EVERY DAY IT IS OPEN TO ATTACK
FROM TWO TYPES OF HOSTILITY. ONE IS EXTERNAL: THE DAILY
BATTLE AGAINST PHYSICAL HARM AND LINGERING GERMS. THE

LYMPH AND IMMUNITY

LYMPH AND IMMUNE SYSTEMS

SEVERAL SYSTEMS OF THE BODY HELP TO DEFEND IT AGAINST VARIOUS HAZARDS – SUCH AS THE SUN'S ULTRAVIOLET RAYS, EXCESSIVE HEAT, HARMFUL CHEMICALS, PHYSICAL DAMAGE, AND THE THREAT OF MICROORGANISMS SUCH AS BACTERIA AND VIRUSES. HOWEVER, THE IMMUNE SYSTEM, INCORPORATING THE LYMPHATIC SYSTEM, IS THE MAIN MEANS BY WHICH THE BODY IS PROTECTED FROM INVASION.

The lymphatic system is an integral part of the immune system and it plays an important part in the body's defence against disease. The active part of the system is lymph fluid, which starts life as the interstitial fluid that collects between cells throughout the body. It drains into networks of tiny capillaries in tissue spaces that unite to form larger vessels called lymphatics. Lymph nodes (lymph glands) are the filtering and storage areas of the system, and they are scattered along the routes of the lymphatics. Unlike blood, lymph is not pumped; instead it moves passively as lymphatics are compressed by contraction of surrounding muscles during movement. Lymph fluid enters the blood circulation via the left and right subclavian veins. Lymphoid organs, including the thymus and spleen, and lymphoid tissue, such as the tonsils and Peyer's patches, complete the system. They contain large numbers of specialized white blood cells, particularly lymphocytes, which protect the body against non-self material such as invading microorganisms.

Adenoids
Or pharyngeal tonsils; situated in rear of nasal cavity; help to filter incoming air and destroy microorganisms

Tonsils
Two pairs of tonsils (palatine and lingual) at back of mouth on either side of pharynx and at base of tongue help guard against inhaled microbes

Cervical (neck) nodes
Collect lymph from right or left side of the face, scalp, nasal chamber, and throat

Axillary (armpit) nodes
Drain lymph from arm, breast, chest wall and upper abdomen

Left subclavian vein
Point at which lymph from left and lower body enters blood after collecting in thoracic duct

Thymus gland
Site of maturation of immune-system T-cells (T-lymphocytes); T-cells develop from stem cells, which migrate here from bone marrow

Spleen
Largest lymph organ; spleen acts as store for some types of lymphocyte and as a major site for filtering blood

Peyer's patch
One of a few clusters of lymphoid nodules in lower part of small intestine; helps to protect against microbes ingested in food

Right lymphatic duct
Collects lymph from upper-right quadrant of body, including right arm and right sides of head and chest

Right subclavian vein
One of two main exit points at which lymph drains into blood system

Thoracic duct
Or left lymphatic duct; collects lymph fluid from both legs, abdomen, left arm, and left sides of head and chest

Cisterna chyli
Enlarged lymph vessel formed from vessels that converge from legs and lower body; eventually narrows into thoracic duct

Supratrochlear node
Collects lymph from hand and forearm

Lumbar lymph nodes
Drains lymph from abdominal organs

External iliac nodes
Receive lymph from organs of lower abdomen

360-DEGREE VIEW

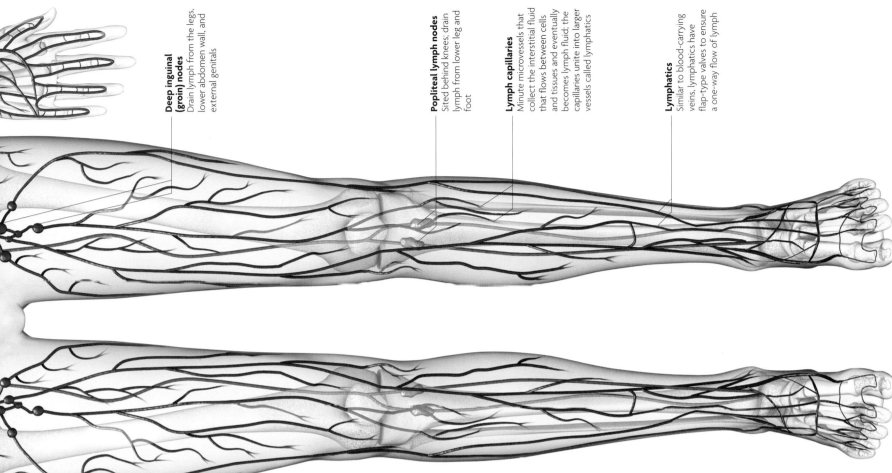

Deep inguinal (groin) nodes
Drain lymph from the legs, lower abdomen wall, and external genitals

Popliteal lymph nodes
Sited behind knees; drain lymph from lower leg and foot

Lymph capillaries
Minute microvessels that collect the interstitial fluid that flows between cells and tissues and eventually becomes lymph fluid; the capillaries unite into larger vessels called lymphatics

Lymphatics
Similar to blood-carrying veins, lymphatics have flap-type valves to ensure a one-way flow of lymph

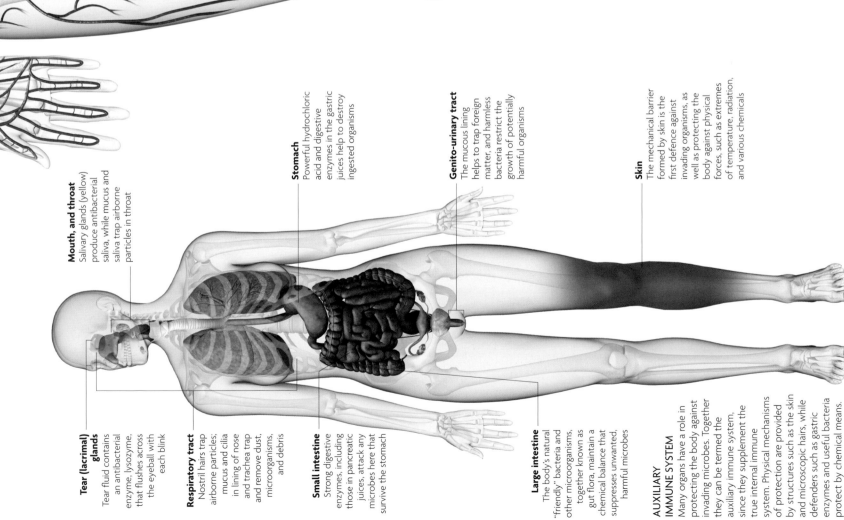

Tear (lacrimal) glands
Tear fluid contains an antibacterial enzyme, lysozyme, that flushes across the eyeball with each blink

Respiratory tract
Nostril hairs trap airborne particles; mucus and cilia in lining of nose and trachea trap and remove dust, microorganisms, and debris

Mouth, and throat
Salivary glands (yellow) produce antibacterial saliva, while mucus and saliva trap airborne particles in throat

Stomach
Powerful hydrochloric acid and digestive enzymes in the gastric juices help to destroy ingested organisms

Genito-urinary tract
The mucous lining helps to trap foreign matter, and harmless bacteria restrict the growth of potentially harmful organisms

Small intestine
Strong digestive enzymes, including those in pancreatic juices, attack any microbes here that survive the stomach

Large intestine
The body's natural "friendly" bacteria and other microorganisms, together known as gut flora, maintain a chemical balance that suppresses unwanted, harmful microbes

Skin
The mechanical barrier formed by skin is the first defence against invading organisms, as well as protecting the body against physical forces, such as extremes of temperature, radiation, and various chemicals

AUXILIARY IMMUNE SYSTEM

Many organs have a role in protecting the body against invading microbes. Together they can be termed the auxiliary immune system, since they supplement the true internal immune system. Physical mechanisms of protection are provided by structures such as the skin and microscopic hairs, while defenders such as gastric enzymes and useful bacteria protect by chemical means.

IMMUNE SYSTEM

THE ADAPTABLE SYSTEM OF BODY DEFENCES CENTRES ON SPECIALIZED WHITE BLOOD CELLS CALLED LYMPHOCYTES. THESE RESPOND TO INVASION BY VARIED MICROORGANISMS. THE COMPLEXITIES OF THE SYSTEM AIM TO CREATE THE CONDITION OF IMMUNITY, IN WHICH, AFTER THE FIRST ATTACK, THE BODY IS PROTECTED OR RESISTANT TO FUTURE INCURSIONS BY EACH PARTICULAR TYPE OF MICROORGANISM.

LYMPH NODES

The lymph nodes (or "glands") are vital to the body's defence system – they produce and harbour immune cells (lymphocytes) that protect the body from disease. Lymph nodes are scattered throughout the body and also concentrated in groups (see p.157). Each node is a mass of lymphatic tissue divided into compartments by partitions of connective tissue known as trabeculae. Lymph fluid from most tissues or organs flows through one or more lymph nodes, where it is filtered and cleaned, before draining into the venous bloodstream. Several smaller lymphatics (vessels) bring lymph to the node, and one larger vessel carries it away. The lymph vessels have valves to ensure a one-way flow of fluid.

INSIDE A NODE
Lymph nodes vary in diameter from 1 to 25mm (¹/₂₅ to 1in), although they can swell during infection or illness. Covered in a fibrous capsule, they contain sinuses, where many scavenging white blood cells, called macrophages, ingest bacteria as well as other foreign matter and debris.

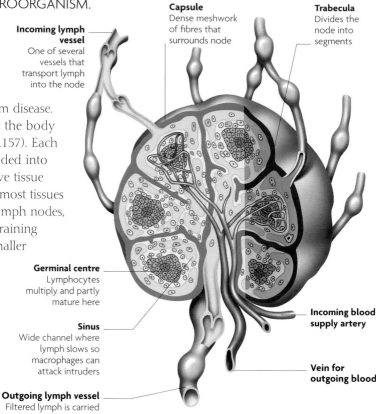

Incoming lymph vessel
One of several vessels that transport lymph into the node

Capsule
Dense meshwork of fibres that surrounds node

Trabecula
Divides the node into segments

Germinal centre
Lymphocytes multiply and partly mature here

Sinus
Wide channel where lymph slows so macrophages can attack intruders

Outgoing lymph vessel
Filtered lymph is carried away by only one vessel

Incoming blood supply artery

Vein for outgoing blood

WHITE CELL TYPES

There are numerous types of white blood cell, known by the general name of leucocytes. Some grow and mature into other types. All are derived from the bone marrow.

Monocyte
Largest cell in the blood, with big and rounded, or indented, nucleus; engulfs pathogens.

Lymphocyte
Chief immune cell, with large nucleus that almost fills the cell; either B or T, depending on development.

Neutrophil
Granulocyte (having many small particles in the cytoplasm) with a multi-lobed nucleus; engulfs pathogens.

Basophil
Circulating granulocyte with lobed nucleus; involved in allergic reactions.

Eosinophil
Granulocyte that is important during allergic reactions; B-shaped nucleus; destroys antigen–antibody complexes.

LOCAL INFECTION

If harmful microbes enter body tissues, both the inflammatory and immune responses act swiftly to limit their spread. The infection may be confined to a naturally defined site, such as the boundary between two sets of tissues. White blood cells and invaders, living and dead, accumulate, along with fluids, toxins, and general debris. The resulting mixture is known as pus, and if it gathers in a localized area, this is an abscess. As the pus collects, it puts pressure on surrounding structures. This may cause discomfort and pain, especially if the surroundings have no flexibility, as in a tooth abscess. The pressure of a brain abscess may have serious consequences for brain functioning.

DENTAL ABSCESS
Microbes gain access through a decayed region of enamel and dentine, infect the pulp, and spread into the root, where pus collects. As pus presses on the pulp nerves, it causes the pain of toothache.

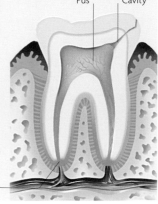

Pus **Cavity**

Abscess

NON-SPECIFIC RESPONSE

The immune responses involve attacks on specific microorganisms or the toxins (harmful substances) they produce, as shown opposite. Non-specific responses react to any kind of damage, such as a physical knock, a burn, extreme cold, corrosive chemicals, and various forms of radiation, as well as living invaders, ranging from microbes to large parasites, such as worms and flukes. The main non-specific defensive response is inflammation (see pp.160–61). Damaged tissue releases chemicals that attract white blood cells. The walls of the capillaries, the smallest blood vessels at the site, become more permeable and porous to allow the passage of white blood cells, defensive chemicals, and fluids, which accumulate as the battle proceeds. The white blood cells surround, engulf, and destroy the invading pathogens. The blood may also clot to form a barrier that not only seals the leak but also prevents further microbial penetration.

INFLAMED TISSUE
The four common signs of inflammation are redness, swelling, increased warmth, and discomfort or pain. They occur after any form of harm such as injury, irritation, or infection, in order to limit the damage and initiate repair and healing.

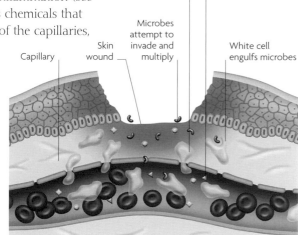

White cells squeeze out of capillary

Defence chemicals diffuse from capillary

Microbes attempt to invade and multiply

Capillary

Skin wound

White cell engulfs microbes

SPECIFIC RESPONSE

Specific responses may occur alongside non-specific reactions such as inflammation, or follow if the infection persists. There are two main types of specific defence: cell-mediated and antibody-mediated (humoral) immunity. Both depend on the actions of lymphoctyes of two different kinds – B and T lymphocytes. B cells make protein antibodies known as gammaglobulins. These react against antigens (foreign protein substances), which differ from the body's own natural proteins. T cells multiply and attack the pathogen cells.

CELL-MEDIATED IMMUNITY

The cellular or cell-mediated type of immunity involves various types of T lymphocyte or T cell, named because they develop inside the thymus gland. Once a T cell recognizes the antigen, it multiplies rapidly and its offspring differentiate into several types. Helper T cells activate both B cells to help antibody-mediated immunity and macrophages to engulf the microbes and debris. Killer (cytotoxic) T cells attack microorganisms as well as any body cells infected with them, using powerful proteins called lymphokines. Suppressor T cells inhibit the response of other cells to the invading microbes.

Transport to lymph node
Macrophages travel in blood and lymph

Invading microbe
Pathogenic (harmful) microorganisms such as bacteria

Antigen

Phagocytosis
Macrophage engulfs microorganisms and their antigens

Lymph node
Macrophages engulf microbes and debris and present antigens to T cells

ANTIBODY-MEDIATED IMMUNITY

Whereas T cells can attack invading organisms directly, the lymphocytes called B cells do so "remotely"' by producing chemicals called antibodies. These are generally Y or T shaped. Each type of antibody acts against a certain microorganism or "non-self" material by attaching to antigens on its surface. The presence of antigens triggers B cells to multiply. Some develop into plasma cells, which are the main antibody-producing cells. As with cell-mediated immunity, memory cells are produced, which can recognize the same antigen and initiate defence many years later.

Memory cell
Some T cells retain memory of the antigen for future defence

Killer T cell
Squeezes into bloodstream and travels to site of infection

Proliferation
Line, or clone, of T lymphocytes, specific to the antigen, multiplies and differentiates into helper, killer, suppressor, and memory cells

Presentation
Macrophage presents antigens from microbe to T cell

Recognition
Preprogrammed T cell recognizes antigen (even if never encountered before)

Helper T-cell
Stimulates antibody-mediated immunity by B cells

Macrophage
Attracted to site by lymphokines

Lymphokines
Proteins toxic to microbes made by killer T cells

Phagocytosis
Macrophage engulfs antigens

Memory B cell
Some B cells retain memory of the antigen from a previous infection

Proliferation
One line, or clone, of B lymphocytes, specific to the antigen, multiplies and differentiates into plasma and other cells

Recognition
Preprogrammed B cell recognizes antigen (even if never encountered before)

Plasma cell
Produces antibodies specific to antigen protein

Antibodies
Float in blood and other fluids

Macrophage
Engulfs antibody–antigen complex and other debris; shares this function with eosinophils

Presentation
Macrophage presents antigens from microbe to B cell

Antibody–antigen reaction
Antibodies stick to antigen sites on microbe, forming antibody–antigen complexes (immune complexes)

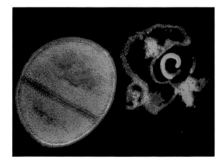

LYSED BACTERIUM
Complement causes dissolving, or lysis, of invaders such as bacterial cells by disrupting their outer membranes (cell shown right).

COMPLEMENT SYSTEM

Circulating in the blood are over 20 proteins and related substances or factors that form the complement system. The complement (or helping and enhancing) proteins are activated by antibodies, certain lymphokines made by the lymphoctyes called T cells (as shown above), bits of cell membrane or DNA, or other products of the battle against invading microorganisms. Once a complement reaction begins, it continues in a "cascade" fashion with one complement protein activating the next, and so on (similar to the cascade reactions of blood clotting). The complement system generally helps to destroy microbes, and prevent them attacking body cells, encourage the activity of white cells such as macrophages, widen blood vessels, and clear away the antigen–antibody complexes.

Additional help
The complement pathways can destroy microbes such as bacteria or viruses by the process of lysis

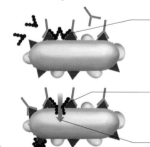

Complement protein binds to complex
Complement attaches to antibody–antigen complex of an invading microorganism

Complement cascade
Sequence of complement reactions produces more complement proteins

Membrane breached
Complement proteins break outer membrane

Swell and burst
Fluid rushes into microbe, which expands and bursts

INFLAMMATORY RESPONSE

INFLAMMATION IS THE BODY'S RAPID, GENERAL RESPONSE TO ANY KIND OF INSULT OR INJURY, SUCH AS PHYSICAL WOUNDS AND FOREIGN OBJECTS, INCLUDING INFECTING ORGANISMS, CHEMICAL TOXINS, HEAT, OR RADIATION.

Unlike the immune response, which is specific against certain invading substances, the inflammatory response is non-specific. It is a fast, generalized reaction that passes through defined phases and involves various types of white blood cells and defensive chemicals. The four cardinal signs of inflammation are redness, swelling, heat, and pain – known by the classical terms of rubor, tumor, calor, and dolor. The process aims to attack, break down, and remove any invading material, living or dead, and dispose of the body's own damaged cells and tissues, as well as initiate healing.

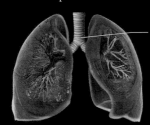

SITE OF DAMAGE
The trachea, or windpipe – the body's main airway

CAUSE OF INFLAMMATION

The respiratory system is under constant threat from tiny inhaled particles of dust and debris and attack by infecting microbes. Here, the lining (epithelium) of the windpipe (trachea) mounts an inflammatory response to dust and bacteria. In reality it usually occurs alongside the specific immune response (see p.158), which targets individual foreign substances.

DEFENSIVE CELLS

Various types of white blood cells (leucocytes) become involved in inflammation, including neutrophils and monocytes. The latter are immature leaving the blood vessels and enter the tissues, but rapidly develop into, active cells called macrophages that replace neutrophils.

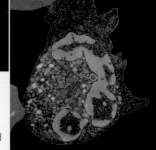

NEUTROPHILS
Among the first cells to take action, these are small but capable of engulfing several pieces of damaged tissue and bacteria.

MACROPHAGE
A single macrophage ("big eater") can consume up to 100 bacteria or similar-sized items before dying.

Red blood cell

Cells of capillary wall

Tufts of cilia
Hair-like projections borne by some cells of the tracheal lining; the cilia beat to remove protective mucus covering the cells

2 Physical damage
As the air current slows, the particles impact the tracheal lining and become trapped in the protective mucus secreted by some of the tracheal lining (epithelial) cells.

1 Causal items
Foreign particles such as micro-shards of glass-fibre and airborne bacteria sweep into the windpipe (trachea) on the current of inhaled air.

3 Physical damage
Sharp particles can fracture the epithelial cells, rupturing the delicate cell membranes.

Surface of epithelium

Foreign particle

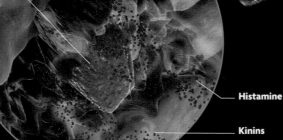

4 Initial spread
Messenger substances, such as histamine and kinins, leak from ruptured cells, especially "mast cells" scattered through the tissue.

Histamine

Kinins

Lung airways
A network of air passages that supply the lungs

PHAGOCYTOSIS

Various kinds of white blood cells can surround, engulf, and ingest smaller items, such as bacteria and cellular debris, in a process known as phagocytosis ("cell eating"). The cell exploits its ability to change shape and move, using the intracellular components of microtubules and microfilaments (see p.26) that form its flexible, mobile internal scaffolding. The ingestion usually takes less than one second, and the consumed material is gradually broken down by enzymes and other chemicals within the cell.

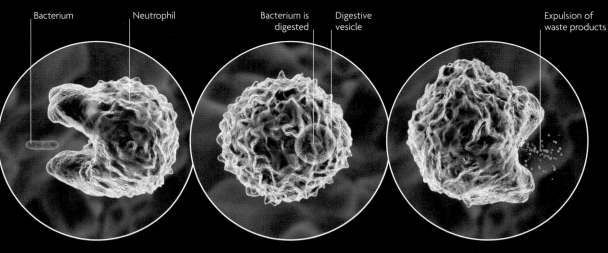

Bacterium   Neutrophil   Bacterium is digested   Digestive vesicle   Expulsion of waste products

1 ENGULFING STAGE
The white cell extends pseudopods ("false feet") towards and around the unwanted items – here a bacterium. The pseudopods merge to engulf them.

2 LYSIS STAGE
The items are trapped in phagocytic vesicles, which with enzyme-containing lysosomes form phagolysosomes, where lysis (breaking down) occurs.

3 EXOCYTOSIS STAGE
Harmless products of cell eating are expelled through the white blood cell's membrane, or in tiny membrane-bound exocytic vesicles to the extracellular fluid.

1 Capillaries dilate
Histamine stimulates vasodilation – the widening of blood vessels, especially capillaries. The cells forming capillary walls stretch to become thinner and narrow gaps appear between them, increasing their permeability – their tendency to allow fluids to pass through.

3 Fluid accumulation
Plasma and escaped fluids from damaged cells gather in tissue spaces, causing swelling. This presses on nerve endings, which helps to cause the fourth sign of inflammation – pain.

4 Neutrophils arrive
Released chemicals attract white blood cells, such as neutrophils. Neutrophils press themselves onto the inner surface of capillaries, a stage called margination. The neutrophils squeeze between the capillary wall cells, in a process called diapedesis, leaving the blood and entering the tissues.

2 Fluid leakage
Increased blood flow produces redness and heat. Plasma (blood's liquid component, pictured as yellow) leaks into the space between the cells, carrying various proteins such as fibrinogen, which helps blood to clot when the skin is broken.

Foreign particle

Bacterium

5 Neutrophils enter tissues
Neutrophils are attracted to the damage the by substances released by the disrupted cells. This chemically-stimulated movement is termed chemotaxis.

Particle
Remains lodged at site of cell damage and continues to release histamine and kinins (red and blue), which flow into the bloodstream

RESPONSE

Once an inflammatory response is triggered, blood flow to the damaged area is increased. The blood vessels, especially capillaries, widen and the capillary walls become thinner and more permeable, allowing plasma and fluid to leak into the space between the cells. Next, white blood cells, such as neutrophils, start to arrive. The neutrophils leave the blood and enter the tissue, drawn to the damaged area by chemicals released by the disrupted cells.

Bronchial tree
May be affected by inflammation, or the problem may remain restricted to a patch of the trachea

FIGHTING INFECTIONS

AN INFECTION OCCURS WHEN MICROSCOPIC ORGANISMS GAIN ENTRY INTO THE BODY, SURVIVE, MULTIPLY, AND DISRUPT NORMAL CELL FUNCTION. THE INFECTION MAY BE LOCALIZED, SUCH AS IN A PATCH OF SKIN OR IN A WOUND, OR SYSTEMIC, IN WHICH THE ORGANISMS ARE CARRIED AROUND THE BODY BY THE BLOOD AND LYMPH TO INVADE MANY PARTS.

VIRUSES

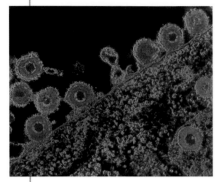

HERPES SIMPLEX VIRUS
An electron micrograph of a cluster of *Herpes simplex* virus (HSV) (orange). HSV1 is responsible for cold sores, and HSV2 for genital herpes.

An important group of harmful microorganisms, or pathogenic microbes (commonly known as "germs" or "bugs"), is the viruses. Viruses are the smallest of all the microbes; millions would cover the head of a pin. Many viruses can remain inactive for long periods and survive freezing, boiling, and chemical attack, yet they can activate suddenly when they have the opportunity of invading a living cell. Viruses are obligate parasites, which means that they must have living cells, or host cells, in order to replicate themselves. The typical virus particle has a single or double strand of genetic material (nucleic acid – either DNA or RNA) surrounded by a shell-like coat of protein, the capsid, and sometimes a protective outer envelope.

VIRUS SHAPES

There are thousands of different types of virus, with shapes such as balls, boxes, polygons, sausages, golfballs, spirals, and even tiny "space rockets". Viruses are classified by their size, shape, and symmetry as well as by the groups of diseases they cause.

Spiral (helical)
The protein coat is corkscrew-like with the genetic material entwined. Examples include myxoviruses and paramyxoviruses.

Protein subunit (capsomer)

Genetic material

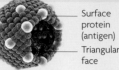

Icosahedral
Twenty equal-sided triangles connect to form a faceted container. Examples include adenoviruses and herpes viruses.

Surface protein (antigen)

Triangular face

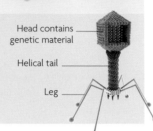

Complex
Like a tiny rocket with "landing legs" that settle on the host cell. They only attack bacteria, so are important in health terms when they attack pathogenic bacteria in the human body. Examples include the T4 bacteriophage.

Head contains genetic material

Helical tail

Leg

LIFE CYCLE OF THE INFLUENZA VIRUS

Viruses have very few genes (typically 100–300). They are not made of cells and have no cellular "machinery" for obtaining energy or raw materials, so they cannot process nutrients or reproduce by themselves. To build copies of itself, a virus invades a host cell, and takes over the cell's own machinery. The host cell dies or functions abnormally.

1 Free virus particle
The complete virus particle, which is capable of independent survival and then infection, is known as a virion.

2 Insertion of virus
Viral surface proteins attach to specific receptor sites on the host cell's surface. After attaching itself, part or all of the virus penetrates the host cell.

3 Nucleic acid insertion
The viral RNA moves to the host cell nucleus and inserts itself into the host's nucleic acid. The result is massive replication of the viral RNA, which then moves towards the cell's surface.

4 Nucleic acid replication
The host cell makes many copies of the viral RNA molecule, using the host's raw materials and sometimes its enzymes. The viral protein subunits are also produced by the host's cellular machinery.

5 Budding virus
The nucleic acid (RNA) strands and protein-coat subunits join to form new virus particles. These form buds in the host cell membrane, using part of the membrane as their outer protective envelope.

6 Release
The buds separate as free virus particles, ready to spread and infect more cells. All eight separate segments of genetic material (RNA) must be present for the virus to successfully carry the infection further.

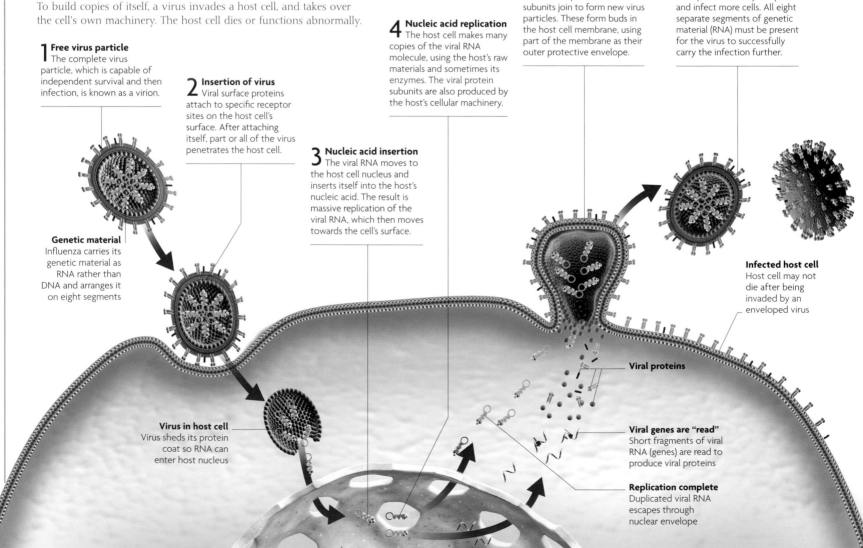

Genetic material
Influenza carries its genetic material as RNA rather than DNA and arranges it on eight segments

Virus in host cell
Virus sheds its protein coat so RNA can enter host nucleus

Viral proteins

Viral genes are "read"
Short fragments of viral RNA (genes) are read to produce viral proteins

Replication complete
Duplicated viral RNA escapes through nuclear envelope

Infected host cell
Host cell may not die after being invaded by an enveloped virus

IMMUNIZATION

As the immune system tackles and defeats most invading microorganisms, some of the white blood cells called lymphocytes become memory cells. They retain the ability to recognize the foreign substances, antigens, on the microbe's surface. If the same microbe invades again, the memory cells stimulate a rapid immune response to destroy the microbes before they take hold. The process of becoming resistant or immune to a particular microbe as a result of infection is natural immunization. Resistance can also be developed artificially. In active immunization (right), dead or weakened (attenuated) versions of the microbe or its toxic products are injected into the body. The immune response occurs, with production of antibodies, but the illness does not develop. In passive immunization, ready-made antibodies are injected into the body.

RAPID RESPONSE

This false-colour microscope image shows a white blood cell (macrophage) engulfing specially weakened bacteria. They are injected into the body to simulate active immunization.

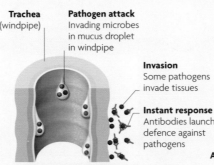

Attenuated bacterium

Macrophage

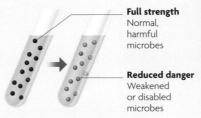

Full strength
Normal, harmful microbes

Reduced danger
Weakened or disabled microbes

1 VACCINE PRODUCTION
A vaccine contains complete or part microbes, or the toxins they make, treated so they will stimulate the immune response without causing symptoms.

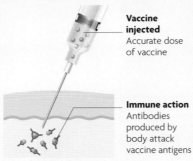

Vaccine injected
Accurate dose of vaccine

Immune action
Antibodies produced by body attack vaccine antigens

2 VACCINE DELIVERY
Introducing the vaccine into the body is called vaccination. It stimulates the immune system to raise antibodies against the antigens on the disease-carrying organisms.

Trachea (windpipe)

Pathogen attack
Invading microbes in mucus droplet in windpipe

Invasion
Some pathogens invade tissues

Instant response
Antibodies launch defence against pathogens

3 IMMUNE RESPONSE
When the body encounters pathogens it has been vaccinated against, the memory cells are already primed and so the immune system can launch an instant defence.

IMMUNIZATION AND PUBLIC HEALTH

Immunization gives individual resistance to infectious diseases, and also group protection, which is an important public health measure. For group protection to occur, a relatively high proportion of people must be immunized to minimize the chance of unprotected people coming into contact with the disease. It may eventually be eradicated. If too few people are vaccinated, the others may not only catch the infection, but also act as hosts for the microbes as they change and mutate into new strains. The existing immunization is not effective against new strains of the disease. Some individuals may be advised to abstain from immunization, due to pre-existing conditions.

RUBELLA VIRUS
This microscope image shows the rubella, or German measles, virus (pink dots) on an infected cell. A combined immunization (MMR) gives lifelong protection to babies.

PASSIVE IMMUNIZATION

Active immunization (left) takes time to develop and works well in healthy people. If urgent protection is needed, or if a person's immune system is weak, passive immunization can be used. Purified antibodies against the microbe are obtained from people or animals who are immune. The antibodies provide swift resistance against the microbes, but they gradually degenerate and are not replaced. The body has no memory for making them again.

Antibodies injected
Purified antibodies from donor

Antibodies released
Antibodies spread in blood

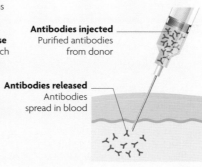

SHORT-TERM PROTECTION
Specific antibodies are given either to treat an existing infection or to provide protection against a disease in the short term.

VIRUSES AND BACTERIA

The two main categories of harmful microorganisms are viruses and bacteria (see p.164). Viruses cannot exist independently except as inactive chemical structures, whereas bacteria have cellular machinery for obtaining energy, processing nutrients, and reproducing themselves. These latter activities make bacteria vulnerable to chemical interference, a feature exploited by antibiotics. Some bacterial infections, such as tetanus, may be prevented by immunization. Viruses are unaffected by antibiotics, but can sometimes can be treated with antiviral drugs. Immunization can also sometimes prevent viral infections.

Disc containing antibiotic

No bacterial growth

ANTIBIOTIC TREATMENT
Bacteria are painted onto a laboratory nutrient dish with discs containing different antibiotics. Lack of bacterial growth around a disc shows which antibiotics are effective.

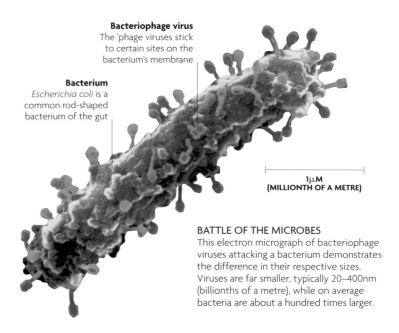

Bacteriophage virus
The 'phage viruses stick to certain sites on the bacterium's membrane

Bacterium
Escherichia coli is a common rod-shaped bacterium of the gut

1μM
(MILLIONTH OF A METRE)

BATTLE OF THE MICROBES
This electron micrograph of bacteriophage viruses attacking a bacterium demonstrates the difference in their respective sizes. Viruses are far smaller, typically 20–400nm (billionths of a metre), while on average bacteria are about a hundred times larger.

BACTERIA

The microorganisms known as bacteria are present almost everywhere – in soil, water, air, food, drink, and on and in our own bodies. Many types of bacteria are harmless; indeed, those present naturally in the human intestines, the "gut flora", have a beneficial effect in helping to extract nutrients from food. However, hundreds of types of bacteria cause infections, ranging from mild to lethal. Bacteria are simpler than other single-cell organisms in that their genetic material (DNA) is free in the cell, rather than contained in a membrane-bound nucleus.

STRUCTURE OF A BACTERIUM

A typical rod-shaped bacterium (bacillus) has a cell membrane enclosing cytoplasm and organelles, such as ribosomes, which are distributed in it. Unlike animal cells, it has a semirigid cell wall outside its cell membrane.

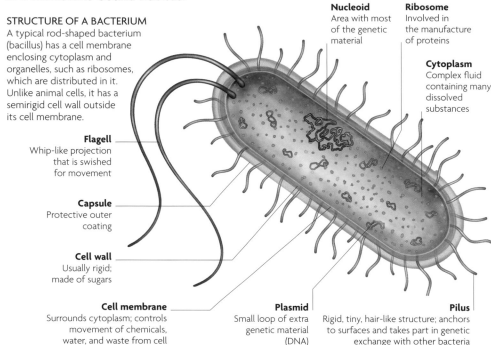

Nucleoid
Area with most of the genetic material

Ribosome
Involved in the manufacture of proteins

Cytoplasm
Complex fluid containing many dissolved substances

Flagell
Whip-like projection that is swished for movement

Capsule
Protective outer coating

Cell wall
Usually rigid; made of sugars

Cell membrane
Surrounds cytoplasm; controls movement of chemicals, water, and waste from cell

Plasmid
Small loop of extra genetic material (DNA)

Pilus
Rigid, tiny, hair-like structure; anchors to surfaces and takes part in genetic exchange with other bacteria

HOW BACTERIA CAUSE DAMAGE

Disease-causing bacteria can enter the body in several ways: via the airways or digestive tract, during sexual contact, or through breaks in the skin. Once inside, some bacteria adhere to and invade body cells, such as the dysentery-causing *Shigella dysenteriae*. Others produce poisonous substances known as bacteriotoxins, or toxins. Many of these alter the biochemical reactions in body cells. The diphtheria toxin from the bacterium *Corynebacterium diphtheriae* damages heart muscle by inhibiting protein production. Some of these toxins are highly dangerous. A bucket of nerve toxin from *Clostridium botulinum* could kill everyone in the world.

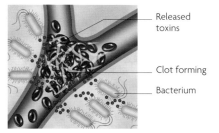

Released toxins

Clot forming

Bacterium

LEAKING VESSELS
Some bacteria release toxins that cause blood to clot in small blood vessels, depriving tissues and organs of their normal blood supply.

SUPERBUGS

Some bacteria pass through their life cycle in less than 20 minutes. This exceptionally fast reproductive rate, coupled with the incredible numbers of bacteria, and the speed at which they pass on genetic information, gives great scope for mutation (see right). A patient taking antibiotics unwittingly provides a testing ground for the bacteria to undergo natural selection for the greatest resistance. Many strains of bacteria resistant to wide-acting, or broad-spectrum, antibiotics have appeared, touted as "superbugs". They may not be resistant to more specialist, narrow-spectrum, antibiotics, but these often have more side effects. Doctors try to reduce this risk by prescribing antibiotics only when necessary.

MRSA
Staphylococcus aureus became resistant to the antibiotic methicillin in the 1960s. It is now known as methicillin resistant *Staphylococcus aureus* (MRSA). In the 1990s, newer strains appeared in hospitals.

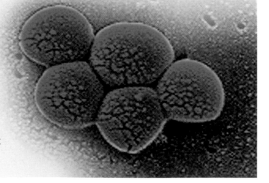

BACTERIAL SHAPES

There are several typical shapes for bacteria, and these, along with the way they are coloured by laboratory stains, are important for classification and working out their origins and relationships. Many thousands of bacterial types are known, with more discovered each year.

Cocci
Generally spherical (shown here in the process of dividing). Examples include *Staphylococcus* and *Streptococcus*.

Dividing cocci bacteria

Bacilli
Oval, or rod-like, with or without surface hairs (pili) or whip-like flagella. Examples are *Streptobacillus* and *Clostridium*.

Pili (hairs) on surface

Spirilla
Spiral or, more accurately, helical (corkscrew-like) in shape, as open or tight coils. Examples include *Leptospira* and *Treponema*.

Open coils

RESISTANCE TO ANTIBIOTICS

Many bacteria are able to develop resistance to antibiotics by changing (mutating) into new strains. Their most effective mechanism is the rapid transfer of plasmids – small loop-like packages of the bacterial genetic material, DNA – between bacterial populations. The gene for antibiotic resistance crops up by accident, and the bacterium possessing it is able to pass the gene to others by the process of conjugation, or "bacterial sex", in which plasmid genetic material is donated or exchanged.

1 ROLE OF PLASMIDS
Plasmids may cause the bacterium to make enzymes against antibiotic drugs, or alter its surface receptor sites, where antibiotics bind. Then, the plasmid duplicates itself.

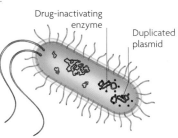

Drug-inactivating enzyme

Duplicated plasmid

2 PLASMID TRANSFER
Plasmid transfer takes place during a process known as conjugation. The plasmid copy is passed from the donor, through a pilus, to the recipient bacterium.

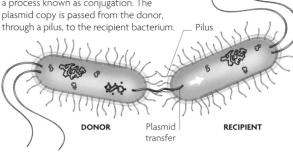

Pilus

DONOR

Plasmid transfer

RECIPIENT

3 DRUG-RESISTANT STRAINS
Recipient bacteria inherit the resistant gene. Plasmid transfer produces populations of bacteria resistant to a range of antibiotics.

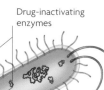

Drug-inactivating enzymes

PROTISTS (PROTOZOA)

Single-celled organisms that have their genetic material inside a nucleus, unlike bacteria (opposite), are known by the general name of protists. The animal-like ones, which can move about, and gain energy by taking in food (rather than capturing energy from sunlight), are sometimes called protozoa. There are thousands of kinds, and most live harmlessly in soil and water. However, some are parasites that cause serious diseases in humans. The protist *Plasmodium* causes the disease malaria, which affects millions of people worldwide. Single-celled parasites employ various mechanisms for evading the body's immune system. The *Leishmania* parasite, for example, which causes the disease leishmaniasis, multiplies within white blood cells that normally destroy such micro-organisms. Many protists have a flexible cell membrane and large nucleus, and may possess tail-like appendages, known as flagella, to aid movement.

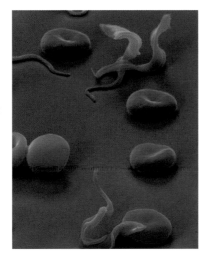

TRYPANOSOMES IN BLOOD
Trypanosomes are worm-like protists (purple), seen here with red blood cells. They cause trypanosomiasis, or sleeping sickness.

MALARIAL LIFE CYCLE

Four types of *Plasmodium* protists cause malaria. They are spread by the bite of the female *Anopheles* mosquito. Malaria produces chills and high fever, which can recur and prove fatal if not treated. Most *Plasmodium* have a similar life cycle, as shown below.

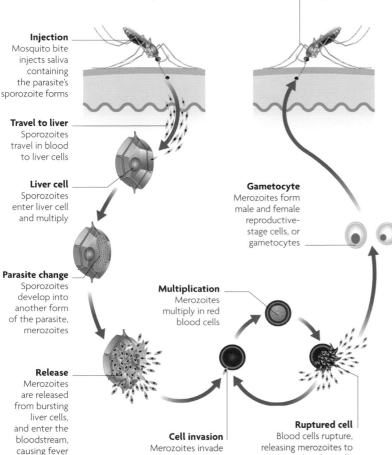

Injection
Mosquito bite injects saliva containing the parasite's sporozoite forms

Travel to liver
Sporozoites travel in blood to liver cells

Liver cell
Sporozoites enter liver cell and multiply

Parasite change
Sporozoites develop into another form of the parasite, merozoites

Release
Merozoites are released from bursting liver cells, and enter the bloodstream, causing fever

Multiplication
Merozoites multiply in red blood cells

Cell invasion
Merozoites invade red blood cells

Ruptured cell
Blood cells rupture, releasing merozoites to invade other cells

Gametocyte
Merozoites form male and female reproductive-stage cells, or gametocytes

Cycle continues
Gametocytes sucked up by mosquito bite mature in insect, and form sporozoites; the cycle continues

FUNGI

Fungi make up one of the great kingdoms of life and include familiar mushrooms and moulds, as well as microscopic single-celled yeasts. They feed on both living and dead organic matter. Disease-causing fungi fall into two main groups: the filamentous fungi, which grow as a network of branching threads called hyphae; and the single-celled yeasts. Some types cause fairly harmless (if unsightly) superficial diseases of the skin, hair, nails, or mucous membranes, for example thrush (candidiasis). Others, such as histoplasmosis, result in potentially fatal infections of certain vital organs, for instance the lungs. Some may be linked to specific occupations such as farming or food production. Other fungal infections, for example ringworm (dermatophytosis), are more likely to affect people with damaged immune systems, such as those with HIV-AIDS.

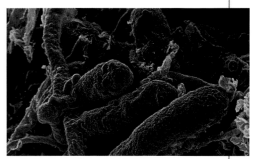

CAUSE OF ATHLETE'S FOOT
Seen here are microscopic threads of the fungus *Epidermophyton floccosum*, which causes the white, itchy skin of athlete's foot.

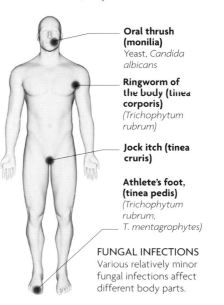

Oral thrush (monilia)
Yeast, *Candida albicans*

Ringworm of the body (tinea corporis)
(*Trichophyton rubrum*)

Jock itch (tinea cruris)

Athlete's foot, (tinea pedis)
(*Trichophyton rubrum*, *T. mentagrophytes*)

FUNGAL INFECTIONS
Various relatively minor fungal infections affect different body parts.

PARASITIC WORMS

Humans, like most other animals, can be infested with parasitic worms that derive all their nutrients from their hosts. At least 20 types of worm-like animals may live in the body as parasites. Most spend at least part of their life cycle in the intestines. Few are members of the segmented worms group, the annelids, which includes common earthworms. Several are roundworms, or nematodes, such as 1cm ($^4/_5$ in) long hookworms *Ancylostoma duodenale*, which live in the gut. Another worm-like group is the flatworms; it includes the tapeworms, such as *Taenia*, which live in the gut, and flukes, such as *Schistosoma*, which cause schistosomiasis, or snail fever.

HOOKWORM
This microscope image shows an adult hookworm's head. The mouth contains several tooth-like structures, which it uses to cling to the intestinal lining of its host.

SCHISTOSOME
Adult flukes, such as this 1–2cm ($^2/_5$–$^4/_5$ in) long *Schistoma*, live in blood vessels. This close-up shows some red blood cells in the fluke's mouth.

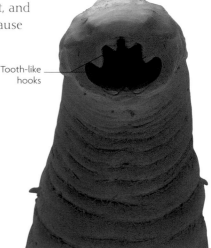

Tooth-like hooks

ALLERGIES

THE IMMUNE SYSTEM NORMALLY DEFENDS THE BODY AGAINST INFECTIONS, CANCER, INJURIES, AND DAMAGING SUBSTANCES SUCH AS TOXIC CHEMICALS. SOMETIMES, HOWEVER, IT OVER-REACTS, ATTACKING A FOREIGN SUBSTANCE THAT IS NORMALLY HARMLESS. THIS REACTION IS AN ALLERGIC RESPONSE. SUCH RESPONSES CAN VARY FROM MILD CONDITIONS TO LIFE-THREATENING DISORDERS.

ALLERGIC RESPONSE

AN ALLERGY DEVELOPS IF THE IMMUNE SYSTEM BECOMES SENSITIZED TO A FOREIGN SUBSTANCE (AN ALLERGEN).

When first exposed to an allergen, such as pollen, nuts, or penicillin, the immune system makes antibodies to fight it. The antibodies coat the surface of mast cells, found in the skin, stomach lining, lungs, and upper airways. If the allergen enters the body again, these cells mount an allergic response.

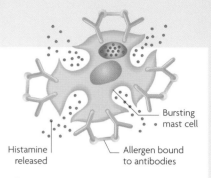

Histamine

Mast cell

Antibody

Cell nucleus

Allergen

1 EXPOSURE TO ALLERGEN
Antibodies bind to the surfaces of mast cells. These cells contain histamine, which normally causes inflammation (see p.158).

Mast cell

Allergen

Antibody

2 ANTIBODIES TRIGGERED
Allergens come into contact with the antibodies. If they link two or more antibodies, they cause the cell to burst.

Bursting mast cell

Histamine released

Allergen bound to antibodies

3 HISTAMINE RELEASED
Granules inside the mast cell release histamine as the cell bursts. Histamine causes an inflammatory response that irritates body tissues and produces the symptoms of an allergy.

ALLERGIC RHINITIS

AIRBORNE ALLERGENS THAT IRRITATE THE LINING OF THE NOSE AND THROAT CAUSE ALLERGIC RHINITIS; THIS ALLERGY MAY BE SEASONAL OR OCCUR ALL YEAR.

In allergic rhinitis, the lining of the nose and throat becomes inflamed after contact with an airborne allergen. One form is hay fever, which is brought on by pollen grains in the spring and summer. Another form, perennial rhinitis, may be caused by house dust mites, bird feathers, or animal fur or skin flakes (dander) and may occur at any time of year. Both forms can cause sneezing, a blocked, runny nose, and itchy, watery eyes, although symptoms tend to be more severe in hay fever.

Often, the cause of rhinitis is easy to identify. If a person cannot avoid contact with the allergen, antiallergy drugs taken before or during an attack may relieve itchy eyes or a blocked nose. Drugs can be applied directly to the inside of the nose or eyes, or taken orally.

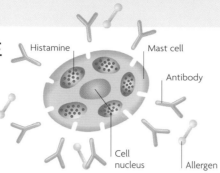

COMMON ALLERGENS
Many people are allergic to pollen grains (above) and suffer from hay fever as a result. The dead bodies and excrement of dust mites (left) can also cause rhinitis.

FOOD ALLERGIES

SOME ALLERGIES ARE CAUSED BY AN EXCESSIVE IMMUNE RESPONSE TO CERTAIN FOODS, MOST COMMONLY NUTS, SEAFOOD, EGGS, AND MILK.

Symptoms of food allergies may appear as soon as the food is eaten or develop over a few hours. Some affect the digestive system, causing swelling and itching in the mouth and throat, nausea and vomiting, and diarrhoea. Others affect the whole body, causing skin rashes, swollen tissues (see angioedema, below), and shortness of breath. In very severe cases, food allergies provoke anaphylaxis (see below left). The only effective treatment is to avoid the problem food.

ANAPHYLAXIS

THIS RARE, BUT POTENTIALLY FATAL, ALLERGIC REACTION RESULTS FROM AN EXTREME SENSITIVITY TO AN ALLERGEN.

Anaphylaxis is a massive immune system response that involves the whole body. Widespread release of huge amounts of histamine causes a sudden fall in blood pressure (shock) and narrowing of the airways, and can be fatal unless treated immediately. Other possible symptoms include a red, itchy, lumpy rash called urticaria, swelling of the face, lips, and tongue (see angioedema, right), and loss of consciousness. Triggers for anaphylaxis include foods such as nuts, drugs such as penicillin, and insect stings. A person

with anaphylaxis needs emergency medical treatment. If someone is known to be at risk of anaphylaxis, his or her doctor may issue syringes of epinephrine (adrenaline) that the person can self-administer as soon as an attack starts. Susceptible people should avoid trigger substances if at all possible.

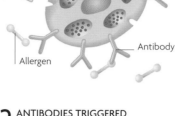

Typical white lumps

URTICARIA
This itchy, red rash, often with white lumps, can result from various allergies. It can also be a symptom of anaphylaxis.

ANGIOEDEMA

SOME ALLERGIC REACTIONS CAUSE SWELLING OF BODY TISSUES, WHICH IS CALLED ANGIOEDEMA.

Swelling usually comes on suddenly, in tissues just under the skin and in mucous membranes. Angioedema often affects the face and lips. It may also occur in the mouth, tongue, and airways, interfering with breathing and swallowing. The most common triggers are foods such as nuts and seafood. Other possible triggers are antibiotic drugs and insect bites. Severe angioedema needs emergency medical treatment. For milder cases, corticosteroid or antihistamine drugs may be given to reduce the swelling.

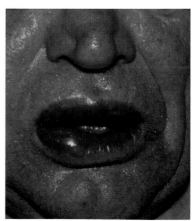

ANGIOEDEMA OF THE LIPS
Sudden, severe swelling of the soft tissues in the face, lips, or larynx is known as angioedema. It is usually caused by an allergic reaction to certain foods.

HIV–AIDS

INFECTION WITH THE HUMAN IMMUNODEFICIENCY VIRUS (HIV) IS ONE OF THE MOST SERIOUS HEALTH PROBLEMS WE FACE TODAY. IT CAN LEAD TO AIDS – ACQUIRED IMMUNODEFICIENCY SYNDROME. IN THIS LIFE-THREATENING CONDITION, THE IMMUNE SYSTEM BECOMES SO WEAK THAT EVEN NORMALLY HARMLESS MICROORGANISMS CAN CAUSE SEVERE INFECTIONS.

HIV INFECTION

HIV IS CARRIED IN BODY FLUIDS, SUCH AS BLOOD, SEMEN, SALIVA, VAGINAL SECRETIONS, AND BREAST MILK. IT IS PASSED ON WHEN INFECTED FLUIDS ENTER THE BODY.

The virus is most commonly transmitted by sexual intercourse. It can also be passed to drug users if they share infected needles, or from a mother to her fetus or newborn baby. Once in the bloodstream, HIV infects cells with structures called CD4 molecules on their surfaces. These cells, CD4+ cells, include white blood cells called CD4+ lymphocytes, which fight infection. The virus multiplies rapidly in CD4+ cells, destroying them in the process. The initial infection may cause a flu-like illness for a few weeks, then there may be no further symptoms for years. If HIV goes untreated, the number of CD4+ lymphocytes eventually falls so low that the immune system is severely weakened, and serious disorders develop.

AIDS

The onset of AIDS is signalled by the development of disorders called AIDS-defining illnesses. Some of these illnesses are opportunistic infections, caused by organisms that are harmless to healthy people but dangerous to those with reduced immunity; one example is infection by *Candida albicans*, which causes thrush. People with AIDS may also develop various types of cancer, notably Kaposi's sarcoma.

KAPOSI'S SARCOMA
Kaposi's sarcoma is characterized by defined, brownish, raised nodules, seen here under the eye. They can occur anywhere in the body, including the internal organs.

HIV REPLICATION
HIV is a type of virus called a retrovirus, which carries its genetic material in the form of RNA. It invades body cells and uses the cells' own processes to multiply.

1 Free HIV particle
The core (capsid) contains two strands of ribonucleic acid (RNA), each carrying a set of genes for the virus. The spikes on the surface are proteins called gp120 antigens (docking protein). They enable the virus to "dock" on the surface of CD4+ cells.

- pg120 antigen (docking protein)
- Membrane
- Protein coat
- Capsid
- Reverse transcriptase
- Integrase
- Viral RNA

2 Binding and injection
The gp120 binds to CD4 molecules and then to co-receptors on the cell surface. The virus fuses with the cell, penetrating the surface. The capsid releases the viral RNA.

3 Reverse transcription
The virus releases an enzyme called reverse transcriptase into the cell. The enzyme converts single strands of viral RNA into double-stranded DNA.

4 Insertion of viral DNA
The viral DNA enters the cell nucleus, where its integrase enzyme incorporates it into the cell's DNA. The cell produces mRNA, which transmits instructions for making new proteins, including HIV proteins.

5 Creation of proteins
The mRNA enters the cell cytoplasm, where it is "read" and chains of HIV proteins and viral RNA are made. These molecules are to become the components of new HIV particles.

6 New HIV created
The HIV constituents gather at the cell wall. An immature virus forms and buds from the cell, taking some cell membrane with it. Enzymes within the virus bring about changes resulting in a mature virus particle.

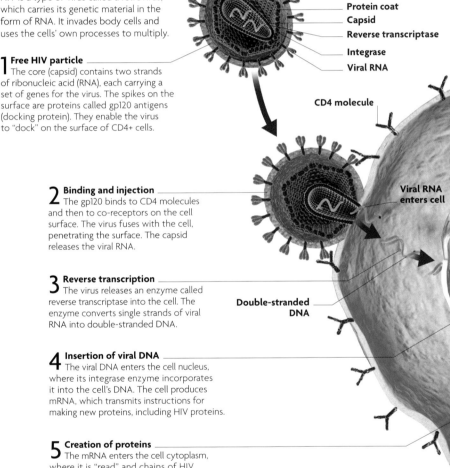

- CD4 molecule
- Viral RNA enters cell
- Double-stranded DNA
- Infected CD4+ lymphocyte
- Cell DNA
- Cell nucleus
- Cytoplasm
- mRNA
- Viral constituents collect at cell
- Infected CD4+ lymphocyte
- Mature HIV particle

Free-floating mature HIV particle repeats the cycle

Immature virus particle

AUTOIMMUNE AND LYMPHATIC DISORDERS

THE IMMUNE SYSTEM NORMALLY PROTECTS THE BODY FROM INFECTIONS, BUT IF IT DOES NOT WORK CORRECTLY ILLNESS MAY RESULT. IN AUTOIMMUNE DISORDERS, A FAULTY IMMUNE RESPONSE IDENTIFIES THE BODY'S OWN TISSUES AS FOREIGN AND PRODUCES ANTIBODIES AGAINST THEM. THE LYMPHATIC SYSTEM DESTROYS INFECTIOUS MICROORGANISMS AND CANCEROUS CELLS, BUT THE SYSTEM ITSELF MAY SUCCUMB TO INFECTION OR CANCER.

LUPUS

A WIDE-RANGING DISORDER, LUPUS OCCURS WHEN THE IMMUNE SYSTEM ATTACKS THE CONNECTIVE TISSUES.

Systemic lupus erythematosus (SLE), or lupus, causes inflammation and swelling of the connective tissues, which hold the skin, joints, and internal organs together. Symptoms vary in severity and may flare up for a few weeks every so often. The cause is unknown, but lupus may be triggered by viral infection, stress, or exposure to sunlight. It is much more common in women and in black or Asian people, and sometimes runs in families. There is no cure; treatment aims to relieve symptoms and control the disease, but in some cases lupus can be fatal.

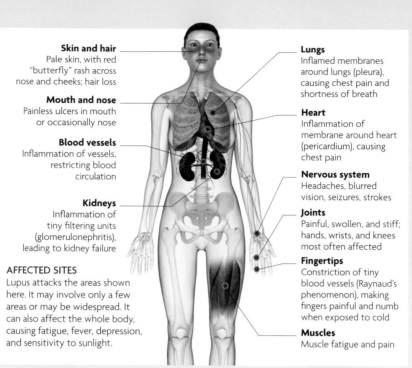

Skin and hair
Pale skin, with red "butterfly" rash across nose and cheeks; hair loss

Mouth and nose
Painless ulcers in mouth or occasionally nose

Blood vessels
Inflammation of vessels, restricting blood circulation

Kidneys
Inflammation of tiny filtering units (glomerulonephritis), leading to kidney failure

Lungs
Inflamed membranes around lungs (pleura), causing chest pain and shortness of breath

Heart
Inflammation of membrane around heart (pericardium), causing chest pain

Nervous system
Headaches, blurred vision, seizures, strokes

Joints
Painful, swollen, and stiff; hands, wrists, and knees most often affected

Fingertips
Constriction of tiny blood vessels (Raynaud's phenomenon), making fingers painful and numb when exposed to cold

Muscles
Muscle fatigue and pain

AFFECTED SITES
Lupus attacks the areas shown here. It may involve only a few areas or may be widespread. It can also affect the whole body, causing fatigue, fever, depression, and sensitivity to sunlight.

SCLERODERMA

IN THIS RARE CONDITION, ANTIBODIES DAMAGE THE SKIN, JOINT TISSUES, AND OTHER CONNECTIVE TISSUES.

Scleroderma is an autoimmune disorder in which the immune system attacks the connective tissues, which hold the body's structures together. The tissues become inflamed and thickened and may harden and contract. The skin is most often affected and may become stiff and tight. The joints, particularly in the hands, may be swollen and painful. The fingers may develop ulcers and hard patches and become painfully sensitive to cold (a condition called Raynaud's phenomenon). The cause of scleroderma is unknown. There is no cure, but treatment may relieve the symptoms and slow the disease.

PULMONARY FIBROSIS

IF ANTIBODIES ATTACK LUNG TISSUE, THEY CAUSE FIBROSIS (THICKENING AND SCARRING) OF THE AIR SACS (ALVEOLI).

In pulmonary fibrosis, an autoimmune reaction causes inflammation of the alveoli in the lungs. The alveolar walls become scarred and less able to take in oxygen. Symptoms include a dry cough and shortness of breath, which may become so severe that the person needs oxygen. The cause is unknown. There is no cure, but corticosteroid drugs may slow the rate of lung damage.

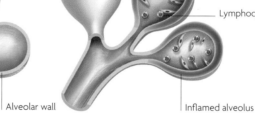

Mucous lining | Alveolar wall

Fibroblast

Lymphocyte

Inflamed alveolus

Thickened alveolar wall

Scar tissue forms

1 NORMAL ALVEOLI
The delicate walls of the alveoli, only one cell thick, easily allow oxygen from the air to pass into the blood and carbon dioxide to leave the body. The inner surfaces of the alveoli are protected by a layer of mucus.

2 INFLAMMATION
Large numbers of disease-fighting cells called lymphocytes enter the alveoli. As they break down, they secrete substances that cause inflammation. This process stimulates cells called fibroblasts to form fibrous tissue.

3 FIBROSIS
The formation of scar tissue (fibrosis) causes the alveolar walls to thicken, and restricts the flow of gases through the walls. Fibrosis gradually destroys the alveoli, and scar tissue may restrict lung expansion.

POLYARTERITIS

THIS RARE BUT SERIOUS AUTOIMMUNE DISORDER CAUSES WIDESPREAD DAMAGE TO SMALL AND MEDIUM-SIZED ARTERIES.

Polyarteritis nodosa is inflammation of artery walls due to an autoimmune reaction, which restricts the blood flow to body tissues. Symptoms include skin lesions and ulcers, abdominal pain, joint pain, and numb fingers and toes. Polyarteritis may also lead to kidney failure or a heart attack. The cause is not known. There is no cure, but corticosteroids may relieve symptoms.

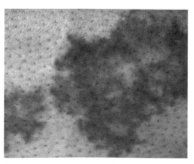

POLYARTERITIS DAMAGE
The purplish areas, seen here on the leg of a person with polyarteritis, indicate tissue starved of blood and oxygen as a result of inflamed blood vessels restricting blood flow.

SARCOIDOSIS

A DISEASE THAT MAY BE ACUTE OR CHRONIC, SARCOIDOSIS CAUSES SORES CALLED GRANULOMAS TO FORM.

Sarcoidosis is thought to be caused by an excessive immune reaction to a chemical or infection in someone with a genetic predisposition to the disease. It most often affects the lungs, causing coughing and shortness of breath but can also develop in the lymph nodes, liver, spleen, kidneys, skin, or eyes. There is no cure, but in most cases, the symptoms disappear by themselves.

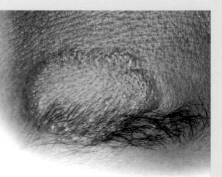

GRANULOMA
This image shows a granuloma above the eye. Granulomas are clusters of disease-fighting cells called macrophages at points where an immune response has been triggered.

ANAEMIA

VARIOUS CONDITIONS, INCLUDING AN ABNORMAL IMMUNE RESPONSE, CAN CAUSE ANAEMIA.

The term "anaemia" is used of disorders in which haemoglobin, the pigment that gives red blood cells their colour, is deficient or abnormal. Haemoglobin carries oxygen in the blood, so if it is deficient it cannot supply enough oxygen to body tissues. There are various types of anaemia. Haemolytic anaemia results from large-scale, rapid destruction of red blood cells (haemolysis). It is most commonly caused by an excessive immune response in which the body produces antibodies that attack red blood cells. This reaction can be due to an autoimmune disorder or may be triggered by drugs, such as penicillin or quinine. The most common type of anaemia is caused by a lack of substances needed to make healthy red blood cells, such as iron. Another type results from inherited disorders that cause the body to produce abnormal forms of haemoglobin – such as sickle-cell disease, in which the red blood cells are distorted into a curved sickle shape. A third type, aplastic anaemia, occurs when the bone marrow fails to produce enough red blood cells.

HAEMOLYSIS
This coloured electron microscope image shows a white blood cell called a macrophage (brown) destroying red blood cells. The loss of red blood cells in this way is called autoimmune haemolytic anaemia.

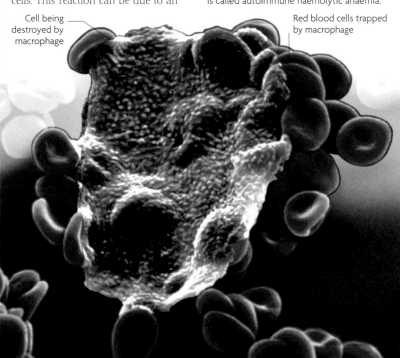

Cell being destroyed by macrophage

Red blood cells trapped by macrophage

LEUKAEMIA

THERE ARE SEVERAL TYPES OF LEUKAEMIA; ALL INVOLVE GROWTH OF CANCEROUS WHITE BLOOD CELLS IN BONE MARROW.

Leukaemia is cancer of the white blood cells. Cancerous cells multiply in the bone marrow, where blood cells are normally made. This process reduces the production of healthy red and white blood cells and of platelets to abnormally low levels. A deficiency of red blood cells causes anaemia (see left). A reduction in normal white blood cells leaves the body unable to fight off infection. A lack of platelets prevents blood from clotting at injury sites, leading to excessive bleeding. The cancerous cells often spread in the bloodstream, causing enlargement of the lymph nodes, spleen, and liver. Leukaemia may be either acute or chronic. It is usually treated with chemotherapy, and sometimes with radiotherapy followed by a stem-cell transplant. The outlook depends on the type and severity, but treatment is more likely to be successful in children.

BLOOD CELL PRODUCTION
All blood cells are produced in bone marrow – soft, fatty tissue in the centre of bones (see p.39). The cells develop from a single type called a stem cell (see p.31). Red blood cells carry oxygen to the tissues. Lymphocytes (a type of white blood cell) fight infection. Platelets help the blood to clot at injury sites, reducing blood loss.

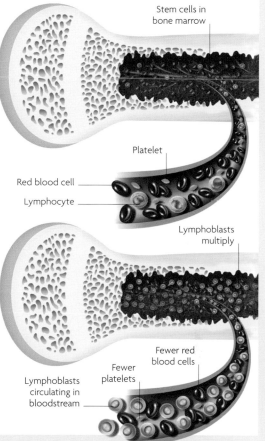

Stem cells in bone marrow

Platelet

Red blood cell

Lymphocyte

Lymphoblasts multiply

ACUTE LYMPHOBLASTIC LEUKAEMIA
In acute lymphoblastic leukaemia (ALL), cancerous, immature lymphocytes, called lymphoblasts, multiply uncontrollably and build up in the bone marrow. As a result, the production of normal blood cells is disrupted, so the levels fall too low. In addition, the lymphoblasts invade the bloodstream, where they multiply further and carry the cancer to other organs and tissues in the body.

Fewer red blood cells

Fewer platelets

Lymphoblasts circulating in bloodstream

LYMPHOMA

ORIGINATING IN THE LYMPHATIC SYSTEM, LYMPHOMA IS A CANCER INVOLVING CELLS CALLED LYMPHOCYTES.

The lymphatic system, like the blood, contains lymphocytes – white blood cells that help the body fight infection. In lymphoma, these cells become cancerous and multiply in a lymph node. The cancer may spread to tissues such as the spleen and bone marrow, and to other nodes. Lymphoma has two main forms: Hodgkin's and non-Hodgkin's. Both may cause swelling of lymph nodes in the neck, armpits or groin, fever, fatigue, and night sweats. Lymphoma in a group of nodes may be treated with radiotherapy; if it is widespread, chemotherapy may be used.

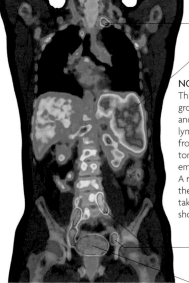

Cancer in lymph node

Cancerous tissue in spleen

NON-HODGKIN'S LYMPHOMA
This image shows malignant growths in a patient's abdomen and chest due to non-Hodgkin's lymphoma. The image is formed from coloured composite computed tomography (CT) and positron emission tomography (PET) scans. A radioactive substance, injected into the patient's bloodstream, has been taken up by the tumours, which show up as patches of intense pink.

Cancerous lymph nodes

Bladder

HODGKIN'S LYMPHOMA

This form of lymphoma involves enlarged, abnormal cells called Reed–Sternberg cells. The cause is not known. Hodgkin's lymphoma usually affects people aged from about 15 to 30 and those from 55 to 70 years old. The most common symptom is enlarged lymph nodes. Others include fatigue, itchy skin, or a rash. Some people have fever, night sweats, weight loss, or pain in the lymph nodes after drinking alcohol. The condition increases vulnerability to infection as the cells of the immune system are unable to function properly. The doctor may carry out blood tests for anaemia and take a biopsy from a swollen lymph node to check for cancerous cells. He or she may also arrange CT scans and a bone marrow biopsy to see if the disease has spread. Treatment includes radiotherapy and chemotherapy.

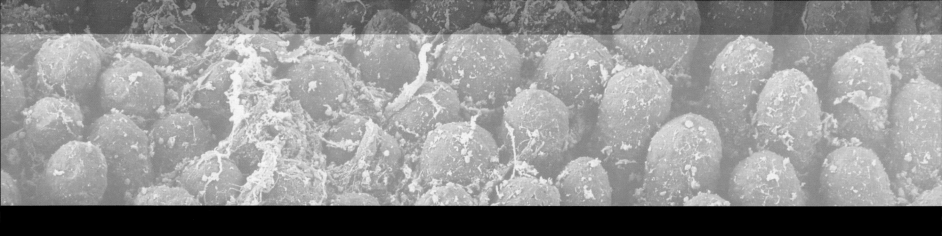

PEOPLE ARE PROBABLY MORE AWARE OF THEIR DIGESTIVE
SYSTEM THAN OF ANY OTHER SYSTEM, NOT LEAST BECAUSE
OF ITS FREQUENT MESSAGES. HUNGER, THIRST, APPETITE,
WIND (GAS), AND THE FREQUENCY AND NATURE OF BOWEL
MOVEMENTS, ARE ALL ISSUES AFFECTING DAILY LIFE.
EATING WELL, ALONG WITH REGULAR EXERCISE, IS ONE

DIGESTIVE SYSTEM

DIGESTIVE ANATOMY

THE DIGESTIVE SYSTEM CONSISTS OF A LONG PASSAGEWAY, KNOWN AS THE ALIMENTARY CANAL OR DIGESTIVE TRACT, AND ASSOCIATED ORGANS, INCLUDING THE LIVER, GALLBLADDER, AND PANCREAS. THE DIGESTIVE TRACT STARTS AT THE MOUTH AND CONTINUES THROUGH THE OESOPHAGUS AND INTESTINES TO THE ANUS. ALONG ITS COURSE FOOD IS BROKEN DOWN AND NUTRIENTS EXTRACTED, WHILE WASTE MATERIALS ARE DISPOSED OF.

After being eaten, or ingested, food embarks on a journey. It can take up to 24 hours to cover a distance of 9m (30ft), through various muscular tubes and chambers. The process begins at the mouth, where food is initially crushed and ground down by the teeth during chewing. The resulting ball, or bolus, of food continues down the throat (pharynx), then travels through the gullet (oesophagus) to the stomach, small intestine, large intestine, and anus. In the small intestine, chemical digestion breaks down food into molecules small enough to absorb into the bloodstream. What cannot be digested is compacted as faeces in the large intestine and eliminated through the anus. Food travels through the system by a process of muscular contraction called peristalsis (see p.181). As well as the digestive tract, the digestive system includes several glands: the spit-making salivary glands; the pancreas, which produces powerful digestive juices; and the body's major nutrient processor, the liver.

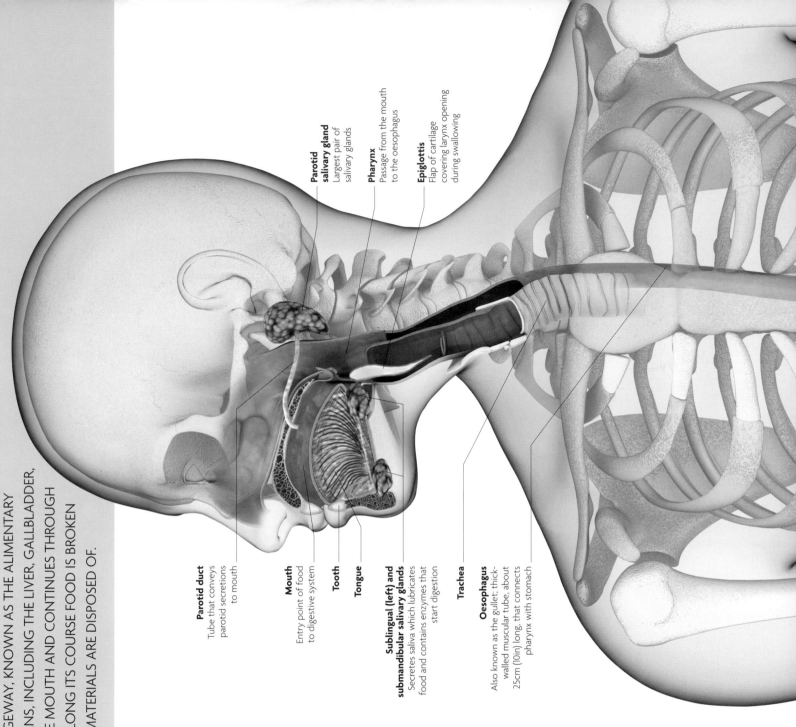

Parotid salivary gland
Largest pair of salivary glands

Pharynx
Passage from the mouth to the oesophagus

Epiglottis
Flap of cartilage covering larynx opening during swallowing

Parotid duct
Tube that conveys parotid secretions to mouth

Mouth
Entry point of food to digestive system

Tooth

Tongue

Sublingual (left) and submandibular salivary glands
Secretes saliva which lubricates food and contains enzymes that start digestion

Trachea

Oesophagus
Also known as the gullet; thick-walled muscular tube, about 25cm (10in) long, that connects pharynx with stomach

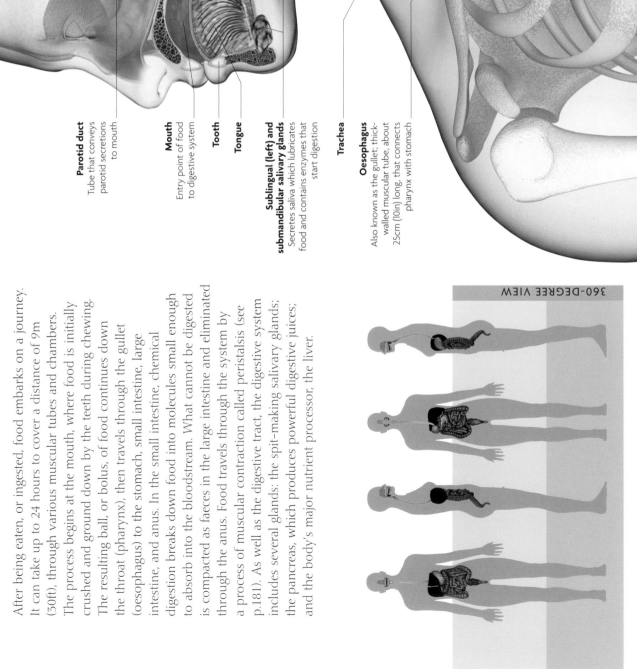

360-DEGREE VIEW

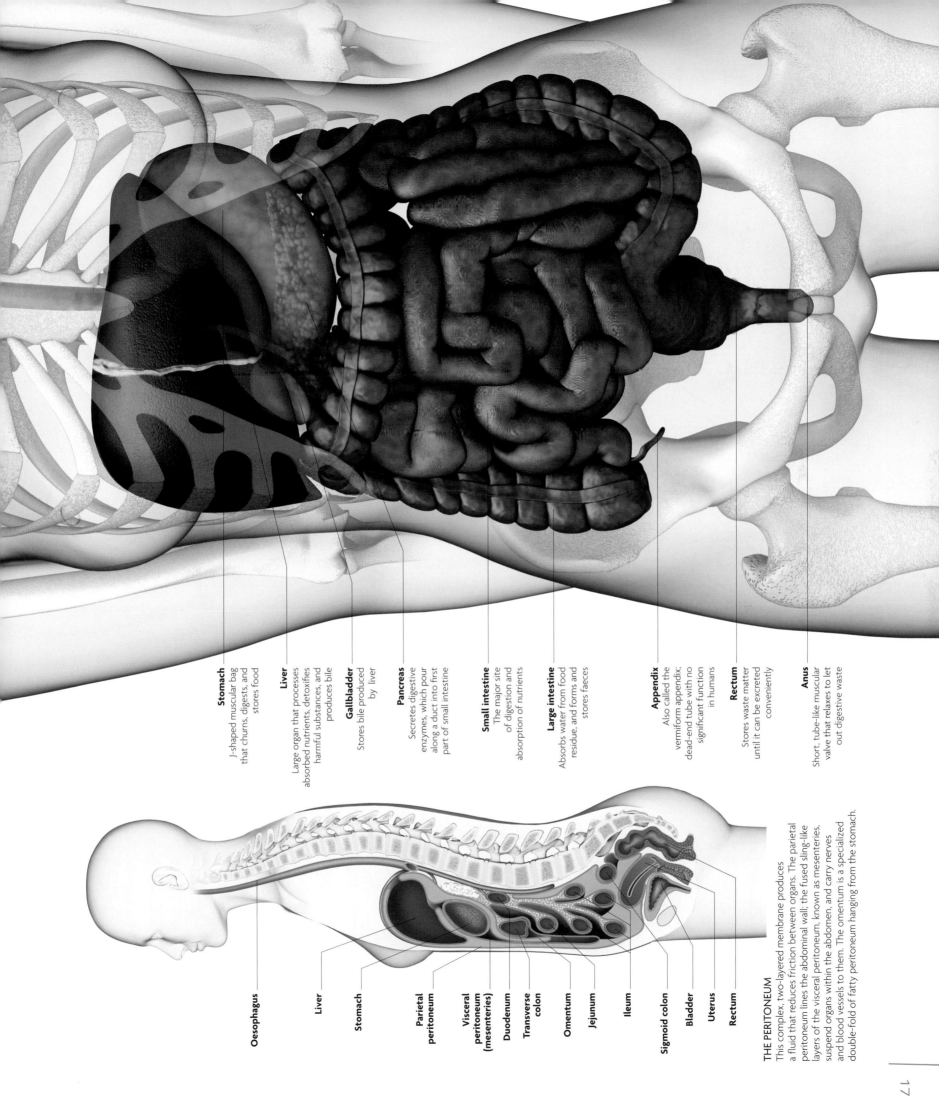

Stomach
J-shaped muscular bag that churns, digests, and stores food

Liver
Large organ that processes absorbed nutrients, detoxifies harmful substances, and produces bile

Gallbladder
Stores bile produced by liver

Pancreas
Secretes digestive enzymes, which pour along a duct into first part of small intestine

Small intestine
The major site of digestion and absorption of nutrients

Large intestine
Absorbs water from food residue, and forms and stores faeces

Appendix
Also called the vermiform appendix; dead-end tube with no significant function in humans

Rectum
Stores waste matter until it can be excreted conveniently

Anus
Short, tube-like muscular valve that relaxes to let out digestive waste

Oesophagus

Liver

Stomach

Parietal peritoneum

Visceral peritoneum (mesenteries)

Duodenum

Transverse colon

Omentum

Jejunum

Ileum

Sigmoid colon

Bladder

Uterus

Rectum

THE PERITONEUM

This complex, two-layered membrane produces a fluid that reduces friction between organs. The parietal peritoneum lines the abdominal wall; the fused sling-like layers of the visceral peritoneum, known as mesenteries, suspend organs within the abdomen, and carry nerves and blood vessels to them. The omentum is a specialized double-fold of fatty peritoneum hanging from the stomach.

MOUTH AND THROAT

THE PROCESS OF DIGESTION STARTS WHEN FOOD ENTERS THE MOUTH. FOOD IS CHEWED, LUBRICATED BY SALIVA, AND MOVED ABOUT BY THE TONGUE. IN ABOUT ONE MINUTE, THE FOOD BECOMES A SOFT, MOIST MASS CALLED A BOLUS. EACH BOLUS IS SWALLOWED THROUGH THE THROAT (PHARYNX) AND PASSES INTO THE OESOPHAGUS.

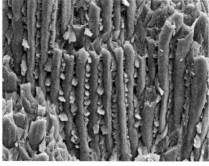

ENAMEL SURFACE
This microscope image shows enamel, which is a hard material made of U-shaped enamel prisms packed with the crystalline mineral substance hydroxyapatite.

TEETH

There are four types of tooth, each of which has a different role. The incisors, at the front, are chisel-shaped with sharp edges for cutting, while the pointed canines or "eye teeth" are designed for tearing. The premolars, with their two ridges, and the flatter molars towards the back of the mouth, which are the largest and strongest teeth, crush and grind food. The portion of the tooth above the gum is the crown; the part embedded in the jawbone is known as the root; and the area where these two meet, at the gum or gingival surface, is called the neck of the tooth. The crown's outside layer is made of a tough bone-like material, called enamel, which is the hardest substance in the body. Beneath it is a layer of softer but still strong tissue called dentine, which is shock-absorbing. At the centre of the tooth, the soft dental pulp contains blood vessels and nerves. Below the gum, bone-like cementum and periodontal ligament tissues secure the tooth in the jawbone.

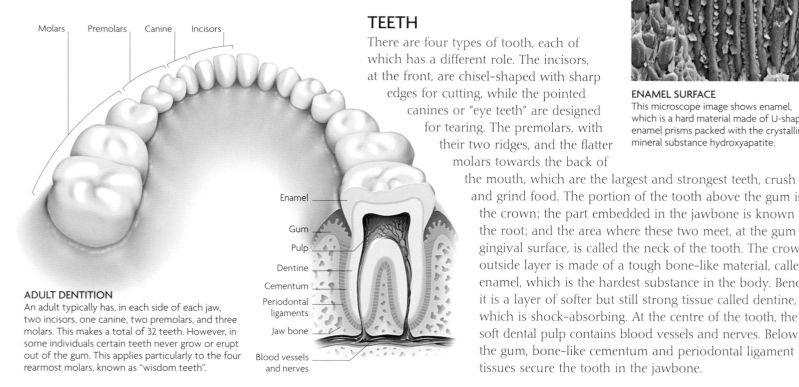

Molars, Premolars, Canine, Incisors

Enamel
Gum
Pulp
Dentine
Cementum
Periodontal ligaments
Jaw bone
Blood vessels and nerves

ADULT DENTITION
An adult typically has, in each side of each jaw, two incisors, one canine, two premolars, and three molars. This makes a total of 32 teeth. However, in some individuals certain teeth never grow or erupt out of the gum. This applies particularly to the four rearmost molars, known as "wisdom teeth".

SWALLOWING

The process of swallowing begins as a voluntary action when a bolus of food is pushed by the rear of the tongue to the back of the mouth. Swallowing usually takes place after a period of chewing; to swallow a solid item such as a tablet without chewing demands concentration. It is easier to swallow a tablet with water, as drinks are usually gulped straight down after entering the mouth. Automatic reflexes control subsequent stages of swallowing, as the muscles of the throat contract and move the bolus rearward and down, and squeeze it into the top of the oesophagus. A flap of cartilage known as the epiglottis prevents food going down "the wrong way" into the larynx and the trachea, where it would cause choking.

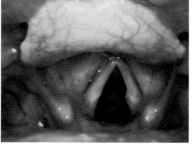

VIEW INTO THE LARYNX
The pale leaf-like flap of the epiglottis is visible at the top of this image. Below it is the inverted "V" of the vocal cords.

BREATHE OR SWALLOW

The pharynx is a dual-purpose passageway: for air when breathing, and food, drink, and saliva when swallowing. Nerve signals from the brain operate the muscles of the mouth, tongue, pharynx, larynx, and upper oesophagus to prevent food from entering the trachea. If food is inhaled, irritation of the airway triggers the coughing reflex to expel inhaled particles and prevent choking. The complex muscle movements of swallowing are a voluntary reflex and also occur when solid matter contacts touch sensors at the back of the mouth.

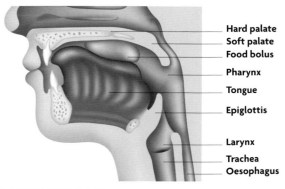

Hard palate
Soft palate
Food bolus
Pharynx
Tongue
Epiglottis
Larynx
Trachea
Oesophagus

1 PHARYNGEAL STAGE
Before the food bolus reaches the back of the mouth, the epiglottis is raised in its normal position, allowing free flow of air from the nasal cavity to the trachea. The oesophagus is relaxed.

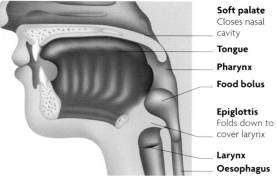

Soft palate
Closes nasal cavity
Tongue
Pharynx
Food bolus
Epiglottis
Folds down to cover larynx
Larynx
Oesophagus

2 OESOPHAGEAL STAGE
The larynx rises and meets the tilted epiglottis, closing the trachea, and the soft palate lifts to close the nasal cavity. Food enters the oesophagus and is pushed downward.

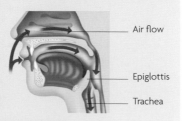

Air flow
Epiglottis
Trachea

DUAL INTAKE
Breathing occurs through the nose or the mouth. Their passageways meet at the throat, and air flows into the trachea.

ANATOMY OF THE MOUTH AND THROAT

The interior of the lips, cheeks, and oral cavity is lined with tough, firmly anchored mucous membrane and a type of tissue called non-keratinized squamous epithelium. Cells here multiply rapidly to replace those rubbed away when biting, chewing, and swallowing. The front underside of the tongue has a fleshy central ridge, the frenulum, which connects to the floor of the mouth. The tongue is the body's most flexible muscle. Within it are three pairs of intrinsic muscles; and outside, three pairs of extrinsic muscles run from the tongue to other parts of the throat and neck. The root of the tongue anchors to the lower jaw (mandible) and to the curved hyoid bone in the neck. The rear of the mouth leads to the middle part of the throat, the oropharynx. The whole throat or pharynx, from its nasal to laryngeal regions, is about 13cm (5in) long in a typical adult.

NOSE, MOUTH, AND THROAT
The roof of the mouth, or oral cavity, is formed by shelves of the maxillary and palatine bones of the skull, together known as the hard palate. This extends rearward as the soft palate, which contains skeletal muscle fibres that allow it to flex when swallowing. The central posterior part of the soft palate extends into a small "finger", the uvula, which can be seen through the open mouth, dangling down from the back, where it helps to direct food downward.

SALIVARY GLANDS

Saliva is produced by three pairs of salivary glands: the parotids, in front of and just below each ear; the submandibulars, on the inner sides of the lower jawbone (mandible); and the sublinguals in the floor of the mouth, below the tongue. In addition, numerous small accessory glands are found in the mucous membranes lining the mouth and tongue. Although composed of 99.5 per cent water, saliva also contains important solutes such as amylase, a digestive enzyme that begins breakdown of starches, and salts. Saliva lubricates food to make chewing and swallowing easier, and it keeps the mouth moist between periods of eating.

SALIVARY GLAND STRUCTURE
Many small, rounded glandular units called acini (brown), separated by connective tissue (pink), discharge their saliva into tiny central ducts. Acinar ducts converge to become the main saliva-carrying glandular ducts.

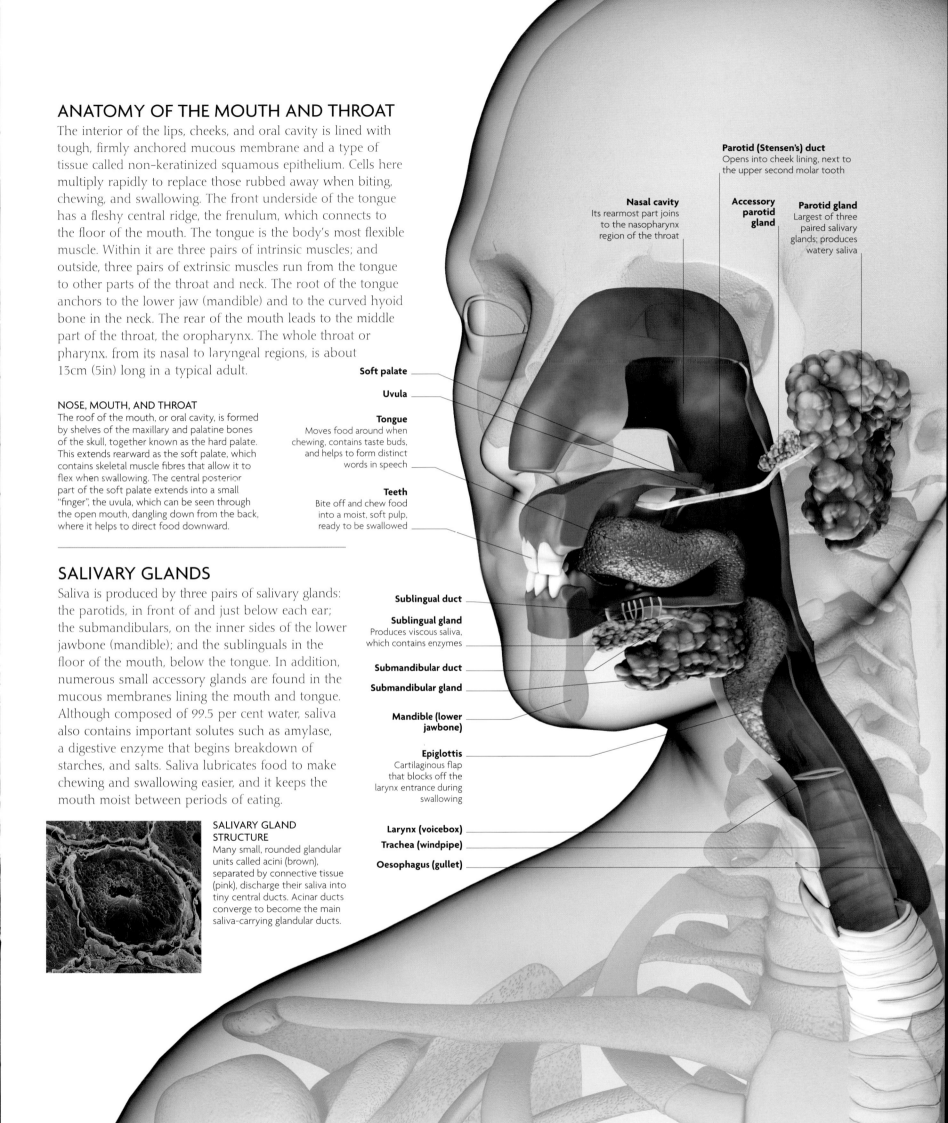

Parotid (Stensen's) duct
Opens into cheek lining, next to the upper second molar tooth

Nasal cavity
Its rearmost part joins to the nasopharynx region of the throat

Accessory parotid gland

Parotid gland
Largest of three paired salivary glands; produces watery saliva

Soft palate

Uvula

Tongue
Moves food around when chewing, contains taste buds, and helps to form distinct words in speech

Teeth
Bite off and chew food into a moist, soft pulp, ready to be swallowed

Sublingual duct

Sublingual gland
Produces viscous saliva, which contains enzymes

Submandibular duct

Submandibular gland

Mandible (lower jawbone)

Epiglottis
Cartilaginous flap that blocks off the larynx entrance during swallowing

Larynx (voicebox)

Trachea (windpipe)

Oesophagus (gullet)

STOMACH AND SMALL INTESTINE

AFTER THE MOUTH, THROAT, AND OESOPHAGUS, THE NEXT MAJOR SECTIONS OF THE DIGESTIVE TRACT ARE THE STOMACH AND THE SMALL INTESTINE. THE STOMACH STORES 1.5 LITRES (2½ PINTS) OR MORE OF FOOD FROM A MEAL AND DIGESTS IT BOTH PHYSICALLY AND CHEMICALLY. THE SMALL INTESTINE CONTINUES THE CHEMICAL BREAKDOWN AND IS THE MAIN SITE FOR ABSORBING THE RESULTING NUTRIENTS INTO THE BLOODSTREAM.

STOMACH STRUCTURE

The stomach is the widest part of the digestive tube. It is a muscular-walled, J-shaped sac in which food is stored, churned, and mixed with gastric juices secreted by its lining. This process begins moments after food enters the stomach from the oesophagus, through the gastro-oesophageal junction. Gastric juices include digestive enzymes and hydrochloric acid, which not only breaks down food but also kills potentially harmful microbes. The smooth muscle layers of the stomach wall contract to combine and squeeze the semiliquid mix of food and gastric juices.

FOLDS AND PITS
With the normal coating of mucus removed in this magnified image (right), the folds (rugae) of the stomach lining are clearly visible.

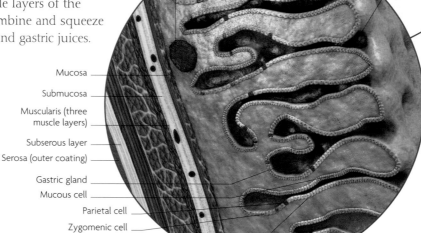

Lymph nodule

Gastric pit

Mucosa

Submucosa

Muscularis (three muscle layers)

Subserous layer

Serosa (outer coating)

Gastric gland

Mucous cell

Parietal cell

Zygomenic cell

Lipase-secreting cell

Enteroendocrine cell

LAYERS OF THE STOMACH WALL
The stomach wall has four main layers: the serosa, muscularis, submucosa, and mucosa. The mucosa has deep infolds (gastric pits) that contain the gastric glands. Mucous cells in the upper part of each pit secrete a mucus lining to stop the stomach from digesting itself. Deeper down are acid-producing parietal cells, and zygomenic (secretes pepsinogen) and lipase-secreting cells for digestion. The enteroendocrine cells secrete the hormone gastrin.

MOVEMENT OF FOOD

Swallowing triggers relaxation of muscles at the gastro-oesophageal junction, enabling food to enter the stomach from the oesophagus. Waves of contractions (peristalsis) of the smooth muscle layers in the stomach wall mix and move food through the stomach. (Similar peristaltic waves propel digestive contents through the whole tract.) The stomach produces up to 3 litres (5 pints) of gastric juices daily. As the food is liquefied, small amounts — just a teaspoonful at a time — are squirted through the stomach's outlet, the pyloric sphincter, into the first part of the small intestine, the duodenum.

PERISTALSIS
Waves of muscle contraction propel food through the tract (see right). The circular muscle contracts and relaxes in sequence producing a "travelling wave" known as peristalsis.

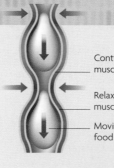

Contracting muscle

Relaxing muscle

Moving food

Duodenum
First and shortest section of the small intestine, about 25cm (10in) long

STOMACH FILLING AND EMPTYING
The stomach expands like a balloon as it fills with food and drink from a meal. Gases produced by chemical breakdown of food, and swallowed air, also collect in and expand the stomach. Those in the highest part of the stomach are expelled by belching (burping or eructation).

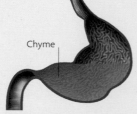

Chyme

1 AFTER A MEAL
Muscles of the stomach wall mix food with gastric juices and churn it to form chyme.

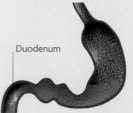

Peristaltic contraction

Pyloric sphincter

2 1–2 HOURS LATER
Peristaltic waves move the liquid stomach contents towards the pyloric sphincter.

Duodenum

3 3–4 HOURS LATER
The pyloric sphincter opens at intervals to let small quantities of chyme into the duodenum.

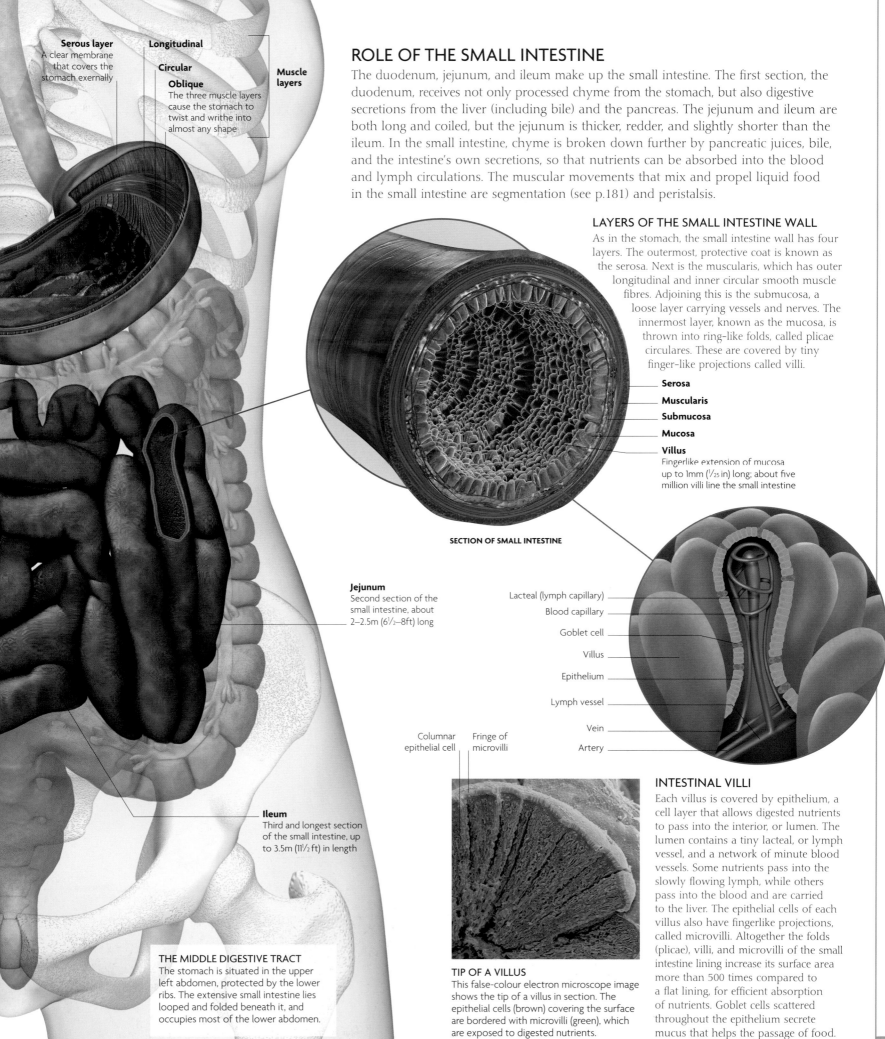

Serous layer
A clear membrane that covers the stomach exernally

Longitudinal

Circular

Oblique
The three muscle layers cause the stomach to twist and writhe into almost any shape

Muscle layers

ROLE OF THE SMALL INTESTINE

The duodenum, jejunum, and ileum make up the small intestine. The first section, the duodenum, receives not only processed chyme from the stomach, but also digestive secretions from the liver (including bile) and the pancreas. The jejunum and ileum are both long and coiled, but the jejunum is thicker, redder, and slightly shorter than the ileum. In the small intestine, chyme is broken down further by pancreatic juices, bile, and the intestine's own secretions, so that nutrients can be absorbed into the blood and lymph circulations. The muscular movements that mix and propel liquid food in the small intestine are segmentation (see p.181) and peristalsis.

LAYERS OF THE SMALL INTESTINE WALL

As in the stomach, the small intestine wall has four layers. The outermost, protective coat is known as the serosa. Next is the muscularis, which has outer longitudinal and inner circular smooth muscle fibres. Adjoining this is the submucosa, a loose layer carrying vessels and nerves. The innermost layer, known as the mucosa, is thrown into ring-like folds, called plicae circulares. These are covered by tiny finger-like projections called villi.

Serosa

Muscularis

Submucosa

Mucosa

Villus
Fingerlike extension of mucosa up to 1mm (1/25 in) long; about five million villi line the small intestine

SECTION OF SMALL INTESTINE

Jejunum
Second section of the small intestine, about 2–2.5m (6½–8ft) long

Lacteal (lymph capillary)

Blood capillary

Goblet cell

Villus

Epithelium

Lymph vessel

Vein

Artery

Ileum
Third and longest section of the small intestine, up to 3.5m (11½ ft) in length

Columnar epithelial cell

Fringe of microvilli

THE MIDDLE DIGESTIVE TRACT
The stomach is situated in the upper left abdomen, protected by the lower ribs. The extensive small intestine lies looped and folded beneath it, and occupies most of the lower abdomen.

TIP OF A VILLUS
This false-colour electron microscope image shows the tip of a villus in section. The epithelial cells (brown) covering the surface are bordered with microvilli (green), which are exposed to digested nutrients.

INTESTINAL VILLI

Each villus is covered by epithelium, a cell layer that allows digested nutrients to pass into the interior, or lumen. The lumen contains a tiny lacteal, or lymph vessel, and a network of minute blood vessels. Some nutrients pass into the slowly flowing lymph, while others pass into the blood and are carried to the liver. The epithelial cells of each villus also have fingerlike projections, called microvilli. Altogether the folds (plicae), villi, and microvilli of the small intestine lining increase its surface area more than 500 times compared to a flat lining, for efficient absorption of nutrients. Goblet cells scattered throughout the epithelium secrete mucus that helps the passage of food.

LIVER, GALLBLADDER, AND PANCREAS

THE LIVER IS THE BODY'S LARGEST INTERNAL ORGAN AND HAS A CRUCIAL ROLE IN THE MANUFACTURE, PROCESSING, AND STORAGE OF MANY CHEMICALS. IT PRODUCES THE DIGESTIVE FLUID BILE THAT IS THEN STORED IN THE GALLBLADDER. THE PANCREAS SECRETES VITAL DIGESTIVE ENZYMES.

STRUCTURE AND FUNCTION OF THE LIVER

Weighing about 1.5kg (3¹/₅lb), the dark red, wedge-shaped liver fills the upper right abdomen below the diaphragm. At a microscopic level, the liver's structural units – lobules – are made up of sheets of liver cells (hepatocytes), tiny branches of the hepatic artery and vein, and bile ducts. Nutrient-rich blood arrives from the intestines via the hepatic portal system (see opposite) and filters through the lobules. The liver has over 250 individual functions, the most important of which are storing and releasing blood sugar (glucose) for energy; sorting and processing vitamins and minerals; breaking down toxins into less harmful substances; and recycling old blood cells.

Hepatic vein
Drains all blood from liver into inferior vena cava

Inferior vena cava
Vein that transports blood from liver and lower body to heart just above

Right liver lobe
Forms around one-seventh of the liver's total bulk

Hepatic duct
Drains bile towards the gallbladder

Hepatic portal vein
Supplies blood from intestinal tract to liver

Gallbladder
Storage bag for liver's bile fluid

Pancreas
Hidden behind lower stomach and transverse colon

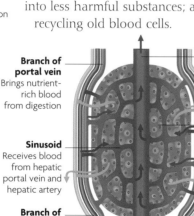

Central vein

Cross-section of lobule

Exterior of lobule

Artery   Bile duct   Vein

Branch of portal vein
Brings nutrient-rich blood from digestion

Sinusoid
Receives blood from hepatic portal vein and hepatic artery

Branch of hepatic artery
Brings oxygen-rich blood to liver

Central vein
Carries away processed blood for waste disposal

Hepatocyte
Filters blood and makes bile

Branch of bile duct
Channels bile fluid away from liver for digestion

LIVER LOBULES
The six-sided lobules nestle together and have blood and bile-collecting vessels around their exteriors.

INSIDE A LOBULE
Hepatocytes filter incoming blood into constituents destined for bile ducts, storage, or waste disposal.

LIVER FUNCTIONS

Most of the liver's tasks are concerned with metabolism. They include: the breakdown of digestive products; the storage of the resulting products; the circulation of substances such as vitamins and minerals; and the construction of complex molecules, such as enzymes.

BILE PRODUCTION	Liver cells secrete bile into small canals called bile canaliculi, which drain into bile ducts running between the lobules. These bile ducts converge to form the common hepatic duct, which conveys bile to the gallbladder for storage.
NUTRIENT PROCESSING	The liver removes nutrients from the blood. It converts simple sugars into glycogen – a process called glycogenesis – and synthesizes amino acids.
GLUCOSE REGULATION	The liver maintains blood glucose levels by converting fat and proteins into glucose. This process is called gluconeogenesis.
DETOXIFICATION	Harmful substances in the blood, such as alcohol and some other poisons, are detoxified. Waste products and unwanted amino acids are converted into urea.
PROTEIN SYNTHESIS	The liver synthesizes blood-clotting proteins and proteins for the fluid part of blood (plasma).
MINERAL AND VITAMIN STORAGE	The liver is a reservoir of minerals such as iron and copper, and the fat-soluble vitamins including A, B_{12}, D, E, and K.
BLOOD WASTE DISPOSAL	Bacteria and general foreign particles are eliminated.
RECYCLING BLOOD CELLS	Old red blood cells are broken down and their constituents reused.

LIVER ARCHITECTURE
In this electron micrograph at a magnification of around 300 times, sheets of hepatocytes can be seen radiating from the central canal. This canal contains the central vein.

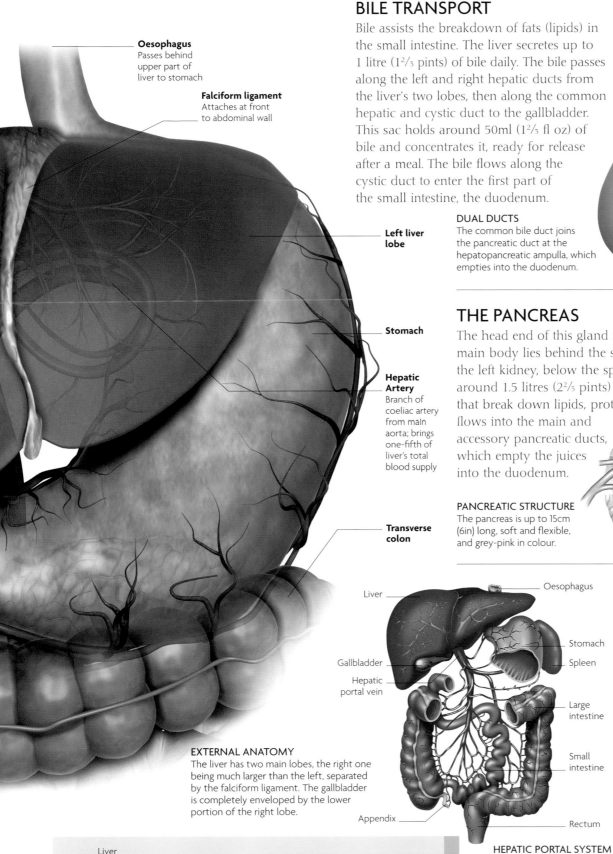

Oesophagus
Passes behind upper part of liver to stomach

Falciform ligament
Attaches at front to abdominal wall

Left liver lobe

Stomach

Hepatic Artery
Branch of coeliac artery from main aorta; brings one-fifth of liver's total blood supply

Transverse colon

BILE TRANSPORT

Bile assists the breakdown of fats (lipids) in the small intestine. The liver secretes up to 1 litre (1²⁄₅ pints) of bile daily. The bile passes along the left and right hepatic ducts from the liver's two lobes, then along the common hepatic and cystic duct to the gallbladder. This sac holds around 50ml (1²⁄₅ fl oz) of bile and concentrates it, ready for release after a meal. The bile flows along the cystic duct to enter the first part of the small intestine, the duodenum.

DUAL DUCTS
The common bile duct joins the pancreatic duct at the hepatopancreatic ampulla, which empties into the duodenum.

Left and right hepatic ducts

Common hepatic duct

Cystic duct from gallbladder

Gallbladder

Common bile duct

Pyloric sphincter of stomach

Pancreas

Hepatopancreatic ampulla (ampulla of Vater)

Duodenum

THE PANCREAS

The head end of this gland nestles in a loop of the duodenum, its main body lies behind the stomach, and its tapering tail sits above the left kidney, below the spleen. Each day, the pancreas produces around 1.5 litres (2²⁄₅ pints) of digestive juice containing enzymes that break down lipids, proteins, and carbohydrates. The fluid flows into the main and accessory pancreatic ducts, which empty the juices into the duodenum.

PANCREATIC STRUCTURE
The pancreas is up to 15cm (6in) long, soft and flexible, and grey-pink in colour.

Pancreatic duct

Head of pancreas

Body of pancreas

Tail of pancreas

EXTERNAL ANATOMY
The liver has two main lobes, the right one being much larger than the left, separated by the falciform ligament. The gallbladder is completely enveloped by the lower portion of the right lobe.

Liver

Oesophagus

Gallbladder

Stomach

Spleen

Hepatic portal vein

Large intestine

Small intestine

Appendix

Rectum

HEPATIC PORTAL SYSTEM
Veins from almost every part of the digestive tract, even the lower oesophagus, converge to form the hepatic portal vein that enters the liver. In this view, some organs have been removed to reveal the blood vessels.

Liver

Pancreas

Gallbladder

FRONT   **RIGHT SIDE**   **REAR**   **LEFT SIDE**

360-DEGREE VIEW

THE HEPATIC PORTAL CIRCULATION

The liver is unusual in that it receives two blood supplies. The hepatic artery delivers oxygen-rich blood to the liver. In addition, the hepatic portal vein supplies the liver with oxygen-poor, nutrient-rich blood from the digestive tract, before this blood returns to the heart and is pumped throughout the body. This enables the liver to stop toxins absorbed in the intestines from reaching the rest of the body, and to regulate the levels of many other substances in the bloodstream. Veins from several organs, including the intestines, pancreas, stomach, and spleen, drain into the hepatic portal vein. It is around 8cm (3in) long and supplies up to four-fifths of the blood into the liver. The flow-rate increases after a meal, but falls during physical activity as blood is diverted from the abdominal organs to skeletal muscles.

LARGE INTESTINE

THE LARGE INTESTINE IS THE FINAL PART OF THE DIGESTIVE TRACT AND COMPRISES THREE MAIN REGIONS – THE CAECUM, COLON, AND RECTUM. THE CAECUM IS A SHORT POUCH THAT LINKS THE SMALL INTESTINE TO THE COLON, WHICH IS AROUND 1.5M (5FT) LONG. THE COLON CHANGES LIQUID DIGESTIVE WASTE PRODUCTS FROM THE SMALL INTESTINE INTO A MORE SOLID FORM THAT THE BODY EXCRETES AS FAECES VIA THE RECTUM AND ANUS.

ROLE OF THE COLON

When the chemical breakdown of food in the small intestine is complete (see pp.176–77), almost all the nutrients vital for bodily functions have been absorbed. The waste product from this process is partially digested, liquefied food (chyme). This passes from the small intestine, through the ileocaecal valve, into the caecum. From there, it reaches the first part of the colon, the ascending colon. The main function of the colon is to convert the liquid chyme into semi-solid faeces for storage and disposal. Sodium, chloride, and water are absorbed through the lining of the colon into blood and lymph, and the faeces become less watery. The colon secretes bicarbonate and potassium in exchange for sodium and chloride. There are also billions of symbiotic or "friendly" microorganisms within the colon.

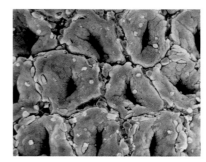

COLONIC GLANDS
This microscope image (magnified 120 times) shows the openings to tubular glands lining the colon. They secrete mucus and absorb water from faeces.

LAYERS OF THE COLON WALL

The colon wall has several layers. The first is an outer coating (serosa). Inside this is the muscularis layer, which comprises two bands of smooth muscle fibres, longitudinal and then circular. These are responsible for colonic movements. The next layer is the submucosa, which has many small lobes of lymphatic tissue called lymphoid nodules. Innermost is the undulating mucosa. This contains goblet cells in intestinal glands, which secrete lubricating mucus to ease the passage of faeces.

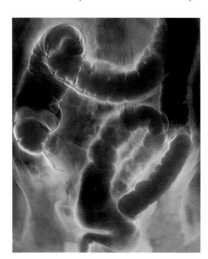

IMAGING THE COLON
This contrast X-ray of the large intestine was made by flowing barium – a fluid opaque to X-rays – into the bowel via the rectum.

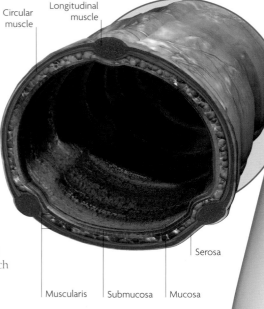

Circular muscle · Longitudinal muscle · Serosa · Muscularis · Submucosa · Mucosa

Ascending colon
Section of colon rising up right side of abdomen

Caecum
Pouch-like entrance to large intestine

Ileocaecal valve
Controls flow of liquefied food from small intestine

Appendix (vermiform appendix)
A finger-like dead-end passage from caecum with no clear major role

PORTIONS OF THE COLON
The three sections of the colon form an almost rectangular "frame", with the loops and coils of the small intestine inside it, the stomach and liver above, and the rectum below.

GUT FLORA

Billions of microorganisms, mainly bacteria, live in the intestinal tract – chiefly in the large intestine. They are known as the gut flora and are normally harmless, provided they do not spread to other parts of the body and are kept in balance. They produce enzymes that break down certain food components, especially the plant fibre cellulose, which human enzymes cannot digest. In this way, the bacteria feed on the undigested fibre in faecal material, provide nutrients that can be absorbed into the body, and help to reduce the amount of faeces. As part of their metabolism, the gut flora also produce vitamins K and B, and the gases hydrogen, carbon dioxide, hydrogen sulphide, and methane. In addition, the flora help to control harmful microbes which may enter the digestive system, and assist the immune system to fight disease by promoting formation of antibodies and the activity of lymphoid tissue in the colonic lining. Overall the gut flora and the body exist in a mutually beneficial partnership (symbiosis). When faeces are excreted, at least one-third of their weight is composed of these bacteria.

BACTERIA IN THE COLON
This electron microscope image (magnified over 2,000 times) shows clusters of rod-like bacteria on the lining of the colon.

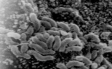

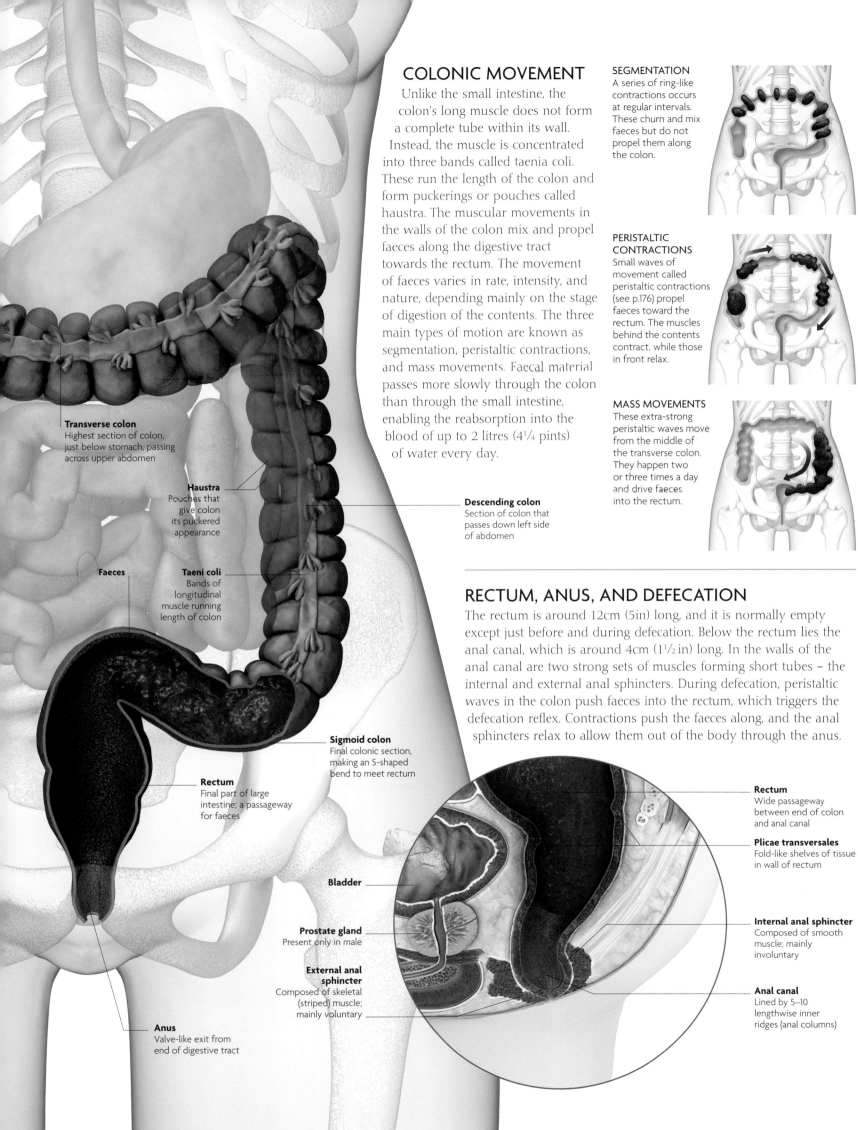

COLONIC MOVEMENT

Unlike the small intestine, the colon's long muscle does not form a complete tube within its wall. Instead, the muscle is concentrated into three bands called taenia coli. These run the length of the colon and form puckerings or pouches called haustra. The muscular movements in the walls of the colon mix and propel faeces along the digestive tract towards the rectum. The movement of faeces varies in rate, intensity, and nature, depending mainly on the stage of digestion of the contents. The three main types of motion are known as segmentation, peristaltic contractions, and mass movements. Faecal material passes more slowly through the colon than through the small intestine, enabling the reabsorption into the blood of up to 2 litres (4¼ pints) of water every day.

SEGMENTATION
A series of ring-like contractions occurs at regular intervals. These churn and mix faeces but do not propel them along the colon.

PERISTALTIC CONTRACTIONS
Small waves of movement called peristaltic contractions (see p.176) propel faeces toward the rectum. The muscles behind the contents contract, while those in front relax.

MASS MOVEMENTS
These extra-strong peristaltic waves move from the middle of the transverse colon. They happen two or three times a day and drive faeces into the rectum.

Transverse colon
Highest section of colon, just below stomach, passing across upper abdomen

Haustra
Pouches that give colon its puckered appearance

Faeces

Taeni coli
Bands of longitudinal muscle running length of colon

Descending colon
Section of colon that passes down left side of abdomen

Sigmoid colon
Final colonic section, making an S-shaped bend to meet rectum

Rectum
Final part of large intestine; a passageway for faeces

Bladder

Prostate gland
Present only in male

External anal sphincter
Composed of skeletal (striped) muscle; mainly voluntary

Anus
Valve-like exit from end of digestive tract

RECTUM, ANUS, AND DEFECATION

The rectum is around 12cm (5in) long, and it is normally empty except just before and during defecation. Below the rectum lies the anal canal, which is around 4cm (1½ in) long. In the walls of the anal canal are two strong sets of muscles forming short tubes – the internal and external anal sphincters. During defecation, peristaltic waves in the colon push faeces into the rectum, which triggers the defecation reflex. Contractions push the faeces along, and the anal sphincters relax to allow them out of the body through the anus.

Rectum
Wide passageway between end of colon and anal canal

Plicae transversales
Fold-like shelves of tissue in wall of rectum

Internal anal sphincter
Composed of smooth muscle; mainly involuntary

Anal canal
Lined by 5–10 lengthwise inner ridges (anal columns)

1 IN THE STOMACH

The stomach lining is dotted with microscopic gastric pits, which contain cells that secrete various substances. Hydrochloric acid, from cells deep in the pits, kills any microbes in swallowed food. Other cells release the enzyme gastric lipase, which begins initial fat breakdown. Digestion of proteins by pepsin begins in earnest. Pepsin is first released in an inactive form (pepsinogen), then it is converted by the stomach's acid. If it was active when released, it would digest the stomach wall itself. A lining of mucus also protects the stomach from digestive enzymes.

Protein

Peptide

Pepsin enzyme

PEPSIN IN ACTION

Pepsin is activated when it meets the acid of the stomach's interior. It splits protein molecules into shorter amino-acid chains called peptides.

Gastric mucosa
Stomach lining

Pepsin
Protein-digesting enzyme

Gastric lipase
Fat-digesting enzyme

Hydrochloric acid

Mucus

Gastric pit
Contains glands secreting enzymes, hydrochloric acid, and mucus

2 IN THE DUODENUM

The part-digested stomach contents, known as chyme, is squirted into the duodenum – the first part of the small intestine. Ducts deliver bile fluid from the liver and gallbladder, and a complex mix of secretions from the pancreas. The pancreatic juices include alkalis, such as bicarbonates, that neutralize the stomach acid, and about 15 enzymes, which work on the three major components of food – carbohydrates, proteins, and fats (lipids).

Bile salt

BILE FUNCTION

Bile contains salts that emulsify large fat droplets, to create an emulsion of tiny fat droplets with a large surface area for enzyme action.

Fat droplet
Containing fat (lipid) molecules

Smaller fat droplet

Wall of duodenum
Lined with finger-like villi

Bile duct from gallbladder

Pancreatic duct from pancreas

Ampulla of Vater

Villus

Protease enzymes

Triglyceride lipid
Fat molecule

Monoglyceride

Bile salts

Lipase

Fatty acid

Lipase

FAT (LIPID) BREAKDOWN

Lipase fat-digesting enzymes break down triglyceride fat (lipid) units to form two fatty acids and a monoglyceride.

Amylase

Starch

Amylase enzyme

CARBOHYDRATE BREAKDOWN

Pancreatic amylase enzyme breaks long-chain carbohydrates, such as starch, into disaccharide (double-sugar) pieces, especially maltose sugar.

Maltose sugar

Peptide

Protein

Protease enzyme

PROTEIN BREAKDOWN

Protease enzymes split proteins into short-chain peptides and amino acids.

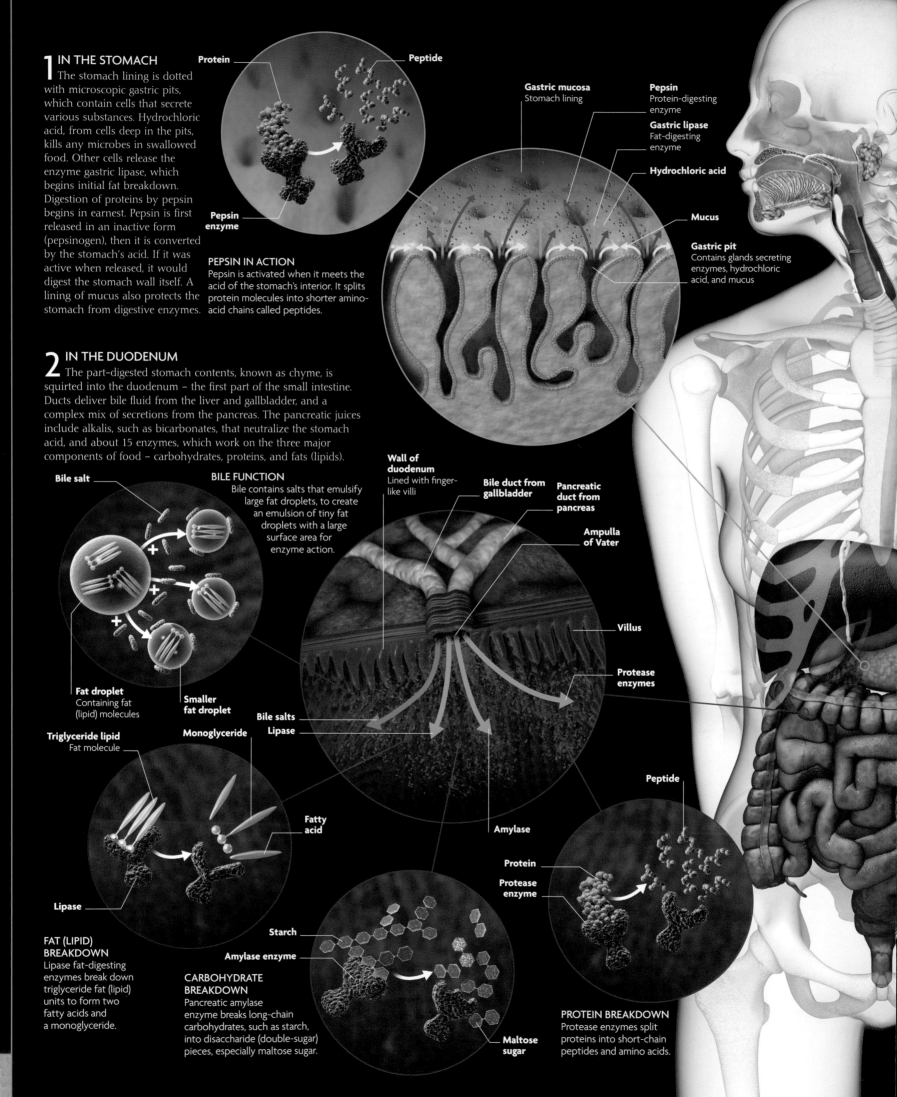

DIGESTION

THE DIGESTIVE PROCESS INVOLVES A SERIES OF PHYSICAL AND CHEMICAL ACTIONS THAT BREAK DOWN THE COMPONENTS OF FOOD INTO NUTRIENT PARTICLES SMALL ENOUGH FOR ABSORPTION.

Vigorous physical digestion of food – mashing and churning – occurs in the mouth, but becomes progressively less important in successive sections of the digestive tract. The stomach also breaks food into small particles physically using muscular movement, but like the mouth, secretes digestive chemicals (enzymes), too. By the time the pulverized food and enzymes (chyme) reach the duodenum (the first part of the small intestine), many food particles are already microscopically small, yet not small enough to pass across cell membranes into the body tissues. Chemical digestion then takes over in importance, with large molecules split into even smaller, absorbable particles that can enter the bloodstream.

HOW ENZYMES WORK

An enzyme is a biological catalyst – a substance that boosts the rate of a biochemical reaction, but remains unchanged. Most enzymes are proteins. They affect the reactions of digestive breakdown, and also the chemical changes that release energy and build new materials for cells and tissues. Each enzyme has a specific shape due to the way its long chains of subunits (amino acids) fold and loop. The substance to be altered (the substrate) fits into a part of the enzyme known as the active site. In the case of digestion, the enzyme may undergo a slight change in 3-D configuration that encourages the substrate to break apart at specific bonds between its atoms.

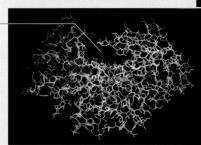

Active site

PEPSIN
A computer model of this digestive enzyme shows the active site as the gap at the top. A protein molecule slots in here and breaks apart.

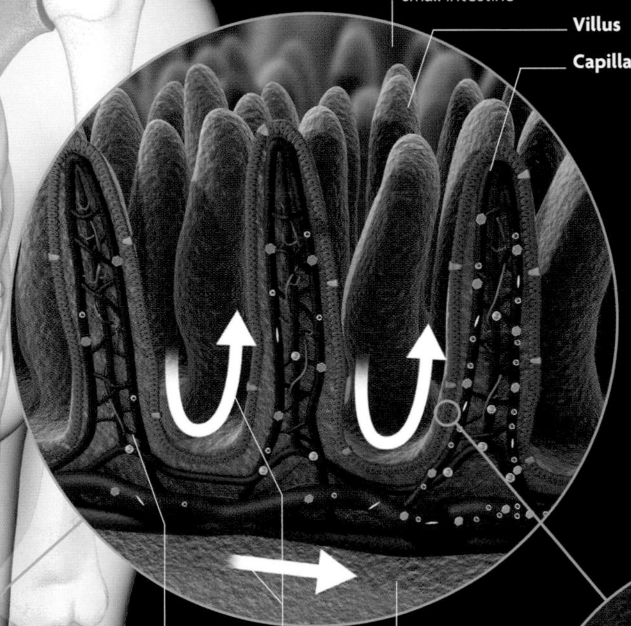

Lumen
Fluid-filled space inside small intestine

Villus

Capillary of villus

3 IN THE SMALL INTESTINE

After the duodenum, the remainder of the small intestine is the site for the final breakdown of food substances and their absorption into the blood and lymphatic fluids. The pancreatic juices and bile fluids continue to work, but the small intestine releases few further enzymes into its inner passage, the lumen. Instead, its enzymes act within the lining cells, and on their surfaces. These enzymes include lactase and maltase, which break down the double (disaccharide) sugars, lactose and maltose, into single-unit glucose and galactose. Intestinal peptidases convert short peptide chains (originally from proteins) into their subunits, amino acids. The fingerlike villi of the intestine lining have surface cells bearing smaller projections of their own (microvilli) where some of the final changes occur.

ABSORPTION ACROSS VILLI
The fingerlike villi (left) of the small intestine lining provide a large area for the absorption of the products of digestion. These substances are shown here accumulating in the bloodstream from left to right.

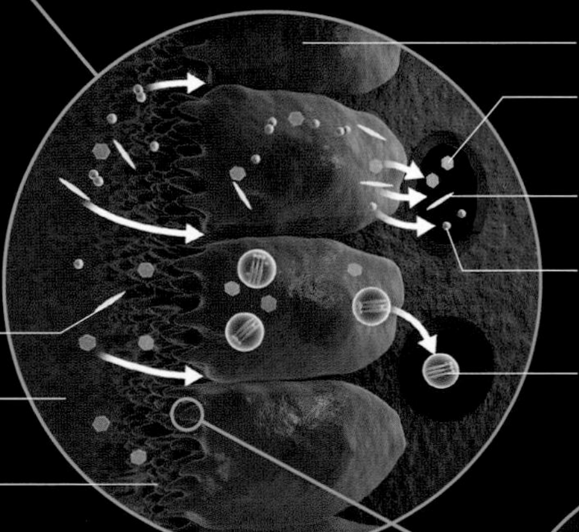

Epithelial (lining) cell of small intestine wall

Glucose

Short-chain fatty acid

Amino acid

EXTREME CLOSE-UP OF CELL MEMBRANE
The enzymes that complete digestion are embedded in the surface membrane of the intestine's epithelial cells (below). The resulting amino acids and sugars are then absorbed through dedicated protein channels in the membrane, while fatty acids simply pass straight through.

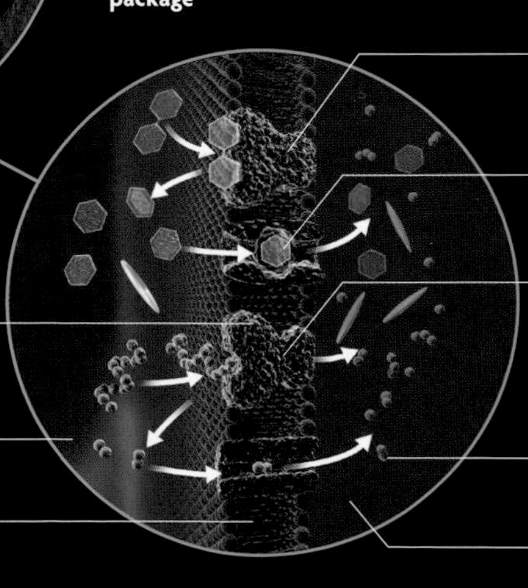

Lipid package

Lacteal
Lymph capillary of villus

Direction of blood flow

Wall of small intestine

Fatty acid

Small intestine lumen

Epithelial cell membrane
Formed into "brush" of microvilli

CLOSE-UP OF VILLUS SURFACE
Short-chain fatty acids, glucose, and amino acids pass through the intestine's epithelial (lining) cells (above) and then into a blood capillary (red). Larger fatty acids are reassembled into triglyceride lipids, packaged, and passed into a lymph capillary (lacteal, purple).

Short-chain fatty acid
Simply diffuses across cell membrane

Small intestine lumen

Epithelial cell membrane

Maltase enzyme
Splits (double) maltose into (single) glucose

Glucose
Passes across membrane through channel protein

Peptidase enzyme
Splits peptides into amino acids

Amino acids
Pass across membrane through channel protein in twos and threes

Epithelial cell interior

DIGESTIVE JOURNEY
Each part of the digestive tract has its own conditions to further the dismantling of food substances into their subunits. Simple salts and minerals, such as sodium, potassium, and chloride, do not need digestion. They are mostly dissolved rapidly and absorbed in the small intestine.

FATES OF NUTRIENTS

The digestive process takes, on average, 12–24 hours. Food is in the stomach for 2–4 hours, and in the small intestine for 1–5 hours. The final stages of digestion and waste compaction in the large intestine may take 12 hours. Different breakdown products are available for absorption at different times.

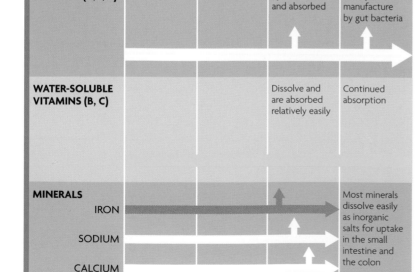

	MOUTH	STOMACH	SMALL INTESTINE	LARGE INTESTINE
PROTEINS		Hydrochloric acid and pepsin break protein into peptide chains	Peptidases snip peptides into amino acids for absorption	
CARBOHYDRATES	Salivary amylase begins starch digestion during chewing	Stomach acid inactivates salivary amylase	Enzymes, such as pancreatic amylase, yield simple sugars	
FAT (LIPIDS)		Gastric lipase splits lipids into fatty acids, and monoglycerides	Pancreatic lipase products enter lacteals	
FIBRE				Soluble fibre broken down – not absorbed
SOLUBLE				
INSOLUBLE				
WATER		Small amounts absorbed by stomach lining	Absorbed by small intestine lining	Most water absorbed by large intestine
FAT-SOLUBLE VITAMINS (A,D,K)			Emulsified by bile salts and absorbed	Further absorption, K manufacture by gut bacteria
WATER-SOLUBLE VITAMINS (B, C)			Dissolve and are absorbed relatively easily	Continued absorption
MINERALS				Most minerals dissolve easily as inorganic salts for uptake in the small intestine and the colon
IRON				
SODIUM				
CALCIUM				

NUTRIENTS AND METABOLISM

THE BODY'S INTERNAL BIOCHEMICAL REACTIONS, CHANGES, AND PROCESSES ARE TERMED METABOLISM. DIGESTION PROVIDES THE NUTRIENTS AS RAW MATERIALS, WHICH ENTER METABOLIC PATHWAYS IN ALL CELLS AND TISSUES.

TAKING IN NUTRIENTS

"Nutrients" encompass all substances that are useful to the body. These include complex chemicals broken down to release energy, chiefly carbohydrates and fats; proteins, which are mainly for building the structural parts of cells; and vitamins and minerals, which ensure healthy functioning. The digestive system absorbs the nutrients into the blood and lymph at different stages along the tract. The blood flow from the major absorption sites of the intestines is along the hepatic portal vein (see p.179) to the liver. This large gland is the chief processor of nutrients. According to the body's needs, the liver breaks down some nutrients into even smaller, simpler molecules, stores others, and releases others into the circulation.

FINAL STAGES OF DIGESTION

The colon (large intestine, see p.180) is the last main site for breakdown and uptake of nutrients, including minerals, salts, and some vitamins. A considerable amount of water, mainly from the digestive juices, is also reabsorbed. Fibre, such as pectin and cellulose, gives bulk to the digestive remnants, and allows the walls to grip the residues as they are compressed into faeces awaiting expulsion. Fibre also helps to delay the absorption of some molecules, including sugars, and so spreads out their uptake through time rather than in one short "rush". In addition, fibre binds with some fatty substances, such as cholesterol, and helps to prevent their overabsorption.

CAECUM
Each day about 100–500 ml (3½–17fl oz) of digestive fluids, undigested leftovers, rubbed-off intestinal linings, and other matter enters the first chamber of the large intestine, the caecum. Considerable amounts of water are resorbed here.

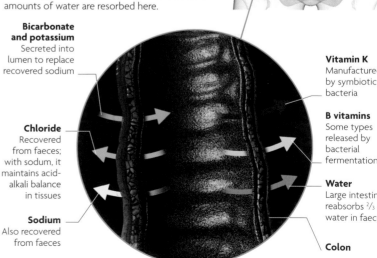

Bicarbonate and potassium
Secreted into lumen to replace recovered sodium

Chloride
Recovered from faeces; with sodium, it maintains acid-alkali balance in tissues

Sodium
Also recovered from faeces

Vitamin K
Manufactured by symbiotic bacteria

B vitamins
Some types released by bacterial fermentation

Water
Large intestine reabsorbs ²/₃ of water in faeces

Colon

BREAKDOWN AND BUILDING UP

Catabolism is the breaking apart of more complex molecules into simpler ones. This happens as part of energy production, for example, when glucose or fats are split apart to release energy. The converse is anabolism, which is the construction of complex molecules from simpler ones. For example, amino acids are linked together to make peptide chains, which then combine to form proteins, as part of protein synthesis (production).

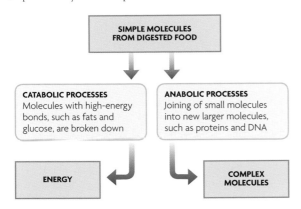

SIMPLE MOLECULES FROM DIGESTED FOOD

CATABOLIC PROCESSES
Molecules with high-energy bonds, such as fats and glucose, are broken down

ANABOLIC PROCESSES
Joining of small molecules into new larger molecules, such as proteins and DNA

ENERGY

COMPLEX MOLECULES

INTERPLAY
Metabolism is a complex interplay of construction and destruction, with many molecules being recycled as they pass between the two processes.

FUNCTIONS OF VITAMINS AND MINERALS

Vitamins are organic substances that are mostly incorporated into coenzymes – molecules that assist and support enzymes in the control of metabolic processes. Regular vitamin intake is required because only a few vitamins can be manufactured in the body. Minerals are simple inorganic substances such as calcium, iron, chloride, and iodine. They are needed both for general metabolism and specialist uses, such as iron for haemoglobin in red blood cells.

BLOOD CLOTTING	BLOOD CELL FORMATION AND FUNCTIONING	HEALTHY TEETH	HEALTHY EYES
Vitamin K	Vitamins B_6 and B_{12}	Vitamins C and D	Vitamin A
Calcium	Vitamin E	Calcium	Zinc
Iron	Folic Acid	Phosphorus	
	Copper	Fluorine	
	Iron	Magnesium	
	Cobalt	Boron	

HEALTHY SKIN AND HAIR	HEART FUNCTIONING	BONE FORMATION	MUSCLE FUNCTIONING
Vitamin A	Vitamin B_1 (Thiamine)	Vitamin A	Vitamin B_1 (Thiamine)
Vitamin B_2 (Riboflavin)	Vitamin D	Vitamin C	Vitamin B_6
Vitamin B_3 (Niacin)	Inositol	Vitamin D	Vitamin B_{12}
Vitamin B_6	Calcium	Fluorine	Vitamin E
Vitamin B_{12}	Potassium	Calcium	Biotin
Biotin	Magnesium	Copper	Calcium
Sulphur	Selenium	Phosphorus	Potassium
Zinc	Sodium	Magnesium	Sodium
	Copper	Boron	Magnesium

HOW THE BODY USES FOOD

The three major food components yield different breakdown products. Carbohydrates (starches and sugars) can be reduced to the simple sugar glucose; proteins are cut into polypeptide chains, peptides, and finally single amino acids; fats (lipids) are reduced to fatty acids and glycerol. The major use of glucose is as the body's most adaptable and readiest source of energy. Uses of fatty acids include forming the bi-lipid membranes around and inside cells (see p.27). Amino acids are reassembled into the body's own proteins, both structural (collagen, keratin, and similar tough substances) and functional (enzymes). However, the body can adapt and divert nutrients to different uses as conditions dictate.

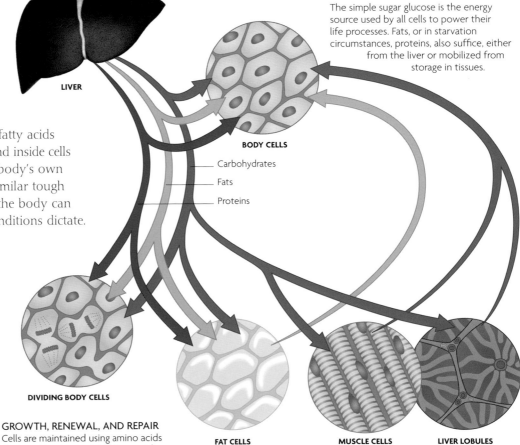

LIVER

BODY CELLS

Carbohydrates
Fats
Proteins

ENERGY PRODUCTION
The simple sugar glucose is the energy source used by all cells to power their life processes. Fats, or in starvation circumstances, proteins, also suffice, either from the liver or mobilized from storage in tissues.

DIVIDING BODY CELLS

FAT CELLS   **MUSCLE CELLS**   **LIVER LOBULES**

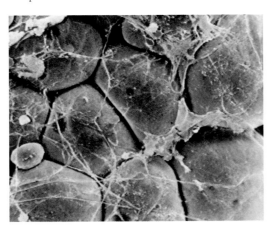

FAT TISSUE
Relatively, fatty substances, or lipids, are the body's most concentrated energy store, producing the most energy when metabolized. Adipose tissue consists of cells replete with fat droplets, stored for times of shortage.

GROWTH, RENEWAL, AND REPAIR
Cells are maintained using amino acids that combine in a variety of ways to build up different protein structures, fats to produce membranes, and glucose to provide the energy. Dividing cells for growth or repair require increased supplies of these nutrients.

ENERGY STORAGE
Surplus glucose is converted into glycogen, which can be stockpiled in the liver and muscle cells. Fatty acids are a concentrated energy store. They are derived either directly from dietary fats, from conversion of excess amino acids, or from conversion of glucose.

UPPER DIGESTIVE TRACT DISORDERS

MANY GULLET (OESOPHAGEAL) AND STOMACH (GASTRIC) PROBLEMS RELATE TO THE CORROSIVE
PROPERTIES OF THE ACIDIC STOMACH CONTENTS. THE UNDERSTANDING AND TREATMENT OF SEVERAL
DIGESTIVE DISORDERS HAS BEEN REVOLUTIONIZED IN THE PAST TWO DECADES BY THE DISCOVERY THAT
THEY ARE LINKED TO THE PRESENCE OF THE BACTERIUM *HELICOBACTER PYLORI*.

GINGIVITIS

INFLAMMATION OF THE GUMS, OR
GINGIVAE, IS ONE OF THE MOST
COMMON OF ALL HEALTH PROBLEMS.

The usual cause of gingivitis is poor
oral hygiene. Dental plaque (deposits of
food particles and other debris) builds
up around the base of the teeth, where
the crowns meet the gum. The gums
become purplish-red and swollen, and
they bleed easily when brushed. Left
untreated, the gum may pull away
from the tooth neck, producing a
pocket where bacteria can collect and
cause infection. The main treatment is
dental attention to remove the plaque.

GASTRIC REFLUX

ACIDIC STOMACH CONTENTS CAN FLOW
BACK INTO THE OESOPHAGUS, CAUSING
DISCOMFORT KNOWN AS HEARTBURN.

Heartburn is a common symptom
and often occurs after overeating
or drinking too much alcohol, or in
pregnant women. Sometimes, however,
the problem persists or increases in
severity and requires medical attention.
If reflux is long term, it can cause
inflammation in the oesophagus.
Obesity and smoking both increase
the likelihood of gastric reflux. The
symptoms can also develop in people
with a hiatus hernia (see opposite).

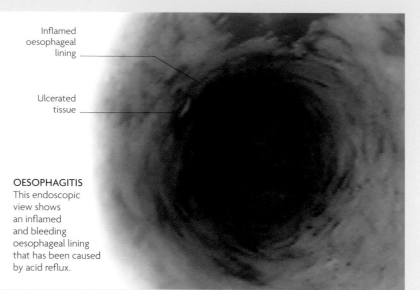

Inflamed
oesophageal
lining

Ulcerated
tissue

OESOPHAGITIS
This endoscopic
view shows
an inflamed
and bleeding
oesophageal lining
that has been caused
by acid reflux.

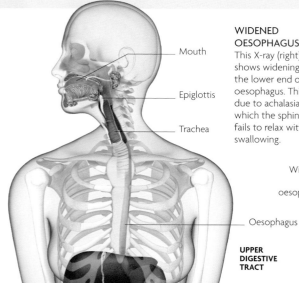

Mouth

Epiglottis

Trachea

Oesophagus

**UPPER
DIGESTIVE
TRACT**

**WIDENED
OESOPHAGUS**
This X-ray (right)
shows widening of
the lower end of the
oesophagus. This is
due to achalasia, in
which the sphincter
fails to relax with
swallowing.

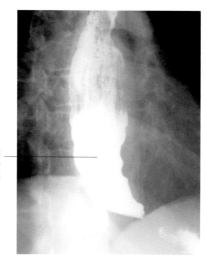

Widened
lower
oesophagus

ACHALASIA

THIS MUSCLE DISORDER OF THE OESOPHAGUS, CAUSES
DIFFICULTY IN SWALLOWING AND DELAYS OR PREVENTS
FOOD PASSING THROUGH TO THE STOMACH.

Achalasia is caused by failure of the muscular ring
(sphincter) at the lower end of the oesophagus to relax
on swallowing, combined with poor coordination
of the contractions in the muscular wall of the
oesophagus that propel food along to the stomach.
Gradually the lower oesophagus distends, causing
symptoms such as difficulty in swallowing, discomfort
or pain behind the breastbone, and regurgitation of
undigested food, especially at night when lying down.
Treatments include widening the sphincter using an
inflatable balloon, drugs to relax the muscles, and
surgery to cut muscle tissue in the lower oesophagus.

CANCER OF THE OESOPHAGUS

A MALIGNANT TUMOUR THAT OCCURS
IN THE OESOPHAGUS IS OFTEN LINKED
TO SMOKING AND EXCESS ALCOHOL.

The symptoms of oesophageal cancer
may not be apparent at first. Difficulty
swallowing solid foods, and then fluids,
is a common symptom. Later, food
may be regurgitated and spill over into
the lungs, causing a cough. Eventually
the cancer may spread through the
oesophagus wall to nearby structures.
Treatment involves surgery to remove
the tumour or to insert a tube in the
narrowed area to help swallowing.

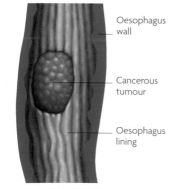

Oesophagus
wall

Cancerous
tumour

Oesophagus
lining

OESOPHAGEAL TUMOUR
An oesophageal tumour physically narrows
or blocks the passageway for swallowed
food. It can be detected by endoscopy
or a barium X-ray.

FOOD POISONING

CONSUMING CONTAMINATED FOOD
OR DRINK CAN RESULT IN DIARRHOEA,
VOMITING, AND ABDOMINAL PAIN.

Most people have had an episode of
food poisoning, often when travelling
overseas. Contaminated food may taste
normal, the symptoms appearing hours
or days later. Mostly, episodes are mild
and clear up in a few days. However,
some more serious infections, such as
salmonella, may require treatment with
antibiotics and rehydration. Careful
preparation, storage, and cooking of
food helps avoid these problems.

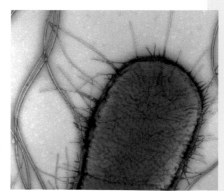

ESCHERICIA COLI BACTERIUM
If *E. coli* bacteria contaminate food, such
as meat or water, they cause an episode
of food poisoning. Infection with *E. coli* can
be serious, particularly in small children.

GASTRITIS

INFLAMMATION OF THE STOMACH LINING, CALLED GASTRITIS, CAUSES DISCOMFORT OR PAIN, AND NAUSEA AND VOMITING.

Sudden onset (acute) gastritis may be caused by over-indulging, especially in alcohol, or by medications known for their effect on the stomach lining, such as aspirin. Chronic gastritis develops over the longer term and may be due to repeated insult to the lining by alcohol, tobacco, or drugs. Another common cause is the bacterium *Helicobacter pylori*. Gastritis usually gets better with medication and by removing the underlying cause.

COMMON CULPRIT
More than 50 per cent of people have *H. pylori* in their stomach lining. If the bacteria cause symptoms, they can be eradicated with antibiotics.

STOMACH CANCER

A CANCEROUS TUMOUR IN THE STOMACH LINING IS MADE MORE LIKELY BY SMOKING, INFECTION WITH *HELICOBACTER PYLORI*, AND A HIGH SALT DIET.

Stomach cancer is more common in people over 50 years of age and in males. This type of cancer spreads (metastasizes) to other parts of the body rapidly and has often done so before the symptoms are noticed. These include upper abdominal discomfort or pain, especially after eating, along with nausea and vomiting, and loss of appetite and weight loss. Anaemia may also develop due to bleeding from the stomach lining. If the cancer is caught early enough, surgical treatment can be successful.

PEPTIC ULCERS

PEPTIC ULCERS ARE ERODED, INFLAMED AREAS EITHER IN THE LINING OF THE STOMACH OR THE FIRST PART OF THE SMALL INTESTINE (THE DUODENUM) THAT CAUSE PAIN.

Most peptic ulcers are associated with *Helicobacter pylori* bacteria. These damage the mucous lining that normally protects against the powerful acidic juices in the stomach and first part of the duodenum. Other contributory factors include alcohol, smoking, certain medications, family history, and diet. Upper abdominal pain is a common symptom. With a duodenal ulcer this is often worse before a meal and relieved by eating; in a gastric ulcer, eating aggravates the pain.

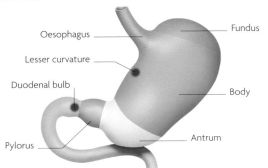

SITES OF PEPTIC ULCERS
A common site for ulcers is in the first part of the duodeum (duodenal bulb). In the stomach, most ulcers develop in the lesser curvature.

EARLY ULCER
If the protective mucous barrier coating the stomach lining breaks down, gastric juices containing strong acid and enzymes come into contact with mucosal cells.

PROGRESSIVE ULCERATION
A true ulcer penetrates the entire lining (mucosal layer) as well as the submucosa and muscle layers. In severe cases, it can perforate the stomach or duodenal wall.

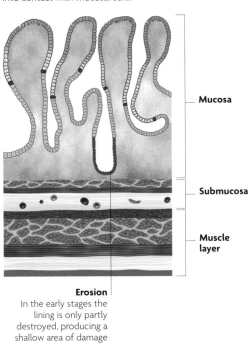

Mucosa

Submucosa

Muscle layer

Erosion
In the early stages the lining is only partly destroyed, producing a shallow area of damage

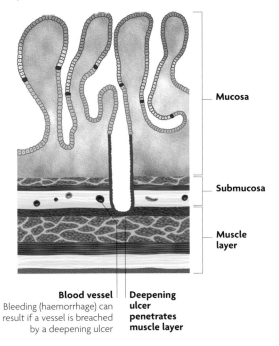

Mucosa

Submucosa

Muscle layer

Blood vessel
Bleeding (haemorrhage) can result if a vessel is breached by a deepening ulcer

Deepening ulcer penetrates muscle layer

HIATUS HERNIA

WEAKNESS IN THE GAP IN THE DIAPHRAGM THROUGH WHICH THE OESOPHAGUS PASSES ALLOWS PART OF THE STOMACH TO PROTRUDE INTO THE CHEST CAVITY.

The diaphragm is a muscular sheet that separates the abdomen from the chest cavity. Normally the stomach lies completely beneath the diaphragm, but in people with a hiatus hernia, its upper section protrudes up through the normally taut aperture, or gap (hiatus) through which the lower oesophagus passes. The hiatus helps the oesophageal sphincter (ring of muscle at lower end of oesophagus) to prevent acidic stomach contents from passing up into the lower oesophagus, and so any symptoms of a hernia are those of gastric reflux (see opposite). There are two types of hiatus hernia: sliding and para-oesophageal. Sliding hernias usually have no symptoms and it is estimated that they are present in around a third of all people over 50. In rare cases, however, para-oesophageal hernias can cause severe pain and require surgery.

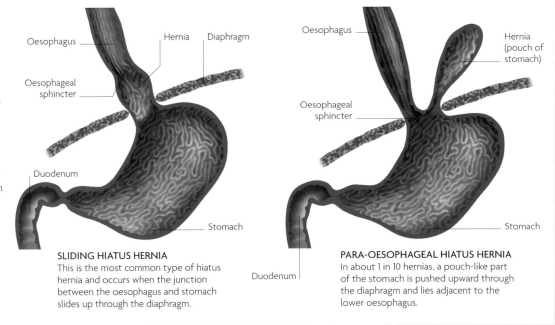

SLIDING HIATUS HERNIA
This is the most common type of hiatus hernia and occurs when the junction between the oesophagus and stomach slides up through the diaphragm.

PARA-OESOPHAGEAL HIATUS HERNIA
In about 1 in 10 hernias, a pouch-like part of the stomach is pushed upward through the diaphragm and lies adjacent to the lower oesophagus.

LIVER, GALLBLADDER, AND PANCREAS DISORDERS

THE LIVER, GALLBLADDER, AND PANCREAS ARE ALL VITAL ORGANS IN THE DIGESTION, ABSORPTION, AND METABOLISM OF FOOD, DRINK, AND DRUGS. AS WITH ALL OTHER ORGANS, THEY ARE VULNERABLE TO INFECTION, TOXIC DAMAGE, AND MALIGNANCY. OFTEN, AS IN THE CASE OF ALCOHOLIC LIVER DISEASE AND HEPATITIS, DISEASES ARE RELATED TO LIFESTYLE BEHAVIOUR AND AS SUCH ARE PREVENTABLE.

ALCOHOLIC LIVER DISEASE

Over a period of many years, regular excessive alcohol consumption can lead to serious liver damage. Men generally drink more heavily than women and should therefore statistically be more likely to develop alcohol-related liver disease. However, women do not metabolize alcohol as efficiently as men and are more vulnerable to its side effects. The toxic effects of certain chemicals in alcohol can damage the liver in different ways, and in some people these toxic effects can increase the risk of developing liver cancer.

PROGRESSION OF THE DISEASE

ALCOHOL CAN CAUSE A WIDE SPECTRUM OF LIVER DISEASES, DEPENDING ON THE NUMBER OF YEARS OF HEAVY DRINKING.

Almost all long-term, heavy drinkers have what is known as a "fatty liver". When alcohol is broken down into its various constituents (metabolized) it produces fat. Globules of fat become lodged in the liver cells, causing them to swell. Fatty liver does not cause any symptoms, but blood-test results may be abnormal. If a person stops drinking at this stage, the fat disappears and the liver may eventually return to normal. However, continued heavy drinking can lead to alcoholic hepatitis, in which the liver becomes inflamed. Symptoms vary from none at all, to acute illness and jaundice. The final stage of alcoholic liver damage is cirrhosis, which can be fatal. Often the only treatment option at this stage is a liver transplant.

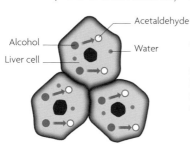

- Acetaldehyde
- Alcohol
- Water
- Liver cell

1 HOW DAMAGE OCCURS
When alcohol (ethanol) is broken down, a substance called acetaldehyde is formed. It is thought that this chemical binds with proteins in the liver cell, which may cause damage, inflammation, and fibrosis.

2 FATTY LIVER
One of the by-products of alcohol metabolism is fat. In excessive drinkers, the liver cells become swollen with globules of fat, which are clearly visible as yellow or white patches if the liver is cut open. The condition is reversible if drinking stops.

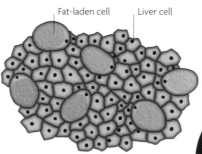

Fat-laden cell — Liver cell

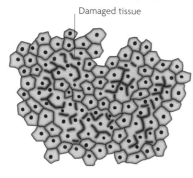

Damaged tissue

3 ALCOHOLIC HEPATITIS
With continued excessive drinking, fatty liver may develop into hepatitis. The liver becomes inflamed and infiltrated with leucocytes (white blood cells). Liver cells may become severely damaged and die.

4 CIRRHOSIS
In this final stage of alcoholic liver disease, the permanent fibrosis and scarring of the liver tissue is life threatening. As the cells are permanently damaged, the liver is unable to carry out its normal functions.

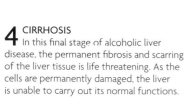

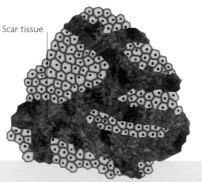

Scar tissue

PORTAL HYPERTENSION

RAISED PRESSURE IN THE BLOOD VESSELS SUPPLYING THE LIVER CAUSES DISTENDED VEINS IN THE OESOPHAGUS AND STOMACH.

One of the complications of liver cirrhosis is portal hypertension. As the tissue becomes progressively scarred and fibrosed, it obstructs the flow of blood into the liver from the portal vein, a large vessel carrying blood from the digestive tract. Pressure builds up in the vein and can cause other vessels "upstream" to become distended. Among these are veins in the abdomen, rectum, and those that supply the oesophagus with blood. The swollen veins, or varices, protrude into the oesophagus and may bleed. In some cases, only slight oozing occurs. In others, a major haemorrhage causes massive vomiting of blood. Not everyone who has liver cirrhosis develops portal hypertension and oesophageal varices. In those who do develop the condition, the varices can be treated with drugs to reduce the blood pressure or injected with a sclerosing (hardening) agent, much like that used to treat varicose veins.

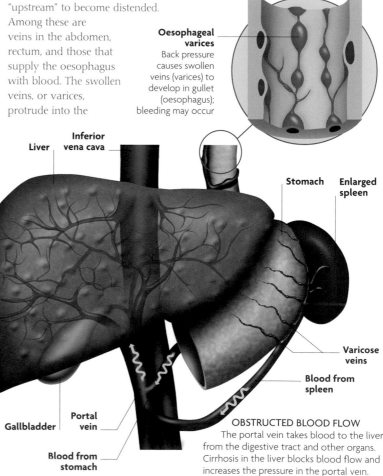

Oesophageal varices
Back pressure causes swollen veins (varices) to develop in gullet (oesophagus); bleeding may occur

- Inferior vena cava
- Liver
- Stomach
- Enlarged spleen
- Varicose veins
- Blood from spleen
- Gallbladder
- Portal vein
- Blood from stomach

OBSTRUCTED BLOOD FLOW
The portal vein takes blood to the liver from the digestive tract and other organs. Cirrhosis in the liver blocks blood flow and increases the pressure in the portal vein. Back pressure causes veins "upstream" and in the oesophagus, to distend.

HEPATITIS

HEPATITIS IS AN INFLAMMATION OF THE LIVER THAT CAN BE CAUSED BY A NUMBER OF DIFFERENT VIRUSES.

Viral hepatitis can be either acute (sudden onset) or chronic (long-term). Although acute hepatitis may resolve in a few weeks, it can progress to the chronic form. The most common type is hepatitis A, which is caused by ingesting contaminated food or water. Hepatitis B is mainly spread via infected blood, but the virus is also found in semen and can be sexually transmitted. Hepatitis C virus is also transmitted through blood and many individuals have been infected by blood transfusions. Most commonly acquired through IV drug use, symptoms vary from feeling mildly unwell to jaundice and liver failure.

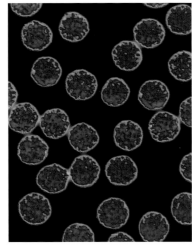

HEPATITIS
This image showing spherical hepatitis B viruses is magnified about 200,000 times. The virus is one of the many causes of the liver disorder, acute hepatitis.

LIVER ABSCESS

A RARE CONDITION IN WHICH PUS-FILLED CAVITIES DEVELOP IN THE LIVER TISSUE, OFTEN DUE TO THE SPREAD OF INFECTION FROM THE ABDOMEN.

A liver abscess can be caused by an amoebic or bacterial infection that spreads from elsewhere in the body via the blood. The origin of the infection varies but may be an infected appendix or gallbladder. However, the cause is often unknown. Some people have very few symptoms and the abscess can go undetected for several weeks. In others, the condition can result in severe pain, vomiting, weight loss, and a high fever. Liver abscesses are usually drained of pus using a large needle. Once the bacterium is identified, the infection is treated with antibiotics.

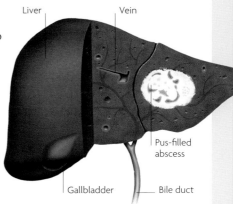

INFECTED ABSCESS
This rare type of abscess can occur alone or in groups. It usually develops following an infection elsewhere in the body, which spreads via the blood to the liver. It can be successfully drained of pus, using a needle and a syringe.

GALLSTONES

SMALL, HARD MASSES FORMED FROM BILE CAN OCCUR IN THE GALLBLADDER. THEY CAUSE PAIN WHEN THEY MOVE ON AND BECOME LODGED IN ADJACENT DUCTS.

In developed countries, the majority of gallstones consist primarily of cholesterol, a fatty substance that is processed in the liver and stored in the gallbladder as one of the constituents of bile. Gallstones can develop if the normal "mix" of bile is altered and the cholesterol content is high. They are far more common in women and are unusual before the age of 30. Most people with gallstones have no symptoms at all. It is only when a stone becomes lodged in one of the ducts leaving the gallbladder that symptoms occur. The main symptom is pain, which varies in intensity and often develops after a fatty meal, when bile is released from the gallbladder to help digestion. For symptomatic gallstones, the treatment is usually a cholecystectomy, or keyhole surgery to remove the gallbladder.

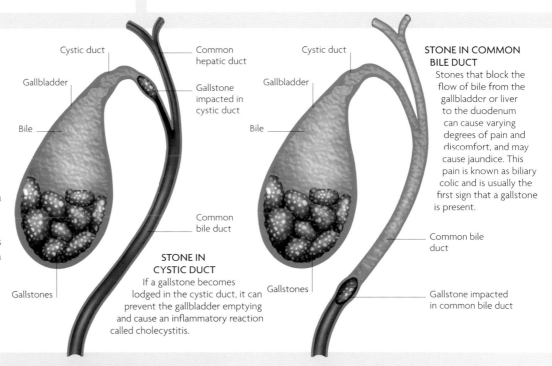

STONE IN CYSTIC DUCT
If a gallstone becomes lodged in the cystic duct, it can prevent the gallbladder emptying and cause an inflammatory reaction called cholecystitis.

STONE IN COMMON BILE DUCT
Stones that block the flow of bile from the gallbladder or liver to the duodenum can cause varying degrees of pain and discomfort, and may cause jaundice. This pain is known as biliary colic and is usually the first sign that a gallstone is present.

CANCER OF THE PANCREAS

AN INCREASINGLY COMMON MALIGNANT TUMOUR, OFTEN LINKED TO SMOKING, RESULTS IN PANCREATIC CANCER.

Tumours of the pancreas are categorized into those that occur in its body or tail of this organ and those that develop in its head. Cancer in the head of the pancreas blocks the flow of bile and is therefore more likely to cause jaundice, while a malignancy in the body or tail commonly produces pain in the upper abdomen. This type of cancer is more common in people who smoke and is seen more often in men. Cancer of the pancreas has a poor prognosis and usually the treatment aims to relieve symptoms.

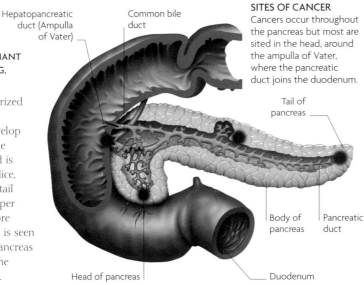

SITES OF CANCER
Cancers occur throughout the pancreas but most are sited in the head, around the ampulla of Vater, where the pancreatic duct joins the duodenum.

PANCREATITIS

A SERIOUS INFLAMMATION OF THE PANCREAS, WHICH CAN BE CAUSED BY DRINKING EXCESSIVE AMOUNTS OF ALCOHOL, OR BY GALLSTONES.

Pancreatitis can be either acute or chronic. In both types, the inflammation is triggered by the enzymes that the pancreas itself manufactures to aid digestion of food in the duodenum. These enzymes become activated while still inside the pancreas and begin to digest the tissue. There are many causes of acute pancreatitis, the most common of which are gallstones, alcohol, some drugs, and certain infections, such as mumps. Chronic pancreatitis is usually associated with long-term alcoholism. In both types, the main feature is pain. In acute pancreatitis this is particularly severe and may be accompanied by nausea and vomiting.

LOWER DIGESTIVE TRACT DISORDERS

INFECTIONS OF THE LOWER DIGESTIVE TRACT – THE COLON, RECTUM, AND ANUS – ARE AMONG THE COMMONEST DIGESTIVE CONDITIONS. THEY ARE A MAJOR CAUSE OF DEATH IN DEVELOPING NATIONS, BUT USUALLY CAUSE ONLY MINOR PROBLEMS IN DEVELOPED COUNTRIES. OTHER DIGESTIVE DISORDERS, SUCH AS CANCER AND INTESTINAL INFLAMMATION, CAUSE MEDICAL PROBLEMS WORLDWIDE.

IRRITABLE BOWEL SYNDROME

THIS COMBINATION OF INTERMITTENT ABDOMINAL PAIN, CONSTIPATION, AND DIARRHOEA AFFECTS AS MANY AS ONE IN FIVE PEOPLE DURING THEIR LIVES.

Often called IBS, this is one of the most common of all digestive complaints. It occurs mainly in people aged 20–30 years, and is twice as frequent in females than males. Its precise cause is unclear, but it is thought to involve abnormal muscular movements within the intestine. The factors that trigger IBS may include a bout of gastroenteritis or sensitivity to particular substances, such as caffeine, alcohol, high-fat foods, or artificial sweeteners. There also seems to be a genetic component, because some families have a history of IBS. The symptoms of IBS include diarrhoea, constipation, abdominal pain, and, in particular, bloating and large quantities of wind (intestinal gas); these problems can be made worse by anxiety, depression, or stress. The pain is often in the lower left area of the abdomen, and it may be relieved by passing gas or faeces. IBS is generally a long-term complaint, but it is usually intermittent and rarely serious.

INFLAMMATORY BOWEL DISEASE

THIS ENCOMPASSES TWO CONDITIONS WITH SIMILAR SYMPTOMS: ULCERATIVE COLITIS AND CROHN'S DISEASE.

Both of these conditions involve serious inflammation of the intestines. There may be an underlying problem with the immune system, which makes it attack the body's own intestinal tissues. There is also a tendency for ulcerative colitis and Crohn's disease to run in families. However, their detailed causes remain unclear. Most cases are long-term and begin between the ages of 15 and 30. Symptoms common to both conditions include abdominal pain, diarrhoea, appetite loss, fever, intestinal bleeding, and weight loss. Treatment involves anti-diarrhoeal and anti-inflammatory drugs, and – especially for sufferers of Crohn's disease – surgery. The operation, called a colectomy, removes the worst affected portions of the large intestine.

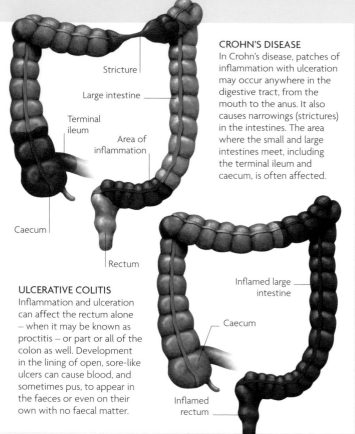

CROHN'S DISEASE
In Crohn's disease, patches of inflammation with ulceration may occur anywhere in the digestive tract, from the mouth to the anus. It also causes narrowings (strictures) in the intestines. The area where the small and large intestines meet, including the terminal ileum and caecum, is often affected.

Stricture
Large intestine
Terminal ileum
Area of inflammation
Caecum
Rectum

Inflamed large intestine
Caecum
Inflamed rectum

ULCERATIVE COLITIS
Inflammation and ulceration can affect the rectum alone – when it may be known as proctitis – or part or all of the colon as well. Development in the lining of open, sore-like ulcers can cause blood, and sometimes pus, to appear in the faeces or even on their own with no faecal matter.

DIVERTICULAR DISEASE

DIVERTICULAR DISEASE INCLUDES DIVERTICULOSIS – POUCHES THAT FORM IN THE WALL OF THE COLON.

Most people with diverticular disease are aged over 50 and have eaten a low-fibre diet for many years, with consequent straining to pass hard stools. The problem becomes more frequent with age. The lowest part of the colon, the sigmoid colon, is most commonly affected, but the whole colon can be involved. In diverticulosis, patches of the intestinal wall bulge outwards into blind-ending pouches known as diverticula. About 95 per cent of people with diverticular disease show no symptoms, but some people have abdominal pain and irregular bowel habits. Diverticulitis occurs when the pouches become inflamed, causing severe pain, fever, and constipation. As in IBD (above), the pain is often in the lower left abdomen and may fade after passing gas or stools.

1 HARD FAECES
Soft, bulky faeces are able to pass easily along the colon. If faeces are hard and dry, usually due to lack of fibre or "roughage" in the diet, the contractions of the smooth muscle layers of the colon must increase in force, putting pressure on the walls of the colon.

Hard, dry faeces
Wall of colon
Blood vessel

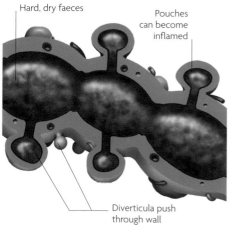

Hard, dry faeces
Pouches can become inflamed
Diverticula push through wall

2 POUCHES FORM
Eventually, the increased pressure pushes small areas of intestinal lining through points of weakness in the muscle of the intestinal wall, often near a blood vessel. The pea- to grape-sized pouches that form easily trap bacteria and may become inflamed.

APPENDICITIS

AN INFLAMED APPENDIX CAUSES ACUTE PAIN THAT USUALLY STARTS IN THE UPPER- OR MID-ABDOMEN, AND IS COMMON IN CHILDREN AND ADOLESCENTS.

Other symptoms of appendicitis include mild fever, nausea, vomiting, and perhaps loss of appetite and frequent urination. In many cases the inflammation progresses so quickly that the sufferer needs urgent hospitalization. Surgical removal of the appendix, called an appendicectomy, is one of the most commonly performed emergency operations. Left untreated, an inflamed appendix can rupture, causing peritonitis (inflammation of the abdominal lining) and abscesses.

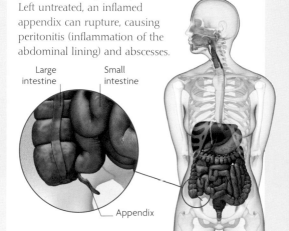

Large intestine
Small intestine
Appendix

COLORECTAL CANCER

CANCER OF THE COLON, RECTUM, OR BOTH, IS ONE OF THE COMMONEST CANCERS IN INDUSTRIALIZED COUNTRIES. RISK FACTORS INCLUDE FAMILY HISTORY AND AGEING.

A malignant tumour in the intestinal wall can often start as a polyp (see right) in the intestinal lining. A high-fat, low-fibre diet, excessive alcohol, lack of exercise, and obesity increase the likelihood of this cancer. Symptoms are a change in bowel habits and stool consistency, abdominal pain, loss of appetite, faecal blood, and a sensation of not fully emptying the bowels. Colorectal cancer can be detected by screening programmes, including faecal tests for blood and colonoscopy. If detected and treated early, the chances of survival of five years or longer are high.

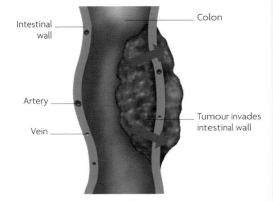

COLONIC TUMOUR
Over time, malignant tumours grow and invade the intestinal wall from where the cancer can spread to other parts of the body via the bloodstream.

INTESTINAL POLYPS

SLOW-GROWING, USUALLY NON-CANCEROUS GROWTHS, LOCATED IN THE LARGE INTESTINE, THAT PROJECT FROM THE MUCOUS MEMBRANE LINING.

These are common in later years – one person in three over the age of 60 may be affected by intestinal polyps. Most people show no symptoms, but polyps may cause diarrhoea, rectal bleeding, and perhaps anaemia. Most cases are successfully detected by colonoscopy and treated, but then need regular checks, since there is an increased risk of colorectal cancer (see left).

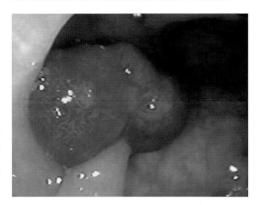

INTESTINAL OBSTRUCTION

OBSTRUCTION OF THE INTESTINE CAUSES ABDOMINAL PAIN AND DISTENSION, ABSENCE OF FAECAL EXCRETION OR GAS, VOMITING, AND SOMETIMES DEHYDRATION.

Digestive material may be prevented from moving along the intestine due to physical blockage or perhaps paralysis of the smooth muscles in the intestinal wall. Causes include pressure from a tumour, or severe inflammation, as in Crohn's disease, that may narrow the intestine so that it is effectively blocked. Some hernias, intussusception (see panel below), and volvulus are further possibilities. Sometimes the muscles fail to contract, perhaps due to mesenteric infarction, serious abdominal peritonitis, or major abdominal surgery. To stabilize the condition and confirm the diagnosis, urgent hospitalization is needed. Treatment includes intravenous fluids, suction of fluid from the stomach, or possibly surgery.

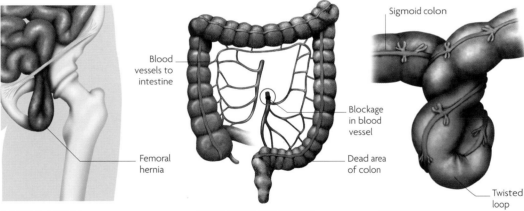

FEMORAL HERNIA
The intestine slips through the narrow femoral canal and becomes trapped, causing an obstruction and severe pain.

MESENTERIC INFARCTION
A segment of intestine, deprived of blood due to blockage of a vessel in the mesentery, soon starts to die.

VOLVULUS
Intermittent intestinal twisting causes severe pain, distension, and vomiting; surgery is needed.

HAEMORRHOIDS

ALSO CALLED PILES, HAEMORRHOIDS ARE VARICOSED (SWOLLEN AND ENGORGED) VEINS THAT PROTRUDE FROM THE RECTAL OR ANAL LINING.

Rectal or anal bleeding and discomfort are commonly associated with haemorrhoids. Causes include constipation from a low-fibre diet, and straining to pass faeces, which may make the blood vessels of the rectum and anus swell. In pregnancy, the growing baby has a similar effect. The symptoms vary greatly in severity, and may include mucus discharge from the anus with anal itching. Treatments include ointments, injections, banding, laser therapy, and surgery.

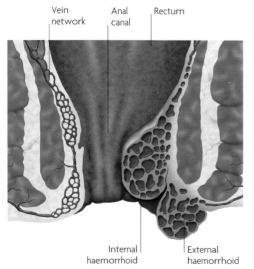

HAEMORRHOIDS
The vein network on the left side of this diagram is normal. The blood vessels to the right are swollen and have formed internal and external haemorrhoids.

INTUSSUSCEPTION

Intestinal obstruction in young children, especially boys under two years of age, can be due to intussusception. Part of the intestine telescopes in on itself, forming a tube within a tube. Symptoms include vomiting, abdominal pain, paler skin, and the passage of bloodstained mucous. The condition progresses rapidly and needs urgent medical attention. It can be both diagnosed and often unblocked by a barium enema.

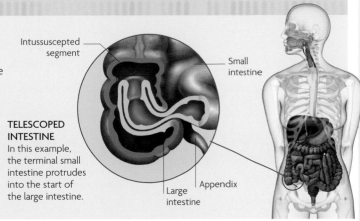

TELESCOPED INTESTINE
In this example, the terminal small intestine protrudes into the start of the large intestine.

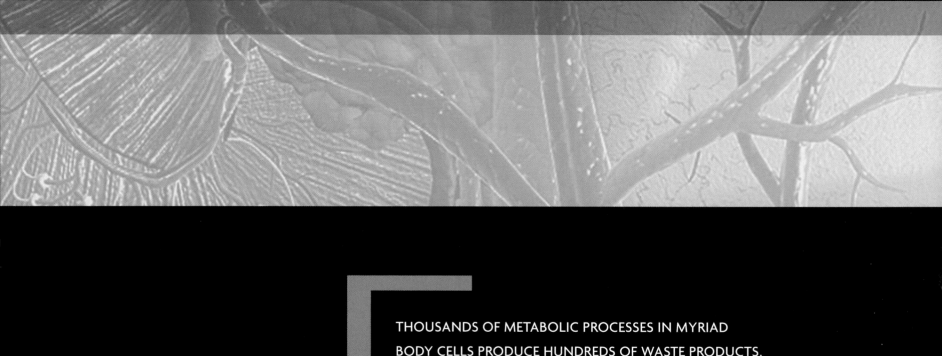

THOUSANDS OF METABOLIC PROCESSES IN MYRIAD
BODY CELLS PRODUCE HUNDREDS OF WASTE PRODUCTS.
THE URINARY SYSTEM REMOVES THEM BY FILTERING
AND CLEANSING THE BLOOD AS IT PASSES THROUGH THE
KIDNEYS. ANOTHER VITAL FUNCTION IS THE REGULATION
OF THE VOLUME, ACIDITY, SALINITY, CONCENTRATION, AND

URINARY SYSTEM

URINARY ANATOMY

THE URINARY SYSTEM IS COMPOSED OF A PAIR OF KIDNEYS, A PAIR OF URETERS, A BLADDER, AND A URETHRA. THESE COMPONENTS TOGETHER CARRY OUT THE URINARY SYSTEM'S FUNCTION OF REGULATING THE VOLUME AND COMPOSITION OF BODY FLUIDS, REMOVING WASTE PRODUCTS FROM THE BLOOD, AND EXPELLING THE WASTE AND EXCESS WATER FROM THE BODY IN THE FORM OF URINE.

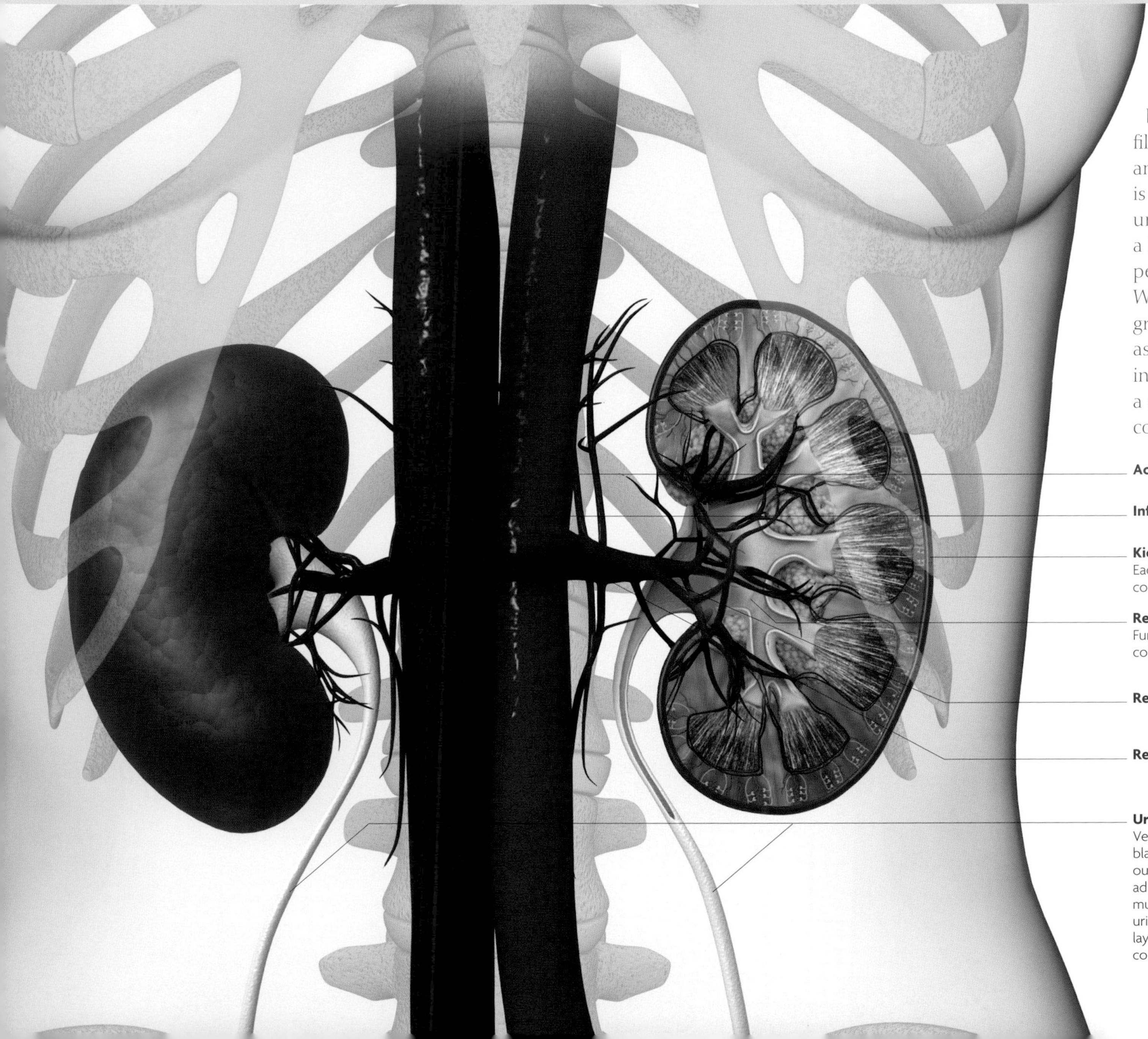

The two kidneys are reddish organs resembling beans in shape that are situated on either side of the abdomen just above the waist and towards the back of the body. The kidneys contain microscopic filtering units that remove waste, unwanted minerals, and excess water from the blood as urine. Each kidney is connected to the bladder by a long tube called a ureter, which transports urine away. The bladder is a hollow, muscular organ situated centrally in the pelvis; it stores urine until it is convenient to release it. When empty, the bladder resembles a deflated balloon, gradually becoming spherical, and then pear shaped, as it fills up. At a certain volume, stretch receptors in its wall transmit nervous impulses that initiate a conscious desire to urinate. The urethra then conducts urine from the bladder to the outside.

Aorta

Inferior vena cava

Kidney
Each is about 10–12.5cm (4–5in) long, and contains about 1 million filtering units

Renal pelvis
Funnel-shaped chamber in which urine collects before passing down the ureter

Renal artery

Renal vein

Ureters
Vessels conveying urine from kidneys to bladder; their walls have three layers: the outer layer, composed of connective and adipose (fat) tissue; the middle layer has muscular fibres, which contract to propel urine to the bladder; the inner, mucosal layer secretes mucus to prevent its cells coming into contact with urine

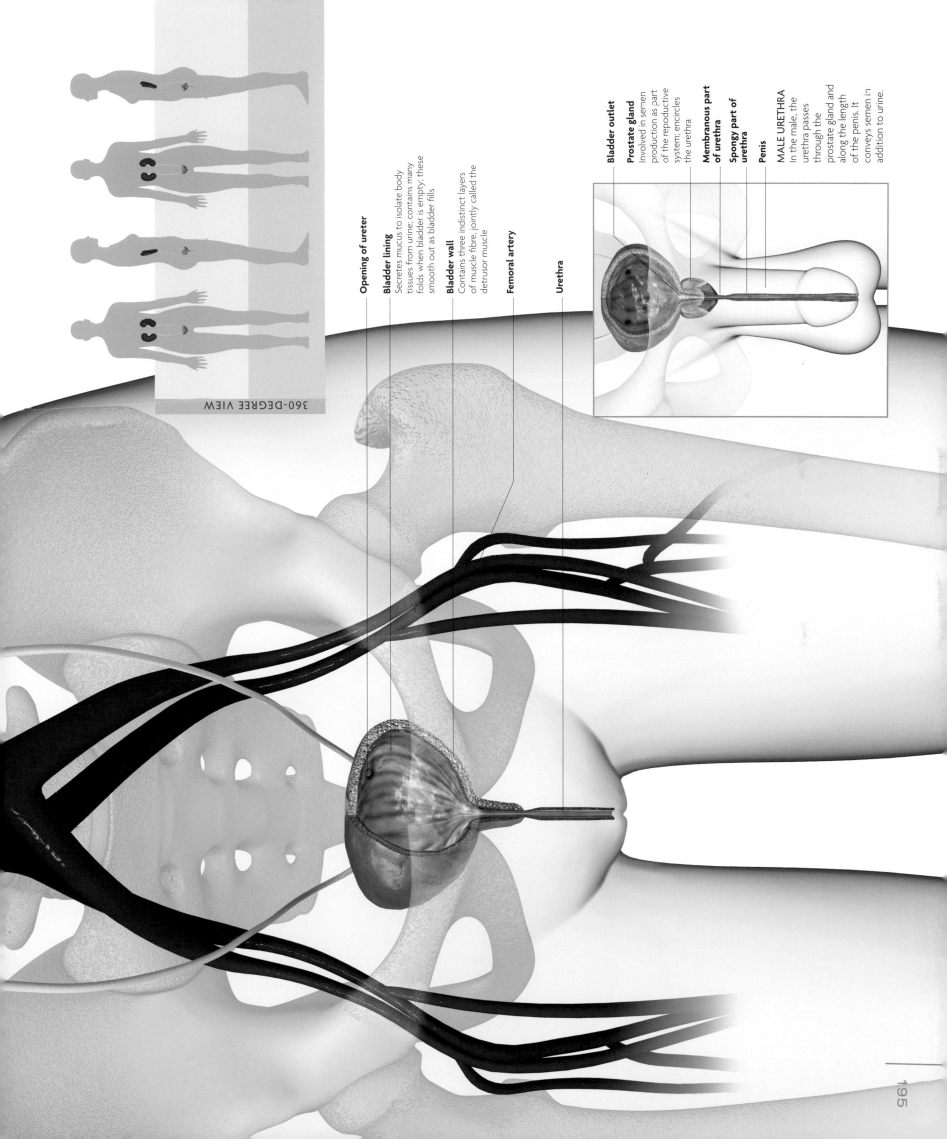

Opening of ureter

Bladder lining
Secretes mucus to isolate body tissues from urine; contains many folds when bladder is empty; these smooth out as bladder fills

Bladder wall
Contains three indistinct layers of muscle fibre, jointly called the detrusor muscle

Femoral artery

Urethra

Bladder outlet

Prostate gland
Involved in semen production as part of the reproductive system; encircles the urethra

Membranous part of urethra

Spongy part of urethra

Penis

MALE URETHRA
In the male, the urethra passes through the prostate gland and along the length of the penis. It conveys semen in addition to urine.

KIDNEY STRUCTURE

THE KIDNEYS ARE PAIRED ORGANS AT THE UPPER REAR OF THE ABDOMINAL CAVITY, ON EITHER SIDE OF THE SPINAL COLUMN. THEIR FUNCTIONS INCLUDE FILTERING WASTE PRODUCTS FROM THE BLOOD. THE WASTE IS EXCRETED – ALONG WITH EXCESS WATER – AS URINE.

INSIDE THE KIDNEY

Each kidney is protected by three outer layers: a tough external coat of fibrous connective tissue, the renal fascia; a layer of fatty tissue, the adipose capsule; and inside this, another fibrous layer, the renal capsule. The main body of the kidney also has three layers: the renal cortex, which is packed full of knots of capillaries known as glomeruli and their capsules; next is the renal medulla, which contains capillaries and urine-forming tubules; and a central space where the urine collects, known as the renal pelvis. The glomeruli, capsules, and tubules are parts of the kidney's million-plus microfiltering units, called nephrons.

GLOMERULUS
In this microscope image the glomerulus is coloured pink. This tangled system of capillaries forms the first part of the nephron, and oozes a filtrate fluid, which is collected by the cup-like Bowman's (glomerular) capsule around it.

NEPHRON
Each microfiltering unit, or nephron, spans the cortex and medulla. The glomerulus, capsule, proximal and distal tubules, and the smaller urine collecting ducts are in the former. The latter contains mainly the long tubule loops of Henle and the larger urine collecting ducts.

Urine-collecting duct
Larger collecting vessel fed by renal tubules

Glomerulus
Ball-shaped capillary mass is the vascular beginning of a nephron

Renal tubule
A long, much-folded, and looped tube where urine is concentrated

Capillaries
These run from the glomerulus and reabsorb essential nutrients, minerals, salts, and water

Loop of Henle

Renal cortex

Renal medulla

Renal artery
Supplies blood to kidney; branches from the aorta (main artery of the body)

Renal vein
Removes cleaned blood, which then drains into inferior vena cava (main lower vein in the body)

Renal hilus
Junction at which the renal blood vessels and ureter pass into the kidney

Interlobular arteries and veins
Branches of the renal artery and vein, which pass through the renal columns

Arcuate arteries and veins
Vessels forming arch-like connections between the cortex and medulla

Ureter
Muscular-walled transport tube for urine, leading down the urinary bladder

Renal papilla
Apex of the renal pyramid

Renal cortex
Outer region of kidney packed with microscopic spherical structures (the capsule-enveloped glomeruli) lending it a granular appearance

Renal medulla
Composed mainly of capillary networks around long loops of renal tubules

Renal column
Regions of cortex tissue separating the renal pyramids

Renal pyramid
Cone-shaped regions of medulla between the renal columns

Major calyx
Several minor calyces (cup-shaped cavities forming the renal pelvis) merge to form major calyces

Minor calyx
Urine from main collecting ducts empties from the renal papilla into a minor calyx

Renal pelvis
Funnel-shaped tube narrowing into upper end of ureter, and into which the major calyces merge

Renal capsule
Thin covering of white fibrous tissue around the whole kidney

KIDNEY CROSS SECTION
This cutaway shows the kidney's main layers, the cortex and the medulla, which form segments known as renal pyramids. The renal artery and vein circulate huge amounts of blood – about 1.2 litres per min (2½ pints/min) at rest, which is up to one-quarter of the heart's total output.

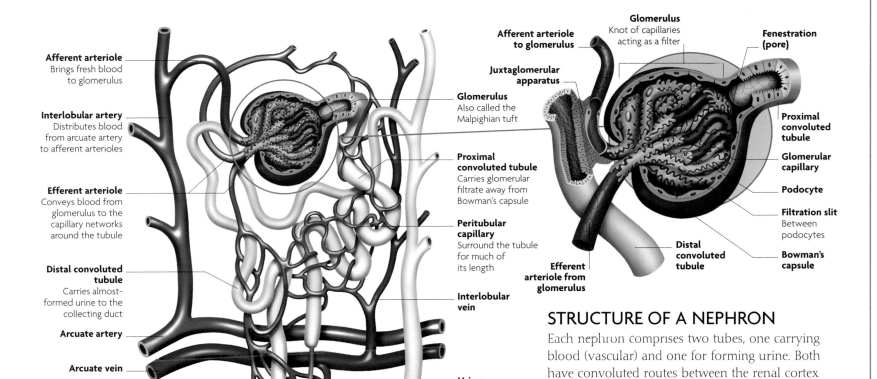

Afferent arteriole
Brings fresh blood to glomerulus

Interlobular artery
Distributes blood from arcuate artery to afferent arterioles

Efferent arteriole
Conveys blood from glomerulus to the capillary networks around the tubule

Distal convoluted tubule
Carries almost-formed urine to the collecting duct

Arcuate artery

Arcuate vein

Capillary network around loop of Henle

Ascending limb

Afferent arteriole to glomerulus

Juxtaglomerular apparatus

Glomerulus
Knot of capillaries acting as a filter

Fenestration (pore)

Glomerulus
Also called the Malpighian tuft

Proximal convoluted tubule
Carries glomerular filtrate away from Bowman's capsule

Peritubular capillary
Surround the tubule for much of its length

Interlobular vein

Urine-collecting duct

Descending limb

Loop of Henle
Positioned in the renal medulla

Proximal convoluted tubule

Glomerular capillary

Podocyte

Filtration slit
Between podocytes

Bowman's capsule

Distal convoluted tubule

Efferent arteriole from glomerulus

BLOOD FILTRATION
One end of the renal tubule is a cup-shaped membrane, Bowman's capsule, which envelops the glomerulus. The other end joins a straight urine-collecting tubule. The capsule is about 0.2mm ($^1/_{125}$ in) in diameter. All of a kidney's tubules end to end would stretch 80km (50 miles). Blood is circulated by the arcuate vessels that run between the renal cortex and medulla.

PODOCYTES
Branching cells on the glomerular surface have filtration slits to restrict the size of molecules passing through the capillary wall.

STRUCTURE OF A NEPHRON
Each nephron comprises two tubes, one carrying blood (vascular) and one for forming urine. Both have convoluted routes between the renal cortex and medulla. The blood vessel starts as an incoming (afferent) arteriole, then forms a tuft of capillary blood vessels, called the glomerulus. This leads to the outgoing (efferent) arteriole, then the peritubular capillaries, and finally a venule that carries the blood away. The renal tube begins with Bowman's capsule. Next, the proximal convoluted tubule dips into the renal medulla and back up to the cortex in a long U-shape – the loop of Henle. Back in the cortex, it winds again as the distal convoluted tubule and joins one of the larger urine-collecting ducts.

MAKING URINE
As blood passes through the nephrons, waste products are removed, while water and other substances are reabsorbed into the bloodstream. By the time the filtrate reaches the collecting duct, it has become urine. The body's total blood plasma is filtered about twice every hour, producing 150 litres (317pt) of glomerular filtrate per day, 99 per cent of which is reabsorbed to yield an average 1.5 litres ($3^1/_5$ pt) of urine daily. Urine production is mainly controlled by hormones, such as the antidiuretic hormone or ADH (vasopressin) from the pituitary gland.

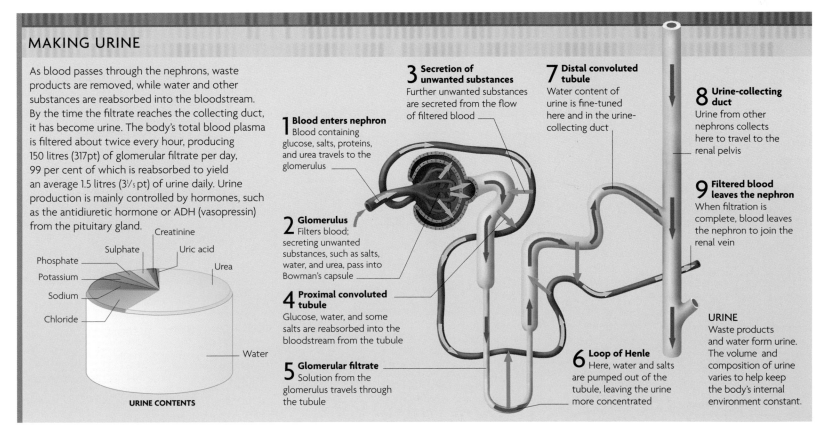

URINE CONTENTS

Creatinine
Sulphate
Uric acid
Phosphate
Potassium
Urea
Sodium
Chloride
Water

1 Blood enters nephron
Blood containing glucose, salts, proteins, and urea travels to the glomerulus

2 Glomerulus
Filters blood; secreting unwanted substances, such as salts, water, and urea, pass into Bowman's capsule

4 Proximal convoluted tubule
Glucose, water, and some salts are reabsorbed into the bloodstream from the tubule

5 Glomerular filtrate
Solution from the glomerulus travels through the tubule

3 Secretion of unwanted substances
Further unwanted substances are secreted from the flow of filtered blood

6 Loop of Henle
Here, water and salts are pumped out of the tubule, leaving the urine more concentrated

7 Distal convoluted tubule
Water content of urine is fine-tuned here and in the urine-collecting duct

8 Urine-collecting duct
Urine from other nephrons collects here to travel to the renal pelvis

9 Filtered blood leaves the nephron
When filtration is complete, blood leaves the nephron to join the renal vein

URINE
Waste products and water form urine. The volume and composition of urine varies to help keep the body's internal environment constant.

URINARY DISORDERS

SOME PARTS OF THE URINARY TRACT ARE SUSCEPTIBLE TO INFECTIONS, RESULTING IN CONDITIONS SUCH AS CYSTITIS. SOME CHRONIC KIDNEY DISEASES ARE ALSO CAUSED BY INFECTION. KIDNEY FAILURE CAN NOW BE TREATED WITH RENAL REPLACEMENT THERAPY, EITHER BY DIALYSIS OR TRANSPLANTATION. HOWEVER, COMMON SYMPTOMS, SUCH AS INCONTINENCE, MAY STILL BE TROUBLESOME.

URINARY TRACT INFECTIONS

ALL ORGANS IN THE URINARY TRACT CAN BE AFFECTED BY INFECTION; ALTHOUGH USUALLY CONFINED TO ONE AREA, IT CAN SPREAD THROUGH THE SYSTEM.

The urine flowing through the urinary tract moves in one direction, from the kidneys through the ureters to the bladder and then through the urethra to leave the body. During urination, the flow from the bladder is rapid and copious, but for long periods urine is stagnant in the bladder. Infections can enter the body through the urethra and spread to the bladder, and sometimes up the ureters to the kidneys. The adult female urethra is 4cm (1½in) long, compared to the male's at 20cm (8in). This short length and the proximity of its outlet to the anus (which means that bacteria from the anal area may enter the urethra) together account for females' greater susceptibility to urinary infection. One of the most common urinary infections is inflammation of the bladder, known as cystitis. Its main symptoms are burning pain and a frequent need to urinate but often with little urine passed on each occasion.

CYSTITIS

In this false-colour micrograph of a bladder lining affected by cystitis, bacteria (yellow rods) colonize the lining's inner surface (blue), causing inflammation. The lining secretes strands of mucus (orange) and may also be damaged so that it leaks blood (red cells), which stains the urine pink.

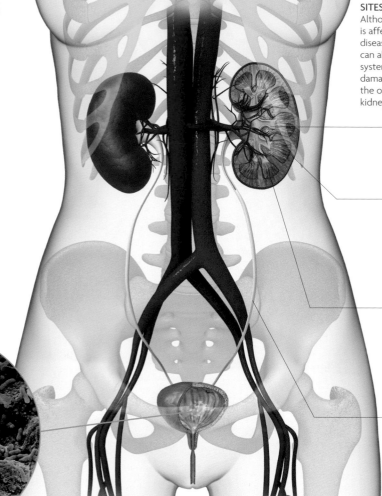

SITES OF DISORDERS

Although each of the urinary organs is affected by its own characteristic diseases, a disorder of any single organ can also affect other parts of the system. For example, kidney stones may damage the ureters, and obstruction to the outflow of urine may damage the kidneys as a result of back pressure.

Pyelonephritis
An acute infection of the urine-collecting system of the kidney

Diabetic nephropathy
Changes to capillaries in the kidneys, which may lead to kidney failure; caused by long-term diabetes mellitus

Glomerulonephritis
Inflammation of the filtering units of the kidney (glomeruli); often related to an autoimmune process

Reflux
The forcing of urine up the ureters by back pressure; can be caused by blockage of the urethra; also occurs in children when the ureters are too lax

INCONTINENCE

A TENDENCY TO LEAK URINE, URINARY INCONTINENCE MOST COMMONLY OCCURS IN WOMEN, ELDERLY PEOPLE, AND THOSE WITH BRAIN OR SPINAL CORD DAMAGE.

Females are susceptible to incontinence because of a weakness in the pelvic floor muscles after childbirth. There are different types. In stress incontinence, weak pelvic floor muscles allow small quantities of urine to escape during exertion, such as running, or activities that raise intra-abdominal pressure, such as coughing. In urge incontinence, the urgent desire to urinate is triggered by irritable bladder muscle that causes the bladder to contract and expel all its urine. In overflow incontinence, a blockage in the urethra or a weak bladder muscle results in build-up of urine that then leaks out. Total incontinence is the complete loss of bladder function due to a nervous system disorder, such as dementia.

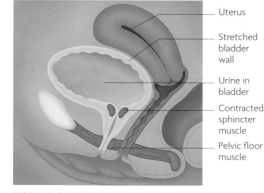

NORMAL BLADDER
A healthy bladder expands like a balloon as it fills with urine. The sphincter muscles and surrounding pelvic floor muscles keep the exit closed. Nerve signals from stretch sensors in the bladder wall travel to the brain, signalling the need for emptying.

Uterus
Stretched bladder wall
Urine in bladder
Contracted sphincter muscle
Pelvic floor muscle

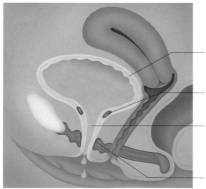

STRESS INCONTINENCE
To empty the bladder, the sphincter and pelvic floor muscles relax, and the detrusor muscle in the bladder wall contracts forcing urine along the urethra. In incontinence, weak muscles may allow this to happen without proper control, so urine leaks out.

Contracted bladder wall
Relaxed sphincter muscle
Urethra
Weakened pelvic floor muscle

KIDNEY STONES

CONCENTRATED SUBSTANCES IN THE URINE MAY FORM CRYSTALLINE DEPOSITS, KNOWN AS KIDNEY STONES OR RENAL CALCULI, WITHIN THE KIDNEY.

Kidney stones are solid, mineral-rich objects that grow due to the coming out of solution (precipitation) of chemicals, such as calcium salts, in urine. Kidney stones can take years to form and grow in various shapes and sizes. A stone may stay in the kidney and cause few problems, but it can increase the risk of urinary tract infection.

DETECTING A KIDNEY STONE

After a dye is injected, an X-ray (pyelogram) can reveal kidney stones. Here, the dense material of a stone is clearly visible in the right kidney (orange, left of image).

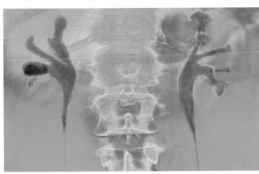

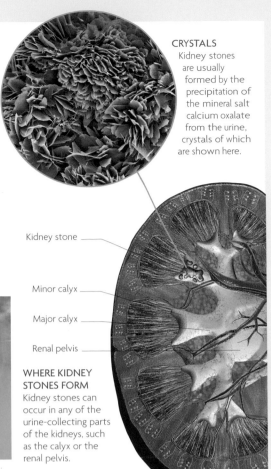

CRYSTALS
Kidney stones are usually formed by the precipitation of the mineral salt calcium oxalate from the urine, crystals of which are shown here.

Kidney stone

Minor calyx

Major calyx

Renal pelvis

WHERE KIDNEY STONES FORM

Kidney stones can occur in any of the urine-collecting parts of the kidneys, such as the calyx or the renal pelvis.

BLADDER TUMOURS

MOST TUMOURS OF THE BLADDER BEGIN AS SUPERFICIAL WART-LIKE GROWTHS, CALLED PAPILLOMAS; UNTREATED THEY CAN BECOME CANCEROUS AND SPREAD.

Bladder tumours are more common in people who smoke, and in men. If they enlarge, they can cause difficulty in urinating, haematuria (blood in the urine), and increased risk of urinary tract infection. If the tumours become cancerous, they may spread to adjacent organs, such as the rectum, and through the bloodstream to more distant parts of the body.

BLADDER TUMOUR

A large bladder tumour (white area, below) may block the outlet from the bladder to the urethra, causing complete retention of urine. This requires urgent medical treatment.

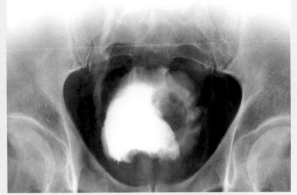

KIDNEY FAILURE

KIDNEY (OR RENAL) FAILURE OCCURS WHEN THE KIDNEY CAN NO LONGER CARRY OUT ITS VITAL FUNCTION OF REMOVING WASTE PRODUCTS FROM THE BLOOD.

There are different types of kidney failure, affecting one kidney or both. Symptoms are caused by build-up of waste products. Acute kidney failure comes on rapidly and may be due to problems such as blood loss, a heart attack, toxins, or a kidney infection. Symptoms include reduced urine output, drowsiness, headache, nausea, and vomiting. Chronic kidney failure develops slowly. It may be due to polycystic kidney disease or long-standing high blood pressure. Symptoms include frequent urination, breathlessness, skin irritation, nausea, vomiting, and muscle twitches and cramps. In end-stage failure, the kidneys have lost all function, and dialysis or kidney transplant is necessary.

POLYCYSTIC KIDNEY

Usually inherited, polycystic kidney disease produces many cysts, or fluid-filled sacs, in the kidney. The kidney enlarges, becomes shaped irregularly, and loses its blood-filtering functions.

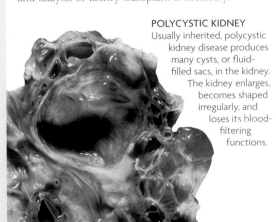

DIALYSIS

Dialysis involves filtering the blood of a person with kidney failure. There are two types of dialysis: haemodialysis, which filters the blood externally, and peritoneal dialysis, in which the peritoneal membrane in the abdomen is used as a filter (see right). In haemodialysis, blood from the body is pumped by a kidney machine through a filter. The filter contains a semi-permeable membrane immersed in a solution known as dialysate. Smaller molecules, such as urea and similar waste products, pass through the membrane into the dialysate while larger, useful molecules such as proteins are retained. The filtered blood returns to the body and the dialysate is discarded. The procedure takes 3 or 4 hours to complete.

Capillary wall

Peritoneal membrane

Red blood cell

Dialysate

Waste product

PERITONEAL DIALYSIS

The peritoneal membrane in the abdomen acts as a filter. Dialysate is flowed into the peritoneal cavity and 4–6 hours later is drained out. Waste products pass from the capillaries of the peritoneal cavity through the peritoneal membrane into the dialysate.

Peritoneal membrane

Dialysate

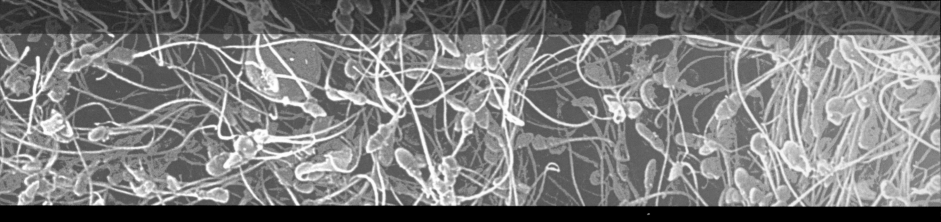

IN BIOLOGICAL TERMS, THE PRIMARY FUNCTION OF THE HUMAN BODY IS TO REPLICATE ITSELF, AND THE SEXUAL AND PARENTING INSTINCTS ARE AMONG THE STRONGEST OF OUR BASIC DRIVES. AS SCIENCE WIDENS THE GAP BETWEEN SEX AND REPRODUCTION, WE CAN CHOOSE MORE WAYS OF HAVING ONE WITHOUT THE OTHER. THESE DEVELOPMENTS, ALONG WITH THE CONTRASTS BETWEEN PROGRESSIVE SOCIETIES AND TRADITIONAL CULTURES, HAVE MULTIPLIED THE ETHICAL ISSUES SURROUNDING SEX AND PREGNANCY. HOWEVER, THE REALITIES OF SEXUALLY TRANSMITTED DISEASES, MALIGNANCIES OF THE REPRODUCTIVE ORGANS,

REPRODUCTION AND LIFE CYCLE

MALE REPRODUCTIVE SYSTEM

OF THE BODY'S MAJOR SYSTEMS, THE REPRODUCTIVE SYSTEM IS THE ONE THAT DIFFERS MOST BETWEEN SEXES, AND THE ONLY SYSTEM THAT DOES NOT FUNCTION UNTIL PUBERTY. THE MALE SYSTEM PRODUCES SEX CELLS (GAMETES) CALLED SPERM. UNLIKE FEMALE EGG MATURATION, WHICH OCCURS IN CYCLES AND CEASES AT MENOPAUSE, SPERM PRODUCTION IS CONTINUOUS, REDUCING GRADUALLY WITH AGE.

THE REPRODUCTIVE ORGANS

In males, the reproductive organs include the penis, the testes, a number of storage and transport ducts, and some supporting structures. The two oval-shaped testes (also termed testicles) lie outside the body in a pouch of skin called the scrotum, where they can maintain the optimum temperature for sperm production – approximately 3°C (5°F) lower than body temperature. Testes are oval-shaped glands responsible for the manufacture of sperm and the sex hormone testosterone. From each testis, sperm pass into a coiled tube – the epididymis – for the final stages of maturation.

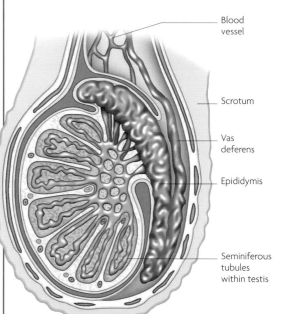

Blood vessel

Scrotum

Vas deferens

Epididymis

Seminiferous tubules within testis

They are stored in the epididymides until they are either broken down and reabsorbed, or ejaculated – forced by movement of seminal fluid from the accessory glands (see opposite) down a duct called the vas deferens.

INSIDE THE SCROTUM
The scrotum contains two testes where sperm are manufactured within tubes called seminiferous tubules, and the two epididymides where sperm are stored. Each epididymis is a tube about 6m (20ft) long, which is tightly coiled and bunched into a length of just 4cm (2in).

SCROTAL LAYERS
Each testis is covered by a thin tissue layer, the tunica vaginalis around which is a layer of connective tissue called fascia. A muscle layer called the dartos muscle relaxes in hot weather to drop the testes away from the body to keep them cool. In cold weather the muscle contracts to draw up the testes so they do not become too chilled. The spermatic cord suspends each testis within the scrotum, and contains the testicular artery and vein, lymph vessels, nerves, and the sperm-carrying vas deferens.

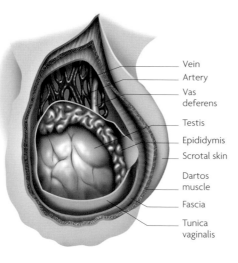

Vein

Artery

Vas deferens

Testis

Epididymis

Scrotal skin

Dartos muscle

Fascia

Tunica vaginalis

PATHWAY FOR SPERM

During ejaculation, waves of muscle contraction squeeze the sperm in their fluid from the epididymis along the loop of the vas deferens. The vas deferens is joined by a duct from the seminal vesicle, one of the male accessory glands, to form the ejaculatory duct. The left and right ejaculatory ducts join the urethra within the prostate, another accessory gland. In the male, the urethra is a dual-purpose tube that carries urine from the bladder during urination and sperm from the

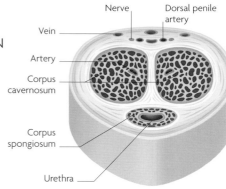

Nerve

Dorsal penile artery

Vein

Artery

Corpus cavernosum

Corpus spongiosum

Urethra

testes. During ejaculation, however, the sphincter at the base of the bladder is closed because of high pressure in the urethra.

PENILE ERECTION
During arousal, large quantities of arterial blood enter the corpus spongiosum and corpus cavernosum, compressing the veins. As a result, blood cannot drain from the penis and it becomes hard and erect.

MAKING SPERM

Each testis is a mass of more than 800 tightly looped and folded vessels known as seminiferous tubules. Inside each tubule, sperm begin as blob-like cells called spermatogonia lining the inner wall. These pass through a larger stage, as primary spermatocytes, then become smaller as secondary spermatocytes, and begin to develop tails as spermatids. As all of this happens, they move steadily towards the middle of the tubule. The spermatids finally develop into ripe sperm with long tails. Thousands of sperm are produced every second, each taking about two months to mature.

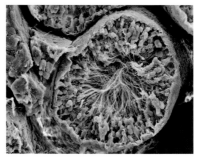

SEMINIFEROUS TUBULE
Sperm take shape as they move towards the centre of the tubule. Their long tails can be seen in this cross-section.

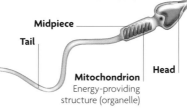

Midpiece

Tail

Mitochondrion
Energy-providing structure (organelle)

Head

SPERM CELL
A sperm is about 0.05mm (1/500 in) long but most of this is a tail. The sperm head is only 0.006mm (1/5000 in), about the same size as a red blood cell.

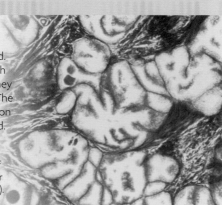

SEMEN

Seminal fluid, or semen, is sperm mixed with fluid added by several glands including the prostate gland. The prostate secretes fluid through tiny ducts to mix with sperm as they are ejaculated down the urethra. The final mix has around 300–500 million sperm in 2–5ml (1/15–1/6 fl oz) of fluid.

PROSTATE GLAND
This microscopic view of a section of prostate gland tissue shows a number of secretory ducts (orange and white).

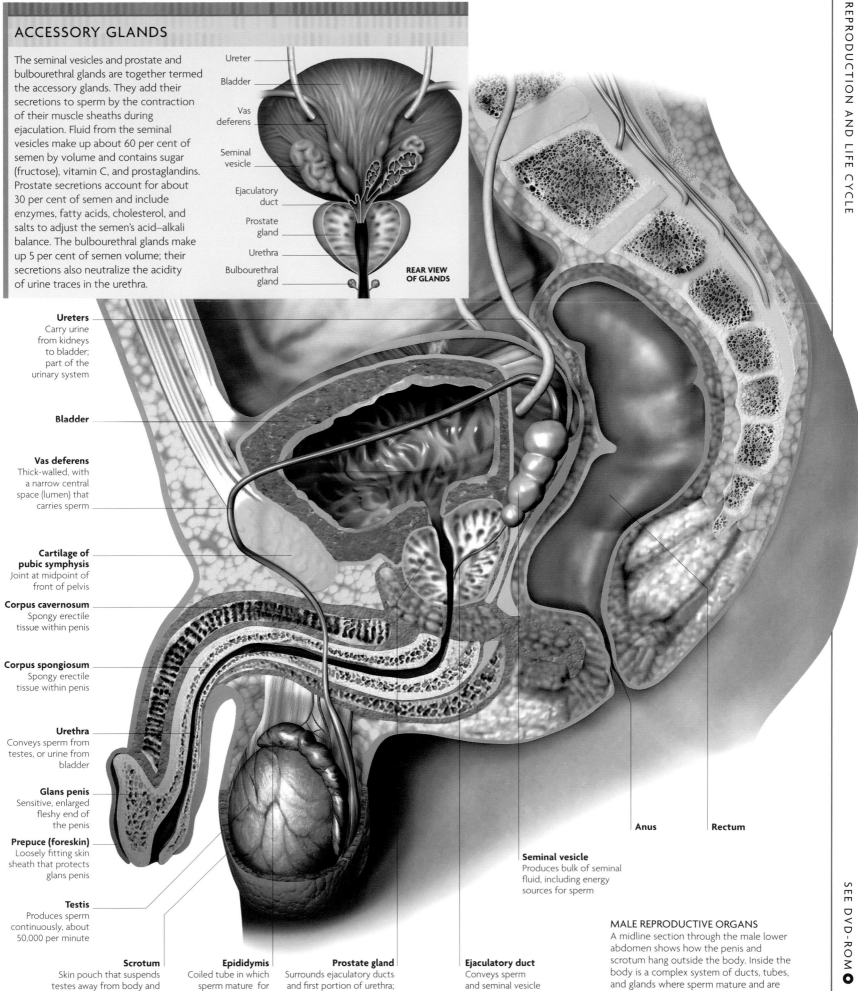

ACCESSORY GLANDS

The seminal vesicles and prostate and bulbourethral glands are together termed the accessory glands. They add their secretions to sperm by the contraction of their muscle sheaths during ejaculation. Fluid from the seminal vesicles make up about 60 per cent of semen by volume and contains sugar (fructose), vitamin C, and prostaglandins. Prostate secretions account for about 30 per cent of semen and include enzymes, fatty acids, cholesterol, and salts to adjust the semen's acid–alkali balance. The bulbourethral glands make up 5 per cent of semen volume; their secretions also neutralize the acidity of urine traces in the urethra.

Ureter

Bladder

Vas deferens

Seminal vesicle

Ejaculatory duct

Prostate gland

Urethra

Bulbourethral gland

REAR VIEW OF GLANDS

Ureters
Carry urine from kidneys to bladder; part of the urinary system

Bladder

Vas deferens
Thick-walled, with a narrow central space (lumen) that carries sperm

Cartilage of pubic symphysis
Joint at midpoint of front of pelvis

Corpus cavernosum
Spongy erectile tissue within penis

Corpus spongiosum
Spongy erectile tissue within penis

Urethra
Conveys sperm from testes, or urine from bladder

Glans penis
Sensitive, enlarged fleshy end of the penis

Prepuce (foreskin)
Loosely fitting skin sheath that protects glans penis

Testis
Produces sperm continuously, about 50,000 per minute

Scrotum
Skin pouch that suspends testes away from body and keeps them cool

Epididymis
Coiled tube in which sperm mature for about 1–3 weeks

Prostate gland
Surrounds ejaculatory ducts and first portion of urethra; produces fluid for semen

Ejaculatory duct
Conveys sperm and seminal vesicle secretions to urethra

Anus

Rectum

Seminal vesicle
Produces bulk of seminal fluid, including energy sources for sperm

MALE REPRODUCTIVE ORGANS
A midline section through the male lower abdomen shows how the penis and scrotum hang outside the body. Inside the body is a complex system of ducts, tubes, and glands where sperm mature and are stored before being ejaculated in semen.

FEMALE REPRODUCTIVE SYSTEM

UNLIKE THE MALE, THE FEMALE REPRODUCTIVE ORGANS ARE SITED ENTIRELY INSIDE THE BODY. THEIR FUNCTION IS TO RIPEN AND RELEASE AN EGG AT REGULAR INTERVALS, AND, IF THE EGG IS FERTILIZED, TO PROTECT AND NOURISH THE EMBRYO AND FETUS. NO EGGS ARE MANUFACTURED AFTER BIRTH – A FEMALE IS BORN WITH A FULL SET.

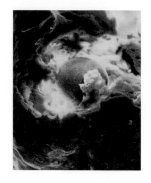

EGG RELEASE
A coloured electron microscope image showing an egg (red) being released from its follicle into the abdominal cavity. Tendrils (fimbriae) at the end of each fallopian tube guide the egg into the tube.

REPRODUCTIVE TRACT

The female reproductive glands (ovaries) are located within the abdomen. From puberty, they mature and release the female sex cells (gametes), known as egg cells or ova. This release occurs roughly once a month as part of the menstrual cycle (see p.219). The ripe egg travels along the fallopian tube to the uterus, the muscular sac in which it develops into an embryo and then fetus. Unfertilized eggs, and the uterine lining, leave via the vagina. The ovaries also make the female sex hormone oestrogen.

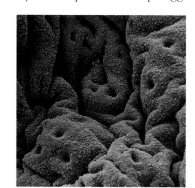

ENDOMETRIUM
An electron micrograph of the thick, folded, glandular endometrium (uterus lining), blood-rich and ready to receive a fertilized egg.

BREASTS

Both females and males have breasts (mammae), which contain modified sweat glands known as mammary glands. In females these are much larger and more developed than in males and produce milk at childbirth. Each breast contains 15–20 lobes of compound areolar glands, each lobe resembling a bunch of grapes on a long stalk. The cells of the glands secrete milk, which flows along merging lactiferous ducts towards the nipple. The breast also contains a widespread drainage system of lymph vessels (see p.156).

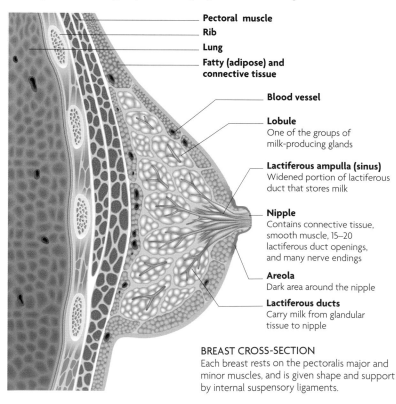

Pectoral muscle
Rib
Lung
Fatty (adipose) and connective tissue

Blood vessel

Lobule
One of the groups of milk-producing glands

Lactiferous ampulla (sinus)
Widened portion of lactiferous duct that stores milk

Nipple
Contains connective tissue, smooth muscle, 15–20 lactiferous duct openings, and many nerve endings

Areola
Dark area around the nipple

Lactiferous ducts
Carry milk from glandular tissue to nipple

BREAST CROSS-SECTION
Each breast rests on the pectoralis major and minor muscles, and is given shape and support by internal suspensory ligaments.

OVULATION

An ovary contains thousands of immature egg cells. During each menstrual cycle, follicle-stimulating hormone (FSH) causes one egg to begin development; this takes place inside a primary follicle. The follicle enlarges as its cells proliferate, and begins to fill with fluid, becoming a secondary follicle that moves to the ovary's surface. It also increases its production of the hormone oestrogen. A surge of luteinizing hormone (LH) causes the follicle to rupture and release the ripe egg – this is ovulation. The lining of the empty follicle thickens into a corpus luteum – a temporary source of hormones.

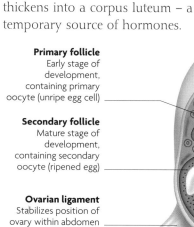

Primary follicle
Early stage of development, containing primary oocyte (unripe egg cell)

Secondary follicle
Mature stage of development, containing secondary oocyte (ripened egg)

Ovarian ligament
Stabilizes position of ovary within abdomen

INSIDE AN OVARY
The ovary contains undeveloped eggs, eggs in follicles at various stages of maturation, and empty follicles forming corpora lutea. The bulk of the glandular tissue surrounding these follicles is known as the stroma.

Egg

Corpus luteum
An empty follicle, filled with hormone-producing cells

VULVA

The external genital parts of the female are together known as the vulva. They are sited under the mons pubis, a mound of fatty tissue that covers the junction of the two pubic bones, the pubic symphysis. Outermost in the vulva are the flap-like labia majora, with the smaller, fold-like labia minora within them. Both are called "labia" due to their resemblance to lips. The labia majora contain fatty and connective tissue, sebaceous glands, smooth muscle, and sensory nerve endings. At puberty their exposed surfaces begin to grow hairs. Within the vulva are the openings to the vagina and the urethra. At the front end of the labia minora is the clitoris. Like the male penis, it is sensitive and engorges with blood during sexual arousal.

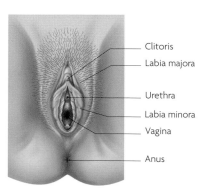

Clitoris
Labia majora
Urethra
Labia minora
Vagina
Anus

EXTERNAL GENITALS
The external genitals have a protective role, preventing infection from reaching the urethra or vagina, but allowing urine to exit.

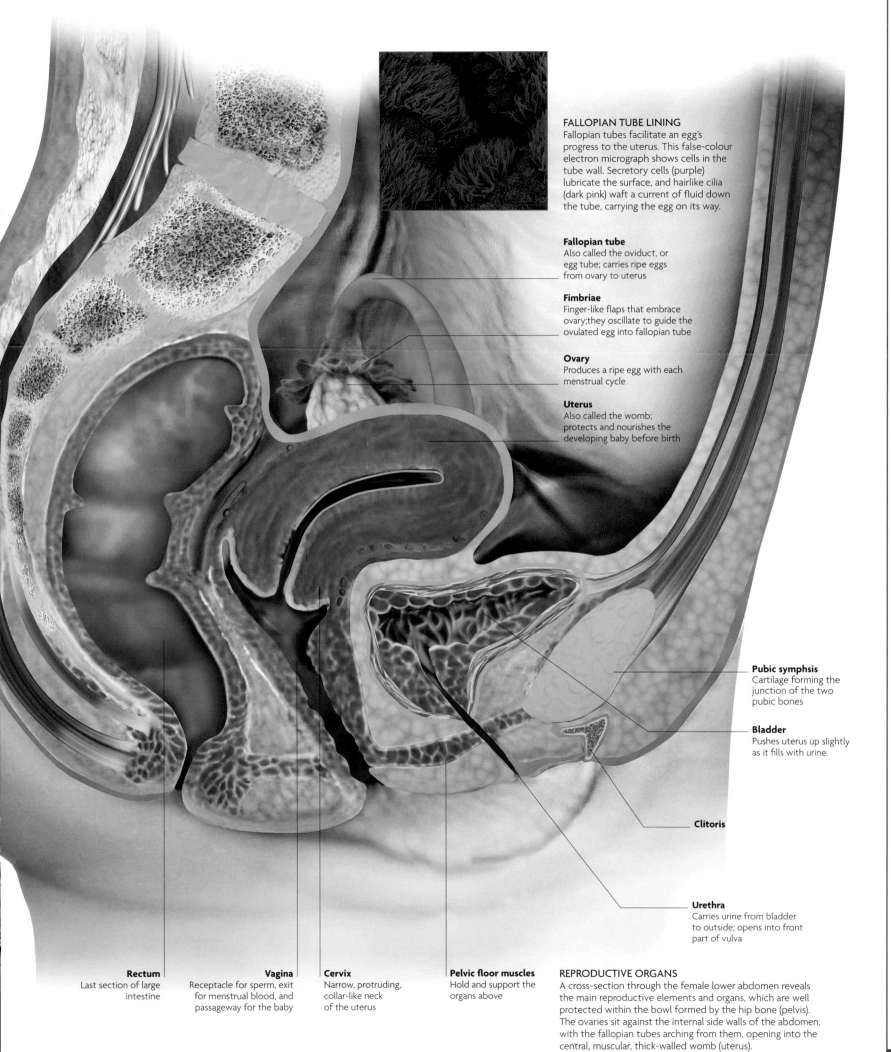

FALLOPIAN TUBE LINING
Fallopian tubes facilitate an egg's progress to the uterus. This false-colour electron micrograph shows cells in the tube wall. Secretory cells (purple) lubricate the surface, and hairlike cilia (dark pink) waft a current of fluid down the tube, carrying the egg on its way.

Fallopian tube
Also called the oviduct, or egg tube; carries ripe eggs from ovary to uterus

Fimbriae
Finger-like flaps that embrace ovary;they oscillate to guide the ovulated egg into fallopian tube

Ovary
Produces a ripe egg with each menstrual cycle

Uterus
Also called the womb; protects and nourishes the developing baby before birth

Pubic symphsis
Cartilage forming the junction of the two pubic bones

Bladder
Pushes uterus up slightly as it fills with urine

Clitoris

Urethra
Carries urine from bladder to outside; opens into front part of vulva

Rectum
Last section of large intestine

Vagina
Receptacle for sperm, exit for menstrual blood, and passageway for the baby

Cervix
Narrow, protruding, collar-like neck of the uterus

Pelvic floor muscles
Hold and support the organs above

REPRODUCTIVE ORGANS
A cross-section through the female lower abdomen reveals the main reproductive elements and organs, which are well protected within the bowl formed by the hip bone (pelvis). The ovaries sit against the internal side walls of the abdomen, with the fallopian tubes arching from them, opening into the central, muscular, thick-walled womb (uterus).

⬤ONCEPTION TO EMBRYO

AFTER THE UNION OF EGG AND SPERM AT FERTILIZATION, THE EMBRYONIC CELLS REPEATEDLY DIVIDE AND IMPLANT INTO THE UTERUS LINING, WHERE THE EMBRYO DEVELOPS ITS OWN SUPPORT SYSTEM, THE PLACENTA.

The first eight weeks of development within the uterus are known as the embryo stage, in which the fertilized egg becomes a tiny human body, no larger than a thumb. The fertilized egg develops into an enlarging cluster of cells, the blastocyst. Some of these cells will form the baby's body, others become the protective membranes or the placenta, which nourishes the embryo and removes waste products.

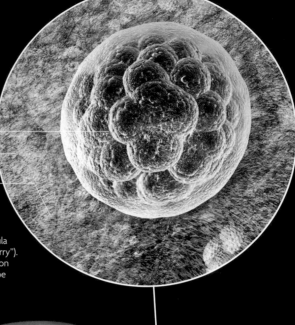

Morula

Fallopian tube lining

Cilia

3 MORULA
The zygote divides several times to form a solid blackberry-like cluster of 16–32 cells, the morula (derived from the Latin for "mulberry"). At around 3–4 days after fertilization the morula leaves the fallopian tube and enters the uterine cavity.

Fallopian tube
Conveys zygote towards uterus

First cleavage
The large zygote splits itself into two cells

Cilia
Microhairs in the fallopian lining that waft the zygote along

Goblet cells
Secrete fluid that fills the fallopian tube

Fallopian tube

Fimbriae

Ovary

Ovarian ligament

2 ZYGOTE
The fertilized egg passes along the fallopian tube. Within 24–36 hours it has divided into two cells, then 12 hours later into four cells, and so on. This process is known as cleavage. At each stage the resulting cells become smaller, gradually approaching normal body cell size.

Ovum (egg cell)
Up to 0.1mm ($^1/_{250}$ in) across (huge compared to other cells); contains 23 maternal chromosomes

Corona cell
Secretes chemicals to aid egg development

Tail of sperm
Lashes to propel sperm towards egg

Sperm head
Contains 23 paternal chromosomes

Acrosome
"Cap" of sperm head that penetrates egg cell membrane

SEXUAL INTERCOURSE

During sexual intercourse, over 300 million sperm are ejaculated into the vagina. Fewer enter the cervix, and fewer still reach the fallopian tubes, with half entering the wrong tube (with no egg released into it). Only a few hundred sperm reach the egg in the other tube – only one can fertilize it.

INTERCOURSE
To penetrate the vagina, the penis becomes erect by engorging with blood. The vagina widens to accept it.

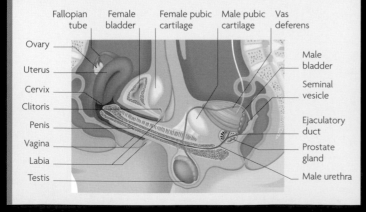

Fallopian tube | Female bladder | Female pubic cartilage | Male pubic cartilage | Vas deferens

Ovary
Uterus
Cervix
Clitoris
Penis
Vagina
Labia
Testis

Male bladder
Seminal vesicle
Ejaculatory duct
Prostate gland
Male urethra

1 FERTILIZATION
Fertilization takes place in the fallopian tube when the head of the sperm cell, or spermatozoon, penetrates the much larger ripe egg cell, or mature ovum. This forms a single cell – the fertilized egg, or zygote, which contains 23 pairs of chromosomes (see p.222).

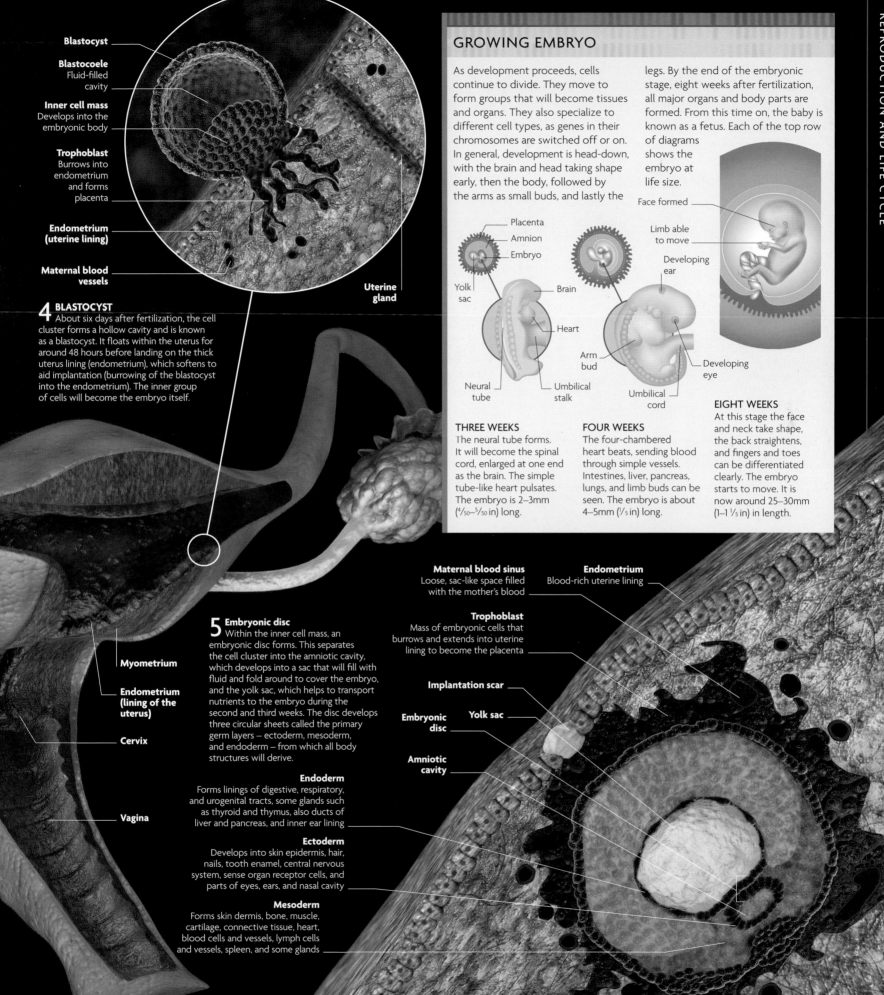

Blastocyst

Blastocoele
Fluid-filled
cavity

Inner cell mass
Develops into the
embryonic body

Trophoblast
Burrows into
endometrium
and forms
placenta

**Endometrium
(uterine lining)**

**Maternal blood
vessels**

**Uterine
gland**

4 BLASTOCYST

About six days after fertilization, the cell cluster forms a hollow cavity and is known as a blastocyst. It floats within the uterus for around 48 hours before landing on the thick uterus lining (endometrium), which softens to aid implantation (burrowing of the blastocyst into the endometrium). The inner group of cells will become the embryo itself.

GROWING EMBRYO

As development proceeds, cells continue to divide. They move to form groups that will become tissues and organs. They also specialize to different cell types, as genes in their chromosomes are switched off or on. In general, development is head-down, with the brain and head taking shape early, then the body, followed by the arms as small buds, and lastly the legs. By the end of the embryonic stage, eight weeks after fertilization, all major organs and body parts are formed. From this time on, the baby is known as a fetus. Each of the top row of diagrams shows the embryo at life size.

Placenta
Amnion
Embryo
Yolk
sac
Brain
Heart
Neural
tube
Umbilical
stalk
Arm
bud
Umbilical
cord
Face formed
Limb able
to move
Developing
ear
Developing
eye

THREE WEEKS
The neural tube forms. It will become the spinal cord, enlarged at one end as the brain. The simple tube-like heart pulsates. The embryo is 2–3mm ($^{4}/_{50}$–$^{5}/_{50}$ in) long.

FOUR WEEKS
The four-chambered heart beats, sending blood through simple vessels. Intestines, liver, pancreas, lungs, and limb buds can be seen. The embryo is about 4–5mm ($^{1}/_{5}$ in) long.

EIGHT WEEKS
At this stage the face and neck take shape, the back straightens, and fingers and toes can be differentiated clearly. The embryo starts to move. It is now around 25–30mm (1–1 $^{1}/_{5}$ in) in length.

Myometrium

**Endometrium
(lining of the
uterus)**

Cervix

Vagina

5 Embryonic disc

Within the inner cell mass, an embryonic disc forms. This separates the cell cluster into the amniotic cavity, which develops into a sac that will fill with fluid and fold around to cover the embryo, and the yolk sac, which helps to transport nutrients to the embryo during the second and third weeks. The disc develops three circular sheets called the primary germ layers – ectoderm, mesoderm, and endoderm – from which all body structures will derive.

Endoderm
Forms linings of digestive, respiratory, and urogenital tracts, some glands such as thyroid and thymus, also ducts of liver and pancreas, and inner ear lining

Ectoderm
Develops into skin epidermis, hair, nails, tooth enamel, central nervous system, sense organ receptor cells, and parts of eyes, ears, and nasal cavity

Mesoderm
Forms skin dermis, bone, muscle, cartilage, connective tissue, heart, blood cells and vessels, lymph cells and vessels, spleen, and some glands

Maternal blood sinus
Loose, sac-like space filled
with the mother's blood

Endometrium
Blood-rich uterine lining

Trophoblast
Mass of embryonic cells that
burrows and extends into uterine
lining to become the placenta

Implantation scar

**Embryonic
disc**

Yolk sac

**Amniotic
cavity**

FETAL DEVELOPMENT

FROM THE EIGHTH WEEK OF PREGNANCY UNTIL BIRTH, AN UNBORN BABY IS KNOWN AS A FETUS. MOST MAJOR DEVELOPMENT HAS ALREADY TAKEN PLACE DURING THE EMBRYO STAGE. THROUGH THE FETAL STAGE, THE BODY GROWS LARGER AND STRONGER, AND SOME DETAILS ARE ADDED TO VARIOUS PARTS.

CHANGES IN THE FETUS

By 12 weeks the fetus has a large head compared with the rest of its body, but its features are distinctly human. All major internal organs are developed, and even tiny nails exist as folds growing on the fingers and toes. The external ears, eyelids, and 32 permanent tooth buds have also formed. One month later, rapid development allows the fetus to move its limbs vigorously, although this is rarely felt by the mother at this stage. The external genitalia are visible, and a fine downy hair (lanugo) grows over the body. As growth continues, the fetus becomes leaner and wrinkly, but by the seventh to eighth month, it starts to accumulate fat and assume the "chubby" appearance of the newborn.

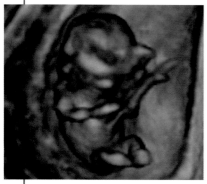

12 WEEKS
This is a 3-D ultrasound scan showing a fetus at 12 weeks. Its eyes will remain closed until around the seventh month.

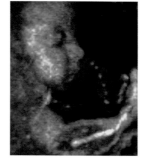

24 WEEKS
By now, movement can be felt by the mother. A fetus at this stage may play with its umbilical cord, as shown here.

36 WEEKS
The fetus is now somewhat restricted by the uterus. The side of the placenta facing the fetus is smooth and circular in outline, with the umbilical cord attached at centre.

Umbilical cord
The structure that connects the placenta and the fetus; provides the immunological, nutritional, and hormonal link with the mother

Amnion
Strong, transparent sac within the chorion; it encloses amniotic fluid

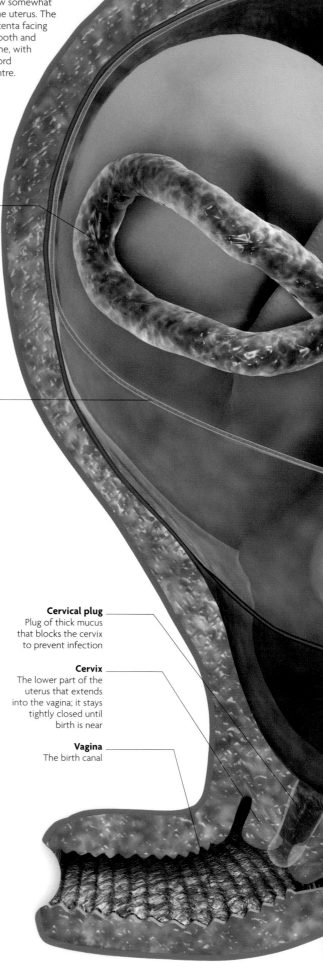

Cervical plug
Plug of thick mucus that blocks the cervix to prevent infection

Cervix
The lower part of the uterus that extends into the vagina; it stays tightly closed until birth is near

Vagina
The birth canal

DEVELOPMENT OF THE PLACENTA

Soon after conception, the embryo develops an organ, the placenta, which produces hormones crucial to continuation of the pregnancy. However, the placenta's main function is to supply the fetus with oxygen and nutrients and to remove waste products via diffusion (movement of a substance from an area of high to low concentration). It also acts as a barrier against harmful microbes and substances that may enter the fetus's body. The placenta derives from the trophoblast – the outer layer of the blastocyst (the mass of cells that results from the fusion of egg and sperm). It begins to form soon after the fertilized egg implants in the uterine lining and is almost fully developed by the fifth month of pregnancy.

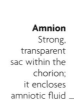

Trophoblast · Maternal artery · Maternal blood sinus · Maternal vein · Lining of uterus (endometrium) · Embryonic cells

1 Specialized cells of the trophoblast layer of the embryo extend into and "invade" nearby blood vessels in the endometrium (uterine lining). Blood from the mother flows from these blood vessels into spaces (maternal blood sinuses) within the trophoblast.

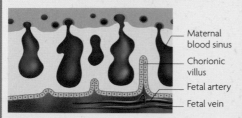

Maternal blood sinus · Chorionic villus · Fetal artery · Fetal vein

2 Other trophoblast layer cells extend finger-like projections, called chorionic villi, into the endometrium. Maternal blood sinuses grow to surround the villi. As the embryo develops, its own blood vessels grow into the chrionic villi.

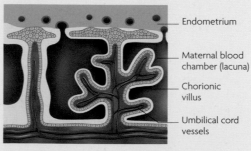

Endometrium · Maternal blood chamber (lacuna) · Chorionic villus · Umbilical cord vessels

3 The trophoblast layer is now establishing itself as a placenta. The villi develop further, sending out more finger-like branches. The maternal blood sinuses also enlarge into lacunae ("lakes") surrounding the villus and supply the placenta with oxygen and nutrients.

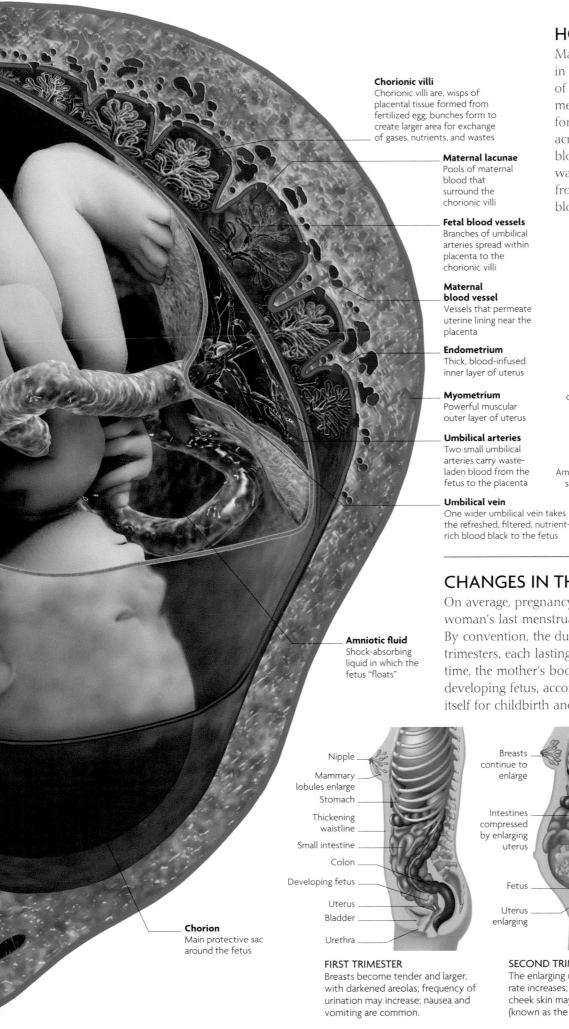

Chorionic villi
Chorionic villi are, wisps of placental tissue formed from fertilized egg; bunches form to create larger area for exchange of gases, nutrients, and wastes

Maternal lacunae
Pools of maternal blood that surround the chorionic villi

Fetal blood vessels
Branches of umbilical arteries spread within placenta to the chorionic villi

Maternal blood vessel
Vessels that permeate uterine lining near the placenta

Endometrium
Thick, blood-infused inner layer of uterus

Myometrium
Powerful muscular outer layer of uterus

Umbilical arteries
Two small umbilical arteries carry waste-laden blood from the fetus to the placenta

Umbilical vein
One wider umbilical vein takes the refreshed, filtered, nutrient-rich blood black to the fetus

Amniotic fluid
Shock-absorbing liquid in which the fetus "floats"

Chorion
Main protective sac around the fetus

HOW THE PLACENTA WORKS

Maternal and fetal blood never make direct contact in the placenta. They are separated by a barrier of cells, which forms on the outermost chorionic membrane. However, this barrier is thin enough for oxygen, nutrients, and some antibodies to pass across it, from maternal blood in the lacunae to fetal blood in the umbilical veins of the placenta. Fetal waste products travel in the opposite direction, from fetal blood in umbilical arteries to maternal blood, to be carried away and disposed of.

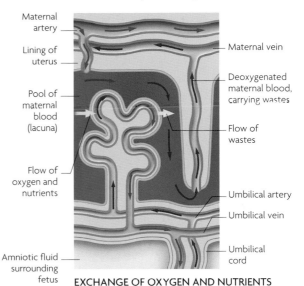

Maternal artery
Lining of uterus
Pool of maternal blood (lacuna)
Flow of oxygen and nutrients
Amniotic fluid surrounding fetus
Maternal vein
Deoxygenated maternal blood, carrying wastes
Flow of wastes
Umbilical artery
Umbilical vein
Umbilical cord

EXCHANGE OF OXYGEN AND NUTRIENTS
Fetal and maternal circulations are separated by a very thin membrane that allows for the passage of gases, nutrients, and waste between them.

CHANGES IN THE MOTHER

On average, pregnancy lasts for 40 weeks from the first day of a woman's last menstrual period (usually 38 weeks from fertilization). By convention, the duration of pregnancy is divided into thirds, or trimesters, each lasting for about three calendar months. During this time, the mother's body undergoes many changes to support the developing fetus, accommodate its increasing size, and prepare itself for childbirth and breast-feeding.

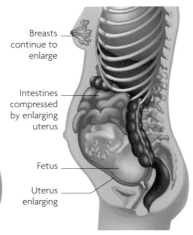

Nipple
Mammary lobules enlarge
Stomach
Thickening waistline
Small intestine
Colon
Developing fetus
Uterus
Bladder
Urethra

Breasts continue to enlarge
Intestines compressed by enlarging uterus
Fetus
Uterus enlarging

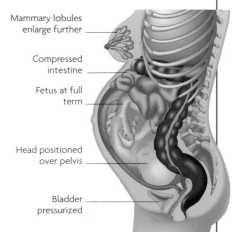

Mammary lobules enlarge further
Compressed intestine
Fetus at full term
Head positioned over pelvis
Bladder pressurized

FIRST TRIMESTER
Breasts become tender and larger, with darkened areolas; frequency of urination may increase; nausea and vomiting are common.

SECOND TRIMESTER
The enlarging uterus shows; heart rate increases; mother's forehead and cheek skin may temporarily darken (known as the "mask of pregnancy").

THIRD TRIMESTER
Skin stretches over the abdomen; slight contractions may be felt; fatigue, back pain, heartburn, and occasional breathlessness may occur.

PREPARING FOR BIRTH

CHANGES OCCUR IN THE BODY DURING LATE PREGNANCY, SIGNALLING THE APPROACH OF CHILDBIRTH. THE HEAD OF THE FETUS DROPS LOWER INTO THE PELVIS; THE EXPECTANT MOTHER MAY EXPERIENCE WEIGHT LOSS; AND THERE MAY ALSO BE SOME EARLY CONTRACTIONS OF THE UTERUS.

MULTIPLE PREGNANCY AND FETAL POSITIONS

The presence of more than one fetus in the uterus is called a multiple pregnancy. Twins occur in about one in 80 pregnancies, and triplets in about one in 8,000. Both events are becoming more common, partly due to improved antenatal care and also increasing use of fertility methods such as IVF (in vitro fertilization). After about 30 weeks, the most common fetal position is head down, facing the mother's back, with the neck flexed forward. Such a position eases passage through the birth canal. However, about 1 in 30 full-term deliveries is breech, in which the baby's buttocks emerge before the head.

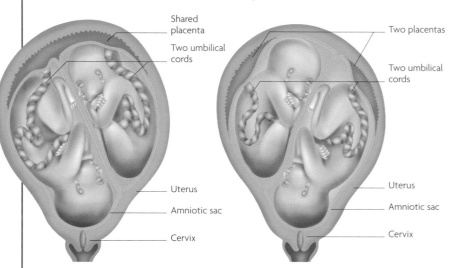

Shared placenta / Two umbilical cords / Uterus / Amniotic sac / Cervix

Two placentas / Two umbilical cords / Uterus / Amniotic sac / Cervix

MONOZYGOTIC TWINS
A single fertilized egg, or zygote, forms an embryo that splits into two. Each develops into a fetus. The two have the same genes and sex and share one placenta. They look alike and are known as "identical" twins.

DIZYGOTIC TWINS
Two eggs are fertilized and develop separately, each with its own placenta. They may be different or the same sex. Also called "fraternal twins", they have the same degree of resemblance as any brothers and sisters.

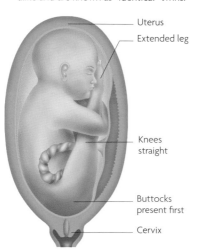

Uterus / Extended leg / Knees straight / Buttocks present first / Cervix

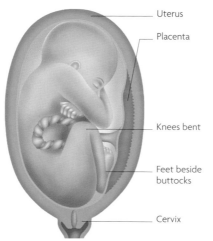

Uterus / Placenta / Knees bent / Feet beside buttocks / Cervix

FRANK BREECH
In frank breech, also called incomplete breech, the baby fails to turn head-down in the uterus. The hips are flexed and the legs are straight, extending alongside the body so that the feet are positioned beside the head.

COMPLETE BREECH
The baby's legs are flexed at the hips and knees, so the feet are next to the buttocks. This occurs less commonly than frank breech. The incidence of breech delivery is much higher among premature babies.

CHANGES IN THE CERVIX

The cervix is the firm band of muscle and connective tissue that forms the neck-like structure at the bottom of the uterus. In late pregnancy, the cervix softens in readiness for childbirth. Sporadic uterine tightenings, known as Braxton–Hicks contractions, help to thin the cervix so that it merges with the uterus's lower segment. Braxton–Hicks contractions are usually painless, and occur through much of pregnancy, becoming noticeable only after mid-term.

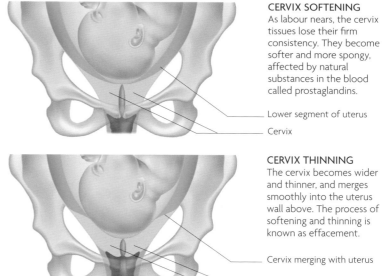

CERVIX SOFTENING
As labour nears, the cervix tissues lose their firm consistency. They become softer and more spongy, affected by natural substances in the blood called prostaglandins.

Lower segment of uterus / Cervix

CERVIX THINNING
The cervix becomes wider and thinner, and merges smoothly into the uterus wall above. The process of softening and thinning is known as effacement.

Cervix merging with uterus / Cervix thinned

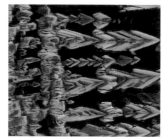

HORMONE CRYSTALS
Intravenous infusion of extra oxytocin hormone (shown here as crystals) can help to induce or speed up labour.

CONTRACTIONS

When pregnancy reaches full-term, the uterus is the largest and strongest muscle in the female body. When its muscle fibres shorten, with the eventual aim of expelling the fetus, it is known as a uterine contraction or simply a "contraction". True contractions, as opposed to Braxton–Hicks contractions, are regular and become steadily more frequent, more painful, and longer-lasting. The main area of contraction is in the uterine fundus (upper uterus), which stretches, causing the lower uterus and cervix to thin. Judging when true labour has started can be difficult due to "false alarms".

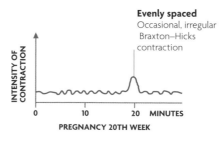

Evenly spaced — Occasional, irregular Braxton–Hicks contraction

PREGNANCY 20TH WEEK

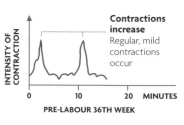

Contractions increase — Regular, mild contractions occur

PRE-LABOUR 36TH WEEK

PROGRESS OF CONTRACTIONS
Through much of pregnancy, gentle, partial contractions occur, but true contractions only begin late in pregnancy. At first, they are well spaced out and relatively low in strength. As labour intensifies, the rate and duration of contractions increase and they put more downward pressure on the baby.

Approaching labour — Interval between contractions decreases

EARLY LABOUR 40TH WEEK

LABOUR

IN MEDICAL TERMS, LABOUR USUALLY MEANS THE FULL
PROCESS OF GIVING BIRTH. IT CAN BE DESCRIBED IN THREE
PHASES OR STAGES: ONSET OF CONTRACTIONS TO FULL
DILATION OF THE CERVIX; DELIVERY OF THE BABY; AND
DELIVERY OF THE PLACENTA (AFTERBIRTH).

ENGAGEMENT

During the last weeks of pregnancy, the baby's presenting part –
the part that will emerge first, usually the head – descends into the
bowl-like cavity of the pelvis. This process is called engagement.
When it happens, many women feel a sensation of dropping and
"lightening". This is because the movement of the baby lowers the
upper uterus, resulting in less pressure on the diaphragm, which
makes it easier for the mother to breathe. Engagement usually takes
place at around 36 weeks during a first pregnancy; however, it may
not happen until the onset of labour during subsequent pregnancies.

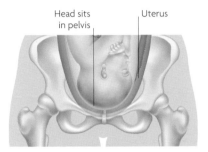

BEFORE THE HEAD ENGAGES
Before the head of the baby engages, the
top of the uterus reaches up to the sternum,
or breastbone. The widest section of the
baby's head has not yet passed through
the inlet of the pelvis into the cavity.

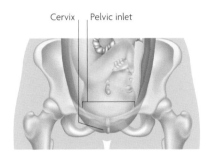

AFTER ENGAGEMENT
The baby's head descends through the inlet
of the pelvis and becomes slotted into,
or engaged, within the pelvic cavity. The
overall position of the uterus drops, and the
baby's head rests against the uterine cervix.

INDUCTION

If a pregnancy continues too long
past the due date – usually 10–14 days
– then labour may need to be
medically induced. This may also be
advised if the health of the mother
or baby, or both, is at risk. There are
several induction methods, depending
partly on the stage of labour. They
include inserting a vaginal pessary,
artificially breaking the waters, or
giving an injection of a hormone that
stimulates contractions of the uterus.

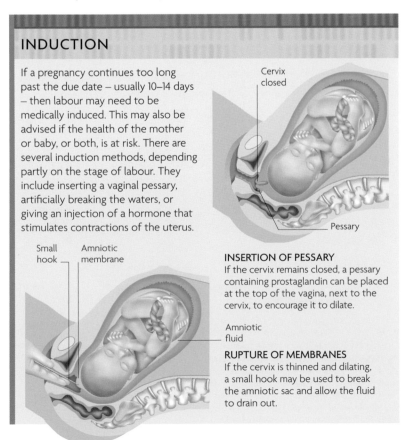

INSERTION OF PESSARY
If the cervix remains closed, a pessary
containing prostaglandin can be placed
at the top of the vagina, next to the
cervix, to encourage it to dilate.

RUPTURE OF MEMBRANES
If the cervix is thinned and dilating,
a small hook may be used to break
the amniotic sac and allow the fluid
to drain out.

CERVICAL DILATION

The first stage of labour begins with the onset of regular, painful
contractions of the uterus, which cause the cervix to dilate. These occur
mainly in the upper uterus so that it shortens and tightens, and this
pulls and stretches the lower uterine segment and cervix. On average,
for a first baby, the cervix dilates at the rate of about 1cm (½in) per
hour; progress is usually more rapid for subsequent babies. In most
women the cervix is fully dilated when it opens to around 10cm (4in).

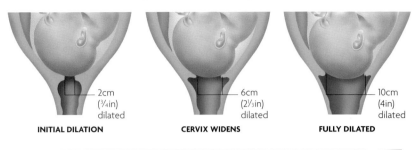

INITIAL DILATION — 2cm (¾in) dilated

CERVIX WIDENS — 6cm (2⅓in) dilated

FULLY DILATED — 10cm (4in) dilated

SIGNS OF EARLY LABOUR

Every woman's experience is
different, but generally there are
three signs that labour is starting:
a "show", contractions, and the
waters breaking. Before labour
begins (usually less than 3 days),
the mucous plug in the cervix,
which acts as a seal during
pregnancy, is passed as a blood-
stained or brownish discharge
(the "show"). As contractions
become stronger and more
regular, the membranes retaining
the amniotic fluid rupture
(break), allowing the fluid (water)
to leak out via the birth canal.

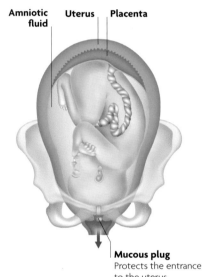

Amniotic fluid | Uterus | Placenta

Mucous plug
Protects the entrance
to the uterus

1 THE "SHOW"
For most of a pregnancy, the mucous
plug in the cervix prevents microbes from
entering the uterus. As the cervix widens
slightly, the plug loosens and falls out.

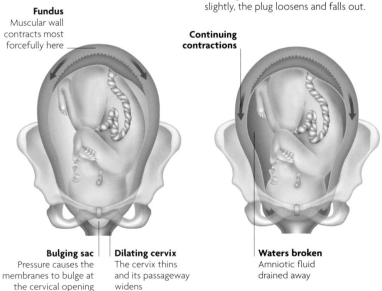

Fundus
Muscular wall
contracts most
forcefully here

**Continuing
contractions**

Bulging sac
Pressure causes the
membranes to bulge at
the cervical opening

Dilating cervix
The cervix thins
and its passageway
widens

Waters broken
Amniotic fluid
drained away

2 CONTRACTIONS
Coordinated muscular contractions
are generated in the upper part of the
uterus, the fundus. This helps to gradually
open, or dilate, the cervix.

3 WATERS BREAK
The amniotic sac (membrane) around
the baby ruptures, or breaks, allowing
colourless amniotic fluid to pass out
through the birth canal.

DELIVERY

THE CULMINATION OF PREGNANCY AND LABOUR, DELIVERY OF THE BABY AND THE PLACENTA INVOLVES A COMPLICATED SEQUENCE OF EVENTS THAT ULTIMATELY SEPARATES CHILD FROM MOTHER, ALLOWING THE START OF THEIR INDEPENDENT RELATIONSHIP.

THREE STAGES OF CHILDBIRTH

The first contractions of labour start in response to the secretion of hormones and, during that first stage of labour, uterine contractions pull the cervix until it is merely a thin sheet of tissue and is fully dilated to approximately 10cm (4in). The membranes of the amniotic sac that protected the fetus in the uterus rupture, a process referred to as the waters breaking. The second stage, delivery, involves synchronized efforts of the mother's contractions and the baby's shifts in position in order to fit its large head into the birth canal and then travel along it to the outside world. After the baby is born and the umbilical cord clamped and cut, is the third stage of labour, in which the placenta, or "afterbirth," is delivered, often with the help of a midwife or obstetrician gently pulling on the cord.

NORMAL DELIVERY
Newborn babies are usually covered with a combination of blood, mucus, and vernix (the greasy covering that protected the fetus in the uterus). This baby's umbilical cord has not yet been clamped and cut.

PELVIC SHAPES

The female pelvis tends to be better adapted to the process of child-bearing and delivery than a man's. Nevertheless, there is a wide variation in shape, with some shapes making childbirth easier than others. A round, shallow shape (gynecoid), the classic "female pelvis" has a generous capacity, and usually results in fewer problems. At the other extreme is a triangular, or android, pelvis which is less spacious and can cause difficulties with childbirth.

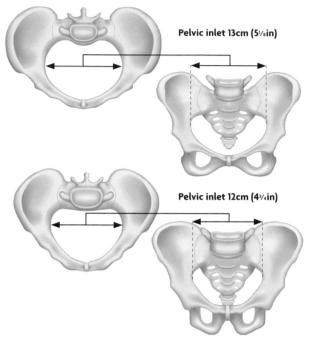

Pelvic inlet 13cm (5⅛in)

GYNECOID PELVIS
A gynecoid pelvis is shallow, allowing the uterus to expand as the fetus grows. The round shape of the wider pelvic inlet provide more room for the head of a fetus to pass through at delivery.

Pelvic inlet 12cm (4¾in)

ANDROID PELVIS
An android (triangular) pelvis is most like a man's in shape. It can be difficult for a woman with this shape of pelvis to have a vaginal delivery unless her baby is small.

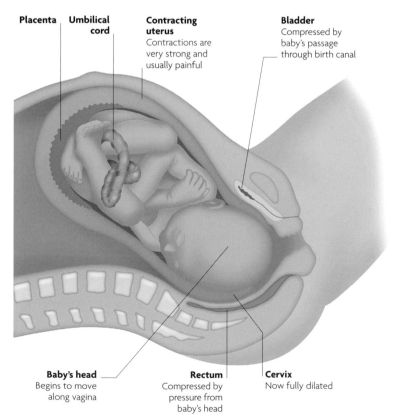

| **Placenta** | **Umbilical cord** | **Contracting uterus** Contractions are very strong and usually painful | **Bladder** Compressed by baby's passage through birth canal |

Baby's head
Begins to move along vagina

Rectum
Compressed by pressure from baby's head

Cervix
Now fully dilated

1 DILATION OF THE CERVIX
Delivery begins when the cervix is completely dilated. The baby turns towards the mother's spine so that the widest part of the baby's skull is aligned with the widest part of the mother's pelvis. As the baby tucks in its chin, it starts moving out of the uterus and into the vagina, which stretches to accommodate the baby's head.

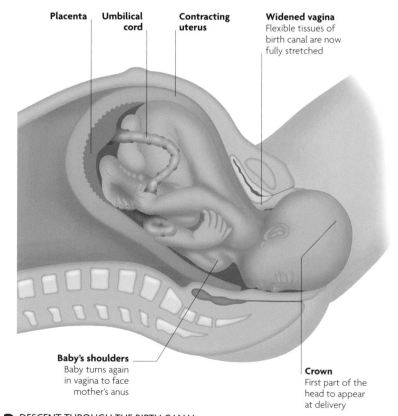

| **Placenta** | **Umbilical cord** | **Contracting uterus** | **Widened vagina** Flexible tissues of birth canal are now fully stretched |

Baby's shoulders
Baby turns again in vagina to face mother's anus

Crown
First part of the head to appear at delivery

2 DESCENT THROUGH THE BIRTH CANAL
As the baby descends through the birth canal, the top of the head appears for the first time. This stage is called "crowning", and the baby has usually turned again, to face the mother's anus this time, so that the emerging head can negotiate the bend in the fully stretched vagina. Birth is usually imminent at this point.

FETAL MONITORING

If delivery is not proceeding as expected, the obstetrician (specialist physician dealing with pregnancy and childbirth) can monitor the heart rate of the fetus to determine whether it is in distress. Fetal monitoring can be done with a stethoscope or, occasionally, Doppler ultrasound scans. To achieve more conclusive results, electronic fetal monitoring (EFM), also known as cardiotocography, can be done, either externally with two devices strapped to the mother's abdomen, or internally with an electrode clipped to the baby's head and hooked up to the electronic fetal monitor. It is now possible to monitor the heart rate remotely so the mother can remain mobile during labour.

MONITORING THE BABY
External electronic monitors record the baby's heart rate and mother's contractions.

Increase in rate with each contraction

Baseline rate 120 bpm

BEATS PER MINUTE

160
140
120
100
80

MINUTES 5 10

FETAL HEART RATE
The response of the baby's heart rate to the mother's contractions is followed with electronic fetal monitoring; the baby's heart rate should increase during uterine contractions.

Regular contractions of uterus

INTENSITY OF CONTRACTIONS

MINUTES 5 10

CONTRACTIONS
This tracing showing the intensity of the mother's contractions, and the one above, for the fetal heart rate, shows that the baby responds to the mother's contractions.

EPIDURAL ANALGESIA

One of the most commonly used methods of pain relief during labour and delivery, epidural analgesia, is delivered via a needle into the space between the vertebrae and the spinal column in the lower (lumbar) region of the back. It affects the nerve fibres that detect contraction pains. A new type of epidural, often called a "walking epidural", reduces pain without removing sensation, allowing women to move around during labour and participate actively in the delivery.

LOCATOR

Spinal cord

Tip of catheter

Vertebra
Fluid

Epidural space

INSERTION OF THE CATHETER
A catheter is passed through a fine needle and inserted into the epidural space. It is left in place, allowing drugs to be topped up throughout labour.

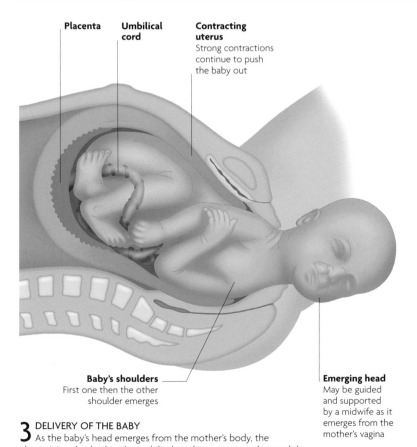

Placenta Umbilical cord

Contracting uterus
Strong contractions continue to push the baby out

Baby's shoulders
First one then the other shoulder emerges

Emerging head
May be guided and supported by a midwife as it emerges from the mother's vagina

3 DELIVERY OF THE BABY
As the baby's head emerges from the mother's body, the obstetrician checks that the umbilical cord is not wrapped around the baby's neck. Mucus is cleared from its nose and mouth so that it can breathe. The baby rotates again so that the shoulders are in position to slip out easily, one shoulder quickly followed by the other one.

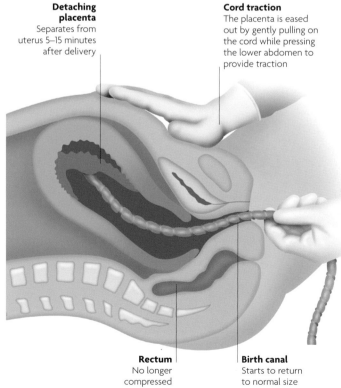

Detaching placenta
Separates from uterus 5–15 minutes after delivery

Cord traction
The placenta is eased out by gently pulling on the cord while pressing the lower abdomen to provide traction

Rectum
No longer compressed

Birth canal
Starts to return to normal size

4 DELIVERY OF THE PLACENTA
The uterus resumes mild contractions soon after the baby is born, sealing shut any blood vessels that are still bleeding. The placenta separates from the lining of the uterus and is eased out by gently pulling on the umbilical cord while pressing on the lower abdomen. The mother may be given a hormonal drug to accelerate this process.

AFTER THE BIRTH

OVER THE SPACE OF 40 WEEKS, THE FERTILIZED OVUM DEVELOPS INTO A COMPLEX, MULTICELLULAR HUMAN BEING, AND HAS PROGRESSED FROM FETUS TO NEWBORN BABY. ALL ORGAN SYSTEMS ARE IN PLACE, BUT SOME WILL QUICKLY ADAPT TO LIFE WITHOUT AN UMBILICAL CORD, WHILE OTHERS WILL NOT COMPLETE DEVELOPMENT UNTIL ADOLESCENCE.

NEWBORN ANATOMY

The anatomy of a newborn baby is characterized by various special features that will facilitate its further growth and development outside the mother's uterus – a baby grows faster in the first year after birth than at any other time in life. Fibrous fontanelles, which separate the skull bones, allow the skull to increase in volume as the brain grows; these fontanelles will start to harden to bone (ossify) at about 18 months, but the process will not be finished until the child is about six years old. Cartilage in the joints and at the end of long bones adapt the skeletal system for rapid growth. At birth, the thymus gland is at its largest relative size, as it has been the centre for development of the immune system in the fetus. Likewise, the liver is enlarged as in the fetus it was the sole producer of red blood cells. This task will now be taken over by the bone marrow.

APGAR SCORE

To assess if a newborn needs emergency care, the Apgar score tests five criteria both one and five minutes after birth. In dark-skinned babies, "colour" refers to the mouth, palms, and soles of the feet.

SIGN	SCORE: 0	SCORE: 1	SCORE: 2
HEART RATE	None	Below 100	Over 100
BREATHING RATE	None	Slow or irregular; weak cry	Regular; strong cry
MUSCLE TONE	Limp	Some bending of limbs	Active movements
REFLEX RESPONSES	None	Grimace or whimpering	Cry, sneeze, or cough
COLOUR	Pale or blue	Blue extremities	Pink

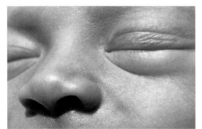

PUFFY EYES
A newborn's eyelids are often puffy. Some babies develop pink eye soon after birth, caused either by a blocked tear duct or by infection with bacteria in the birth canal.

VERNIX
This greasy white substance over the fetus' body stops the skin from wrinkling due to exposure to amniotic fluid while in the uterus. It is washed or wiped off after birth.

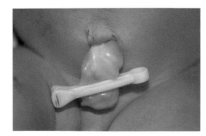

UMBILICAL CORD
The link between fetus and maternal placenta, the umbilical cord, has two arteries and a vein in a jelly-like covering. It is clamped and cut shortly after birth.

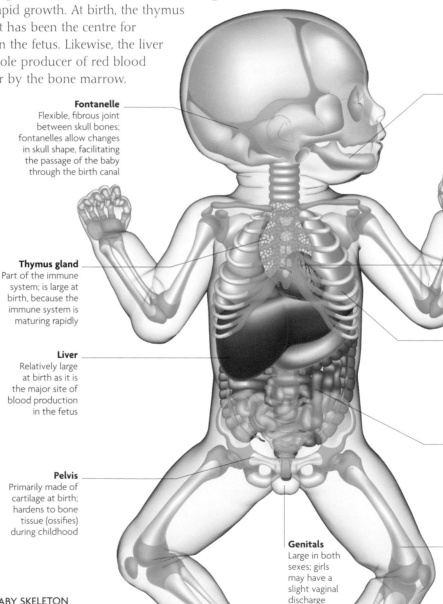

Jaw
Contains fully formed primary (milk) teeth within jawbone; in most cases, teeth do not start to erupt until the baby is six months old

Fontanelle
Flexible, fibrous joint between skull bones; fontanelles allow changes in skull shape, facilitating the passage of the baby through the birth canal

Heart
Changes in structure at birth to enable blood to circulate through the lungs rather than through the placenta

Thymus gland
Part of the immune system; is large at birth, because the immune system is maturing rapidly

Liver
Relatively large at birth as it is the major site of blood production in the fetus

Lung
With the first breath, the baby's lungs fill with air, expand, and regular breathing (respiration) begins

Intestines
Excretes the first faecal material as a thick, sticky, greenish-black mixture of bile and mucus, called meconium

Pelvis
Primarily made of cartilage at birth; hardens to bone tissue (ossifies) during childhood

Genitals
Large in both sexes; girls may have a slight vaginal discharge

Femur
Long bone of the thigh; only the shaft has hardened into bone at birth; the ends are still cartilage to allow for growth

BABY SKELETON
At birth, a baby has some 300 bones, but some of these fuse during childhood and adolescence, leaving adults with only 206. Cartilaginous areas of the baby's skeleton are shown in blue and those composed of bone are shown in off-white. A few areas remain cartilage throughout the person's life.

Foot
At birth, most of the bones in the foot are cartilage, and the foot may be turned in or out depending on the baby's position in the uterus

CIRCULATION IN THE UTERUS

As the placenta provides oxygen and nutrients, fetal circulation has anatomical variations ("shunts") to allow blood to bypass not–yet–functioning liver and lungs. The ductus venosus shunts incoming blood through the liver to the right atrium, which shunts it through a gap, the foramen ovale, to the left atrium (mostly bypassing the right ventricle) and onwards to the body. Blood that makes it into the right ventricle passes into the pulmonary artery but is shunted into the aorta by the ductus arteriosus, thus bypassing the lungs.

CIRCULATION AT BIRTH

At birth, the baby takes its first breaths and the umbilical cord is clamped. This forces the circulatory system into a monumental response – to convert itself immediately to obtain its oxygen supply via the lungs. Blood is sent to the lungs to retrieve oxygen, and the pressure of this blood returning from the lungs into the left atrium forces shut the foramen ovale between the two atria, thus establishing normal circulation. The ductus arteriosus, the ductus venosus, and the umbilical vein and arteries, close up and become ligaments.

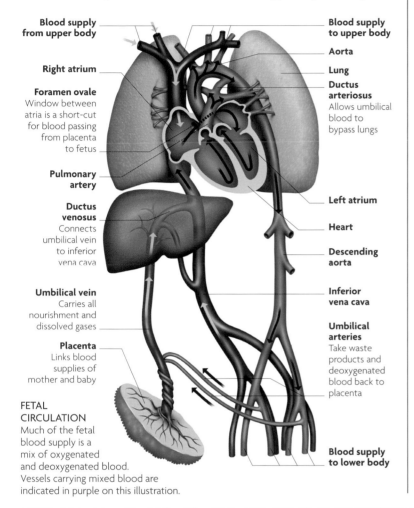

Blood supply from upper body

Right atrium

Foramen ovale
Window between atria is a short-cut for blood passing from placenta to fetus

Pulmonary artery

Ductus venosus
Connects umbilical vein to inferior vena cava

Umbilical vein
Carries all nourishment and dissolved gases

Placenta
Links blood supplies of mother and baby

Blood supply to upper body

Aorta

Lung

Ductus arteriosus
Allows umbilical blood to bypass lungs

Left atrium

Heart

Descending aorta

Inferior vena cava

Umbilical arteries
Take waste products and deoxygenated blood back to placenta

Blood supply to lower body

FETAL CIRCULATION
Much of the fetal blood supply is a mix of oxygenated and deoxygenated blood. Vessels carrying mixed blood are indicated in purple on this illustration.

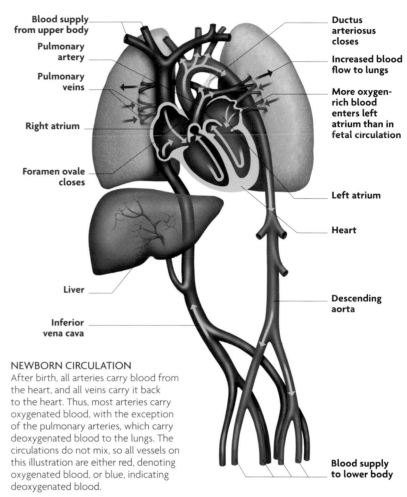

Blood supply from upper body

Pulmonary artery

Pulmonary veins

Right atrium

Foramen ovale closes

Liver

Inferior vena cava

Ductus arteriosus closes

Increased blood flow to lungs

More oxygen-rich blood enters left atrium than in fetal circulation

Left atrium

Heart

Descending aorta

Blood supply to lower body

NEWBORN CIRCULATION
After birth, all arteries carry blood from the heart, and all veins carry it back to the heart. Thus, most arteries carry oxygenated blood, with the exception of the pulmonary arteries, which carry deoxygenated blood to the lungs. The circulations do not mix, so all vessels on this illustration are either red, denoting oxygenated blood, or blue, indicating deoxygenated blood.

CHANGES IN THE MOTHER

As with a newborn baby, many physiological changes take place in the mother after birth that the body prepares for during the pregnancy. The process of enhancing breast tissue in anticipation of breast-feeding begins early in the pregnancy: the breasts enlarge visibly and the alveoli in each of the milk-producing glands (lobules) swell and multiply. From three months into the pregnancy, the breasts are able to produce colostrum, a fluid rich in antibodies (that help protect a newborn from allergies and respiratory and gastrointestinal infections), water, protein, and minerals. After the birth, colostrum supplies a breast-fed baby with nutrition until the mother's milk begins to flow several days later. Soon after birth, the uterus begins to shrink to its pre-pregnancy size – a process that is helped along by breast-feeding.

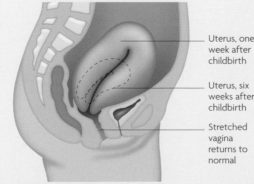

Uterus, one week after childbirth

Uterus, six weeks after childbirth

Stretched vagina returns to normal

UTERUS SHRINKS
After delivery of the baby and the placenta in the second and third stages of labour, hormones in the mother's body cause her uterus and vagina to shrink back to their normal size and position in her body.

Lobule

BEFORE PREGNANCY

New and enlarged lobule

DURING PREGNANCY AND LACTATION

LACTATION
During pregnancy, lobules (milk-producing glands) increase in size and number in preparation for breast-feeding the baby. By the end of the first trimester, they can produce colostrum, the yellow fluid that provides antibodies to protect against allergy and respiratory and gastrointestinal infections in the newborn.

GROWTH AND DEVELOPMENT

DURING THE EARLY YEARS, INFANTS AND YOUNG CHILDREN DEVELOP
BASIC PHYSICAL SKILLS SUCH AS WALKING AND TALKING. AS CHILDHOOD
PROGRESSES, AGILITY IMPROVES AND INTELLECTUAL ABILITIES INCREASE.
PHYSICAL GROWTH IS VERY RAPID DURING INFANCY, THEN OCCURS AT A
FAIRLY STEADY RATE UNTIL GROWTH RATE SPEEDS UP AGAIN AT PUBERTY.

BONE GROWTH

Body growth depends on the increasing size of its internal
framework, the skeleton. The long bones of the legs are responsible
for most of the increase in height, and for changing proportions
through childhood. Most of the long bones develop from cartilage
precursors, by a sequence of changes (ossification). The process
starts before birth at primary ossification centres in the bone shafts.
After birth, secondary ossification centres develop near the bone
ends. Growth ceases when ossification is complete, at 18–20 years.

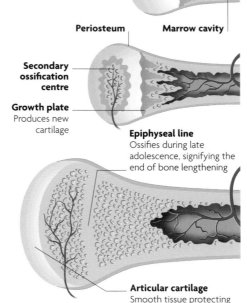

Epiphysis
Bone end, made
of cartilage

Growth plate

Blood vessel

Shaft

LONG BONE OF A NEWBORN
The shaft, or diaphysis, is turning
to hard bone from the primary
ossification centre, and has a
marrow cavity. The bulbous
end or head, the epiphysis, is
all cartilage, and relatively soft.

Periosteum

Marrow cavity

Secondary ossification centre

Growth plate
Produces new
cartilage

Epiphyseal line
Ossifies during late
adolescence, signifying the
end of bone lengthening

LONG BONE OF A CHILD
A secondary ossification centre
inside the head begins to change
the surrounding cartilage to
hardened, mineralized bone
tissue. An elongating growth area
(epiphyseal growth plate) forms
between the shaft and head.

Articular cartilage
Smooth tissue protecting
the bone end

LONG BONE OF AN ADULT
By about 18–20 years, all zones
have hardened into true bone,
with the epiphyseal growth plate
represented by a line of dense
bony tissue. The only remaining
cartilage is smooth, slippery
articular cartilage, which covers
the head inside the joint.

BONE DEVELOPMENT
This X-ray shows bone growth in
the hand – bone tissue is pink/blue.
The hands of the 1 and 3 year olds
show wide spaces of cartilage
between each finger bone. Wrist
bones appear absent in the 1 year
old as they are made of cartilage;
wrist bone formation has begun at
3 years. In the hand of the 20 year
old, all the bones are fully formed.

 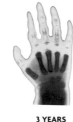 

1 YEAR   **3 YEARS**   **20 YEARS**

CHANGING PROPORTIONS

If the body's height at different ages is superimposed onto a grid,
the dramatic changes in body proportions that take place from
birth to adulthood are clearly demonstrated. In a newborn infant,
the head is relatively large, being wider than the shoulders and
representing about one-quarter of the baby's total height; the
legs are about three-eighths of the baby's total height. As the
child grows, the head and then the torso do so at a lesser rate,
while the arms and then the legs "catch up". By the age of two
years the head accounts for about one-sixth of the child's total
height. When final adult size
is reached during adolescence,
the head represents only about
one-eighth of body length, and
the legs one-half.

HEAD–BODY PROPORTIONS
The overall growth trend is for
the head to lead, growing first and
fastest. Then the other body regions
catch up, first the torso, followed by
the arms and finally the legs.

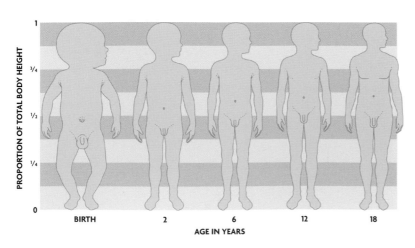

PROPORTION OF TOTAL BODY HEIGHT

1
3/4
1/2
1/4
0

BIRTH   **2**   **6**   **12**   **18**

AGE IN YEARS

SKULL AND BRAIN

At birth, the brain is a quarter of its adult size. It has almost its
full complement of nerve cells (neurons), but they have not yet
developed large numbers of interconnections. A baby's skull is
partly cartilage and there are gaps (fontanelles) and seams (sutures)
between its bones to allow for expansion. By two years, the brain
has enlarged to four-fifths of its adult size, and
neurons are forging links
into networks.

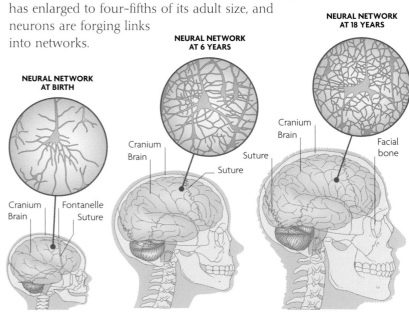

**NEURAL NETWORK
AT 18 YEARS**

**NEURAL NETWORK
AT 6 YEARS**

**NEURAL NETWORK
AT BIRTH**

Cranium
Brain

Facial
bone

Cranium
Brain

Suture

Cranium
Brain

Suture

Suture

Cranium
Brain

Fontanelle
Suture

BIRTH
The cranium and brain are
huge in comparison to the
small facial bones. Almost
all the neurons are present,
but their links are limited.

SIX YEARS
The cranial bones are fusing
at sutures. Neurons rapidly
extend their projections
(dendrites and axons) and
their interconnections.

ADULT
The cranium is a solidly
fused braincase. The brain
is full sized and new links
(synapses) form less often
between neurons.

DENTAL DEVELOPMENT

The first set of teeth, known as the primary or deciduous dentition, erupts through the gums in a set order, from about six months into the third year. In general, apart from the canines, the teeth appear from front to back. However, the exact times and order vary, and

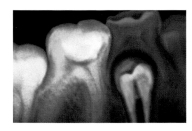

TOOTH ERUPTION
A coloured X-ray of a permanent, or adult, tooth (green) erupting under a child's milk, or deciduous, teeth.

occasionally a baby is born with one or more teeth. These primary teeth loosen and fall out as the adult, or permanent, dentition erupts through the gums. This starts at about six years of age. The set of 32 permanent teeth is complete when the third molars (wisdom teeth) appear in the late teens or early twenties. In some people, however, the third molars never make an appearance above the gum.

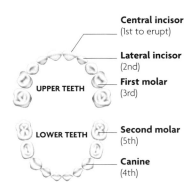

Central incisor (1st to erupt)
Lateral incisor (2nd)
First molar (3rd)
UPPER TEETH
LOWER TEETH
Second molar (5th)
Canine (4th)

DECIDUOUS DENTITION
The baby teeth consist of two incisors, one canine, and two molars, in each half of each jaw, totalling 20 teeth. Teeth are shed from front to back, with the rearmost lost by 10–12 years of age.

Central incisor (2nd to erupt)
Lateral incisor (3rd)
Canine (4th)
First molar (1st)
UPPER TEETH
LOWER TEETH
Third molar (7th)
Second molar (6th)
Second premolar (joint 5th)
First premolar (joint 5th)

ADULT DENTITION
The central (medial) incisors are first to show through the gum, at 6–8 years. There are 32 teeth in the complete set.

STAGES OF DEVELOPMENT

Babies are born able to see, hear, and perform reflex actions, such as grasping, urination, and defaecation. Gradually, the infant learns to bring these reflexes under conscious control. As the eyes start to focus clearly, the baby watches his or her hands, and learns how conscious movements formulated in the brain result in actual movement. During early childhood, these basic motor skills are refined. The child also gains a range of social developmental skills, such as smiling, to elicit a response

from those around. For most children, development takes place in a fairly predictable sequence, for example standing must occur before walking. However, there is great variation in the ages at which stages are reached; acquiring a skill early does not always mean the skill will become greater later. Some babies and children miss stages and go straight on to the next.

NEONATAL GRASP
A newborn's grasp, when its palm is touched, is one of the primitive reflexes, which disappear in a few months.

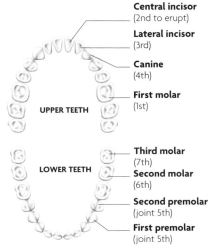

AGE IN YEARS

	0	1	2	3	4	5

MOTOR SKILLS
Basic motor coordination progresses initially by "trial and error". The infant watches its body parts and associates a particular movement pattern with its mental intention to make the movement, as a series of motor nerve signals. Muscles gradually become coordinated as the brain learns to combine patterns of movements by reinforcing and linking the neural pathways that control them.

- Can lift head to 45°
- Can walk without help
- Can hop on one leg
- Can bear weight on legs
- Can roll over
- Can walk upstairs without help
- Can stand by hoisting up own weight
- Can balance on one foot for a second
- Can sit unsupported
- Can pedal a tricycle
- Can crawl
- Can kick a ball
- Can catch a bounced ball

VISION AND MANUAL DEXTERITY
A new baby is near-sighted, able to focus clearly only on objects up to a metre away. After six months, focusing is more varied and items several metres away are clear. The eyes move together in a more coordinated way, rather than occasionally squinting. Hand–eye coordination soon develops as the baby watches its fingers and senses what they touch.

- Holds hands together
- Likes to scribble
- Can copy a circle
- Plays with feet
- Can draw a straight line
- Can copy a square
- Reaches out for a rattle
- Can pick up a small object
- Can grasp object between finger and thumb
- Can draw a rudimentary likeness of a person

SOCIAL AND LANGUAGE SKILLS
After a few weeks, a baby starts to turn the head towards sounds. Language develops from listening and associating sounds with objects, and by practising first words. In the second year, the young child learns words at an astonishing rate, sometimes several a day, although they may not be fully understood. Social skills develop in tandem with language skills.

- Can drink from a cup
- Stays dry at night
- Smiles spontaneously
- Stays dry in the day
- Squeals
- Says "dada" and "mama" to parents
- Knows first and last names
- Can put two words together
- Can dress without help
- Starts to learn single words
- Can talk in full sentences

0	2	4	6	8	10	12	14	16	18	20	22	24	26	28	30	32	34	36	38	40	42	44	46	48	50	52	54	56	58	60

AGE IN MONTHS

PUBERTY

AT PUBERTY, HORMONAL CHANGES STIMULATE PHYSICAL GROWTH, ALTERATIONS IN BEHAVIOUR, AND THE DEVELOPMENT OF SEX ORGANS. THESE CHANGES ARE TRIGGERED WHEN GONADOTROPIN-RELEASING HORMONE (GNRH) FROM THE HYPOTHALAMUS ACTS ON THE ANTERIOR PITUITARY GLAND. IN BOTH SEXES, EMOTIONAL AND PSYCHOLOGICAL CHANGES ALSO OCCUR.

FEMALE PUBERTY

In girls, the physical changes of puberty start at around 10 or 11 years. Most show some signs of development by age 13 and no further changes tend to take place after age 16. Changes to the female body are caused by the action of two hormones, oestrogen and progesterone. It is still unclear what causes the hypothalamus to start releasing GnRH, the hormone that switches on puberty, but social and psychological factors as well as diet may play a part. Puberty occurs

earlier than it used to. In 1890, most girls had their first periods at 15, today they start at around 12–13. The first sign of puberty is breast development, then hair starts to grow in the armpits and pubic area. Leg hair thickens and body shape changes, with body fat increasing. Hair and skin become oily, which may cause acne. Finally, menstruation (the period) begins. Girls may experience fatigue, mood swings, and irritability.

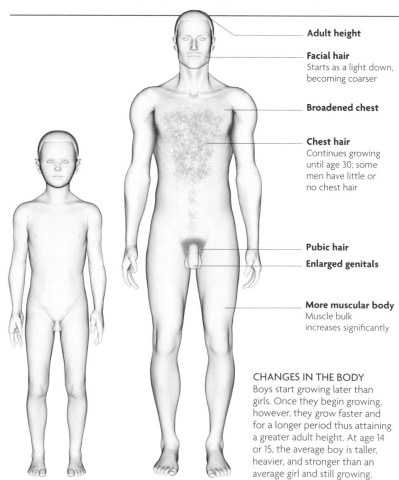

FOLLICLES IN AN OVARY
At puberty, the ovaries start to form mature follicles (collections of blue cells), each containing a ripe egg (red).

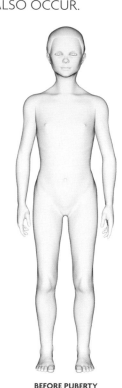

Adult height
Girls reach half adult height just before their second birthdays; the growth spurt at puberty begins two years earlier in girls than boys

Armpit hair

Breast development
Area around nipple swells and becomes a mound with a small amount of breast tissue underneath

Broadened hips
Pelvis and hips widen and waist narrows due to fat redistribution influenced by female hormones

Pubic hair

BEFORE PUBERTY   **AFTER PUBERTY**

CHANGES IN THE BODY
The growth rate is fastest early in puberty, before periods start, and peaks at about age 12, when girls grow up to 9cm (3½in) a year. Growth slows, usually stopping between the ages of 14 and 16, when the sex hormones cause the epiphysial growth plates (see p.216) in long bones to ossify so they are no longer influenced by growth hormones.

Adult height

Facial hair
Starts as a light down, becoming coarser

Broadened chest

Chest hair
Continues growing until age 30; some men have little or no chest hair

Pubic hair

Enlarged genitals

More muscular body
Muscle bulk increases significantly

BEFORE PUBERTY   **AFTER PUBERTY**

CHANGES IN THE BODY
Boys start growing later than girls. Once they begin growing, however, they grow faster and for a longer period thus attaining a greater adult height. At age 14 or 15, the average boy is taller, heavier, and stronger than an average girl and still growing.

MALE PUBERTY

In boys, the physical changes of puberty start later than in girls, at around age 12 or 13. Most show signs of development by age 14, and complete the changes of puberty by age 17 or 18. The testicles and penis get bigger first, then hair grows in the pubic area and armpits. Muscles increase in bulk, and some breast tissue might also develop. Testosterone causes the cartilage in the voice box to grow larger and thicker, which results in the vocal cords getting longer and thicker. This causes the cords to vibrate at a lower frequency so the voice becomes deeper. Finally, facial hair appears, which may be accompanied by acne. Boys are more likely than girls to experience problems with oily skin and perspiration. The sign of sexual maturation for boys is ejaculation. Although capable of having an erection at birth, boys only produce sperm when the hormone testosterone begins circulating in their bodies. It is then that they are able to ejaculate for the first time.

SPERM PRODUCTION
Sperm develop in the testes – sperm cells gradually move away from the supporting cells and mature as they pass through the seminiferous tubule and epididymis. The process takes about 74 days.

MALE HORMONE CONTROL

Hormone production is often regulated by feedback, when the amount of a substance in a system controls how much of it is made. Sperm production and male hormones are controlled by feedback loops involving the testes, hypothalamus, and pituitary gland. The pituitary controls testis function, producing follicle-stimulating hormone (FSH) and luteinizing hormone (LH). Pituitary production depends on gonadotropin-releasing hormone (GnRH) from the hypothalamus. The process is governed by negative feedback – high levels of testosterone act on the pituitary to slow the release of LH and FSH.

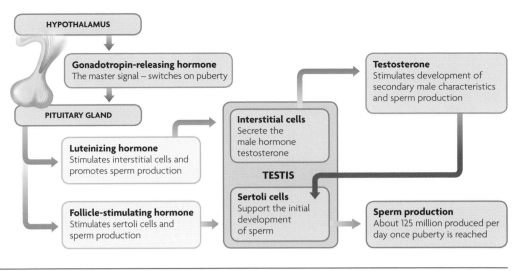

FEMALE HORMONE CONTROL

Female hormones are also tightly regulated by the hypothalamus and pituitary gland. The biological clock that regulates the female cycle consists of the rhythmic release of gonadotropin-releasing hormone (GnRH) from the hypothalamus. GnRH regulates release of the luteinizing hormone (LH) and follicle-stimulating hormone (FSH) in the anterior pituitary gland. These hormones also send feedback to the hypothalamus and the pituitary. Disturbances in the release of GnRH or in the pituitary gland can result in inadequate production of FSH and LH, and abnormal function of the ovaries.

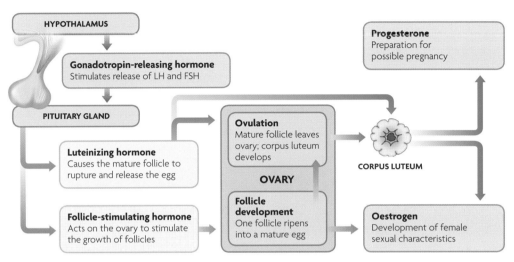

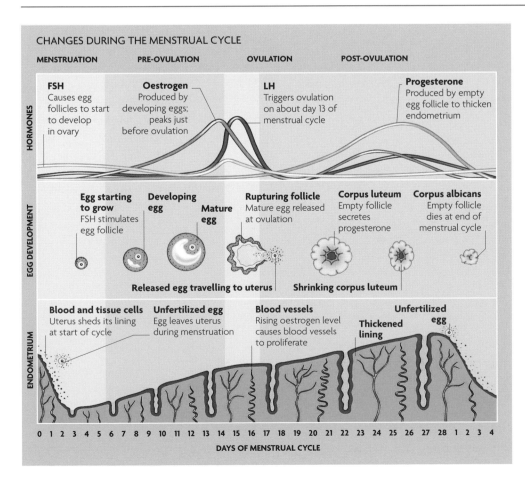

THE MENSTRUAL CYCLE

The principal sign that a girl is becoming sexually mature is the onset of menstruation. For a few days each month, termed the period, bleeding occurs from the vagina, as the lining of the uterus is shed at the start of each cycle. Afterwards the lining thickens again to prepare for the implantation of a fertilized egg. At the start of the cycle, FSH is released by the pituitary gland, which stimulates egg follicles in the ovary. The follicles secrete oestradiol, a form of oestrogen. This triggers the release of LH, which matures the egg and weakens the wall of the follicle, allowing release of the now mature egg (ovum). Whether the right or left ovary ovulates is entirely random. If fertilized, the embryo is implanted into the uterine wall, and signals its presence by releasing human chorionic gonadotropin (HCG), the hormone measured in pregnancy tests. This signal maintains the corpus luteum and enables it to continue to produce progesterone. In the absence of a pregnancy and without HCG, the corpus luteum dies and progesterone levels fall. Progesterone withdrawal leads to menstrual bleeding and, as FSH levels rise, a new crop of follicles is formed – the cycle begins again.

AGEING

ALL LIVING CREATURES HAVE A NATURAL LIFESPAN. FOR HUMANS, THIS
IS AROUND 75–85 YEARS, ALTHOUGH SOME PEOPLE LIVE MUCH LONGER. THE
BRAIN, MUSCLES, JOINTS, EYES, AND OTHER ORGANS ALL DECLINE WITH AGE,
BUT CHANGES ARE USUALLY SMALL UNTIL AFTER THE AGE OF 60. GENETICS
AND LIFESTYLE ARE MAJOR CONTRIBUTORS TO A PERSON'S LIFESPAN.

CELLULAR DETERIORATION

Cells, the basic building blocks of all tissues, change as they become older. It has been
shown that cells can only divide a fixed number of times (known as the Hayflick limit),
after which they lose their ability to function properly. Connective tissue becomes
increasingly stiff, making the organs, blood vessels, and airways more rigid, so that
they do not function as efficiently. Cell membranes change, so tissues have more
trouble receiving oxygen and nutrients and getting rid of carbon dioxide and wastes,
causing an increase in pigments and fatty substances inside cells. One theory, known
as the "wear and tear" hypothesis, claims
ageing is caused by a lifetime accumulation
of little faults in the cells. Others view
ageing as a predetermined, genetically
controlled process. How quickly a person's
cells deteriorate, and therefore how long he
or she lives, is a balance between how fast
things go wrong
with cells and how
efficiently the body
functions to prevent
damage building up.

AGEING GRACEFULLY
Skin is one of the most
visible signs of ageing.
Creased and sagging skin,
seen as wrinkles, can be
predetermined by genes.

Epidermis
Thick layer
confers strength

Dermis
Well supplied
with elastic and
collagen fibres

Fatty layer
Gives strong support
to upper skin layers

YOUNG SKIN
A thick top layer, many elastic and collagen fibres in the
deeper layers, good layers of supporting fat, and plenty
of sebaceous glands producing oil help to maintain the
smoothness and suppleness of young skin.

Liver spots
Pigmentation patches in
areas exposed to sun

Wrinkles
Creased, sagging skin
that gives a lined
appearance

Dermis
Thinner; contains fewer
collagen fibres, causing
reduced elastic recoil

Fatty layer
Thicker relative to
dermis, although may
also be thinner with age

OLDER SKIN
A thinner outer layer and fewer elastic fibres and
collagen in the deeper layers result in skin that
appears loose, with deeper creases and wrinkles.

NERVOUS SYSTEM

As people age, the brain and nervous system undergo
changes, losing nerve cells. Nerve cells transmit
messages more slowly than previously.
As nerve cells break down, senses may be affected.
Reflexes may be lost, leading to problems with
movement and safety. Waste products may collect in
the brain tissue. Some slowing of thought, memory,
and thinking occurs, but keeping the mind active
may help preserve brain function.

VISION

Older people are susceptible to a number of visual
disorders (see p.101). In a cataract, the normally
transparent lens of the eye becomes cloudy.
Meanwhile, macular degeneration can affect
the retina, causing detailed vision to deteriorate.

COMMON EYE PROBLEMS
A range of eye and visual disorders is
more likely to occur with increasing age.
Presbyopia, which is the loss of the
ability to adjust the eye for near
vision, is almost universal.

Lens degeneration
Lens usually stiffens
due to presbyopia, so
loses ability to focus; or
a cloudy lens (cataract)
can lead to poor vision

HEARING

More than half of people over 60 have
difficulties hearing. Problems are caused
by changes in the cochlea, a structure
found in the inner ear, shaped like a
snail's shell. It contains tiny hair cells,
which move in response to vibrations
passed from the small bones in the
middle ear. Movement of hair cells
generates signals that are transmitted to
the brain. At birth, there are about
15,000 hair cells in the inner ear, but
they gradually reduce with age, and the
body is unable to generate new cells.

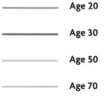

Semicircular canals
Detect movement
and balance

Cochlear nerve

Cochlea
Hair cell reduction
affects hearing

HEARING LOSS
Loss of hair cells in the cochlea, which results in
hearing loss, is likely to be due to a combination
of excessive exposure to noise, side-effects
from medications, and genetic predisposition.

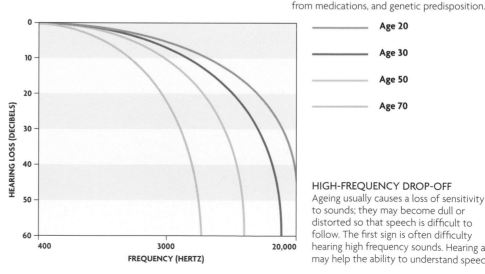

Age 20

Age 30

Age 50

Age 70

HIGH-FREQUENCY DROP-OFF
Ageing usually causes a loss of sensitivity
to sounds; they may become dull or
distorted so that speech is difficult to
follow. The first sign is often difficulty
hearing high frequency sounds. Hearing aids
may help the ability to understand speech.

HEARING LOSS (DECIBELS)

0
10
20
30
40
50
60

400   3000   20,000
FREQUENCY (HERTZ)

METABOLISM

Metabolism is the sum of all the chemical reactions taking place in the body, and basal metabolic rate (BMR) is the energy expended for basic body functions at rest, including functioning of the brain, heart, lungs, and other organs. It is the number of joules a body requires for lying still and breathing. Additional joules are needed for activities such as eating, walking, and digesting. Metabolism declines with age. Adults typically experience a 2–3 per cent drop in metabolism with every 10 years, mostly due to the increased body fat that accrues with age. As each kilo of body fat uses an estimated 42 joules (5 calories per pound) per day and each kilo of lean muscle burns about 460 joules (50 calories per pound) per day, losing muscle and laying down fat slows metabolism drastically and often leads to weight gain. Human growth hormone is also responsible for building and maintaining lean muscle mass, and as it diminishes, the body has a harder time maintaining its muscle.

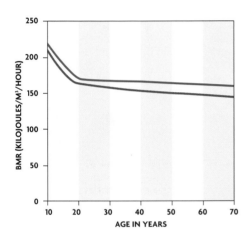

DECLINE IN BMR WITH AGE
As a result of the decline in BMR, older adults need fewer kilojoules per kilogram of bodyweight than younger people. Due to decreased digestive secretions, enzyme activity, and the absorption of nutrients from the intestine, the elderly may need vitamin and mineral supplements.

CHANGES TO THE SKELETON

Osteoporosis, in which bones become fragile, is a common disease of old age (see p.48). It develops as a result of a decline in bone tissue renewal with age. When oestrogen is reduced in older women, bone is broken down faster than it is replaced. Bones are significantly thinned, and a fall is more likely to cause the wrist, the hip, or other vulnerable bones to break. Often people do not know they have osteoporosis until they have a fracture. Osteoarthritis (see p.52), in which the cartilage that lines the joints gradually degenerates, is a joint ailment that commonly affects elderly people.

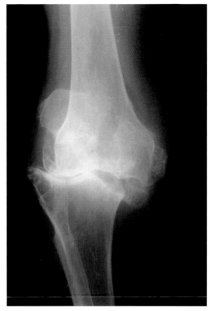

KNEE WITH OSTEOARTHRITIS
This X-ray shows a knee joint in which the cartilage has thinned through decades of wear and tear. The bone ends rub painfully.

ORGAN FUNCTION

Age affects all body organs, including the heart, lungs, kidney, liver, and brain. Most have a "reserve" – an ability to function beyond their usual needs. With age, this reserve is lost. Organs that age fastest in one individual may not age so quickly in another. This suggests genes, lifestyle, and disease all affect the rate of ageing, and that several distinct processes are involved. Often, people have one organ that ages fastest, which becomes the "weakest link", and causes death. Studies of supercentenarians (people over 110) suggest the organs of these people age uniformly, so they do not have a weakest link.

THE MENOPAUSE

The menopause signals the end of a woman's fertile life, and results from decreasing production of sex hormones. In developed countries, the average age for the menopause is 51 years. Women experience variable symptoms, some of which are due to lack of oestrogen, including hot flushes, night sweats, insomnia, headaches, and a dry vagina that may cause discomfort during sexual intercourse. Psychological difficulties often accompany these physical changes and falling oestrogen levels can cause depression. Many women experience symptoms and irregular periods for several years up to the menopause (known as the perimenopause). Menopause is complete when a woman has not had a period for one year. Hormone replacement therapy (HRT) can relieve symptoms of menopause, but long-term HRT has been linked to an increased risk of breast cancer, heart disease, and stroke.

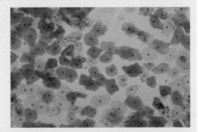

PREMENOPAUSAL CERVICAL SMEAR
Before the menopause, the vaginal lining is thick and well lubricated. The smear reveals large cells with small nuclei.

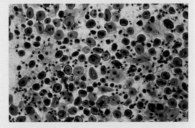

POSTMENOPAUSAL CERVICAL SMEAR
Declining oestrogen levels cause the vaginal lining to thin. The smear reveals fewer cells (which clump together) with larger nuclei.

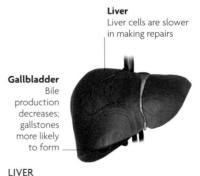

Liver
Liver cells are slower in making repairs

Gallbladder
Bile production decreases; gallstones more likely to form

LIVER
Ageing reduces enzymes produced by the liver, affecting the body's ability to metabolize certain drugs, so that dosages may need to be reduced for older people.

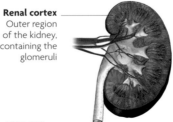

Renal cortex
Outer region of the kidney, containing the glomeruli

KIDNEY
Glomeruli (tiny coils of capillaries supplying blood to the kidneys) decrease in number with age. By 80 years of age, people only have half the normal complement.

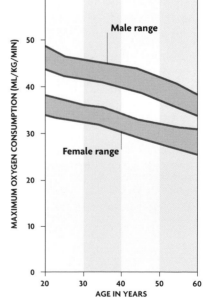

HEART AND LUNG PERFORMANCE
Heart muscle thickens with age, resulting in reduced pumping ability. The amount of air that can be drawn into the lungs in a single breath also declines. Overall heart-and-lung performance can be measured by maximum oxygen consumption per minute, and this declines with age.

INHERITANCE

THE PASSING OF GENETIC INFORMATION FROM
PARENT TO CHILD IS KNOWN AS INHERITANCE.
THE INFORMATION IS IN CHEMICAL CODES
CARRIED BY DEOXYRIBONUCLEIC ACID (DNA)
IN THE SEX CELLS (EGGS AND SPERM).

INHERITANCE OF GENES

Everything needed to specify a person is passed
on in our genes. Every gene carries a "blueprint"
to make a particular product. Some gene products
have a distinctive effect on a person's appearance
or biology – skin pigmentation or eye colour, for
instance. However, gene products can combine
(for example, one can control or regulate the
production of another) to produce a complex trait,
such as athletic ability. Simple features controlled
by single genes are inherited in predictable
patterns (see pp.224–25). However, complex traits,
such as athletic ability, are controlled by many
genes. Their inheritance is not always predictable:
tall parents tend to have tall children – but not
always. The way information is copied in physical
form and passed from parent to offspring is much
more clearly understood.

SEQUENCING THE GENOME

The Human Genome Project was set up in 1990 to
identify all the base pairings along all the strands of DNA,
in all the chromosomes of the genome. In 2003, a
complete list, comprising over three billion base pairs, was
published. A major technique used in DNA sequencing is
gel electrophoresis. DNA is extracted from cells, purified,
and broken into smaller fragments of known length by
chemicals known as restriction enzymes. The DNA
fragments are then placed in a gel substance through
which an electric current passes. The fragments move
at different speeds and separate out through the gel
according to their size and electrical charge. They are
then stained by chemical dyes and show up as dark
stripes, like the bar codes seen below. Computers can
read these bar codes and reveal the base pair sequences.

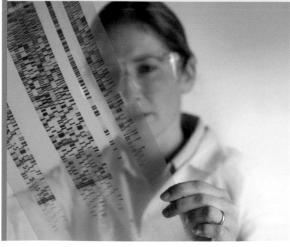

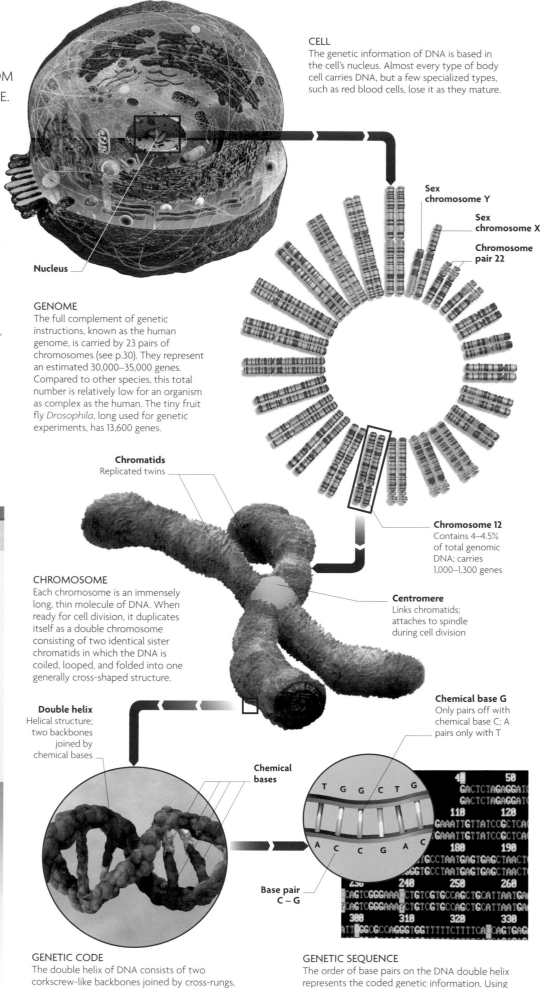

CELL
The genetic information of DNA is based in
the cell's nucleus. Almost every type of body
cell carries DNA, but a few specialized types,
such as red blood cells, lose it as they mature.

Nucleus

Sex chromosome Y

Sex chromosome X

Chromosome pair 22

GENOME
The full complement of genetic
instructions, known as the human
genome, is carried by 23 pairs of
chromosomes (see p.30). They represent
an estimated 30,000–35,000 genes.
Compared to other species, this total
number is relatively low for an organism
as complex as the human. The tiny fruit
fly *Drosophila*, long used for genetic
experiments, has 13,600 genes.

Chromatids
Replicated twins

Chromosome 12
Contains 4–4.5%
of total genomic
DNA; carries
1,000–1,300 genes

CHROMOSOME
Each chromosome is an immensely
long, thin molecule of DNA. When
ready for cell division, it duplicates
itself as a double chromosome
consisting of two identical sister
chromatids in which the DNA is
coiled, looped, and folded into one
generally cross-shaped structure.

Centromere
Links chromatids;
attaches to spindle
during cell division

Double helix
Helical structure;
two backbones
joined by
chemical bases

Chemical base G
Only pairs off with
chemical base C; A
pairs only with T

Chemical bases

**Base pair
C – G**

GENETIC CODE
The double helix of DNA consists of two
corkscrew-like backbones joined by cross-rungs,
which are pairs of chemical bases, of four kinds,
adenine (A), thymine (T), guanine (G), and cytosine
(C). The bases always pair in a specific way.

GENETIC SEQUENCE
The order of base pairs on the DNA double helix
represents the coded genetic information. Using
chemicals to separate the DNA strands and
identify the bases, DNA sequencing machines
can show the data on screen as lists of letters.

DNA REPLICATION

Apart from carrying genetic information in chemically coded form, as its sequences of base pairs, DNA has another key feature. It can make exact copies of itself – a process known as replication. It does this by separation of the two backbone strands and the bases attached to them, at the bonds between the base pairs. Then each strand acts as a template to build a complementary partner strand. DNA replication takes place before cell division (see right).

1 SEPARATION
The two strands of the double helix separate at the base pair links. This exposes each base, ready to latch onto its partner in the newly constructed strand.

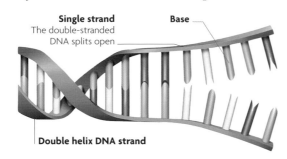

Single strand
The double-stranded DNA splits open

Base

Double helix DNA strand

2 BASES JOIN
Free nucleotides each one a base combined with a potion of DNA backbone, join to the two sets of exposed bases. This can only happen in the correct order since A always pairs with T, and C with G.

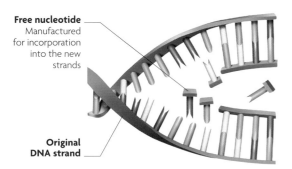

Free nucleotide
Manufactured for incorporation into the new strands

Original DNA strand

3 TWO STRANDS FORM
More nucleotides join, linked by a new backbone. Each strand now has a new "mirror-image" partner, giving two double-helices, which are identical to each other and to the original.

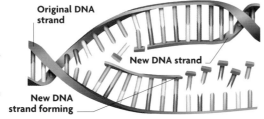

Original DNA strand

New DNA strand

New DNA strand forming

MUTATIONS

DNA replication usually works well. However, factors such as radiation, or certain chemicals, may cause a fault, where one or more base pairs do not copy exactly. This change is a mutation. The new base sequence may result in a different protein being built from it, which could cause a problem in the body.

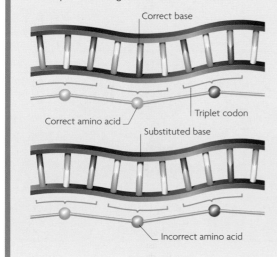

Correct base

Correct amino acid

Triplet codon

NORMAL GENE
Each set of three base pairs (a triplet codon) specifies which amino acid should be added to the series of amino acids that make normal protein for that gene.

Substituted base

Incorrect amino acid

MUTATED GENE
In a point mutation, one base pair is altered. A different amino acid may be specified, which will disrupt the protein's eventual shape and function.

MAKING NEW BODY CELLS

The process by which a cell divides into two identical daughter cells is known as mitosis. First, all the genetic material is duplicated by DNA replication, and each chromosome becomes two identical units or chromatids (see opposite). These double–chromosomes line up across the cell's middle, then separate and move apart, one member migrating to each end of the cell as it splits into two. Mitosis occurs constantly to produce new cells for growth, maintenance, and repair.

1 PREPARATION
DNA strands replicate and form double-chromosomes. The nuclear membrane breaks down.

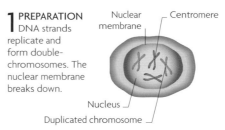

Nuclear membrane

Centromere

Nucleus

Duplicated chromosome

2 ALIGNMENT
Double-chromosomes line up; thread-like fibres create a spindle that connects to the centromere of each.

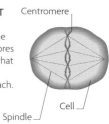

Centromere

Cell

Spindle

4 SPLITTING
The spindle disappears, and nuclear membranes form around the two groups of chromosomes.

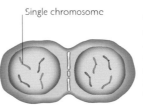

Single chromosome

Single chromosome

3 SEPARATION
The centromere splits so that one single chromosome moves to each end of the cell.

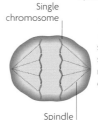

Spindle

5 OFFSPRING
The cytoplasm divides and the cell splits into two. Each of the body cells has a full set of chromosomes (23 pairs) with all the genetic information. Only two pairs are shown here for clarity.

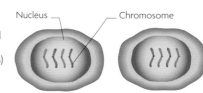

Nucleus

Chromosome

MAKING SEX CELLS

Cell division by meiosis produces sex cells – eggs and sperm. It is similar to mitosis, above, but has an extended series of stages that separate each pair of chromosomes, ending with four daughter cells that have half the normal number of chromosomes, with only one member of a chromosome pair in each. At fertilization, when egg and sperm unite, the chromosome number (23 pairs) is restored. All subsequent cell divisions of the fertilized egg are by mitosis.

1 PREPARATION
DNA strands replicate and coil up in the nucleus, forming X-shaped double-chromosomes.

Duplicated chromosme

2 PAIRING
The matching (homologous) pairs align, make contact, and exchange genetic material.

Matching pair of chromosomes

4 TWO OFFSPRING
Each cell has one double-chromosome of each pair, as a random choice during separation.

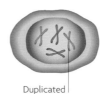

Duplicated chromosomes

3 FIRST SEPARATION
The thread-like spindle pulls one of each pair to each end as the cell splits.

Spindle

Chromosome pair separates

5 SECOND SEPARATION
The double-chromosome splits, each half moving to one end of the dividing cell.

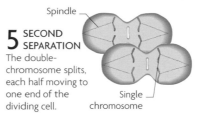

Spindle

Single chromosome

6 FOUR OFFSPRING
The four sex cells differ from each other and the parent cell in their genetic composition.

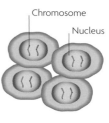

Chromosome

Nucleus

PATTERNS
OF INHERITANCE

GENES ARE PASSED FROM ONE GENERATION TO THE NEXT, IN
A VAST SEQUENCE OF INHERITANCE. THEY ARE RESHUFFLED
AT EACH STAGE SO THAT OFFSPRING ARE UNIQUE, BUT THERE
ARE PATTERNS IN THE MODE OF INHERITANCE.

VERSIONS OF GENES

Each cell in a body has a double-set of genetic material, as 23 pairs
of chromosomes. One chromosome of each pair, and the genes on
it, come from the mother. The other chromosome is from the father.
So there are, in effect, two versions of every gene in the set – one
maternal and one paternal. These versions of genes are called alleles.
Inheritance patterns vary depending on how these two versions
interact, because they may be identical or slightly different.

TWO BY TWO
Chromosomes have the same
sets of genes. But the individual
allele on one chromosome may
differ slightly from its equivalent
allele on the other chromosome.

GENERATIONAL SEQUENCE

In the double-set of genes of each person, one single set was
inherited from the mother, and one set from the father. In
turn, each of the parents had inherited one single set from one
grandparent and one from the other grandparent – and so on.
The versions of the genes (alleles) are mixed, or reshuffled, at each
generation. So, in effect, a child has one-quarter of its genes from
each grandparent. This is why a child's inherited features strongly

MIXED, BUT NOT BLENDED
Genes are "units" of inheritance that are
shuffled at each generation into different
combinations. Individual genes do not blend
with each other to create new versions.

resemble a mixture of the
features of the parents, but
those of the grandparents
less markedly, and so on.

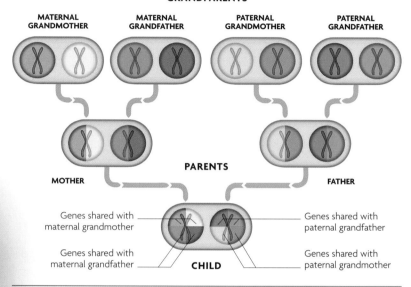

INHERITANCE OF GENDER

The gender of offspring is determined by the two sex chromosomes,
numbered as pair 23. In a female, both of these chromosomes are
X, and have the same sets of genes. A male has one X chromosome,
and the other is the much smaller Y, with male genes. When egg
cells form, they each contain an X. When sperm cells form, half their
number receive an X, and the other half, a Y. An egg fertilized by
an X-carrying sperm has an XX sex chromosome pairing, so the

BOY OR GIRL?
Gender is determined by the
inheritance of sex chromosomes,
X and Y (the other 22 chromosome
pairs are not shown here).

baby is female. If the sperm contains
a Y, the pairing is XY, and the baby
is male. The gender of offspring is
always determined by the father.

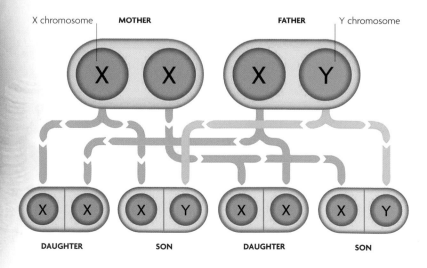

RECESSIVE AND DOMINANT GENES

Each gene in a cell exists in two versions, one inherited from each parent. In some cases these gene versions, or alleles, are different, and produce slightly different results. One allele may be dominant and "overpower" the other, which is recessive. An example is eye colour, although this is not so simple as depicted below.

RECESSIVE AND RECESSIVE

Each parent has two alleles for eye colour. Here both parents have only "blue" alleles. When both alleles are the same, the individual is said to be "homozygous". Their children can only inherit "blue" alleles, and so all have blue eyes.

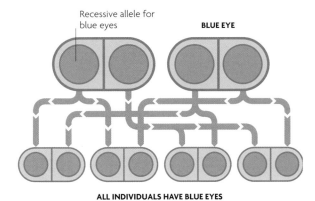

Recessive allele for blue eyes   BLUE EYE

ALL INDIVIDUALS HAVE BLUE EYES

Recessive allele for blue eyes   BLUE EYE   BROWN EYE   Dominant allele for brown eyes

RECESSIVE AND MIXED

One parent has two "blue" alleles, the other one "blue" and one "brown" allele. "Brown" is dominant and takes over when it occurs with "blue". So the chance is 1 in 2 that each offspring has brown eyes.

BLUE EYES   BROWN EYES   BLUE EYES   BROWN EYES

MIXED AND MIXED

Each parent has a "brown" and a "blue" allele. Individuals such as these, who carry two different alleles, are "heterozygous." Only one of the four possible combinations leads to offspring with blue eyes.

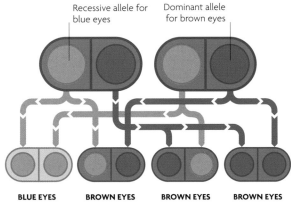

Recessive allele for blue eyes   Dominant allele for brown eyes

BLUE EYES   BROWN EYES   BROWN EYES   BROWN EYES

Recessive allele for blue eyes   Dominant allele for brown eyes

DOMINANT AND RECESSIVE

One parent has two "blue" alleles, the other two "brown" alleles. The four possible combinations all produce brown eyes, but all four still carry "blue" alleles.

ALL INDIVIDUALS HAVE BROWN EYES

SEX-LINKED INHERITANCE

The pattern of inheritance changes when the alleles for a body feature are carried on the pair of sex chromosomes instead of the ordinary chromosomes. In the case of a female, XX, any dominant and recessive alleles can interact, as shown to the left. But in the male, an allele on the X chromosome may not have its equivalent on the Y chromosome, and vice versa. This means a single allele can be the only one to determine the feature. An example is colour-impaired vision, where the problem allele is on the X chromosome.

COLOUR-BLIND FATHER AND UNAFFECTED MOTHER

Sex chromosomes combine in four possible ways, governed by chance. Here, any daughter will inherit the colour-impairment allele, and will be a carrier, but also has the normal allele on her other X chromosome, to give normal vision. No sons can be affected, nor can they be carriers.

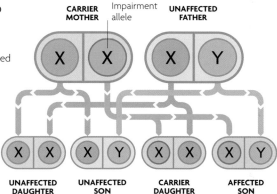

UNAFFECTED MOTHER   Impairment allele   AFFECTED FATHER

CARRIER DAUGHTER   UNAFFECTED SON   CARRIER DAUGHTER   UNAFFECTED SON

CARRIER MOTHER AND UNAFFECTED FATHER

The four possible combinations give one-quarter each for unaffected sons and daughters. There is a one-in-four chance a daughter is a carrier, or that a son inherits the colour-impairment allele. He has no second X chromosome and therefore no normal allele, so the result is impaired colour vision.

CARRIER MOTHER   Impairment allele   UNAFFECTED FATHER

UNAFFECTED DAUGHTER   UNAFFECTED SON   CARRIER DAUGHTER   AFFECTED SON

MULTIPLE-GENE INHERITANCE

Some body traits follow clear single-gene inheritance patterns. However, the situation becomes more complex in two ways. First, there may not be only two alleles of a gene with a simple dominant-recessive interaction between them. There may be three alleles or more in existence in the general population, although each person can have only two of them. An example is the blood group system with alleles for A, B, and O. Second, a trait may be influenced by more than one gene. These two situations mean a trait can be governed by multiple genes, and for each of these genes, by multiple alleles of the gene — added to which, the genes may interact in different ways, according to which alleles are present in each of them. In such cases, the numbers of possible combinations multiply, making multi-gene inheritance exceptionally difficult to unravel.

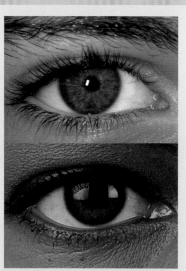

MORE THAN ONE GENE
Eye colour was originally viewed as a simple case of single-gene inheritance. But research shows there are at least three genes for eye colour and probably more (see page 29).

FEMALE REPRODUCTIVE DISORDERS

PROBLEMS CAN ARISE IN ANY PART OF THE FEMALE REPRODUCTIVE TRACT AS WELL AS IN ONE OR BOTH BREASTS. MANY OF THE DISORDERS ARE HARMLESS, AND SOME ARE EVEN SYMPTOMLESS. HOWEVER, THE COMPLEX STRUCTURES OF THE FEMALE REPRODUCTIVE SYSTEM ARE SUBJECTED TO ENORMOUS HORMONAL FLUCTUATIONS. THE PHYSIOLOGICAL STRESSES OF PREGNANCY AND CHILDBIRTH ARE ALSO SUSCEPTIBLE TO SOME MORE SERIOUS DISORDERS, INCLUDING VARIOUS TYPES OF CANCER.

BREAST LUMPS

A BREAST LUMP IS ANY SOLID OR SWOLLEN AREA THAT CAN BE FELT OR SEEN IN THE BREAST TISSUE; ONLY ABOUT 1 IN 10 BREAST LUMPS IS DUE TO CANCER.

Breast lumps are an extremely common problem and very few women can claim not to have suffered from them at some time. Generalized breast lumpiness is especially common when breasts change shape during puberty, pregnancy, and in the days before menstruation. Non-specific

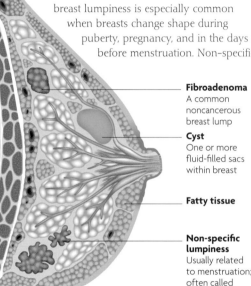

Fibroadenoma
A common noncancerous breast lump

Cyst
One or more fluid-filled sacs within breast

Fatty tissue

Non-specific lumpiness
Usually related to menstruation; often called fibrocystic disease

lumpiness may be associated with tenderness and is usually related to the hormonal fluctuations of the menstrual cycle; this is often known as fibrocystic disease. A single breast lump may be a fibroadenoma, which is an overgrowth of one or more milk-producing lobules; this condition is noncancerous. A more defined lump may be a breast cyst, which is a fluid-filled sac in the breast tissue. A painful lump in the breast may be an abscess, a collection of pus, caused by an infection. Only a small percentage of lumps are a symptom of breast cancer. It is very important for all women to become aware of their breast shape and how it changes through the menstrual cycle. Ideally, breast familiarity should start around the age of 20 and continue throughout life. There is no evidence that formalized self-examination has greater benefits in terms of detecting cancer than a more relaxed approach of awareness. The emphasis is on knowing what is normal for the individual, looking and feeling for changes, knowing what to be aware of, and reporting any changes immediately. From the age of 50, women should attend regular screening.

TYPES OF BREAST LUMP
Different types of breast lump cause varying amounts of pain and tenderness; often they are symptom-free. They may occur individually or in groups, and more than one type of lump may be present at the same time. Many types of noncancerous breast lumps do not require treatment.

BREAST CANCER

Cancer of the breast is the most common female cancer. The risk increases with age, doubling every 10 years. The causes are unclear, but a number of risk factors have been identified. The female hormone, oestrogen, plays a role and women with higher exposure, for example through having an early puberty, late menopause, or no children, have a higher risk. Age is significant, with many more cases occurring over the age of 50. Faulty genes are also a known cause. A breast lump, usually painless, is often the first sign of breast cancer.

Cancerous tumour
Ragged, uneven borders are typical of a cancerous growth

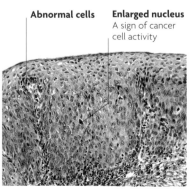

BREAST CANCER
Mammogram of a female breast showing a tumour (white mass). Mammography is a special X-ray technique used to visualize breast tissue as a means of cancer screening.

ENDOMETRIOSIS

ENDOMETRIAL TISSUE FROM THE UTERUS CAN BECOME ATTACHED TO OTHER ORGANS IN THE PELVIC CAVITY.

Endometriosis is a common condition, affecting many women of childbearing age. It can cause debilitating pain and very heavy periods; in severe cases, the condition can lead to fertility problems. The endometrium, the lining of the

uterus, is shed approximately once every month as part of the menstrual cycle. Endometriosis causes small pieces of the uterine lining to become attached to other nearby organs, such as the ovaries or large intestine. These pieces of tissue respond to hormonal changes and bleed during menstruation. Since the blood cannot leave the body through the vagina, its normal exit, it irritates nearby tissues, causing pain and eventually forming scars. The cause of the disorder is unknown.

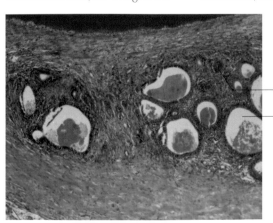

Bleeding

Enlarged gland

ENDOMETRIOSIS
A light micrograph view shows a section through the vaginal lining. The abnormal tissue responds to hormones and bleeds during menstruation.

CERVICAL CANCER

CANCER OF THE CERVIX IS A MALIGNANT GROWTH THAT OCCURS IN THE LOWER END OF THE CERVIX (NECK OF UTERUS).

Cancer of the cervix is one of the most common cancers diagnosed in women. Risk factors include unprotected, early-age sex, having many partners, and genital warts (HPV infection). Early cell changes display no symptoms but later on there may be abnormal vaginal bleeding. However, cell changes are detectable at an early, precancerous stage, so the condition can be treated and its spread prevented. Various degrees of cell change (dysplasia) can be picked up by a routine cervical (Pap) smear test long before cells become cancerous. Regular screening is a vitally important preventive measure. The precancerous states are known as cervical intraepithelial neoplasia (CIN) and range from mild abnormality (CIN1), through moderate (CIN2), to severe (CIN3). CIN1 cells have the

potential to return to normal, whereas CIN3 can progress to cancer if left untreated. Precancerous cells are most commonly found in women under 35, and because it takes many years for progression to full-blown cancer, cervical cancer is more common in an older age group of women.

CERVICAL (PAP) SMEAR
This microscope image shows squamous cell carcinoma of the cervix. Irregular cells in the surface epithelium and large nuclei confirm the presence of cancer.

Abnormal cells

Enlarged nucleus
A sign of cancer cell activity

OVARIAN CYSTS

FLUID-FILLED SWELLINGS THAT GROW ON OR IN ONE OR BOTH OF THE OVARIES ARE TERMED OVARIAN CYSTS.

Most ovarian cysts are noncancerous swellings filled with fluid that occur on or within an ovary. They are a common problem and are most likely to occur in women of childbearing age. Small cysts are often symptom-free, but if they grow they can press on nearby structures, causing problems such as abdominal pain and a frequent need to pass urine. Many cysts disappear of their own accord, but larger ones, particularly if they are causing symptoms, may require surgical removal. Different types of cyst occur, but the most common is a follicular cyst. This occurs in one of the egg-producing follicles within the ovary and may grow to be 5cm (2in) across. Another type occurs in multiple form and is called polycystic ovary syndrome. Other less common forms are also found. Occasionally there

are complications that require urgent medical attention. For example, the cyst may rupture or become twisted; it may grow extremely large, causing massive abdominal distension; or, very rarely, a cyst may undergo cell changes and develop into ovarian cancer.

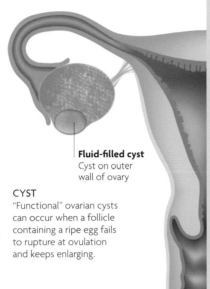

Fluid-filled cyst
Cyst on outer wall of ovary

CYST
"Functional" ovarian cysts can occur when a follicle containing a ripe egg fails to rupture at ovulation and keeps enlarging.

OVARIAN CANCER

CANCER OF THE OVARY IS A MALIGNANT GROWTH THAT MAY DEVELOP IN EITHER ONE OR BOTH OVARIES.

Although cancer of the ovary is not the most common cancer of the female reproductive tract, it causes many more annual deaths than any of the other types. This is because symptoms tend to occur only when the disease is advanced and has spread to other parts of the body. This makes treatment more complex and less likely to succeed. When symptoms do occur, they may include pain and swelling in the abdomen and the need to pass urine frequently. The cancer is

more common between the ages of 50 and 70, and is extremely rare in women under the age of 40. Women who have never had children and those with a close relative with the disease are most at risk. Rarely, an ovarian cyst may develop into cancer. Presently, there is no effective screening for ovarian cancer. However, women in the high risk groups will be carefully monitored so, should the disease develop, it is caught at an early and treatable stage.

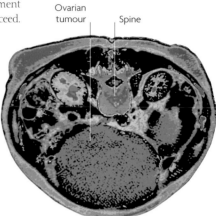

Ovarian tumour   Spine

CANCER OF THE OVARY
A CT scan of a section through a woman's body showing a large ovarian tumour (green, lower centre). Also seen are the kidneys (yellow), spine (pink, centre), ribs (pink at edges), and body fat (blue). A cancer of this size would cause symptoms due to pressure on surrounding structures and suggests that the disease has spread.

FIBROIDS

NONCANCEROUS TUMOURS THAT OCCUR WITHIN THE WALL OF THE UTERUS ARE CALLED FIBROIDS.

Fibroids are very common, occurring in about one-third of women of childbearing age. They can occur singly or in groups and range in size from pea-sized to as large as a grapefruit. Small fibroids are unlikely to cause any problems, but larger ones may result in prolonged and heavy menstrual bleeding, and increasingly severe period pain. Large fibroids can distort the uterus, which may cause infertility, or put pressure on other organs, such as the bladder or rectum.

SITES OF FIBROIDS
Fibroids can occur in any part of the uterus wall and are named according to their site, for example in the cervix, or in the tissues they occur in.

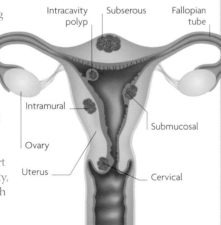

Intracavity polyp
Subserous
Fallopian tube
Intramural
Submucosal
Ovary
Uterus
Cervical

UTERINE CANCER

CANCER OF THE UTERUS OCCURS WHEN A TUMOUR ORIGINATES IN THE LINING OF THE UTERUS (THE ENDOMETRIUM).

Uterine cancer is most likely to affect women between the ages of 55 and 65. Although the causes are unclear, there are definite risk factors, which include

being overweight, a late menopause (after age 52), and not having children. In premenopausal women, symptoms are heavier-than-normal menstrual bleeding, or bleeding between periods or after intercourse; postmenopausal women may have renewed bleeding. In most cases, the treatment for cancer of the uterus is a hysterectomy.

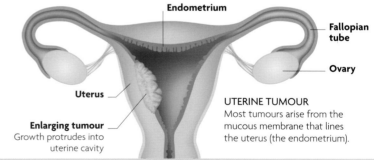

Endometrium
Fallopian tube
Ovary
Uterus
Enlarging tumour
Growth protrudes into uterine cavity

UTERINE TUMOUR
Most tumours arise from the mucous membrane that lines the uterus (the endometrium).

PROLAPSED UTERUS

PROLAPSE OF THE UTERUS OCCURS WHEN THE LIGAMENTS AND MUSCLES HOLDING IT IN PLACE ARE WEAKENED, ALLOWING IT TO DISPLACE DOWNWARD.

Prolapse of the uterus is more likely to occur after the menopause when low oestrogen levels affect the ability of the ligaments to retain the uterus. Childbirth, obesity, and straining while coughing or opening the bowels are contributing factors. The uterus protrudes down into the vagina, and in severe cases may travel as far as the vulva. Symptoms may include a feeling of fullness in the vagina, pain in the lower back, and difficulty passing urine or faeces.

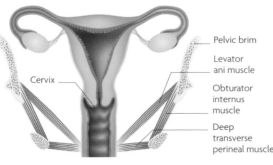

Pelvic brim
Levator ani muscle
Obturator internus muscle
Deep transverse perineal muscle
Cervix

NORMAL UTERUS
The uterus is kept in place by muscles and ligaments. Regular pelvic floor exercises are important to maintain their strength and avoid prolapse.

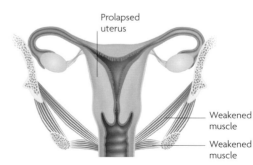

Prolapsed uterus
Weakened muscle
Weakened muscle

PROLAPSED UTERUS
In this case of uterine prolapse, the uterus has slipped down into the vagina. The wall of the vagina may also prolapse.

MALE REPRODUCTIVE DISORDERS

THE MALE REPRODUCTIVE TRACT IS SUBJECT TO A RANGE OF DISORDERS. THOSE AFFECTING THE
EXTERNAL, VISIBLE PARTS ARE USUALLY APPARENT AT AN EARLY STAGE. HOWEVER, PROBLEMS AFFECTING
INTERNAL PARTS OF THE SYSTEM, SUCH AS THE PROSTATE GLAND, MAY NOT BE NOTICED UNTIL
A LATER STAGE, WHEN TREATMENT AND A SUCCESSFUL OUTCOME MAY BE MORE DIFFICULT TO ACHIEVE.

HYDROCELE

THE MEMBRANE SURROUNDING THE
TESTIS CAN BECOME FILLED WITH FLUID
CAUSING SWELLING, OR A HYDROCELE.

Each testis is surrounded by a
double-layered membrane, which
under normal conditions contains a
small amount of fluid. In a hydrocele,
an excessive amount of fluid forms,
causing the testis to appear swollen.
The condition occurs most frequently
in infants and elderly people. The cause
of hydrocele is not usually known,
although infection, inflammation, or
injury to the testis are possible triggers.
A hydrocele does not usually cause
any pain, but a dragging sensation due
to the increased size and weight of the
scrotum may be apparent. In younger
sufferers, the condition often gets
better without the need for treatment.
However, if the condition is causing
discomfort, the hydrocele may be
surgically removed or, for those who
are not fit enough for surgery, the fluid
may be drained from the area using
a needle and syringe.

SWOLLEN TESTIS
A hydrocele is the result of
excess fluid filling the double-
layered membrane that surrounds
the testis; it causes the scrotum
to appear swollen.

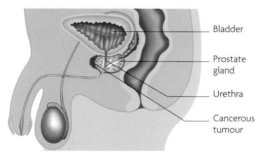

Scrotum

Testis

Fluid
Fluid accumulates
around the testis

TESTICULAR CANCER

CANCEROUS TUMOURS GROWING
WITHIN ONE OF THE TESTES COMMONLY
AFFECT YOUNG MEN.

Cancer of the testis is one of the most
commonly occurring cancers in men
aged between 20 and 40. Although it is
easily curable if discovered at an early
stage, the cancer can spread to the
lymph nodes and to other parts of
the body if not treated. Symptoms
of testicular cancer include a hard,
painless lump in the testis; a
change in the size and
appearance of the testis; or a dull ache
in the scrotum. There are three different
types of testicular tumour (germ cell
tumour, stromal cell tumour, and
secondary testicular tumour), all of
which develop in the sperm-producing
cells of the testis. As early treatment of
the cancer is vital and has a very high
cure rate, all men should regularly
examine their testes; any swellings
or changes in the scrotal skin should
be reported urgently. Soft lumps
or painful swellings are likely
to be caused by a cyst or infection.

TUMOUR ON TESTIS
A tumour of this size
on the outer wall of the
testis would be clearly
felt through the thin outer
skin and layers of the scrotum.

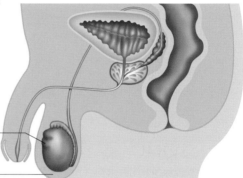

Tumour
A tiny growth on
the testis

Scrotum

PROSTATE DISORDERS

CONDITIONS THAT AFFECT THE PROSTATE GLAND RANGE
FROM INFLAMMATION AND BENIGN ENLARGEMENT TO
SERIOUS DISORDERS, SUCH AS CANCER.

The prostate gland lies just beneath the bladder and
surrounds the upper part of the urethra (the tube that
connects the bladder with the penis). This chestnut-
sized organ produces secretions that are added to the
sperm-containing fluid, semen. Disorders affecting the
prostate are very common and tend to occur in the
middle and later years of a man's life. The most serious
condition, prostate cancer, is a tumorous growth
within the gland. Although potentially life threatening,
it tends to occur most commonly in elderly men, in
whom it often grows slowly and may never cause
symptoms. However, new screening techniques mean
the condition is being detected in much younger men
who need to receive treatment. Enlargement of the
prostate gland is extremely common, and most men
over the age of 50 have some degree of such growth.
Although considered part of the ageing process, the
condition can cause distressing urinary symptoms
if the gland constricts the urethra. Symptoms may
include frequent urination, delay in starting to urinate,
weak flow, dribbling, and a feeling of incomplete
emptying. Prostatitis (see right) is a common
condition, often caused by infection.

Bladder

Prostate
gland

Urethra

Cancerous
tumour

PROSTATE CANCER
A cancerous tumour of this size growing on the prostate
gland is unlikely to cause immediate problems; but as it
grows it may put pressure on the urethra, causing urinary
symptoms, and may spread to other parts of the body.

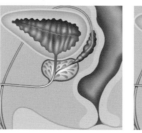

NORMAL PROSTATE

ENLARGED PROSTATE

ENLARGED PROSTATE
A normal prostate gland fits snugly
around the urethra and abuts the bladder;
enlargement can squash the urethra.

Enlarged
prostate
presses on
urethra

PROSTATITIS

Inflammation of the prostate gland, or prostatitis,
can be acute or chronic. The acute type is less
common; severe symptoms come on suddenly,
but these usually clear up quickly. Symptoms may
include fever, chills, and pain around the base of
the penis, in the lower back, and during defecation.
Chronic prostatitis features longstanding but often
mild symptoms that are difficult to treat, such as
groin and penis pain, pain on ejaculation, blood in
semen, and painful urination. Possibly caused by a
bacterial infection from the urinary tract, both types
are most common in men between 30 and 50 years.

CAUSATIVE BACTERIUM
This electron micrograph shows the bacterium
Enterococcus faecalis, implicated in prostatitis. It
is a normal, harmless inhabitant of the human gut.

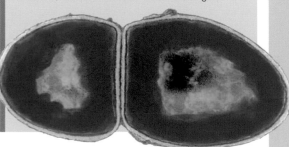

SEXUALLY TRANSMITTED INFECTIONS

SEXUALLY TRANSMITTED INFECTIONS (STIs), ALSO KNOWN AS SEXUALLY TRANSMITTED DISEASES (STDs), ARE INFECTIONS THAT ARE PASSED FROM PERSON TO PERSON BY SEXUAL ACTIVITY. GENITAL, ANAL, AND ORAL SEX CAN ALL PASS ON AN INFECTION TO ANOTHER PERSON. STIs CAN USUALLY BE SUCCESSFULLY TREATED WITH DRUGS, AND "SAFE SEX" IS AN IMPORTANT PREVENTIVE MEASURE.

GONORRHOEA

GENITAL INFLAMMATION CAUSED BY THE BACTERIUM *NEISSERIA GONORRHOEAE* IS KNOWN AS GONORRHOEA.

Although gonorrhoea tends to be more prevalent among males, it can also affect women. The main sites of infection are the urethra and, in women, the cervix. Symptoms often do not appear, but if they do commonly include a discharge of pus from the penis or vagina and pain on urination. Women may also experience lower abdominal pain and irregular vaginal bleeding. Occasionally the infection spreads to other parts of the body, such as the joints (via the bloodstream). If the disease is left untreated, it can cause infertility in women.

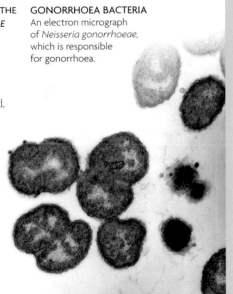

GONORRHOEA BACTERIA
An electron micrograph of *Neisseria gonorrhoeae*, which is responsible for gonorrhoea.

PELVIC INFLAMMATORY DISEASE (PID)

IN PID, THE FEMALE REPRODUCTIVE TRACT BECOMES INFLAMED, USUALLY AS A RESULT OF AN STI.

PID is a common cause of pelvic pain in young women; other possible symptoms are fever, heavy or prolonged periods, and pain during intercourse. Sometimes, there are no symptoms. Usually it is the result of an STI such as chlamydia or gonorrhoea.

Infection after childbirth or a pregnancy termination are also possible causes. The inflammation starts in the vagina and spreads to the uterus and fallopian tubes. In severe cases, the ovaries are also infected. Left untreated, there may be damage to the fallopian tubes, causing infertility and an increased risk of ectopic pregnancy (see p.232).

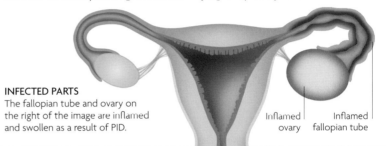

INFECTED PARTS
The fallopian tube and ovary on the right of the image are inflamed and swollen as a result of PID.

Inflamed ovary | Inflamed fallopian tube

NON-GONOCOCCAL URETHRITIS

ALSO CALLED NON-SPECIFIC URETHRITIS, THIS MALE STI IS CAUSED BY AN INFECTION OTHER THAN GONORRHOEA.

Non-gonococcal urethritis (NGU) is one of the most common STIs affecting men the world over. Typically, features include inflammation of the urethra (the tube leading from the bladder to the tip of the penis), with or without a discharge of pus; inflammation and soreness at the end of the penis; and pain on passing urine, particularly when the urine is concentrated first thing in the morning. In about half

of all cases, the agent that is responsible for causing NGU is the bacterium *Chlamydia trachomatis*; this bacterium can also infect women, leading to chlamydial infection. Other possible causes of NGU include the bacterium *Ureaplasma urealyticum*; a protozoan *Trichomonas vaginalis*; the fungus *Candida albicans*; the genital warts virus (human papillomavirus, HPV); and the genital herpes viruses (herpes simplex viruses HSV1 and HSV2). It is important for both partners to seek treatment to prevent reinfecting one another. In order to effectively prevent STDs, sexually active people should limit the number of their sexual partners, and use a condom for penetrative sex.

SYMPTOMS OF NGU
The main problem is inflammation of the urethra, which causes pain and soreness at the external opening on the penis and painful urination. If the infection spreads, the testis and epididymis may also become swollen.

Urethra
Inflammation of urethra causes pain on passing urine

Testis
May become swollen if infection spreads

Epididymis
Sometimes also becomes inflamed

SYPHILIS

A BACTERIAL INFECTION OF THE GENITAL ORGANS, SYPHILIS CAN AFFECT BOTH MALES AND FEMALES.

Infamous in history, syphilis has declined dramatically in the years since antibiotics became available. The causative bacterium, *Treponema pallidum*, enters the body by the genital routes and affects the reproductive organs; it spreads to other parts of the body and,

if left untreated, can cause death. The first sign is a highly infectious sore (chancre) on the penis or vagina, along with swollen lymph nodes. The next stage involves a rash and wart-like patches on the skin, with flu-like symptoms. With no treatment, it can proceed to a final, possibly fatal, stage characterized by personality changes, mental illness, and nervous system disorders. Today, the disease rarely progresses to this stage.

CHLAMYDIA INFECTION

INFECTION BY THE BACTERIUM *CHLAMYDIA TRACHOMATIS* CAUSES CHLAMYDIAL INFECTION IN WOMEN.

Chlamydial infection is a very common STI. It occurs only in women, although the same bacterium causes non-gonococcal urethritis in men. Invasion by bacteria causes inflammation of the reproductive organs, and symptoms include vaginal discharge, a frequent urge to urinate, lower abdominal pain, and pain during intercourse. Chlamydial infection can lead to pelvic inflammatory disease, if left untreated, and may then cause infertility. A swab taken from the cervix can reveal the presence of the bacteria.

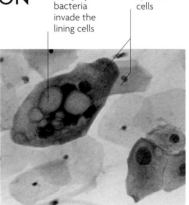

Chlamydia bacteria invade the lining cells | Epithelial cells

BACTERIA IN CERVICAL SMEAR
This micrograph (x400) of a cervical smear shows *Chlamydia trachomatis* bacteria (pink cells within large blue cell).

INFERTILITY DISORDERS

IF A COUPLE IS UNABLE TO CONCEIVE AFTER A YEAR OF HAVING UNPROTECTED SEX, ONE OR BOTH PARTNERS MAY HAVE A FERTILITY PROBLEM. THE LIKELIHOOD OF FERTILITY DISORDERS INCREASES WHEN COUPLES WAIT UNTIL THEY REACH THEIR 30s OR 40s TO START A FAMILY, BY WHICH TIME NATURAL FERTILITY IS IN DECLINE. FOR COUPLES UNWILLING TO ACCEPT CHILDLESSNESS, DIFFERENT TYPES OF FERTILITY ASSISTANCE AND TREATMENT ARE AVAILABLE.

CAUSES OF FEMALE INFERTILITY

In about a third of infertility cases, the problem lies with the woman's reproductive system. There may be a physical problem, such as damage to a fallopian tube that prevents the egg reaching its destination; ovulation problems, in which an egg is not released on a monthly basis; implantation problems, in which the uterus has abnormalities that are incompatible with supporting a fetus; or the cervix may be inhospitable to sperm. However, the cause may be unknown or it may be a combination of problems.

DAMAGED FALLOPIAN TUBE

FALLOPIAN TUBE DAMAGE, WHICH RESULTS IN SCARRING AND DISTORTION, CAN PREVENT MOVEMENT OF EGGS.

The fallopian tube may become blocked as a result of endometriosis, in which fragments of the uterine lining (endometrium) become embedded in the tube tissue. Pelvic inflammatory disease (PID), often caused by a sexually transmitted infection, such as chlamydia (see p.229), may go unnoticed at the time of infection but scarring due to the inflammation can cause problems with fertility later. An intrauterine contraceptive device can increase the risk of PID developing. Usually, only one tube is affected, which means that every other month the woman has a chance to conceive.

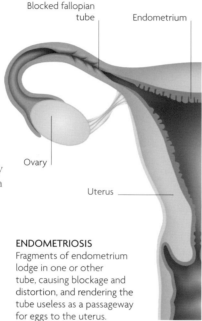

ENDOMETRIOSIS
Fragments of endometrium lodge in one or other tube, causing blockage and distortion, and rendering the tube useless as a passageway for eggs to the uterus.

ABNORMALITIES OF THE UTERUS

IMPLANTATION OF THE FERTILIZED EGG MAY BE PREVENTED IF THERE IS A PHYSICAL PROBLEM WITH THE UTERUS.

Although structural abnormalities of the uterus are rare, they have the potential to cause problems with fertility. The uterus may not have developed correctly during the fetal stage and may be misshapen or malformed as a result. Large and numerous noncancerous tumours (fibroids) in the muscular wall of the uterus can encroach on the space within the organ and cause the uterus to become distorted. Surgery on the uterus or pelvic inflammatory disease can also affect the structure of the uterus and possibly lead to problems with conception later.

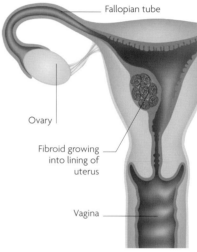

FIBROID
A very large, benign (noncancerous) growth is seen pushing the uterine wall inward with the result of reducing the size of the cavity within the uterus and distorting the shape of the organ.

CERVICAL PROBLEMS

THE CERVIX CAN CAUSE FERTILITY PROBLEMS BY BEING HOSTILE TO SPERM OR BECAUSE IT HAS A PHYSICAL DEFECT.

The cervix, or neck of the womb, produces mucus that is usually thick; just before ovulation, when the level of oestrogen increases, the mucus turns less viscous to allow sperm to penetrate. If oestrogen levels are low or if there is infection within the reproductive tract, the mucus may remain thick and impregnable to sperm. Another problem that may make the cervix inhospitable is that sometimes a woman's immune system forms antibodies to her partner's sperm, which will then damage or kill the sperm in the cervix. Polyps, fibroids, narrowing (stenosis), and distortion are other problems of the cervix that may be related to infertility.

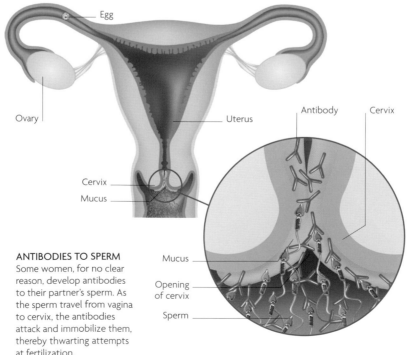

ANTIBODIES TO SPERM
Some women, for no clear reason, develop antibodies to their partner's sperm. As the sperm travel from vagina to cervix, the antibodies attack and immobilize them, thereby thwarting attempts at fertilization.

OVULATION PROBLEMS

EGGS MAY NOT BE RELEASED AT ALL OR ONLY INTERMITTENTLY, CAUSING DIFFICULTY WITH CONCEPTION.

Ovulation is the release of a mature egg ready for fertilization. Normally, an egg is released from alternate ovaries approximately every month. Any deviation from this pattern has the potential to cause problems with fertility. The precise problem can range from complete absence of egg release to infrequent release. The problem is common because it depends on a complex interaction of hormones. Factors that influence the hormones include pituitary and thyroid gland disorders, polycystic ovary syndrome, long-term use of oral contraceptives, being very overweight or underweight, excessive exercise, and stress. Premature menopause is another possible cause.

CAUSES OF MALE INFERTILITY

As with female infertility, male causes account for around a third of cases (with the remainder having no known cause). The problem may be with the quality of the sperm or with the transportation of sperm from the testes via the epididymides and the vas deferens before ejaculation. Problems with ejaculation, which may be a result of illness or psychological problems, prevent sperm from reaching the vagina either because erection cannot be achieved or maintained, or because of retrograde ejaculation.

PROBLEMS WITH SPERM PRODUCTION

SPERM MAY BE PRODUCED IN LOW QUANTITIES OR MAY BE DEFORMED OR UNABLE TO SWIM PROPERLY; ALL REDUCE THE LIKELIHOOD OF CONCEPTION.

Huge numbers of sperm must be produced in order for fertilization to occur; men in whom this does not happen are said to have a low sperm count. Microscopic examination can reveal this problem and can also look at the size, shape, and movement (motility) of individual sperm. Problems in any of these areas can cause reduced fertility. If only a small volume of semen is produced per ejaculation, fertility may also be reduced.

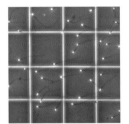 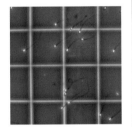

NORMAL SPERM COUNT   **LOW SPERM COUNT**

DIFFICULT PASSAGE OF SPERM

DISTORTION OR BLOCKAGE OF ANY OF THE TUBES THAT CARRY SPERM FROM TESTIS TO PENIS CAN REDUCE FERTILITY.

Sperm has a long and tortuous journey from its source in the testis until it is ejaculated. Narrowing, blockage, or other distortion of any of the tubes, including the epididymis and vas deferens, that make up this network can slow or completely block the passage of sperm. Causes of this problem are various, but infection of the male reproductive system is most likely. Some sexually transmitted infections (STIs, see p.229), most notably gonorrhoea, can cause inflammation of the tubes, which leaves scar tissue that can distort their structure and affect their sperm-carrying ability.

Narrowed lumen of vas deferens

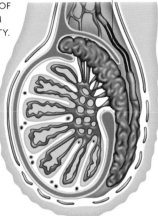

INFLAMED VAS DEFERENS
Damage to the vas deferens, one of the tubes that transports sperm, can prevent or slow down its passage. Infection, usually by a sexually transmitted infection, can be responsible for such damage.

EJACULATION PROBLEMS

ERECTILE DYSFUNCTION AND RETROGRADE EJACULATION CAN BOTH AFFECT FERTILITY.

A number of ejaculation problems prevent sperm from arriving in the vagina by the normal means, making fertilization impossible. The most common of these is erectile dysfunction (difficulty in achieving or maintaining an erection) which may be a result of diabetes mellitus, a spinal cord disease, impaired blood flow, certain drugs, or psychological problems. Another problem, retrograde ejaculation, causes semen to flow back into the bladder because of faulty valves; this can be a complication of surgery for partial or complete removal of the prostate gland. Various treatments are available that can help reduce erectile dysfunction, depending on the nature of the problem.

IN-VITRO FERTILIZATION

A METHOD OF ASSISTED CONCEPTION, IN-VITRO FERTILIZATION BRINGS SPERM AND EGG TOGETHER OUTSIDE THE BODY.

Since the first "test-tube baby" was born through in-vitro fertilization (IVF) in 1978, this method of assisted conception has become commonplace. IVF is performed if th e fallopian tubes are blocked or if the cause of infertility cannot be found or treated. The method involves extracting eggs from an ovary. Eggs are artificially ripened by the use of hormones so that more than one is available for fertilization, increasing the chance of success. The eggs are then mixed with a sample of sperm from the woman's partner, or a donor, and incubated at normal body temperature for 48 hours. Up to three fertilized eggs are then injected directly into the woman's uterus through a thin tube that passes through the vagina and cervix. Treatment is successful if one or more of the eggs implants in the uterine wall. IVF results in pregnancy in around 15 per cent of attempts.

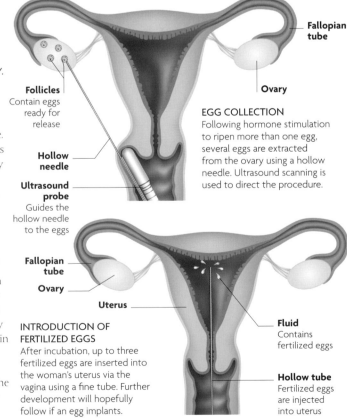

Fallopian tube

Follicles
Contain eggs ready for release

Ovary

Hollow needle

Ultrasound probe
Guides the hollow needle to the eggs

EGG COLLECTION
Following hormone stimulation to ripen more than one egg. several eggs are extracted from the ovary using a hollow needle. Ultrasound scanning is used to direct the procedure.

Fallopian tube

Ovary

Uterus

Fluid
Contains fertilized eggs

Hollow tube
Fertilized eggs are injected into uterus

INTRODUCTION OF FERTILIZED EGGS
After incubation, up to three fertilized eggs are inserted into the woman's uterus via the vagina using a fine tube. Further development will hopefully follow if an egg implants.

INTRACYTOPLASMIC SPERM INJECTION

A refined version of IVF, intracytoplasmic sperm injection (ICSI) can be used in male infertility when conventional assisted techniques have failed. A sperm cell is injected directly into a single mature egg in a laboratory. The procedure is very delicate and involves the use of micro-instruments under a microscope. Success rates are 10–15 per cent in one menstrual cycle, and only one embryo develops.

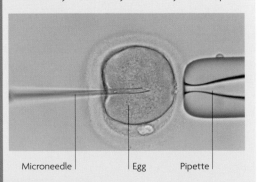

Microneedle   Egg   Pipette

SPERM INJECTION
This micrograph shows a sperm being injected into an egg. The round egg cell is being injected with a microneedle. The tip of a pipette holds the egg securely in place.

PREGNANCY AND LABOUR DISORDERS

THE MAJORITY OF PREGNANCIES AND BIRTHS PROCEED WITHOUT ANY MAJOR PROBLEMS AND RESULT IN HEALTHY, FULL-TERM BABIES. HOWEVER, PROBLEMS CAN ARISE IN NORMALLY HEALTHY WOMEN DURING THIS TIME, WHICH MAY ENDANGER BOTH THE MOTHER'S AND THE BABY'S HEALTH. FEW DISORDERS OF PREGNANCY AND LABOUR HAVE ANY PERMANENT PHYSICAL EFFECT ON EITHER MOTHER OR BABY.

ECTOPIC PREGNANCY

AN ECTOPIC PREGNANCY IS ONE THAT BEGINS IN A SITE OUTSIDE THE UTERUS, USUALLY IN A FALLOPIAN TUBE.

About 1 per cent of pregnancies are ectopic; they are more common in women under 30. The fertilized egg does not implant in the uterine lining but develops in one of the fallopian tubes, or more rarely in another area. Normal embryonic development is not possible and the pregnancy usually fails. The embryo must be surgically removed to avoid rupture of the fallopian tube and internal bleeding.

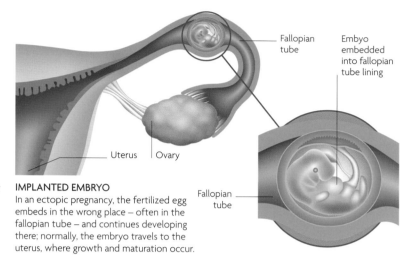

IMPLANTED EMBRYO
In an ectopic pregnancy, the fertilized egg embeds in the wrong place – often in the fallopian tube – and continues developing there; normally, the embryo travels to the uterus, where growth and maturation occur.

PRE-ECLAMPSIA

HIGH BLOOD PRESSURE AND FLUID RETENTION ARE CHARACTERISTIC OF THIS CONDITION OF PREGNANCY.

A condition that occurs in 5–10 per cent of pregnancies, pre-eclampsia is particularly common in the weeks leading up to the birth. Features include high blood pressure, fluid retention, and protein in the urine. Pre-eclampsia is usually easy to treat but if left unchecked can proceed to a life-threatening problem called eclampsia, which can cause headaches, visual disturbances, seizures, and eventually a coma.

PLACENTAL PROBLEMS

FUNCTIONAL OR POSITIONAL PROBLEMS OF THE PLACENTA PRIOR TO DELIVERY ARE TERMED PLACENTAL PROBLEMS.

Two main problems can affect the placenta: placenta praevia, in which the placenta covers the opening of the cervix out of the uterus; and placental abruption, in which the placenta separates from the uterine wall. The degree of severity in placenta praevia

PLACENTA PRAEVIA
Complete placenta praevia, as shown here, is a serious condition in which the cervix is covered entirely by the placenta. A less severe form involves a low-lying placenta that only partially obstructs the exit from the uterus.

depends on how much of the cervix is covered; it ranges from marginal, which may cause few problems, to complete, which is a serious conditon. Placental abruption usually comes on suddenly and can be life-threatening for the fetus because essential supplies are compromised. Both conditions can cause vaginal bleeding, but in less severe cases, symptoms may go unnoticed.

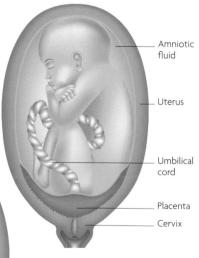

Amniotic fluid
Uterus
Umbilical cord
Placenta
Cervix

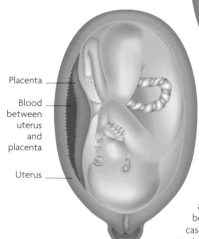

Placenta
Blood between uterus and placenta
Uterus

PLACENTAL ABRUPTION
Premature separation of the placenta from the uterine wall may be concealed, as shown here, in which case blood collects between the uterus and placenta. In other cases, the blood escapes and leaves the body via the vagina, revealing the problem.

MISCARRIAGE

ALSO CALLED SPONTANEOUS ABORTION, MISCARRIAGE IS THE UNINTENDED END OF A PREGNANCY BEFORE WEEK 24.

Miscarriage is very common, occurring in 25 per cent of all pregnancies. Most miscarriages occur in the first 14 weeks of pregnancy and over half of these are due to a genetic or fetal abnormality. Later miscarriages have a variety of causes, ranging from physical problems with the cervix or uterus to severe infection. Smoking, alcohol, or drug abuse may also be factors. If three or more occur consecutively, it is known as recurrent miscarriage.

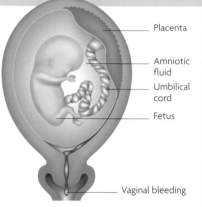

Placenta
Amniotic fluid
Umbilical cord
Fetus
Vaginal bleeding

THREATENED MISCARRIAGE
The fetus remains alive and the cervix is closed although there is some blood loss. It may proceed to full miscarriage, when the fetus dies, or a successful birth.

POLYHYDRAMNIOS

THIS CONDITION CAN OCCUR WHEN AN EXCESSIVE AMOUNT OF AMNIOTIC FLUID BATHES THE FETUS WITHIN THE UTERUS.

In polyhydramnios, excess amniotic fluid builds up in the uterus, causing abdominal pain or discomfort. The problem may be chronic, with fluid accumulating slowly after week 32, or acute, in which the problem develops over a few days from around 22 weeks. The acute form may be associated with identical twins. The excess fluid allows the baby to move more, increasing the likelihood of an abnormal presentation, and the chances of a premature labour.

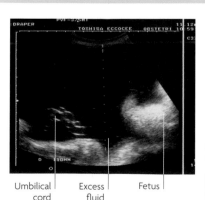

Umbilical cord
Excess fluid
Fetus

EXCESS AMNIOTIC FLUID
This ultrasound scan of a fetus indicates an excess of amniotic fluid, which can cause problems for both mother and baby.

ABNORMAL PRESENTATION

ANY DEVIATION FROM THE HEAD-DOWN, BACKWARD-FACING DELIVERY POSITION OF THE BABY IS CONSIDERED ABNORMAL.

Eighty per cent of babies adopt the normal position for birth with the head down and facing towards the mother's back. The baby usually achieves this by week 36. Other babies are in a position that may cause problems during labour. Breech (see p.210) and occipitoposterior positions (see right) are the most common. In a breech birth, the baby's buttocks present first. Some presentations may allow the umbilical cord to drop through the birth canal and cause fetal distress. The cervix and vagina are more vulnerable to tears if the presentation is abnormal.

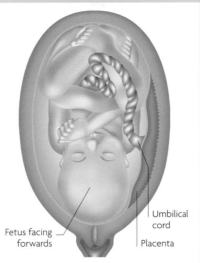

Fetus facing forwards

Umbilical cord

Placenta

OCCIPITOPOSTERIOR POSITION
Although the baby's head is facing down, as is normal, the baby is turned 180° towards the front. The majority move to face the mother's back during the course of labour.

PRETERM LABOUR

LABOUR THAT BEGINS BEFORE THE 37TH WEEK OF PREGNANCY IS CALLED PRETERM, OR PREMATURE, LABOUR.

Most pregnancies last for about 40 weeks, but delivery during the final three weeks is considered full term. Labour occurring before 37 weeks is preterm and results in a premature baby. Premature labour rarely causes maternal problems, but the earlier the birth, the greater the problems encountered by the baby. The cause is not always known, but multiple births, polyhydramnios (see opposite), and urinary tract infection are known trigger factors. Sometimes premature labour can be halted or delayed, giving the baby more time in the womb.

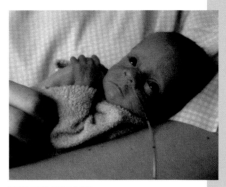

PREMATURE BABY
This premature baby is being fed through a nasogastric tube because his sucking reflex has not yet developed and swallowing ability is poor. Other features are his tiny size, wrinkled and yellow skin, and disproportionately large eyes.

PROBLEMS DURING DELIVERY

SEVERAL PROBLEMS CAN LENGTHEN THE SECOND STAGE OF LABOUR OR PREVENT THE PROGRESSION OF NORMAL DELIVERY.

The second stage of labour, or delivery, starts when the cervix has reached full dilation at 10cm (4in) and ends with the birth of the baby. Problems at this stage are common, particularly in a first pregnancy. Some originate in the first stage of labour. These include weak uterine contractions and abnormal presentation, so that the fetus cannot put pressure on the cervix to help dilation. Also, a lengthy first stage can exhaust the mother to such an extent that she has little strength to push in the second stage. Other problems arise in the second stage itself. The baby's passage through the birth canal may be delayed because it is not in the optimal position for delivery. There may be a problem with the baby actually passing through the pelvis; this could be because the baby is especially large or because the mother has a small or irregular pelvis. Once the baby has reached the vaginal opening, problems with delivery may occur if the tissues cannot stretch sufficiently to let the head out. In spite of these potential problems, a normal or assisted vaginal delivery is often possible; however, under certain circumstances, a caesarean section (see right) may be the only option.

CAESAREAN SECTION

If delivery is proving difficult, if it is a multiple birth, or if the mother has a good medical reason for avoiding vaginal delivery, a caesarean section is performed. This involves removing the baby and the placenta from the uterus through an incision in the lower abdomen. The procedure is often carried out under epidural anaesthesia so that the mother remains conscious and can interact with her baby soon after birth.

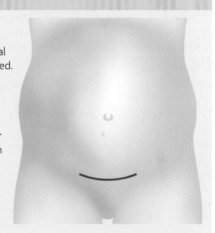

HORIZONTAL INCISION
An incision is made just below the pubic hairline, through which the surgeon can remove baby and placenta.

ASSISTED DELIVERY

IF DELIVERY IS NOT PROCEEDING SMOOTHLY OR QUICKLY ENOUGH, ONE OF TWO TYPES OF ASSISTED DELIVERY, EITHER VACUUM SUCTION OR FORCEPS, MAY BE USED.

Assisted delivery means physically helping the baby out of the womb through the birth canal. It may be necessary if the mother is too exhausted to push the baby out or if the baby becomes stuck or distressed. The possible methods involve vacuum suction or forceps. In each case, the instrument is used to pull the head clear of the vaginal opening, after which the delivery will proceed as normal. To enlarge the birth opening to allow entry of the instrument and make extracting the head easier, an episiotomy is usually performed. Under local anaesthetic, an incision is made in the perineum (the tissue between the vagina and anus). Cutting the tissue avoids the ragged tear that may result in the absence of intervention. The cut is made at an angle in order to avoid the anus.

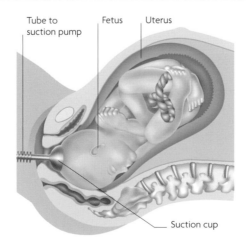

Tube to suction pump

Fetus

Uterus

Suction cup

VACUUM SUCTION DELIVERY
A suction cup is placed on the baby's head and its connecting tube attached to a pump that is switched on. With each contraction, the doctor gently pulls the baby towards the outside world.

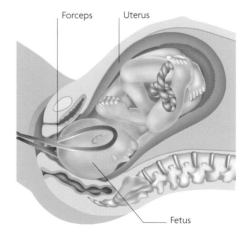

Forceps

Uterus

Fetus

FORCEPS DELIVERY
Spoon-shaped obstetric forceps are carefully placed around the baby's head. As the mother pushes, the doctor pulls gently on the forceps until the baby's head reaches the vagina.

INHERITED DISORDERS

INHERITED DISORDERS ARE CAUSED BY DEFECTIVE GENES OR ABNORMAL CHROMOSOMES THAT
ARE PASSED FROM PARENTS TO CHILDREN. IN CHROMOSOME DISORDERS, THERE IS A PROBLEM IN
THE NUMBER OR STRUCTURE OF CHROMOSOMES, WHEREAS IN GENE DISORDERS, THERE IS A FAULT
IN ONE OR MORE OF THE GENES THAT ARE CARRIED ON INDIVIDUAL CHROMOSOMES.

CHROMOSOME DISORDERS

Chromosome disorders are inherited disorders that result from either an incorrect number of chromosomes (numerical disorders) being passed on from parent to child or from an alteration in the structure of some of the chromosomes (structural disorders).

Mosaicism is a type of numerical disorder but not every single cell is affected, so the problem may not manifest itself. Errors occur before fertilization when genetic material is swapped during the cell division involved in egg and sperm production.

NUMERICAL

A MISTAKE DURING CELL DIVISION IN EGG OR SPERM CELLS (MEIOSIS) CAN RESULT IN ONE CELL HAVING TOO MANY CHROMOSOMES AND THE OTHER TOO FEW.

This is the most common type of chromosome anomaly, with two-thirds of disorders falling into this group. In many cases, extra or missing chromosomes result in miscarriage. However, there are a few exceptions in which the fetus survives. The most common is Down's syndrome, also known as trisomy 21 because the disorder is caused by an extra chromosome 21. Abnormalities in the sex chromosomes have a less severe effect on the embryo, and there may not be any obvious signs of a problem. A girl with an extra X chromosome or a boy with an extra Y chromosome will probably go unnoticed. However, a boy with an extra X chromosome (XXY) will have Klinefelter's syndrome, which becomes apparent at puberty with the failure of secondary sexual characteristics to develop. A girl born with only one X chromosome has Turner's syndrome.

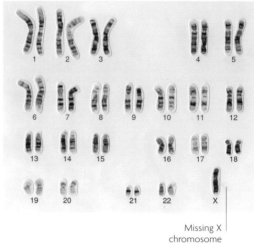
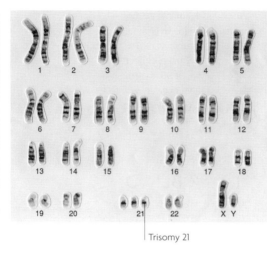

Missing X chromosome

Trisomy 21

TURNER'S SYNDROME
This set of chromosomes (karyotype) from a female with Turner's syndrome shows only one X chromosome rather than the two that are normal for a female. Although they are of normal intelligence and have normal life expectancy, girls with this condition have short stature and are usually infertile.

DOWN'S SYNDROME
This karyotype is from a male with Down's syndrome, indicated by an extra chromosome 21, known as trisomy 21. This is the most common chromosomal abnormality and causes a characteristic physical appearance, learning difficulties, and often abnormalities of the heart.

STRUCTURAL

DURING CELL DIVISION IN EGG OR SPERM CELLS (MEIOSIS), A SMALL SECTION OF CHROMOSOME MAY BECOME MISPLACED.

During the natural exchange of genetic material between chromosomes, a small section may be deleted, duplicated, or inserted the wrong way round, or inverted. Such structural abnormalities often result in miscarriage, but if the pregnancy proceeds to full term, there may be birth defects depending on the amount and type of altered genetic material. Another problem – translocation – happens when material is swapped between two different chromosomes. If there is no net loss or gain of material, it is known as a balanced translocation, and outward problems are unlikely. In unbalanced translocation, the extra and missing information can lead to defects or, if severe, miscarriage.

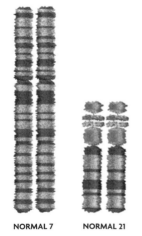

NORMAL 7   **NORMAL 21**

PAIRED CHROMOSOMES
In normal chromosomes, the pairs are equally matched; arms are of equal length and the positions of the genes are exactly the same for each of the 23 pairs. This occurs whether the chromosome is long (as in chromosome 7) or if it is much shorter (as in chromosome 21).

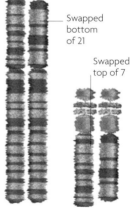

Swapped bottom of 21

Swapped top of 7

TRANSLOCATED 7   **TRANSLOCATED 21**

BALANCED TRANSLOCATION
In a typical translocation, a large part of one chromosome is joined to another; here most of chromosomes 7 and 21 are joined. In a balanced translocation, such as this, no genetic material is lost or gained and no outward abnormality is seen.

MOSAICISM

MOSAICISM IS A MIXTURE OF BODY CELLS, SOME CONTAINING A NORMAL NUMBER OF CHROMOSOMES AND OTHERS CONTAINING AN ABNORMAL NUMBER.

The presence of more than one type of cell in an individual is known as mosaicism. For example, some cells may have the normal number of 46 chromosomes, while others have an extra one, giving a total of 47 chromosomes. If only a few cells have an abnormal number of chromosomes, there are unlikely to be any outward signs of disease and the abnormality would be detectable only by an analysis of a blood sample. With a greater proportion of incorrect cells, disorders may occur. These disorders are the same as with straightforward numerical abnormalities. For example, Down's syndrome can be a result of mosaicism if a large number of cells have an extra chromosome 21 (making a total of 47 chromosomes). However, this is a rare cause of numerical disorders, being responsible for only 1–2 per cent of cases. Other syndromes, such as Turner's and Klinefelter's, can also develop as a result of mosaicism.

GENE DISORDERS

Many disorders result from inheriting faulty genes. Defective genes may have mild, moderate, or potentially fatal consequences, or they may have no effect at all. Some genetic disorders are apparent soon after birth or in early life whereas others, such as Huntington's disease, are not discovered until adult life. Types of inheritance (see p.225) include dominant, where only one parent has to carry the defective gene; recessive, where both parents are carriers; and X-linked, where the faulty gene is on the X chromosome.

HUNTINGTON'S DISEASE

A DOMINANT GENE DISORDER, HUNTINGTON'S DISEASE CAUSES DEGENERATION OF PART OF THE BRAIN.

Huntington's disease is caused by an abnormal dominant gene. Also called Huntington's chorea, the disease causes involuntary movements, personality changes, and progressive dementia. Deterioration occurs over 15–20 years. Symptoms do not usually develop until over the age of 30, by which time the gene may have been passed to the next generation. For this reason, genetic testing and counselling is offered if a relative suffers from the disease.

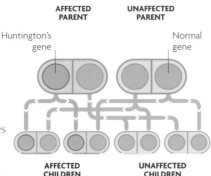

AFFECTED PARENT — Huntington's gene
UNAFFECTED PARENT — Normal gene
AFFECTED CHILDREN
UNAFFECTED CHILDREN

DOMINANT INHERITANCE
In this example, one of the parents has the abnormal gene and the other parent is unaffected. Each child has a 1 in 2 chance of inheriting the faulty gene and therefore of developing the disorder in adulthood.

ALBINISM

A DISORDER CHARACTERIZED BY A LACK OF THE BROWN PIGMENT MELANIN, ALBINISM CAUSES VERY PALE FEATURES.

Albinism is caused by a recessive gene, which means that a child has to inherit a defective gene from each parent. The gene causes a fault in an enzyme that is essential for melanin production. The condition is rare with an incidence of about 1 in 20,000. Affected individuals have little or no pigment in the skin, hair, and eyes; skin is pale, hair is white, and eyes range from pink to very pale blue. The eyes are very sensitive to bright light, and visual impairment is common.

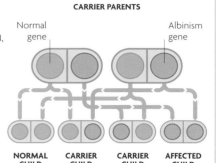

CARRIER PARENTS — Normal gene / Albinism gene
NORMAL CHILD
CARRIER CHILD
CARRIER CHILD
AFFECTED CHILD

RECESSIVE INHERITANCE
In this example, both parents carry the abnormal gene but do not have the disorder. Their children may be unaffected (1 in 4 chance), may be carriers of the faulty gene (1 in 2), or may have the condition (1 in 4).

COLOUR BLINDNESS

COLOUR BLINDNESS AFFECTS THE ABILITY TO DISTINGUISH BETWEEN TWO COLOURS, NOTABLY RED AND GREEN OR, LESS COMMONLY, BLUE AND YELLOW.

A colour-blind person has difficulty distinguishing between two colours because of a defect in the cones in the retina. The disorder is inherited by a faulty gene carried on the X chromosome. The more common type of colour blindness, red–green, affects males because they have only one X chromosome, and any defect carried is likely to be expressed. In a female, who has two X chromosomes, a fault on one will be over-ridden by the other, and she becomes a carrier. This type of inheritance is called X-linked recessive. Blue–yellow colour blindness is also inherited but not linked to the X chromosome.

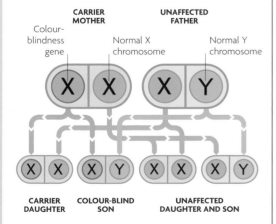

CARRIER MOTHER — Colour-blindness gene / Normal X chromosome
UNAFFECTED FATHER — Normal X chromosome / Normal Y chromosome
CARRIER DAUGHTER
COLOUR-BLIND SON
UNAFFECTED DAUGHTER AND SON

X-LINKED RECESSIVE INHERITANCE
In this example, a mother carries the abnormal gene on the X chromosome but is unaffected. The sons have a 1 in 2 chance of inheriting the disorder and the daughters have a 1 in 2 chance of being carriers but will not have the disorder.

CYSTIC FIBROSIS

IN CYSTIC FIBROSIS THE MUCUS-SECRETING GLANDS PRODUCE ABNORMALLY THICK SECRETIONS THAT CAUSE PROBLEMS IN MANY PARTS OF THE BODY.

Cystic fibrosis is a common, severe, inherited disease that causes various health problems and a reduced life expectancy. Symptoms are due to excess mucus in the body, notably in the lungs and pancreas. This causes repeated lung infections and problems digesting food, causing failure to put on weight or grow at the normal rate. Cystic fibrosis is caused by an abnormal gene carried on chromosome 7. It is a recessive disorder, which means a defective gene has to be received from each parent. Prenatal genetic testing and genetic counselling will be offered to parents of one affected child if they are considering having more.

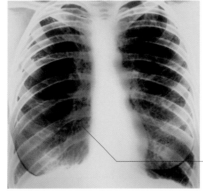

DAMAGE TO LUNGS
In this coloured chest X-ray of the lungs of a patient with cystic fibrosis, the bronchial walls (orange) on either side of the spine (white, centre) are thickened as a result of repeated infection caused by excess production of mucus in the body.

Thickened bronchial walls

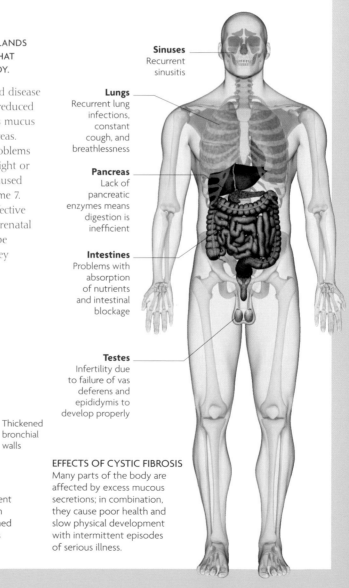

Sinuses
Recurrent sinusitis

Lungs
Recurrent lung infections, constant cough, and breathlessness

Pancreas
Lack of pancreatic enzymes means digestion is inefficient

Intestines
Problems with absorption of nutrients and intestinal blockage

Testes
Infertility due to failure of vas deferens and epididymis to develop properly

EFFECTS OF CYSTIC FIBROSIS
Many parts of the body are affected by excess mucous secretions; in combination, they cause poor health and slow physical development with intermittent episodes of serious illness.

CANCER

CANCER IS NOT A SINGLE DISEASE, BUT A LARGE GROUP OF DISORDERS WITH DIFFERENT SYMPTOMS. NEARLY ALL CANCERS HAVE THE SAME BASIC CAUSE: CELLS MULTIPLY UNCONTROLLABLY BECAUSE THE NORMAL REGULATION OF THEIR DIVISION HAS BEEN DAMAGED. THE FAULTY GENES AT THE ROOT OF THE PROBLEM – AND THERE MUST BE MORE THAN ONE OF THESE GENES – MAY BE INHERITED, OR THEY MAY BE CAUSED BY KNOWN CARCINOGENS (CANCER-CAUSING AGENTS) OR THE AGEING PROCESS.

CANCEROUS (MALIGNANT) TUMOURS

A CANCER IS A GROWTH OR LUMP THAT DAMAGES SURROUNDING TISSUES AND ORGANS, AND THAT MAY SPREAD TO OTHER PARTS OF THE BODY.

Normally, cells divide and replace themselves at a controlled rate. A malignant, or cancerous, tumour is a mass of abnormal cells that divide excessively quickly and do not carry out the normal functions of their tissue. These cells are often irregular in size and shape and bear little resemblance to the normal cells from which they arose. This irregular appearance is often used to diagnose cancer during microscopic examination of a small sample of tissue taken from a tumour. A tumour gradually enlarges, crowding out normal cells, pressing on nerves, and infiltrating blood and lymph vessels. It is important to distinguish a malignant tumour from a non-malignant one, because cancerous cells can spread to other parts of the body.

CANCER CELLS DIVIDING
In this magnified image, a cancerous cell is dividing to form two cells that contain damaged genetic material. If left untreated cancer cells multiply uncontrollably.

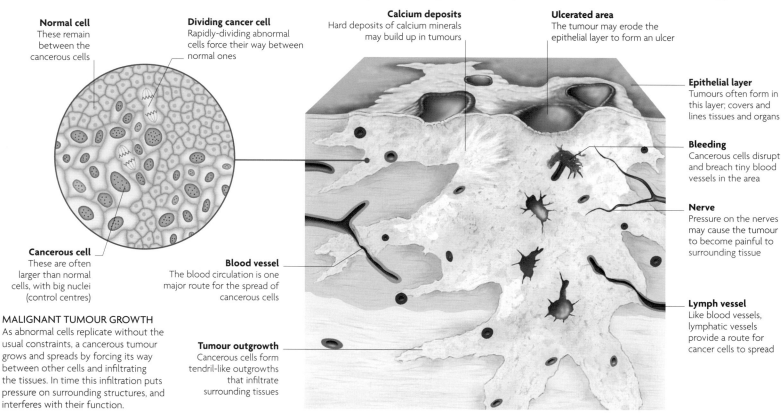

Normal cell
These remain between the cancerous cells

Dividing cancer cell
Rapidly-dividing abnormal cells force their way between normal ones

Calcium deposits
Hard deposits of calcium minerals may build up in tumours

Ulcerated area
The tumour may erode the epithelial layer to form an ulcer

Epithelial layer
Tumours often form in this layer; covers and lines tissues and organs

Bleeding
Cancerous cells disrupt and breach tiny blood vessels in the area

Nerve
Pressure on the nerves may cause the tumour to become painful to surrounding tissue

Cancerous cell
These are often larger than normal cells, with big nuclei (control centres)

Blood vessel
The blood circulation is one major route for the spread of cancerous cells

Lymph vessel
Like blood vessels, lymphatic vessels provide a route for cancer cells to spread

MALIGNANT TUMOUR GROWTH
As abnormal cells replicate without the usual constraints, a cancerous tumour grows and spreads by forcing its way between other cells and infiltrating the tissues. In time this infiltration puts pressure on surrounding structures, and interferes with their function.

Tumour outgrowth
Cancerous cells form tendril-like outgrowths that infiltrate surrounding tissues

NON-CANCEROUS (BENIGN) TUMOURS

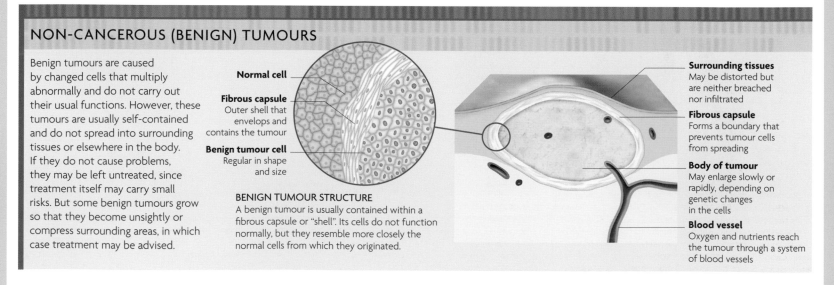

Benign tumours are caused by changed cells that multiply abnormally and do not carry out their usual functions. However, these tumours are usually self-contained and do not spread into surrounding tissues or elsewhere in the body. If they do not cause problems, they may be left untreated, since treatment itself may carry small risks. But some benign tumours grow so that they become unsightly or compress surrounding areas, in which case treatment may be advised.

Normal cell

Fibrous capsule
Outer shell that envelops and contains the tumour

Benign tumour cell
Regular in shape and size

BENIGN TUMOUR STRUCTURE
A benign tumour is usually contained within a fibrous capsule or "shell". Its cells do not function normally, but they resemble more closely the normal cells from which they originated.

Surrounding tissues
May be distorted but are neither breached nor infiltrated

Fibrous capsule
Forms a boundary that prevents tumour cells from spreading

Body of tumour
May enlarge slowly or rapidly, depending on genetic changes in the cells

Blood vessel
Oxygen and nutrients reach the tumour through a system of blood vessels

HOW CANCER STARTS

CANCERS ARE OFTEN TRIGGERED BY CARCINOGENS (SUCH AS TOBACCO SMOKE AND CERTAIN VIRUSES). HOWEVER, INHERITANCE OF FAULTY GENES ALSO PLAYS A PART.

Cancer-causing agents – carcinogens – damage specific genes (sections of DNA) known as oncogenes that regulate vital processes such as cell division and growth, repair of damaged genes, and the ability of faulty cells to self-destruct. Most damaged genes are repaired as part of normal cell metabolism. But some can gradually be altered, or mutated, by regular exposure to a carcinogenic agent so that they fail to carry out their functions. Damage to oncogenes may cause them to make altered versions of their chemicals within the cell. These work like molecular locks or keys that "trick" the cell into functioning abnormally; eventually the cell may become cancerous and divide to form a tumour.

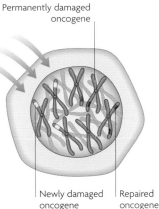

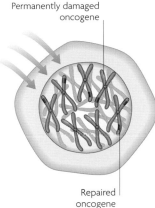

1 DAMAGE FROM CARCINOGENS
Carcinogens continually bombard cells and may eventually affect genes on the chromosomes. Usually new damage to oncogenes is limited and soon repaired.

Carcinogen | Normal gene | Newly damaged oncogene
Outer cell membrane | Chromosome | Nucleus

2 PERMANENT DAMAGE
Damage to oncogenes and repair continue, but with time or higher-than-normal exposure to carcinogens, some of the oncogenes suffer permanent harm.

Permanently damaged oncogene
Newly damaged oncogene | Repaired oncogene

3 CELL BECOMES CANCEROUS
Eventually, a number of oncogenes are permanently altered. Key cell functions are irreparably affected and the cell "tips over" into cancerous mode.

Permanently damaged oncogene
Repaired oncogene

FORMATION OF A TUMOR

It takes just one cell to undergo cancerous changes for a tumour to form. This unchecked cell divides into two cells, which each do the same, and so on. All resulting cells inherit the cancerous changes. The total cell number doubles on each division. A solid tumour is detectable after 25–30 doublings, when it contains about one billion cells.

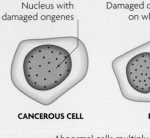

Nucleus with damaged ongenes | Damaged ongenes passed on when cell divides

CANCEROUS CELL | **FIRST DOUBLING**

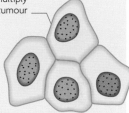

Abnormal cells multiply to form a solid tumour

TUMOUR GROWTH
After just four doublings, there are 16 cells, and after ten doublings, more than 1,000. The doubling time varies according to the tumour type but ranges from one month to two years.

SECOND DOUBLING

HOW CANCER SPREADS

THE DEFINING FEATURE OF A MALIGNANT TUMOUR IS ITS ABILITY TO SPREAD, NOT ONLY LOCALLY INTO NEIGHBOURING TISSUES, BUT ALSO TO DISTANT SITES.

The spread of cancerous cells to distant body locations is known as metastasis. The initial tumour is called the primary tumour, and those that develop in remote sites are known as secondary tumours or metastases. Secondary tumours do not arise randomly; for example, breast cancer tends to spread to the bones and lungs. To metastasize, cancerous cells must overcome many obstacles, such as scavenging white blood cells and other weapons of the body's immune system. However, once they penetrate healthy tissue, the malignant cells set up their own blood system by invading existing blood vessels and by producing chemicals that stimulate blood vessels to infiltrate the tumour (angiogenesis). The main routes of spread are the body's two "highways" for distributing nutrients and collecting wastes: the blood and lymph systems.

Spread by lymph

The lymphatic system is a network of vessels, which contain lymph fluid, and nodes (glands), which contain white blood cells. Cancerous cells enter a lymph vessel and travel to a lymph node, where they may develop into a tumour; some cells may be destroyed by the immune system, temporarily halting the spread.

Spread by blood

Primary cancer often spreads to sites that have a good blood supply, such as the lungs and brain. The liver is a particularly common site as it receives a plentiful supply from the heart and from the intestines via the portal vascular system (see p.179). When the cancerous cells reach small blood vessels, they can push between cells of the vessel wall and invade the tissues beyond.

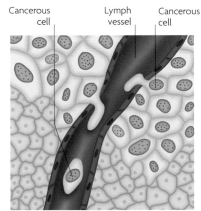

Cancerous cell | Lymph vessel | Cancerous cell

1 LYMPH VESSEL BREACHED
As the primary tumour grows, its cells invade adjacent tissues – and the small vessels of the lymphatic system are rarely far away. Cancerous cells enter the lymph fluid and pass along it to the nearest lymph node.

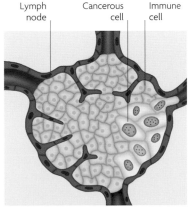

Lymph node | Cancerous cell | Immune cell

2 TUMOUR IN LYMPH NODE
Just one cancerous cell entering a local lymph node can start to divide and grow into a secondary tumour (metastasis). Immune cells here may destroy some of the cancer cells and stop the spread temporarily.

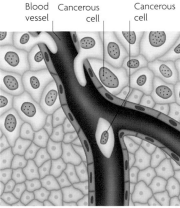

Blood vessel | Cancerous cell

1 BLOOD VESSEL WALL RUPTURED
As a primary tumour expands and infiltrates, some of its cells rupture the walls of blood vessels. The cancerous cells can now detach, to be swept away by the blood and flow around the circulatory system.

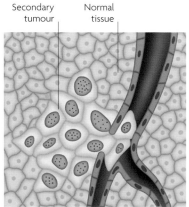

Cancerous cell | Secondary tumour | Normal tissue

2 SECONDARY TUMOUR FORMED
Cancerous cells are often bigger than red blood cells and become lodged in narrow vessels distant from the primary site. Here the cells divide, push into surrounding tissues, and establish a secondary tumour.

GLOSSARY

Text terms in *bold italics* refer to other items that appear in the glossary.

A

Abscess
A walled cavity containing *pus*, surrounded by inflamed or dying *tissue*.

Accommodation
The process by which the eyes adjust to focus on nearby or distant objects.

Acoustic neuroma
A *tumour* on the *nerve* that connects the ear and brain.

Acquired immune deficiency syndrome (AIDS)
A condition resulting from infection with the *human immuno-deficiency virus* (HIV), which is spread by sexual intercourse or infected blood. AIDS results in the loss of resistance to infections and some *cancers*.

Acute
A condition that begins abruptly and may last for a short time. Contrasts with *chronic* conditions.

Adenoids
Clusters of *lymphoid tissue* on each side of the back of the upper part of the throat.

Adipose tissue
Tissue made of specialized cells that store fatty (*lipid*) substances, for energy, physical "padding", and insulation.

Allele
Form or version of a *gene*. For example, the *gene* for eye colour has blue and brown alleles.

Allergen
Any substance causing an allergic reaction in a person previously exposed to it.

Alveolus (pl. alveoli)
One of many tiny air sacs in the lungs. Gases diffuse in and out of blood through alveolar walls.

Alzheimer's disease
A progressive *dementia* due to loss of *nerve* cells in the brain affecting more than 10 per cent of people over 65.

Amino acid
One of about 20 kinds of building-block subunits of *protein*.

Amniocentesis
The process of withdrawing a sample of fluid from the *uterus* to obtain information on the health and genetic make-up of the *fetus*.

Anaemia
A group of conditions in which the amount of *haemoglobin* in the blood is reduced.

Aneurysm
A swelling of an *artery* caused by damage to or weakness in the vessel wall.

Angina
Pain or tightness in the centre of the chest brought on by exertion; caused by an inadequate blood supply to the heart muscle.

Angiography
A method of imaging blood vessels in which *X-rays* are taken after a *contrast medium* has been injected.

Angioplasty
Any process used to widen the bore of an *artery* that is narrowed by disease. See also *Balloon angioplasty*.

Antibiotic
A medical drug that acts chiefly against *bacteria*; it has little or no effect against *viruses*.

Antibody
A soluble *protein* that attaches to body invaders, such as *bacteria*, and helps to destroy them.

Anticoagulant
A drug used to limit any tendency for blood to clot within *arteries* or *veins*.

Aorta
The central and largest *artery* of the body. It arises from the heart's left *ventricle* and supplies oxygenated blood to all other *arteries* except the pulmonary *artery*.

Aortic valve
A triple-cusped valve at the origin of the *aorta* that allows blood to leave the left *ventricle* of the heart but prevents backward flow.

Appendix
The worm-like structure attached to the large intestine. It has no known function.

Aqueous humour
The fluid filling the front chamber of the eye between the back of the *cornea* and front of the iris and *lens*.

Arrhythmia
An irregular heartbeat, due to a defect in the electrical impulses or pathways that control contractions.

Arteriole
A small terminal branch of an *artery* leading to even smaller *capillaries*, which link to the *veins*.

Artery
An elastic, muscular-walled tube that transports blood away from the heart to other body parts.

Arthritis
Inflammation in a joint, causing varying degrees of pain, swelling, redness, and restriction of movement.

Articulation
A joint, or the way in which jointed parts are connected.

Asthma
A disease in which the airways narrow so that breathing becomes intermittently difficult.

Atherosclerosis
A degenerative disease of arteries in which raised plaques of fatty material limit blood flow and cause local blood clotting.

Atrial fibrillation
A disorder in which the *atria* beat very rapidly.

Atrial septal defect
A hole in the wall (the septum) between the upper two chambers of the heart.

Atrium (pl. atria)
One of two thin-walled, upper chambers of the heart.

Autoimmune disease
A disease caused by a defect in the immune system, which attacks the body's own tissues.

Autonomic nervous system (ANS)
The portion of the nervous system controlling unconscious functions such as heartbeat and breathing.

Axon
The long, fibre-like process of a *nerve* cell that conducts nerve impulses to or from the cell body; bundles of axons form nerves.

B

Bacterium (bacteria *pl.*)
A type of microorganism with one cell. Only a few of the many species of bacteria cause disease.

Balloon angioplasty
The use of a catheter with an inflatable tip to widen an *artery*.

Basal ganglia
Paired masses, or nuclei, of *nerve* cell bodies lying deep in the brain; concerned with control of movement.

Base
In *nucleic acids* (*DNA, RNA*), nitrogen-containing chemical units or nitrogenous bases (adenine, thymine, guanine, cytosine, uracil) the order of which carries genetic information.

Benign
Mild and with no tendency to spread; contrasts with a *malignant* condition.

Beta-blocker
A drug that blocks the action of adrenaline (epinephrine). This slows the *pulse* and reduces blood pressure.

Bile
A greenish-brown fluid from the *liver* that is concentrated and stored in the *gallbladder*; helps the digestion of fats.

Biliary system
The network of *bile* vessels formed by the ducts from the *liver* and the *gallbladder*, and the *gallbladder* itself.

Biopsy
A sample of *tissue* from any part of the body that is suspected of disease, taken for microscopic examination.

Blood clot
A mesh of *fibrin*, *platelets*, and blood cells that forms when a blood vessel is damaged.

Boil
An inflamed, *pus*-filled area of skin, which is usually an infected *hair follicle*.

Bolus
A chewed-up quantity of food ready to be swallowed; also, a drug rapidly injected into the bloodstream.

Bone marrow
The fatty *tissue* within bone cavities, which may be red or yellow. Red bone marrow produces *red blood cells*.

Bradycardia
A slow heart rate. This is normal in athletes but may signal disorders in others.

Brainstem
The lower part of the brain; houses the centres that control vital functions, such as breathing and the heartbeat.

Breech delivery
A buttock-first birth; carries a slightly higher risk to the *fetus* than a head-first birth.

Bronchial tree
The trachea and the branching system of air tubes in the lungs; consists of progressively smaller *bronchi* and bronchioles.

Bronchitis
Inflammation of the lining of the breathing tubes, resulting in a cough that produces large amounts of sputum (phlegm).

Bronchus (pl. bronchi)
One of the larger air tubes in the lungs. Each lung has a main bronchus that divides into smaller branches.

C

Calcium-channel blocker
A drug that limits movement of dissolved calcium across cell membranes; it is used to treat high blood pressure and heart *arrhythmias*.

Cancer
A localized growth, or *tumour*, caused by abnormal, uncontrolled reproduction of cells that invade surrounding tissue. It can spread to other parts of the body (see *metastasis*) if left untreated.

Capillary
One of the tiny blood vessels that link the smallest *arteries* and smallest *veins*.

Carcinoma
A *cancer* of either the inner or the outer surface layer (*epithelium*). Carcinomas commonly occur in the skin, linings of the air tubes, large intestine, breast, *prostate gland*, and *uterus*.

Cardiac
Relating to the heart.

Carpal tunnel syndrome
Numbness and pain in the thumb and middle fingers. It results from pressure on the median *nerve* where it passes through the gap under a *ligament* in front of the wrist.

Cartilage
Common type of connective *tissue*, usually tough and resilient, forming some structural parts, such as the ear and nose, and lining bones inside joints.

Central nervous system (CNS)
The brain and spinal cord; receives and analyses sensory data, and initiates a response.

Cerebellum
The region of the brain located behind the *brainstem*. It is concerned with balance and the control of fine movement.

Cerebrospinal fluid
A watery fluid that bathes the brain and spinal cord.

Cerebrum
The largest part of the brain; made up of two cerebral hemispheres. It contains the *nerve* centres for thought, personality, the senses, and voluntary movement.

Chemotherapy
Treatment involving powerful chemical drugs, often used to kill cancerous or *malignant* cells.

Chlamydia
Small *bacterium* that causes the eye disease trachoma and *pelvic inflammatory disease*.

Cholecystitis
Inflammation of the *gallbladder*; commonly the result of obstructed outflow of *bile* by a *gallstone*.

Cholecystography
X-ray of the *gallbladder* after a *contrast medium* has been introduced into it.

Cholestasis
A slowing or cessation of the flow of *bile* in the *liver*.

Chorionic villus sampling
Removal of a small piece of *tissue* from the *placenta* for *chromosome* or *gene* analysis; allows for early detection of fetal abnormalities.

Chromosome
A threadlike structure, present in all nucleated body cells, that carries the genetic code for the formation of the body. During cell division, chromosomes coil into "X" shapes. A normal human body has 23 pairs of chromosomes.

Chronic
A persistent medical condition that usually lasts more than six months and may result in a long-term change in the body; contrasts with *acute*.

Cirrhosis
Replacement of *liver tissue* by fine fibrous *tissue*, which results in hardening and impaired function; may be caused by excessive alcohol consumption or infection.

Cochlea
The coiled structure in the inner ear that contains the *organ* of Corti, which converts sound vibrations into *nerve* impulses for transmission to the brain.

Collagen
The body's most important structural *protein*, present in bones, *tendons*, *ligaments*, and other connective *tissues*. Collagen fibrils are twisted into bundles called fibres.

Colon
The part of the large intestine that extends from the caecum to the rectum. Its main function is to conserve water by absorbing it from the bowel contents.

Congenital
Present at birth. Congenital disorders may be hereditary or may result from diseases or injuries that occur during fetal life or the birth itself.

Contrast medium
A substance through which *X-rays* are unable to pass.

Cornea
The transparent dome at the front of the eyeball that is the eye's main focusing *lens*.

Coronary
A term meaning "crown". Refers to the arteries that encircle and supply the heart with blood.

Corpus callosum
The wide, curved band of about 20 million *nerve* fibres that connects the two hemispheres of the *cerebrum*.

Corticosteroid
A drug that simulates the natural steroid *hormones* of the outer zone (*cortex*) of the adrenal glands.

Cortex
Outer layer in various *organs*, such as the cerebral cortex (brain), *renal* cortex (*kidney*), and adrenal cortex.

Cranial nerves
The 12 pairs of *nerves* emerging from the brain and *brainstem*. They include the *nerves* for smell, sight, eye movement, facial movement and sensation, hearing, taste, and head movement.

Crohn's disease
An inflammatory disease that affects the *gastrointestinal tract*. Symptoms may include pain, *fever*, and diarrhoea.

Cyst
A walled cavity, which is usually spherical, filled with fluid or semi-solid matter; usually benign.

Cystadenoma
A harmless, *cyst*-like growth of glandular *tissue*.

Cystitis
Inflammation of the urinary bladder, usually caused by infection. Produces frequent, painful urination and, in some cases, incontinence.

Cytoplasm
Watery or jelly-like substance that fills the bulk of a cell; it contains many *organelles*.

D

Defibrillation
A strong pulse of electric current applied to the heart to restore its normal rhythm.

Dementia
The loss of mental powers and *memory* as well as the ability to look after oneself; dementia is often a result of degenerative brain disease.

Dermis
The thick inner layer of skin made of connective *tissue*; contains structures such as sweat glands.

Dialysis
The basis of artificial *kidney* machines that separate dissolved substances. A system of filtration across a semi-permeable membrane. Permits waste excretion and preservation of essential nutrients.

Diaphragm
The dome-shaped muscular sheet that separates the chest from the abdomen. When the muscle contracts, the dome flattens, increasing chest volume and drawing air into the lungs.

Diastole
The period in the heart cycle when all four chambers are relaxed and the heart is filling with blood.

Diffusion
The natural tendency of fluid substances to spread out, especially when in solution, to give an even concentration.

Digestive system
The mouth, *pharynx*, oesophagus, stomach, and intestines. Associated *organs* are the *pancreas*, *liver*, and *gallbladder* and their ducts.

Diverticular disease
The presence of diverticula – small sacs that are created by protruson of the intestine's inner lining through the wall.

DNA (Deoxyribonucleic acid)
A chemical with a double-helix structure that carries genetic information in the form of the sequence of its subunits (*bases*).

Dominant
In genetics, when one form (allele) of a *gene* is "stronger" than another (the *recessive allele*), and it takes over.

Dopamine
A chemical messenger (neurotransmitter) in the brain that is involved in the control of body movement.

Down's syndrome
A genetic disorder in which a person's cells contain an extra *chromosome* 21 (three instead of the usual two). For this reason the condition is also known as trisomy 21.

Diaphragm
The C-shaped first part of the small intestine, into which the stomach empties. Ducts from the *gallbladder*, the *liver*, and the *pancreas* all enter the duodenum.

Duodenum
The C-shaped first part of the small intestine, into which the stomach empties. Ducts from the *gallbladder*, the *liver*, and the *pancreas* all enter the duodenum.

Dura mater
A tough membrane, the outer layer of the *meninges*, which covers the brain and the spinal cord. It lies over the arachnoid and pia mater and adheres closely to the inside of the skull.

E

Eardrum
The membrane separating the outer ear from the *middle ear* that vibrates in response to sound.

Ectopic pregnancy
Implantation of a fertilized egg in a site other than the uterine lining.

Electrocardiography
Recording and study of the heart's electrical activity.

Electroencephalography
Recording and study of the brain's electrical signals.

Embolus (pl. emboli)
Any material, such as *blood clots*, air bubbles, *bone marrow*, fat, or *tumour* cells, carried in the bloodstream.

Embryo
The developing baby from conception until the eighth week of pregnancy.

Endocarditis
An inflammation that affects either the inner lining of the heart wall or a *heart valve*.

Endocrine gland
A gland that produces *hormones* (chemical messenger substances), which are released directly into the blood rather than along tubes or ducts.

Endorphin
A morphine-like substance produced by the body in times of pain and stress, and also during exercise.

Endoscopy
Insertion of a viewing device into the body, through a natural orifice or incision, to study the interior, take samples, or carry out treatment.

Enzyme
A *protein* that accelerates a chemical reaction.

Epidermis
The outer layer of the skin; its cells become flatter and scalier towards the surface.

Epiglottis
A leaflike flap of *cartilage* located at the entrance of the *larynx*, which covers the opening of the airways during swallowing and helps to prevent food or liquid from entering the windpipe (*trachea*).

Epilepsy
A disorder featuring episodes of unregulated electrical discharge throughout the brain or in a specific area.

Epithelium
Covering or lining *tissue* that forms sheets and layers around and within many *organs* and other *tissues*.

Eustachian tube
The tube that connects the back of the nose to the cavity of the *middle ear* and equalizes air pressure.

F

Fallopian tube
One of the two tubes along which an *ovum* travels to the *uterus*, after release from an *ovary*: the most common site of an *ectopic pregnancy*. Also known as a uterine tube.

Fertilization
The union of a sperm and an egg, after sexual intercourse or artificial insemination, or in a laboratory test tube.

Fetus
The developing baby from about the eighth week after *fertilization* until the time of birth. See *embryo*.

Fever
A body temperature that registers above 37°C (98.6°F), measured in the mouth, or 37.7°C (99.8°F) in the rectum.

Fibreoptics
The transmission of images through bundles of flexible, glass or plastic threads. Some types of endoscope use fibreoptic transmission to view directly and treat structures that are located far within the human body.

Fibrin
An insoluble *protein* that is converted from the blood *protein* fibrinogen to form a fibrous network – a stage in the creation of a *blood clot*.

Fibroid
A *benign tumour* of fibrous and muscular *tissue* growing in the wall of the *uterus*, usually in women over 30. Fibroids are often multiple and may cause symptoms.

Fibrosis
An overgrown scar or connective *tissue* that is formed as the body's natural healing response to any wound or burn. Fibrous *tissue* may modify an *organ's* structure, and thereby impair its effectiveness.

Fistula
An abnormal channel that lies between any part of the interior of the body and the surface of the skin, or between two internal *organs*.

G

Gallbladder
The small, fig-shaped bag lying under the *liver*, into which *bile* secreted by the *liver* passes to be stored.

Gallstone
An oval or faceted mass of cholesterol, calcium, and *bile* pigment, that forms in the *gallbladder*. Gallstones vary in size and are more common in women than in men.

Ganglion
Lump-like group of cell bodies of *nerve* cells (*neurons*) with many interconnections; also, a localized, *cyst*-like, fluid-filled lump near a *tendon*, joint, or bone.

Gastric juice
A mixture produced by thecells of the stomach that contains hydrochloric acid and digestive *enzymes*.

Gastritis
An inflammation of the stomach lining from any cause, including infection or alcohol.

Gastrointestinal tract
The muscular tube that extends from the mouth, through the *pharynx*, oesophagus, stomach, and small and large intestines to the rectum.

Gene
A distinct section of a chromosome that is the basic unit of inheritance. Each gene consists of a segment of deoxyribonucleic acid (*DNA*) containing the code that governs the production of a specific *protein*.

Genome
The full set of *genes*, or hereditary information, for a living organism; the human genome consists of 30,000–35,000 *genes*.

Glaucoma
An abnormal rise in the pressure of the fluids within the eye, that if left untreated, causes internal damage to the eye that may result in blindness.

Glial tissue
A *nerve* cell that provides support for *neurons*.

Glucose
A simple sugar obtained by breakdown of long-chain carbohydrates, such as starch, in the diet. Glucose is also known as blood sugar and is the main form of energy within the body.

Glue ear
A disorder in which sticky fluid accumulates in the *middle ear* impeding movement of the *ossicles*.

Gonorrhoea
A sexually transmitted disease that may cause pelvic inflammation in women and narrowing of the urine outlet tube in men. If untreated, the disease may spread to other parts of the body.

Gout
A metabolic disorder causing attacks of *arthritis*, usually in a single joint.

Grey matter
The darker coloured regions of the brain and spinal cord that are composed mainly of *neuron* cell bodies as opposed to their projecting fibres, which form *white matter*.

H

Haematoma
An accumulation of blood within any part of the body, caused by a torn blood vessel.

Haemoglobin
The *protein* in *red blood cells* that combines with oxygen, carrying it from the lungs throughout the body.

Haemophilia
An inherited bleeding disorder caused by deficiency of a clotting *protein*.

Haemorrhage
The escape of blood from a blood vessel, usually as a result of an injury.

Haemorrhoids
Ballooning of *veins* in the lining of the anus (external haemorrhoids) or in the lower part of the rectum (internal haemorrhoids).

Hair follicle
A pit on the surface of the skin from which hair grows.

Heart-lung machine
A pump and oxygenator that performs the functions of the heart and the lungs during *cardiac* operations.

Heart valve
One of four structures of the heart that allow passage of blood in one direction only.

Hemiplegia
Paralysis of one half of the body, from damage to the motor areas in the brain, or to the *nerve* tracts that connect these motor areas to the spinal cord.

Hepatic
Concerning the liver.

Hepatitis
Inflammation of the *liver*, usually as a result of a viral infection, excess alcohol, or toxic substances. Symptoms include *fever* and *jaundice*.

Hepatocyte
A type of *liver* cell with many functions.

Hernia
Displacement of an organ or tissue out of the cavity in which it usually lies. The most common type is a *hiatus hernia*.

Hiatus hernia
The sliding upward of part of the stomach through the opening in the *diaphragm*.

Hippocampus
A structure in the brain concerned with learning and long-term *memory*.

Homeostasis
Active processes by which an organism maintains constant internal conditions.

Hormone
A chemical released by the *endocrine glands* and some *tissues*. Hormones act on specific receptor sites in other parts of the body.

Human immunodeficiency virus (HIV)
The virus that causes AIDS and destroys cells of the immune system, thereby undermining its efficiency.

Hypothalamus
A small structure located at the base of the brain, where the nervous and hormonal systems of the body interact. It is linked to the *thalamus* above and *pituitary gland* below.

I–K

Ileum
The final segment of the small intestine, where most absorption of nutrients takes place.

Immune deficiency
Any failure of the function of the immune system from causes such as AIDS, *cancer* treatment, or ageing.

Immunity
Resistance or protection against disease, especially infection.

Immunosuppressant
A drug that interferes with the production and activity of certain *lymphocytes*.

Interferon
A *protein* produced by cells to defend against viral infections and some *cancers*.

In vitro fertilization
Fertilization of *ova* in a laboratory container by the addition of sperm or sperm *nuclei*; the resulting *embryos* are introduced into the woman's *uterus*.

Irritable bowel syndrome
Recurrent gas, abdominal discomfort, and alternating constipation and diarrhoea. It is often associated with stress.

Jaundice
A yellowing of the skin and whites of the eyes that is due to deposition of *bile* pigment. Jaundice results from altered *liver* function.

Kaposi's sarcoma
A slow-growing *tumour* of blood vessels that affects some people with AIDS. Scattered bluish-brown nodules occur on the skin and internally.

Kidney
One of two bean-shaped organs in the back of the abdominal cavity that filter blood and remove wastes, particularly urea.

Killer T cells
White blood cells that can destroy damaged, infected, or *malignant* body cells.

L

Laparoscopy
The visual inspection of the interior of the abdomen, through a narrow optical and illuminating device, and often using a video camera.

Larynx
The structure in the neck at the top of the *trachea*, known as the voice box, that contains the *vocal cords*.

Lens
The internal lens of the eye, also called the crystalline lens; it fine-focuses vision by adjusting its curvature. The outer lens is called the *cornea*.

Leukaemia
A group of blood disorders in which *malignant white blood cells* grow in *bone marrow* and invade *organs* elsewhere in the body.

Ligament
A band of *tissue* consisting of *collagen* – a tough, fibrous, elastic *protein*. Ligaments support bones, mainly in and around joints.

Limbic system
A collection of structures in the brain that plays a role in the automatic (involuntary) body functions, emotions, and the sense of smell.

Lipid
Fatty or oily substance, insoluble in water, with varied roles in the body, including formation of *adipose tissue*, cell membranes (phospholipid), and steroid *hormones*.

Liver
The large *organ* in the upper right abdomen that performs vital chemical functions, including processing of nutrients from the intestines, manufacture of sugars, *proteins*, and fats; detoxification of poisons; and conversion of waste to *urea*.

Lobe
A rounded projection or subdivision forming part of a larger structure such as the brain, lung, or *liver*.

Lymphatic system
An extensive network of transparent lymph vessels and *lymph nodes*. It returns excess *tissue* fluid to the circulation and combats infections and *cancer* cells.

Lymph node
A small, oval gland packed with *white blood cells* that acts as a barrier to the spread of infection. Nodes occur in series along lymph vessels.

Lymphocyte
White blood cell that is part of the immune system; it protects against *virus* infections and *cancer*.

Lymphoid tissue
A *tissue* rich in *lymphocytes* found in *lymph nodes*, the *spleen*, intestines, and *tonsils*.

M

Macula
Any small, flat, coloured spot on the skin; also the central region of the *retina*; also a structure in the ear vestibule.

Malignant
Refers to a cancerous *tumour* that may spread throughout the body, causing death; contrasts with *benign*.

Mammography
The *X-ray* screening of the breasts, using low-radiation *X-rays*; used to detect breast *cancer* at an early stage.

Mastectomy
Surgical removal of part or all of the breast. It is usually performed to treat breast *cancer* and is often followed by *radiotherapy*.

Mastitis
Inflammation of the breast, usually resulting from an infection acquired during breast feeding. *Bacteria* enter through cracks in the nipples. Symptoms include *fever*, and hardening or tenderness of the breast.

Medulla
The inner part of an *organ*, such as the *kidneys* or adrenal glands. Also refers to the part of

the *brainstem* lying immediately above the start of the spinal cord, just in front of the *cerebellum*.

Meiosis
The stage in the formation of the sperm and eggs when chromosomal material is randomly redistributed and the number of *chromosomes* is reduced to 23 instead of the usual 46 found in other body cells.

Memory
The data store for recent and remote experience. Short-term memory stores are small and the contents are soon lost unless repeatedly refreshed. Long-term memory stores are very large but are not always readily accessible.

Meninges
The three membrane layers around the brain and spinal cord, the pia mater on the inside, arachnoid and *dura mater* next to the skull.

Meningitis
An inflammation of the *meninges*, sometimes as a result of a *virus* infection.

Meniscectomy
Surgical removal of a torn or displaced *cartilage* (*meniscus*) from the knee joint; usually carried out with the use of a fibreoptic viewing tube, which is inserted into the joint, and a TV monitor.

Meniscus
A crescent-shaped pad of *cartilage* found in the knee and some other joints.

Menopause
The end of the reproductive period in women, when the *ovaries* have ceased their production of eggs and menstruation has stopped.

Metabolism
The sum of all the physical and chemical processes that take place in the body.

Metastasis
The spread or transfer of any disease, but especially *cancer*, from its original site to another site where the disease process continues.

Microscopy
Examination by a microscope, often to make a diagnosis. Simple techniques use focused light rays and magnifying lenses; in order to achieve higher magnifications, beams of electrons are used.

Middle ear
The air-filled cleft within the temporal bone between the *eardrum* and the outer wall of the inner ear; contains *ossicles*. Also called the tympanic cavity.

Migraine
The effects of narrowing and then widening of some of the *arteries* of the scalp and brain, usually on one side. The symptoms include visual disturbances, nausea, and severe headache.

Miscarriage
A spontaneous ending of a pregnancy before the *fetus* is mature enough to survive outside the *uterus*.

Mitochondrion (pl. mitochondria)
A cell *organelle* containing genetic material; it is also involved in the production of energy for cell functions. It is covered with a double-layered membrane.

Mitosis
The process by which a cell *nucleus* divides to produce two daughter cells, each of which has the identical genetic makeup of the parent cell.

Mitral valve
The valve that lies between the left *atrium* and the left *ventricle* of the heart.

Mole
Any birthmark, pigmented spot, growth, or *congenital* blemish, whether flat, raised, and/or hairy, on the skin.

Molecule
A group of atoms joined, or bonded, together. Water (H_2O) has three atoms, two hydrogen (H) and one oxygen (O); large molecules such as *proteins* and *DNA* have millions.

Motor cortex
The part of the surface layer of each hemisphere of the *cerebrum* in which voluntary movement is initiated. The motor *cortex* can be mapped into areas that are linked to particular parts of the body.

Motor neuron
A *nerve* cell that carries the impulses to muscles that cause its movement.

Motor neuron disease
A rare disorder in which *motor neurons* suffer a progressive destruction, resulting in a corresponding loss of movement.

Mucocoele
A *cyst*-like abnormal sac filled with mucus that arises from a *mucous membrane*.

Mucous membrane
The soft, skin-like, mucus-secreting layer lining the tubes and cavities of the body.

Muscular dystrophy
One of several herditary muscle disorders featuring gradual, progressive muscle degeneration and weakening.

Mutation
Change in the genetic material, usually by alteration of one or more *nucleic acid* bases.

Myocardium
The special muscle of the heart, The fibres form a network that can contract spontaneously.

Myofibril
Cylindrical elements within muscle cells (fibres) that consist of thinner filaments, which move to produce muscle contraction.

Myofilament
Long, thread-like *proteins* within *myofibrils* of muscle cells.

N

Nephron
The *kidney's* filtering and tubular system, consisting of a filtration capsule, the glomerulus, and a series of tubules that reabsorbs or excretes water and wastes to control fluid balance.

Nerve
The thread-like projections of individual *neurons* (nerve cells) held together by a fibrous sheath. Nerves carry electrical impulses to and from the brain and spinal cord and other body parts.

Neuron
A single *nerve* cell, the function of which is to transmit electrical impulses.

Nociceptor
A *nerve* ending responding to painful stimuli.

Noninvasive
Any medical procedure that does not involve penetration of the skin or an entry into the body through any of the natural openings.

Nucleic acid
Deoxyribonucleic acid (*DNA*) or ribonucleic acid (*RNA*); chains of *nucleotides*, with genetic information in the order of the *nucleotides* bases.

Nucleotide
Building-block subunit of a *nucleic acid* (*DNA*, *RNA*) consisting of a sugar, phosphate, and a nitrogen-containing base.

Nucleus (pl. nuclei)
The control centre of a cell, containing the genetic material, *DNA*. It is bounded by a nuclear membrane.

O

Oesophagitis
An inflammation that affects the oesophagus, often caused by the reflux of stomach acid into the oesophagus.

Oestrogen
A sex *hormone* that prepares the uterine lining for an implanted fertilized egg and stimulates the development of a female's secondary sexual characteristics.

Olfactory nerve
One of two *nerves* of smell that run from the olfactory bulb in the roof of the nose directly into the underside of the brain.

Optic nerve
One of the two *nerves* of vision. Each one has about one million *nerve* fibres running from the *retina* to the brain, carrying visual stimuli.

Organ
Discrete body part or structure with a vital function, for example, the heart, *liver*, brain, or *spleen*.

Organelle
A tiny part inside a cell that has a specific role. The *nucleus*, *mitochondria*, and ribosomes are examples.

Ossicle
One of three tiny bones (the incus, malleus, and stapes) of the *middle ear* that convey vibrations from the *eardrum* to the inner ear.

Ossification
The process of formation, renewal, and repair of bone. Most bones in the body develop from *cartilage*.

Osteoarthritis
A degenerative joint disease that features damage to the *cartilage*-covered, weight-bearing surfaces of the joint.

Osteomalacia
Bone softening caused by defective mineralization, which usually results from poor calcium absorption due to a deficiency of vitamin D.

Osteon
The rod-shaped unit, also called a haversian system, that is the building block of cortical bone.

Osteoporosis
Loss of bone substance, due to bone being reabsorbed faster than it is being formed. The bones become brittle and are fractured easily.

Osteosarcoma
A highly *malignant* form of bone *cancer* that mainly affects adolescents. It often develops near the knee.

Osteosclerosis
Increased bone density that may result from a severe injury, osteoarthritis, or osteomyelitis. It is detected on an X-ray film as an area of extreme weakness.

Otitis media
Inflammation in the middle-ear cavity, often caused by infection that has spread from the nose or throat.

Otosclerosis
A hereditary bone disease affecting the inner ear, in which the foot of the inner *ossicle* becomes fused to the surrounding bone.

Ovary
One of two structures lying at the end of the fallopian tubes on each side of the *uterus*. They store ovarian follicles, release the mature *ova*, and produce the female *sex hormones* (*oestrogen* and *progesterone*).

Ovulation
The release of an *ovum* from a mature follicle in the *ovary* about midway through the menstrual cycle; if not fertilized, the egg is shed before menstruation.

Ovum (pl. ova)
The egg cell; if *fertilization* occurs, the ovum develops into an *embryo*.

P

Pacemaker
An electronic device implanted in the chest that delivers short electric pulses via electrodes to regulate the heartbeat.

Paget's disease
A disease that causes bone to become weaker, thicker, and distorted.

Pancreas
A gland behind the stomach that secretes digestive *enzymes* and *hormones* that regulate *glucose* levels.

Paralysis
Loss of the power of movement of part of the body due to a *nerve* or muscle disorder.

Paraplegia
Paralysis of the lower limbs, usually from injury or disease to the spinal cord or brain.

Parasite
An organism that lives in or on another organism (the host), and benefits at the host's expense.

Parasympathetic nervous system
One of the two divisions of the *autonomic nervous system*; it maintains and restores energy, for example by slowing the heart rate.

Parathyroid glands
Two pairs of yellowish *endocrine glands*, located behind the thyroid gland, that help control the level of calcium in the blood.

Parietal

A term referring to the wall of a body cavity, rather than its contents.

Parkinson's disease

A neurological disorder that features involuntary tremor, muscle rigidity, slowness of movements, tottering steps, and small handwriting. The intellect is not affected.

Parotid glands

The large pair of salivary glands situated, one on each side, above the angles of the jaw just below and in front of the ears.

Pelvic inflammatory disease

Infection of the reproductive *organs* of the female. The cause may be unknown, but it often occurs following a sexually transmitted disease.

Pelvis

The basin-like ring of bones to which the lower end of the *spine* is attached and with which the thigh bones articulate. The term is also used to refer to the soft *tissue* contents.

Peptic ulcer

The local destruction of the lining of the oesophagus, stomach, or *duodenum* from the effects of the *bacterium Helicobacter pylori*, stomach acid, and digestive *enzymes*.

Pericarditis

An inflammation of the membranous *pericardium* that surrounds the heart. It may cause pain and the accumulation of fluid, called pericardial effusion.

Pericardium

The layers of membrane surrounding the heart. The outer fibrous sac encloses the heart, and roots of the major blood vessels emerging from it. The inner layer attaches to the heart wall.

Periosteum

The tough *tissue* coating all bone surfaces except joints, from which new bone can be formed; it contains blood vessels and *nerves*.

Peripheral nervous system

All the *nerves* with their coverings that fan out from the brain and spinal cord, linking them with the rest of the body. The system consists of *cranial nerves* and *spinal nerves*.

Peristalsis

A coordinated succession of contractions and relaxations of the muscular wall of a tubular structure, such as the intestines, that moves the contents along.

Peritoneum

The double-layered membrane that lines the inner wall of the abdomen. The peritoneum covers and partly supports the abdominal *organs*. It also secretes a fluid that lubricates the movement of the intestines.

Peritonitis

An inflammation of the *peritoneum* due to *bacteria*, *bile*, pancreatic *enzymes*, or chemicals; sometimes the cause may be unknown.

Phagocyte

A *white blood cell* or similar cell that surrounds and engulfs unwanted matter, such as invading microbes and cellular debris.

Pharynx

The passage leading down from the back of the nose and the mouth to the oesophagus; it consists of the nasopharynx, the oropharynx, and the laryngopharynx.

Pituitary gland

A gland hanging from the underside of the brain. It secretes *hormones* that control many other glands in the body and is regulated by the *hypothalamus*.

Placenta

The disc-shaped *organ* that forms in the *uterus* during pregnancy. It links the blood supplies of the mother and baby via the *umbilical cord* and nourishes the growing embryo.

Plasma

The fluid part of the blood from which all cells have been removed; contains *proteins*, salts, and various nutrients.

Platelet

A fragment of large cells called megakaryocytes that is present in large numbers in the blood and necessary for blood clotting.

Pleura

A double-layered membrane, the inner layer of which covers the lung and the outer layer lines the chest cavity. A layer of fluid lubricates and enables movement between the two.

Pleural effusion

Accumulation of excessive fluid between the layers of the *pleura*, which separates them and compresses the underlying lung.

Pleurisy

Inflammation of the *pleura*, usually from a lung infection such as *pneumonia*; may lead to adhesion between the *pleural* membranes, causing pain on inhalation.

Plexus

A network of interwoven *nerves* or blood vessels.

Pneumoconiosis

Any lung-scarring disorder due to inhalation of mineral dust; scarring causes the lungs to be less efficient in supplying oxygen to the blood.

Pneumocystis pneumonia

A lung infection with the opportunistic microorganism *Pneumocystis carinii*; occurs mainly in *immune deficiency* disorders.

Pneumonia

Inflammation of the smaller air passages and *alveoli* of the lungs due to infection or contact with inhaled irritants or toxic material.

Pneumothorax

The presence of air in the space between the *pleura*, which causes the lung to collapse.

Primary

A term describing a disorder that has originated in the affected structure.

Progesterone

A female sex *hormone* secreted by the *ovaries* and *placenta* that allows the *uterus* to receive and retain a fertilized egg.

Prostaglandin

One of a group of fatty acids made naturally in the body that act like *hormones*.

Prostate gland

A male accessory sex gland situated at the base of the bladder and opening into the *urethra*. It secretes some of the fluid in semen.

Prosthesis

Any artificial replacement for a part of the body, internal or external, whether its purpose is functional or cosmetic.

Protein

Huge *molecule* composed of chains of *amino acids*; the basis of many structural materials (keratin, *collagen*), *enzymes*, and antibodies.

Pulmonary artery

The *artery* that conveys deoxygenated blood from the right *ventricle* of the heart to the lungs to be re-oxygenated.

Pulse

Rhythmic expansion and contraction of an *artery* as blood is forced through it.

Pus
A yellowish-green fluid that forms at the site of a bacterial infection; contains *bacteria*, dead *white blood cells*, and damaged *tissue*.

Q–R

Quadriplegia
Paralysis of both arms, both legs, and the trunk, usually caused by severe spinal cord damage in the neck region.

Radiotherapy
Treatment with radiation, such as *X-rays* or radioactive implants, usually against cancerous or *malignant* cells.

Recessive
In genetics, when one form (*allele*) of a *gene* is "weaker" than another (*dominant allele*) and is taken over by it.

Red blood cells
Biconcave, disc-shaped cells, without nuclei, that contain *haemoglobin*. There are 4–5 million red cells in 1 millilitre (1/500 pints) of blood.

Renal
Relating to the *kidneys*.

Respiration
1. Bodily movements of breathing.
2. Gas exchange of oxygen for carbon dioxide in the lungs.
3. Similar gas exchange in the *tissues* (cellular respiration).
4. Breakdown of *molecules* such as *glucose* to release their energy for cellular functions.

Reticular formation
Nerve cells scattered throughout the brainstem that are concerned with alertness and direction of attention to external events.

Retina
A light-sensitive layer lining the inside of the back of the eye that converts optical images to *nerve* impulses, which travel to the brain via the *optic nerve*.

Rheumatoid arthritis
A disorder that causes joint deformity and destruction. It typically affects smaller joints first.

Ribosome
Ball-like *organelle* within cells involved in building *proteins* from *amino acids*.

RNA
Ribonucleic acid, different forms of which carry out various functions, including transfer of genetic information and manufacture of *proteins*.

Rubella
A mild viral infection, also known as German measles; if it affects a woman in early pregnancy, it can cause serious harm to the *fetus*.

S

Saccharide
The basic unit that makes up carbohydrates.

Saliva
A watery fluid secreted into the mouth by the salivary glands to aid in chewing, tasting, and digestion.

Sarcoma
A *cancer* that arises from connective *tissue* (such as bone), muscle, fibrous *tissue*, or blood vessels.

Sciatica
Pain caused by pressure on the sciatic *nerve*; felt in the buttock and back of thigh.

Secondary
A term describing a disorder that follows or results from another disorder (known as the primary disorder).

Septal defect
An abnormal opening in the central heart wall that allows blood to flow from the right side to the left or vice versa.

Sex hormones
Steroid substances that bring about the development of bodily sexual characteristics. Sex hormones also regulate sperm and egg production and the menstrual cycle.

Sinoatrial node
A cluster of specialized muscle cells in the right *atrium* that acts as the heart's natural *pacemaker*.

Sinus bradycardia
An abnormally slow, but regular, heart rate resulting from a low rate of pacing by the *sinoatrial node*.

Sphincter
A muscle ring, or local thickening of the muscle coat, surrounding an opening in the body.

Spinal fusion
A surgical operation to fuse two or more adjacent *vertebrae* in order to stabilize the *spine*.

Spinal nerves
The 31 pairs of combined motor and sensory *nerves* that emerge from and enter the spinal cord.

Spine
The column of 33 ring-like bones, called *vertebrae*, that divides into seven cervical *vertebrae*, 12 thoracic *vertebrae*, five lumbar *vertebrae*, and the fused *vertebrae* of the sacrum and coccyx.

Spleen
A lymphatic *organ* situated on the upper left of the abdomen that removes and destroys worn-out *red blood cells* and helps to fight infection.

Stapedectomy
An operation to relieve deafness caused by *otosclerosis*.

Stem cell
Generalized type of cell, usually fast-dividing, with the potential to become many different kinds of specialized cells.

Steroid drugs
Drugs that simulate the actions of the natural *corticosteroids* or the *sex hormones* of the body.

Stroke
Damage to the brain by deprivation of its full blood supply or leakage of blood from a ruptured vessel; may impair movement, sensation, vision, speech, or intellect.

Subarachnoid haemorrhage
Bleeding from a ruptured *artery* or *aneurysm* lying under the arachnoid layer of the *meninges*.

Subdural haemorrhage
Bleeding between the *dura mater* and arachnoid layers of the *meninges*.

Sublingual glands
The pair of salivary glands in the floor of the mouth.

Submandibular glands
The pair of salivary glands that lie immediately under the jawbone near its angle.

Suture
A surgical stitch used to close a wound or incision.

Sympathetic nervous system
One of the two divisions of the *autonomic nervous system*. It prepares the body for action, for example by constricting the intestinal and skin blood vessels, widening the pupils of the eyes, and increasing the heart rate.

Synapse
The junction between two *nerve* cells, or between a *nerve* cell and a muscle fibre or a gland. Chemical messengers are passed across a synapse to produce a response in a target cell.

Synovial fluid
Thin, slippery, lubricating fluid within a joint.

Synovial joint
A mobile joint with a membrane that produces a lubricating fluid.

Syphilis
A sexually transmitted or *congenital* infection that, if untreated, passes through three stages and can involve serious damage to the nervous system. *Congenital* syphilis is very rare.

T

Taste bud
A spherical nest of receptor cells found mainly on the tongue; each responds most strongly to a sweet, salty, sour, or bitter flavour.

Tendinitis
Inflammation of a *tendon*, causing pain and tenderness, usually from injury.

Tendon
A strong band of *collagen* fibres that joins muscle to bone and transmits the pull caused by muscle contraction.

Tenosynovitis
Inflammation of the inner lining of a *tendon* sheath, usually from excessive friction due to overuse.

Testis (pl. testes)
One of a pair of the sperm- and *hormone*-producing sex glands in the scrotum.

Testosterone
The principal male sex *hormone* produced in the *testis* and in small amounts in the adrenal *cortex* and *ovary*.

Thalamus
A mass of *grey matter* that lies deep within the brain. It receives and coordinates sensory information.

Thorax
The part of the trunk between the neck and the abdomen that contains the heart and the lungs.

Thrombolytic drug
A drug that dissolves *blood clots* and restores blood flow in blocked *arteries*.

Thrombus (pl. thrombi)
A *blood clot* that usually results from damage to a vessel lining.

Tissue
Structure of similar cells with one main function.

Tonsils
Oval masses of *lymphoid tissue* on the back of the throat on either side of the soft palate; help protect against childhood infections.

Trachea
The windpipe. A muscular tube lined with *mucous membrane* and reinforced by about 20 rings of *cartilage*.

Transient ischaemic attack (TIA)
A "mini-stroke" that passes completely in 24 hours. An attack can imply danger of a full *stroke*.

Tumour
A *benign* or *malignant* swelling, especially a mass of cells resulting from uncontrolled multiplication.

U

Umbilical cord
The structure that connects the *placenta* to the *fetus*. It provides the immunological, nutritional, and hormonal link with the mother.

Urea
A waste product of the breakdown of *proteins*; the nitrogen-containing component of urine.

Urethra
The tube that carries urine from the bladder to the exterior; much longer in the male than in the female.

Urethritis
Inflammation of the lining of the *urethra* that is usually caused by a sexually transmitted disease.

Urinary tract
The system that forms and excretes urine; made up of the *kidneys*, ureters, bladder, and *urethra*.

Uterus
A hollow muscular structure in which the *fetus* grows and is nourished until birth.

V

Vagina
The passage from the *uterus* to the external genitals that stretches during sexual intercourse and childbirth.

Vagus nerves
The tenth pair of *cranial nerves*; helps to control automatic functions such as heartbeat and digestion.

Vas deferens
One of a pair of tubes that lead from the *testis* carrying sperm, which mix with fluid before entering the *urethra*.

Vasectomy
A surgical procedure for male sterilization in which each *vas deferens* is cut and tied.

Vein
A thin-walled blood vessel that returns blood at low pressure to the heart.

Vena cava
One of the two large *veins*, the superior and inferior, that empty into the right *atrium*.

Ventricle
A chamber or compartment, usually fluid-filled. For example, the two *cardiac ventricles* of the heart and four cerebral *ventricles* in the brain.

Vertebra (pl. vertebrae)
One of the 33 bones of the vertebral column (*spine*).

Virus
The tiniest form of infecting particle (germ). It takes over a cell to produce copies of itself.

Vocal cords
One of two sheets of *mucous membrane* stretched across the inside of the *larynx* that vibrate to produce voice sounds when air passes between them.

W–Z

Wart
A contagious, harmless skin growth that is caused by the human papilloma *virus*.

White blood cell
Any of the colourless blood cells that play various roles in the immune system.

White matter
Nerve tissue formed mainly of the projecting fibres, or *axons*, of *neurons* (*nerve* cells).

X chromosome
A sex *chromosome*. Body cells of females have two X chromosomes.

X-ray
Very short-wavelength, invisible electromagnetic energy which, if not carefully controlled, can penetrate and damage body *tissues*; used for imaging and treatment (*radiotherapy*).

Y chromosome
A sex *chromosome*. Its presence is necessary for the development of male characteristics. Body cells of males have one Y and one *X chromosome*.

Zygote
The cell produced when an egg is fertilized by a sperm; contains genetic material for a new person.

INDEX

ACKNOWLEDGMENTS

Dorling Kindersley would like to thank several people for their help in the preparation of this book. Anna Barlow contributed valuable comments on the cardiovascular system. Peter Laws assisted with visualization and additional design work was done by Mark Lloyd. 3-D illustrations were created from a model supplied by Zygote Media Group, Inc. Ben Hoare, Peter Frances, and Ed Wilson all provided editorial assistance. Marianne Markham and Andrea Bagg contributed to the initial development work.

The Human Body Book Picture Credits

The publisher would like to thank the following for their kind permission to reproduce their photographs:

(Key: a–above; b–below/bottom; c–centre; f–far; l–left; r–right; t–top)

Abbreviations
Alamy: Alamy Images; **DK:** DK Picture Library www.dkimages.com; **SPL:** Science Photo Library; **Wellcome:** The Wellcome Institute Library, London.

Sidebar Images: 34–53 Skeletal System – Wellcome: Professor Alan Boyde; **54–65 Muscular System – SPL:** Eye of Science; **66–101 Nervous System – SPL:** Nancy Kedersha; **102–111 Endocrine System – Wellcome:** University of Edinburgh; **112–127 Cardiovascular System – Wellcome:** EM Unit / Royal Free Med. School; **128–143 Respiratory System – SPL:** GJLP; **144–153 Skin, Hair, and Nails – SPL:** Steve Gschmeissner; **154–169 Lymph and Immunity – SPL:** Francis Leroy, Biocosmos; **170–191 Digestive System – SPL:** Eye of Science; **200–237 Reproduction and Life Cycle – SPL:** Susumu Nishinaga.

6 SPL: Sovereign, ISM. **10–11 SPL:** Francois Paquet-Durand. **12 Alamy:** Phototake Inc. (c); Rob Walls (br). **SPL:** CNRI (bl). **Wellcome:** Prof. R. Bellairs (cr); K. Hodivala-Dilke & M. Stone (tr). **13 Alamy:** Chad Ehlers (bl). **Getty Images:** Science Faction / L. Steinmark – CMSP (br). **SPL:** CNRI (bc); GJLP (cl); Wellcome Dept. of Cognitive Neurology (cr); Zephyr (tr, cra). **Wellcome:** Mark Lythgoe & Chloe Hutton (tc). **16 SPL. 17 DK:** Andy Crawford (cl). **SPL:** Steve Gschmeissner (bc). **18 Still Pictures:** PHONE Labat J.M. / F. Rouquette (crb); Volker Steger (ca). **19 SPL:** Francois Paquet-Durand. **20 SPL:** CNRI. **22 SPL:** Adam Hart-Davis (cr); Adam Hart-Smith (crb). **23 SPL:** Richard Wehr / Custom Medical Photo. **25 Corbis:** Visuals Unlimited (tl). **27 SPL:** Professors P. Motta & T. Naguro (bl/Golgi, bl/Endoplasmic, bl/Mitochondrion); Volker Steger (cla). **28 SPL:** Lawrence Livermore Laboratory (cra). **29 Alamy:** Bjanka Kadic (cr). **30 SPL:** Biophoto Associates (ca); L. Willatt, East Anglian Regional Genetics Service (tr). **31 SPL:** Alain Pol, ISM (cr). **Wellcome:** Annie Cavanagh (bl). **32 Alamy:** Phototake Inc. (br). **SPL:** Nancy Kedersha / UCLA (cl). **Still Pictures:** Ed Reschke (bl). **33 Corbis:** Visuals Unlimited (bl). **SPL:** Innerspace Imaging (tr); Claude Nuridsany & Marie Perennou (cl). **Still Pictures:** Ed Reschke (tl, cr). **Wellcome:** David

Gregory & Debbie Marshall (br). **38 SPL:** Steve Gschmeissner (bl). **Wellcome:** Professor Alan Boyde (c). **39 SPL:** Biophoto Associates (c); Prof. P. Motta / Dept. of Anatomy / University "La Sapienza", Rome (bl). **Wellcome:** M.I. Walker (cra). **40 DK:** Philip Dowell / Courtesy of The Natural History Museum, London (tr). **Wellcome:** (ca). **41 SPL:** Eye of Science (tl); GJLP (bc). **42 SPL:** Simon Brown (cl). **43 SPL:** Anatomical Travelogue (cl). **46 SPL:** Sovereign, ISM (cr). **47 Wellcome:** (tl). **48 Wellcome:** (tr). **49 SPL:** CNRI (br); GCa (cr). **Wellcome:** (tc, tr/Above, tr/Below). **50 SPL:** CNRI (tc); Zephyr (bc). **Wellcome:** (cr). **51 SPL:** Biophoto Associates (tl); St Bartholomew's Hospital, London (tr). **52 SPL:** Princess Margaret Rose Orthopaedic Hospital (ca); Antonia Reeve (br). **53 Mediscan:** (bc). **SPL:** CNRI (tl). **59 SPL:** (bl/Smooth). **Wellcome:** M.I. Walker (bl/Striated, bl/Cardiac). **60 Getty Images:** Stone / Catherine Ledner (bc). **Still Pictures:** Ed Reschke (cl). **61 SPL:** Neil Borden (cla). **62 SPL:** Steve Gschmeissner (cl). **64 SPL:** Biophoto Associates (br). **65 Mediscan:** (bl). **Wellcome:** (ca). **70 Wellcome:** Dr Jonathan Clarke (cla). **71 Wellcome:** (tr); Prof. Peter Brophy (cla). **75 Alamy:** allOver Photography (bl/Willis). **SPL:** Zephyr (bl/Blood Supply). **Still Pictures:** Alfred Pasieka (cla). **76 SPL:** Alexander Tsiaras (cla). **77 SPL:** Bo Veisland, MI&I (bl); Zephyr (tc). **78 SPL:** Sovereign, ISM (bl). **80 Alamy:** Phototake Inc, (cl). **83 SPL:** CNRI (c). **84 SPL:** Steve Gschmeissner (tr). **85 Wellcome:** (cl, c). **86 Still Pictures:** Volker Steger (tc). **87 Corbis:** Visuals Unlimited (c). **88 SPL:** Eye of Science (cl). **89 Alamy:** Phototake Inc. (bc). **SPL:** Pascal Goetgheluck (tl). **91 DK:** (bc). **SPL:** Susumu Nishinaga (tc). **92 SPL:** Prof. P. Motta / Dept. of Anatomy / University "La Sapienza", Rome (tc). Louise Thomas: (br/Above, br/Below). **93 DK:** (bc). **95 SPL:** Dr. G. Ravily (bl). **96 SPL:** Simon Fraser / Royal Victoria Infirmary, Newcastle Upon Tyne (br); Alfred Pasieka (bl). **97 SPL:** Alfred Pasieka (cr). **98 Alamy:** Medical-on-Line (br); Phototake Inc. (fbl, bl). **99 SPL:** Ctesibius, ISM (c). **100 SPL:** Bo Veisland (tc); Professor Tony Wright, Institute of Laryngology & Otology (clb). **Wellcome:** (cr). **101 SPL:** Sue Ford (br). **107 SPL:** Steve Gschmeissner (br); Manfred Kage (bc). **109 Alamy:** Medical-on-Line (cr). **Wellcome:** (br). **110 DK:** (br). **Still Pictures:** Ed Reschke (cl). **111 Alamy:** Scott Camazine (crb). **Wellcome:** (cr). **116 DK:** Steve Gorton (cl). **118 DK:** Dave King (c). **119 SPL:** CNRI (bl); Manfred Kage (tr). **120 Alamy:** Phototake Inc. (tr). **122 SPL:** BSIP VEM (cra); Alain Pol, ISM (br). **123 SPL:** CNRI (cb); Prof. P. Motta / G. Macchiarelli / University "La Sapienza", Rome (tc). **124 Alamy:** Medical-on-Line (bl). **SPL:** (br). **125 SPL:** Professors P.M. Motta & G. Macchiarelli (bl). **126 SPL:** James King-

Holmes (br). **132 Alamy:** Phototake Inc. (bc). **DK:** Dave King (c). **Mediscan:** (cl). **SPL:** BSIP, Cavallini James (tr). **136 SPL:** Zephyr (cl). **137 SPL:** CNRI (cra, fcra); Dr Gary Settles (br). **138 SPL:** Dr Gopal Murti (br); Dr Gary Settles (cl). **Wellcome:** R. Dourmashkin (bc). **139 Alamy:** Scott Camazine (cl). **SPL:** CNRI (cr). **140 Alamy:** Phototake Inc. (cl). **SPL:** CNRI (bl). **Wellcome:** (cr). **141 istockphoto:** (bc); Daniel Fascia (cl). **142 SPL:** (br); Biophoto Associates (c); CNRI (bc). **143 SPL:** ISM (tr); James Stevenson (crb). **146 SPL:** Sheila Terry (cl). **148 Alamy:** Phototake Inc. (crb). **SPL:** J.C. Revy (ca). **149 SPL:** Steve Gschmeissner (clb); Prof. P. Motta / Dept. of Anatomy / University "La Sapienza", Rome (cr, br). **150 DK:** Steve Gorton (tr); Susanna Price (cb/Light); Jules Selmes and Debi Treloar (ca, cb/Dark, cb/Intermediate). **SPL:** Alfred Pasieka (c). **151 Alamy:** Medical-on-Line (bl). **Mediscan:** (cl). **Wellcome:** (c, bc). **153 Alamy:** Ian Leonard (cra); Medical-on-Line (bl); SHOUT (clb); WoodyStock (cla). **SPL:** BSIP, Laurent (crb); Dr P. Marazzi (br). **159 SPL:** CNRI (bl). **160 Alamy:** Phototake Inc. (cra/Macrophage, cra/Neutrophil). **162 Alamy:** Phototake Inc. (cla). **163 SPL:** (clb); Eye of Science (br); NIBSC (cra). **Wellcome:** (bl). **164 Alamy:** Scott Camazine (bc). **165 SPL:** Eye of Science (cla); NIBSC (bc); David Scharf (tr, br). **166 Alamy:** Phototake Inc. (cl). **SPL:** (br); Dr P. Marazzi (br). **Wellcome:** Annie Cavanagh (cr). **167 SPL:** Sue Ford (cra). **168 SPL:** CNRI (br). **Wellcome:** (bl). **169 SPL:** ISM (bc); Manfred Kage, Peter Arnold Inc. (cl). **175 SPL:** Dr T. Blundell, Dept. of Crystallography, Birkbeck College (cra). **177 Corbis:** Frank Lane Picture Agency (bl). **178 SPL:** CNRI (c); Eye of Science (tr). **179 SPL:** Steve Gschmeissner (bl). **180 SPL:** Eye of Science (ca). **181 Alamy:** Phototake Inc. (bc). **182 SPL:** Prof. P. Motta / Dept. of Anatomy / University "La Sapienza", Rome (br). **184 SPL:** Prof. P. Motta / Dept. of Anatomy / University "La Sapienza", Rome (ca); Professors P. Motta & F. Carpino / University "La Sapienza", Rome (bc); Alain Pol, ISM (cl). **186 Mediscan:** (c). **SPL:** David M. Martin, MD (cra). **Wellcome:** David Gregory & Debbie Marshall (br). **187 SPL:** P. Hawtin, University of Southampton (cla). **189 SPL:** Alfred Pasieka (tc). **191 SPL:** David M. Martin, MD (cra). **196 Wellcome:** David Gregory & Debbie Marshall (cl). **197 SPL:** Manfred Kage (c). **198 SPL:** Professor P.M. Motta et Al (cl). **199 SPL:** CNRI (bl); Steve Gschmeissner (tc); Alain Pol, ISM (cla); Zephyr (cr). **202 SPL:** Steve Gschmeissner (bl); Parviz M. Pour (br). **204 SPL:** Professors P.M. Motta & J. Van Blerkom (tr). **Wellcome:** Yorgos Nikas (ca). **205 Alamy:** Phototake Inc. (tc). **208 Mediscan:** Chineze Otigbah (br). **SPL:** CIMN, ISM (c). **210 SPL:** Alfred Pasieka (c). **212 SPL:** Keith / Custom Medical Stock Photo (cl). **213 SPL:**

BSIP, Laurent (tl). **214 Alamy:** Pavel Filatov (cl); Ross Marks Photography (clb); SHOUT (bl). **216 SPL:** (cl). **217 Corbis:** Jose Luis Pelaez, Inc. (cr). **SPL:** BSIP VEM (tl). **218 SPL:** Professor P.M. Motta, G. Macchiarelli, S.A, Nottola (cl); Susumu Nishinaga (br). **220 Alamy:** Chad Ehlers (cl). **SPL:** (clb). **221 SPL:** (bl). **Wellcome:** (tr). **222 Corbis:** Andrew Brookes (bl). **SPL:** Philippe Plailly (br). **225 Alamy:** Albert Biest (crb). **DK:** Jules Selmes and Debi Treloar (br). **226 SPL:** Dr Isabelle Cartier, ISM (br); CNRI (bl); Sovereign, ISN (cr). **227 SPL:** GJLP (cra). **228 SPL:** CNRI (br). **229 Mediscan:** CDC (cla). **SPL:** (br). **231 SPL:** James King-Holmes (fcl, cl). **Still Pictures:** Jochen Tack (br). **232 Mediscan:** Chineze Otigbah (br). **233 Alamy:** Janine Wiedel Photolibrary (tr). **234 Wellcome:** Wessex Reg. Genetics Centre (c, cr). **235 SPL:** Simon Fraser (bc). **236 SPL:** Steve Gschmeissner (tr)

Endpapers: **Wellcome:** K. Hardy.

All other images © Dorling Kindersley
For further information see:
www.dkimages.com

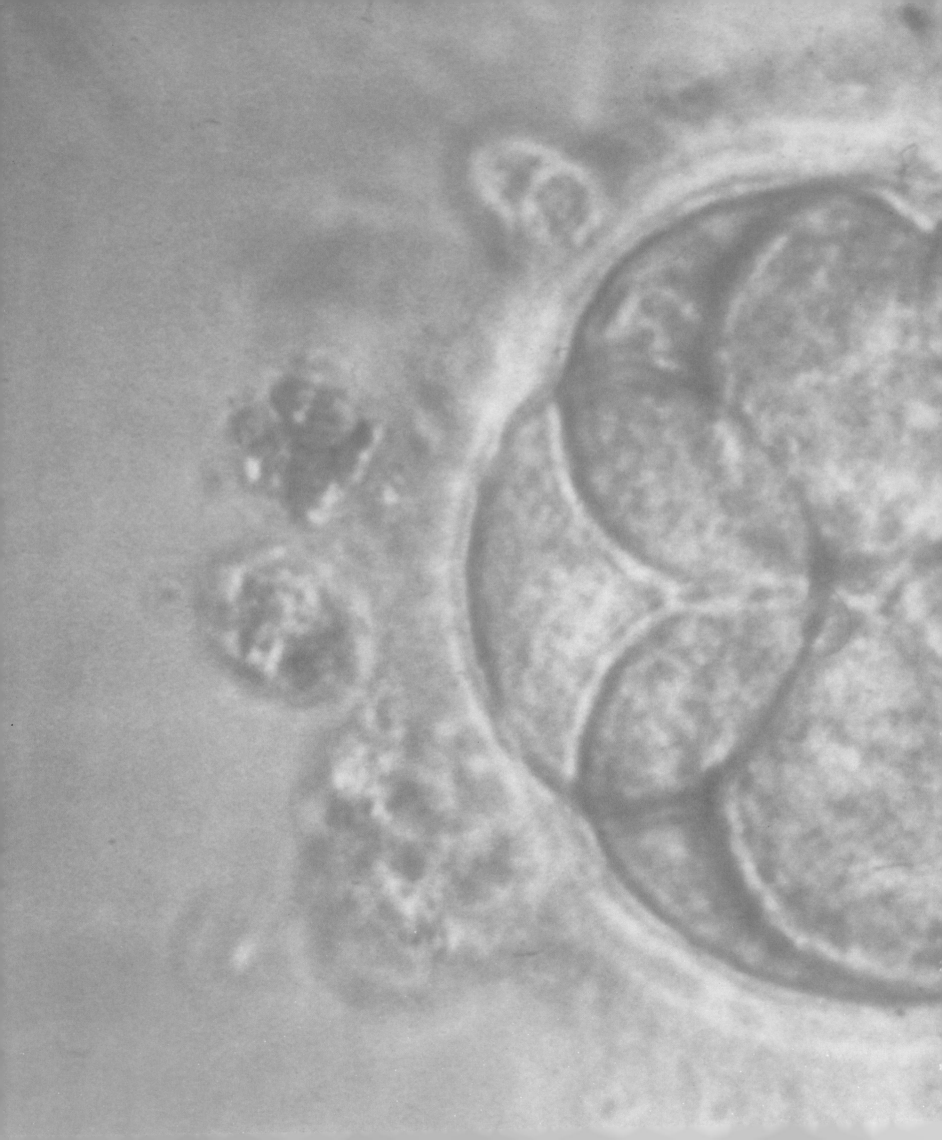